Modern Battlefield Warplanes

Modern Battlefield Warplanes

General Editors
David Donald and Daniel J. March

AIRtime Publishing Inc.

United States of America

Published by AIRtime Publishing Inc.
120 East Avenue, Norwalk, CT 06851
Tel (203) 838-7979 • Fax (203) 838-7344
email: airpower@airtimepublishing.com
www.airtimepublishing.com

ISBN 1-880588-76-5

Editors
  David Donald, Robert Hewson and Daniel J. March

Authors
  Thomas Andrews, Yefim Gordon, Robert Hewson, Jon Lake and
  Rick Stephens

  Additional material by David Donald and Daniel J. March

Artists
  Mike Badrocke, Chris Davey, Zaur Eylanbekov, Keith Fretwell,
  Alexey Mikheyev, John Weal

Jacket Design
  Zaur Eylanbekov

Controller
  Linda DeAngelis

Operations Director
  E. Rex Anku

Retail Sales Director
  Jill Brooks

Sales Manager
  Joy Roberts

Publisher
  Mel Williams

PRINTED IN SINGAPORE

To order more copies of this book or any of our other titles call toll free
within the United States 1 800 359-3003, or visit our
website at: *www.airtimepublishing.com*

Other books by AIRtime Publishing include:
  United States Military Aviation Directory
  Carrier Aviation Air Power Directory
  Superfighters The Next Generation of Combat Aircraft
  Phantom: Spirit in the Skies Updated and Expanded Edition
  Tupolev Bombers
  Black Jets
  Century Jets
  Air Combat Legends Vol. 1

New books to be published during 2004 include:
  Russian Military Aviation Directory Vols 1 and 2,
  Air Combat Legends Vol. 2, Warplanes of the Fleet

Retail distribution via:

Direct from Publisher
AIRtime Publishing Inc.
120 East Ave., Norwalk, CT 06851, USA
Tel (203) 838-7979 • Fax (203) 838-7344
Toll-free 1 800 359-3003

USA & Canada
Specialty Press Inc.
39966 Grand Avenue, North Branch
MN 55056
Tel (651) 277-1400 • Fax (651) 277-1203
Toll-free 1 800 895-4585

UK & Europe
Midland Counties Publications
4 Watling Drive
Hinckley LE10 3EY
Tel 01455 233 747 • Fax 01455 233 737

INTRODUCTION

This unique book is based on highly detailed reports first published in *World Air Power Journal* and *International Air Power Review*. They have been updated with new sections to cover recent events. Together they provide a comprehensive review of the main close support aircraft and attack helicopters currently in use over today's battlefield.

Modern Battlefield Warplanes

CONTENTS

A-10

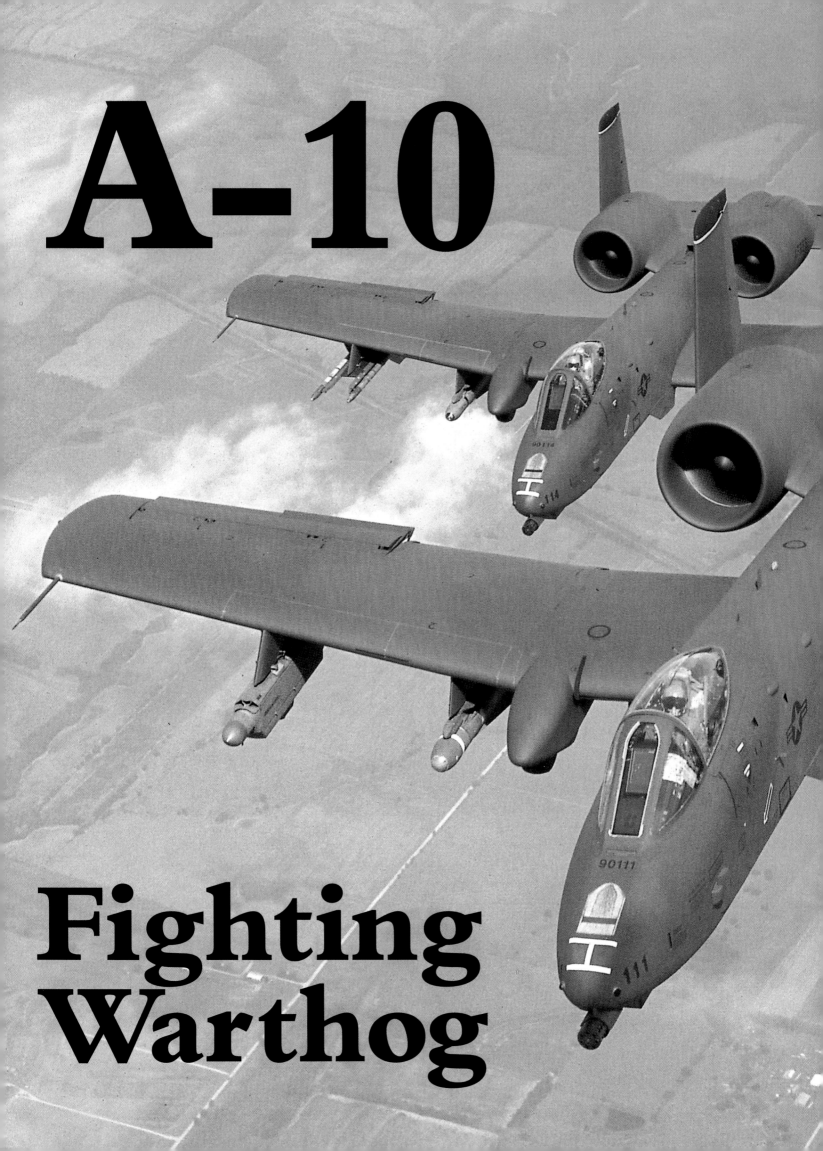

Fighting Warthog

Main picture: Big, ugly and awkward, the Warthog is far from blessed with outstanding performance, but it makes up for it by being able to carry a heavy load right into harm's way, deliver a deadly punch, and escape from the most dangerous situations.

Above: The A-10 has always been an fierce performer in both peacetime exercise and real combat situations. Its pilots are perhaps the last of the 'real' fighter pilots, flying aggressively to wring the most from their low-tech mount in a fashion more akin to World War II flying than to their contemporaries.

Seemingly destined for the scrap heap by 1991, the A-10 earned itself at least a few more years of front-line service when the 1991 Gulf War showed that it was not too old, too slow and too vulnerable to operate in a modern battlefield. Never a beauty queen, and the butt of many jokes to the effect that it was the 'only airplane vulnerable to rear hemisphere birdstrikes', it more than makes up for these shortcomings in rugged character and performance on the battlefield. During the Gulf War it quickly became a favourite of the press and public, much to the mortification of generals who desperately wanted to replace it with more F-16s.

Above: Gulf veteran 'Hogs' from the 706th TFS 'Cajuns' cavort for the camera. Despite their powerful contribution to the Gulf War, the A-10 is slowly on the way out. This New Orleans-based Reserve fighter unit has recently re-equipped with the Lockheed F-16.

Right: The A-10 was designed with virtually no relaxed stability. Until LASTE provided an autopilot, this meant that the aircraft had to be flown 'hands-on' the entire flight, but on the plus side it gave tremendous agility. To A-10 pilots, this attribute means the ability to survive on the battlefield, jinking and rapid turns remaining the A-10's foremost defence.

Right: A 355th FW A-10 peels away from the tanker. Inflight refuelling was not a major factor in the A-10's original tasking, as it was expected to operate mainly from forward bases. However, tanking is regularly practised as it is used regularly on deployments.

The genesis of the A-10 dates from before the Vietnam War, during which some of the Navy's ancient Douglas A-1 Skyraiders were pressed into service by the Air Force as close air support (CAS) and search and rescue (SAR) aircraft after the conventional solution of using retired fighters (in this case the F-100 Super Sabre) or dedicated interdictors (such as the F-4 or F-105) proved expensive, inaccurate and largely ineffective, while purpose-built lighter aircraft, from the U-10 to the brand-new OV-10, lacked punch and the speed necessary to survive in a high-threat environment.

Although the design dated from World War II and was thought to be too old and too slow to survive in the 'modern battlefield', the 'Spads' (as they were called) proved remarkably successful. Learning that speed can sometimes be a liability, and that ruggedness and reliability count for a lot in combat, the Air Force's Attack Experimental (AX) programme set out to develop a replacement which would have a similarly simple but strong airframe, many weapons pylons, great battle damage resistance and excellent low-speed agility. It was determined that during any war in Europe there would generally be 4,000 ft (1219 m) of runway left in operation after an anti-airfield strike. This distance was therefore written into the requirement as the maximum ground roll of a fully armed aircraft. A more lightly loaded aircraft would have to be able to take off in 1,000 ft (305 m). Today this seems ridiculously optimistic, and restrictive, but in the early 1960s it seemed to be a very stringent requirement. The new aircraft was also to be designed to survive in the 'anticipated ground fire environment of the 1970s and 1980s', which suggested a hitherto-unknown level of armour protection and systems redundancy.

Initially it seemed that a twin turboprop with a wing replete with high lift devices, and packed with cheap, reliable, combat-survivable and maintainable systems, would be the ideal solution, rather than accepting the carrier-optimised A-7 Corsair II, although this aircraft was procured for USAF service in the interdictor role. Politically the requirement for a dedicated CAS aircraft was important, since the Air Force wanted to secure the role as a USAF mission, to foil efforts by the US Army and Marine Corps to try to acquire their own CAS types.

The Attack Experimental programme was launched in June 1966 and a requirement was issued in that September. The Air Force issued the request for proposal (RFP) to 21 companies for AX design studies on 6 March 1967. Before these could be submitted, follow-on study contracts were issued to General Dynamics, Grumman, Northrop and McDonnell on 2 May 1967, calling for detailed research on exactly how armour should be configured and located, how

fuel, hydraulics and other systems should best be protected and routed and, where necessary, duplicated. It was reasoned that these larger companies would have the resources and computer power to achieve this research, which would then be made available to all AX contenders.

Most studies were still of B-57 Canberra-sized twin turboprops of between 40,000 and 60,000 lb (18144 and 27216 kg) weight, and with a unit cost, including R&D, of about $1.5 million. By 1969, however, the target weight had been reduced to 35,000 lb (15876 kg) and the cost to $1 million, and twin fanjets had started to look like a sensible powerplant option, especially since studies were showing that very high bypass fans were likely to be more economical than turboprops. The use of turbofan engines also offered other advantages. The lack of propellers meant that such engines could be located closer to the aircraft centreline (with the attendant reduction of asymmetric handling problems) and were easier to install and maintain, with fewer complex components (e.g., propeller and reduction gear). The bypass air helped reduce IR signature, and the engine is also exceptionally quiet.

Performance requirement

The final draft requirement left engine choice to industry, but recommended the use of turbofans of between 7,000 and 10,000 lb (31.1 and 44.5 kN). Sufficient fuel was to be provided for a mission radius of 250 miles (402 km), with a loiter time of two hours while carrying a warload of 9,500 lb (4309 kg). Take-off distance was set at 4,000 ft (1219 m) or less. The requirement demanded a high level of agility, sufficient to manoeuvre below a 1,000-ft (305-m) cloud base. Another vital requirement was for 'ease of maintenance at austere forward bases', while the AX would have to embody all these attributes while remaining 'low-cost'. The requirement also reflected the process by which the AX had gone from being a general-purpose bomb-truck to a more specialised, cannon-armed tankbuster.

Melvin Laird, Robert MacNamara's eventual successor as Secretary for Defense, abandoned the former's use of fixed-price contracts in favour of a cost-plus (incentive) scheme, while also abandoning the concept of concurrence under which all new items required are developed simultaneously. The emphasis on a low-cost aircraft, together with the new Secretary's 'good housekeeping' measures, allowed serious consideration of a 'fly-before-buy' policy evaluating rival prototypes. It also imposed a requirement to use off-the-shelf hardware wherever possible and to abandon any thoughts of using the advanced composite materials then being developed.

Competitive prototype RFPs were issued to 12 companies on 7 May 1970, specifying an anticipated programme of 600 aircraft at a unit price of $1.4 million constant 1970 dollars, with a contingency inflation allowance of 15 per cent. Responses were received from Boeing, Cessna, Fairchild, General Dynamics, Lockheed and Northrop on 10 August 1970, the other companies approached (Beech, Bell, Grumman, LTV, McDonnell and North American Rockwell) declining to bid because of the very low price being offered. Northrop and Fairchild-Republic were declared the winners of this 'fly-before-buy' prototype competition on 18 December 1970, each winning the right to build two prototypes. The new aircraft received their official designations on 1 March 1971: the Northrop YA-9 and Fairchild-Republic YA-10. The first YA-10 flew from Edwards AFB on 10 May 1972, in the hands of Republic Division chief test pilot Howard 'Sam' Nelson, with the YA-9 flying on 30 May 1972, also from Edwards, in the hands of the unrelated Lew Nelson. The second YA-10 made its first flight on 21 July 1972.

Fly-off competition

The Air Force's formal evaluation of the prototypes lasted from 10 October until 9 December 1972, with the YA-9s logging 307.6 hours, and the YA-10s 328.1. Generally preferred by the evaluation pilots (three from AFSC and two from TAC, who each flew both types after role familiarisation in the A-37), the real advantage of the YA-10 was the ease of access to its underwing hardpoints. Other factors stated included the shorter, easier transition from prototype to production aircraft, the Fairchild aircraft having been built to what amounted almost to a production standard, at least structurally. The use of an existing engine (the TF34 being used by the Navy's S-3 Viking) was also

Warthog in its element: A-10 pilots feel happiest with their nose in the mud and trees, where the aircraft can use its agility to the full to keep hidden behind terrain. For Maverick attacks, the aircraft does have to pop up to acquire and lock-on the target.

Left: The main disadvantage of the high bypass ratio turbofans is not the lack of speed, but the lack of acceleration. However, with good energy management, the A-10 pilot can wring acceptable performance from his mount, and the tight turning radius can cause a nasty shock for opposing fighters.

vitally important. The A-10's superior MMH/FH figures and better redundancy were crucial factors.

As always, political considerations were very important, and awarding the AX contract to Fairchild meant much-needed employment for the company and the region, which was a less urgent need at Northrop or for southern California. The defeated YA-9 was not without advantages, the most notable being its unique side-force control system that linked the split airbrakes and the rudder and allowed the pilot to track a ground target without worrying about bank angle or fuselage direction. Both aircraft exceeded the specification, and while the Northrop aircraft was judged to have superior handling characteristics, with significantly less roll inertia, this was felt to be counterbalanced by the maintainability and survivability of the A-10. The decision, thus, was far from being a foregone conclusion.

Pre-production order

Fairchild-Republic was announced the winner on 18 January 1973, and set about building 10 pre-production YA-10As after signing the $159.2 million pre-production contract on 1 March 1973; simultaneously, General Electric received a $27.6 million contract for TF34 engines for these aircraft. This engine contract was not a foregone conclusion either, since there had been careful studies of a proposed Avco-Lycoming F102-powered A-10. The F102 was a significantly cheaper engine, and had greater growth potential. Eventually, as a result of the more advanced stage that the TF34 had reached, and a desire for commonality with a then-proposed eight TF34-engined AWACS, General Electric received the order.

This is perhaps not being entirely fair to the TF34.

Derived from the C-5 Galaxy's TF39, the new engine has a novel nickel alloy combustor which gives a long, maintenance-free life, while the fuel injection system uses a two-stage swirler which vaporises the fuel before ignition. The TF34 had a limited life, its use being confined to the A-10 and Viking and, in a civil form, the Canadair Challenger 601, but in many ways it formed the basis of the success of the later F404 and F110 fighter engines.

Modifications to the engine to suit it to the A-10 were very minor, being largely confined to modifications to meet the USAF's left/right interchangeability requirements, although jetpipes are angled upwards to reduce trim changes when the power is adjusted. The prototype A-10s flew with Navy-standard engines, but pre-production machines received the heavier, cheaper TF34-GE-100. Harder-than-anticipated use, dictated by more low-level hard-turning flight than had been envisioned, resulted in greater-than-expected hot section wear and tear. As a result, engines were upgraded in service to TF34-GE-100A standards with a modified combustor and high pressure turbine. This doubled hot section life to 2,000 hours, including 360 hours at maximum power. The Fairchild company took the contract very seriously, vice president and Farmingdale general manager Donald Strait, an experienced P-47, F-84 and F-105 pilot, setting up a 'Tiger Works' (modelled on the Lockheed 'Skunk Works').

In July 1973, when the Air Force was slow to act on a congressional recommendation that the new aircraft be evaluated against the A-7D, funding for four of the YA-10As was cut. From 16 April until 10 May 1974, the fly-off was held at McConnell AFB, in Wichita, Kansas. The second YA-10 and an A-7D were flown by four Air Force

pilots with combat experience in F-100s and F-4s. Because of its design, the YA-10 was found to be more survivable, more lethal because of its yet-to-be-fitted 30-mm cannon, and less expensive to operate. Perhaps its most remarkable coup over the venerable SLUF was when the YA-10 was able to spend two hours 'on station', 260 nm (299 miles/481 km) from base, with 18 500-lb (227-kg) bombs. The A-7D was only able to spend 11 minutes. This evaluation finally killed off the proposed A-7DER, a stretched, re-engined, rebuilt Corsair II incorporating the GAU-8 Avenger cannon. 1974 was not an entirely happy year for the A-10, a USAF committee expressing its concern with production progress forcing the acquisition of new numerically controlled machine tools, and the placing of contracts for some critical components with sub-contractors. This was hardly surprising, since Farmingdale had not run a major programme since the closure of the F-105 production line more than 10 years earlier.

The first prototype, 71-1369, was placed in flyable storage on 15 April 1975, after completing 467 sorties and 590.9 hours of flight time. The second YA-10, 71-1370, finished the 37-month prototype programme when it was placed in flyable storage on 13 June 1975, after completing 354 flights and 548.5 flying hours. It later became an Air Force recruiting display, before being turned over to the Air Force Museum.

Development

The pre-production YA-10As joined the test programme from February 1975. Although obviously similar to the YA-10s, a number of subtle external changes were incorporated in these aircraft, mostly around the wings. Fixed leading-edge slats and trailing-edge fairings, which were found to be necessary to avoid stalling the engines when the wing stalled, were standardised, although a moveable slat was later added to production aircraft. Ventral strakes that had been added to the YA-10s to smooth airflow around the underfuselage weapon pylons were also incorporated. The wingspan was increased slightly outboard of the ailerons, and maximum flap deflection was cut from 40° to 30° (and eventually just 20° on production aircraft). Finally, the vertical tails were reshaped, an air refuelling receptacle was added in the nose, as was an internal boarding ladder, and the gun was depressed 2°, while provision was made for an undernose pylon to carry the 'Pave Penny' laser spot tracker.

These six aircraft were each tasked with specific parts of the test programme. Aircraft No. 1, 73-1664, was the last A-10 to make its first flight from Edwards AFB, on 15 February 1975, and was used to test performance and handling. The second aircraft, 73-1665, was the first aircraft to make its first flight from Fairchild's Farmingdale, Long Island, facility, on 26 April 1975, and was tasked with armament and weapons certification. The third pre-production aircraft, 73-1666, made its maiden flight on 10 June 1975, and tested subsystems and weapons delivery. The fourth aircraft, 73-1667, first flew on 17 July 1975, and conducted initial operational test and evaluation (IOT&E) and propulsion testing. The No. 5 aircraft, 73-1668, first flew on 9 August 1975 and assisted with IOT&E and stores certification testing. The final pre-production aircraft, 73-1669, made its first flight on 10 September 1975, and was the climatic test aircraft. Although these were their primary duties, the aircraft sometimes performed other testing. While it was testing a new gun propellant on 8 June 1978, both of 73-1669's engines flamed out and failed to restart. Its pilot had his ejection filmed by a chase plane and broadcast on the nightly news (both the prototype and pre-production aircraft used the Douglas ESCAPAC, while production aircraft switched to the standard McDonnell ACES II).

Since there were only six YA-10As, instead of the required 10, testing gradually fell behind schedule, although the test and evaluation programme was generally very successful. The first production aircraft, 75-0258, flew on 10 October 1975 and was delivered to the Air Force on 5

Above: This view of the prototype YA-10 reveals some important design features. The ability to survive in a hostile groundfire environment was partly due to the redundancy inherent in the design. It has oft been quoted that the A-10 could continue to fly with one of its tails or one of its engines shot away. The low-set tailplane and high-set engines meant that the exhaust fumes were largely shielded from the shoulder-launched heat-seeking missiles which proliferate on the modern battlefield.

Below: 71-1370 was the second YA-10 prototype, here seen at Edwards fitted with spin parachute in the tailcone, and painted in a charcoal grey with white surfaces.

Fairchild A-10

Above: 73-1665 was the first of the pre-production YA-10As to take to the air from the Farmingdale facility, and was used for weapons work. It was later fitted with these revised nose contours.

Right: This was the fourth pre-production airframe, and was assigned to operational evaluation. Like all the pre-production aircraft, it featured the GAU-8/A gun from the outset. The long nose boom was for test instrumentation.

November 1975. It and the next three production A-10As joined the testing effort. This shortage of aircraft delayed the delivery of the first operational A-10A to the 355th TFW until March of 1976, five months behind the original schedule. Apart from this delay, the only thing to mar the A-10's early success was the fatal crash of an aircraft at the 1977 Paris Air Salon at Le Bourget. Sam Nelson was killed when he hit the ground during a series of low-level loops on 3 June 1977, a grave loss to the programme.

The 355th TFTW conducted the final operational test and evaluation, flying a handful of their aircraft to Farnborough for the SBAC show and then on for a tour of Europe, which included compatibility checks with new-generation HASs. While in Europe, the aircraft took part in exercises. The wing also conducted Arctic tests (Operation Jack Frost) from Eielson in January 1977, and in April and May four aircraft from the wing's 333rd TFTS took part in Operation Red Flag at Nellis AFB, operating from an advanced strip on a dry lakebed. Later in 1977 the A-10 took part in a series of trials known as JAWS (Joint Attack Weapons System), which were critical in defining the role and tactics that would be followed by the new aircraft, in particular the ways in which it would operate in conjunction with Army attack helicopters.

A-10 nomenclature

The A-10 was christened the 'Thunderbolt II' by the Pentagon bureaucracy during the delivery of the 100th aircraft, 76-0553, on 3 April 1978, perpetuating a trend begun by McDonnell's very successful Phantom II. The ceremony was suitably grand, and was centred around a static display comprising the A-10 and its illustrious namesake. One can be excused for musing about the reasons for this now-maddening habit: maybe 'the brass' think tacking 'II' on a name will make a new design successful, or that reusing a previously-used name is safe and 'politically correct' (disguised as knowledge of a manufacture's past successes), or perhaps it is just a combination of laziness and lack of imagination. The truth of the matter is probably a combination of all of the above but, thankfully, this disease has not infected the lieutenants and captains who actually fly aeroplanes for a living.

As early as 1973, noting the new aircraft's not-so-smooth lines, and taking into account its not-so-high flying mission,

the Tactical Air Warfare Center, recalling the 'Groundhog' nickname of the F-84, the 'Superhog' of the F-84F and the F-105's 'Ultra-Hog', had proposed a far more appropriate name: 'Warthog'. However, hating the complexity of a word with two syllables, this was eventually shortened to simply 'Hog' (correctly pronounced 'Hawg'). No one closely associated with the A-10 calls it by that 'other name'. ('Hog' drivers' wives have observed that the best way to differentiate between a 'Hog' and its driver is that the former stops whining when the flight is over.) In one way, the official name is more appropriate than the brass intended. Like the original Thunderbolt, the A-10 is a rugged, dependable ground attack aircraft, and like its namesake its official name is virtually ignored in favour of an affectionate but more derogatory nickname.

The first pre-production aircraft, 73-1664, was bailed to Fairchild-Republic in 1978 for conversion into the two-seat YA-10B, commonly known as the Night/Adverse Weather (N/AW) A-10. Development was funded partly by the company, which put in $2 million, and partly by the DoD, which put in an amount variously reported as $5 million or $7.5 million. The possibility of conversion to two-seat configuration had been stipulated in the original concept. In addition to the second seat, the major change to this aircraft was the addition of 20 in (51 cm) to the top of the vertical tails. A pod-mounted ground-mapping radar was mounted on the left fuselage pylon, with a FLIR pod on the right fuselage pylon. Had the A-10B been produced, these sensors would have been installed in the front of the respective main landing gear pods. The aircraft was also fitted with an LN-39 INS and AN/APN-194 radar altimeter but, extraordinarily, armour was not extended to the rear seat.

In any event, the Air Force was not interested in either this night-attack version or a two-seat trainer (pilots usually

Above: The first service unit to receive the A-10 was the 355th Tactical Fighter Wing, which was established as the training unit (and later redesignated as a TTW to reflect its primary role). The wing had previously been an A-7 operator, and it was this type which was the first to be displaced by the Warthog in USAF service.

Left: In operational service, it was the 354th TFW at Myrtle Beach AFB which became the first to swap its Corsair IIs for Warthogs. These were soon busy on deployments around the US outposts, this pair being seen over Hawaii.

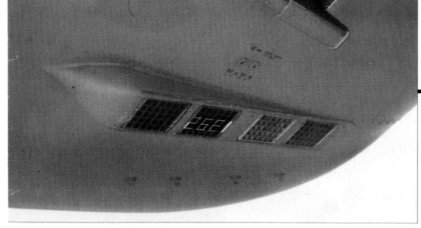

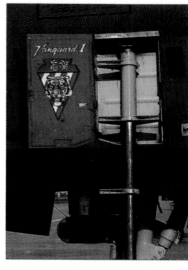

Operating in an intense battlefield scenario, the A-10 needs all the defences it can carry. An important deterrence against shoulder-launched SAMs are infra-red decoy flares. These are carried in ALE-40 dispensers (which can also eject radar-defeating chaff) mounted under the turned-down wingtips (above) and in the rear of the undercarriage fairings (left).

Above: Minor maintenance can be performed on the TF34 engine with the large side-access panel hinged down. However, for more work the engine is very easily removed.

Left: A close-up of the AAS-35 Pave Penny laser spot tracker. This is mounted on a special pylon below the aircraft's nose, giving it an excellent 'look' ahead of the aircraft. The sensor can be programmed to pick up coded laser 'sparkles'.

Above: The A-10 has the capability to operate from austere locations. The most basic of needs is for the pilot to be able to access the aircraft without any support equipment. A door on the port side covers a sturdy telescopic entry pole, with attached steps. Ground crew quickly found the step door as the ideal place to carry on their art.

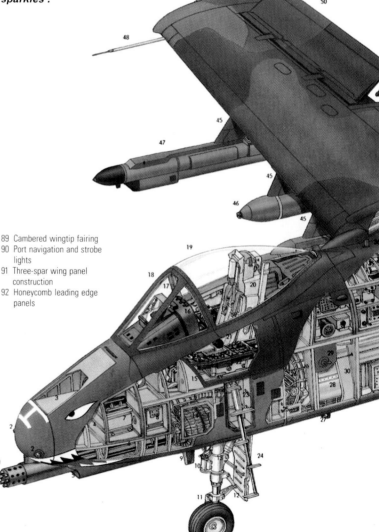

Fairchild A-10A Thunderbolt II

1 Cannon muzzles
2 Radar warning antennas
3 Flight refuelling receptacle, open
4 Nosewheel bay offset to starboard
5 Gun bay venting intake
6 Cannon barrels
7 Electrical equipment compartment
8 Battery
9 UHF aerial
10 Nosewheel hydraulic steering unit
11 Forward-retracting nose undercarriage
12 Nosewheel hydraulic steering unit
13 Shock absorber leg strut
14 Ammunition feed chutes
15 Titanium armour cockpit 'bathtub' enclosure
16 Instrument panel shroud
17 Pilot's head-up display
18 Armoured windscreen panels
19 Upward-hinged canopy cover
20 McDonnell Douglas ACES 2 ejection seat
21 Engine throttle lever
22 Side console panel
23 Ladder stowage compartment
24 Retractable boarding ladder
25 Emergency canopy release
26 Ammunition feed hydraulic drive
27 VHF homing aerial
28 Ammunition magazine, 1,174 rounds

29 Incidence vane
30 Ammunition magazine armour plating
31 Electrical system test and servicing panel
32 Ventral strake
33 Cartridge case return chute
34 Avionics equipment bays
35 Aerial selector switches
36 IFF aerial
37 Fuselage top longeron
38 Lateral control and cable ducts
39 Fuselage bag-type fuel tanks
40 Tank access panel
41 Anti-collision light
42 UHF/TACAN aerial
43 Integral wing tank fire suppressant foam filling
44 Gravity filler cap
45 Starboard wing stores pylons
46 Mk 20 Rockeye II cluster bomb
47 AN/ALQ-119 ECM pod
48 Pitot head
49 Starboard navigation and strobe lights
50 Split aileron/deceleron
51 Aileron tab
52 Two-segment Fowler-type flaps
53 Starboard engine nacelle
54 Fan face
55 General Electric TF34-GE-100 turbofan engine
56 Engine oil tank
57 Cantilevered engine mounting beams
58 By-pass (fan air) duct

59 Core engine exhaust nozzle
60 One-piece horizontal tailplane
61 Endplate tailfin
62 Starboard rudder
63 Starboard elevator
64 Elevator hydraulic actuators
65 Tail navigation light
66 Radar warning antennas
67 Rudder and elevator honeycomb composite construction
68 Three-spar fin construction
69 Rudder hydraulic actuator
70 Formation light
71 Radar warning antennas
72 VHF/AM aerial
73 Port engine nacelle exhaust ducts
74 Engine mounting bulkhead
75 APU exhaust
76 APU bay, fireproof container
77 Air conditioning equipment
78 Conditioned air delivery duct
79 Wingroot fillet
80 Trailing-edge flap shroud ribs
81 Flap track and guide rail
82 Flap hydraulic jacks
83 Synchronising linkage
84 Port single-slotted Fowler-type flaps
85 Flap and aileron honeycomb construction
86 Aileron hydraulic actuator
87 Split aileron/deceleration hydraulic jack
88 Port split aileron/deceleron, open

89 Cambered wingtip fairing
90 Port navigation and strobe lights
91 Three-spar wing panel construction
92 Honeycomb leading edge panels

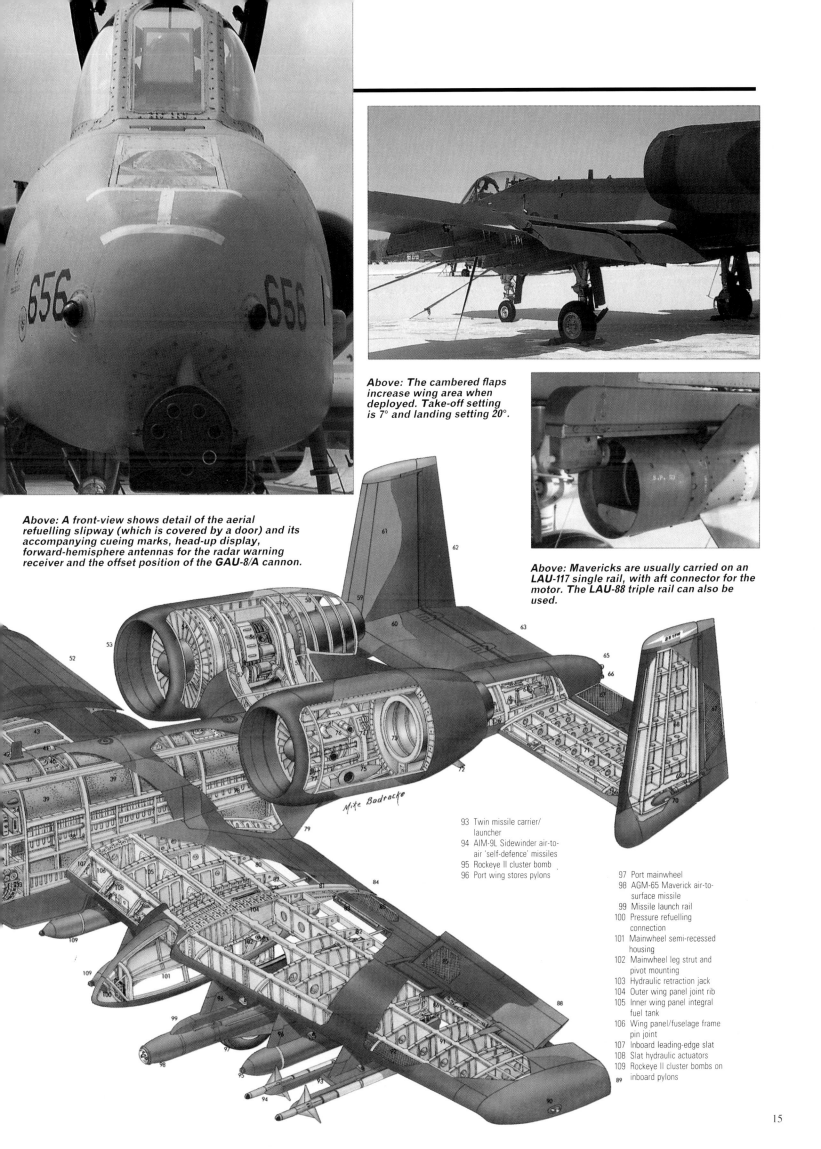

Above: A front-view shows detail of the aerial refuelling slipway (which is covered by a door) and its accompanying cueing marks, head-up display, forward-hemisphere antennas for the radar warning receiver and the offset position of the GAU-8/A cannon.

Above: The cambered flaps increase wing area when deployed. Take-off setting is 7° and landing setting 20°.

Above: Mavericks are usually carried on an LAU-117 single rail, with aft connector for the motor. The LAU-88 triple rail can also be used.

Mike Badrocke

93 Twin missile carrier/launcher
94 AIM-9L Sidewinder air-to-air 'self-defence' missiles
95 Rockeye II cluster bomb
96 Port wing stores pylons

97 Port mainwheel
98 AGM-65 Maverick air-to-surface missile
99 Missile launch rail
100 Pressure refuelling connection
101 Mainwheel semi-recessed housing
102 Mainwheel leg strut and pivot mounting
103 Hydraulic retraction jack
104 Outer wing panel joint rib
105 Inner wing panel integral fuel tank
106 Wing panel/fuselage frame pin joint
107 Inboard leading-edge slat
108 Slat hydraulic actuators
109 Rockeye II cluster bombs on inboard pylons

Right: Fairchild bailed back the first pre-production YA-10A to produce the Night/Adverse Weather A-10 (designated YA-10B). This added a second seat for a weapon systems officer and night sensors.

Far right: The YA-10B remained a one-off as the USAF had no interest in its night capabilities (or in its potential as a conversion trainer). It has remained at Edwards AFB, and is now part of the base museum collection.

The YA-10B carried its FLIR and radar sensors in pods, but had a production order for the night version been ordered, the sensors would have been relocated into the 'kneecaps' of the main undercarriage fairings.

compare the A-10's flying qualities to the T-37 trainer, calling it a 'Big Tweet'), although Fairchild energetically marketed the aircraft as a combat-ready trainer, pointing out huge cost savings to be made by removing the need for an instructor's chase aircraft on many A-10 conversion and tactical training sorties. Fairchild also promoted the basic YA-10B as the basis for defence suppression, battlefield co-ordination and interdictor versions. Unfortunately, these relied on the LANTIRN system, which was also slated for the higher priority F-15E and F-16C. The YA-10B was evaluated during 1979, but night attack with the A-10 did not become reality until 12 years later.

As a final, desperate attempt to save the two-seater, Fairchild marketed it in the Pacific area as a maritime strike aircraft, carrying Harpoon or Exocet, but these attempts came to nothing. There have been other stillborn A-10 variants. In 1976, Fairchild showed a model of the A-10 with long, slim nacelles housing unreheated versions of the J101 or RB.199, trading endurance for higher speed in an attempt to win export orders. This would have given a speed increase in the order of 50 kt (57 mph; 92 km/h) in low-level flight with weapons, but was not sufficient to overcome the prejudices of the intended customers, who regarded a 450-kt (517-mph; 831-km/h) attack aircraft as little more than an obsolete anachronism.

Designed during the long war in Vietnam, the A-10 was always intended for use in Europe, and the first aircraft were delivered to the USAFE's 81st TFW during January 1979. The Connecticut ANG became the first Guard users of the

aircraft that April (and also the first Guard unit to receive a fighter not 'handed down' by the regulars), while the Reservists at Barksdale became the first AFRES recipients of the type in June. Never exclusively a CONUS/USAFE type, A-10As were also sent to PACAF and Alaska in November and December 1981.

One tough customer

The A-10 is an extremely unusual shape by comparison with other contemporary military aircraft, but its configuration is dictated by its role. The high aspect ratio unswept wing has a large thickness/chord ratio and is highly cambered for high lift, which allows great strength at relatively light weight. The outer panels incorporate some 7° of dihedral, but are tipped by anhedral Hoerner wingtips that reduce induced drag and reduce wingtip vortices, as well as improving aileron effectiveness at low speeds. The low wing loading gives good turn performance, and a single slotted Fowler flap can be used to further enhance agility. The cockpit is set high on the fuselage and is carried well forward, giving good visibility forward and down − a prerequisite for a successful ground attack aircraft. The cockpit itself is remarkably austere, a TV monitor for the EO Maverick being the only major feature that would not be immediately familiar to an F-84 pilot.

Realising that operations in direct support of ground forces in the Central European theatre of NATO would expose the A-10 to withering ground fire, keynotes of the new design became survivability in a combat environment,

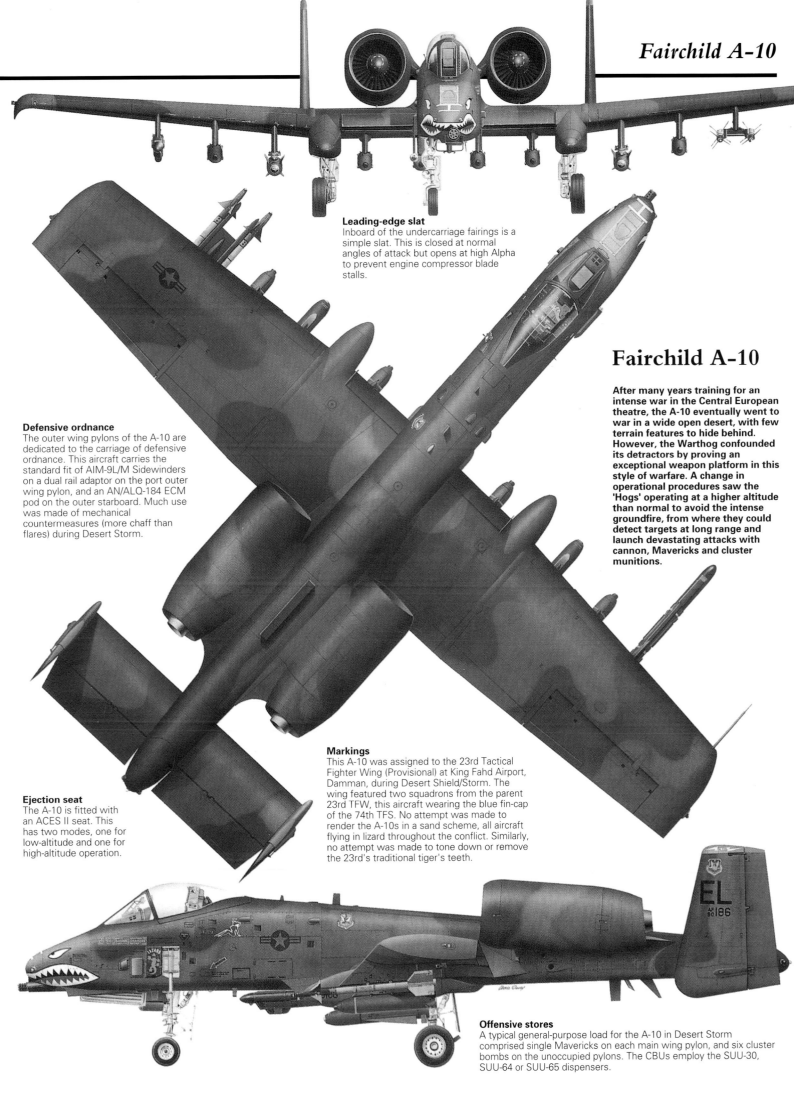

Leading-edge slat
Inboard of the undercarriage fairings is a simple slat. This is closed at normal angles of attack but opens at high Alpha to prevent engine compressor blade stalls.

Fairchild A-10

After many years training for an intense war in the Central European theatre, the A-10 eventually went to war in a wide open desert, with few terrain features to hide behind. However, the Warthog confounded its detractors by proving an exceptional weapon platform in this style of warfare. A change in operational procedures saw the 'Hogs' operating at a higher altitude than normal to avoid the intense groundfire, from where they could detect targets at long range and launch devastating attacks with cannon, Mavericks and cluster munitions.

Defensive ordnance
The outer wing pylons of the A-10 are dedicated to the carriage of defensive ordnance. This aircraft carries the standard fit of AIM-9L/M Sidewinders on a dual rail adaptor on the port outer wing pylon, and an AN/ALQ-184 ECM pod on the outer starboard. Much use was made of mechanical countermeasures (more chaff than flares) during Desert Storm.

Ejection seat
The A-10 is fitted with an ACES II seat. This has two modes, one for low-altitude and one for high-altitude operation.

Markings
This A-10 was assigned to the 23rd Tactical Fighter Wing (Provisional) at King Fahd Airport, Damman, during Desert Shield/Storm. The wing featured two squadrons from the parent 23rd TFW, this aircraft wearing the blue fin-cap of the 74th TFS. No attempt was made to render the A-10s in a sand scheme, all aircraft flying in lizard throughout the conflict. Similarly, no attempt was made to tone down or remove the 23rd's traditional tiger's teeth.

Offensive stores
A typical general-purpose load for the A-10 in Desert Storm comprised single Mavericks on each main wing pylon, and six cluster bombs on the unoccupied pylons. The CBUs employ the SUU-30, SUU-64 or SUU-65 dispensers.

On Tactical Air Support Squadrons, the OA-10 replaced Cessna OA-37Bs. This pair illustrates the hand-over for the 103rd TASS, Pennsylvania ANG.

For several units in the ANG, the delivery of their new A-10s spelled goodbye to the venerable North American F-100 Super Sabre. The Warthog offered much greater persistence and accuracy in the close air support role.

remain controllable enough after sustaining damage to their flight controls to usually reach a relatively safe bail-out area; their new A-10 had a set of back-up flight controls designed in from the start, using cables rather than rods, which could jam more easily. Battle damage resistance was extensively trialled, tests including firing multiple 23-mm shells at representative structural units while also blasting these with a 400-kt airflow. The A-10's battle damage resistance and get-you-home abilities were designed not only to produce an aircraft which could be repaired and returned to the fray; an extensively damaged aircraft could serve as a spares source for other A-10As, such is the left/right and aircraft-aircraft interchangeability of parts and components.

To protect the 'Hog' drivers from anti-aircraft artillery (AAA), the A-10A's cockpit was surrounded with a 'bathtub' of titanium armour designed to withstand hits from 23-mm projectiles from the Soviet ZSU-23-4, and even to withstand some 57-mm shell strikes. The bathtub is not a casting, as the name might suggest, but consists of massive plates of titanium alloy bolted together and lined with a multi-layered nylon spall which prevents splinters from entering the cockpit even if the bathtub's integrity is compromised. Titanium was chosen after in-depth evaluation of ceramic and aluminium armour. This single unit represents 47 per cent of the weight of armour carried, with 37 per cent more protecting the fuel system.

The main fuel tanks form a cross in the centre-section, close to the centre of gravity, obviating the need for fuel transfers. The tanks, which are tear-resistant and self-sealing, can therefore be made into separate, independent units that can be isolated from one another. If all are holed, a pair of self-sealing sumps contains sufficient fuel for a 200-nm (230-mile/370-km) flight. The tanks are protected by rigid, reinforced fire-retardant foam, with a layer of reticulated flexible foam inside that. The foam is designed to minimise spillage of fuel, to prevent airflow through a holed tank and to inhibit fire. Tests which involved firing 300 rounds of high-explosive incendiary (HEI) ammunition into the tanks failed to cause an explosion.

followed closely by maintainability. Single point failures were 'designed out' of the aircraft, accounting for its two engines and tails, and for the profusion of duplicated systems, hydraulic and fuel lines, etc. The dual hydraulic, electrical and pneumatic systems are widely separated and carried in protected ducts. The wings and horizontal tailplanes each have triple spars, giving an astonishing degree of structural redundancy. The main landing gear is housed in pods to avoid the need for a wheel well inside the wing, which would necessitate breaks in the wing structure. The engines are set high to avoid FOD ingestion during operation from semi-prepared strips, and are widely spaced to avoid a hit on one causing damage and debris which could 'take out' the second. Double curvature is avoided wherever possible, the bulk of the A-10A's skin consisting of flat plates, simple cylinders or cones which require no expensive and time-consuming stretch-forming during manufacture and which are easier to repair in the field.

Two-thirds of all battle damage was designed to be repairable in the field within 12 hours, and three-quarters within 24 hours. During the Vietnam War, Fairchild-Republic had been forced to make emergency modifications to its F-105 Thunderchiefs (a.k.a. 'Thuds') to allow them to

Terrain masking

Agility makes a major contribution to survivability, since it allows the A-10 to make maximum use of terrain masking and to avoid exposing itself to hostile fire. At the A-10A's low speed, relatively low *g* turns produce a small turn radius and high turn rate. An A-10 making a 3.5 *g*, 180° turn at 320 kt will complete the turn in 16 seconds, and use a radius of 2,700 ft (823 m), while an F-16 travelling at 600 kt and pulling 6 *g* will take 17 seconds with a radius of 3,620 ft (1103 m).

Unlike its faster brethren, the A-10 has no tailhook or drag chute (virtual necessities on second-generation jet fighters). No provisions were made in the original design for an inertial navigation system (INS) or weapon delivery computer, a reflection of the miserable performance and reliability of the 'advanced avionics' used during the aircraft's design period.

Another aspect of a modern war is its incredibly high tempo of operations. To minimise its need for support equipment, the A-10 was designed with an auxiliary power unit (APU) to negate the need for externally assisted starting, and to allow systems to be run-up or checked without starting the engines. The APU's intake was located on the right side of the aircraft, underneath the engine, with the exhaust on the opposite side, where it leaves a stain on the bottom of the left engine nacelle. Reflecting a style of warfare where pilots fly several sorties without getting out of their cockpits, it was also fitted with a single point refuelling receptacle to allow it to be 'hot-pit' refuelled without shutting down its engines.

One of the most enduring qualities of Douglas's 'Spad' was its endurance. To replicate this feature in a jet designed

Left: One special capability of the A-10 is to use short, semi-prepared strips. The extending flaps and split wingtip airbrakes keep landing run short, and take-off distance is equally impressive.

Below: A pair of 138th TFS A-10As breaks for landing. The pair is the basic tactical formation, one aircraft providing cover while the other makes an attack. A-10 crews call it mutual support, and it allows maximum safety and the minimum of time between attacks.

for use at low altitude required the use of high-bypass turbofan engines. The 9,065-lb (40-kN) static thrust General Electric TF34 was chosen. Aside from endurance, the bypass air of this engine cooled the exhaust plume, reducing the A-10's vulnerability to IR-guided missiles. To further reduce the threat from surface-launched IR missiles (the SA-7 'Grail' had just been fielded), the engines were positioned high on the aft fuselage, just in front of and above the tail. This configuration formed a 'box' which hid the exhaust gases for several more feet, allowing them additional time to cool before becoming clearly visible from the ground. The combination of large frontal area (i.e. drag) and slow spool-up time of the engines resulted in the A-10 having poor acceleration characteristics. This lack of acceleration in a combat scenario was what really concerned crews, although higher speed was always seen as 'nice to have', especially on ferry flights. In the late 1970s, some consideration was given to replacing the turbofans with turbojets to cure this problem, but modification costs were determined to be too expensive.

Long endurance

Internal fuel capacity was about 1,650 US gal (7958 litres), which weighed about 10,700 lb (4853 kg). The combination of fuel-efficient engines and relatively generous fuel supply allowed the A-10 to spend one hour on station, 150 miles (241 km) from base – 10 times longer than any other aircraft. This could be supplemented for ferry flights only by up to three 600-US gal (2536-litre) external fuel tanks, holding about 3,900 lb (1773 kg) of fuel. The external

fuel tanks were the same as those used by the F-111; because they were not used frequently, their reliability was always suspect, and it was not uncommon to have tanks function on test flights prior to a deployment only to have them balk 'on the day'. Only three pylons were plumbed for fuel tanks, with a single tank carried on the centreline being the most common ferry configuration.

The AAS-35 Pave Penny target identification set, laser (TISL) is carried by the A-10A from a special pylon on the front right portion of the fuselage. TISL is not a laser designator, but instead senses coded energy pulses reflected from targets designated with lasers by ground troops. It then projects a symbol on the HUD to help the pilot locate his target more quickly, so he can then attack it with a Maverick, 'dumb' bombs, or cannon.

A design originated for work in the steamy jungles of South East Asia, the A-10 has operated with equal success in many different climates. At far left CONUS-based Warthogs arrive in Egypt for a Bright Star exercise, while at left an Alaska-based A-10 from the 18th TFS land at Kotzebue to practise operations in an austere Arctic climate. The latter has a soluble white paint applied for operations over snow.

Fairchild A-10

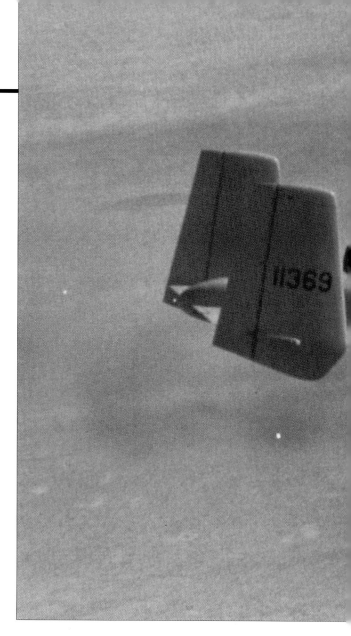

The YA-10 prototypes were initially fitted with the 20-mm M61A1 Vulcan cannon because the definitive production cannon was not ready. The RFP for this weapon had been issued six months after the AX RFP, and resulted in two new gun designs and four types of ammunition. General Electric (inventors of the modern Gatling-type cannon) and Philco Ford developed separate prototypes under $12.1 million development contracts, while Hughes licensed the Oerlikon 304RF-30 as an 'insurance policy'. Test firings began in 1972 and the General Electric cannon was selected in June 1973.

Seven-barrelled Gatling

The first prototype was retrofitted with the production model's seven-barrelled GAU-8 Avenger 30-mm cannon in February 1974 (the losing Philco Ford cannon had been a six-barrelled weapon). Test firings were conducted against 15 tanks, including US M48s and Soviet T-62s acquired from Israel. The use of seven barrels allowed a very high rate of fire to be achieved without exceeding the temperature limits of the barrels, since each barrel actually

Nose detail of a 103rd FS A-10A reveals the cooling sleeve around the rotary cannon. Several attempts have been made to divert gun gases away from the aircraft, including a vaned collar which was fitted to most A-10s for some time. However, this was not ideal, and the plain barrel end has been retained.

fires at a relatively slow rate. Each barrel is effectively a simple non-repeating 30-mm rifle, with its own breech and bolt, joined together into a single rotor revolving on a common axis, with firing mechanisms outside the moving rotor.

Proving the value of prototyping, this test programme, which ran through July, pronounced the cannon/aeroplane combination compatible, but not before discovering that the cannon's 10,000-lb (45-kN) recoil would force the production nose to be redesigned. This required moving the nose gear slightly to the right of the aircraft's centreline, which allowed the cannon's recoil to be directed down the centreline. Because only one barrel fires at a time (while the other six 'cool' as they rotate), the gun still appears to be offset slightly to the left. Even with any asymmetric recoil force cancelled out, firing the gun has a very noticeable effect. The muzzle horsepower of 17,700 compares with MHP figures of less than 100 for wartime aircraft cannons, and reduces the air speed by several knots. MHP is a factor of muzzle velocity, projectile mass and rate of fire, and gives an excellent idea of the power being generated.

The development of the GAU-8 was not always trouble-free. Much effort had to be expended in trying to eradicate the build-up of explosive gases during firing, and one aircraft was actually lost when both engines flamed out after ingesting such gases, as related above. Fortunately, the pilot was able to eject safely, while being filmed by his photo-chase wingman. An early solution was to weld onto the nose massive square-section vents but, while this allowed firing trials to continue, it clearly would not be an acceptable fix for production aircraft. A double flame-out is still extremely serious in an A-10, since the

Above: The first YA-10A lets fly with the GAU-8/A after having been retrofitted with the weapon. A cumbersome rig is fitted around the nose of the aircraft to ensure that the blast and gases are directed beneath the aircraft. During gun firing, the recoil slows the aircraft coinsiderably, so a long burst is not advisable.

Left: The tiger growls – an A-10 from the 25th TFS in a typical aggressive 'Hog' pose. The GAU-8/A emits an unforgettable sound when fired, one which is audible from several miles away. The psychological impact must be considerable to all occupants of hostile vehicles.

engine relight speed of the TF34 is higher than the aircraft's maximum level speed. At high altitudes, the aircraft can be dived to achieve relight speed, but at low level the pilot has no option but to eject.

The GAU-8 is actually the gun part of the A/A 49E-6 gun system which, with a gross weight of 4,200 lb (1910 kg), includes a drum normally containing 1,174 rounds of ammunition. The whole unit is about the same size and

weight as a Cadillac.

Although there are different types of ammunition available, the most common load is called 'combat mix' (CM) and consists of a single 1.5-lb (0.68-kg) PGU-13 HEI round mixed in with five 1.65-lb (0.75-kg) PGU-14 armour-piercing incendiary (API) rounds. The depleted uranium (DU) projectile from the PGU-14 weighs 0.94 lb (0.43 kg) and leaves the gun travelling at 3,240 ft (988 m)

A-10 weapons

As successor to the legendary Skyraider, the A-10 was provided with an excellent range of weapons, and 11 hardpoints from which to carry it. The stations are numbered from port outer to starboard outer, with Station 6 being the centreline. Stations 2 and 10 are often removed to save weight and drag.

A-10A ORDNANCE LOADS

Sta 1	Sta 11	Sta 2/10	Sta 3/9	Sta 4/8	Sta 5/7	Sta 6	Remarks
2 AIM-9	ECM pod	removed	1 AGM-65	2 Mk 82	removed	empty	flat-TER
2 AIM-9	ECM pod	1 Mk 82	1 AGM-65	1 Mk 82	1 Mk 82	empty	
2 AIM-9	ECM pod	removed	1 AGM-65	3 Mk 82	removed	empty	
2 AIM-9	ECM pod	empty	2 AGM-65	1 Mk 82	1 Mk 82	empty	slant-LAU-88
2 AIM-9	ECM pod	1 Mk 82	3 AGM-65	1 Mk 82	1 Mk 82	empty	
2 AIM-9	ECM pod	1 SUU-25	1 AGM-65	3 Mk 82	empty	empty	(night)
2 AIM-9	ECM pod	1 SUU-25	2 AGM-65	3 Mk 82	empty	empty	(night)
2 AIM-9	ECM pod	empty	1 AGM-65	1 Mk 84	empty	empty	oil feeder lines
2 AIM-9	ECM pod	1 LAU-68	1 LAU-68	3 Mk 82	empty	empty	oil trenches
2 AIM-9	ECM pod	empty	2 AGM-65	empty	empty	empty	ground war
2 AIM-9	ECM pod	removed	1 AGM-65	2 SUU-30	removed	empty	flat-TER
2 AIM-9	ECM pod	empty	1 SUU-30	1 SUU-30	1 SUU-30	empty	
2 AIM-9	ECM pod	empty	1 AGM-65	3 SUU-30	empty	empty	
2 AIM-9	ECM pod	1 SUU-30	1 AGM-65	1 SUU-30	1 SUU-30	empty	
2 AIM-9	ECM pod	1 SUU-25	1 AGM-65	3 SUU-30	empty	empty	(night)
2 AIM-9	ECM pod	1 SUU-25	2 AGM-65	1 SUU-30	1 SUU-30	empty	(night)
2 AIM-9	ECM pod	empty	1 AGM-65	1 SUU-64	1 SUU-64	empty	Gator
2 AIM-9	ECM pod	empty	1 AGM-65	1 SUU-65	1 SUU-65	empty	CEM & SFW
2 AIM-9	ECM pod	removed	1 AGM-65	2 Mk 20	removed	empty	slant-TER
2 AIM-9	ECM pod	removed	1 AGM-65	2 Mk 20	removed	empty	flat-TER
2 AIM-9	ECM pod	empty	1 Mk 20	1 Mk 20	1 Mk 20	empty	
2 AIM-9	ECM pod	1 Mk 20	1 AGM-65	2 Mk 20	1 Mk 20	empty	flat-TER
2 AIM-9	ECM pod	1 SUU-25	1 AGM-65	3 Mk 20	empty	empty	(night)
2 AIM-9	ECM pod	1 SUU-25	2 AGM-65	3 Mk 20	empty	empty	(night)

OA-10A ORDNANCE LOADS

Sta 1	Sta 11	Sta 2/10	Sta 3/9	Sta 4/8	Sta 5/7	Sta 6	Remarks
1 AIM-9	ECM pod	1 LAU-68	1 LAU-68	empty	empty	empty	
1 AIM-9	ECM pod	1 LAU-68	empty	1 Mk 82	empty	empty	
1 AIM-9	ECM pod	1 LAU-68	1 LAU-68	1 Mk 82	1 Mk 82	empty	

Above and below: The massive gun takes up a considerable amount of space in the forward fuselage. A special trolley loads the ammunition automatically into the large armoured drum tank.

Above: An A-10 fires its GAU-8/A Avenger cannon in a shallow dive. With the right elevation fixed, the pilot can 'walk' the gunfire along a line of, say, trucks, using the rudders.

Right: A long firing pass from an 81st TFW A-10. The kinetic energy released by firing the gun slows the aircraft appreciably.

Left: A short muzzle blast signals a round leaving the cannon. Several different blast deflectors have been applied to the cannon, but the A- has reverted to a standard open bar arrangement.

Above: An A-10 lays down retarded bombs at low level. This option is only used in a relatively threat-free environment.

Right and below: For destroying area targets, the cluster bomb is highly effective, but the need to directly overfly puts the A-10 at great risk from groundfire. These are *CBU*-87s.

Above: During its development, the A-10 was tested with precision weapons, such as the Paveway *LGB* and Hobos *EOB*.

The *AGM-65 Maverick* (below) is the principal ordnance carried by the A-10, used for stand-off precision attacks. Shown above are the two seeker heads for the imaging infra-red version (upper) and *TV* scene magnification (lower).

Above and left: For self-defence, the A-10 usually carries an *ECM* pod on one outer pylon (*AN/ ALQ-131* illustrated above) and twin *AIM-9Ls* on the opposite.

Above: Standard ordnance for the OA-10A is the *LAU-68* rocket pod, each pod containing seven rockets for marking targets. The rockets are *Mk 66* motors, usually with white phosphorus warheads.

23

Fairchild A-10

per second, and can kill a main battle tank from as far away as 21,600 ft (6584 m), depending on the tank. The kill mechanism of this projectile is interesting: it is specifically designed to have enough energy to penetrate tank armour - once. Once inside the tank, it stays there; the reader is left to imagine the consequences. The use of depleted uranium led to predictable (and groundless) howls of anguish from the USSR, which described the shell as an atomic weapon. In fact, the radioactivity of the shells is negligible, and they can be safely handled. Their use did put the gun into a special export category, and this is understood to be one of the major factors which prevented a purchase of the A-10 by Thailand. All projectiles use an aluminium cartridge case for lightness and have plastic instead of copper bands on the shell itself. These save weight and cost, and save wear on the barrel, extending life and acting as crude barrel cleaners.

The Avenger system is capable of firing either 2,100 (normally) or 4,200 nearly 1-ft (31-cm) long 30-mm cannon shells per minute, powered by dual hydraulic motors. About 1987 the rate was fixed at 3,900 rpm in preparation for a gun gas deflector modification (which was later cancelled). The USAF specified a minimum barrel life of 21,000 rounds per gun. Rounds are stored radially, pointing in towards the axis of the ammunition drum, their bases slotted into lengthways grooves in the inside of the drum. This system requires a specialised piece of ground support equipment for loading (the only such equipment needed by the A-10) and can simultaneously unload spent cases and reload new ones, changing a full load in 13 minutes. Since most bursts are only a few seconds long, it is more practical to think in terms of 35 and 65 rounds per second (although in the first second, 'only' 50 bullets exit the cannon since it takes a half second for it to reach maximum speed). During Desert Storm, 940,254 rounds of combat mix (CM) were fired (an average of 119 per sortie, just a 2-second burst). An

Warthog paint schemes

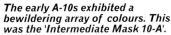

The early A-10s exhibited a bewildering array of colours. This was the 'Intermediate Mask 10-A'.

Few aircraft have had such a variety of paint schemes applied, or been so associated with just one, as the A-10A. The YA-10s were initially overall federal standard number (FSN) 36473 Aircraft Grey, and later repainted FSN 36118 Gunship Grey. The first YA-10A, 73-1664, was also Gunship Grey. Pre-production aircraft two, five and six (73-1665, -1668, and -1669) had a mottled pattern of white sprayed over a black base coat. Aircraft three (73-1666) was overall FSN 36320 Dark Compass Ghost Grey. Aircraft four (73-1667) was the first to have a paint similar to the first production scheme applied. It was overall 40 per cent MASK-10A, a light greenish-grey which reflected 40 per cent of the light hitting it. (The MASK-10A paints were never assigned FSN numbers.)

The seventh aircraft, which was the first production A-10A (75-0258), was overall FSN 36375 Light Compass Ghost Grey with a gloss overcoat, while the eighth and ninth (75-0259 and -0260) were the same colour but lacked the overcoat. Aircraft number 10 (75-0261) had its top painted like 75-0259, but had its underside painted 50 per cent MASK-10A. The 11th aircraft (75-0262) had 40 per cent MASK-10A on the upper surfaces, with a Dark Compass Ghost Grey underside. Aircraft 12 through 30 (75-0263 through 75-0281) had what became known as the 'Intermediate MASK-10A' scheme, with an asymmetric pattern of 30 per cent MASK-10A and the lighter 50 per cent MASK-10A. From aircraft 31 through 145 (75-0282 through 77-0230), a symmetrical pattern of improved-quality 30 per cent and 50 per cent MASK-10A, along with a 'false canopy' on the belly in Gunship Grey, was applied.

After the Joint Attack Weapons System (JAWS) exercise in 1977, which tested tactics for the use of A-10As with

Army attack and scout helicopters, it was discovered that the MASK-10A scheme was very visible to Aggressor F-5Es. To counter this prior to the follow-on JAWS II in November 1977, at least four aircraft assigned to Nellis in late 1977 (75-0258, -0259, -0260, and -0262) were painted in mottled camouflage patterns, which became collectively known as the JAWS schemes. Although effective, these schemes were difficult to maintain. However, the point had been made that the air-to-air threat in a 'NATO' war would outweigh the surface-to-air threat for the 'Warthog'.

In September 1978, a prototype 'Charcoal Lizard' scheme was applied in a wraparound pattern to 75-0266 of the 422nd FWS using FSN 34092 Dark Green, 34102 Medium Green and 36231 Medium Grey. Its evaluation proved successful and, after darkening the grey to FSN 36081, was selected to replace the two-tone 'MASK-10A' grey scheme, beginning with the 148th production airframe, 77-0223. These aircraft began to show up in Europe in April 1979, after about 30 grey aircraft had been delivered to the 81st TFW. A small factor in this decision may have been a tiff between the Air Force and aviation artist Keith Ferris over the legal rights to the false canopy painted on the belly of the grey aircraft, a feature not seen on Air Force aircraft since. The 917th TFW at Barksdale painted at least one A-10A (78-0552) in an experimental sand, tan and light green camouflage pattern, and another (76-0530) in a similar camouflage of medium, dark and extra dark greys. Neither scheme was adopted for the fleet.

In 1992, after evaluating the lessons of Desert Storm and in light of the demise

of the Warsaw Pact, it was decided that the surface-to-air threat was again predominant for any foreseeable operation in which the A-10 might be involved. A scheme using Dark Compass Ghost Grey upper surfaces and Light Compass Ghost Grey under surfaces was devised and applied. The first aircraft to be painted in this scheme was 81-0956, which first flew from RAF Bentwaters, UK, on 12 June 1992.

Above: Both prototypes were repainted in this Gunship Grey to reduce conspicuity.

During 1991 the 917th TFW applied two experimental camouflage schemes, a grey concoction (above) and a desert scheme (below).

Left: Most associated with the A-10 is the Charcoal Lizard scheme.

Below: Compass Ghost is the current standard A-10 scheme.

Above: The six squadrons of the 81st manned forward-operating locations in Germany, to which pilots regularly deployed so that they could get to know the terrain well. Likely choke-points were well surveyed as these would be the prime killing areas for the 'Hogs'.

additional 16,360 rounds of HEI were fired by 23rd TASS OA-10As, which did not use combat mix (an average of only 18 per sortie).

European operations

The A-10 was designed during Vietnam, but intended for combat in Europe. It did not take long to discover that flying in Germany by the seat of one's pants at low altitude was not easy, that relying on line-of-sight TACAN was impractical at very low level and to realise that combat would not make the task easier (something just about anyone who had ever flown there could have attested to). The stability augmentation system ('Hog' drivers have nothing as sophisticated as an autopilot) helps reduce workload, and has been upgraded in service, but its function is to ensure consistent control responses and warn of

excessive angles of attack or an impending stall.

Bowing to reality, the Air Force finally began production installation of an AN/ASN-141 inertial navigation system (INS) with the 391st aircraft (79-0127). This also required the installation of a modified HUD with a new, more powerful symbology generator. To get INS-equipped aircraft to Europe as quickly as possible, a swap of all 81st TFW aircraft was conducted. Aircraft at RAF Woodbridge and Bentwaters were flown to Sacramento Air Logistics Center (SM-ALC), at McClellan AFB in California, and dropped off for programmed depot maintenance (PDM) where modification to install the INSs were made. Meanwhile, the pilots flew to Fairchild-Republic's A-10A production facility in Hagerstown, Maryland, picking up factory-fresh INS-equipped aircraft, and returned them to England. Once that process was complete, PDM for European A-10As was shifted to RAF Kemble.

The A-10A's European operations were built around the main operating bases (MOBs) at RAF Bentwaters and RAF Woodbridge in England, supporting several forward operating locations (FOLs) in Germany. (Although the focus was Germany, Europe-based A-10As were also prepared to deploy in support of other NATO allies, such as Norway or Italy.) The FOL concept allowed the A-10As to be responsive to the CAS requirements of NATO ground forces. Small detachments rotated through the FOLs on a continual basis, allowing pilots to be intimately familiar with the people they might have to defend, as well as their territory, including probable avenues of Soviet attack plus the friendly units along them. Over time, experienced crews actually became able to work their 75/100-nm long and 20-nm deep sectors of responsibility without referencing maps.

There were six FOLs, three under the control of each Allied Tactical Air Force (ATAF) in Germany. Only Sembach, Norvenich, Ahlhorn and Leipheim actually hosted squadron detachments; the other two FOLs would have only been activated had war broken out. Although the FOLs were capable of minor maintenance and emergency repairs, aircraft would have had to return to the MOBs for major maintenance. Had an FOL's runway been bombed, the A-10s, capable of taking off in three-quarters of a mile, could have used part of the runway or a taxiway, or even deployed to emergency airstrips using straight sections of autobahn (A-10As were sometimes allowed to practise this technique on new stretches of the roadway before they were opened to the public).

Each squadron was assigned its own FOL, with two squadrons assigned to the inactive detachments that were stationed at two other squadrons' FOLs one week out of three. This arrangement resulted in each squadron having eight of its aircraft deployed two weeks out of three, keeping 32 A-10As in Germany. In late 1988, when the

Above: Some of the European training centred on operations from dispersed and well-camouflaged sites. Ground crews trained at hiding the A-10 and its equipment under woods.

Right: In time of war all NATO airfields would have been prime targets during the first round of WarPac air strikes, so the A-10 would have most likely fought from stretches of autobahn. Hides could have been in forests, or in supermarket car parks!

509th and 511th TFSs transferred to the 10th TFW, the number of 81st TFW aircraft in Germany at any given time dropped to 24, with the other eight belonging to the 10th TFW. From an individual pilot's perspective, a normal rotation was composed of two weeks at the FOL, flying about twice a day, followed by four weeks at home, flying about twice a week.

FOLs were split into 2nd ATAF (northern half of Germany) and 4th ATAF (southern half). In the former were Det 3 at Ahlhorn (activated 1 July 1979, assigned to 91st TFS pre-1989, 509th after), Norvenich (activated 1 October 1979, deactivated 19 March 1992, assigned to 78th TFS pre-1989, 510th TFS after) and Jever, which was only a planned FOL (509th TFS assigned pre-1989 and 511th after). In 4th ATAF, there was Sembach (activated 1 September 1978, deactivated 3 May 1991, assigned to 510th TFS pre-1989, 78th TFS after), Leipheim (activated 1 April 1979, deactivated 25 September 1992, assigned to 92nd TFS pre-1989, 91st TFS after) and the planned FOL at Wiesbaden (assigned to 511th TFS pre-1989 and 92nd TFS after).

If the Cold War had ever turned hot, 18 aircraft would have deployed to each FOL. During combat operations, three two-ship formations from each FOL would have been

in contact with Warsaw Pact forces, with three more en route to the battle, while the remaining six aircraft would have been on the ground being rearmed. Co-ordination between ground forces and the A-10As would have been provided by OV-10A Bronco forward air controllers operating just behind the battlefield. A FAC could have remained 'on station', just behind the forward edge of the battle area, for up to four hours, maintaining the 'corporate memory' which would allow him to co-ordinate the air-to-ground battle to maximum effect.

Top: Not particularly effective over snow, the Charcoal Lizard scheme nevertheless was highly effective in hiding the A-10 from the attentions of MiGs over the forest and fields of Central Europe.

Above: Today the A-10 is deployed in several composite wings. The 23rd Wing is dedicated to support of the army at Fort Bragg, and a squadron of A-10s provides close air support.

Like the F-111, the A-10 has long been a subject for hot debate. Its vulnerability on the battlefield has been called into question since it was first procured, yet its results in combat and exercises maintain it as a force to be reckoned with.

Inside the A-10

Specification
Fairchild A-10A

Powerplant: two General Electric TF34-GE-100 turbofans, rated at 9,065 lb (40.3 kN) each

Wing span: 57 ft 6 in (17.53 m)
Length: 53 ft 4 in (16.26 m)
Height: 14 ft 8 in (4.47 m)
Wing area: 506 sq ft (47.01 m2)
Tailplane span: 18 ft 10 in (5.74 m)
Wheel track: 17 ft 2 ½ in (5.25 m)
Wheelbase: 17 ft 8 ¾ in (5.40 m)

Empty weight: 21,541 lb (9771 kg)
Operating empty weight: 24,959 lb (11321 kg)
Forward airstrip weight: 32,771 lb (14865 kg)
Maximum take-off weight: 50,000 lb (22680 kg)
Internal fuel: 10,700 lb (4853 kg)
Maximum ordnance: 16,000 lb (7258 kg)
Maximum ordnance with full internal fuel: 14,341 lb (6505 kg)

Maximum speed at sea level: 439 mph (706 km/h)
Cruising speed: 387 mph (623 km/h) at 5,000 ft (1525 m)
Rate of climb: 6,000 ft (1828 m) per minute at sea level
Take-off distance: 4,000 ft (1220 m) at MTOW, 1,450 ft (442 m) at forward airstrip weight
Landing distance: 2,000 ft (610 m) at MTOW, 1,300 ft (396 m) at forward airstrip weight
Ferry range: 2,454 miles (3950 km)
Combat radius: 288 miles (463 km) with 20-minute reserve and 1.7-hour loiter, 620 miles (1000 km) with 20-minute reserves and no loiter

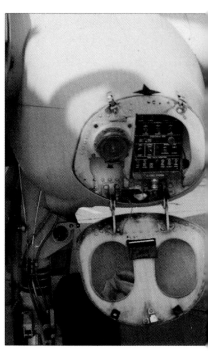

Above: The tasked mission of the A-10 dictates rapid turn-rounds between sorties. Ground troops regularly practise the art of refuelling and rearming 'Hogs' in a matter of minutes. To aid the former task, the A-10 has a single-point refuelling point in the port 'kneecap' of the undercarriage fairing, and a control panel.

Above and left: The 'office' of the 'Warthog' is quite simple compared to other fighters. The head-up display provides standard combat data, aiming cues provided by the Pave Penny laser spot tracker and CCIP information. The central panel is dominated by the attitude indicator and navigation display. On the right, at top, is the display screen for Maverick imagery, below which are engine instruments. On the left at top is the RWR display, below which is the armament panel. The right-hand panel is mainly for communications, while the left panel (left) has system controls.

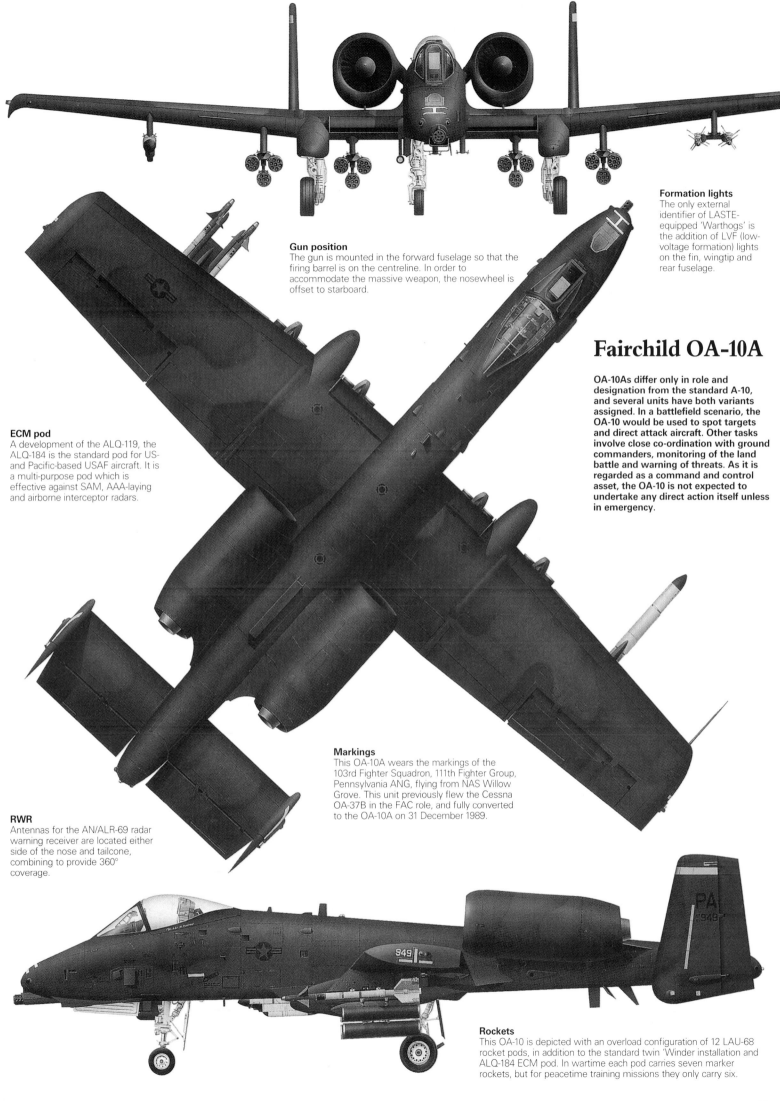

Gun position
The gun is mounted in the forward fuselage so that the firing barrel is on the centreline. In order to accommodate the massive weapon, the nosewheel is offset to starboard.

Formation lights
The only external identifier of LASTE-equipped 'Warthogs' is the addition of LVF (low-voltage formation) lights on the fin, wingtip and rear fuselage.

Fairchild OA-10A

OA-10As differ only in role and designation from the standard A-10, and several units have both variants assigned. In a battlefield scenario, the OA-10 would be used to spot targets and direct attack aircraft. Other tasks involve close co-ordination with ground commanders, monitoring of the land battle and warning of threats. As it is regarded as a command and control asset, the OA-10 is not expected to undertake any direct action itself unless in emergency.

ECM pod
A development of the ALQ-119, the ALQ-184 is the standard pod for US- and Pacific-based USAF aircraft. It is a multi-purpose pod which is effective against SAM, AAA-laying and airborne interceptor radars.

Markings
This OA-10A wears the markings of the 103rd Fighter Squadron, 111th Fighter Group, Pennsylvania ANG, flying from NAS Willow Grove. This unit previously flew the Cessna OA-37B in the FAC role, and fully converted to the OA-10A on 31 December 1989.

RWR
Antennas for the AN/ALR-69 radar warning receiver are located either side of the nose and tailcone, combining to provide 360° coverage.

Rockets
This OA-10 is depicted with an overload configuration of 12 LAU-68 rocket pods, in addition to the standard twin 'Winder installation and ALQ-184 ECM pod. In wartime each pod carries seven marker rockets, but for peacetime training missions they only carry six.

Above: Long considered a day attack platform, the A-10 picked up some night capability with the LASTE mod, which added an NVG-compatible cockpit and radar altimeter.

Far right: The rocket pods under the wing denoted the adoption of the forward air control mission under the guise of the OA-10A. In fact the OA-10A does not differ in the slightest from a standard A-10. However, the aircraft is not normally used in direct action as it is classified a command and control asset by the USAF, and is accorded a high value.

Below: A sight more associated with maritime patrol aircraft, an A-10 gets a wash-down at Myrtle Beach. The aircraft is a 354th TFW(P) Gulf veteran, displaying its kill scoreboard on the starboard side below the cockpit.

Air liaison officers, pilots operating with Army ground units, would have translated their needs into 'pilot speak', relaying this information to the FACs, who would have passed it on to the 'Hogs' and Army helicopters for 'appropriate action'. The transfer of information would have occurred by means of a technique called the 'nine-line brief'. These pieces of information would tell the pilot everything he needed to know to attack the target. They included the: initial point (IP), the place from which to begin the attack, usually a visual landmark; magnetic heading from the IP to the target; distance from the IP to the target; elevation of the target area; description of the target; geographical co-ordinates of the target; position of friendly forces; direction to egress the target area, should the aircraft be damaged during the attack; and any other significant information.

Tactics developed during the JAWS exercises were refined and renamed joint air attack team (JAAT). The A-10As would have initially attacked an armoured column from just above 100 ft (31 m), hitting its AAA and SAM defences with Mavericks, before dropping behind terrain cover. With these defences suppressed, the attack helicopters would have attacked the tanks from less than 100 ft (31 m) with BGM-71 TOWs and cannon fire, taking turns with the reattacking A-10As. As the 'Hogs' cleared the area, the helicopters would have risen from their cover to continue the battle and cover the A-10As' departure. In this complimentary team, the A-10As had the speed, survivability and firepower, while the helicopters could remain on station, co-ordinate artillery, and land, if necessary, to co-ordinate with ground commanders.

Obviously, any war in Central Europe would have involved serious losses. NATO planning depended heavily on reinforcements arriving from the US to sustain the war effort. To improve their knowledge of European flying conditions, terrain and procedures, without the time and expense of deploying entire squadrons, Continental US A-10 units would conduct periodic exchanges of a few pilots with the 81st TFW in England. This operation, called Boar Swap, also allowed UK-based crews to visit US units, reinforcing the cohesion of the 'Warthog' community.

By the late 1980s, the Vietnam-vintage OA-37Bs and OV-10As were reaching the end of their useful lives. In the eyes of the Air Force, so was the A-10, as far as front-line combat operations were concerned. Beginning in 1987, selected 'Hogs' were redesignated as OA-10As, the firtst serving with the 23rd TASS. In keeping with the increasingly politicised and bizarre way in which American combat aircraft are designated, F-16s with different engine/inlet combinations and primary missions (day versus night attack with LANTIRN) are all called F-16C/Ds, while the lowly A-10A got a whole new designation because of a mission change. There is no physical difference between an A-10A and a 'fast FAC' OA-10A. Because they only employ rockets for target marking and do not use most of the rest of the A-10A's arsenal, the OA-10A costs about $45 (£30) less per hour to operate than an A-10A. In these days of ever-decreasing defence budgets, every penny counts.

Desert Shield/Storm

The 23rd TFW(P) and 354th TFW(P) formed the two halves of the 144-aircraft A-10A/OA-10A force (informally known as the 'Fahd Squad') which operated from King Fahd International Airport, near the city of Damman in north-eastern Saudi Arabia. Readers interested in a fascinating account of the A-10A's role in the Gulf War are encouraged to read William Smallwood's book, *Warthog*.

During Desert Storm the OA/A-10A force flew 19,545.6 hours in 8,755 sorties (16.5 per cent of the 53,000 sorties flown by the coalition), of which 7,445 delivered weapons (85 per cent of A-10 sorties flown, 18 per cent of the coalition's 41,000 strike sorties). Overall A-10 weapon system reliability during Desert Storm was 98.67 per cent (this was the percentage of times weapons were successfully expended when the trigger was squeezed or the 'pickle' button depressed). Targets listed as 'confirmed kills' included 1,106 trucks, 987 tanks (25 per cent of all destroyed, plus perhaps as many more hit, but not claimed), 926 artillery pieces (again, about 25 per cent of the war's total, with perhaps twice this number believed actually hit, but not claimed), 501 armoured personnel carriers (about 30 per cent of the total destroyed during the war), 249 command vehicles, 112 military structures, 96 radars, 72 bunkers, 51 'Scud' missile launchers (revisionist arguments about the number of those actually destroyed aside), 50 AAA sites, 28 command posts, 11 'FROG' missile launchers, 10 parked fighters, nine surface-to-air missile (SAM) sites, eight fuel tanks and two air-to-air helicopter kills.

Three sorties a day

Combat operations of both wings were very similar. Typical operations from King Fahd involved flying a sortie, landing at the King Khalid Military City (KKMC) FOL to re-arm, flying another sortie back to KKMC, then flying one last sortie to recover back at King Fahd. This resulted in about eight hours of flying time during a 12-hour duty day. However, if the missions involved 'Scud' hunting, the flying time would increase to about 10 hours. Search and rescue strip alert was another A-10A mission at KKMC. Each wing had a squadron designated for night combat. For the 354th, this was the 355th TFS, which developed most of the night tactics used by A-10As during the war. The 'Falcons' flew only about a dozen daytime missions against GCI sites during the first two days of the air war, and then flew exclusively at night for the rest of the war. After the first

two weeks of the air war, the 74th TFS became the dedicated night squadron for the 23rd TFW(P).

A second FOL was operated by the 917th TFW for the 23rd TFW(P) at Al Jouf, in far northern Saudi Arabia. Known as 'Cajun West', 10 aircraft at a time were deployed there for five days before rotating back to King Fahd. Despite very primitive living conditions, the flying there was relatively low threat and target rich. While their primary missions focused on 'Scud' hunting and support of special operations, other targets of opportunity soon presented themselves. These included 'Home Depot' (a massive complex of munition storage bunkers and warehouses just north of the Baghdad-to-Amman highway in south-western Iraq), 'Hicksville' (another munitions storage area, even larger than 'Home Depot', just south of the Euphrates River between Ramadi and the Syrian border, and named after Captain Al 'Gator' Hicks, who discovered it), 'The Villas' (yet another munitions storage area just north of 'Home Depot'), and 'East and West Tac' (named after two bombing ranges at Nellis AFB, Nevada, these were concentrations of armour from the 55th Infantry Brigade guarding a strategic road intersection near the town

Above: Ground troops sweated blood to keep the A-10 sorties generated during Desert Storm. Armourers loaded CBUs, 30-mm ammunition and, as here, Mavericks at a phenomenal rate. A-10 pilots expended them as rapidly, amassing a huge kill tally.

Below: A 'Combat Hogdriver' on the tanker. KC-135s extended the ability to range over much of Iraq.

Warthog nose art

During their time in Saudi Arabia, most of the 144 A-10s picked up nose art. Much of it was applied after the end of the war, along with kill tally scoreboards.

Even the tails of some aircraft received decoration, this being 77-0205 of the 706th TFS, part of the 23rd TFW(P).

Fightin' Irish 80-0157/354th TFW(P)

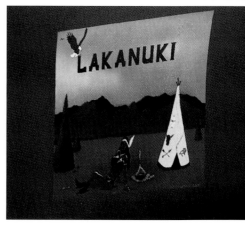

Lakanuki 80-0170/354th TFW(P)

Stephanie Ann/Bayou Babe 76-0531/23rd TFW(P)

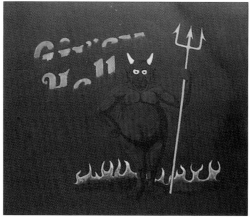

Giv'em Hell 81-0953/354th TFW(P)

Have Sun Will Travel 79-0224/354th TFW(P)

Randi Lauren/Brenda Beth 77-0240/23rd TFW(P)

New Orleans Lady 77-0274/23rd TFW(P)

Poo! 80-0144/354th TFW(P)

of Nukhayb). Early in the war, pilots would hit one of these area targets on their way home from 'Scud' hunting; later, as 'Scuds' became more difficult to find, they would expend most of their bombs on the area targets, reducing weight and drag so they could spend more time hunting for 'Scuds' with their Mavericks. All these targets, combined with Colonel Bob Efferson's leadership style, made tours at Al Jouf a sought-after and rewarding experience.

Both of the A-10A's air-to-air kills during Desert Storm were made using the GAU-8. The first was scored by the 706th TFS 'Cajuns' Captain Bob Swain over what may have been a BO 105 (there really was not much left to identify) on 6 February 1991 in 77-0205, later named 'Chopper Popper' and now displayed at the USAF Armament Museum at Eglin AFB, Florida. The other was by the 511th TFS 'Vultures' Captain Todd 'Shanghai' Sheehy, who shot down an Mi-8 on 15 February 1991 in 81-0964. (On another occasion two 23rd TFW(P) aircraft were the only aircraft available to AWACS to confront an Iraqi 'Flogger'. When

they turned towards the MiG, it used its speed advantage over its opponents and ran.) Unfortunately, also on 15 February when Captain Sheehy scored his kill, two A-10As were shot down by IR SAMs and another badly damaged. As part of the tactical changes implemented the next day to help prevent similar losses, gun use was suspended until 23 February, when the ground war began.

A-10 ordnance

Like the A-1 Skyraider that was its inspiration, the A-10 employs a fascinating and varied array of air-to-ground ordnance. Most of these weapons were used with devastating effect during Operation Desert Storm in early 1991. There are 11 stores pylons on the aircraft, with number one at the left wingtip and number 11 on the right. Stations five, six and seven are on the fuselage, with stations four and eight inboard of the main landing gear sponsons. The other stations are outboard of these sponsons. The pylons on stations 2/10 and 5/7 can be removed in high threat areas to

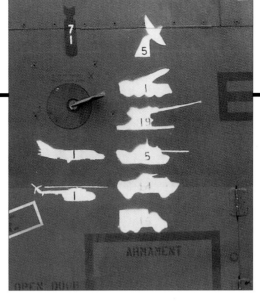

Kill marks were displayed on the starboard side on 23rd aircraft (left), and on the port for 354th (above). The machine above (81-0964) wears a helicopter for an air-to-air kill, and a 'Fitter' silhouette for an Su-22 destroyed on the ground. The other symbols are for radar sites, 'Scuds', artillery pieces, tanks, APCs and other vehicles.

Iraqi Nightmare 77-0266/23rd TFW(P)

Camel Jockey 77-0255/23rd TFW(P)

Holy *~...+! 77-0271/23rd TFW(P)

Desert Rose 77-0273/23rd TFW(P)

Yankee Express 79-0220/354th TFW(P)

Crawfish logo for 706th TFS 77-0260/23rd

Desert Belle 81-0947/354th TFW(P)

improve manoeuvrability. During Desert Storm, this appears to have been done on all aircraft during the early stages of the air campaign. The centreline pylon (station 6) is not loaded for combat operations, and is most often used to mount a 600-US gal (2271-litre) fuel tank (P/N 7540863-10) for ferry operations (the same tank used by the F-111). While two more of these tanks can be carried from stations 4/8, this is not often done.

The primary defensive armament of the A-10 is composed of two AIM-9L/M Sidewinders. These are mounted to LAU-105 or LAU-114 launcher rails mounted on an Air National Guard-developed dual rail adapter (DRA). This assembly is usually mounted on the left outboard wing station (number one), unless there is a wiring problem on that particular aircraft, in which case it can be mounted on the opposing station. A-10s inadvertently fired three AIM-9s during Desert Storm, two by the 23rd TASS and one by the 74th TFS. Also, 23rd TASS 'Nail FACs' were only noted to have carried one AIM-9 during Desert Storm.

Of more practical, if less apparent, importance are the defensive avionics. An ECM pod is mounted on the wing station opposite the AIM-9s (usually number 11). During the time frame of Desert Storm, US-based aircraft normally carried an ALQ-119(V)-15 pods, while Shallow ALQ-131s were carried on overseas-based aircraft. The ALQ-184(V)-1 and Deep ALQ-131 are also authorised, although they do not appear to have been used during the war. In addition to ECM pods, A-10As carry ALE-40 chaff and flare countermeasures dispensers under their wingtips and at the back of the main landing gear sponsons. During Desert Storm, OA/A-10As expended 355,381 bundles of chaff and 108,654 flares in self-defence (an average of over 40 bundles of chaff and 12 flares per sortie).

During Desert Storm, A-10As launched 5,013 AGM-65 Mavericks – 90 per cent of the Air Force total (it is ironic that, following the war, the Air Force immediately moved to replace the Mavericks, while making plans to retire the only aircraft that used them effectively). These missiles are only

Fairchild A-10

Above: A-10s from the 23rd TFW seen soon after their arrival at King Fahd. The ferry tanks are used only for deployment flights, being stressed for too light a load for combat operations. They are the same type as used by the F-111.

Right: Dark green A-10s look somewhat incongruous in the searing light of Saudi Arabia. Among the important missions was 'Scud'-hunting.

Below: During the latter stages of the conflict, the A-10s worked closely with the Army. This 511th TFS aircraft lands at King Khalid past a row of OV-1 Mohawk battlefield surveillance platforms, which occasionally spotted targets for A-10s.

carried on stations 3/9, just outboard of the landing gear sponsons. The primary method of carriage is from single rail LAU-117 launchers, although triple-rail LAU-88s can also be used. When LAU-88s were used during Desert Storm, it was only with slant-loads of two missiles, even though virtually any symmetrical combination was authorised. (Some reliability problems were experienced with LAU-88s, causing them to be used less frequently than they might have been otherwise.) Typically, a mix of $22,000 AGM-65B 'Scene Magnification' electro-optical (EO) and $141,000 AGM-65D imaging infra-red (IIR) missiles were carried (if LAU-88s were used, EO missiles were loaded on one wing, with IIRs on the other). Both missiles were equipped with 125-lb (57-kg) shaped charge warheads, ideal for use against armour. AGM-65Bs were used exclusively for daytime missions, with 1,682 being fired during the war. IIR versions used included 3,128 of the AGM-65Ds, and 203 of the $150,000 AGM-65Gs, which were fitted with 300-lb (136-kg) blast warheads, and used against targets such as GCI and

SAM sites (the latter could only be used from LAU-117). Lacking any night vision equipment, the two night squadrons improvised by using their IIR Mavericks to hunt for targets.

Bomb loads

Gravity bombs of less than 1,000 lb (454 kg) can be parent-loaded on any station except the centreline, but only one type of bomb is carried per mission. Generally though, they are only loaded on stations 5/7, 4/8 and 2/10. During Desert Storm, A-10As delivered 14,184 Mk 82 LDGP 500-lb (227-kg) bombs while flying missions from Fahd and the KKMC FOL. Cluster bomb usage included 2,278 Mk 20 Rockeye IIs, three versions of the SUU-30H dispenser (including 1,852 CBU-52 fragmentation cluster bombs, 2,326 CBU-58, and 278 CBU-71 frag/incendiary cluster mines). Other Mk 82-based weapons include the Mk 82 SE, Mk 82 AIR, Mk 36 Destructor mines, and BDU-50 inert practice bombs.

Above: Refuelling during a training sortie, this Maryland 'Hog' carries an inert Maverick for target acquisition purposes, and practice bombs which imitate the ballistics of a Mk 82. The Maverick imagery is recorded on video, allowing a playback for debriefing purposes.

Left: Two shots as A-10s from Barksdale undertakes a low-level live bomb drop. For work at this altitude an AIR retarded weapon is advisable so that it does not explode right underneath the aircraft.

Triple ejector racks (TERs) have been used with all of the weapons in the previous paragraph. Although cleared for use on stations 3/9, since those are always occupied by Mavericks the only stations TERs are usually carried on with live bombs are 4/8, just inboard of the landing gear sponsons. (Stations 5/7 are also authorised for TERs, but in practice they are only used when BDU-33 practice bombs are being dropped.) While they can carry three bombs, the normal combat load during Desert Storm was two, usually flat-loaded, although a few slant-loads were also seen. Only the 354th TFW(P) used TERs, while the 23rd TFW(P) preferred pylon-mounted weapons.

Current-generation cluster bombs can also be used. During Desert Storm 1,033 CBU-87 combined effects munitions (CEMs), which use the SUU-65 version of the tactical munitions dispenser (TMD), were used from the Al Jouf and KKMC FOLs. The A-10 is also authorised to employ a second TMD weapon, the CBU-89 'Gator' mine, which uses the SUU-64 dispenser. In mid-1993 it was reported that it would also be qualified to deliver loads of four of another TMD weapon, the SUU-65-based CBU-97 sensor fused weapon (SFW). Again, while authorised from Maverick stations, these cluster bombs are normally only parent-mounted to stations 4/8 and 5/7.

Just prior to the Desert Storm ground campaign, 1,976 Mk 84 LDGP 2,000-lb (907-kg) bombs were used to cut lines intended to feed oil-filled trenches the Iraqis planned to use as a defensive measure. This weapon is carried on the

Fairchild A-10A Thunderbolt II
510th Fighter Squadron
52nd Fighter Wing
Spangdahlem AB, Germany
November 1993

Airbrakes
The large hydraulically-powered ailerons bestow an excellent roll rate on the Warthog, but also split above and below the wing to act as airbrakes. These are deployed on landing to reduce the roll, and can also be used to stabilise the aircraft for aiming in a dive.

Once the mainstay of NATO's anti-armour force ranged against the massed tanks of the Warsaw Pact, by late 1993 the A-10 served with only one squadron in Europe, part of a composite wing alongside 'Wild Weasel' F-4s and F-16s. In 1994 its most likely combat scenario was not in a high-tech tank battle on Europe's Central Front, but in the hills and forests of former Yugoslavia, rooting out isolated artillery positions. Like other A-10 units, the 510th Fighter Squadron also had OA-10As on strength, and would use these in a fast-FAC role in support of the regular A-10s and attack aircraft from other units. The regular A-10As would be used in a traditional anti-armour role, as ResCAP aircraft to cover combat rescue attempts and on non-fragged close air support missions. The latter is the modern version of the old 'cab-rank' tactic, heavily armed A-10s loitering in or near the battle area waiting for ground commanders to call on their talents.

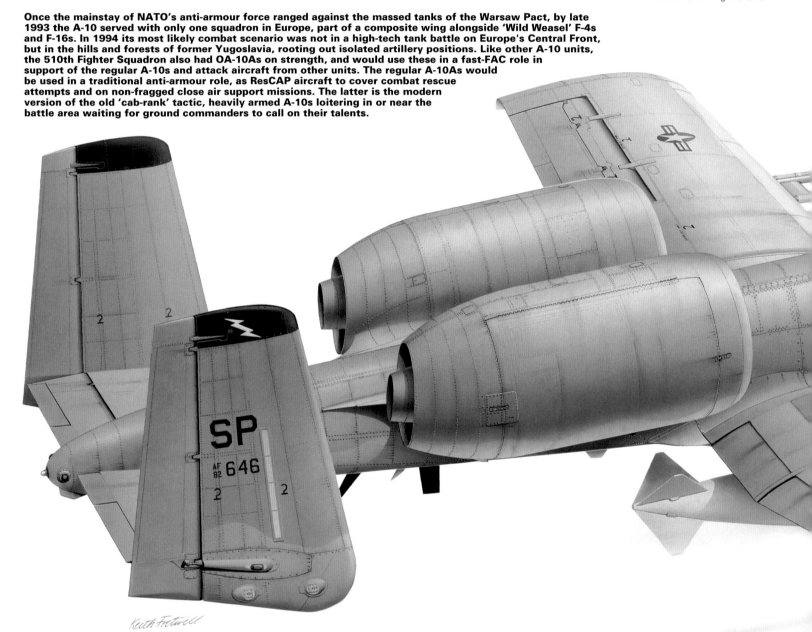

Keith Fretwell

Lights
The A-10 has standard daytime formation lights on the extreme tailcone, lower fins, wingtips, spine and belly. The LASTE mod adds LVF 'slime' lights to the wingtips, fin, and spine (just aft of the cockpit). Floodlights are incorporated in the inner face of the outer pylons to light the nose area for night refuelling.

Fuel tanks and protection
Positioned in the shape of a cross, close to the A-10's centre of mass, the main fuel tanks provide an internal fuel capacity of some 1,650 US gal (7958 litres). This generous fuel allowance, combined with the relatively low-burn nature of the General Electric TF34-GE-100 turbofans, bestows the aircraft with a combat endurance far exceeding that of contemporary close-air support types. At distances of over 100 miles (161 km) from base, with a standard weapons load, the A-10 can remain over the battlefield for well over an hour. For protection from groundfire the A-10A's fuel tanks are tear-resistant and self-sealing and are protected by a twin layer of reinforced fire-retardant foam and reticulated flexible foam. In addition, armour plating, capable of stopping a 23-mm cannon round, is positioned below the fuel tanks.

Markings

After having spent most of its career in a 'Charcoal Lizard' scheme to foil interception from aircraft above, the A-10s began reverting to a grey scheme to protect against surface threats. There are two shades of grey, and the scheme is known as 'Compass Ghost'. All other markings are in black, and consist of 'SP' tailcode for the 52nd Wing, serial number, stencilling, national insignia and squadron fin-tip markings for the 510th FS 'Buzzards'.

LASTE

A major improvement to the A-10, the Low Altitude Safety and Target Enhancement programme added an autopilot to the A-10, among other improvements. These include a radar altimeter and a continually-computed impact point for high accuracy in bombing and gun aiming, NVG-compatible cockpit and night formation lights.

Pave Penny

On the pylon under the starboard side of the nose is the AAS-35 Pave Penny laser seeker. This is a marked target seeker, which spots targets that have been designated by other sources (usually ground or heliborne FACs). Aiming cues are then provided on the HUD.

Ammunition

Three types of ammunition are provided for the GAU-8/A. The PGU-13/B is an HEI (high explosive, incendiary) round, and is mostly suitable against soft targets and non- or lightly-armoured vehicles. It has a jacket of naturally fragmenting material and standard explosive filling. The PGU-14/B is the API (armour piercing, incendiary) round, and is of greatest effect against armour. A lightweight aluminium body surrounds a depleted uranium core which penetrates through armour. Although radioactivity is minimal, the uranium is nevertheless incendiary, and creates heat once inside the tank shell. Finally the PGU-15/B is a TP (training practice) round, and has no explosive filling. It matches the ballistics of the HEI round for aerial marksmanship. For normal combat sorties, the HEI and API are carried in a ratio of 1:5, or Combat Mix. The rounds are fed from the drum on to a continuous belt, and taken to the gun. Spent cartridge cases or unfired rounds are returned via the belt to the drum.

GAU-8/A Avenger

The massive Avenger is a seven-barrelled rotary cannon driven by two hydraulic motors. It is spun up to its full firing rate of 4200 rounds per minute in 0.55 seconds, and has a maximum capacity of 1,350 rounds of 30-mm ammunition on a linkless feed system. The ammunition is held in a drum that is 1.85 m (6 ft 1 in) long and 0.85 m (2 ft 9 in) in diameter. The feed system weighs in at 1548 kg (3,412 lb) when loaded, to which can be added 281 kg (620 lb) for the gun itself. The gun and feed system is over 4 m long, of which 2.30 m (7 ft 6i n) is barrel.

ECM pod

The AN/ALQ-131 is the standard ECM pod for USAFE tactical aircraft, and is carried by the A-10 on one of the outboard pylons. The pod is a modular system, allowing it to be adapted to various scenarios. Each module can slot into the pod structure without complete dissembly. A digibus connects the various modules, which are controlled by a digital computer. Cooling is provided by a self-contained freon/ram air system, which has no moving parts and requires no power.

Maverick missile

Although the gun is the most powerful such weapon ever fitted to a tactical aircraft, it is the Maverick that is the weapon of choice for the anti-armour mission to which the A-10 is so well adapted. The missile is 2.49 m (8ft 2in) long, and has a wing span of 0.72 m (2ft 4in). Two versions are in general use on the A-10 for anti-armour work, the AGM-65B with TV scene magnification seeker, and the AGM-65D with an imaging infra-red seeker. The former has a launch weight of 210 kg (463 lb) and the latter weighs 220 kg (485 lb). Both of these versions have a 57-kg (125-lb) shaped-charge high explosive warhead, which penetrates armour easily. One further Maverick variant is used by the A-10 – the AGM-65G. This is an IIR weapon with revised seeker so that the pilot can designate a specific point within a larger heat source. It is used principally against radar or SAM sites, and incorporates a 136-kg (300-lb) blast penetration warhead. To launch a Maverick, the pilot must climb to get a good view of the target, select a missile and then use the image supplied by the seeker head to acquire and designate. The image is presented on a screen in the cockpit. Once the target is designated, using cross-hairs on the screen, the missile can be launched. It holds the designated image in its own memory, guiding itself to impact and allowing the launch aircraft to escape immediately.

81st TFW inactivation process

Inactivation of the 81st TFW was announced in late May 1991. Indicative of how quickly events had overtaken the best laid of Cold War plans, the announcement was made at the opening ceremonies of the wing's brand new community centre. It, along with several other major new buildings and nearly 300 new houses, had been started as part of a much-needed facelift for a facility that would be needed indefinitely. Less than two years from the closure announcement, the last A-10As left RAF Bentwaters, and what had been the largest wing in the US Air Force only a couple of years earlier had ceased to exist. The 81st TFW did not go out with a whimper, however. It supported operational missions until less than four months before the final transfers took place; on 17 December 1992, it simultaneously put 20 A-10As

into the air for the final time in what was called 'Hog Joust 92'.

'Harvesting' a major flying operation is a complex task, especially when the unit is still supporting operational missions and upgrading aircraft. The process can be a confusing one; while each of these increasingly common inactivations is unique, most involve retiring some aircraft and transferring the rest to other units. Flying time must be carefully controlled so that gaining units do not receive a group of aircraft requiring major maintenance inspections at the same time. The need to transfer aircraft of similar ages leads to the need to rearrange the wing's aircraft assignment among its squadrons, since old and new aircraft are normally mixed so all the new ones do not belong to one squadron. A look at what happened with the 81st TFW makes similar events

One of the first aircraft to be repainted grey, 81-0964 took part in Provide Comfort. It is one of the few Bentwaters 'Hogs' to remain in Europe with the 52nd Fighter Wing at Spangdahlem.

easier to understand.

On 5 February 1992, the 81st TFW reassigned its aircraft so that squadron inactivations and aircraft transfers would mesh. Aircraft designated to undergo the LASTE modification process had been selected sometime before, and that modification programme was half-completed when the realignment took place. All aircraft sent to the 52nd FW not destined to be aircraft battle damage repair (ABDR) training aircraft were modified at RAF Bentwaters.

As the time to transfer an aircraft

approached, it was placed in 'transfer dock' where all necessary inspections were accomplished. Transfers to the US happened when groups of about six aircraft had gone through this process. All transfers were planned to avoid transatlantic flights during the winter, partly because of the generally inclement weather at that time of year but especially because of the strong headwinds. A-10As do not fly very fast in the best of weather, and none of the aircraft transferring had autopilots (aircraft not going to AMARC were to be modified with LASTE in the US). A long-planned February participation in an 'Air Warrior' exercise at Nellis AFB, Nevada, resulted in the first eight aircraft transferring about a month early. The final transatlantic transfer occurred in November 1992, with the final deliveries to Spangdahlem AB, Germany, beginning on 12 January and finishing on 23 March 1993.

No attempt was made to repaint aircraft with their new squadron colours; if an aircraft remained in the squadron it belonged to prior to 5 February, it retained its colours. However, if it changed units, the old colours were usually painted over with camouflage 'touch up' paint. The wing commander's aircraft was changed from 80-181 to 82-655 when the former went into transfer dock in June 1992. Based on lessons learned during Desert Storm, all aircraft used in Operation Provide Comfort were repainted in a new grey scheme during the late summer of 1992. It was later decided to repaint all aircraft being transferred to Spangdahlem, which were also the aircraft which had been LASTE-modified. The last aircraft to be painted was the commander's 'flagship', in late January 1993.

Right: Mavericks are easily transported in crates, ready for immediate use with the minimum of attention. Note the tiger's teeth on this 23rd TFW aircraft's ECM pod.

Below: Jinking violently, an A-10 releases a flare as it escapes from the target area. The use of flares and chaff is mandatory in most combat scenarios when an aircraft operates close to enemy defences.

same stations used by TMDs.

The two night squadrons, the 74th and 355th TFSs, were the exclusive users of SUU-25 dispensers during Desert Storm. Noted with unusual hemispherical nose caps, these dispensers were used to drop 5,488 flares and target markers, with eight loaded in each of these modified LAU-10 rocket pods. Allowable flares include Mk 24 or LUU-2 (which burn at 2 million candlepower for three and five minutes respectively), and the MJU-3 (modified LUU-2) IRCM flare. Target markers are the LUU-1 (red), LUU-5 (green), or LUU-6 (fuchsia). They differ from flares in that they burn for 30 minutes at 1,000 candlepower. SUU-25s are parent-mounted from stations 2/10, although they are also authorised on the Maverick stations.

Target marking

White phosphorous (WP), or 'Willy Pete', 2.75-in rockets were primarily used by the 23rd TASS OA-10As during Desert Storm, which used 2,748 for target marking. While official records indicate the OA-10As carried no other weapons (save their GAU-8 and AIM-9L/Ms), photographs from the war show them also carrying Mk 82s. An additional 138 rockets were used just prior to the beginning of the ground war during unsuccessful attempts by the 353rd TFS to ignite the oil already in Iraqi defensive trenches. The rocket configuration was M156 warheads mounted on Mk 66 wrap-around fin aircraft rockets (WAFARs). They were carried in either LAU-68 or similar LAU-131 seven-tube pods. Although TER carriage was authorised, primary carriage was to parent-mount the pods from stations 2/10, 3/9 and 4/8.

Records from Desert Storm show an unexplained entry, labelled '69', which may have been an additional FOL or an operation unrelated to OA/A-10As. The only munitions

81st TFW Warthogs in happier days. The wing flew F-84s, F-101s and F-4s prior to A-10s.

Aircraft	Before Feb 92	After Feb 92	Transferred	New Unit
76-514	510 TFS	510 TFS	23 Nov 92	AMARC
76-522	78 TFS	510 TFS	23 Nov 92	AMARC
76-550	91 TFS	510 TFS	9 Nov 92	52 FW ABDR
76-553	92 TFS	510 TFS	14 Sep 92	52 FW ABDR
79-217	78 TFS	510 TFS	23 Nov 92	AMARC
79-218	92 TFS	510 TFS	23 Nov 92	AMARC
79-221	510 TFS	510 TFS	23 Nov 92	AMARC
79-225	91 TFS	510 TFS	30 Oct 92	355 FW
80-143	78 TFS	78 TFS	28 Apr 92	355 FW
80-145	92 TFS	78 TFS	25 May 92	355 FW
80-147	510 TFS	78 TFS	24 Feb 92	602 ACW
80-155	510 TFS	510 TFS	20 Sep 92	355 FW
80-158	91 TFS	91 TFS	1 Aug 92	442 TFW
80-159	92 TFS	78 TFS	25 Sep 92	355 FW
80-160	510 TFS	510 TFS	30 Oct 92	355 FW
80-167	78 TFS	78 TFS	24 Feb 92	602 ACW
80-168	92 TFS	78 TFS	25 Sep 92	355 FW
80-169	510 TFS	78 TFS	24 Feb 92	355 FW
80-171	91 TFS	91 TFS	23 Jul 92	442 TFW
80-179	78 TFS	78 TFS	24 Feb 92	355 FW
80-180	91 TFS	91 TFS	8 Sep 92	442 TFW
80-181	92 TFS	91 TFS	23 Jul 92	442 TFW
80-192	92 TFS	91 TFS	15 Aug 92	442 TFW
80-195	510 TFS	510 TFS	30 Oct 92	355 FW
80-203	78 TFS	78 TFS	28 Apr 92	355 FW
80-204	91 TFS	91 TFS	25 May 92	355 FW
80-205	91 TFS	91 TFS	13 Sep 92	442 TFW
80-206	78 TFS	78 TFS	24 Feb 92	602 ACW
80-207	92 TFS	78 TFS	24 Feb 92	355 FW
80-215	510 TFS	91 TFS	22 Jul 92	442 TFW
80-216	510 TFS	510 TFS	10 Sep 92	355 FW
80-217	92 TFS	91 TFS	15 Aug 92	442 TFW
80-220	91 TFS	91 TFS	14 Sep 92	355 FW
80-228	510 TFS	91 TFS	15 Aug 92	442 TFW
80-233	78 TFS	78 TFS	28 Apr 92	355 FW
80-234	91 TFS	91 TFS	25 May 92	355 FW
80-235	78 TFS	78 TFS	24 Feb 92	355 FW
80-236	78 TFS	78 TFS	28 Apr 92	355 FW
80-270	78 TFS	78 TFS	28 Apr 92	355 FW

Aircraft	Before Feb 92	After Feb 92	Transferred	New Unit	Aircraft	Before Feb 92	After Feb 92	Transferred	New Unit
80-271	91 TFS	91 TFS	21 Nov 92	355 FW	81-988	510 TFS	510 TFS	13 Jan 93	52 FW
80-272	92 TFS	91 TFS	1 Aug 92	442 TFW	81-991	91 TFS	92 TFS	21 Dec 93	52 FW
80-274	510 TFS	91 TFS	1 Aug 92	442 TFW	81-992 *	92 TFS	92 TFS	19 Feb 93	52 FW
80-276	92 TFS	91 TFS	1 Aug 92	442 TFW	82-646 *	510 TFS	510 TFS	9 Oct 92	52 FW
80-278	78 TFS	78 TFS	26 Sep 92	355 FW	82-649 *	91 TFS	510 TFS	29 Jan 93	52 FW
80-279	510 TFS	91 TFS	22 Jul 92	442 TFW	82-650	510 TFS	510 TFS	13 Jan 92	52 FW
80-280	91 TFS	91 TFS	28 Apr 92	355 FW	82-654 *	78 TFS	92 TFS	1 Mar 93	52 FW
80-281	92 TFS	78 TFS	25 May 92	355 FW	82-655 *	91 TFS	92 TFS	23 Mar 93	52 FW
81-941	78 TFS	78 TFS	24 Feb 92	602 ACW	82-656	92 TFS	92 TFS	21 Dec 93	52 FW
81-942	91 TFS	91 TFS	30 Oct 92	355 FW	82-658	78 TFS	92 TFS	19 Feb 93	52 FW
81-943	92 TFS	78 TFS	25 May 92	355 FW					
81-944	510 TFS	91 TFS	15 Aug 92	442 TFW					
81-950	78 TFS	78 TFS	25 May 92	355 FW	(*If asterisked, LASTE modification occurred before the realignment.)				
81-951	91 TFS	92 TFS	10 Feb 93	52 FW					
81-952 *	510 TFS	510 TFS	5 Mar 93	52 FW					
81-954 *	92 TFS	92 TFS	13 Jan 93	52 FW					
81-956	91 TFS	92 TFS	29 Jan 93	52 FW					
81-960 *	78 TFS	92 TFS	12 Mar 93	52 FW					
81-961	92 TFS	92 TFS	5 Mar 93	52 FW					
81-962 *	91 TFS	92 TFS	18 Feb 93	52 FW					
81-963	92 TFS	92 TFS	22 Jan 93	52 FW					
81-965	510 TFS	510 TFS	19 Mar 93	52 FW					
81-966 *	510 TFS	510 TFS	10 Feb 93	52 FW					
81-976	91 TFS	92 TFS	13 Jan 93	52 FW					
81-977 *	92 TFS	92 TFS	18 Feb 93	52 FW					
81-978	78 TFS	92 TFS	1 Mar 93	52 FW					
81-980	510 TFS	510 TFS	9 Oct 92	52 FW					
81-982 *	78 TFS	92 TFS	23 Mar 93	52 FW					
81-983 *	91 TFS	92 TFS	22 Jan 93	52 FW					
81-984 *	78 TFS	92 TFS	12 Mar 93	52 FW					
81-985	92 TFS	92 TFS	19 Mar 93	52 FW					

Above: 80-0147 lands at Nellis during an exercise. It stayed in the US afterwards, with the 602nd ACW.

Below: 76-0550 is one of two ex-81st aircraft used for battle damage repair training at Spangdahlem.

loaded at '69' were 3,071 Mk 82s, 653 Mk 84s, 298 CBU-58, 713 CBU-87, 87 CBU-89 and 6,959 bundles of chaff (these numbers are omitted in the previously mentioned totals). Significantly, no 30-mm ammunition, Mavericks or flares were loaded at this location.

Other weapons certified for carriage, but seldom, if ever, seen on operational aircraft include all versions of the GBU-10 and GBU-12 laser-guided bombs (LGBs) based on the Mk 84 and Mk 82 warheads (and carried on the same stations), BLU-52 tear gas bombs (all stations but 1/6/11), CTU-2 resupply containers (stations 3/9), BL755 cluster bombs (all stations but 6), and M117 LDGPs (all stations but 6). MXU-648 travel pods can be carried on stations 3/9, 4/8 and the centreline.

Although it was qualified on the A-10 (stations 3/9 and 4/8), the GBU-8 electro-optical guided bomb (EOGB) was never used operationally. Also, despite numerous publicity photos showing the aeroplane carrying 'everything but the kitchen sink', the need for maximum manoeuvrability over the battlefield resulted in much more modest combat loads. For the Central European scenario, tactics were to attack armoured column defensive vehicles with AGM-65 Mavericks, then to attack the offensive vehicles with bombs and the massive GAU-8/A 'Avenger' cannon.

LASTE

In the late 1980s the low-altitude safety and targeting enhancement (LASTE) programme was initiated to install several high-technology improvements into the rather basic A-10 avionics suite. The first addition was a radar altimeter (coupled with a voice warning system) to improve the pilot's situational awareness at low altitude. If the pilot descended beneath a preselected altitude or at too steep an angle to recover, the system would warn him in time to avoid hitting

the ground,. The second major change was the installation of the same weapons delivery computer used by the F-16. Even though the 'Warthog' lacks the radar ranging of the F-16, the computer dramatically improved bombing accuracy. In addition to displaying a continuously computed impact point (CCIP) bombing solution on the head-up display (HUD), it also provided a projection of the bullet trajectory to the A-10 pilots for the first time. Competing against other fighters with the help of these improvements for the

A pair of LASTE-equipped A-10s from the evaluation unit, the 57th Fighter Wing. Grumman has taken over as the product support contractor for the A-10 in its final years.

Fairchild A-10

Above: Following the end of the Gulf War, A-10s were sent from Bentwaters to Incirlik in Turkey to take their place on the Provide Comfort detachment protecting the Kurds in northern Iraq. Operations mostly consisted of armed reconnaissance and attack cover for helicopters and transports.

Right: The new-look A-10 sports the light grey camouflage it was born with. With the addition of LASTE and much experience behind it, it is now a far more effective warplane.

first time in the 1991 Gunsmoke bombing competition, the 'Warthogs' of the 175th Tactical Fighter Group (ANG) from Baltimore, Maryland, won the semi-annual contest. Although the victory was extremely satisfying for all 'Hog' drivers, it garnered only grudging recognition from Air Force officials.

LASTE added more than the two improvements from which it got its name; the 'Hog' finally got an autopilot. For the first time ever, the 'call of nature' ceased to be an emergency procedure in the A-10, and pilots were no longer required to hand-fly the airplane all of the time. In addition to making 'necessary chores' easier, this would also allow an OA-10A FAC to take his hands off the controls for a few moments to jot down vital notes for his nine-line briefs while directing CAS operations.

In recognition of the growing importance of night combat, LASTE also installed vastly improved cockpit

lighting that made the A-10 compatible with night-vision goggles (NVGs). Finally, to improve the safety of flying formation at night, strip lighting was added which, along with some 'warts' on the tail, provides the only external evidence of the modification. Fleet modification to the LASTE standard did not begin in earnest until mid-1991, after Desert Storm. While most of the LASTE modifications were installed at the SM-ALC, some aircraft were modified by 'speed lines' set up at overseas bases.

Into the Balkans

In July 1993 the deteriorating situation in Bosnia led to the deployment of 12 A/OA-10As from the 510th Fighter Squadron of the 52nd Fighter Wing, based at Spangdahlem, Germany, to Aviano in northern Italy. Operation Deny Flight had begun in April under UN Protection Force (UNPROFOR) leadership, establishing a 'No-Fly Zone' over the republic in an attempt to contain the fighting. On the ground, however, UN peacekeeping forces and aid convoys were coming under regular attack and, by the end of July 1993, some 100 attack aircraft from four NATO nations were conducting fully-armed missions. Their task was to provide close air support against any Bosnian, Serb or Croat aggression. Armed with LAU-97 target-marking rockets, Spangdahlem's OA-10As were particularly active searching for aggressive Serbian forces, however, active engagement of ground units would not commence until the following year.

Opposite page: 'Slime' lights glowing, a pair of A-10s flies into the sunset. Once considered as totally obsolete, the change in world conflicts has ensured a limited place for the Warthog for some years yet.

Right: Defence against groundfire was the driving concern for putting the 'Hogs' back into grey, although the false cockpit is intended to deceive opposing fighters. Proven against helicopters, just quite how the A-10 would fare in air-to-air combat has never been put to the test in combat.

Fairchild A-10

Above: The drawdown of the A-10 fleet in the early 1990s saw many examples retired to the AMARC facility at Davis Monthan. The surviving 390 examples remained in active duty, ANG and Air Force Reserve service throughout the remainder of the decade. Despite limited upgrades, the AGM-65 (as carried here) remains the type's principle stand-off weapon.

The sole remaining USAFE OA/A-10A unit was called on time and again for operations over Bosnia and Kosovo in the 1990s. Operation Allied Force in 1999 saw the 81st Fighter Squadron initially deploy to Aviano AB, Italy, where combat operations commenced in early April. Wearing the squadron's Panther emblem on the cowling, one of the 81st's A-10s (above right) departs Aviano on 5 April for a strike mission against Serbian armour. Initial operations from Aviano required significant tanker support due to the transit distance to the conflict zone, as demonstrated by this pair of 81st FS A-10s departing the tanker en-route to Kosovo (far right). With Serbian ground units well hidden during the hours of daylight, dawn and dusk operations were regularly mounted in an attempt to catch the enemy in the field (right).

Deliberate Force

Throughout the winter of 1994-95 NATO aircraft continued to patrol Bosnian airspace. The hard-pressed USAFE A-10s had been relieved by Air National Guard units, including the 118th FS and the 172nd Fighter Squadron, from August 1994 and it was these aircraft that were to participate in Combat SAR operations during strikes against Udbina airfield and Serbian SAM sites throughout Bosnia. If a NATO aircraft was downed the A-10s were tasked with preventing enemy forces reaching the aircrew, using its powerful 30-mm cannon and AGM-65 missiles. These limited operations continued until August 1995, when a Serbian mortar attack on a market in Sarajevo prompted the UN to finally let the NATO air forces off the leash in Operation Deliberate Force.

At the commencement of the operation the A-10 unit in place at Aviano was the 131st FS, 104th FG of the

Massachusetts ANG. On 29 August offensive action began, with firstly radar and SAM sites targeted using USAF SEAD aircraft. Once the airspace had been 'sanitised', strike packages containing aircraft from many NATO air arms pounded ammunition dumps, command bunkers and troop barracks throughout the country, with operations centring on targets around Sarajevo. Expecting a response from the Bosnian-Serb army, a close air support (CAS) presence was constantly maintained over the city, the bulk of the daytime operations being conducted by pairs of A-10s. Under instructions from UN forward air controllers (FACs) in and around the city, the A-10s used AGM-65 Maverick missiles along with their internal cannon to attack Serb artillery, mortar, anti-aircraft artillery and bunker positions. Over the following weeks the OA/A-10A once again proved invaluable over a complicated battlefield, proving its 'low and slow' CAS credentials have no equal in the western world. As the hostilities diminished towards the end of September, the A-10s returned to armed policing sorties and were to remain in theatre until a peace deal was finally brokered. Less than four years later, however, the A-10 was to return to the region as Serbian aggression in Kosovo led to full-scale conflict.

A-10s in Allied Force

In early 1999 President Slobodan Milosevic began a pre-planned action against ethnic Albanians in Kosovo. Amidst worrying claims of genocide and ethnic cleansing, NATO issued an ultimate for Serbian troops and special police to withdraw from the area. In mid-March NATO's patience ran out and a plan to remove the Serbian forces by the use of air power was instigated under the name Operation Allied Force. Air arms from 11 NATO nations conducted the first strikes on 24 March with the aim of disrupting, degrading and, if necessary, eventually destroying Serbia's forces and its facilities. With strikes against fixed targets failing to shift Serbia's position, on 30 March eight OA/A-10As of the 81st Fighter Squadron, based at Spangdahlem, were redeployed to Aviano, Italy, in preparation for strikes against Serbian troops and armour in Kosovo itself. Joined at Aviano by four A-10s from the US-based 23rd Fighter Group, offensive operations began in the first week of April.

Despite being hampered by the weather and strict rules of engagement, the A-10s, working over Kosovo alongside US and Dutch F-16s and RAF Harriers, hit numerous troops and vehicles. As the fighting intensified during the following week and NATO deployments of combat aircraft increased, the A-10 force was re-located to Gioia del Colle, the closest Italian base to Kosovo, and was supplemented by four more aircraft from the 81st FS. Over the following weeks the A-10s, principally carrying Mk 82 bombs, AGM-65 Mavericks and target-marking rockets, flew intensive combat sorties over Kosovo seeking and attacking identified Serbian armour, vehicles and troops. The task was not an easy one. The Serbian army was well dispersed and hidden within both the mountainous terrain and the pockets of towns and villages. With pilots having to seek permission to attack, the quarry could often disappear before engagement permission had been

granted. By mid-May 1999 the Serbian forces were showing no signs of withdrawal and an earlier NATO estimate that some 40 per cent of its fighting capability in Kosovo had been destroyed was proving to be massively over-optimistic. A new method of engaging the enemy on the ground was initiated.

Kosovan 'kill boxes'

Searching for enemy positions among burning and deserted villages and thick forests had proved an extremely difficult mission. To increase the effectiveness of NATO patrols, Kosovo was split into designated 'kill boxes', each one controlled by an airborne forward air controller (AFAC). The OA-10 was used extensively in the AFAC role, identifying and designating targets for other A-10s, F-16s and Harriers to attack. In mid-May counter attacks on the ground by the KLA forced more of the Serbian units into the open during the day, and the A-10s profited accordingly, causing massive damage to the Serbian warfighting capability. Having again proven to be one of the USAF's most valuable assets in a regional conflict, further A-10s arrived in Italy in mid-May in the form of the 104th Expeditionary Operations Group, comprising Air National Guard (ANG) aircraft and pilots from the 104th, 110th and 124th Fighter Wings. The 18 A-10s were based at Trapani-Birgi AB, Italy, and were active over Kosovo until the hostilities ceased in mid-June.

In addition to its regular AFAC and CAS roles during Allied Force, three A-10As were deployed to Taszar AB, Hungary, to act as CSAR support for the co-located US Marine Corps F/A-18D Hornets.

During the 80 days of NATO combat missions the A-10 had once again confounded its critics and proved of more use than many of its much-vaunted hi-tech brethren.

'Warthog' fleet

Despite a reprieve from the the USAF's misguided plans to axe the aircraft from the inventory in the wake of the 1991 Gulf war, the A-10 active fleet still saw a dramatic reduction in numbers. More than 260 A-10As were dispatched to the Aerospace Maintenance and Regeneration

Center (AMARC) at Davis-Monthan AFB. Active service A-10 units were drastically cut, with the remaining 390 aircraft being primarily distributed to Air National Guard and Air Force Reserve units.

By 1994 the majority of the A-10 fleet was approaching the original service life of 8,000 hours. Along with the improvements incorporated under the LASTE programme, a wider-ranging service life extension programme (SLEP) was initiated allowing continued operations until at least 2008.

Deployments to Arabia

Following the end of the 1991 Gulf War, protective no-fly zones were established in the north and south of Iraq to protect the Kurdish and Shia Muslim populations from air attack. A-10s mounted periodical deployments to the region to help enforce the UN-mandated action. In December 1998 A-10s participated in the most serious combat action taken against Iraq before Operation Iraqi Freedom was mounted in 2003. Desert Fox involved precision strike packages of USAF, US Navy and RAF aircraft attacking suspected WMD sites and other important military targets, as access difficulties for UN weapons inspectors proved insurmountable. While B-1Bs, B-52s, F-15Es, F-16s, F-14s, F/A-18s and Tornado GR.Mk 1s pounded their selected targets, A-10s were used to drop leaflets telling sections of the regular Iraqi army that they were not under attack and to remain in position, and distributing others to reassure the civilian population that they would not be targeted. In the end, the four-day operation did little to weaken Saddam Hussein's resolve and would eventually result in the invasion of Iraq five years later. Meanwhile, A-10s continued to play a vital role in Southern Watch operations, with regular, ANG and reserve units taking their turn to deploy to Kuwait.

A trio of 355th Wing Thunderbolt IIs, based at Davis Monthan AFB, formates close to the Barry M. Goldwater range complex south of Tucson, Arizona. As well as the combat-assigned 354th Fighter Squadron, the 355th Wing also incorporates the training element of USAF A-10 operations in the form of the 357th and 358th Fighter Squadrons. Davis Monthan and the nearby range offer an average of 360 clear flying days per year, making it an ideal location for 'Hog' pilots to learn their trade. In addition to its two full squadrons of aircraft, the 355th Wing's training facilities also include two A-10 simulators capable of creating realistic combat scenarios and all manner of in-flight emergencies, and an NVG training classroom equipped with a three-dimensional illuminated terrain board to simulate realistic night-flying images.

Below left: Despite the thawing of the Cold War, the USAF maintains an active duty A-10A squadron in Alaska in the form of the 355th FS 'Fighting Falcons'. As seen on this example the A-10 regularly flies with AIM-9 Sidewinder missiles on the outer wing pylon for self-defence and interception of enemy helicopters.

Below: A fully 'tooled-up' A-10A from the Spangdahlem, Germany-based 81st Fighter Squadron poses for the camera in February 2000. The unit will be among the first to receive the 'Hog Up' upgraded airframes.

Fairchild A-10

Operation Enduring Freedom

Within hours of the terrorist atrocities committed in the US on 11 September 2001 the prime suspect emerged as Osama bin Laden's al-Qaeda network. Four weeks later the US, supported by forces from the UK, launched Operation Enduring Freedom with the aims of smashing the terrorist network, capturing bin Laden and removing the host Taliban regime from power in Afghanistan. The first month of the war involved the destruction of the Taliban's fighting capability and the bombing of suspected ground combatants using both US Navy, USAF and RAF bomber and strike aircraft. In November the first coalition troops entered the country and by the end of December the major objectives of this one sided conflict had been achieved and the Taliban had been removed from power. However, pockets of resistance remained, particularly in the mountainous regions in the south and east of the country.

The mopping-up operation was to prove as dangerous and complex as the early action. In early March 2003 12 A-10s on assignment with the 332nd Air Expeditionary Group were relocated from Al Jaber AB in Kuwait, to Pakistan to begin combat operations. Other A-10s from the 74th Fighter Squadron and the 706th Fighter Squadron were relocated 'in country' at Bagram airfield. From here the aircraft would take part in the heavy fighting associated with Operation Anaconda. With US ground forces facing fierce resistance in the Shah-i-Kot mountain stronghold, A-10s were repeatedly called on to provide close air support to the beleaguered troops. Only a combined force of A-10s, AH-64s and AC-130s prevented the US positions from being overwhelmed. The A-10 once again proved able to destroy enemy forces in close proximity to friendly troops using a combination of Maverick missiles, rockets and its 30-mm cannon.

Throughout the remainder of the year A-10s remained in Afghanistan, searching for and attacking the elusive Taliban and al-Qaeda remnants. In 2004 Afghanistan remained a regular deployment for reserve, ANG and regular A-10 squadrons as the quest to eliminate any remaining terrorist activity and resistance continues.

Back to Iraq

With the main thrust of military action in Afghanistan largely completed, the US and a number of coalition parties turned their attention to Iraq, citing its breach of UN Security Council Resolution 1441 as justification for military action. With diplomacy failing and the UN split regarding the legality of military action, the US and a number of coalition allies, including the UK, began a rapid build-up of forces in the region in late 2002/early 2003. A 17 March 2003 deadline for Iraq to comply with UNSCR 1441 was issued and, following non-compliance, a 48-hour extension granted. With the passing of this final deadline military action commenced on 20 March 2003 with an attempted decapitation strike by a pair of 49th FW F-117As.

A total of around 60 OA/A-10As was in place in the Middle East at the outbreak of Iraqi Freedom. Although only a small percentage of the 863 USAF aircraft (293 of which were fighters) committed to the action, the 'Hog' once again made an impact of greater proportion than its modest numbers. The units deployed as the conflict began were the 75th, 190th, 172nd and 303rd Fighter Squadrons, based at Ahmed Al Jaber, Kuwait, and the 118th Fighter Squadron positioned at Azraq, Jordan. Initially, the main bulk of the OA/A-10 force was committed primarily to destroying the most capable Iraqi ground units, including the elite Republican Guard. The 50 aircraft operating from Kuwait were integrated as a 'super squadron', allowing the maximum amount of airframes to be available to any of the squadron pilots without having to wait for spares, support equipment and ground staff from their own units to become available. As the ground force advanced rapidly through Iraq the amount of close air support taskings rapidly increased and pilots were often called on to fly two or more missions each day.

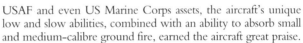

Once again proving to be the 'Army's best friend', a week after combat commenced upwards of 80 per cent of the requests for a specific aircraft type asked for the A-10. Ideally suited to visually identifying and attacking enemy ground forces in a rapidly moving battlefield, the A-10 made extensive use of AGM-65 Maverick missiles, dumb bombs and its GAU-8B cannon to obliterate the opposition. The infrared-guided AGM-65D Maverick did suffer acquisition problems during the heavy sandstorms that disrupted the first 12 days of the advance, but this was more than compensated for by the excellent record of the AGM-65H, using enhanced low-light TV guidance. This weapon regularly found its target at ranges in excess of 15 miles (24 km).

A-10 'Scud hunters'

While the main A-10 force was achieving much publicised success, the 118th Fighter Squadron, operating in secrecy from Jordan, was completing equally valuable missions in the deserts to the west of Baghdad. It was from here that the coalition feared Saddam Hussein may order the launch of Scud missiles at Israel, as had happened in the 1991 conflict. Operating alongside British and US Special Forces, the A-10s not only helped neutralise the 'Scud threat' (although this was less than initially feared), but also interdicted enemy ground forces in the area, helping prevent any counter attack on the flank of the coalition advance.

As the advance gathered pace the Kuwait based OA/A-10s were able to relocate to Tallil air base, near Nasiriya. From here the aircraft flew numerous CAS missions as the advance reached the outskirts of Baghdad. OA-10As were also in continuous use in the forward air control (FAC) role. Flying as a lead element for A-10 attack missions, or working with other

USAF and even US Marine Corps assets, the aircraft's unique low and slow abilities, combined with an ability to absorb small and medium-calibre ground fire, earned the aircraft great praise.

Search and destroy

One of the more important tasks was 'road reconnaissance', involving fastidious searches for hidden Iraqi forces that could threaten the coalition ground forces on their advance to Baghdad. These unbriefed and 'open' missions against an enemy that could well possess portable surface-to-air missiles were among the most hazardous of the war, especially after the ground forces entered Baghdad and the searches were conducted over an urban environment. Unsurprisingly, a number of A-10s were subject to intensive groundfire, yet only one aircraft was shot down in the course of the war – the pilot being rescued by a nearby US Army unit. Three other A-10s were seriously damaged, however, all managed to return to base.

Top and above left: The A-10A's effectiveness in Iraqi Freedom was vastly improved when Tallil Air Base, deep inside Iraq, became available for combat operations. Initially the aircraft used the base for 'hot refuellings', returning to Kuwait in the evening. Later, A-10s were permanently based at the airfield.

Above: Two views show a 75th FS A-10A attacking Iraqi insurgents near Kirkuk in November 2003 with its 30-mm cannon, before releasing defensive flares.

Right: One of a number of A-10As to receive severe battle damage during combat missions over Iraq is loaded onto a shipping cradle for transport back to the US.

Below: The damage to Capt. Kim Campbell's 172nd FS A-10A on 7 April 2003 is readily apparent. The fact that she managed to nurse her crippled aircraft back to base astonished even the A-10's harshest critics.

Above: A pair of 131st FS, 104th FW, A-10As from the Massachusetts Air National Guard is seen on its way to the Gulf for participation in Iraqi Freedom. Both aircraft are equipped with a single large auxiliary fuel tank beneath the fuselage to increase ferry range. Once in theatre, the Kuwait-based A-10 units were incorporated as part of the 332nd Air Expeditionary Wing. With the US still smarting from the 11 September 2001 terrorist attacks the nearest aircraft wears the emotive 'Let's Roll' artwork on the forward fuselage. Other OA/A-10A units already deployed to Kuwait for Iraqi Freedom comprised the 75th, 118th, 172nd, 190th and 303rd Fighter Squadrons.

Above right: The Air Force Reserve Command was represented in Iraqi Freedom by the 'KC Hawgs' belonging to the 303rd Fighter Squadron, 442nd Fighter Wing, normally based at Whiteman AFB, Mo. The unit was in the thick of the fighting from the outset of combat and is seen here forward deployed at Tallil Air Base in April 2003. The A-10 earned great praise for its record during Iraqi Freedom. As one 'Hog' advocate put it: "The A-10s are the only aircraft carrying the weapons necessary to fight the close-in fight. Laser-guided bombs and JDAMs are wonderful weapons, but cannot usually be used on a fast moving battlefield when friendlies are as close as 100 m from the enemy. There is no aircraft that can match the A-10's standard load including 30-mm cannon and Maverick missiles".

Indestructible 'Hog'

The damage sustained to one of these A-10s produced the most publicised fixed-wing hero of the conflict. On 7 April Capt. Kim 'KC' Campbell was part of a two-ship 'road reconnaissance' mission operating over the Baghdad suburbs. Whilst in a hard turn to port her aircraft was hit by a SAM (probably an SA-14 or SA-16). The impact not only took out the starboard engine and port horizontal stabiliser, but also rendered both primary and secondary hydraulic control systems inoperable. As the aircraft rolled to port and descended Capt. Campbell had just seconds to make a decision as to whether to eject or stay with the badly damaged aircraft. Fighting to bring the wings level Campbell managed to nurse the A-10 into a gentle climb and follow the flight leader back to Al Jaber. Without the aid of boosted controls, Campbell performed a safe single-engined landing, using the emergency braking system to bring the aircraft to a halt. On the ground Campbell's reaction to seeing the rear end of her aircraft was "Wow. For the amount of damage this jet took it's amazing it reached home". Capt. Campbell returned to operational missions the following day.

Other missions for the A-10 during Iraqi Freedom included some 32 leaflet dropping missions, using M129 leaflet dispensers, and combat search and rescue (CSAR) escort missions, plus precision strike missions using a small number of A-10s fitted with the Litening targeting pod and laser-guided weapons.

As before the A-10 had stood up to its critics within the Air Force and the Pentagon. The small force flew more sorties than any other type of combat aircraft during the campaign and posted a healthy 85 per cent mission capable rate. Once again USAF officials in Washington, who were considering cancelling proposed A-10 upgrade programmes and scheduling an early retirement for at least a portion of the fleet, were forced to reconsider following the acclaim the type received from both theatre commanders and ground forces.

Following the official end of the conflict the A-10 remained in Iraq, flying missions in the ongoing attempt to quell the growing insurgency that has threatened to destabilise the country.

Upgrades and life-extension

From the end of the 1991 Gulf War the A-10A has periodically been slated for retirement. USAF Generals, enamoured with the faster, high-technology F-16, sought to use the funds allocated to the 'Warthog' fleet to procure more F-16s. However, in times of conflict, the A-10 time and again proved its worth in the close air support role, posting impressive serviceability and survivability figures and claiming more than its fair share of ground 'kills'. The LASTE upgrade programme added much-needed night-attack and modern weapons delivery capabilities, but if the surviving A-10s were to serve well into the 21st Century more comprehensive upgrades were necessary.

Following the LASTE programme, initiated in the early 1990s, from 1999 the A-10 fleet has begun the process of additional systems upgrades, including integration of a sophisticated embedded global positioning system/inertial navigation system (EGI) and a new control display unit (CDU). An upgraded multi-function display replaces the TV screen in the upper right corner of the instrument panel and is designed to provide the pilot with an electronic moving map.

With USAF planners now conceding that the A-10A is a vital part of the inventory, current life projections schedule the aircraft to remain viable until 2028, by which time each surviving airframe will have accumulated between 18,000 and 24,000 hours. To allow this significant life extension a multi-stage improvement programme has been initiated, consisting of two major elements.

'Hog Up' and 'Hog Cupid'

Lasting some eight years, and due for completion in FY2009, the 'Hog Up' programme will extend the available airframe hours to meet the redefined needs. As aircraft pass through regular Programmed Depot Maintenance they are reworked in accordance with the Aircraft Structural Improvement Program (ASIP). During ASIP the outer wings on all 362 examples in the inventory will receive new outer wings, and 240 A-10s will additionally receive new centre wing panels. The programme is split into three phases of which the first of which has already been completed. In Phase 1 A-10s in storage at AMARC provided centre and outer wings. These were then 'zero-houred' ready for fitment to operational aircraft. Phase 2 is the test and evaluation element, conducted by Northrop Gruman and involving stresses being placed on two of the 'zero-hour' wings, simulating the equivalent of 10 years service. Phase 3, which is now underway, involves the strengthening of the centre-sections of the new wings with stainless steel straps before they are fitted to their allocated aircraft at the Ogden ALC facility.

Running concurrently with the 'Hog Up' programme is 'Hog Cupid'. Designed to modernise the aircraft's combat capabilities, 'Hog Cupid' incorporates an upgrade of the LASTE system to include an Integrated Flight Fire and Control Computer (IFFCC) and associated portable mission planning system to support LASTE and the EGI. For added protection, the A-10s are also receiving the Common Missile Warning System (CMWS) and automated chaff and flare dispensing systems. All aircraft are slated to have received the 'Hog Cupid' upgrade by 2005.

Despite a strong affection for their mount, 'Warthog' pilots have always bemoaned the aircraft's lack of available thrust and sedate acceleration and maximum speed. Consideration is currently ongoing to replace the A-10's General Electric TF34-100 turbofan engines with a unit providing more power. General Electric has already put forward its improved TF34-101, providing an additional 400 lb (1.7 kN) of thrust per engine. The application of new engines would provide a significant engineering challenge, as any additional weight would alter the aircraft's centre of mass. Rectification could only come with repositioning the engine nacelle or adding ballast to the aircraft. In addition, extra power would add to the already noticeable 'nose-down' pitch movement when power is rapidly applied. It is certainly possible that if the A-10

Above and left: Weapons training and tactics is taught by the 357th and 358th Fighter Squadrons at Davis Monthan AFB. The aircraft above carries a pair of AGM-65 Maverick training rounds, while left a pair of 357th FS A-10As practices strafing a ground target. Along with the training syllabus at Davis Monthan, frontline A-10 squadrons are regular visitors to Nellis AFB for Red and Green Flag and Air Warrior large-scale exercises.

Below: Despite its impressive combat record the 'Hog' community has always had to operate under the imminent threat of the axe. Recent action in Iraq has given hope that the aircraft will receive the much-needed upgrades to keep the type in the frontline inventory well into the third decade of the century. Here an A-10A rolls to mark a target with simulated M-156 white phosphorus rockets, as part of an aerial demonstration for visiting US civic, business, and industry leaders at RAF Mildenhall in 2003.

is to receive a new powerplant it would be derated to current thrust levels to ensure an almost limitless service life. No final decision on if, or when, an engine upgrade will be implemented has yet been taken.

Precision attack

In 2002 the USAF conducted a series of eight test flights at Davis Monthan AFB, Arizona, using an A-10A equipped with a Northrop Grumman AN/AAQ-28 Litening Extended Range (ER) targeting and navigation pod. This much needed boost to the A-10 programme at last gave the aircraft the capability of designating and delivering laser-guided bombs. The multi-sensor Litening II pod features an advanced FLIR camera, charge-coupled device (CCD) television camera, laser spot tracker/range finder and an infrared marker and laser designator. After the evaluation, the aircraft participated in a successful joint force experiment at Nellis AFB, Nevada, its success determining that the pod was used in limited numbers but with great success in the soon to be launched Operation Iraqi Freedom.

The single squadron equipped in-theatre with the Litening, although lacking the real-time datalink fitted to their US Marine Corps AV-8B brethren, reported that weapon delivery accuracy and ability to engage certain targets was much higher than the rest of the deployed A-10 units. A-10s from the Spangdahlem-based 81st Fighter Squadron were also temporarily equipped with the baseline Litening pod during a six-month deployment to Afghanistan in support of Operation Enduring Freedom in 2003. The ability to self designate targets for precision-guided munitions has added a powerful bow to the A-10's armament and reduced risk over hostile territory, where the risk from groundfire is high.

The integration of Litening II is just one facet of the planned Precision Engagement Upgrade Program. Initial plans call for around 125 active-duty aircraft to be equipped with modern reconnaissance and targeting systems and a range of precision-guided weapons by 2007. In early 2004 the programme had entered the engineering and manufacturing development (EMD) phase with flight testing due to run until the end of 2005. Provided by Lockheed Martin Systems Integration-Owego, the precision engagement modifications will enable all updated aircraft to operate with either the Litening II/AT or Lockheed Martin Sniper XR reconnaissance and targeting pods and deploy a range of laser- and GPS-guided munitions,

including the Boeing Joint Direct Attack Munition (JDAM) and the Lockheed Martin Wind-Corrected Munitions Dispenser (WCMD). Modification to a number of key systems within the aircraft's architecture is required, including an upgraded power system, the incorporation of the 1760 weapons databus and digital stores management system along with the addition of two multifunction displays assisting the pilot with situational awareness.

Future of the 'Hog'

Experiences in Iraqi Freedom demonstrated that the few A-10s fitted with the Enhanced Precision Location Reporting System - Situational Awareness Data Link (EPLRS-SADL) were at a distinct advantage, being able to link with both the US Army and through the NATO Link 16 standard datalink. Advanced datalinking abilities will inevitably form a major part of the upgrade process. Further into the future the A-10 is likely to gain a 'blue force' tracking capability to help prevent instances of friendly fire.

Despite the best efforts of Air Force chiefs to 'kill' the A-10 in the 1990s it now seems highly likely that this pugnacious and versatile warplane will see half a century of frontline service.

Air Combat Command

Air Combat Command, formed on 1 June 1992, operates all of the USAF's bombers and combat-coded fighters, as well as attack, combat rescue and reconnaissance platforms. As well as incorporating the direct-reporting A-10 units of the Air Warfare Center, ACC is also responsible for the US-based active-duty A-10 squadrons and gains responsibility for all A-10 Air National Guard and Air Force Reserve Command units for operational situations. Each active-duty A-10 unit has a complement of around 24 aircraft. Reserve and ANG units have a typical complement of around 18 OA/A-10As.

AIR WARFARE CENTER

Reporting directly to ACC is the US Air Force's Air Warfare Centre (AWC). This includes the 53rd Wing headquartered at Eglin AFB in Florida and the 57th Wing based at Nellis AFB, Nevada.

53RD WING, 53RD TEG

Established in 1995 the 53rd Wing is responsible for the test and evaluation of a wide range of frontline USAF aircraft and is headquartered at Eglin AFB, Florida. The 53rd TEG operates its aircraft from a range of bases across continental USA.

422nd TES 'Green Bats'   Nellis AFB, Nevada   'OT'
The 422nd Test and Evaluation Squadron is tasked with evaluating new weapons systems, exploiting foreign technologies, and conducting operational tests for upgrades and new hardware for five aircraft types: A-10, F-15C/D, F-15E, F-16C/D and HH-60G.

NINTH AIR FORCE (ACTIVE DUTY)

4TH FIGHTER WING, 23RD FG

The 4th Fighter Wing is one of two rapid response aerospace expeditionary wings in the USAF and is headquartered at Seymour Johnson AFB, North Carolina. The 4th Fighter Wing is unusual in having two Operational Groups flying different aircraft at different bases. The 4th OG, based at Seymour Johnson, comprises two training and two frontline F-15E Strike Eagle squadrons. The 23rd FG operates two frontline OA/A-10A squadrons from Pope AFB, North Carolina.

74th FS 'Flying Tigers'   Pope AFB, North Carolina   'FT'
Named in honour of the famous American Volunteer Group 'Flying Tigers', which operated in China during World War II and were eventual incorporated into the USAAF as the 23rd Fighter Group, the 74th Fighter Squadron received its first A-10As in December 1980. The squadron received the Air Force Outstanding Unit Award in 1991 following its distinguished performance in Operation Desert Shield/Storm. After a brief period flying the F-16 in the mid-1990s, the 74th FS transitioned back to the A-10 and was heavily involved in Operation Enduring Freedom missions from Bagram AB in Afghanistan.

57TH WING

The 57th Wing is tasked with providing advanced training to instructor level for the frontline USAF combat types. In addition, the 57th Wing oversees all flying operations from Nellis AFB, including Red and Green Flag and Air Warrior exercises.

USAF Weapons School A-10 Division   Nellis AFB, Nevada   'WA'
On 1 October 1977, the 66th Fighter Weapons Squadron was reactivated to assume responsibility for the A-10 Fighter Weapons Instructor Course (FWIC) at Nellis AFB. Tactical Air Command, as it was then, assigned eight A-10As to the squadron and tasked the unit with preparing 24 fighter weapons instructors annually. The squadron remained responsible for the mission until a reorganisation on 11 May 1981 created the A-10 division, which operates as part of the USAF Weapons School at Nellis today.

Each USAF Weapons School division has its own commander and cadre of instructors. Only the top 2-3 per cent of all USAF pilots are deemed good enough for the Weapons School. The A-10 course comprises 35 missions and some 350 hours of classroom work.

Left: The 422nd A-10As (coded 'OT') spend much of the time testing new equipment or weapons in a simulated combat environment. The unit was heavily involved in the development of the A-10 NVG system and the fielding of the improved AGM-65H Maverick missile.

75th FS 'Sharks'   Pope AFB, North Carolina   'FT'
The 75th Fighter Squadron relinquished its A-7Ds for the A-10A in 1981 while stationed at England AFB, Louisiana. Along with the 74th FS, the 75th FS relocated to its present base at Pope AFB, North Carolina in June 1992. Although not assigned to combat during Operation Desert Storm in 1991, the unit saw combat in the region in 2003, forming a significant part of the OA/A-10A assets operating from Kuwait and inside Iraq during Operation Iraqi Freedom.

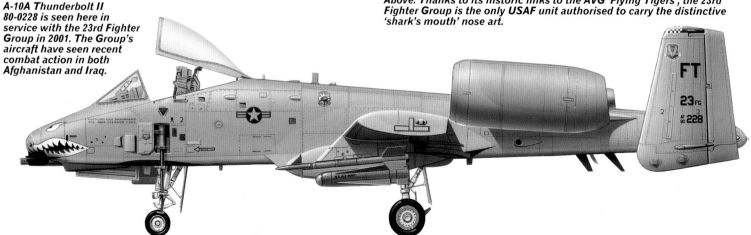

Above: Thanks to its historic links to the AVG 'Flying Tigers', the 23rd Fighter Group is the only USAF unit authorised to carry the distinctive 'shark's mouth' nose art.

A-10A Thunderbolt II 80-0228 is seen here in service with the 23rd Fighter Group in 2001. The Group's aircraft have seen recent combat action in both Afghanistan and Iraq.

NINTH AIR FORCE (GAINED ANG UNITS)

103RD FIGHTER WING, 103RD OG

Based at Bradley ANGB, Connecticut, the 103rd Fighter Wing is a combat ready unit comprising one A-10 squadron and several operational support groups. Under the charge of the Connecticut Air National Guard, the Wing's assets are placed in the hands of ACC's Ninth Air Force at times of operational need.

118th FS 'Flying Yankees'   Bradley IAP/ANGB, Connecticut   'CT'
In May 1979, the 118th Tactical Fighter Squadron became the first Air National Guard unit to convert to the A-10A, having previously flown the F-100D. In doing so, it become the first ANG unit to ever receive new aircraft directly from the manufacturer. The unit saw service from Aviano AB in 1996 in support of the UN-mandated Deny Flight operation. Originally slated to receive the F-16 in the mid-1990s, this plan was cancelled and today the 12 A-10As and six OA-10As continue to serve with the unit. In 2003 the 118th FS was dispatched to Jordan for operations in Iraqi Freedom. Operating over the desert to the west of Baghdad, one of the many tasks was to seek and destroy any Scud missiles threatening Israel.

Above: In November 2003 the 118th FS applied this special scheme to one of its A-10As to celebrate its 80th anniversary.

104TH FIGHTER WING, 104TH OG

Wearing the unit's established red fin stripe adorned with five stars, this 131st FS A-10A is one of 17 of the type currently allocated to the unit.

An important element of the Massachusetts Air National Guard, the 104th Fighter Wing operate both the OA-10A and A-10A in the FAC and CAS roles. The unit are also equipped to conduct night attack operations.

131st FS 'Death Vipers'   Barnes MAP/ANGB, Massachusetts   'MA'
The 'Death Vipers' converted from the F-100D to the A-10A in July 1979 and have been based at Barnes ANGB since that time. As with all ANG A-10 units, the 131st has seen its fair share of overseas deployments, participating in Operation Deny Flight over Bosnia as well as Southern Watch duties in Kuwait. Elements from the squadron have also participated in Iraqi Freedom operations from mid-2003.

110TH FIGHTER WING, 110TH OG

Assigned to the Michigan Air National Guard, the 110th Fighter Wing was established in 1947 at its present base. A relative latecomer to A-10 operations, the 110th FW did not replace its OA-37B aircraft with the 'Warthog' until mid-1991.

172nd FS 'Mad Ducks'   Battle Creek ANGB, Michigan   'BC'
The 172nd Fighter Squadron is currently assigned 17 OA/A-10As and in its 13-year existence has seen a range of combat action. In 1999 the unit was amalgamated into the 104th Expeditionary Operations Group for action in Operation Allied Force over Kosovo. In 2000 the unit conducted an extended tour in support of Southern Watch.

111TH FIGHTER WING, 111TH OG

The 111th Fighter Interceptor Wing came into being in July 1955 having previously operated as the 103rd Bomb Squadron allocated to the Pennsylvania ANG. The Wing moved to its present base at NAS Willow Grove in 1963.

103rd FS 'Black Hogs'   NAS Willow Grove JRB, Pennsylvania   'BC'
Nicknamed the 'Black Hogs' the 103rd Fighter Squadron received its first A-10s in 1988 and completed the conversion process from the OA-37B in 1990. Since that time the unit has been a regular visitor to Al Jaber AB in Kuwait for Operation Southern Watch duties.

175TH WING, 175TH OG

Maryland Air National Guard's 175th Wing is comprised of two flying units; the 104th FS flying the OA/A-10A and the 135th Airlift Squadron, which recently converted to the C-130J. Both units are co-located at Martin State Airport.

104th FS   Martin State Airport/Warfield ANGB, Maryland   'MD'
In October 1980 the 104th Tactical Fighter squadron converted from the A-37B to the A-10A. The unit has won several honours since operating the A-10, including winning the 'Gunsmoke' bombing competition at Nellis AFB in 1991.

Below and bottom: 104th FS A-10As wear the 'MD' tailcodes recognising their assignment to the Maryland Air National Guard.

TWELFTH AIR FORCE

355TH WING, 355TH OG

Located at Davis Monthan AFB, Arizona, the 355th Wing is the unit responsible for training A/OA-10 aircrews for assignment to operational units around the world. The two training units have a higher than usual complement of some 28 aircraft, while the combat-coded 354th FS has a more usual complement of 22 aircraft.

354th FS 'Bulldogs'   Davis-Monthan AFB, Arizona   'DM'
Formed in November 1942, the 354th FS operated the P-47 and P-51 in Europe during the remainder of World War II. After periods in the 1950s and 1960s flying the F-86, F-94 and F-105 the unit reformed in 1971 with the A-7, becoming a training unit for the type until 1993. The squadron is now the sole combat-coded A-10 unit in the 355th Wing and is on alert for rapid deployment anywhere in the world.

357th FS(FTU) 'Dragons'   Davis-Monthan AFB, Arizona   'DM'
Following a distinguished combat history in both World War II and Vietnam, the 'Dragons' spent the majority of the 1970s as an A-7 training unit. In October 1979 the unit began to receive the A-10 and since that time has operated as a training unit for the type. The 357th FS flies an average of 6,000 sorties a year and is capable of training up to 65 pilots, along with further training for prospective A-10 instructors.

358th FS(FTU) 'Lobos'   Davis-Monthan AFB, Arizona   'DM'
Formed during World War II, the 'Lobos' completed tours in both Korea and Vietnam before transitioning to the A-7D. In 1978 the unit received the A-10 and took on the training role, which it continues to this day. The unit was assigned to the newly activated 355th OG in May 1992 and currently flies around 11,000 hours annually.

Davis Monthan can now rightly be regarded as the home of the A-10, with more of the type based here than at any other location. All instructors with the 355th Wing regularly participate in exercises such as Air Warrior and are allocated places at the Fighter weapons School at Nellis AFB to ensure their skills are maintained at the highest level.

TWELFTH AIR FORCE (GAINED ANG UNITS)

124TH WING, 124TH OG

Based at Boise Air Terminal-Gowen Field, Idaho, the 124th Wing is a major component of the Idaho Air National Guard. The Wing was equipped with the F-4 Phantom in the 'wild weasel' role for many years, before the type was retired from Idaho ANG service in 1996. Since that time the wing has operated the A-10s of the 190th FS and C-130Es belonging to the 189th Airlift Squadron.

190th FS   Boise Air Terminal-Gowen Field, Idaho   'ID'
The 190th Fighter Squadron has operated the A-10 for less than a decade but has already seen significant combat action. In 1993 the unit was integrated into the 'super squadron' at Ahmed Al Jaber AB in Kuwait for participation in Operation Iraqi Freedom. The unit flew continuous combat sorties for over two months and were credited with destroying numerous Iraqi tanks, vehicles and surface-to-air missile sites.

Carrying the 190th FS 'ID' tailcodes, a 124th Wing A-10 carrying a Maverick training round beneath the port wing and an ACMI acquisition pod beneath the starboard wing departs Nellis AFB during a Red Flag exercise. The unit was to put this training to good use over Iraq in 2003.

Air Force Reserve Command

TENTH AIR FORCE (GAINED BY ACC)

442ND FIGHTER WING, 442ND OG

Located at Whiteman AFB, Missouri, the 442nd Fighter Wing is one of three Air Force Reserve Command Tenth Air Force A-10 Wings, which are gained by ACC in times of operational need. The unit can call on a over 1,000 personnel.

303rd FS 'KC Hawgs'   Whiteman AFB, Missouri   'KC'
With the squadron name taken from the 'KC' tail code from its time based at Richard-Gebaur AFB, near Kansas City, the 303rd Fighter Squadron began conversion from the C-130E to the A-10A in June 1982. In June 1994 the unit relocated to Whiteman AFB and four years later deployed to Kuwait to provide anti-armour support for Operation Southern Watch. In November 1999 the unit was once again deployed to the Middle East as part of Air Expeditionary Force 1, providing close air support and CSAR cover over southern Iraq. Combat operations were finally conducted in 2002 when the unit deployed to Bagram AB, Afghanistan in support of Operation Enduring Freedom. A year later the 303rd FS was in action during Operation Iraqi Freedom.

917TH WING, 917TH OG

The 917th Wing, based at Barksdale AFB, Louisiana, is a composite wing operating both the OA/A-10A and the B-52H Stratofortresses of the 93rd Bomb Squadron. The 917th Wing had originally formed at Barksdale in 1963 as the 917th Troop Carrier Group equipped with C-124 transports.

47th FS 'Termites'   Barksdale AFB, Louisiana   'BD'
Reactivated as the 47th Tactical Fighter Squadron in 1973, under the 917th Tactical Fighter Group, and equipped with the A-37B, the 'Termites' re-equipped with the A-10 in October 1980. From December 1993 until 1996 the unit participated in Operations Deny Flight and Decisive Edge over Bosnia.

The 303rd Fighter Squadron has seen more recent combat action than any A-10 unit, participating in operations in Afghanistan and Iraq during 2002-03.

926TH FIGHTER WING, 926TH OG

Operating both OA-10A and A-10A variants the NAS New Orleans-based 926th Fighter Wing adopted the type in early 1982. The aircraft carry an 'NO' tail code and red fin flashes.

706th FS 'Cajuns'   NAS New Orleans JRB, Louisiana   'NO'
Having replaced its A-37Bs with new A-10As in 1982, the 706th TFS trained for the typical Cold war scenario before being called to action in 1991 to participate in Operation Desert Storm. Operating as part of the 23rd TFW(P), the unit distinguished itself during its five month deployment. In early 2002 the unit again saw combat action, this time operating from Bagram AB, Afghanistan, during Operation Enduring Freedom.

Air Force Materiel Command

AIR ARMAMENT CENTER

46TH TEST WING, 46TH OG

The Air Armament Center, headquartered at Eglin AFB, Florida., is one of four product centres in Air Force Materiel Command. Serving as the focal point for all Air Force armaments, the centre is responsible for the development, acquisition, testing, deployment and sustainment of all air-delivered weapons. The 46th Test Wing is responsible for the test and evaluation (T&E) of non-nuclear munitions, electronic countermeasures, and navigation/guidance systems for the Air Armament Center. In addition to the A-10, the unit also operates F-16s, F-15s an NC-130A and a UH-1N from its Eglin headquarters.

40th FLTS   Eglin AFB, Florida   'ET'
The 40th FLTS is responsible for operating all the various types allocated to the 46th Test Wing. Normally allocated a single A-10A, the aircraft is periodically significantly modified from the baseline version in support of the test and evaluation duties conducted.

Wearing large 'ET' codes associated with aircraft operated by the 40th FLTS, this A-10 has been modified with an extended instrumentation boom fitted to the nose of the aircraft.

Pacific Air Forces (PACAF)

SEVENTH AIR FORCE

51ST FIGHTER WING, 51ST OG

For the majority of the Cold War the Korean peninsula was an area of great tension with the communist North at loggerheads with US-supported South Korea. Despite the collapse of the USSR, the US maintains a large military presence in South Korea to deter any aggression from the North. The 51st Fighter Wing encompasses two frontline squadrons based at Osan AB. The 25th FS operates 24 OA/A-10As and the 36th FS is equipped with the F-16C/D Block 40.

25th FS 'Assam Dragons'   Osan AB, South Korea   'OS'
The 25th TFS transferred from the 18th TFW at Kadena AB, Okinawa, to the 51st Composite Wing (Tactical) on 1 February 1981. Initially based at Suwon AB the unit received its A-10As from January 1982. In 1990 the unit moved to its present base at Osan AB and from that time has conducted day and night close air support, interdiction, forward air control and CSAR duties.

ELEVENTH AIR FORCE

354TH FIGHTER WING, 354TH OG

While based at Myrtle Beach AFB, SC, the 354th TFW became the first operational A-10 unit when the 353rd TFS began conversion to the type in late 1976. The wing was declared operational in October 1978 when all three squadrons had re-equipped. After participating in Operation Desert Storm the Wing was deactivated in March 1993, before re-emerging at Eielson AFB, Alaska, in August that year. Today the unit operates one A-10 squadron and one F-16C/D squadron (18th FS).

355th FS 'Fighting Falcons'   Eielson AFB, Alaska   'AK'
The 355th FS was the last of the Wing's squadrons to re-equip with the A-10 in 1978 and participated in Operation Desert Storm. Redeploying to Alaska, the unit is currently the only A-10 unit in the Eleventh Air Force and in the late 1990s conducted two operational tours in support of Operations Southern Watch and Desert Fox.

Both types operated by the 354th FW formate for the camera over snow-covered mountains during a sortie from Eielson AFB.

United States Air Forces in Europe (USAFE)

THIRD AIR FORCE

52ND FIGHTER WING, 52ND OG

As the most versatile wing within the USAFE, the 52nd FW operates two squadrons of Block 50 F-16C/Ds (22nd and 23rd FS) and a single squadron of OA/A-10As (81st FS). The Spangdahlem-based Wing is the sole USAF frontline unit now stationed in Germany, and in the 1990s performed numerous deployments in support of operations over Bosnia and Kosovo.

81st FS 'Panthers'   Spangdahlem AB, Germany   'SP'
Now the sole Thunderbolt II unit permanently based in Europe, the 81st Fighter Squadron reformed as an A-10 unit following the withdrawal of the UK-based A-10s in the wake of the 1991 Gulf War. The unit was particularly hardworked during Operation Allied Force in 1999, conducting FAC, CAS and Combat SAR operations over the war torn region. As one of the dwindling number of active duty squadrons, the 81st FS is likely to be among the first units to receive upgraded aircraft following the 'Hog Up' and 'Hog Cupid' programmes.

Harrier II

AV-8B/Night Attack, AV-8B Plus, GR.Mk 5 & GR.Mk 7

Above: The US Marine Corps ultimately accepted 286 AV-8B Harrier IIs into service, between 1982 and 1992. The first production aircraft flew on 19 August 1983, but by then four FSD aircraft had already been delivered to VX-5 for Naval Preliminary Evaluation and Initial Operational Test and Evaluation. On 12 January 1984 VMAT-203 formally accepted the first AV-8B into service. This aircraft is wearing the markings of VMA-223 'Bulldogs' which became the third unit to transition to the Harrier II in 1987, when its A-4M Skyhawks were withdrawn.

Above right: This is the first prototype YAV-8B, converted from the 11th airframe of the pre-production batch of 12 AV-8As. It first flew in its new configuration in 1978 and was later passed to NASA.

The story behind the genesis and deployment of the first-generation Harrier was outlined in *World Air Power Journal* Volume 6 just as the RAF's Harrier GR.Mk 3s were being withdrawn from service, and as the new GR.Mk 5, GR.Mk 7 and AV-8B were working up. These second-generation Harriers have now matured, having overcome early teething troubles, and represent some of the most advanced and effective attack aircraft in service today. At first sight, first- and second-generation Harriers look very similar, but, in fact, the new aircraft enjoys considerably greater capability, flexibility and effectiveness, and has assumed new roles and responsibilities.

The basic RAF Harrier GR.Mk 1 had never been intended to be much more than an interim STOVL fighter-bomber, originating after the cancellation of the supersonic, all-weather P.1154. The aircraft emerged as a timely, slick, glib, clever, compromise combination of the prototype P.1127/Kestrel airframe, with some elements of the cancelled aircraft's nav-attack system. The basic airframe/engine combination was unsophisticated, making the Harrier little more than a VTOL Hunter. Unlike aircraft like the Hunter and A-4 Skyhawk, however, the Harrier's limitations and high vibration levels made it certain that it would have only a relatively short service life, and Hawker Siddeley (later BAe) never stopped looking at more advanced Harriers as potential replacements for the original aircraft. Despite its limitations, the Harrier's unique capabilities made it a useful combat aircraft, and the type won a vital export order from the US Marine Corps. In service, the Harrier was a slightly frustrating enigma, pointing clearly to what might be possible, while being itself too constrained by its limitations. On Europe's Central Front, the Harrier's ability to operate from forward sites made it a useful CAS/BAI tool, and won it the affection of its pilots. Nonetheless, it was never very capable, carrying too small a warload over too short a radius of action. It was often dismissed (sometimes with good humour) as a VTOL Hunter.

UK/US plans for the future

By 1975, the Harrier GR.Mk 1 and the US Marines' AV-8A were looking decidedly tired, their primitive avionics severely limiting operational capability. The addition of a Ferranti LRMTS and a radar warning receiver to produce the GR.Mk 3 was no solution to the underlying

(80 miles; 130 km) short of the A-4's normal radius, but with less than half of the Skyhawk's 4,000-lb (1814-kg) payload. The Skyhawk did require much more of an airfield, however. Comparisons with the lightweight Skyhawk revealed that what was actually needed was a VTOL or STOVL strike fighter with the payload and range of aircraft like the F-105 or A-7, or perhaps even the F-111. The era of fast-jet CAS was coming to an end, and future jet fighter-bombers would need to strike further behind the front line.

The search for a 'Super Harrier'

Hawker Siddeley had examined a plethora of advanced Harrier designs, most notably the P.1184 'Super Harrier' with increased thrust and wing area giving improved payload capability. McDonnell Douglas had explored an advanced Harrier for the US Navy under the designation AV-8C (later reapplied to a simple SLEP-type upgrade to USMC AV-8As). Finally, in 1973, Hawker Siddeley and McDonnell Douglas teamed to examine Harrier derivatives, primarily to meet the US Navy Air Systems Command HIPAAS (High Performance Attack Aircraft System) requirement for a new STOVL or VTOL strike fighter. The aircraft was also intended to fulfil an RAF requirement for a Harrier replacement, a US Marine requirement for a Skyhawk and first-generation Harrier replacement, and to serve aboard the Royal Navy's new through-deck cruisers and the US Navy's projected Sea Control Ships. A Joint Management Board was established in 1972, with co-chairmen, project managers, financial and engine specialists from both countries. A 26-volume, jointly financed, eight-month project definition phase began on 12 April 1973 and was presented to the two governments on 13 December 1973. A Phase I specification was set out in 1974.

problems of lack of sophistication, range and payload capability. In the US, some people claimed that the AV-8A could not carry "a pack of cigarettes the length of a football field." Using STOL techniques, the AV-8A could tote 1,500 lb (681 kg) over a 380-nm (437-mile; 703-km) radius, with a 1,200-ft (365-m) take off run – only 70 nm

Above: The first of four FSD AV-8Bs is seen here outside its St Louis birthplace, where it was rolled out on 16 October 1981. The years leading up to this had been fraught with difficulty for the AV-8B programme as pro- and anti-Harrier factions battled over funding in the US Congress. The Harrier's 'foreign' origins, and somewhat biased criticism of the AV-8A's performance, led to a long drawn out debate as to whether the programme should proceed – despite the fact that the AV-8B under discussion would be far superior to the earlier Harriers. The coming to power of the Reagan administration cleared away many of the funding obstacles as the AV-8B no longer had to compete for cash against other acquisition programmes.

Below: The arrival of the radar-equipped AV-8B Harrier II Plus in 1995 brought with it an even greater transformation than that from AV-8A to AV-8B.

In 1969 McDonnell Douglas had been granted a licence to manufacture the Harrier in the United States when the USMC placed its first order for the aircraft, and in 1971 Pratt & Whitney received a similar licence for production of the Pegasus engine. In fact, the USMC's 112 AV-8As and eight TAV-8As were all built at Kingston (as were the 10 AV-8S and two TAV-8S Matadors delivered to the Spanish navy) and were merely assembled by McDonnell Douglas. Although the option of building Harriers in the US was not exercised, the same agreement had provided for collaboration between Hawker Siddeley and McDonnell Douglas in future V/STOL and Harrier developments.

The aim of the study was to produce a minimum-change, minimum-cost derivative of the Harrier, taking advantage of the new 24,500-lb (108.99-kN) Pegasus 15 engine and a new advanced wing design to produce what became known as the AV-16A Advanced Harrier. The unofficial AV-16A designation was applied to indicate the programme's objectives, which were to develop a Harrier with twice the payload/range capability. Specifically, the partners sought a VTO gross weight of 21,500 lb (9752 kg), or 25,000 lb (11340 kg) with a 320-ft (97-m) deck run, with a VTO payload of 2,000 lb (907 kg) over a 300-nm (345-mile; 555-km) radius, or of 4,000 lb (1814 kg) over the same radius after a short take-off (STO).

The new aircraft was also known as the AV-8X. It would have a wider fuselage to accommodate the new engine, with its increased diameter fan (2¾ in; 7 cm larger), bigger intakes, a raised cockpit, strengthened undercarriage and new avionics. Although the Pegasus engine's huge fan and 'four-poster' nozzle configuration gave it a huge frontal area, factions in the US and the UK continued to press for a supersonic Harrier, although the aircraft's inherently large frontal cross-section made such a development difficult, if not unlikely. A supersonic version, known variously as the AV-16S-6 or P.1185, was drawn up at much the same time as the AV-8X, incorporating Plenum Chamber Burning and relatively minor airframe improvements.

An engine demonstrator using only the fan of the proposed Pegasus 15 had run at 24,900 lb (110.74 kN) in 1972, revealing that increased thrust was quite possible. Similar McDonnell Douglas and Hawker Siddeley wing designs were evaluated and tunnel tested for the new design. Both proved to have superior drag and lift co-efficient characteristics to the original Harrier wing, despite their lower sweep, wider span, extra hardpoints and thicker skins.

UK pull-out leads to AV-8B

The AV-16A was finally halted in 1975, when the British government pulled out of the project, ostensibly because there was insufficient common ground between the USMC, USN and RAF requirements, but also because the Pegasus 15 engine promised to be too expensive to develop, requiring, as it did, a new high-pressure section and an estimated $250 million (or even $500 million) R&D programme. The overall costs of the AV-16A programme

were estimated at $31 billion or more, and this was simply too much for the politicians in both countries to bear. It was a bad time for any advanced military programme, with the oil crisis in full flow, and with a massive need for public expenditure cuts.

McDonnell Douglas continued to work on an advanced Harrier, although it, the AV-8A Plus (later AV-8B), was less ambitious than the AV-16 – to the delight of the US Marines, who wanted the Harrier to be kept simple, serviceable and survivable. The US Navy turned away from

the project altogether, looking instead to the Rockwell XFV-12. Powered by a Pegasus Mk 105 (derived from the Sea Harrier's Mk 104, with a Digital Engine Control System), the new Harrier II combined the raised cockpit of the AV-16 (itself developed from the raised Sea Harrier cockpit) with the McDonnell Douglas-designed, increased-span, increased-area, supercritical wing, of mainly composite construction, albeit with metal tips, leading edges, pylon and outrigger attachment points. It was the largest single airframe component ever manufactured in

Above: The AGM-65 is an important AV-8 weapon and the Marines employ a unique version of the missile – the AGM-65E – to meet their special (close air support) requirements. Unlike previous versions of the Maverick, which relied on TV or imaging infra-red guidance, the AGM-65E has a laser seeker head. Though the AV-8B cannot self-designate a target, it can attack targets designated by Marines on the ground. This allows the Harrier/ Maverick combination to operate very close to the forward line of troops but with a much reduced risk of fratricide. It also gives the Harrier pilot a measure of stand-off distance and even allows him to attack targets he cannot see.

Left: The addition of APG-65 radar should have opened up a whole new range of weapons to the Harrier II Plus. In principle, the aircraft is now capable of carrying a BVR missile, like the AIM-120 AMRAAM, and long-range air-to-surface weapons, like the AGM-84 Harpoon. However, integration of these weapons has proceeded at a very slow pace and none is yet cleared for use on the Harrier II Plus. As a result, the most capable Harriers in the world are still using the old fashioned ordnance of earlier versions, such as the dumb bombs seen here on these VMA-223 aircraft.

epoxy resin composites and promised to be corrosion-proof, fatigue resistant and 400 per cent stronger than an equivalent alloy wing. It demanded new construction techniques, in which laminated sheets were heated to 500°F (260°C) in an autoclave, under 200 psi (1379 kPa) pressure. The new wing was fitted with massive single-slotted positive circulation flaps, which lowered to 61° and added 7,600 lb (3447 kg) to STO lift.

The new wing had a 4° reduction in sweepback but had increased span and a higher thickness/chord ratio, going from 8.5 per cent to 10 per cent. This thicker wing provided increased internal fuel tankage, equivalent to 30 minutes more of on-station time. Portions of the upper wing skin were detachable for servicing, but the whole lower skin was fixed. It was 330 lb (150 kg) lighter than an equivalent metal wing.

Pegasus developments

The new Pegasus engine for the AV-8B was developed from 1980 by Rolls-Royce at Patchway, with assistance from Smiths Industries and Dowty. The DECS was fitted to a GR.Mk 3 (XV277) and successively improved systems and development engines were flown in the aircraft between 11 March 1982 and 1987. Software was refined and fine-tuned to solve the problem of slow throttle response, and the engine was able to reliably provide 100 per cent thrust on take-off (on earlier Pegasus engines there was a tendency for thrust to stagnate at 92 per cent). An important by-product of the DECS was that it allowed engines to be changed without requiring full-power run-ups, making engine changes in the field easier to accomplish. A development Mk 105 Pegasus 11-21 with DECS was ready in time to be installed in the first development Harrier GR.Mk 5, ZD318, which first flew on 23 April 1985.

The need to provide a 'deck alert' capability made McDonnell Douglas determined to improve VTO and hover performance; the company designed a new retractable air dam which helped trap a cushion of air between the gun pods or newly designed ventral strakes. They were closely based on new Lift Improvement Devices

(LIDs) designed by Hawker Siddeley (like the big flaps) but not adopted by the British company during the period in which increased thrust seemed to offer the best way forward. The LIDs trapped a cushion of air below the fuselage, and helped prevent reingestion of recirculated air from the nozzles, adding the equivalent of 1,200 (5.34 kN) of extra lift. The company also reduced aircraft weight, by making extensive use of composites in the wing and forward fuselage.

YAV-8B into the air

Naval Air Systems Command demanded a 'full-scale' wind tunnel model of the new AV-8B wing, and a simple boilerplate replica of the new wing, intakes and flaps (together with an instrumented Pegasus 3) were fitted to the grounded second AV-8A (158385) for tests in NASA's vast 80 x 40-ft (24.4 x 12.2-m) wind tunnel at the Ames Research Center. These tests were successful, and flight-worthy examples of the new wing were fitted to two more AV-8As (158394 and 158395) which became the YAV-8B prototypes. The first made its maiden flight on 9 November 1978, and the second followed on 19 February 1979. The second aircraft was subsequently lost on 15 November, when the pilot ejected following a flame-out. As well as the new wing, the two YAV-8Bs were fitted with the new YF402-RR-404 engine that featured distinctive extended zero-scarf forward nozzles, which were more fully enclosed and which prevented the jet efflux from 'splaying outwards'.

The YAV-8B proved to be much 'draggier' than the original AV-8A, even after modifications to the wingroot fairing, intake cowl, and inboard underwing pylons. This made the aircraft significantly slower, although it did have much better payload/range characteristics. The USMC finally could look forward to a Harrier which could fly more than a '20-minute sortie'. Brief consideration was given to retrofitting the new wing to existing AV-8As, but this option was soon rejected, since it gave an unacceptable increase in tailplane loads. The new LIDs were incorporated in 47 AV-8As, which underwent a SLEP to become AV-8Cs.

The enhanced performance of the YAV-8Bs was sufficient to prompt the US DoD to fund a Full Scale Development batch of four Harrier IIs in FY79. They were powered by F402-RR-404 engines. The F402-RR-404 or Pegasus 11 had a nominal short lift wet (brief take-off/hover rating, with water injection) of 21,500 lb (95.62 kN), or a dry rating of 20,500 lb (91.17 kN). Either is available for only 15 seconds per flight, and in standard operations a normal lift rating of 19,500 lb (86.72 kN) for up to 150 seconds per flight is more significant. In conventional wingborne flight the engine is limited to 16,750 lb (74.49 kN) (for up to 15 minutes), with a maximum continuous rating of 13,500 lb (60.04 kN). McDonnell test pilot Charlie Plummer took the first FSD AV-8B on its initial hover check on 5 November 1981, by which time the British had signed up to buy the aircraft, as described below, so they all had British-built rear fuselages.

Wing and fuselage changes

These aircraft also introduced MDD's entirely new nose and revised, extended centre fuselage. The new forward fuselage was of composite construction, and weighed 25 per cent less than the equivalent section of the AV-8A. The pilot's seat and cockpit floor were raised, giving more internal volume for systems and equipment, while a new rear-view canopy covered the raised cockpit, with a wrap-round windscreen in front. The rear fuselage was extended to compensate for extra weight forward, and the tailplane was redesigned, with an aluminium leading edge and a detachable trailing edge of honeycomb construction.

From the second FSD aircraft, all AV-8Bs were fitted with the smaller '70 per cent' version of the British-designed LERX, although, interestingly, the larger 100 per cent LERX eventually was adopted on later aircraft. Four of the seven pylons were plumbed for the carriage of auxiliary fuel tanks.

Although McDonnell Douglas had pressed on alone to develop the AV-8B, the programme was never given an easy ride in Washington, DC. Its British origins were always a major stumbling block, while the limited payload range characteristics of the AV-8A were dragged up again and again. Throughout the life of the programme, various politicians repeatedly attempted to withhold funds from the AV-8B, usually in favour of further production of the F/A-18 Hornet.

Such opposition was not really justified, as test results started to show. During one early FSD sortie, for example, Charlie Plummer carried seven 500-lb (227-kg) bombs over a range of 422 miles (679 km) after a 700-ft (213-m) take-off run, returning to Patuxent River with 1,800 lb (816 kg) of fuel. He then flew a CAS profile with 12 500-lb

bombs, taking off after a 1,200-ft (365-m) roll and attacking a target 185 miles (298 km) away, returning for a vertical landing with 600 lb (272 kg) of reserves. By comparison with the AV-8A, the new version carried double the payload with much enhanced accuracy.

When the USMC procured its first-generation Harriers it did so on the basis that the aircraft was an 'off-the-shelf item, and while some systems were replaced during service

The Harrier GR.Mk 7 upgrade brought the RAF Harrier force up to the same standard as the USMC's AV-8B (NA)s. These No. 20(R) Sqn aircraft are seen recovering from an attack training mission over Scotland.

Second-generation Harriers

Above: The GR.Mk 7 Harrier is fitted with a GEC-Marconi 1010 FLIR in a new overnose housing. The same system is being fitted to the Tornado as part of the GR.Mk 4 upgrade and to the Jaguar if that part of the GR.Mk 3 upgrade is approved. This aircraft is carrying two AIM-9L Sidewinders and two 500-lb bombs.

Above right: The Canadian-built Bristol CRV-7 rocket system is now replacing the earlier SNEB rockets long associated with British Harriers. This aircraft is firing a full LAU-5003 pod of the 2.75-in rockets, in a 30° dive over the Holbeach range, in Lincolnshire.

Opposite right: This No. 20 (R) Squadron is seen dropping a load of four (inert) 1,000-lb bombs, from 150 ft (45 m), over the Tain range, on Dornoch Firth in northeastern Scotland. These bombs are fitted with the Type No. 117 retarding tail unit, which was specially designed for UK 1,000-lb bombs. It features a 1.9-m (6.23-ft) diameter ribbon parachute and four metal airbrakes which pop out from the tail section. On release, a timer is triggered by a lanyard. The timer deploys the retarding system which is pulled into place by aerodynamic force. The system is linked to the bomb's fuse, ensuring that the weapon only becomes live when correctly deployed – an essential safety measure for low-level operations.

to optimise the aircraft for its USMC role, others had to be retained until the advent of a 'clean piece of paper' in the shape of the Harrier II. They included the aircraft's INAS (the Marines preferring to use TACAN), the use of LOX (instead of an OBOGS) and the need for a laser designator. The USMC was particularly keen to replace the Harrier's twin 30-mm cannon, since they were logistically difficult to support (using ammunition which was unique in the US forces) and were not adequately protected against electromagnetic interference onboard ship. For the AV-8B, McDonnell Douglas replaced the twin ADEN guns with a single GAU-12/A Equalizer 25-mm Gatling gun. The gun was housed in the port cannon pod, with ammunition (300 rounds of linkless Oerlikon KBA) layered in the starboard pod, and supplied to the gun across a 'bridge' which doubled as a lift enhancer. The new gun enjoyed a very rapid rate of fire, being driven by engine bleed air at up to 9,000 rpm and firing 3,600 rpm. The new gun was optimised for strafing ground targets.

AV-8B systems

Unlike the AV-8A and AV-8C, the AV-8B featured almost from the start the Hughes AN/ASB-19(V)-2 Angle Rate Bombing System, proven in the A-4M Skyhawk. It was optimised for dive attack profiles and was linked to the new AN/AYK-14 mission computer and the SU-128/A HUD. The first two FSD aircraft initially flew with 'solid' noses and extended test instrumentation probes, but later aircraft had the distinctive glass nose associated with ARBS.

Inside the cockpit, the AV-8B was a very different aircraft to any of its predecessors. Whereas the original Harrier cockpit had been entirely analog (unkindly described by some as an ergonomic slum), the AV-8B used a cockpit based on that designed for the F/A-18 Hornet, which in the 1980s was regarded as the benchmark modern fighter cockpit with its HOTAS controls and large MFDs.

The Harrier II was made easier to fly in an effort to reduce the high attrition rate. Advances in technology allowed the use of a sophisticated three-axis Sperry Stability Augmentation and Attitude Hold System (SAAHS), linked to a Departure Resistant System (DRS), minimising pilot workload in the hover and during the transition to and from the hover. The SAAHS even allowed hands-off vertical landings to be made, demonstrated by Bill Lowe in February 1983.

A USMC report entitled "Frosty Nozzle" had addressed the EW and secure communications shortcomings of the original AV-8A, and as a result the AV-8C had incorporated a KY-28/TSEC secure voice radio, AN/ALE-39 dispensers, ALR-67 RWR, and provision for the ALQ-126C DECM pod. These systems were used from the start by the AV-8B, which was also planned to use the troubled ASPJ jammer.

The first FSD aircraft was used primarily for the evaluation of general flying characteristics, and the second for engine and intake testing, proving of the fuel system and inflight refuelling. The third FSD aircraft undertook avionics and weapons testing, and subsequently underwent spin testing, while the fourth (closest to the intended production standard) concentrated on the new gun.

A pilot production batch of 12 F402-RR-404A-engined AV-8Bs was ordered in FY82, the first of which flew on 29 August 1983. Like the four FSD aircraft, the pilot production AV-8Bs were originally delivered with a double row of suction relief doors on the intake lips, but they were deleted when the intake was refined to improve airflow. Early aircraft were subsequently retrofitted with the new single row of intake doors. FY83 saw a limited production batch of 21 aircraft, towards a planned total of 328 aircraft, a number that was soon reduced to 286, including the FSD aircraft and three aircraft transferred to Italy. The pilot production aircraft were the last delivered with F402-RR-404A engines, subsequent aircraft (delivered from mid-1985) being powered by the F402-RR-406 (Pegasus 11-21).

The F402-RR-406 cured early surge problems, and gave a longer life, with a hot-end inspection at 500 hours and a TBO of 1,000 hours. The engine had a maximum lift rating of 22,800 lb (101.40 kN), though a combat rating gave a maximum rating of 24,500 lb (108.96 kN) in level flight. The new engine's turbine section ran about 10°-20°F cooler, improving component life.

The Harrier II attained its Naval Preliminary Evaluation in June 1982, opening the way for an Initial Operational

Test and Evaluation (IOT&E) by VX-5. The AV-8B began to enter service in December 1983, initially with VMAT-203, the Harrier training unit, which received the first of the pilot production batch on 12 January 1984. The first of eight front-line ('gun') squadrons, VMA-331, was formally commissioned on 30 January 1985.

Early DACT training showed a tendency to depart if the aircraft was pushed past its brochure limits, and from BuNo. 162081 the SAAHS was refined. Only lingering fuel leak and AN/ARC-182 radio problems prevented the squadron from beating the USMC maintenance requirements of 15.9 MMH/FH, a 1.9 hour mean repair time, and a 75 per cent mission ready rate.

TAV-8B for the Marines

Although the Marines had suffered from a high accident rate during Harrier pilot training before the introduction of the TAV-8A, the service initially decided that it had no need for a dedicated trainer version of the AV-8B. This decision was quickly reversed, but it was still three years between the introduction of the first VMAT-203 AV-8Bs and the induction of the squadron's first TAV-8B. In the interim, trainee Harrier pilots first flew in the all-analog 1960s cockpit, then transitioned to a first solo in the digital cockpit of the AV-8B. Apart from the radical difference in operating environment, the new variant also had dramatically different handling characteristics, justifying design and development of a two-seat Harrier II – the TAV-8B. The first TAV-8B was the 65th Harrier II, and first flew (in the hands of Bill Lowe) on 21 October 1986.

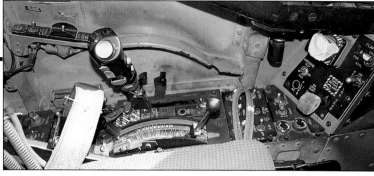

The cockpit of the US Marine Corps' AV-8B Night Attack Harrier (left) is built around the Unisys CP-1429/AYK-14(V) mission computer. The HUD (right) is a Smiths Industries SU-128/A dual combiner HUD, which can display FLIR imagery. The two CRTs are Kaiser IP-1318/A digital display indicators. The right-hand screen can show a digital moving map system – a moving map was never fitted to the Marines' original AV-8As. Allowing for its sophisticated HOTAS controls, the basic Harrier cockpit remains the same. Nozzle position and throttle controls for the F402-RR-408 Pegasus engine are located on the left side panel (above).

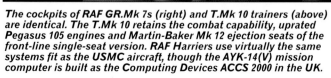

The cockpits of RAF GR.Mk 7s (right) and T.Mk 10 trainers (above) are identical. The T.Mk 10 retains the combat capability, uprated Pegasus 105 engines and Martin-Baker Mk 12 ejection seats of the front-line single-seat version. RAF Harriers use virtually the same systems fit as the USMC aircraft, though the AYK-14(V) mission computer is built as the Computing Devices ACCS 2000 in the UK.

Harrier GR.Mk 7
No.1 (F) Sqn, RAF
(Operation Deliberate Guard)
Gioia del Colle

RAF Harriers served as part of NATO's Operations Deny Flight/Decisive Endeavour/Deliberate Guard (enforcing the 'No-Fly Zone' over Bosnia) from July 1995 until February 1997. When aircraft from No. 1 Sqn deployed to Gioia, in 1996, they became the first to wear unit markings in-theatre. The Bosnian Harrier detachment operated under the RAF codename of Joint Endeavour.

NATO operations in Bosnia

Operation Deny Flight was initiated by NATO AIRSOUTH on 12 April 1993 to enforce the 'No-Fly Zone' over Bosnia-Herzegovina. This followed UN Resolution 816, passed when the threat from Bosnian Serb forces to UNPROFOR troops and the UN declared 'safe havens' became extreme. Serbian provocation led to the Operation Deliberate Force air strikes of August 1995. With the implementation of the Dayton peace agreement, the assets of Deny Flight were transferred to Operation Decisive Endeavour, on 20 December 1995 – in support of IFOR. On 21 December 1996 those forces were transferred to Operation Deliberate Guard, in support of SFOR. At time of writing, 144 aircraft from 11 countries (plus NATO's own E-3s) were still deployed for operations in the region.

RAF airborne designation

Harrier GR.Mk 7s (from No. IV Squadron) dropped 1,000-lb Paveway II laser-guided bombs against Serbian targets in Bosnia, using laser designation provided by RAF Jaguar GR.Mk 1As. The Jaguar can carry the GEC-Marconi TIALD (Thermal Imaging Airborne Laser Designator) pod which uses a combination of FLIR and TV sensors to track a target and a laser designator to guide weapons. It is the only such combined system currently available and is surprisingly compact. The pod weighs 210 kg (463 lb) and is only 2.9 m (9.51 ft long). Harrier GR.Mk 7s have completed fit testing with TIALD, but the system has not yet been integrated with the Harrier.

Harrier ECM

The ARI 23333/1 Zeus electronic countermeasures system is a joint development between GEC-Marconi and Northrop Grumman. It is specific to RAF Harriers and features an integrated radar warning and ECM fit to protect against all known ground and airborne radar threats. Each GR.Mk 7 has four receiver and four transmitter antennas for Zeus, and the system is linked to the onboard chaff/flare dispensers which it activates automatically.

RAF laser-guided bombs

RAF Harriers are only cleared to use the 1,000-lb Paveway II LGB. The British version of this weapon is a joint development between Texas Instruments and Portsmouth Aviation Ltd. In RAF service it is known as the CPU-123/B. The more advanced Paveway III is being integrated with the Tornado and is a future weapons option for the Harrier GR.Mk 7.

BOL chaff dispenser

The BOL 300 dispenser has been developed by Sweden's CelsiusTech to be fitted to standard missile launch rails (such as the US LAU-7 or the UK's CRL) and replace dedicated chaff pods (such as the Phimat previously carried by the Harrier). This frees up valuable hardpoints for weapons carriage. BOL has been adopted by the Harrier and Tornado F.Mk 3. Each BOL launcher can carry 160 chaff 'packets'.

ZD380

28

Above and opposite right: For many years the French-built TDA 68-mm rocket has been a prime RAF Harrier weapon. More popularly known as SNEB rockets, a Harrier can carry four 19-round MATRA 155 'SNEB pods'. This No. 20 Squadron aircraft (above) is firing a full load of rockets over the Salisbury range. The second aircraft, another GR.Mk 7 from the same squadron, gives a clearer view of the empty pods. SNEB rockets can be fitted with a variety of warheads. The 253 ECC rocket relies on a Type 23 HEAT (High-Explosive Anti-Tank) warhead to penetrate up to 400 mm (16 in) of armour. The 256 EAP rocket has a Type 26P high-explosive/ fragmentation warhead for anti-personnel attacks. An inert practice round (the 253.3XF2) and a practice smoke marker round (the 252.5XF3) are also available, and an ECM/decoy warhead has been developed. From its optimum launch height a SNEB rocket has a maximum range of 4 km (2.48 miles). SNEB is now being replaced in the UK inventory by the CRV-7 rocket, which is a more modern design with a much higher impact velocity.

The TAV-8B features a lengthened forward fuselage (by 3 ft 11 in/1.19 m to 50 ft 3 in/15.32 m) housing stepped tandem cockpits for the student (front) and instructor (rear). They are fitted with full dual controls. The aircraft has a taller fin (by 17 in/43 cm) with a 'filled in' leading edge, giving increased chord and area for improved directional stability, and the environmental control system is modified to cope with the demands of two cockpits. Unlike the TAV-8A, the new trainer does not have an extended tailcone. The TAV-8B was not designed to have an operational front-line role, so it has only two external hardpoints, intended principally for the carriage of auxiliary fuel tanks, training weapons or practice bombs. Twenty-four TAV-8Bs were ordered, two for Italy and the rest for VMAT-203.

From 1986, production Harriers began to receive a new digital engine control system developed by Dowty Smiths Industries. Engines fitted with DECS received an A-suffix to their designations. The TAV-8B prototype (162747) was actually the first aircraft to be so-equipped. The second TAV-8B was delivered to VMAT-203 on 24 July 1987.

Britain orders the AV-8B

After pulling out of the AV-16A, it was certainly not a foregone conclusion that Britain would produce a STOVL or VSTOL aircraft to replace the Harrier. The future of the McDonnell Douglas Harrier II was by no means assured, and a successful Kingston second-generation Harrier could even sell to the USMC. Air Staff Target 403 (AST.403) drew competing proposals from BAe at Warton (the STOL P.96) and from Kingston, which proposed a new STOVL type with a PCB Pegasus and a ventral intake. This eventually led to the Eurofighter, but a new Harrier began to take shape in response to Air Staff Requirement 409 (ASR.409).

Britain's original plan for a second-generation Harrier was to modify existing Harrier GR.Mk 3s with Kingston's new 'big wing', which differed from the new McDonnell Douglas wing primarily in its composition, being of conventional alloy construction and thus known as the 'tin wing'. This derisive nickname was unfortunate, since the wing was aerodynamically very advanced and reflected BAe's advanced wing design experience gathered in the Hawk and Airbus programmes. Opponents of the indigenous design averred that the McDonnell design was 'more advanced', and that the Kingston 'big wing' was in some way 'inferior'. This was a gross over-simplification, and the American wing was probably less advanced, except in its use of advanced (and arguably less battle damage tolerant) materials. In many respects, during the early and mid-1970s, the upgrade of existing Harriers with a new metal wing made more sense than the production of an all-new design with a carbon-fibre wing.

Utilisation of the RAF's GR.Mk 3s continued apace, and it soon became clear that to rewing the aircraft (some of which had amassed 4,000 flying hours by 1988) would not be cost-effective. Ever optimistic, BAe suggested producing new-build big-winged aircraft as Harrier GR.Mk 5s, making extensive use of GR.Mk 3 or Sea Harrier production tooling, and incorporating a Sea Harrier-type forward fuselage, with its raised cockpit. By this time the GR.Mk 5(K) incorporated the YAV-8B's revised intakes, zero scarf nozzles and AV-8B type LIDs (known in the UK as CADs). The Kingston wing would almost certainly have given lower drag than the McDonnell Douglas wing at high speed, and, despite its heavier weight, the GR.Mk 5(K), as it became known, would have been faster than the AV-8B. It would also have enjoyed an equivalent or better low-level radius of action and payload capability. The company eventually hoped to retrofit Sea Harriers with the new 'big wing', though this improvement died when the RAF ordered the AV-8B.

UK needs versus US reality

The RAF's requirement for second-generation Harriers was always perceived as being quite small, since it was thought that the Harrier GR.Mk 3 needed replacing only in RAF Germany, and that the UK-based squadron could soldier on with upgraded GR.Mk 3s. Unfortunately, a 60-aircraft order to equip two front-line squadrons was insufficient to launch production of the GR.Mk 5(K), particularly in the face of competition from the US AV-8B, which already had 330 firm orders. Moreover, the new British Conservative government was firmly committed to the Trident missile, and to massive Tornado procurement, and yet wanted to keep a tight reign on defence expenditure. Against such a background, the Harrier programme was not accorded a high priority. Finally, the technical merits of the lightweight composite supercritical American wing became increasingly apparent, while the low unit price of the AV-8B proved even more attractive to the politicians. It was soon considered inevitable that if the RAF were to acquire a second-generation Harrier, then that aircraft would be the American AV-8B. A Memorandum of Understanding signed in August 1981 provided for the abandonment of British 'big wing' Harrier development, and for the acquisition of AV-8Bs for the RAF. This was something of a kick in the teeth to BAe, whose Kingston Division (as Hawker) had designed the original Harrier configuration, and who would now only be expected to build some sub-assemblies and components of an American refinement of its own design, rather than its own Harrier derivative.

Fortunately, the AV-8B and the cancelled Kingston 'big wing' Harrier shared a host of common features, including a relocated outrigger undercarriage, which actually reduced

wheeltrack from 22.18 to 16.99 ft (6.76 to 5.18 m), despite its wider span. This allowed either aircraft to taxi on single track roads.

The RAF order for 62 AV-8Bs won BAe a substantial share in the programme, which initially included 336 aircraft for the US Marines and 12 for Spain. The aircraft were designated as Harrier GR.Mk 5s, reusing the designation associated with Kingston's original 'tin wing' Harrier. BAe gained the contract to build the vital reaction control system for all Harriers, together with all aft and aft-centre fuselage sections, fins and carbon-fibre rudders, and all

Left and far left: The AIM-9L Sidewinder is carried by the Harrier GR.Mk 7 as a self-defence weapon. Crews regularly practise with captive seeker heads but each pilot can expect to fire a live missile once per tour (approximately every three years). The UK's main missile firing ranges are over the Irish Sea off the Welsh coast. Trials are conducted over the Aberporth ranges using Jindivik target drones (towing flares) flown from Llanbedr. The launch seen here (left) – of an AIM-9G – was conducted as part of a Qualified Weapons Instructor course. It is a 'look-up' launch, in a head-to-head engagement, with the aircraft climbing at 30° to 40°. The view through the HUD of a second aircraft (far left) gives some idea of more typical launch parameters, at a target crossing left to right. The trail aircraft is flying at 387 kt (Mach 0.64) and a height of 5,780 ft. The aircraft is turning right in a 17° climb (approximately) while pulling 1.3 g.

Second-generation Harriers

Above: Air-to-air refuelling capability is an essential element in the US Marine Corps doctrine of rapid deployment/self deployment. As part of the major airframe changes and performance improvements of the AV-8B, the Harrier II acquired a more permanent tanking capability than the AV-8A. The early Harriers could mount an ungainly add-on refuelling probe above the port engine intake. With the AV-8B (and Harrier GR.Mk 5/7) came a retractable probe in a streamlined fairing. This probe is often described as 'bolt-on' but is virtually a permanent fixture on all aircraft. This AV-8B is a VMA-542 aircraft, refuelling from a KC-130.

Above right: The Marine Corps has four versions of the Hercules tanker: the KC-130F, KC-130R, KC-130T and KC-130T-30. The basic KC-130F was based on the C-130B, with uprated T56-A-16 engines and a new wing. It entered service in 1960. The KC-130R/T was based on the C-130H airframe, and has additional transferable fuel capacity. The KC-130T is intended as a quick-change tanker/transport. The latest version, the KC-130T-30, is the only stretched Hercules variant in US military service. Based on the KC-130T, it incorporates the 15-ft (4.57 m) fuselage stretch of the C-130H-30. The two Harriers here tanking from this KC-130F are both carrying the little-seen AN/ALQ-164 ECM pod on their centreline stations. This Harrier-specific pod has been in USMC service since 1995.

centreline stores pylons; this represented 40 per cent of the work on USMC and RAF aircraft, and BAe was promised 25 per cent of final assembly for deliveries to third countries. BAe also built carbon-fibre tailplanes for all RAF aircraft. A separate assembly line was established at Dunsfold for the final assembly of all RAF Harriers.

Even after the decision was taken to procure a BAe-built version of the US-designed AV-8B, there were pressures to change various items of equipment in order to better suit the aircraft to RAF needs, and to create more jobs for British industry. This approach has transformed the AV-8B from a cheap, fully-integrated, off-the-shelf aircraft into what was effectively a new weapons system, albeit in an existing airframe. It was probably inevitable that the RAF would require a more highly specified aircraft than the Marine Corps. USMC AV-8As had been equipped with a simpler weapons aiming computer than the RAF's Harriers, reflecting the USMC's less demanding role and more demanding maintenance requirements.

Unfortunately, the integration of many of the new RAF-specific systems did not go quite as planned, causing severe delays and cost escalation. Some people wondered why the RAF simply could not have acquired AV-8Bs to the same standards as the USMC, pointing to the cost and timescale benefits which would have accrued. This observation completely overlooked the fact that the basic USMC AV-8B simply did not meet the RAF's requirement, and that changes were not a luxury but a necessity.

UK systems for the GR.Mk 5

Although the US Marine Corps AV-8Bs were optimised for medium-level operation, the RAF expected its Harriers to continue to operate primarily at ultra-low level, and in the most dangerous threat environment in the world – the North German Plain, the inevitable battleground of the Cold War. The basic AV-8B was entirely unable to meet the RAF's stringent 1-lb (0.45-kg) bird, 600-kt (690-mph; 1110-km/h) impact requirement, and leading-edge skin thicknesses were increased, while the intake lips and wrap-round windscreen were also strengthened. The Hughes Angle Rate Bombing System (used on late-mark A-4 Skyhawks and optimised for medium-level attacks) was retained on the RAF's Harrier GR.Mk 5, although many thought that a Ferranti Laser Rangefinder and Marked Target Seeker (as used in the original Harrier GR.Mk 3, Jaguar and Tornado) would have been more useful. The ARBS uses collimated TV and laser spot trackers, and is optimised for medium-level use. The ARBS can be used to give a x6 magnification view ahead of the aircraft, presented on one of the MFDs.

For navigation at low level, the RAF demanded a moving map display, selecting a Ferranti projected map display similar to the equipment used in the Tornado, and

linking it to the Ferranti FIN 1075 INAS. The Ferranti moving map incorporated a 5.18-ft (1.57-m) film strip which was equivalent to 600 sq ft (56 m²) of charts and which was interfaced to the digital navigation computer. The system had provision for frames showing airfield approach charts, target details or FRCs. To enhance survivability, the aircraft was designed to incorporate a new Zeus internal ECM system (replacing the AV-8B's AN/ALR-67 RHAWS and podded AN/ALQ-164(V) jammer). Zeus detects and analyses radar frequencies, using an onboard library of more than 1,000 known emitters, displaying threats by direction and type, and assigning threat priorities. Threats can be jammed or countered automatically. The aircraft was also fitted with a Plessey Missile Approach Warning radar system in the tailcone, and with TACDS V-10 (AN/ALE-40) flare dispensers under the fuselage. The MAWS was essentially a small Doppler radar, and thus differed from the UV/IR-detector-based missile approach warner eventually fitted to USMC AV-8Bs. The RAF Harriers' integrated EW installation was also intended to incorporate CelsiusTech BOL chaff dispensers. They carried small packets of 160 0.3-in (8-mm) thick 'slices' of chaff, which would be ejected from the outrigger, 'blooming' rapidly in the wingtip vortices.

The RAF Harrier IIs received a new IFF transponder, replacing the Bendix AN/APX-100 used by the AV-8B with a Cossor IFF.4760, broadly compatible with the US Mk XII system. The GR.Mk 5 also introduced a GEC Avionics AD.3500 radio, giving secure voice capability.

Hardpoint changes

The RAF's brief combat experience in the Falklands had pointed to the need for extra pylons for the carriage of defensive AAMs, which otherwise used invaluable hard-points, two of which might already be required for the carriage of fuel tanks. If two more were used for AIM-9 Sidewinders, only two would be available for offensive weapons. This led the RAF to regard the standard AV-8B six-pylon wing as being wholly inadequate (the Kingston 'big wing' had incorporated wingtip launch rails). The decision was therefore taken to add two dedicated Sidewinder pylons to the wings of RAF Harriers, and the

addition of local strengthening within the wing structure for the new pylons was achieved without difficulty. The shallow new pylons did not interfere with weapons or tank carriage on the existing pylons and were neatly added to the forward end of the outrigger undercarriage fairings, which had to be fitted with a ceramic tile to protect them from damage by a Sidewinder's rocket efflux on launch.

The other underwing pylons were also redesigned to be able to accommodate the BL755 CBU, then perceived as being the RAF Harrier's primary weapon. The BL755 is heavier and bulkier than the Mk 82, around which the USMC AV-8B was designed.

The RAF's Harriers had always had a limited reconnaissance capability, with all aircraft carrying a port oblique F95 camera in the nose. No. IV Squadron in Germany and

No. 1417 Flight in Belize used a reconnaissance pod. The Harrier GR.Mk 5 was expected to retain a similar capability, and the most apparent external difference between USMC AV-8Bs and RAF Harrier GR.Mk 5s was the addition of a shallow fairing below the noses of the British aircraft. It was meant to accommodate a BAe MIRLS (Miniature/Militarised Infra-Red Linescan), adapted from the linescanner developed for the Tornado GR.Mk 1A, which was itself developed from commercial equipment. Intended to have a broad 200° field of view (from above the horizon to above the other), perhaps with a limited forward oblique coverage, the equipment was linked to a Computing Devices reconnaissance management system. It was intended that all GR.Mk 5s would be capable of carrying the equipment, but that only one squadron would be fully

The tail flash on this VMA-542 Harrier II Plus is evidence of the subtle return of squadron markings to the Marines' universally grey Harrier fleet. VMA-542 'Flying Tigers' transitioned to the AV-8B in 1986 and, in 1993, it became the first Harrier II Plus unit. The 'Flying Tigers' are one of the longest-standing Marine AV-8 units, having swapped their F-4Bs for AV-8As in June 1970.

Since its inception the AV-8B Harrier has been a product of the McDonnell Aircraft Company, a division of McDonnell Douglas Aerospace, itself a division of the McDonnell Douglas Corporation. In February the 10,00th military jet (an F/A-18) was rolled out of its famous St Louis factory. This total included 286 AV-8Bs and TAV-8Bs for the Marines plus another 33 export aircraft – not including those for the RAF. In early 1997 the momentous news emerged that the Boeing Corporation was planning to acquire all the assets of McDonnell Douglas Aerospace to form an unprecedented aviation industry giant with 220,000 employees. On 1 July 1997 the Federal Trade Commission approved the merger, which some observers had said raised serious anti-trust or monopoly concerns. The European Commission made a formal statement of objection to the merger in May, but this was primarily concerned with the civil aircraft market. The AV-8B programme is now the responsibility of the Boeing-owned McDonnell Aircraft and Missile Systems, which oversees all of the fixed-wing, rotary-wing and tactical missile projects previously run by various off-shoots of McDonnell Douglas. They include the AH-64, F-15, F/A-18, SLAM and JASSM. In addition, several Boeing projects including the RAH-66 Comanche, V-22 Osprey and CH-46 Sea Knight have been added to its portfolio. Full integration of the two firms will be achieved in 1998.

equipped, thereby directly replacing the reconnaissance-roled Harrier GR.Mk 3s which had flown only with No. IV Squadron. In the event, the MIRLS failed to appear, and GR.Mk 5s flew with ballast in their undernose fairings.

New gun for the RAF

The original Harrier GR.Mk 3 (and the AV-8A/C) had carried a pair of 30-mm ADEN cannon. These slow-firing weapons were very different to the fast-firing but small-calibre 20-mm M61A1 used by most US service aircraft, and were bound to be replaced in the second-generation Harrier II. In designing the AV-8B, McDonnell Douglas replaced them with a single new GAU-12/A Equalizer 25-mm gun. After evaluation, the RAF decided that the new US weapon was not suitable for the RAF's GR.Mk 5, which was instead designed to carry a pair of 25-mm Royal Ordnance revolver cannons. They, it was felt, would offer a similar rate of fire (a combined rate of 1,650-1,850 rpm) to the single GAU-12, while delivering three times the kinetic energy of the old 30-mm cannon, with a muzzle velocity of 3,450 ft (1051 m) per second. Each pod contained 100 rounds of ammunition, which could include AP (armour piercing), HE (high explosive), APDS (AP discarding sabot), APHE incendiary and MP (multi-purpose) rounds, with disintegrating links. The new British weapon was thought to be more versatile, with better air-to-air performance, and the complete installation promised a weight saving of around 200 lb (90 kg). The British weapon could also fit inside slightly slimmer pods, which offered aerodynamic advantages, giving lower drag and allowing them to function more effectively as LIDS.

The RAF judged that the AV-8B's instantaneous rate of turn (about 15° per second) was inadequate (AST.409 required 20° per second). The USMC had pioneered the use of the Harrier in the air-to-air role, developing the technique of 'viffing' (VIFF – Vectoring In Forward Flight). The Corps had wired the outboard underwing pylons of its aircraft for the carriage of Sidewinders from an early stage, so it was extraordinary that it was a British invention (the LERX, first tested on the second P.1127 RAF, XV277) that transformed the turning ability of the second-generation Harrier. The LERX was originally designed for retrofit on the GR.Mk 3, and the surface adopted for the AV-8B was a smaller and less effective compromise.

It has been reported in several sources that British Harrier GR.Mk 7s dispensed with water injection, appropriating some of the weight/capacity of the water tank to increase internal fuel, but this is completely in error.

Production deliveries were originally scheduled to begin in mid-1986, with squadron deliveries beginning in 1987. Wittering did not receive a GR.Mk 5 until 1 July 1987, and operational flying began in March 1988. No. 1 (F) Squadron only reached its established strength in February 1989.

The first delay came about as the result of a freak accident to the sixth production Harrier GR.Mk 5, whose ejection seat drogue gun fired inadvertently, separating the pilot from the seat and dragging him, and his main parachute (shredding it in the process), through the broken canopy. The pilot fell to his death near Boscombe Down, while the Harrier flew on for 500 miles (805 km), and was intercepted by a USAF C-5 Galaxy during its flight. The Harriers were grounded while the cause of the accident was investigated. Doubt was cast on the seat (a Martin-Baker Mk 12H, which was one of the GR.Mk 5 specific items of equipment, replacing the US Stencel seat), leading to a prolonged grounding at a critical point in the programme. Completed aircraft awaited flight testing at Dunsfold, where they required the provision of new 'inflatable' hangars. The accident was eventually traced to a loose article which distorted the firing rod of the manual override when the pilot lowered his seat, so steps were taken to protect the rod against damage in the future.

More delays ensued because the British-specified tyres proved susceptible to 'creep', and had to be replaced. The new Sidewinder outrigger pylons initially proved impossible to use, since their nitrogen cooling bottles could not be replaced with the missile in place and the undercarriage down. Early RAF Harriers used AIM-9Gs on the pylons for publicity photos and the like, but when a powered-up missile or acquisition round was required, it was carried on a Sidewinder launch rail fitted to the outboard underwing pylon.

A slow service start

Even more seriously, the Ferranti FIN.1075 INS did not live up to expectations. Employing a floated, rate-integrating gyro platform, Ferranti's FIN.1075 was extremely advanced, but even in 1989 was insufficiently mature for service use. The equipment initially was of so little utility that the RAF were forced to equip the first batch of aircraft with the USMC-specified Litton ASN-130 INS sets. It then had to procure 32 more Litton sets to give additional aircraft (the first RAF Germany machines) a measure of operational capability. Fortunately, the FIN.1075 eventually came good, and now is regarded as a superb piece of equipment, fitted to all Harriers. From late 1992, some aircraft had GPS added, and their INSs were modified to FIN.1075G standard, with the facility to be automatically updated using inputs from the GPS. In the early days of the programme, though, many Harriers were delivered straight to storage at RAF Shawbury while the problems were addressed.

The delayed deliveries of Harrier GR.Mk 5s meant that the aircraft had a 'slow start'. A Harrier Conversion Team (with three pilots who had trained on the AV-8B simulator with the USMC at Cherry Point) was established within No. 233 OCU in February 1987, but did not begin flying

TAV-8B
1 Gruppo Aereo
Marina Militare
Grottaglie

Italy joined the Harrier club in May 1989 when it ordered two TAV-8Bs for initial pilot training, to be conducted in the United States. A front-line force of 16 Harrier II Plus aircraft followed. The TAV-8Bs were delivered in August 1991, at a reported cost of $25 million each.

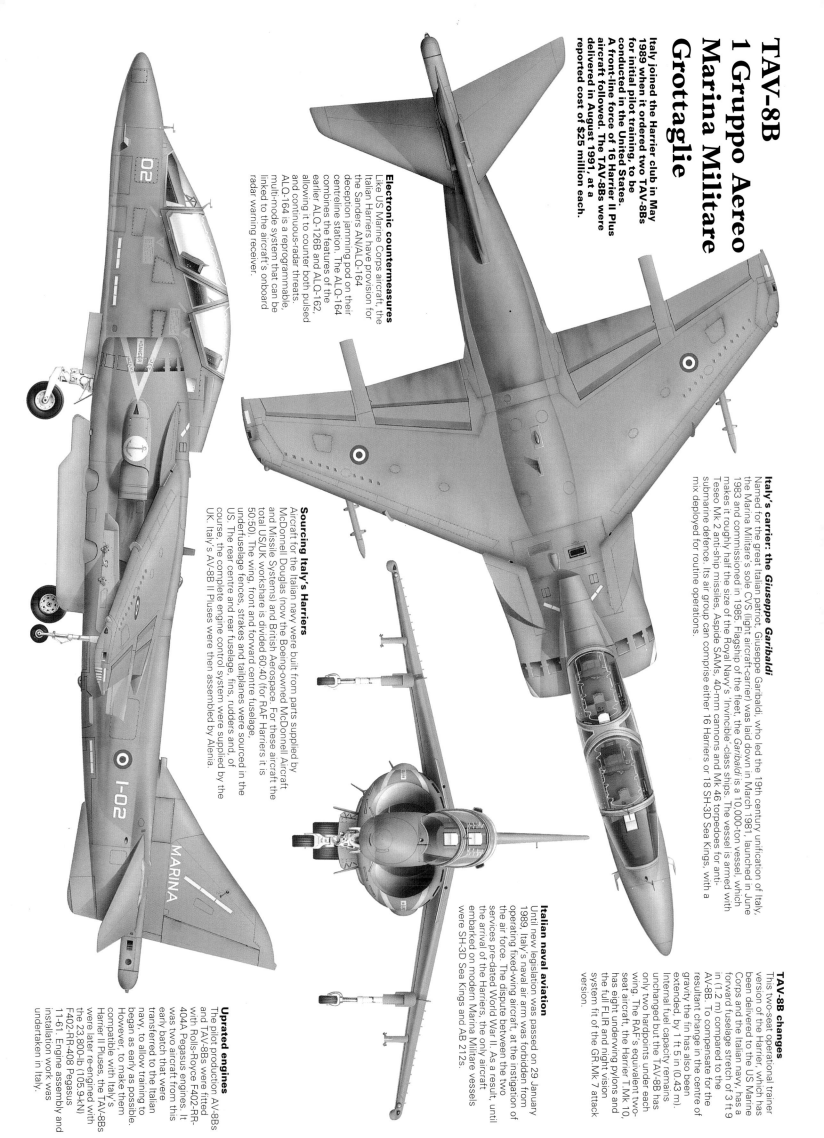

Italy's carrier: the Giuseppe Garibaldi
Named for the great Italian patriot, Giuseppe Garibaldi, who led the 19th century unification of Italy, the Marina Militare's sole CVS (light aircraft-carrier) was laid down in March 1981, launched in June 1983 and commissioned in 1985. Flagship of the fleet, the Garibaldi is a 10,000-ton vessel, launched which makes it roughly half the size of the Royal Navy's 'Invincible'-class ships. The vessel is armed with Teseo Mk 2 anti-ship missiles, Aspide SAMs, 40-mm cannons and Mk 46 torpedoes for anti-submarine defence. Its air group can comprise either 16 Harriers or 18 SH-3D Sea Kings, with a mix deployed for routine operations.

TAV-8B changes
This two-seat operational trainer version of the Harrier, which has been delivered to the US Marine Corps and the Italian navy, has a forward fuselage stretch of 3 ft 9 in (1.2 m) compared to the AV-8B. To compensate for the resultant change in the centre of gravity the fin has also been extended, by 1 ft 5 in (0.43 m). Internal fuel capacity remains unchanged but the TAV-8B has only two hardpoints under each wing. The RAF's equivalent two-seat aircraft, the Harrier T.Mk 10, has eight underwing pylons and the full FLIR and night vision system fit of the GR.Mk 7 attack version.

Italian naval aviation
Until new legislation was passed on 29 January 1989, Italy's naval air arm was forbidden from operating fixed-wing aircraft, at the instigation of the air force. The dispute between the two services pre-dated World War II. As a result, until the arrival of the Harriers, the only aircraft embarked on modern Marina Militare vessels were SH-3D Sea Kings and AB 212s.

Sourcing Italy's Harriers
Aircraft for the Italian navy were built from parts supplied by McDonnell Douglas (now the Boeing-owned McDonnell Aircraft and Missile Systems) and British Aerospace. For these aircraft the total US/UK workshare is divided 60:40 (for RAF Harriers it is 50:50). The wing, front and forward centre fuselage, underfuselage fences, strakes and tailplanes were sourced in the US. The rear centre and rear fuselage, fins, rudders and, of course, the complete engine control system were supplied by the UK. Italy's AV-8B II Pluses were then assembled by Alenia.

Electronic countermeasures
Like US Marine Corps aircraft, the Italian Harriers have provision for the Sanders AN/ALQ-164 deception jamming pod on their centreline station. The ALQ-164 combines the features of the earlier ALQ-126B and ALQ-162, allowing it to counter both pulsed and continuous-radar threats. ALQ-164 is a reprogrammable, multi-mode system that can be linked to the aircraft's onboard radar warning receiver.

Uprated engines
The pilot production AV-8Bs and TAV-8Bs were fitted with Rolls-Royce F402-RR-404A Pegasus engines. It was two aircraft from this early batch that were transferred to the Italian navy, to allow training to begin as early as possible. However, to make them compatible with Italy's Harrier II Pluses, the TAV-8Bs were later re-engined with the 23,800-lb (105.9-kN) F402-RR-408 Pegasus 11-61. Engine assembly and installation work was undertaken in Italy.

Second-generation Harriers

Above: This VMFA-542 AV-8B is seen on 27 February 1991, on what is reputed to be the last Harrier mission of Operation Desert Storm – before delivering its load of Mk 7 CBUs. The first combat action for the AV-8B came on 17 January 1991 when Iraqi troops invaded the Saudi town of Khafji. Four alert Harriers (from VMA-311 and VMA-542) were scrambled to support Marines at risk in the area – the AV-8B's first combat mission. For most of the war the Harriers did not fly the CAS missions for which they had trained, but they did form scout/gun teams with airborne FACs. Initially, these missions were flown with OV-10s, but then F/A-18D 'fast FACs' arrived – which made the job of the FAC a lot less risky. Harriers generated huge sortie rates to deliver 6 million lb (2.72 million kg) of ordnance. Five AV-8Bs were lost in combat.

on the GR.Mk 5 until March 1988. The first conversion course began on 18 July 1988, using the Spanish EAV-8B simulator at Rota. The course provided eight days of ground school, teaching pilots the new aircraft's systems, followed by 16 flying sorties, five of which were range sorties using ARBS. Most of the initial trainees were long-time Harrier GR.Mk 3 pilots, who required little training, and ground began to be made up. About six flying hours were dedicated to handling, four to formation flying, and five to ARBS work plus simulated attack profiles.

Although serious, the Harrier GR.Mk 5's problems were viewed as being temporary teething troubles, and a further order for 34 more Harrier IIs was placed in early 1988. This order brought the total to 96, and promised to allow the re-equipment of all the RAF's Harrier squadrons, not just those at RAF Gütersloh in Germany. Original plans had called for the retention of the 'youngest' GR.Mk 3s at Wittering, where they were to have operated after receiving a comprehensive upgrade that would have included modifications to extend fatigue life, a small LERX, enlarged fuel tanks, twin Sidewinder launch rails, a nav-attack system upgrade, new ECM equipment and a new anti-armour weapon. However, procurement of the extra 34 Harrier IIs brought the GR.Mk 3's career to a premature close. This was perhaps just as well, since no convincing solution had been found to the problem of the GR.Mk 3's very limited remaining fatigue life, which was pegged at a modest 3,000 flying hours.

No. 1 (F) Squadron (originally to have retained GR.Mk 3s) was declared operational in the autumn of 1988, and No. 3 Squadron began its transition to the new aircraft from May

1989. Unable to drop full-scale live ground attack weapons, No. 1 (F) Squadron went on Missile Practice Camp at RAF Valley in July 1989, and mounted a deployment to Bardufoss, Norway, its aircraft wearing a temporary coat of disruptive white camouflage. No. IV Squadron (originally scheduled to have been the RAF's first GR.Mk 5 unit) soldiered on with GR.Mk 3s until 7 December 1990, when it transitioned straight to the more advanced GR.Mk 7.

As the second-generation Harrier began to enter service, it assumed a subtly different role to that undertaken by its predecessor, with more emphasis on hitting targets further behind the front line. What had been a pure CAS (close air support) mission shifted to become a BAI (battlefield air

interdiction) and FOFA (follow on forces attack) role. This alteration in role inferred operating at longer ranges, but also necessitated improved night-attack capability, since enemy reinforcements were most likely to 'move up' under cover of darkness. The new batch of aircraft (to be designated as GR.Mk 7s) were to feature additional night-attack capability, although they used different equipment to the McDonnell Douglas-developed Night Attack Harrier II for the US Marine Corps. The aircraft was not intended to operate as an all-weather, day/night attack aircraft, since its sensors were essentially clear air capable only, with even light rain severely degrading FLIR performance. Night navigation remained difficult until the introduction of GPS.

The Nightbird programme

Development of equipment for the night-attack role had gathered pace during the 1980s, most notably under the joint RAE/DRA Nightbird programme. Initially, rudimentary night-vision goggles were flown aboard a variety of aircraft, from Andovers to Hunters and Harrier T.Mk 4As. From 1988, lighter, balanced helmet/NVG combinations were developed and flown. Under a programme known as Penetrate, FLIR imagery was projected onto a raster HUD. GEC developed a terrain-referenced navigation system and a new digital map display. Under the Nightbird programme, various equipment was flown 'tactically' aboard an A&AEE Buccaneer, a Tornado, the 'Nightcat' Jaguar T.Mk 2A, and a pair of Harrier T.Mk 4As. The latter aircraft had NVG-compatible cockpits, and featured an experimental FLIR in their extended LRMTS nosecones, together with a developmental Ferranti 4510 cursive/raster HUD. The first Nightbird Harrier was initially used by the RAE's Flight Systems department, then by the SAOEU at Boscombe Down, where it was joined by the second modified T.Mk 4A. The Nightbird programme provided a steep learning curve for its participants, supplying general lessons in the limitations of NVGs,

and the difficulties imposed by poor weather, brightly lit urban areas and even a full moon. It also revealed the difficulties imposed by flying a fast jet while looking through relatively narrow field of view NVGs, and of the problems posed by monochromatic vision and the lack of depth perception. Equipment was refined, improved and even invented as the scientists reacted to the pilots' findings. For VTOL operations, RAE Bedford invented a cheap, simple night landing light system (the Bedford Experimental Lighting System), which used standard 240-V household fluorescent light tubes, powered by a 12-V battery. This made them invisible to the naked eye, but bright enough to mark the hover position to a pilot wearing NVGs.

GR.Mk 5 gives way to GR.Mk 7

The RAF's first 41 Harriers were built as GR.Mk 5s, followed by 21 built to an interim GR.Mk 5A standard. This incorporated wiring for the FLIR and certain fittings and was intended to allow easy conversion to full GR.Mk 7 standards. All but three GR.Mk 5As were delivered straight to storage at RAF Shawbury, ZD433 going to Wittering as a ground instructional maintenance trainer, ZD466 to Rolls-Royce at Filton, and the last GR.Mk 5A, ZD470, to Boscombe Down on 19 June 1990. The GR.Mk 5As were followed by the 34 production GR.Mk 7s. A total of 58 surviving GR.Mk 5s and GR.Mk 5As was retrofitted to GR.Mk 7 standards, the number being held low by attrition.

The first GR.Mk 7s were two rebuilt Development Batch GR.Mk 5s, ZD318 and ZD319, which retained the earliest grey colour scheme. ZD318 made the GR.Mk 7's maiden flight on 29 November 1989, transferring to Boscombe Down for service trials on 30 May 1990, just as the first 'production' GR.Mk 7s began rolling off the Dunsfold production line. Conversions of existing aircraft began with GR.Mk 5 ZD380, redelivered to Dunsfold on 9 January 1990, and delivered to No. IV Squadron on 21 December. The £16 million contract to update 58 GR.Mk 5/

Above: Many of the improvements integrated into the AV-8B Harrier II Plus came as a result of experience during Operation Desert Storm.

Far left: Marine Corps Harriers flew 7.7 per cent of all US combat sorties during Operation Desert Storm – 3,380 sorties were made by 86 aircraft. When Iraq invaded Kuwait the AV-8B(NA) was not yet fully operational so the squadrons that deployed to the Gulf were all equipped with AV-8Bs. The first to arrive were MAG-13's VMA-311, along with VMA-542. The Harriers travelled to Shaikh Isa air base, in Bahrain, but transferred to the King Abdul Aziz base in Saudi Arabia. VMA-231 arrived in December 1990, followed by a detachment from VMA-513. VMA-331 arrived with MAG-40, 4th MEB, embarked aboard the USS Nassau. A dark grey disruptive pattern was painted over the Harrier's basic grey camouflage, as seen on this aircraft overflying the burning Al Burgan oil fields, west of Kuwait City.

AV-8B Harrier II Plus
VMA-542 'Flying Tigers'
Marine Air Group 14
2nd Marine Air Wing
MCAS Cherry Point

AV-8B cockpit
When McDonnell Douglas and British Aerospace were (re)designing the AV-8B Harrier II, substantial changes were made to the forward section of the aircraft. In addition to a completely revised airframe shape, the cockpit was totally rebuilt around the new computerised navigation/attack suite and multi-function displays. The new cockpit was dubbed the 'advanced crew station'. The most obvious difference over earlier Harriers was the much improved field of vision for the pilot, courtesy of the single-piece wraparound bubble canopy. The pilot also sat much higher in the AV-8B than in the AV-8A, with an eye-line raised by some 10.5 in (26.7 cm). The new seat position also provided much improved 'over-the-shoulder' vision.

US avionics upgrade programme
In September 1997 the US Navy awarded a $14 million COTS (Commercial-Off-The-Shelf) contract to Smiths Industries Aerospace, for an upgrade to the Weapons Management and Control System (WMCS) of the AV-8B. The upgrade is known as OSCAR (Open Systems Core Avionics Requirements) and will be conducted in association with the Boeing Company – McDonnell Aircraft and Missile Systems. OSCAR is an important part of any future advanced weapons integration for the Marine Corps' Harriers, as it will allow new air-to-air and air-to-ground systems to be more easily 'plugged in' to the WMCS.

AN/APG-65 multi-mode radar for the Harrier II Plus
When the AN/APG-65 radar (developed and built by the Hughes Aircraft Company) was introduced in the F/A-18 Hornet, it revolutionised airborne radar technology. The new radar offered a combination of multi-mode, all-digital performance in the air-to-air and air-to-ground roles coupled with an extremely compact size. AN/APG-65 possesses a velocity search function which provides the maximum detection range against (fast) oncoming targets. A range-while-scan mode displays all-aspect targets within a shorter range bracket. A track-while-scan mode provides any aircraft fitted with AN/APG-65 to 'fire-and-forget' radar-guided BVR missiles such as the AIM-7 Sparrow and AIM-120 AMRAAM. Single-track target, and gun modes are also provided. For close-in air combat manoeuvring the AN/APG-65 has three 'dogfight' modes. The radar can 'look' at an area equivalent to that seen through the pilot's HUD and lock the gunsight onto any target found within a given range. The radar can scan vertically within a narrow beam, lock onto the first target found and provide sighting cues. Finally, the pilot can 'boresight' the radar to lock onto a specific target at which the aircraft is pointing directly. For air-to-ground missions the range of APG-65 modes is equally impressive, and the radar performs with ease over both land or water. The radar can update the aircraft's onboard navigation system, provide terrain avoidance information for low-level flight, locate moving targets on the ground, provide precise range to targets, and also has a specific sea surface mode to locate ships in all weather conditions. The success of APG-65 has led to an even better radar for the Hornet, the AN/ APG-73. Now that this newer set is being retrofitted to US Navy F/A-18Cs, the surplus APG-65s are being used as part of the AV-8B Harrier II Plus upgrade for the US Marine Corps. A $181 million radar integration and production contract for the Harrier II Plus programme was signed between McDonnell Douglas and British Aerospace in January 1991. This covered the conversion of a prototype for test and development work plus the 27 new-build Harrier II Plus aircraft authorised as part of the FY91 budget. The II Plus prototype first flew in September 1992 and the aircraft is now operational with several Marine Corps Harrier squadrons.

ASTOVL and JSF testbed

The YAV-8B Harrier, operated by NASA's Ames Research Center, has been engaged in extensive flight test development for the USAF/USN/USMC JSF (Joint Strike Fighter) programme. Previously known as the JAST (Joint Advanced Strike Technology) programme, and before that as ASTOVL (Advanced Short Take-Off and Vertical Landing), the JSF programme seeks to provide a stealthy, affordable, single-seat fighter that will replace a wide range of US aircraft including the A-10, F-16, F/A-18 and AV-8B, while supplementing the F-15, F/A-22 and F/A-18E/F. JSF has evolved with a STOVL version and so Harrier experience will play an essential part in its development. The most important advance to be made for any future STOVL fighter is blending the Harrier's independent, and somewhat complicated, set of lift and flight engine controls into one seamless system, allowing the pilot to translate from vertical to level flight with ease. A substantial amount of development of just such a system has already been done in the UK with the VAAC (Vectored-thrust Advanced Aircraft flight Control) Harrier – a modified Harrier T.Mk 2 – now flown by QinetiQ. The VAAC Harrier has been flying since 1983 with a variety of fly-by-wire control systems and other advancd controls. In the US, the NASA YAV-8B began flying in 1995 with a new HUD and flight control system that allowed pilots to make blind landing into very confined spaces, at night if necessary. The modified Harrier has been dubbed the VSRA (Vertical Systems Research Aircraft) and has been flown by pilots from the US Navy's Air Warfare Center, NASA and the UK's QinetiQ. The VSRA uses modified stick and throttle controls with newly developed HUD displays to cue and control deceleration into the hover and landing.

AGM-65E Maverick

The USMC has introduced a specialised version of the Maverick missile, the AGM-65E, which is a semi-active, laser-guided version of the original TV-/IR-guided Maverick. This version was developed specifically for the Marines to be used as a precision weapon for close air support missions where friendly troops are in contact with enemy forces. AGM-65E was based on development work done during the 1970s on the AGM-65C version, which was intended for the Navy and the Air Force, but never entered production. The AGM-65E introduced a new 300-lb (136-kg) blast penetrator warhead, compared to the previous 125-lb (57-kg) shaped charge warhead, optimised for anti-armour missions. The AGM-65E entered service in 1985. All 'E-model' Mavericks are painted grey.

AV-8B Harrier Armament System

The gun fitted to the AV-8B is a development of the GAU-12/U 'Equaliser' 25-mm cannon, developed by General Electric. The gun was first trialled on a Harrier in 1980 and entered service with the USMC in 1984. The pods have been fitted with strakes to improve their aerodynamic effect. When the cannon are not fitted, Harriers are flown with long ventral strakes replacing each entire pod. The gun is part of a two-pod system. Each pod is 3.34 m (10.95 ft) long, 350 mm (13.7 in) wide and 470 mm (18.5 in) deep. The starboard pod contains 300 rounds of ammunition on a linear linkless feed system which is connected, at the rear, to the cannon breach system in the port pod. The rotary cannon is driven by a pneumatic system that uses engine bleed air. The motor spins at 9,000 rpm but this is geared down for the cannon. The cannon can speed up to its maximum rate of fire, 3,600 rounds per minute, in 0.4 seconds. The GAU-12 can fire a range of high-explosive incendiary, armour-piercing and armour-piercing (discarding sabot) rounds.

Rolls-Royce Pegasus engine

The Pegasus engine is a two-shaft turbofan, designed purely for the Harrier. It provides lift and thrust for forward flight through four swivelling exhaust nozzles. The Pegasus entered service on the Harrier in 1969, as the Pegasus 11, rated at 21,500 lb (95.64 kN) thrust. When the AV-8B entered development, an uprated version of the engine, the Pegasus 11-21, was introduced (in 1984). In addition to providing a little extra power (the Pegasus 11-21 is rated at 21,750 lb/96.75 kN), the new engine boasted much improved reliability and reduced maintenance times. From 1986 onwards all Pegasus 11-21s were delivered with FADEC (Full Authority Digital Engine Controls) systems to further improve their performance. The US designation for this engine was F402-RR-406A. The 11-21 has now been further improved to Pegasus 11-61 standard, offering 15 per cent more thrust (23,800 lb/106 kN) even at higher outside air temperatures and twice the overhaul life of the 11-21. In US service the Pegasus 11-61 is designated as the F402-RR-408A. As the leading expert on VTOL engine design and operation, Rolls-Royce is now heavily involved in the JSF programme. Rolls-Royce's American partner on the F402 programme has been Pratt & Whitney, for over 20 years. A variant of Pratt & Whitney's F119 engine (which powers the F/A-22) – the F119/JSF – was used as the baseline powerplant in both Boeing and Lockheed Martin's competing JSF proposals, with Rolls-Royce responsible for the lift fan. However, Rolls-Royce also had a formal partnership with General Electric and Allison (which it later acquired as a US subsidiary) to develop an alternative JSF engine, based on General Electric's YF120. Development of the F120 has been funded – Rolls-Royce is therefore heavily involved in both JSF engine alternatives.

Right: The Marine Corps' experience with the Harrier in Desert Storm was generally a good one, and underlined the aircraft's ability to rapidly deploy to austere locations and maintain a high tempo of operations. After the fighting had ceased, tentative requirements for a Harrier 3 were put forward. They centred around the uprated Pegasus 11-61 engine which had been test flown in a special British Harrier GR.Mk 5 testbed in 1989. Interest in a new engine was accelerated by problems with the existing Pegasus -404 and -406 engines, particularly with the digital engine control-equipped Pegasus -406/As fitted to the AV-8B (NA). These engines had to be modified with new control software.

Above: The Marine Corps' requirement for a further improved Harrier evolved into the Harrier II Plus (a designation which some sources have incorrectly ascribed to the Night Attack version). The II Plus was built around the uprated Pegasus -408 engine which had been introduced in the AV-8B(NA). With this engine, however, the Marines rediscovered an old Harrier problem – titanium fires in overstressed turbine blades which led to the loss of one aircraft. This phenomenon had already been encountered by one of the P.1127s in the early 1960s. It was countered in the AV-8B by the substitution of steel blades.

5As with FLIR, NVG-compatible cockpits and digital moving maps was announced shortly before ZD380 was delivered, on 11 November 1990. The first GR.Mk 5A to be upgraded was ZD430, which was delivered from Shawbury in September 1990, and left for No. IV Squadron on 9 April 1991. The conversion programme was completed in 1994.

GR.Mk 7 for night attack

Introduction of the GR.Mk 7 was astonishingly rapid. One distinguished analyst commented, "Not for 40 years has one mark of RAF combat aircraft so swiftly been replaced by another of the same design. No sooner had the…GR.5 entered service with 1 and 3 Squadrons and 233 OCU, then it was giving way to the GR.7." This was true, at least insofar as the physical disposition of GR.Mk 7 airframes was concerned, although it was many months before pilots worked up to become 'night combat ready' and before the new variant could actually be used operationally in its intended night-attack role.

The Harrier GR.Mk 7 is the RAF's equivalent to the USMC's Night Attack model, and is for the most part similarly equipped, although almost every individual new item

of equipment is different to the equivalent item in the US variant. The new variant received a new GEC-Marconi colour map display and revised software for the Computing Devices ACCS 2000 (Unisys AN/AYK-14) mission computer. An off-the-shelf GEC Avionics FLIR is mounted in front of the cockpit, as close to the pilot's eye level as is possible without obscuring forward vision. This minimises parallax problems when the FLIR image is projected in the HUD, although the image is usually presented in the starboard MFD. To allow the presentation of FLIR imagery in the HUD, the GR.Mk 7 has a new Smiths Industries wide-angle HUD. A HOTAS button on the throttle allows the pilot to select either a hot-equals-black or reversed polarity picture. The FLIR incorporates other 'clever' features, including V-shaped arrow markers which can point towards hot spots in the picture (e.g., vehicle engines), drawing attention to what may be a target. The temperature differential required is not huge, and on the ground pilots sometimes find the FLIR markers pointing at bald ground crew, whose heads tend to give off more heat!

GEC-Ferranti Nightbird NVGs complement the fixed FLIR, allowing the pilot to 'look into a turn' or to scan areas outside the FLIR coverage, and are image intensifiers, not reliant on IR to obtain a picture. As such, the pilot can see objects which may not show up in the FLIR. Flying with NVGs is not easy, since the image is monocular, with no depth and no colour. The pilot must move his head constantly to compensate for the very narrow field of view (no more than 40°), which can be disorientating. The pilot will usually 'read' the HUD symbology through the NVGs, but glances below them to look at the moving map or FLIR picture. The NVGs are mounted on a swivel, and can be hinged upwards out of the way when not in use. When flying with NVGs, a clear visor held on with press-studs usually replaces the normal twin-visor arrangement. On the GR.Mk 7, the Martin-Baker Mk 12 ejection seat is modified to Type 12 Mk 2 standards to allow automatic jettison of the NVGs, using compressed gas, actuated by a 'pulse' of energy through the pilot's helmet 'pigtail'. If a pilot ejected with the NVGs in place there would be a strong possibility of him breaking his neck, and although it is preferable to remove the goggles and stow them prior to ejection, an automatic disconnect is provided.

Externally, the GR.Mk 7 differed from the GR.Mk 5 very little, with an almost impossibly small fairing for the

FLIR above the lengthened nose (a 9-in/23-cm extension was incorporated, giving a more graceful profile). The MIRLS fairing below the nose was finally deleted and replaced by a pair of prong-like fairings (sometimes referred to as 'tusks') on each lower 'corner' of the nose, which house forward hemisphere antennas for the Zeus ECM .

The new nose shape was, inexplicably, one of the 'slowest ships' in the package of improvements which formed the GR.Mk 7 'convoy', and delayed tests aimed at ascertaining the effect of the new nose contours on the airflow into the intakes, and especially on engine stall margins. The problem was one of plastic filler breaking off, a potentially dangerous FOD hazard. When they eventually finished, the trials demonstrated that the new nose shape had no appreciable effect on handling or intake airflow.

Although designed and built for night-attack duties, the first GR.Mk 7s entered service in the day CAS/BAI role. No. IV Squadron re-equipped with GR.Mk 7s from September 1990, trading up directly from first-generation GR.Mk 3s and becoming the first GR.Mk 7 squadron. It was 18 months before the GR.Mk 7 flew a representative sortie at night, and No. 1 (F) Squadron was destined to become the first night-attack declared RAF Harrier unit.

Flying with NVGs began (with the SAOEU at Boscombe Down) on 11 December 1990. Subsequently, the SAOEU detached three aircraft to MCAS Yuma, Arizona in March-April 1991, where they flew 150 hours with and alongside the new Night Attack AV-8Bs of VMA-211. A three-man night-attack trials cadre of Wing Commander Keith Grumbley, Flight Lieutenant Paul Gunnell and Flight Lieutenant Steve Hawkins began intensive night trials on their return, dropping practice

Above and left: The Marine Corps had an unfunded requirement for a radar-equipped Harrier since 1988 – influenced no doubt by the dramatic successes of the Royal Navy's Sea Harrier FRS.Mk 1s and their Blue Fox radar. As part of the Harrier II Plus project definition, a radar was added to the design. This was made possible by two factors. The first was the radar itself, the multi-mode Hughes AN/APG-65, which had been developed for the F/A-18 Hornet. APG-65 is an all-digital radar which had been specifically designed to fit the small radome of the Hornet. By reducing the antenna diameter by a further 2 in (5.08 cm) it was possible to adapt the radar to the AV-8B, without a serious loss of performance. The second factor in favour of the new radar was availability. Most post-Block 12 Hornets are now having their APG-65 sets replaced by the improved APG-73, potentially providing a ready supply of second-hand, but still very capable, radars for the Harriers. The reprofiled nose of the Harrier II Plus has been extended by 1 ft 5 in (0.43 m) to house the radar and the night attack FLIR system has been repackaged. The striking new lines of the II Plus are obvious on the VMA-223 aircraft (left) compared to the AV-8B(NA) of VMA-214 (above).

Above and top: The RAF's UK Harrier force is based at RAF Wittering, in Cambridgeshire, which provides a wide range of operating environments. On the northern side of the airfield a 1,000-ft x 100-ft (305-m x 30.5-m) runway is provided to practise short-strip/road operations (top). The Vigo Wood site (above) allows year-round rough field training, though operations are curtailed by wet winter ground which requires 'tin strips' to be laid. Full deployment exercises are conducted 'in the field', including weapons handling and even NBC procedures, over one/two-week stints, once or twice each year.

bombs from heights as low as 200 ft (60 m). Finally, on 19 February 1992, Gunnell and Hawkins flew a fully representative night-attack profile from West Freugh to Garvie Island, where they dropped live 1,000-lb (454-kg) bombs. One of the aircraft was equipped with a modified FIN.1075G, receiving inputs from a spine-mounted GPS, giving much enhanced navigational accuracy.

The SAOEU did much more than test the GR.Mk 7's new sensors and systems, however, developing the tactics, techniques and doctrine necessary to fully exploit the aircraft's potential. They included operating in conjunction with Tornado GR.Mk 1s, which could use their radar to shepherd Harriers through patches of poor weather.

Starting with ZG506 (the 17th new-build GR.Mk 7, and the 77th Kingston-built Harrier II), RAF Harriers finally received the larger 100 per cent LERX (100 per cent of the size of the LERX originally designed for retrofit to the GR.Mk 3). The new 7.5 sq ft (0.7 m²) LERX curved down towards its leading edge, and was deeper in cross-section, fairing smoothly into the upper wing surface contours. The original 4.85 sq ft (0.45 m²) LERX, by contrast, was a simple flat plate, which left a step down from the top of the wing leading edge. Surprisingly, retrofit

of the new LERX has been slow, and many RAF Harriers (including the T.Mk 10s) retain the early, smaller LERX. When the new LERXes are retrofitted, minor adjustments have to be made to the Honeywell AN/ASW-46(V)2 SAAHS (Stability Augmentation and Attitude Hold System) to allow the increased tailplane movement which counters the destabilising effects of the increased surface area forward of the centre of pressure.

Deliveries of the GR.Mk 7 were rapid, but the aircraft took longer to be ready for front-line service. On 30 July 1991 the entire RAF Harrier II fleet was grounded following three inflight electrical fires in a period of only two months, one having caused the loss of an aircraft. The RAF declined to accept new GR.Mk 7s while modifications were made to the RAF Germany Harriers, resulting in the delivery of only 13 aircraft in 1991, and the imposition of penalties on BAe of £40,000 per aircraft per month.

Snags in service

The cause of the inflight fires was traced to chafing of Kapton wiring insulated with carbon – a problem discovered and dealt with by the USMC in 1987. The wiring wore, causing arcing, while the rectifier was already working at maximum capacity and thus was unable to cope with power surges. Tags were added to separate wires, and lightweight Tefzel wiring was substituted for Kapton. Finally, the power-switching panel in the rectifier was improved. Half of the fleet were flying again by late September after an interim repair (priority being given to repairs to the Germany-based aircraft) and deliveries of GR.Mk 7s recommenced on 4 November 1991. New wiring looms were installed during Majors and Mk 5 to Mk 7 conversions.

As if the wiring problems were not enough, fatigue cracks to frames 31 and 32 were discovered in 1991. They were caused by acoustic stresses adjacent to the rear nozzles, but proved to be reasonably minor. Accordingly, the RAF produced its own interim repair (a metal patch which took each aircraft out of service for some three weeks), before BAe produced a definitive repair incorporated during GR.Mk 7 conversion. This involved rebuilding the affected area with thicker titanium skins and doubled stringers.

More seriously, when it entered service the GR.Mk 7 was hardly an operational aircraft, and was virtually unable to carry any meaningful weapon load. At a press facility

Above: Deployments to Norway have been routine for the RAF's Harriers for many years. As part of the Arctic Express exercises, Harriers have spent several weeks operating from Bodø, sometimes with Jaguars and Tornados. On previous Arctic deployments No. 1 Squadron has camouflaged its Harrier GR.Mk 5s with a temporary white overlay, but this has not been adopted by the GR.Mk 7s.

Left: The Harrier has been based in Germany since 1970, but in 1998 the two squadrons – Nos 3 and IV – will return to RAF Cottesmore. This is a result of the post-Cold War defence cuts and also of the virtual elimination of all low-level flying training in Germany; the latter was undertaken universally in 'the good old days' and is essential for aircrew to maintain operational effectiveness. All RAF units in Germany have been forced to transit to the UK for any low-level flying. These No. 3 Squadron aircraft are seen tanking from a VC10 tanker, in 1996, having made the trek from RAF Laarbruch to conduct a four-ship low-level exercise over Scotland. Refuelling is essential as its gives the aircraft full tanks with which to begin, and one and half hours' flying time over the lakes and mountains.

marking the Harrier GR.Mk 5's service entry, years before, the press release had stated that the new aircraft could carry Hunting BL755 CBUs, MATRA rocket pods, laser-guided Paveway II bombs, conventional HE bombs and a pair of 25-mm ADEN cannon, along with AIM-9s. In fact, few of the listed weapons had been cleared for carriage by the aircraft then, and some would not be available to the Harrier force for another 10 years. Even by February 1991 (when USMC Harriers were at war in the Persian Gulf), RAF GR.Mk 5s and GR.Mk 7s were cleared only to drop 6.6-lb (3-kg) practice bombs and to fire AIM-9Ls, although trials were reportedly then proceeding well with Phimat chaff dispensers (first carried during a March-April deployment to Norway), slick and retarded 1,000-lb bombs and MATRA 155 SNEB rocket pods. All these weapons had been cleared by BAe, but not necessarily by the RAF.

No. 1 (F) Squadron had been declared to SACEUR's Strategic Reserve (with GR.Mk 5s) on 2 October 1989, though quite how useful the aircraft could have been

remains open to question. Harrier QWIs had very little to do in those earliest days, except to long for some solutions to the problems which hamstrung their aircraft.

The problems were essentially due to poor software integration, although they were exacerbated by delays to various equipment items. The sudden appearance of Phimat, for instance, was indicative of delays to the Harrier's advanced internal EW suite, which had been intended to incorporate BOL chaff dispensers inside the outrigger Sidewinder launch rails. Their unavailability led to the interim use of the French-built Phimat pods, usually carried below the port outboard underwing pylon.

Zeus itself was not cleared for use by the first GR.Mk 7s, but underwent extensive trials at NAS China Lake. The MAWS was similarly delayed, and was extensively tested at China Lake (on a GR.Mk 5) during 1989 under Operation Horsefly. Clearance trials stretched into 1994, integrating the various elements in order that (for example) the MAWS could automatically trigger the appropriate countermeasures.

Squadron worked out that pilots spent an average of 180 days away from base, most of it in the UK for low-flying training. As RAF Germany shrank in size, the Harriers moved west from Gütersloh to the clutch airfield at Laarbruch, but this did nothing to help the situation. No. 3 Squadron moved on 16 November 1992, and No. IV followed on 27 November. This was made possible by the increased range of the Harrier GR.Mk 7.

Expanded capabilities, further deployments

By late 1992, the Harrier GR.Mk 7 was a much more useful operational aircraft, capable of carrying a range of weapons, including BL755 CBUs, 1,000-lb bombs, and MATRA 155 rocket pods containing 18 68-mm SNEB rockets. During 1991, No. 3 Squadron completed re-equipment with the GR.Mk 7, and the GR.Mk 5s were concentrated at Wittering, pending their turn in the conversion process. No. 1 (F) Squadron began flying GR.Mk 7s in June 1992, and had completed conversion to the new variant by November 1992. In that month, five No. 1 (F) Squadron aircraft were fitted with GPS (like the SAOEU GPS 'prototype'), opening the door to long-distance overseas deployments, operations over featureless and unfamiliar terrain, and long-range overwater flights. This capability was exploited during a deployment by four aircraft to MCAS Yuma in April 1993, following a No. 3 Sqn deployment to Kuantan, Malaysia in September 1992.

Once re-equipped with GR.Mk 7s, No. 1 (F) Squadron rapidly transitioned to the night-attack role. Original plans had provided for the establishment of a single specialist flight (with six aircraft and eight pilots) within No. 1 (F) Squadron, but instead the whole squadron transitioned to the role, and all without down-declaring from its SACEUR Strategic Reserve Commitment. An experienced SAOEU and Nightbird Harrier pilot, Squadron Leader Mike Harwood, was posted in as OC Night, reporting to the Squadron CO. The squadron soon had six GPS-equipped aircraft (ZD431, 435, 437, 438, 463 and 464), and ZD469 was fitted with a video recorder for debriefing training flights.

No. 1 (F) Squadron's pilots worked up in their new role from the autumn of 1992, practising all types of take-off and landing, medium-level formation flying, navigation and weapons delivery, low-level lay-down, dive and rocket attack missions, and inflight refuelling (with and without NVGs). Nos 3 and IV Squadrons in Germany received 'switch-on clearance' for their night-attack systems and sensors in early 1993, but did not begin training until No. 1 (F) Squadron completed its second night-attack training session in April 1994. This was largely as a result of German

Life on the Harrier GR.Mk 7 squadrons was different to life on the Harrier force in GR.Mk 3 days. The introduction of the longer-range Harrier GR.Mk 7 allowed operations from bases further back from the front line, while the need to carry heavier loads led to increased emphasis being placed on prepared, harder surfaces. The shifts from CAS to BAI and FOFA and from GR.Mk 3 to GR.Mk 7 prompted a shift from rural to urban forward operating bases. Operations from supermarket car parks (with aircraft using large retail units as hides) had always been envisaged but could not be practised in peacetime. As Cold War tensions abated, it became increasingly difficult to use even rural sites, as environmentalists and local people began to object to the disruption caused. Moreover, from 1990 Germany imposed successively more stringent limitations on low flying, lifting the base height from 250 to 500 ft (76 to 152 m), and extending a 250-ft limit from 15 minutes to the final IP-to-target run. It then imposed a low flying ban below 400 ft (122 m), then eventually below 1,000 ft (305 m), forcing the Gütersloh-based Harriers to export most of their low-flying training back to the UK. The Tornado Turnaround Facility at RAF Leuchars was expanded to provide support to RAF Germany Harriers 'popping over for the day'. By 1994, one pilot on No. IV

civilian sensibilities, which made night flying training in Germany virtually impossible. The period May-September was not used for night-attack training, since skies were not dark enough. No. 3 Squadron then converted to the night role, each pilot flying some 25 sorties, mainly from Wittering. Ten of the squadron's GR.Mk 7s deployed to Marham in December 1994 for intensive night-flying practice and training, and more aircraft then deployed to Leeming in December. No. IV Squadron was scheduled to undergo a similar night conversion programme in the winter of 1995-96, but a deployment to Italy to support operations over Bosnia delayed this. Thus No. IV, which had been the first squadron to receive GR.Mk 7s, became the last to actually operate in the night-attack role for which the aircraft had been optimised.

Operation Warden

In 1992 deployments had been made to Chile (for participation in the FIDAE air show) and Nellis AFB (for a Red Flag). 1993 saw an even more significant overseas deployment: Operation Warden. Although billed as an operation protecting the Kurds in northern Iraq, Operation Provide Comfort (Operation Warden being the British element of the US-led mission) did little more than monitor Saddam Hussein's breaches of the UN-declared safe area. During the GR.Mk 3 era, No. 1 (F) Squadron had always been the Harrier squadron tasked with fulfilling and maintaining 'out-of-area' commitments (especially NATO SACEUR Strategic Reserve duties), with the exception of the detachment in Belize (a purely national commitment), which was always shared between the three squadrons. When it became necessary to replace Jaguars on Operation Warden, all three Harrier squadrons were on the verge of being declared to NATO's Reaction Force (Air) and it was the RAF Germany squadrons that provided the aircraft, and the majority of personnel, for the detachment (with each of the three front-line squadrons taking a two-month turn at manning the deployment). The Jaguar force had been maintaining an almost constant overseas detachment since the build-up to the Gulf War, and needed a rest. Nine Laarbruch-based GR.Mk 7s were fitted with FIN.1075G and had their dark green camouflage over-painted in washable medium grey ARTF (Alkali Removable Temporary Finish); eight deployed to Incirlik to take over from the eight-aircraft Jaguar detachment, operating primarily in the armed reconnaissance role. A total of 18 aircraft eventually received the Warden modifications.

New reconnaissance mission

Giving the Harrier GR.Mk 5/7 a reconnaissance capability has taken many years. The originally specified MIRLS has never materialised, and the undernose MIRLS fairing of the GR.Mk 5 only ever carried ballast, and later Zeus LRUs. The Harrier force effectively lost its reconnaissance commitments in the run-up to the retirement of the

GR.Mk 3. Nos 1 and IV Squadrons lost their reconnaissance intelligence and exploitation facilities in May 1989. When the RAF's second-generation Harriers did need to carry out reconnaissance missions over northern Iraq, they had to be hastily modified to carry GR.Mk 3 pods that had been withdrawn from service. This modification required the provision of a great deal of new wiring and took 650 man-hours per aircraft. These old pods contained a fan of four F.95 cameras giving horizon-to-horizon coverage, with a single forward oblique F.135. Readoption of the reconnaissance role also necessitated intensive training for the pilots involved. During the course of the Harriers' commitment in Turkey, the old pods were replaced by newly-procured and more modern reconnaissance pods.

Operation Warden ushered in a new era for the RAF's Harrier force. The aircraft gained a much improved reconnaissance role (top). This GR.Mk 7 is carrying a test camera pod. 'W' series codes were applied (above) to signify the Warden duty. The Harriers were replaced by Jaguars in April 1995. This AIM-9L-armed Harrier (below) is seen on its last Warden flight, in 1995.

A number of reconnaissance pods were evaluated by the SAOEU even before the Harriers deployed to Incirlik to participate in Operation Warden. They included the Vinten Vicon 18 Series 403, a Vinten-owned flight trials pod quoted by some sources as containing a Type 753 panoramic camera and a Type 4000 linescan. The pod can contain various sensor configurations, and has flown with a number of new-generation EO- and IR-based sensors, usually with an optical panoramic camera to establish 'ground truth'. Reports that the Harrier has carried the massive Vicon 57 multi-sensor pod are entirely erroneous, for the pod is much too large for the Harrier.

Harrier recce pods

For Warden, the Harrier augmented the old GR.Mk 3 pods by using the Vicon 18 Series 603 LOROP pod (three of which were acquired for use by the Jaguars during the Gulf War, and handed over when the Jaguars left Incirlik). The Series 603 contained a single F.144 (Type 690) camera with a 900-mm/36-in (7° FoV) lens, but had no space for a panoramic camera for image cross-referencing. This meant that a 603-equipped Harrier would usually operate in conjunction with an aircraft carrying the original pod.

Later, the Harrier was cleared for use with the Vicon 18 Series 601 GP-1 pod, which contains a single Type 690 (F.144) camera with a 450-mm lens, plus a Type 900B (F.152) panoramic camera with a 3-in lens aft. Eight GP-1s were acquired to meet an Urgent Operational Requirement for additional medium-level reconnaissance capability, six primarily for use by the Tornado GR.Mk 1 and GR.Mk 1A, and two for the Harrier force. (Four more pods were subsequently acquired for the Jaguar.) Aircraft carrying the pods were either those originally modified to carry the GR.Mk 3 pods, or new aircraft with the same wiring changes.

During Operation Warden flights, Harriers usually operated in pairs, each aircraft carrying a reconnaissance pod on the centreline, with AIM-9Ls, two CBU-87 cluster bombs, a Phimat pod and two 250-Imp gal (1136-litre) external fuel tanks. They tended to launch in waves of six aircraft, with each pair assigned between 12 and 18 targets and supported by VC10 tankers. Clearances for the CBU-87 and the CRV-7 rocket (in 19-round LAU-5003B/A pods) were obtained specifically for the medium-altitude role, as practised in Operation Warden. The Harrier GR.Mk 7 could carry its load farther than could a Jaguar, but the aircraft was considerably less maintainable, and to sustain the same tempo of operations required more aircraft and more personnel.

The switch from CAS-type operations with the first-generation Harrier to longer-range interdiction missions with the GR.Mk 7 led to a requirement for enhanced mission planning equipment. This led to an order for 50 Advanced Mission Planning Aids from EDS Scicon (for a reported £50 million) similar to the system planned for the Tornado GR.Mk 4. The AMPA computer receives the incoming ATM (Air Tasking Message) and generates a provisional route, taking advantage of known enemy defences and using terrain masking where possible. The route is complete with waypoints, fuel, timings and speeds to meet the Time on Target (ToT) specified in the ATM. Pilots can view a synthetic three-dimensional view of any feature, pictured from the direction of approach and shaded realistically to simulate sun or moonlight at the planned time. The system can also store reconnaissance imagery. The pilot can amend the route as necessary, before downloading the plan into a portable electronic data store from which it would then be loaded into the aircraft.

By the mid-1990s, the Harrier GR.Mk 5/GR.Mk 7 had left many of its problems behind, though one legacy of the early difficulties (particularly the software problems) was a huge backlog of clearances for various weapons, systems and items of equipment. When he retired in 1997, the

Above: This GR.Mk 7 is fitted with the 70 per cent **LERX** that is still widespread on **RAF** Harriers.

Below left: This VMA-331 AV-8B, on deployment to Norway, is carrying a 'live' gun pod and ALQ-164 ECM pod.

outgoing Chief of the Air Staff, Air Chief Marshal Sir Michael Graydon, admitted that "the Harrier GR.7 is relatively new – the aircraft is still getting clearances." Three years earlier, in 1994, the clearance of new equipment was probably at its peak. When the then-CAS, Sir Peter Harding, visited Bosnia and found the RAF being sidelined because of its lack of PGM capability, his directive to provide more TIALD-carrying aircraft to fill the gap had been intended to result in the integration of the TIALD designator on the Harrier GR.Mk 7. In fact, such was the pressure and workload being experienced with integrating other equipment and weapons on the Harrier that the

Jaguar was selected to use TIALD instead, and, with supreme irony, the supposedly high-tech Harrier acted as a simple bomb-truck, toting the Paveway II LGBs which were guided to their targets by the ancient but superbly-equipped Jaguar GR.Mk 1Bs.

Harrier and Jaguar

This was perhaps unfortunate for the Harrier force, since the success of the Jaguar/TIALD combination resulted in a renaissance for that aircraft and in the launch of the Jaguar 96 and Jaguar 97 upgrades. Under these upgrades, the ageing Jaguar will become the first RAF aircraft to deploy

Opposite, above: The RAF's T.Mk 10 trainers are fully combat-capable, unlike the Marines' TAV-8Bs. These three clean-winged aircraft wear the markings of No. 20 (R) Sqn, the Harrier OEU.

Opposite, below: This GR.Mk 7 is carrying a centreline baggage pod and a single Sidewinder acquisition round. Harrier launch rails are now being equipped with a CRL fitted with an integral CelsiusTech BOL chaff dispenser.

The nose of the GR.Mk 7 Harrier is filled with the dual-mode TV/laser target seeker/tracker of the AN/ASB-19(V2) Angle Rate Bombing Set (ARBS). Above it is the GEC-Marconi FLIR. Below the nose are the twin housings for the Zeus ECM system.

The Night Attack AV-8B uses the same ARBS and FLIR combination as the RAF aircraft, in a slightly repackaged form. The AV-8B relies on the AN/ALR-67(V)2 RWR and has provision for an AN/ALQ-164 ECM pod, which is rarely seen.

In the AV-8B Harrier II Plus the 'old-fashioned' ARBS, and its functions, have been completely replaced by the multi-mode AN/APG-65 radar. The addition of an all-new radome and extended nose has led to the FLIR system being repositioned.

McDonnell Douglas AV-8B Harrier II Plus

1 Glass-fibre radome
2 Planar radar scanner
3 Scanner tracking mechanism
4 Radar mounting bulkhead
5 Forward-Looking Infra-Red (FLIR)
6 APG-65 radar equipment module
7 Forward pitch control reaction air nozzle
8 Pitot head, port and starboard
9 Cockpit front pressure bulkhead
10 Pitch feel unit and trim actuator
11 Yaw vane
12 Single piece wrap-round windscreen
13 Instrument panel shroud
14 Rudder pedals
15 Underfloor avionics bay, air-data computer and inertial navigation equipment
16 Electro-luminescent and covert night vision goggle (NVG) formation lighting strips
17 Control column
18 Engine throttle and nozzle angle control levers
19 Instrument panel with full-colour multi-function CRT displays
20 Pilots head-up display (HUD)
21 Sliding cockpit canopy with miniature detonating cord (MDC) emergency breaker
22 UPC/Stencil lightweight ejection seat
23 Cockpit section framing, all-composite forward fuselage structure
24 Sloping seat mounting rear pressure bulkhead
25 Intake boundary layer separator
26 Port air intake
27 Landing/taxiing light
28 Levered suspension nosewheel, shortens on retraction
29 Intake suction relief doors, free floating
30 Hydraulic nosewheel retraction jack
31 Hydraulic system accumulator
32 Demountable flight refuelling probe
33 Cockpit air conditioning pack

34 Intake boundary layer air spill duct
35 Heat exchanger ram air intakes
36 Rolls-Royce F404-RR-408 Pegasus 11-61 turbofan engine
37 Full authority digital engine control (FADEC) unit
38 Upper formation lighting strips
39 Accessory equipment gearbox
40 Alternator
41 Engine oil tank
42 Forward fuselage fuel tank
43 Hydraulic system ground connectors and engine monitoring and recording equipment
44 Fuselage lift improvement device (LID), lateral strake
45 Forward zero-scarf (fan air) swivelling exhaust nozzle
46 Centre fuselage fuel tank
47 Nozzle bearing
48 Gas turbine starter/auxiliary power unit
49 Leading-edge root extension (LERX)
50 Engine bay venting air intake
51 Wing centre-section integral fuel tank
52 Starboard wing integral tank
53 Fuel feed and vent piping
54 Starboard weapons pylons

55 RWR antenna
56 Starboard navigation light
57 Roll control reaction air valve, upper and lower surface vents
58 Wingtip formation lights
59 Fuel jettison
60 Starboard aileron
61 Outrigger wheel fairing
62 Starboard outrigger wheel, retracted position
63 Slotted flap
64 Articulated flap vane
65 VHF/UHF antenna
66 Anti-collision beacon
67 De-mineralised water tank
68 Engine fire suppression bottle
69 Water filler
70 Rear fuselage fuel tank
71 Electrical system distribution panels, port and starboard
72 Chaff/flare launchers
73 Heat exchanger ram air intake
74 Rudder hydraulic actuator
75 Starboard all-moving tailplane

76 Formation lighting strip
77 Fin conventional light alloy structure
78 MAD compensator
79 Temperature probe
80 Broad-band communications antenna
81 Glass-fibre fin-tip antenna fairing
82 Radar beacon antenna
83 Rudder
84 Honeycomb composite rudder structure
85 Yaw control reaction air valve, port and starboard nozzles
86 Rear RWR antennas
87 Rear pitch control reaction air nozzle

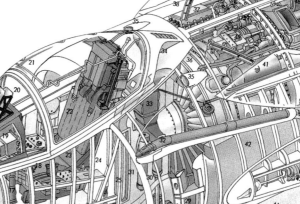

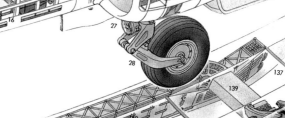

88 Port all-moving tailplane
89 Carbon-fibre composite multi-spar tailplane structure
90 Tail bumper
91 Lower broad-band communications antenna
92 Tailplane hydraulic actuator
93 Heat exchanger exhaust
94 Avionics equipment air conditioning pack
95 Tailplane control cables
96 Conventional rear fuselage light alloy structure
97 Rear fuselage avionics equipment bay
98 Avionics bay access hatch, port and starboard
99 Formation lighting strip
100 Ventral airbrake panel
101 Airbrake hydraulic jack
102 Port slotted flap
103 Carbon-fibre composite flap structure
104 Flap hydraulic jack
105 Exhaust nozzle shroud

106 Outboard flap hinge and vane interconnecting link
107 Port outrigger fairing
108 Port aileron
109 Aileron carbon-fibre composite structure
110 Fuel jettison
111 Port wingtip formation lights
112 Roll control reaction air valve, upper and lower surface vents
113 Port navigation light
114 RWR antenna
115 Port wing stores pylons
116 Port outrigger wheel
117 Pylon attachment hardpoints
118 Outer wing panel dry bay
119 Aileron hydraulic actuator
120 Outrigger wheel strut
121 Hydraulic retraction jack
122 Port wing integral fuel tank
123 Aileron control rod
124 Intermediate missile pylon
125 AIM-9L/M Sidewinder air-to-air missile

126 Missile launch rail
127 Wing leading-edge fence
128 Carbon-fibre composite 'sine wave' multi-spar structure
129 Rear, hot stream, swivelling exhaust nozzle
130 Rear nozzle bleed-air cooled bearing housing
131 Hydraulic reservoir, dual system, port and starboard
132 Pressure refuelling connection and control panel

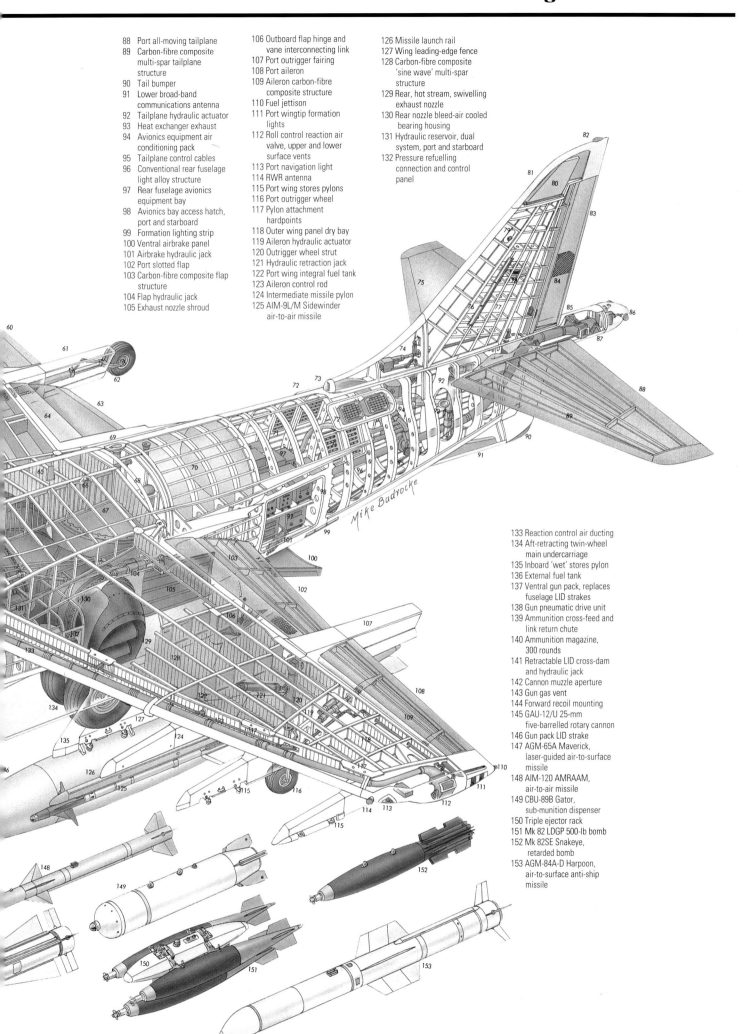

Mike Badrocke

133 Reaction control air ducting
134 Aft-retracting twin-wheel main undercarriage
135 Inboard 'wet' stores pylon
136 External fuel tank
137 Ventral gun pack, replaces fuselage LID strakes
138 Gun pneumatic drive unit
139 Ammunition cross-feed and link return chute
140 Ammunition magazine, 300 rounds
141 Retractable LID cross-dam and hydraulic jack
142 Cannon muzzle aperture
143 Gun gas vent
144 Forward recoil mounting
145 GAU-12/U 25-mm five-barrelled rotary cannon
146 Gun pack LID strake
147 AGM-65A Maverick, laser-guided air-to-surface missile
148 AIM-120 AMRAAM, air-to-air missile
149 CBU-89B Gator, sub-munition dispenser
150 Triple ejector rack
151 Mk 82 LDGP 500-lb bomb
152 Mk 82SE Snakeye, retarded bomb
153 AGM-84A-D Harpoon, air-to-surface anti-ship missile

Second-generation Harriers

helmet sights, ASRAAM missiles, a PC-based mission planner with embedded TRNS, and other equipment which might otherwise have made its debut on the Harrier. Even nine years after the service introduction of the Harrier GR.Mk 5, the RAF's Harrier IIs lacked much of their planned equipment. For example, despite what were said to have been successful trials during Operation Horsefly at the Naval Weapons Center, China Lake, in 1989, the Plessey MAWS has still not been fully cleared.

Operation Deny Flight

After being relieved from the Operation Warden commitment by Tornados, from July 1995 the Harrier force found itself providing a rotational detachment to Gioia del Colle. From there, the aircraft again replaced Jaguars, this time supporting NATO's Operation Deny Flight, attempting to enforce UN resolutions which aimed to damp down the fratricidal conflict between Bosnian, Serb and Croat forces. No. IV Squadron deployed with 12 'deployment pool' aircraft (fresh from an EW upgrade at Dunsfold) to Gioia del Colle, where they became operational on 1 August 1995. This allowed most of the Jaguars to return home to Coltishall, although a detachment of two TIALD-equipped aircraft was maintained at Coltishall, on standby to operate alongside the Harriers.

Some of the aircraft operated by No. IV Squadron wore the same medium grey ARTF colour scheme they previously had worn for Operation Warden, but most wore a new two-tone dark grey colour scheme, with a very high demarcation between the bulk of the aircraft (in medium sea grey) and the darker (dark sea grey) topsides. The new colour scheme used LIR (low infra-red) polyurethane paint with a lower IR signature than 'normal' paint. Squadron markings were not carried. The detachment to Italy marked the first public appearance of the new LAU-71 missile launch rail on the dedicated 'winder pylon. Distinguished by a black domed front end, incorporating a HIPAG gas generator, the new launch rail was packed with BOL chaff packages, and this allowed the aircraft to routinely operate without a Phimat pod. The Harriers usually operated with large underwing tanks inboard, AIM-9L Sidewinders on their dedicated pylons, and CPU-123/B Paveway II LGBs on the centre underwing pylons, and with the outboard pylons empty. They could have been used to allow the carriage of two more AIM-9s had there been a significant air threat, or for the carriage of CRV-7 rockets, CBU-87s or other offensive weapons. Operating in the reconnaissance role, the Harriers carried a GP.1 or Vicon 18 Series 603 pod, sometimes with CBU-87s replacing the LGBs. Harriers also operated in the SUCAP (cab rank) role, usually with CBU-87s or 1,000-lb HE bombs, but none was dropped in anger.

Combat over Bosnia

The RAF Harrier II had its baptism of fire over Bosnia, only one month after arriving at Gioia del Colle, participating in Operation Deliberate Force, the UN's pre-prepared response to the inevitable violations of humanitarian agreements. The operation was triggered by a Bosnian Serb mortar attack on the centre of Sarajevo on 28 August. Between 30 August and 14 September, NATO flew 3,000 sorties, with another brief period of strikes flown between 8 and 10 October. The Harriers attacked an ammunition dump at Lukavica and an arms factory at Vugosca before dawn on 30 August, as part of the second wave of strikes. They tended to operate in fours, with a Jaguar GR.Mk 1B accompanying each pair.

In the CAS role over Bosnia, the Harrier GR.Mk 7s were inevitably accompanied by (or could call upon)

AGM-88 HARM-equipped USN/USMC F/A-18s or EA-6Bs. There was inevitable speculation that the aircraft might eventually gain an autonomous SEAD (Suppression of Enemy Air Defences) capability, probably with the BAe ALARM missile.

An ongoing area of concern in the Harrier GR.Mk 7 is the continued unavailability of the 25-mm ADEN cannon. By 1996 published sources were stating that the cannon were still not in use, and that the starboard pod now accommodated a GEC-Marconi ARI 23333 Zeus RF spectrum ECM system. Certainly empty (or cannon-less) pods are routinely carried in place of ventral strakes, acting as LIDs, and cannon may have only ever been fit-checked in one development batch Harrier GR.Mk 5. It is not known if the weapons have been flown on a Harrier, though no photos have ever been released showing the guns fitted to a flying aircraft. The presence of the gun is immediately obvious, since the end of the barrel projects some way from the gun pod, unlike those of the GR.Mk 3 or USMC AV-8B.

Harrier at sea

The Harrier's STOVL capabilities make it ideally suited for shipboard operations. The earliest prototypes flew demonstrations and trials aboard a number of ships, culminating in shipboard operations by the USMC's AV-8As, and in the development of the dedicated Royal Navy Sea Harrier. RAF Harriers deployed aboard HMS *Hermes* during 1982, playing a significant role in the operation to retake the Falklands Islands. Their inclusion in the Task Force was as much due to a shortage of Sea Harriers and pilots as to any unique capability, however, and apart from a series of deployment exercise by No. 1 (F) Squadron (the first aboard *Illustrious* in 1984, another on *Ark Royal* in 1987), shipborne operations were not routinely practised by the RAF's Harrier force.

Above: AV-8Bs wear a two-tone overall grey scheme, and most of the fleet still wear toned-down markings. This AV-8B(NA) carries the ram's head badge of VMA-214 'Black Sheep'. Note also the AN/ALE-39 chaff/flare launchers in the rear upper fuselage.

Below: There are few more ear-splitting sounds than a Harrier in the hover. The column of black smoke under this 'Flying Nightmares' aircraft is a sure sign that its Pegasus -408 is working hard.

Above: The Spanish
naval air arm had
acquired 11 AV-8S
Matadors (service
designation VA.1), plus
two TAV-8As (VAE.1), by
1980. In March 1983 a
follow-on order for 12
AV-8Bs was placed, and
the first of these aircraft
was delivered in 1987.
The early model Harriers
have now been
withdrawn from use, and
sold to the Thai navy.

Right: Spain joined the
Harrier II Plus
programme in 1990,
signing an agreement
with the USA and Italy
on 28 September. The
first II Plus was
delivered in 1996 and
entered service with 9ª
Escuadrilla .

Pilots from No. 3 Squadron undertook training on Yeovilton's ski-jump in early 1994; this proved to be something of a 'false dawn', although it did provide a useful indication of the aircraft's inherent suitability for carrier operations. Carrier trials of the GR.Mk 7 (again aboard *Illustrious*) were finally undertaken by the Strike Attack OEU during June 1994. Following ski-jump take-off training at RNAS Yeovilton, Wing Commander Nick Slater led five pilots in the trials, which involved three GR.Mk 7s. Flight Lieutenant Chris Norton became the first RAF pilot to land a GR.Mk 7 aboard ship on 27 June 1994, flying ZG745. The GR.Mk 7 was cleared to operate from the ship's 13° ski-jump even at maximum AUWs of 32,000 lb (14515 kg), and carrying up to 13,325 lb (6044 kg) of external stores and weapons. Such heavyweight take-offs required about two-thirds of the deck length, reaching a take-off airspeed of 105 kt (120 mph; 193 km/h), which often represented a ground (deck) speed of 70 kt (80 mph; 130 km/h), with the wind and the carrier's forward speed taken into account. These loads represented much more than has ever been achieved by a Sea Harrier. The trials

included 40 sorties lasting 44 flying hours, and established detailed clearance limits, GR.Mk 7 deck interface and maintenance requirements. They also tested for electro-magnetic interference from and with the ships systems.

The RAF goes to sea

Following these trials, in 1995 the RAF formally signed an agreement to reinstate the maritime capability of its GR.Mk 7s. In early 1997 No. 1 (F) Squadron deployed four aircraft operationally aboard HMS *Illustrious* as part of Operation Ocean Wave '97. In Exercise Hot Funnel the four aircraft flew aboard on 28 February 1997, off the coast of Oman. The four pilots were each making their first deck landing, though all had made two day and two night ski-jump take-offs at Yeovilton prior to the deployment. Wing Commander Mark Leaky (OC No. 1 (F) Squadron) led a detachment of nine pilots, 60 ground crew and three engineer officers, and conducted maritime operations from the ship for two weeks, disembarking in Malaysia. Each pilot flew around 20 hours during the period, including NVG deck landings.

This was not the first time RAF Harrier GR.Mk 7s have deployed aboard a Royal Navy carrier, but it marks the start of a new era for joint-service Harrier operations, with RN Sea Harrier F/A-2s and RAF GR.Mk 7s operating together as a mixed fighter force (Sea Harrier – OCA/DCA, and GR.Mk 7 – CAS) in support of the UK's new Joint Rapid Deployment Force. The RAF aircraft bring a new level of night-attack capability and ground attack/offensive support expertise to the carrier air wing.

The four aircraft (ZD400, 461, 462 and 468) received a number of modifications to make them better suited to carrier operations. A GPS was added, and the INS was brought up to FIN.1075G standards, with new software to reduce the likelihood of toppling while the platform aligned on the (moving) carrier deck. For interoperability

Top: Spain's flagship, the carrier **Príncipe de Asturias (R-11), was based on a US Navy design for the Sea Control Ship, a multi-role, low-cost ship. The US Navy abandoned the project but the Spanish navy considered it to be an ideal way to replace its vintage carrier SNS** Dédalo. *A 12° ski-jump plus additional accommodation for flag staff were added, as* **Príncipe de Asturias would function also as a command and control ship. The ship was laid down on 8 October 1979, launched on 22 May 1982 and commissioned on 30 May 1988. The maximum aircraft/helicopter capability is 29 machines, 17 in the hangar deck and 12 on the flight deck.**

Above: Italy's Harrier II Plus acquisition has given the naval air arm a modern fighter (for the first time) that is arguably more capable than anything in the air force inventory. Like the Spanish and USMC aircraft, however, the Italian AV-8B II Pluses are hampered by the lack of progress in weapons integration.

with Royal Navy Sea Harrier F/A-2s and Sea King AEW.Mk 2s, the RAF aircraft were also fitted with an I-band IFF transponder. The water replenishment point was moved to inside the undercarriage bay, saving the ground crew from having to clamber onto the slippery wings on a rolling deck.

The use of the Harrier GR.Mk 7 by a number of units, in slightly different roles and locations, has led to the incorporation of a number of temporary modifications using STFs. This, in turn, has led to a certain lack of standardisation and commonality across the fleet, although the configuration remains more common than those of the Tornado GR.Mk 1 or the Jaguar. A common configuration and equipment fit is being achieved through the Mod 95 programme, which effectively gives all aircraft the 100 per cent LERX and the

RAF Germany NVG cockpit, and incorporates the operational war fit as deployed for Operations Warden and Deliberate Force. If the Harrier is to serve until its currently planned out-of-service date, the aircraft will almost certainly receive more ambitious modifications and upgrades. The medium- and high-level roles have become increasingly important since the end of the Cold War, while peace-keeping or limited war scenarios have made the avoidance of collateral damage a pre-eminent consideration. These factors have led to a growing emphasis on the use of laser-guided bombs and other PGMs. The Harrier can already carry LGBs, of course, but still cannot 'mark' or designate its own targets. Acquisition of the TIALD laser designator pod (briefly trialled, or at least fit-checked by the SAOEU) is now very likely, perhaps with Terprom or another TRN (terrain-referenced navigation) system. The Jaguar force has shown that TIALD operation is possible in a single-seat cockpit, but many believe that if it were delivered to the Harrier force, the pod would be most likely to be fitted to twin-stick T.Mk 10s. With only 12 surviving T.Mk 10s under-taking a heavy training commitment, this seems unlikely, however.

US night attack

The retirement of the Marines' last A-6Es in April 1993 left the Corps without a dedicated long-range all-weather heavy attack aircraft. The Corps, did, however, enjoy a considerably expanded medium-range night/all-weather capability with its squadrons of F/A-18Ds, and with its night-attack-capable Lot 12 F/A-18Cs. The enhanced capability of the Harrier II placed increased emphasis on longer range and night operations, in just the same way that the RAF found itself requiring greater night-attack capabilities in its Harriers, and at much the same time.

McDonnell Douglas was awarded a $2.1 million design definition contract for a night-attack Harrier in late 1985.

This aircraft was originally known as the AV-8D, although it subsequently became the Night Attack AV-8B. A trial at the NWC, China Lake, flew a podded GEC Marconi FLIR on a TA-7C, with the pilots wearing Cats Eyes NVGs. It was decided that the proposed Night Attack AV-8B would be similarly equipped.

Night Attack FLIR system

In 1989 GEC Sensors received an initial £10 million contract for FLIRs for the new Harrier variant. MDD designed a neat installation for it above the nose, allowing ARBS to be retained. The Hughes AN/ASB-19(V) ARBS is a daylight-only device, and is therefore redundant during night operations. The new US night-attack aircraft had a new expanded field of view HUD (20° azimuth by 16°, from 14° azimuth) to allow 1:1 correlation of the FLIR picture (20° azimuth by 13°) overlaid on the HUD. The aircraft also featured a new multi-purpose colour display, and a CRT-based digital map display, which retrieved data from an optical compact disc in the Hamilton Standard AN/ASQ-194 data storage set. The pilot was provided with GEC Cats Eyes Generation III NVGs (with a field of view of 40° in azimuth by 30°) giving better peripheral vision, outside the 22° cone covered by the FLIR. The Cats Eyes NVGs featured prisms below the image intensifiers. No provision is made for NVG disconnect on USMC AV-8Bs, so use during take-off and landing is prohibited.

The Night Attack Harrier also took advantage of a new engine, the Pegasus 11-61, known in the US as the F402-RR-408. This engine was developed directly from Britain's XG-15 engine technology demonstration programme, which had been jointly funded by the British MoD and Rolls-Royce on a 70:30 basis. The new engine had improved fan aerodynamics, and single crystal turbine blades, among a host of improvements and modifications. The hot end inspection cycle was doubled to 1,000 hours, and lifecycle cost was asserted to have been reduced by 40 per cent. Engine thrust was dramatically improved, with Rolls-Royce claiming a short lift wet rating of 23,800 lb (105.85 kN), and McDonnell Douglas claiming 24,500 lb (108.96 kN). The USMC rating was 23,400 lb (104.07 kN). Despite its British origins, the 11-61 was not adopted for retrofit on RAF Harriers, though its testbed was a black-painted GR.Mk 5, ZD402. This aircraft first flew its new engine on 9 June 1989 and was subsequently used to set a series of Class-H time-to-height records. Rolls-Royce chief test pilot Andy Sephton set records of 36.38 and 81 seconds to 3000 and 9000 m (9,842 and 29,527 ft), respectively, while BAe Dunsfold's Heinz Frick reached 6000 and 12000 m (19,685 and 39,370 ft) in 55.38 and 126.63 seconds, respectively. Very significantly, the AV-8B(NA) was fitted with four extra Tracor AN/ALE-39 chaff/flare dispensers above the rear fuselage, giving the aircraft a total of 180 flares or chaff cartridges, compared to 60 on the standard, baseline AV-8B.

AV-8B(NA) deliveries to the Corps

The 87th single-seat AV-8B was built as the first AV-8B(NA) prototype, flying on 26 June 1987 and beginning a three-month evaluation at China Lake. The first production AV-8B(NA) was the 167th single-seater, the second FY89 aircraft. From then until the introduction of the Harrier II Plus, all single-seaters built were AV-8B(NA)s. VMA-214 was the first squadron to receive the Night Attack Harrier from September 1989, and all four Yuma-based units were re-equipped by September 1992. Only two units had started to transition to the variant by the time the Gulf War broke out, and, with only about 15 aircraft delivered, it was not worth sending them to the theatre of operations. Moreover, the AV-8B(NA) was then suffering from engine problems. When the engine casings cooled rapidly, but the core heated, the clearance between fan and casing reduced. If the pilot then made a high-*g* pull-up the fan could distort

Right: The standard RAF GP bomb is the Royal Ordnance-developed Mk 10/13/18/20 1,000-lb bomb. All basic bomb shapes are identical in appearance, but the Mk 13 has a filling of 180 kg (399 lb) of RWA 4 high explosive, while the others use slightly differing amounts of Torpex explosive. The (live) bombs seen on the GR.Mk 7 above are fitted with the No. 114 'slick' tail, while the dummy bombs seen here on this SAOEU Harrier are fitted with the No. 117 retarding tail unit.

Left: RAF Harriers employed their Paveway II LGB capability in Bosnia. In British service, the Paveway II seeker system is mated with the Mk 10 (RWA 4), Mk 13 (RWA 4) or Mk 18 (Torpex) 1,000-lb bomb body plus a No. 120 pop-out tail fin unit. RWA 4 explosive is designed to be more resistant to kinetic heating induced by low-level high-speed flight. The most recently developed Mk 20 bomb shape is also Paveway II-compatible.

Right: During Operation Warden the most commonly carried air-to-ground weapon was the US-supplied CBU-87/B Combined Effects Munition (CEM). The CEM was acquired by the RAF during the Gulf War, in preference to its own BLU 755 cluster bomb, which is optimised for low-level deliveries. The CBU-87/B carries 202 BLU-97 sub-munitions which each combine an anti-armour, anti-materiel (fragmentation) and incendiary warhead in a single bomblet.

Below: The key to the AV-8B(NA) and GR.Mk 7's all-weather attack credentials are their combination of FLIR and NVG systems. Each operator uses a slightly differing night vision goggle fit, including (from left to right): GEC-Marconi Cats Eyes (USMC), GEC-Marconi Nightbird (RAF) and Cats Eyes (Spain).

Harrier Weapons

Above: The latest model of the AGM-65 Maverick to be integrated into the USMC inventory is the AGM-65E semi-active laser homing model. AGM-65E was specially developed for the Marines to allow it to be used in close support of friendly troops.

Left: This early production AV-8B drops 500-lb bombs fitted with the Snakeye retarding tail, which is still a standard fit with the USMC and USN, but not the USAF.

Above: The Marines opted for a podded version of the General Electric (now Lockheed Martin Armament Systems) GAU-12/U Equaliser 25-mm cannon. The gun is carried to port, while the starboard pod carries 300 rounds of ammunition.

Below: This VMA-223 AV-8B is carrying four 1,000-lb Mk 83 AIR (Air Inflatable Retard) bombs fitted with the Goodyear Aerospace BSU-85 ballute tail fin.

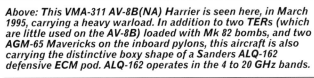

Above: This VMA-311 AV-8B(NA) Harrier is seen here, in March 1995, carrying a heavy warload. In addition to two TERs (which are little used on the AV-8B) loaded with Mk 82 bombs, and two AGM-65 Mavericks on the inboard pylons, this aircraft is also carrying the distinctive boxy shape of a Sanders ALQ-162 defensive ECM pod. ALQ-162 operates in the 4 to 20 GHz bands.

Above: Seen at MCAS Yuma, this VMA-311 AV-8B(NA) is carrying four Mk 7 dispensers, which are most commonly used in their Mk 20 Rockeye II cluster bomb form, containing 247 Mk 118 bomblets. The Mk 7 can also carry the CBU-59 APAM and CBU-78 Gator sub-munitions families.

Left: This VMA-223 AV-8B Harrier II Plus is carrying six inert Mk 83 bombs with the standard low-drag conical fins. Such heavy bombs are usually restricted to the two innermost hardpoints on the AV-8B's wing.

downwards and the blade tips could touch the abrasive coating inside the engine casing. The solution was simple, and included the replacement of titanium fan blades by steel ones, alteration of the abradable inner coating, and an increase in the fan-blade clearance. While the modifications were made the AV-8B(NA)s continued in use, powered by retrofitted F402-RR-406A engines. Then the Cherry Point squadrons started to transition, beginning with VMA-223.

Harrier T.Mk 10 trainer

The introduction of the AV-8B(NA) complicated the training task for VMAT-203, but the decision was taken not to procure a night-attack-configured two-seater for the USMC, on the basis that operational role conversion could be carried out at squadron level using the single-seater and the simulator. Had the USMC not already bought its two-seat Harrier IIs, the decision might have been different. The RAF was in a different situation, since it had failed to buy a two-seat trainer version of the second-generation Harrier.

When the RAF's front-line Harrier was the GR.Mk 5, the old T.Mk 4 was adequate (though by no means ideal) for basic conversion training, demonstrating the particular techniques necessary for successful STOVL operations. A dedicated two-seat trainer was available in the shape of the TAV-8B, though this was ruled out on cost grounds. Instead, in April 1988, it was announced that no new two-seaters would be procured, and that instead a handful of T.Mk 4s would be modified to T.Mk 6 configuration.

The increasing sophistication of the RAF's single-seat Harriers and the increasing age of its first-generation two-seat T.Mk 4s led to a 1990 £200 million order for 14 two-seat

Harrier T.Mk 10s (to meet a requirement originally stated to be for 10 aircraft), similar to the US TAV-8B, but incorporating the night-attack features of the GR.Mk 7. This order was announced on 28 February 1990, although it was later reduced to 13 aircraft. Plans to convert T.Mk 4s to T.Mk 6 standard, with FLIRs and NVGs, were abandoned as not being cost-effective. The T.Mk 4s were old, and were becoming increasingly difficult to support, while the first-generation Harrier trainer was barely representative of the second-generation single-seater in its handling characteristics or in its systems, cockpit layout, and operating procedures. This became critical once the Harrier started operating by night.

The first T.Mk 10 was built at Dunsfold from components produced at Brough, Kingston and in St Louis, but the rest were assembled at Warton, moving from Dunsfold because the latter facility was full of Sea Harriers being converted to F/A-2 standards, and Harrier GR.Mk 7s. The Dunsfold-built T.Mk 10 prototype (TX-01, ZH653) made its maiden flight (planned for 16 March) on 7 April 1994. The first aircraft to be delivered to the RAF was ZH657, which went to Wittering on 30 January 1995, and the new variant was formally introduced to service on 1 March 1995.

Introduction of the Harrier T.Mk 10 simplified the Harrier conversion training programme, during which the first GR.Mk 7 sortie (preceded by T.Mk 4 and simulator work) previously required an instructor flying chase, with two more radio-equipped instructors strategically located on the airfield. Unlike the USMC's TAV-8Bs, the RAF's Harrier T.Mk 10 is fully operationally capable, with the same equipment as the GR.Mk 7 and the full quota of

eight underwing pylons (TAV-8Bs have only two). The prime user of the T.Mk 10 was No. 20 (Reserve) Squadron, with seven aircraft on charge during 1996/97. Each front-line squadron also received a single T.Mk 10.

The heavyweight T.Mk 10 is considered by some people to be short of 'grunt', and the variant would be a prime candidate for re-engining with the Pegasus 11-61, as used by Italian two-seaters. Without it, hover performance is marginal at best, especially in warmer summer temperatures.

The cancellation of rewinged A-6F Intruders and the continued non-appearance of the Bell Boeing V-22 Osprey was a significant factor in the funding of extra Harriers and Harrier upgrades. The AV-8E did not appear (it was an improved aircraft with a more powerful engine and large LERXes) largely because it was overtaken by events – and chiefly by the Harrier II Plus.

The Harrier has many detractors within the Marine Corps, most of whom point to the longer range, greater payload, and higher speed of the F/A-18, and its ability to fire radar-guided AAMs; they loudly assert that the USMC needs more Hornets, instead of the 'second-rate' Harriers. Opponents are sceptical about forward basing (which brings increased vulnerability to enemy air attack, and difficulties with security and logistics support) and are dismissive of the aircraft's relatively heavy maintenance requirements and single-engined vulnerability. Critics felt that their position was justified and endorsed by operational experience during Operation Desert Storm, during which Harrier IIs proved less flexible than the Corps' F/A-18s and a great deal more vulnerable to ground fire, especially by heat-seeking SAMs, which tended to home onto a spot between the four nozzles. F/A-18s sometimes limped home with damage to the extremities of their engine nozzles, but when Harriers were hit they were inevitably hit amidships and downed. Had the aircraft been fitted with AN/AAR-44(V) MAWS, it has been estimated that four of the five aircraft lost in the war would have survived.

USMC Harriers in the Gulf

The Harrier played a crucial role in Desert Storm, and was the first Marine Corps tactical aircraft in-theatre. The 86 aircraft deployed flew 3,380 sorties (4,112 combat flying hours) and delivering more than 6 million lb (2.7 million kg) of ordnance in 42 days of operations. During the war the Harriers operated from a disused air base, a forward airstrip

and from USS *Nassau* (LHA-6), all options unavailable to other types. General Schwarzkopf specifically named the Harrier as being one of seven weapons systems that had made a significant contribution to the quick victory. The only other aircraft mentioned were the F-117A and AH-64.

Units deployed to the Gulf were VMA-542 (recently returned from Iwakuni), VMA-331, VMA-513 and VMA-311. The bulk of VMA-231 was at Iwakuni, but sent aircraft to the Gulf after being replaced by VMF-513. VMA-211 and VMA-214 were converting to the Night Attack version (which was suffering problems with its F402-RR-408 engine) and remained in the US, and VMA-223 deployed to Rota for possible use. Thus, five of the eight

This page: Marine Corps Harriers have made several Adriatic deployments in support of ongoing NATO air operations over Bosnia. These VMA-231 aircraft are seen on board the USS Wasp (LHD-1) as part of composite squadron HMM-264 in December 1995. Note the 'EH' tailcodes and black pawn badge of CH-46F unit HMM-264, which has been applied to the Harrier detachment. In such cases, the full-strength helicopter squadron becomes the parent aviation unit of the MEU. All were active participants in the IFOR peacekeeping operation in the region.

Second-generation Harriers

'gun' squadrons were involved in the war, either wholly or in part. The Harriers flew mainly in the BAI role against targets in Kuwait, primarily using the Mk 7 CBU (and especially its Mk 20 Rockeye II anti-armour version), the Mk 77 Mod 5 napalm bomb, Mk 82 500-lb bombs, Mk 83 1,000-lb bombs and AGM-65E semi-active laser homing Maverick ASMs (with OV-10s and later F/A-18Ds providing designation). AIM-9M Sidewinders were carried singly in the early days but, with no real air threat, were discarded in favour of using the pylons for offensive weaponry. Aircraft in each formation would usually carry a Sanders AN/ALQ-164 deception jammer, which proved effective, but were in short supply.

Most of the deployed units flew from King Abdul Aziz, moving closer to the action when Sheikh Isa became too overcrowded as the US build-up continued. Even this was not as near to the front line as the Harrier force was used to, and a basic forward operating location was established at Tanajib, an oil company airfield only 45 miles (72 km) from the Kuwaiti border. It could handle 12 aircraft. The AV-8B's war was a busy one, and included CAS of engaged Marines at Khafji on 17 January. Aircraft tended to fly in pairs rather than more unwieldy four-aircraft divisions. ARBS worked fairly well most of the time, though lack of contrast was a problem, and smoke and haze could also severely degrade the system's effectiveness.

Radar-equipped Harrier

The Harrier force was unlucky not to be able to field the more advanced AV-8B Harrier II Plus in the war, since the radar-equipped Harrier might have proved more versatile and might have silenced some of the critics, although (in truth) all USMC fast jets in Desert Storm were used almost exclusively in the air-to-ground role, principally by day. Quite apart from its enhanced air-to-air potential, the Harrier II Plus was described by McDonnell Douglas as having a 74 per cent improvement in day attack capability and a 31 per cent improvement by night. One of the radar's stated purposes was to feed slant range information to the AN/ASB-19(V)2/3 ARBS, which was retained, although its nose-mounted TV tracker was obviously supplanted by the radar antenna and radar. The radar could also be used for terrain-mapping, target location, acquisition and identification, and terrain avoidance.

Design of a radar-equipped Harrier began in 1988, after a joint announcement by BAe and McDonnell Douglas in June 1987 that they intended to develop a radar-equipped variant, initially as a private venture. The US Marine Corps became increasingly interested in the new Harrier derivative, as did Spain and Italy, leading to the September 1990 signature of a tripartite Memorandum of Understanding between the four nations to develop the new variant. Alenia and CASA each gained 15 per cent shares in the programme. It was announced at that stage that the aircraft would use a Hughes AN/APG-65 pulse-Doppler radar, almost identical to the radar used by the F/A-18 Hornet, albeit with a

smaller (24 x 28-in/60 x 71-cm) scanner to fit the Harrier's smaller nose contours and 34-in (86-cm) diameter radome. The software was also modified, and a new circuit card was provided for the target data processor. Some black boxes were redistributed within the fuselage, but the installation was as much like that in the Hornet as was possible. The radar could provide range and bearing information for anti-ship missiles like Harpoon or Sea Eagle. The radar had a range of air-to-ground modes for ranging, moving target indication, mapping and navigation, and nine air-to-air modes (all fairly academic until a BVR missile could be funded). In essence, McDonnell Douglas hoped to transform the AV-8B into a STOVL clone of the Night Attack F/A-18C – an understandable desire when two of the initial three customers were already Hornet operators, and since the primary operator, the USMC, was increasingly relying on the Hornet. Anything which brought increased commonality between Harrier and Hornet was useful.

Choice of radar

Had this not been a major consideration, it might have made more sense to adopt the GEC-Marconi Blue Vixen radar as used by the British Sea Harrier F/A-2, a radar already being considered as an APG-65 replacement in some proposed F/A-18 upgrades. Blue Vixen was already integrated with AMRAAM in the Sea Harrier, with test firings beginning in March 1993.

Addition of the new APG-65 radar added a 1,000-lb (454-kg) weight penalty, but this was relatively insignificant since all Harrier II Pluses were powered by the more powerful 23,800-lb (105.85-kN) F402-RR-408 (Pegasus 11-61) engine. Other changes to the II Plus included adoption of the RAF-type wing, with a 100 per cent LERX and, most significantly, four pylons per side, including the dedicated AAM pylons on the undercarriage outriggers. The combination of uprated engine and LERX, in particular, improves performance by a significant margin. Inside the cockpit, the new variant has an additional MFD to allow the display of radar data.

The Harrier II Plus was based on the Night Attack AV-8B, and retained full night-attack capability and standard night-

attack equipment, although the aircraft had a redesigned
overnose FLIR fairing (of more angular and more constant
cross-section) which was reportedly more aerodynamically
efficient and easier to manufacture. Like the Night Attack
aircraft, the II Pluses had the 100 per cent LERX, with
twin Goodyear AN/ALE-39 chaff/flare dispensers on each
side of the upper rear fuselage and with a lengthened ram
air intake at the base of the fin. The aircraft also had a new
overwing UHF antenna, which also served as the antenna
for the AN/APX-100 IFF set. Provision was made for the
future carriage of a reconnaissance pod on the centreline.
Gross take-off weight was increased to 31,000 lb (14062 kg),
with 7,759 lb (3519 kg) of internal fuel and 13,200 lb (5987 kg)
of stores, while fatigue life was increased to 6,000 hours.

The second FSD AV-8B served as the aerodynamic
prototype for the Harrier II Plus, and carried inert AIM-120
AMRAAMs, which have yet to be funded. The aircraft was
also intended from the start to operate with a BVR anti-ship
missile – AGM-84 Harpoon is the obvious choice.

MDD modified the 205th single-seater (164129) to serve
as the FSD Harrier II Plus after receiving a $20 million
contract from Naval Air Systems Command. The aircraft
first flew on 22 September 1992, a month ahead of
schedule, in the hands of McDonnell Douglas test pilot
Jackie Jackson. The aircraft was delivered to the NAWC-AD
for testing, before transfer to the NAWC-Weapons Division
at China Lake. It was joined by the first production
Harrier II Plus from 23 April 1992. The second went to
VX-5 for OT&E and the third to VMA-542 after briefly
undergoing carrier suitability trials.

Harrier II Plus orders

The US Navy originally ordered 27 new-build radar
Harriers, and intended to order 48 more, followed by 192
conversions from earlier versions. The aim was to bring all
surviving Harriers to II Plus standards. In the event, the
second batch of new-build aircraft was cancelled, although
the total in the first batch later rose to 31 new-build

airframes. The first of them was funded from the 20 FY89 single-seaters, with six more coming from the 22 FY90 aircraft. All 21 FY91 single-seaters and all six aircraft from FY92 (Gulf War attrition replacements) were also delivered with radar. The new-build Harrier II Pluses were delivered to the three front-line squadrons at Cherry Point, which initially operated a mix of old day-attack AV-8Bs and brand-new radar-equipped Harriers. In the mixed squadrons, all pilots typically fly one week per month in the new variant, usually night cycle NVG training.

Eight new-build Harrier II Plus aircraft were procured by the Spanish Navy (which have also had the surviving basic AV-8Bs brought up to the same standards). Sixteen were ordered by the Italian navy, 13 of which were to be assembled locally, by Alenia.

Even if the Harrier II Plus production run was cut short, large numbers of earlier AV-8Bs were upgraded to the same standards. Four conversions were funded in FY94, four more in FY95, eight in FY96, 12 in FY97, 13 in 1998 and 18 in 1999, against an initial requirement for 72-75 rebuilds. The rebuild programme was worth about $1.7 billion, and was completed in October 2003.

The remanufacture of a standard or Night Attack AV-8B to Harrier II Plus configuration is reported to cost about two-thirds of the price of a new aircraft. It is an extremely extensive process, using an entirely new fuselage, a new -408A engine, new radar and FLIR, and brand-new cockpit displays, and reworking of the undercarriage, tail unit, wing, gun pod and pylons. McDonnell Douglas (now Boeing) and the Naval Aviation Depot at Cherry Point shared the work: aircraft were disassembled and inspected at NADEP, which also incorporated most of the necessary structural modifications, and McDonnell Douglas (Boeing) built the new fuselage and performed final assembly work. Reused components were fatigue tested but are not zero-lifed. The first of a total of 72 remanufactured AV-8Bs was flown by Jackie Jackson on 29 November 1995.

Even without AMRAAM and Harpoon (often thought to be the *raison d'être* of the upgrade programme), the radar of the II Plus significantly increased the aircraft's usefulness, since it is effective in conditions that would blind the AV-8B(NA), whose FLIR cannot cope with mist, haze, rain or smoke.

Improvements to the AV-8B

A number of improvements to the AV-8B were funded in the late 1990s. These included the OSCAR (Open Systems Core Avionics Requirements) programme, which improved avionics interfaces, and, by using COTS (Commercial Off-The-Shelf) items, reduced costs. Launched in conjunction with Spain and Italy, OSCAR features new mission and weapons management computers and a GPS/INS suite, allowing new systems and weapons to be integrated on the aircraft. OSCAR 1.1 allowed the carriage of AMRAAM missiles by Spanish and Italian AV-8B Harrier II Plus aircraft. Other stages of OSCAR included the integration of the Litening II targeting pod (for delivery of GBU-12 and GBU-16 LGBs). Plans also call for the aircraft to be cleared to carry JDAM missiles for additional stand-off precision strike capability. The programme allowed integration of other new weapons, and provided an overall reducton in weight. The aircraft also received an automatic target hand-off system (ATHS), AN/ARC-210, a new defensive aids package including AN/ALE-47, a video fatigue recorder, a digital flap controller and a flight incident recorder, and the aircraft was made MIL STD 1760B compatible.

From the 1990s the USMC concentrated its power projection in the form of the Marine Expeditionary Unit (Special Operations Capable) structure. The Harrier has suffered problems in becoming truly integrated into this flexible and hard-hitting approach. The small-deck ships

from which the USMC Harriers operate lack the precision approach radars found on the larger US Navy carriers. This severely limits the ability of the aircraft to operate in poor weather conditions. At times operations are even cancelled in fine weather when the risk of changing conditions could threaten the returning aircraft. These limitations were exposed during action against Serbia in 1999.

Harriers over Kosovo

In early 1999 a total of eight AV-8Bs of VMA-231 was deployed aboard USS *Kearsage* as part of the 26th Marine Expeditionary Unit (Special Operations Capable). By mid-April 1999 the 26th MEU(SOC) was ready to contribute to Operation Noble Anvil – the name given to US participation in Operation Allied Force. Initial USMC operations in the Adriatic had been conducted by the 24th MEU(SOC), operating from USS *Nassau*, and despite the arrival of *Kearsage*, *Nassau* was to remain on station to support the aid for refugees efforts.

The eight AV-8Bs aboard *Kearsage* only played a limited role in the air campaign, the lack of a dedicated designating pod and the poor weather during much of the operation reducing the effectiveness of the small AV-8B force. Much

of the flying involved training missions, ready to support a ground offensive if this had become neceassry.

On 1 May one of the aircraft was lost, crashing into the Adriatic while recovering to the carrier. The pilot was rescued by a 'plane-guard' CH-46. At the cessation of hostilities in June 1999, the USS *Kearsage* and its AV-8Bs remained on station into the autumn months, in support of the Kosovo Stabilisation Force.

RAF deployment

Royal Air Force Harriers did, however, play a much more meaningful role in the conflict. On 15 February 1999 eight Harrier GR.Mk 7s of No. 1(F) Squadron, RAF, deployed to Gioia del Colle, Italy, in support of the Kosovo Verification Mission. The unit took over from No. IV(AC) Squadron, which had conducted Operation Deliberate Forge operations since the autumn of 1998.

In March 1999 the deteriorating situation in Kosovo and the increasing evidence of Serb repression of Kosovar Albanians saw a massive increase in available NATO air assets, in preparation for military action. With Serbian President Slobodan Milosevic showing no signs of halting the ethnic cleansing in the Kosovo region, NATO launched Operation

Above and below: A furious pyrotechnics display at the 1996 Aspen air show (above) provides a dramatic background for this VMA-211 AV-8B(NA). The Harrier has now undergone its own trial by fire in several major conflicts and emerged as a reliable combat aircraft that can undertake any task required of it. The four GR.Mk 7/AV-8B operators around the world should, by rights, have been joined by many others who need the Harrier's unique capabilities. What is required is a little extra faith in those abilities and a little extra money to ensure the Harrier II's potential does not go unfulfilled.

Above: In 1993 VMA-542 became the first operational USMC squadron to receive the radar-equipped AV-8B Harrier II Plus. This pair of aircraft is seen later in the decade operating from MCAS Cherry Point. The unit continues to operate the AV-8B from Cherry Point to this day as part of the 2nd Marine Aircraft Wing (2nd MAW). Other Cherry Point-based Harrier units comprise VMA-223 'Bulldogs', VMA-231 'Ace of Spades' and the training unit VMAT-203 (FRS) 'Hawks'.

Right: Three views of RAF Harrier GR.Mk 7s at Gioia del Colle, Italy, while conducting combat operations during Operation Allied Force in 1999. No. 1(F) Squadron flew over 800 missions during the 11-week conflict, the majority of sorties concentrating on the discovery and destruction of hostile Serbian ground units within Kosovo. In contrast to the heavily publicised application of precision-guided munitions, much of the ordnance dropped by the Harriers over Kosovo was of the unguided type. Use of the RBL 755 cluster bomb and 500-lb (227-kg) and 1,000-lb (454-kg) 'dumb' bombs was particularly prevalent – the latter seen here on trolleys before loading onto the aircraft (far right).

Allied Force on 24 March 1999. No. 1(F) Squadron Harriers were immediately in action, attacking targets both within Serbia and Kosovo. Two RAF TriStar tankers were also deployed to provide the Harriers with an in-theatre air-to-air refuelling capablitiy.

On 28 March four additional Harriers were dispatched to Gioia del Colle, joined by another four examples on 7 April – bringing No. 1(F) Squadron's total compliment of aircraft to 16. To allow such a sizeable force to operate, additional pilots and groundcrew, predominantly from No. 20(R) Squadron, were also provided.

In the 78-day operation No. 1(F) Squadron flew over 850 combat sorties, accounting for some 12 per cent of all

NATO strike missions flown. The majority of weapons used during the 11-week campaign were numerous unguided bombs and over 500 RBL 755 cluster munitions, as well as Paveway II laser-guided bombs. The performance of the TIALD/Paveway II used by both the Harriers and Tornado GR.Mk 1s proved disappointing, with a success rate of only 65 per cent. This compared with the combination's success rate of 85 per cent over Bosnia in 1995 and 100 per cent in the 1991 Gulf War. A lack of training experience with LGBs and poor weather was put forward by a number of Harrier pilots for the unsatisfactory performance of the system during the conflict. Using the RBL 755 cluster bombs the Harriers achieved a 40 per cent success rate, with 31 per cent missing the target and 29 per cent unaccounted for.

For their action in Allied Force No. 1(F) Squadron commander Wing Commander A. Golledge was awarded the DSO and three other squadron pilots received the DFC.

In July 1999 No. 3 Squadron took over from No. 1(F) Squadron at Gioia del Colle, and the three operational squadrons continued their rotational deployments in support of the subsequent policing operations, known as Operation Deliberate Forge, until the Harrier force was withdrawn from the area in April 2001.

An MCAS Cherry Point-based AV-8B Harrier II Plus, with an AIM-9L Sidewinder missile fitted on the outer wing pylon, is refuelled at a designated 'hot pit' on the flightline. The ability to rapidly refuel and turnaround the aircraft was put to good use in Operation Iraqi Freedom, where USMC AV-8Bs used Tallil airfield as a forward refuelling point to allow numerous combat missions to be conducted each day.

Joint Force Harrier

Following action in Operation Allied Force, the RAF's operational Harrier units prepared for a major reorganisation that would define their role for the following decade.

The UK government's Strategic Defence Review, published in July 1998 committed to re-align the Royal Navy's Sea Harrier squadrons and the RAF Harriers under a new force named Joint Force Harrier (JFH). Designed to enable a flexible force to be rapidly deployed anywhere in the world, JFH enabled RAF Harriers, Sea Harriers or a mixture of both to deploy aboard the Royal Navy's aircraft-carriers and/or to deploy to ground bases abroad, and was formed on 1 April 2000. In August of that year No. 1(F) Squadron moved from its long-term base at RAF Wittering to join the other two RAF front-line Harrier units (Nos 3 and 4 Squadrons) at RAF Cottesmore, both of which had returned from Germany in 1999. With the imminent retirement of the Sea Harrier, JFH will be concentrated at RAF Cottesmore and Wittering with Harrier GR.Mk 9/9As and T.Mk 12s until the arrival of the planned Joint Strike Fighter in 2012.

The first test for the newly-established JFH came in May 2000, as No. 3 Squadron was embarked aboard HMS *Illustrious* for Exercise Linked Seas. The deteriorating situation in Sierra Leone saw the carrier and its air group redeploy to the area to support British Army efforts to restore stability. The Harriers flew numerous missions in support of the ground forces before relative calm was eventually restored.

From the time of the JFH reorganisation, continuing Northern Watch commitments saw regular deployments of all three operational RAF Harrier units to Incirlik in Turkey. The aircraft were used for reconnaissance duties and as close air support assets, helping deter Iraqi aggression against the Kurdish population in the north of Iraq.

AV-8B II Plus in Spain and Italy

Following the delivery of the last of 13 Italian Navy AV-8B Harrier II Plus aircraft in December 1997, the Spanish Navy took delivery of the last of five remanufactured Harrier II Plus aircraft on 5 December 2003. This delivery marked the end of Harrier II production by Boeing, with the only work on new variants now being the RAF's upgrade of its fleet to GR.Mk 9/9A standard. Spanish and Italian AV-8B Harrier II Plus's have since received modifications to carry the Litening II targeting pod, allowing the aircraft to deploy GBU-12 and GBU-16 laser-guided munitions.

In mid-2000 a joint test programme for both Spanish and Italian AV-8B Plus radar-equipped variants was conducted at the China Lake test facility in the USA, removing the restrictions placed on the flight envelope in which the AMRAAM missile can be released. The Italian Navy began to field the weapon on its aircraft in 2003.

Grounding the fleet

The AV-8B's service history has not been without its controversies. The mission-capable rates posted by the aircraft have never quite matched expectations and, in July 2000, all AV-8Bs fitted with the Rolls-Royce F402-RR-408 engine were grounded following the third crash involving engine malfunction within a few months. The latest incident had occurred on 21 June 2000 when the pilot of an AV-8B on a training mission from Twenty-Nine Palms, Ca, suffered an engine fire and ejected. Examination of the wreckage pointed to a fault with the number three engine bearing assembly and rectification of all affected units would be necessary. In conjunction with Rolls-Royce, the Naval Aviation Depot and various parties at NAS Cherry Point, Naval Air Systems Command approved the modifications to solve the problem, involving major engine repairs and other systems enhancements. A total of 105 AV-8Bs was affected by this action, of which 11 were operationally deployed at the time of the grounding. The remainder of the fleet, powered by the F-402-RR-406 version of the engine, remained unaffected.

The loss of a large portion of the available AV-8B airframes was obviously a big blow to the USMC and a desperate reallocation of the Harrier's commitments was instigated. Over the following 12 months aircraft availability gradually improved as the aircraft passed through the modification process until, by mid-July 2002, the USMC Harrier force was back to full strength.

Extra training and pilot proficiency courses were conducted to regain sufficient qualified aircrew, the numbers having rapidly dropped during the grounding. With the engine fault cured, Harrier squadrons once again deployed at sea in the latter half of 2001, commencing with the 31st MEU in the western Pacific.

Below: The final Spanish AV-8B Harrier II Plus was delivered to the customer by Boeing in December 2003. All Spanish and Italian examples of this variant are now cleared to carry both the Litening II designation pod, for the application of precision-guided bombs, and the AMRAAM missile for beyond visual range (BVR) air-to-air combat.

Bottom: USMC AV-8Bs often participate in joint training exercises with other US military forces. Here a VMA-231 example readies for take-off at Nellis AFB, Nevada, while supporting a phase of the A-10 Division, US Weapons School course in November 2002.

Above: Following the conclusion of the Operation Enduring Freedom campaign, USMC assets continued to be deployed to the region in support of ongoing operations against remaining pockets of Taliban and al-Qaeda fighters in the mountainous areas bordering Afghanistan. Here a Harrier II Plus, armed with a pair of GBU-12 LGBs, prepares to launch from USS Wasp in August 2002, while operating as part of the 22nd MEU(SOC).

Right and above right: The first USMC Harriers into action during Operation Enduring Freedom were the six AV-8B(NA)s attached to the 15th MEU(SOC) aboard USS Peleliu. During the first raids on 3 November 2001 the AV-8Bs delivered Mk 82 'dumb' bombs, as seen on this aircraft departing the carrier as part of that first strike package (right). In the following days further strikes were launched from Peleliu (above right).

Below: An AV-8B of VMA-513 is seen at rest at Bagram, Afghanistan, in October 2002. The ability to operate fom inside the country allowed the Harriers to support the ground forces much more effectively.

Taking aside the problems associated with the faulty engine bearing, the introduction of the F402-RR-408 engine has not only offered much improved power safety margins, but also has a longer time between major overhauls and an Engine Monitoring System to self-diagnose any faults. The AV-8B does unquestionably have a chequered safety record in USMC service, with some 42 Marine pilots having perished in crashes since the Harrier II's introduction. As squadron pilots point out, however, the AV-8B's record since the engine modification programme was completed has been superior to the F/A-18 Hornet in USMC service. The upgrading of the AV-8B flight simulators and changes to the training course are also cited as reasons for the AV-8B's improving safety record.

The fact that the aircraft still tops the mishap rate per 100,000 flying hours is as much a function of the nature of the shorter endurance missions flown by the AV-8B force and the inherent danger of shipboard operations than any particular shortcoming with the aircraft, according to the USMC. Despite a pervading opinion in the US DoD that the AV-8B is one of the US military's most unsafe

airframes, the pilots who fly the aircraft are of a different opinion. Critics also point to the aircraft having insufficient range and speed, but this is not the case according to Lt Col. Rob Kuckuk of VMA-214: "It goes too slow for what? Find me an F-15 guy who drops his weapons while supersonic. I can run a Hornet out of gas every time. It's simply untrue to say we don't have the legs".

Operation Enduring Freedom

Following the 11 September 2001 terorist attacks on New York and Washington, the US immediately began to plan its 'War on Terror'. The first phase involved the attempted destruction of the al-Qaeda terrorist organisation and the death or capture of its leader, Osama bin Laden. The terrorist organisation had based itself in Afghanistan, with the blessing of the fundamental Taliban regime that governed the country. Having hastily drawn together a coalition of partners for military action, the US assembled a large military force for an aerial attack, with the aim of removing the Taliban from power and disabling all al-Qaeda operations in the country under the operation name Enduring Freedom. Offensive operations commenced on 7 October 2001 with both USAF and carrier based US Navy aircraft attacking command and control facilities, airfields and other sites of strategic importance.

The USMC was not involved in the first weeks of the operation. However, on 3 November 2001 15th Marine Expeditionary Unit AV-8Bs launched from USS *Peleliu* to begin bombing missions on al-Qaeda and Taliban command and control positions in southern Afghanistan. The aircraft, armed with 500-lb (227-kg) Mk 82 unguided bombs, returned to the parent ship four hours later. The 15th MEU(SOC) had deployed to the Arabian Sea area on 28 September 2001, equipped with six AV-8Bs.

As the air action intensified, AV-8Bs, including radar-equpped AV-8B Harrier II Plus aircraft from USS *Bataan*'s

26th MEU(SOC), joined the attacks. Further missions were flown throughout November and December, the majority being supported by USMC KC-130 tanker aircraft.

By January 2002 the objective of removing the Taliban had been achieved and both ground and air bases had been set up within the country to conduct the extensive 'mopping up' operations. Many Taliban and al-Qaeda remnants had fled to the inhospitible White Mountain region in the east of the country and it was here, in March 2002, that the US forces would conduct their bloodiest battle of the war.

Named Operation Anaconda, US commanders planned to surround and capture or destroy what was believed to be a few hundred enemy fighters in the Upper Shah-i-Kot valley. Launched on 2 March, the operation immediately went awry as US Army troops came under heavy fire during insertion by helicopter. Other US troops on the ground also came under attack as it became readily apparent that the strength of the enemy had been underestimated. Close air support by US Army AH-64s and USAF A-10s, F-16s and F-15Es was immediately called in, supported by additional strikes by US Navy F-14s and F/A-18s and USAF B-52s, B-1s and AC-130 gunships. Additional aid was requested, and the 13th MEU(SOC) aboard USS *Bon Homme Richard* was rushed to the conflict area from the coast of Oman. Arriving on 4 March 2002, the 13th MEU immediately dispatched its AH-1W gunships and CH-53E transport helicopters to support the operation. In addition, USS *Bon Homme Richard* also sent its AV-8B Harriers into action. Over the next few days the AV-8Bs flew over 100 combat missions in support of Operation Anaconda, dropping 32 GBU-12 500-lb (227-kg) LGBs and two unguided 500-lb (227-kg) bombs in support of the US forces on the ground.

With the conclusion of Anaconda, the USMC maintained a presence in the region, using its AV-8Bs for reconnaissance and strike missions against pockets of enemy fighters as, and when, they were detected.

As operations continued in Afghanistan, in August 2001 the last 'vanilla' day-attack AV-8Bs were retired from front-line service, leaving all operational units equipped with the AV-8B(NA) and AV-8B Harrier II Plus versions. Day attack versions, however, continued to serve with the Harrier Training Squadron at MCAS Cherry Point.

Top: The remit of the USMC expeditionary force has ensured that AV-8Bs have deployed to points all around the globe. The situation in Sierra Leone in 2003 saw the AV-8Bs of the 398th Air Expeditionary Group cover personnel recovery and emergency evacuation operations, operating from Freetown International Airport.

Above: As part of the US-led 'War on Terror', both current variants of the AV-8B have been operating from Djibouti as part of the Combined Joint Task Force (the counter-terrorism operation in the Horn of Africa). Here, a pair of AV-8Bs prepare to depart Djibouti's international airport in June 2003.

Left: The USMC retain an AV-8B presence in Japan with the 1st Marine Air Wing at MCAS Iwakuni. Here a 'Plus' of VMA-231 prepares to conduct a sortie from the base in November 2003.

Right: The 3rd Marine Air Wing centralised its AV-8B assets for Iraqi Freedom, instead of allocating them to medium helicopter squadrons as per the norm. Here, a Harrier II Plus launches from USS Nassau on 7 April 2003 for a pre-planned strike using a single GBU-16 LGB (port wing), guided to its target using a Litening II targeting pod (starboard wing).

Below: Carrying a pair of AGM-65 Mavericks, a VMA-214 AV-8B II Plus prepares to depart Ahmed Al Jaber AB in Kuwait on 12 April 2003.

Below: USMC AV-8Bs operated from both sea and land during Iraqi Freedom. With a lack of available air-to-air refuelling assets, large underwing auxiliary fuel tanks were a necessity, giving the aircraft sufficient endurance to patrol their allocated 'kill box' for over an hour.

Below centre: The GBU-16 was the weapon of choice for many of the AV-8B combat sorties, and linked to the Litening targeting pod proved highly effective. With the US still smarting over the '9/11' terrorist attacks, this example has been adorned with a World Trade Centre memorial sticker on its GBU-16.

Below right: An AV-8B II Plus is manoeuvred on the deck of USS Tarawa during the conflict. Tarawa was one of the two LHDs in theatre.

Iraqi Freedom Harriers

Operation Telic, the British name for the action against Iraq in 2003, involved the deployment of 12 aircraft from Nos 1(F) and IV(AC) Squadrons, to Ahmed Al Jaber AB in Kuwait, based alongside USMC F/A-18Ds and AV-8Bs, and USAF F-16Cs and OA/A-10As. The Harrier GR.Mk 7s used a variety of weapons to attack both fixed and mobile targets including RBL 755 cluster bombs, AGM-65 Maveick missiles and both Paveway II and GPS-equipped Enhanced Paveway laser-guided bombs. The latter was only fitted as an emergency measure shortly before the conflict began to allow the Harriers to attack targets where designation using the TIALD system was unreliable. It also allowed the weapons to be deployed from a greater stand-off range and higher altitude as added protection from groundfire and SAMs. Among the many 'kills' attributed to the Harrier GR.Mk 7 was the delivery of a 1,000-lb (454-kg) Enhanced Paveway III directly into the Ba'ath party headquarters building in Basra.

Many sorties invovled air-to-air refuelling and the accuracy of the strikes was considered above average. The Enhanced Paveway was particularly effective on its operational debut on the Harrier, proving more accurate than US-delivered JDAMs. A number of No. IV(AC) Sqn's sorties involved the detection and destruction of surface-to-surface missiles as part of the RAF's Time Sensitive Targeting mission.

Formations of Harriers self-designated targets, with one or more of the attack formation carrying a BAE Systems TIALD pod. Although the performance of TIALD could not match more advanced systems, such as the Litening II, the strict rules of engagement ensured that the majority of targets were hit avoiding collateral damage. Night attack missions were also conducted using night vision goggles.

As the US-led advance progressed rapidly through the south and central regions of Iraq, both USMC and RAF Harriers were able to operate 'cab rank' operations almost at will due to the total air supremecy. Harriers were often called on to provide close air support to both US and British ground forces at very short notice as the battlefield rapidly changed as the advance progressed at great speed. Positive identification of targets before attack was vitally important and the lead pilot during RAF Harrier missions used hand-held binoculars by day and the TIALD pod by night to confirm the target was hostile before any weapons were delivered. When not operating attack missions, the RAF GR.Mk 7s also flew numerous valuable reconnaissance missions using the Joint Reconnaissance Pod.

Scud-hunters

In addition to Nos 1(F) and IV(AC) Squadrons, based in Kuwait, eight aircraft from No. 3 Squadron were deployed to Azraq in Jordan. Joining USAF OA/A-10As, F-16s and AC-130 gunships, the Jordan-based Harriers were tasked with destroying any Iraqi Army units operating in the deserts to the west of Baghdad and hunting down and destroying any mobile Scud missile launchers, which could threaten Israel. This would allow the US/British forces to establish bases in the west of the country as the campaign unfolded. As the conflict progressed and the Scud threat diminished the Harriers were employed in support of the final advance into Baghdad.

In fact, the Harriers were by no means restricted to supporting one area or one force in-theatre. About 30 per cent of the Harrier's missions were flown in support of British and US Marine action, with the remaining 70 per

cent of close air support sorties being in support of the US Army's drive to Baghdad. During the 22 days of the main campaign No. 3 Squadron's eight aircraft alone flew over 1,000 hours of combat time – the equivalent of two aircraft being permanently airborne 24 hours a day.

Marines in the Gulf

As the war unfolded the close air support and battlefield air interdiction efforts of both RAF and USMC Harriers were concentrated on the 'kill box' method of attack. Aircraft approaching the battlefield were directed by E-2 or E-3 AWACS aircraft to their assigned 'box'. On entering the engagement the aircraft were then controlled by an assigned Forward Air Controller, usually another Harrier or an OA-10A, and queued up to be assigned targets by the Joint Terminal Air Commanders.

The USMC Harrier force, operating mainly in the first days of the conflict from the two amphibious warfare ships USS *Tarawa* and USS *Nassau*, and latterly mainly from Ahmed Al Jaber in Kuwait, numbered a total of 70 aircraft. The benefit of the AV-8B upgrade to incorporate the Litening II targeting pod immediately became apparent. Using a recently fitted datalink to provide real-time video coverage to Marine combat unit headquarters, via a Pioneer UAV ground station, the AV-8B could be dual-roled for close air support and reconnaissance duties with ease. Allowing commanders to assess real-time images of the battlefield from a remote location was a major advantage, enabling attacks to be planned and strategies conceived as the AV-8Bs were on station. The Litening pod, when used for designating for precision-guided munitions, also performed beyond expectations, with a target destruction success rate well above anything achieved by the AV-8B before.

A typical load for an AV-8B would encompass four 1,000-lb (454-kg) LGBs and two CBU-99 cluster munitions. Lead aircraft in each element would replace one of the LGBs

RAF groundcrew go to work on a GR.Mk 7 under the hot Kuwaiti sun. In no small part thanks to the hard work completed by the ground support, the GR.Mk 7s demonstrated a higher mission-capable rate than the USMC AV-8Bs.

with the Litening II pod. Litening-equipped AV-8Bs were also used extensively as Forward Air Contollers for USMC F/A-18Ds, acquiring targets for the latter to attack using JDAMs.

The AV-8Bs proved highly adaptable as the conflict progressed, as Maj. Gen. James Amos of the 3rd MAW explained: "I had my Harriers flying off highways and bombed-out runways as we advanced on Baghdad for the final show-down. I simply could not have been more pleased with the reliability of the airplane and its weapons systems…and in the courage and discipline of my AV-8 pilots".

Both RAF Harriers and USMC AV-8Bs made good use of the latest version of the Maverick missile – the AGM-65G2. New software allowing the AV-8Bs to uncage the IR-seeker head and determine the coordinates of a target before launch helped drastically reduce the likelihood of fratricide incidents. Harrier GR.Mk 7s also used the weapon against point targets, such as naval craft, in the Basra area.

The fielding of the AV-8B during Iraqi Freedom was not, however, all good news. The aircraft's servicibility was again called into question, reinforced by the fact that the USMC AV-8Bs had the lowest mission-capable rate of any combat aircraft used in the conflict at just 67.3 per cent. The figure is without doubt an effect of operating a

Above: Unlike in the previous Gulf War USMC AV-8Bs had both the systems and weapons to conduct effective night operations. Numerous after dark sorties were flown from Ahmed Al Jaber (above left) and from the amphibious carriers in the Persian Gulf (above).

Below: Harrier GR.Mk 7 operations during Operation Telic were concentrated at Ahmed Al Jaber, Kuwait. Below two typical weapons layouts are demostrated: two Paveway II LGBs, two RBL 755 cluster bombs and two AIM-9L Sidewinder missiles (below); a pair of British 1,000-lb (454-kg) dumb bombs and two AIM-9L Sidewinders (bottom).

Above: A pair of No. 1(F) Squadron Harrier GR.Mk 7s is seen here in transit to Bardufoss, Norway, for Exercise Snow Falcon in January 2004. Seven of the squadron's aircraft received the 'winter' camouflage for the duration of their deployment, in which they flew affiliation sorties with Royal Norwegian Air Force F-16s and conducted Ground Forward Air Control (GFAC) work with the Royal Marines and the Norwegian Army. Training for combat operations in any environment is an important element of ensuring the expeditionary nature of Joint Force Harrier is as effective as possible.

Right: The Harrier GR.Mk 9/9A upgrade is designed to provide the RAF with a weapons platform capable of fulfilling the needs of Joint Force Harrier until the introduction of the Joint Strike Fighter sometime after 2012. In February 2004 BAE Systems took the opportunity to undertake the variant's first carrier-borne trials aboard HMS Ark Royal. The primary aim was to assess the performance of the Mk 9's new inertial navigation unit (INS/GPS) on a moving platform. The trials involved undertaking the various types of inertial align while on the carrier, and then flying ashore to measure the resultant drift between alignment and landing at a known, fixed position. The deployment coincided with the last embarkation at sea of No. 800 NAS's Sea Harrier FA.Mk 2s – the unit disbanding in March 2004.

complex aircraft, often from small carriers, at the end of an extremely long logistical chain. However, questions will still remain about the suitability of the aircraft for expeditionary air warfare if such mission-capable rates are expected to be the norm. In addition, the AV-8Bs suffered from a lack of air-to-air refuelling support, as US Navy and US Air Force air assets had first call on the tankers, leaving the Harriers without sufficient endurance to be fully effective over the battlefield. Despite these faults the AV-8B did perform creditably during the conflict and, when operating from the forward refuelling point at Tallil air base inside Iraq during the final days of the main campaign, was one of the coalition's most vital weapons in detecting hidden Iraqi ground forces in an urban or semi-urban environment as the advance reached Baghdad.

By the end of the main phase of Iraqi Freedom all eight operational AV-8B units had participated in some form in either Enduring Freedom or Iraqi Freedom, elements from VMA-211, -223, -231, -311 and -542 seeing action in the latter conflict. Remarkably, given the aircraft's record in service, not a single airframe was lost during either operation, proving that the reliability and capability of the AV-8B had reached new levels.

Harrier GR.Mk 9

The entire RAF Harrier fleet is slated to undergo a limited avionics upgrade to sustain and enhance its capabilities and

add smart weapon-delivery capabilities. The single-seat version will then become known as the Harrier GR.Mk 9 and the two-seater allocated the designation T.Mk 12.

In addition, in December 1999 the long-awaited and much-needed decision to provide a more powerful engine for the Harrier was approved under a £100 million contract with Rolls-Royce. Budgetery constraints, however, have limited the procurement to just 30 engines for 20 aircraft. Existing Pegasus 105 engines will be 'returned to works' for modification to Mk 107 standard, increasing the engine rating from 21,750 lb (96.75 kN) to 23,800 lb (105.87 kN). Once all upgrades have been completed re-engined single-seat aircraft will be designated GR.Mk 9A, with aircraft retaining the old Pegasus 105s becoming GR.Mk 9s. Examples fitted with the new engine, but yet to receive avionics and weapons upgrade have been designated GR.Mk 7A.

The first GR.Mk 7A made its maiden flight at BAE System's Warton airfield on 20 September 2002. The aircraft, along with the rest of the fleet, are planned to receive new rear fuselage sections to eliminate exhaust induced fatigue problems. The additional power increases the aircraft's all-up weight from 32,000 lb (14515 kg) to 34,000 lb (15422 kg), allowing a greater weapons load and improving 'bring back' capabilities when operating from warships or land. The first two Harrier GR.Mk 7As were delivered to No. 3 Squadron at RAF Wittering in October

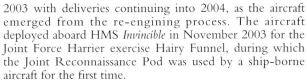

2003 with deliveries continuing into 2004, as the aircraft emerged from the re-engining process. The aircraft deployed aboard HMS *Invincible* in November 2003 for the Joint Force Harrier exercise Hairy Funnel, during which the Joint Reconnaissance Pod was used by a ship-borne aircraft for the first time.

New weapons, new capabilities

The systems upgrade to GR.Mk 9/9A/T.Mk 12 standard is officially known as the Integrated Weapons Programme (IWP). Central to the IWP is the integration of new precision-guided weapons, including Brimstone and the new GPS guidance-capable Paveway IV laser-guided bomb. To facilitate the use of these 'smart' weapons the MIL-STD-1760 Stores Management System (SMS) is to be integrated, which, when linked to a new onboard open system mission computer and new high order language operational flight programme software, will permit the aircraft to effectively 'talk' to the weapons. In addition, the upgrade will include a new Inertial Navigation System/GPS, which will provide the weapons with navigation data via the 1760 interface, and new secure communications systems. Cockpit improvements include the addition of a new head-down display (HDD) and video map generator. To enhance the Harrier's flight safety envelope a Ground Proximity Warning System (GPWS) is also planned. For operations in Iraqi Fredom a number of Harrier GR.Mk 7s were fitted with inboard weapons pylons capable of deploying the GPS-guided Enhanced Paveway bomb as an emergency measure.

The first contract for the multi-phase upgrade was issued on 2 December 1999 encompassing the initial development, with a follow-on contact, signed in January 2003, covering mainly software refinement and flight test work. On 30 May 2003 the first GR.Mk 9 (serial ZD320) to complete the IWP upgrade made its maiden flight at Warton. At that time the first 24 deliveries were due to the RAF by the end of 2004, however, delays to the programme have ensured that this target is unlikely to be met. On 21 April 2004 the second GR.Mk 9 joined the flight test programme, with the third example – this time a GR.Mk 9A – due to make its maiden flight by mid-2004. Operational release for the GR.Mk 9/9A is anticipated in 2006, although this date is again under scrutiny. The integration of the MBDA Brimstone is still yet to commence and, following the earlier cancellation of Storm Shadow and ASRAAM integration, the future of carrying the weapon on the Harrier is still not assured.

With the flight test programme in progress, the second phase of the IWP upgrade, designated Capability C2 and worth around £100 million to prime contractor BAE Systems, was awarded in January 2004. Capability C2 incorporates the integration of the Paveway IV bomb and improves the integration of infrared- and TV-guided versions

of the AGM-65 Maverick missile already fielded on the GR.Mk 7. The need for the Harrier force to be equipped with the Maverick had been highlighted by the shortcomings during Operation Allied Force, and in 2000-01 a programme was initiated to integrate the missile to the current GR.Mk 7 fleet. Initial Operating Capability (IOC) with the weapon was declared in March 2001 and full operational clearance was granted in time for the Harriers to employ the weapon during Operation Iraqi Freedom in 2003. Capability C2 also includes the addition of the Successor Identification Friend or Foe (SIFF) system, decreasing the aircraft's vulnerability in an operational environment.

With the planned phase-out of the Royal Navy's Sea Harrier FA.Mk 2 in 2004-06, Joint Force Harrier will be solely equipped with Harrier GR.Mk 9/9A and T.Mk 12 aircraft. Two operational squadrons will be flown by RAF aircrew and two by Royal Navy pilots under the control of AOC 3 Group, RAF. A training squadron will incorporate the majority of the two-seat T.Mk 12s.

TAV-8B modification

Following the introduction of the AV-8B Harrier II Plus and the implementation of the OSCAR upgrade programme, the USMC TAV-8B two-seat trainers somewhat lagged behind in terms of capability, and were becoming increasingly unsuitable for training pilots in the methods of attack employed by the frontline squadrons. This has been addressed by the TAV-8B Harrier Trainer Upgrade Program (TUP), a joint project between Naval Air Systems Command and Boeing. Lacking any upgrade since introduction, the modification package includes all-new wiring, incorporation of enhanced night vision capabilities and fitment of the more powerful F402-RR-408 engine. With each TUP upgrade taking around 18,000 man hours, a total of 14 aircraft will be modified. The first aircraft to full TUP standard was delivered to VMAT-203 at MCAS Cherry Point in July 2003, with the last aircraft due to emerge from the upgrade process in 2007. TUP modifications will bring the aircraft up to a similar standard to the front-line aircraft and will allow operational squadrons to spend less time bringing new pilots up to mission readiness standard.

Waiting for JSF

With the last of the 72 Harrier IIs rebuilt to AV-8B Plus standard delivered on 30 September 2003 to VMA-231 'Ace of Spades', the USMC was at full strength with eight front-line AV-8B squadrons operational. Both the USMC and British-operated Harriers will continue to provide vital close air support, so important in recent conflicts, until the advent of the Lockheed Marin JSF, destined to enter service in both countries in the middle part of the next decade.

Jon Lake and Daniel J. March

Above: During deployments with Marine Expeditionary Units, the Harrier contingent is usually allocated to the lead Helicopter Squadron. Here an AV-8B Harrier II Plus of VMA-542 'Flying Tigers' conducts a sortie from the deck of USS Wasp when assigned to the CH-46 unit HMM-266 (Reinforced). The aircraft were embarked as part of the 22nd MEU(SOC) in October 2003, conducting PHIBRON/MEU integration training. With the integration of the Litening II targeting pod now complete, the AV-8B force is looking-forward to the integration of the JDAM to further enhance its strike capablities.

Above left: An AV-8B Harrier II Plus approaches the deck of USS Saipan on 1 April 2004. Allocated to the deployment's lead squadron HMM-263 (Reinforced), the Harriers conducted an intensive Expeditionary Strike Group/MEU pre-deployment work-up as part of the 24th MEU(SOC). During deployments, aircraft and crews may come from more than one Harrier squadron and mixed assets of both the AV-8B(NA) and AV-8B Harrier II Plus are common.

AH-64A/D Apache and AH-64D Longbow Apache

The Apache is the world's premier attack helicopter. Its long, and sometimes controversial, early history was crowned by a combat record in Operation Desert Storm which swept away any lingering doubts about the Apache's supremacy – doubts which none of its crews shared. Once a product of Hughes Helicopters and then McDonnell Douglas, the Apache is today the responsibility of the Boeing Corporation. To them now falls the responsibility of fielding the AH-64D Longbow Apache, an attack helicopter so advanced it will revolutionise the future battlefield.

AH-64 Apache and Longbow Apache

At 02:37:50, in the early darkness of 17 January 1991, First Lieutenant Tom Drew thumbed the radio switch in the pilot's seat of his AH-64A and initiated Operation Desert Storm with the laconic words "party in 10." Today it is a fact well-known, but still worth repeating, that the first shots of the war against Iraq were fired not by US Air Force F-117s, 'Secret Squirrel' B-52s or Tomahawk-toting US Navy vessels, but by AH-64A Apaches of the 101st Airborne Division, US Army. On that first night, eight Apaches operating as Task Force Normandy headed north from Al Jouf in Saudi Arabia, over the border and through the Iraqi front line, to destroy two key air-defence radar sites inside Iraq. First with Hellfires, and then with rocket and gun fire, the two teams of Apaches obliterated the Iraqi positions in a mission that would prove to be the template for all subsequent AH-64 operations in Desert Storm – supremely effective and deadly accurate.

There is no denying that the Task Force Normandy operation, planned and executed by Lieutenant Colonel Dick Cody and the men of the 1st Battalion, 101st Aviation Regiment, 101st Airborne Division, was the long-awaited vindication of the AH-64 as a weapon, in its first true combat test. The Apache and its crews had come in for more than their fair share of criticism since the first AH-64s were fielded in 1986. Teething troubles – some serious, some not – led to damaging speculation and Congressional scrutiny that proved, to the Apache community, that mud sticks. Furthermore, the personnel of the 15 Apache battalions deployed to the Gulf, along with their friends and families at home, had to suffer the assault of a prime-time American current affairs programme which damned the aircraft and forecast doom for those about to go to war in it. None of their prophecies came true. As recorded below, the AH-64 had an exceptional operational debut and notched up many firsts for US Army aviation, and for the combat helicopter as a whole. In Operation Desert Storm the Apache finally proved its claim to be the best attack helicopter in the world, a claim which no-one could begin to dispute, except perhaps those involved with the AH-64D Longbow programme.

This is not to say that the Apache is invincible, and one need look no further than the success of TF Normandy to discern some of the weaknesses that still hinder the AH-64A. While the Apaches performed with finesse their task of killing their first night targets, it is an unpalatable fact (for some) that they could never had found those targets without the help of USAF AFSOC Pave Low III MH-53Js which led the Apache teams to the right place with their GPS and TFR systems. The Apache's own navigational fit was simply not up to the job. As an aircraft of the 1970s the Apache is an analog, not a digital, warrior. The mission-planning effort required for any Apache mission today, let alone one as important as TF Normandy, is immense, because every eventuality must be foreseen, sketched out and planned on paper before the aircraft are in the air. Apaches fight as a team and if the cohesion of that team is lost, so is the mission. More than most, Apache crews know the truth of von Clausewitz's maxim that 'no plan survives contact with the enemy'. This places immense strain on the crews, who have to call on the skill and experience gained from hundreds of hours of training. Communication of new ideas or new intelligence is difficult, if not impossible, after launch, so Apache crews have to fly and fight in one of the most stressful combat environments imaginable, hoping that all the answers have been worked out before the shooting starts.

This will soon change. At present, the US Army is in the early stages of fielding the AH-64D Longbow Apache, a combat helicopter for the digital battlefield of the 21st century. These are not mere buzz-words. The US Army is probably further ahead than any other branch of the US armed forces in planning to make maximum use of new technology in weapons, sensors, intelligence gathering and C^3 (command, control, communications) on the future battlefield. Army aviation and McDonnell Douglas have designed the Longbow to fight and win the intelligence war, which again is not an empty phrase but one which describes a combat situation where the AH-64D crew will be all-seeing, all-knowing and all-powerful. That, at least, is the plan. Before examining the Apache of the future we should discuss the Apache of the present, and why it is the benchmark against which all others are measured.

Although the lineage of the attack helicopter in United States service can be traced to Southeast Asia, the roots of the Apache lie firmly in Europe. The Bell AH-1G Huey-Cobra had a highly successful combat career in Vietnam after its introduction in August 1967. The Hughes BGM-71 TOW (Tube-launched, Optically-tracked, Wire-guided) missile ultimately gave the sleek 'Snake' unprecedented hitting power against armoured targets, coupled with secure stand-off ranges (though initial results of airborne TOW firings in Vietnam were poor). In Europe, where the 'real' war would be fought, the arrival of the AH-1 paved the way for the second generation of US attack helicopters that would be firmly dedicated to killing Soviet tanks in Germany. However, the AH-1 was originally only a stop-gap – developed in haste to cover delays in the Army's 'big plan' for armed helicopters.

Prehistory of the AH-64

After the successful debut of the armed UH-1, the US Army initiated the Advanced Aerial Fire Support System programme to develop a new combat helicopter for gunship, escort and fire support tasks. The result was a 1966 contract with Lockheed to develop 10 prototypes of the immense AH-56A Cheyenne. The Cheyenne was one of countless aircraft which appear as a footnote to the story of others but deserve an entire account of their own. It was conceived not as a manoeuvrable armed helicopter for nap-of-the-earth (NoE) flying, but as a large weapons platform for Vietnam-era gun and missile attacks. The Cheyenne had a General Electric T64 turboshaft driving a four-bladed main rotor, coupled with a conventional tail rotor and a decidedly unconventional pusher propeller at the end of the tailboom. The first AH-56A made its maiden flight on 21 September 1967, chalked up a startling maximum speed of 220 kt (407 km/h, 253 mph), and in January 1968 the US Department of Defense signed a contract for an initial batch of 375. The Air Force took issue with the Army for

acquiring this 'close-support aircraft'. The first prototype crashed on 12 March 1969 (killing the pilot), technical delays and hitches abounded and, finally, the advent of the shoulder-launched SAM, in the shape of the SAM-7 'Grail' (9K32 Strella-2), sealed the fate of the Cheyenne. To survive from then, any new helicopter would have to

Above: Lockheed's AH-56 Cheyenne was an over-complex design that was ultimately defeated by the small infantry SAMs that emerged in the late 1960s. As a result the Cheyenne became just a museum exhibit.

Right: In 1972 Lockheed became one of the five bidders for the Army's Advanced Attack Helicopter (AAH) competition with its proposed CL-1700. Owing much to the Cheyenne, the CL-1700 was one of the more unwieldy AAH designs.

Right: Boeing's AAH entrant featured a novel side-by-side, yet staggered, cockpit arrangement offering "four eyes forward to find and fight," as the brochure put it. Ironically, Boeing is now at the helm of the AH-64 Apache.

Right and below right: When the winners of the AAH initial evaluation were announced it was not surprising that Bell was selected as one of the two finalists. The wooden mock-up that Bell first produced was completely camouflaged; even the blades were painted. In contrast, the two prototypes wore an overall drab green scheme. Bell's YAH-63 design drew on all the company's experience with the AH-1 HueyCobra. It was beaten into the air by its Hughes rival, by a single day, in September 1975. The YAH-63 had an unhappy development and one of the two flying prototypes was lost in a crash. The other prototype, like the Cheyenne before it, survives today as an exhibit in the US Army Aviation Museum, at Ft Rucker, Alabama.

operate at less than tree-top height and be supremely agile. What was needed was a gunboat and not an ironclad, and so the US Army retired to generate another specification.

The space left by the cancellation of what might have been up to 1,000 Cheyennes still needed to be filled. With a eye on the Central European front, the US Army's next requirement coalesced around an aircraft that would better the AH-1 in terms of range, performance and firepower which still being manoeuvrable enough to fly NoE missions through, around and under forests, hills and power lines. The AH-1/TOW combination was still the best available and held the line in Europe for a decade, but it obviously could be improved.

Birth of the AAH

In August 1972 the official Request for Proposals (RFP) for the Advanced Attack Helicopter (AAH) was announced. It specified an aircraft that would cruise at 145 kt (269 km/h, 167 mph) with a full load of eight TOW missiles (or a minimum expendable ordnance load of 1,000 lb/ 454 kg) for a mission duration of 1.9 hours. Performance demands were set, surprisingly, in (Middle Eastern) terms of 4,000 ft (1220 m) altitude at an ambient temperature of 95° F (35°C). By way of comparison, conditions for 'NATO hot day' operations were defined as 2,000 ft (610 m) at 70°F (21°C). Maximum speed was to be 175 kt (323 km/h, 201 mph) and maximum vertical rate of climb 500 ft/min (152 m/min). The new helicopter would have to have operational g limits of +3.5 and -1.5 and be structurally resistant to hits from 12.7-mm armour-piercing incendiary rounds. In addition, the rotorhead (and the entire aircraft) had to remain flyable after a hit from a 23-mm high-explosive incendiary shell, the then-standard Warsaw Pact AAA calibre. A sign of the prescience of these requirements is that they would not be seen as unreasonable, or inadequate, today. The SAM threat to the aircraft was perhaps even a higher priority and the AAH would have to prove that its IR signature, and thus its vulnerability to shoulder-launched infantry SAMs, could be reduced to an acceptably low level. Such passive countermeasures would be backed up by chaff/flare dispensers. Crew survivability was placed at a premium – far too many crews had been lost in Vietnam in fragile helicopters. The AAH crew must be able to survive a crash at 30 mph (48 km/h) – a vertical impact of 42 ft/s (12.8 m/s) – with a forward speed of 15 kt.

Of course the key to survivability on the battlefield would be to allow the AAH to kill its targets outside the air defence envelope that could be expected around an advancing armoured column. The alarming Israeli experience of the 1973 Yom Kippur war showed that this might no longer be possible when faced with Soviet weapons such as the ZSU 23-4 Shilka radar-directed mobile AAA system or SA-8 'Gecko' and SA-9 'Gaskin' mobile SAMs. The TOW missile was becoming progressively less able to outreach these defences and its method of employment left the launch aircraft exposed for an unacceptable length of time.

Bell's rival and the YAH-64

While this issue was emerging as a serious challenge to the AAH concept, the US Army was faced with five competing submissions for the new helicopter – from Bell, Boeing-Vertol (teamed with Grumman Aerospace), Hughes, Lockheed and Sikorsky. Bell Helicopter Textron, not surprisingly, saw itself as the front-runner. It had amassed the most relevant experience of any of the competitors and its resultant YAH-63 (Bell Model 409) had the appearance of a thoroughbred. Boeing-Vertol, whose YUH-61A design was about to go head-to-head with Sikorsky for the US Army's UTTAS transport helicopter fly-off, offered a large AAH design, reminiscent of the Cheyenne, with some unusual features. It had a reversed tricycle undercarriage, podded engines, four-bladed rotor and large forward fuselage. The crew sat in tandem, but in

separate off-set cockpits. Lockheed, determined not to be left behind after the success, and failure, of the Cheyenne, developed the Cheyenne-lookalike CL-1700, powered by a Lycoming PLT-27 engine. Sikorsky (which would ultimately win the UTTAS competition in December 1976 with the UH-60 Blackhawk) came up with a development of the S-67 Blackhawk – however, like Boeing-Vertol, the ongoing UTTAS competition made it an unlikely candidate for AAH victory.

The final competitor was Hughes Helicopters, of Culver City, California. Hughes Helicopters was founded on 14 February 1934 by the great Howard R. Hughes Jr, as the aviation division of his Hughes Tool Company. Hughes had supplied the much-loved and respected OH-6A Cayuse, the 'Loach', to Army aviation units in Vietnam, where the type had proved to be a very tough and reliable performer, even though substantial numbers were lost in combat. For the AAH competition Hughes looked first to its OH-6 experience and took that type's small size and damage-tolerant structure as its guiding principles. An OH-6-inspired design soon proved to be far too small to meet the Army's AAH requirements and so Hughes's designers proffered the angular and awkward-looking Model 77 which, to the US Army, became the YAH -64.

Defining the future battlefield

As planning for the AAH competition advanced so, too, did US Army doctrine for the attack helicopter, as a concept and a weapon. The philosophy during the 1960s and 1970s had been one of 'whoever brings the most to the party wins' – victory in battle would be decided by the size of the force one side could apply to the battlefield. By the 1970s advancing technology – and clear Soviet numerical superiority – transformed this credo to 'win at night'. The interim Army aviation solution, the AH-1/NVG combination, was not proving successful in Europe. The Cobra had only maps rather than Doppler navigation, limited comms, limited reach and limited combat effectiveness. The emergence of the doctrine of 'active defence', where units would move laterally along the battlefield to reinforce each other, defined the AAH as an aircraft that must be able to conduct regimental operations at night. The objective was for an attack helicopter regiment to be capable of destroying an armoured corps. As a result, the AAH fell into line with other Army battlefield systems destined for

service in the 1980s (and then under development), such as the XM1 which became the Abrams MBT and the MICV which became the M2 Bradley IFV. The AAH became a platform for electro-optical sensors that would allow it to locate, identify and target the enemy in darkness when their combat performance was rightly seen as degraded, and then engage them from concealed positions. As the AAH competition progressed so did the development of this system, the heart of the Apache, which emerged under the unrevealing acronym of TADS/PNVS.

On 22 June 1973 the US Department of Defense announced that the Bell YAH-63 and Hughes YAH-64 had been chosen as the AAH competitors. This launched Phase 1 of the competition whereby both firms would build and fly two prototypes, plus a Ground Test Vehicle (GTV) for a competitive fly-off in mid-1976. Following the Phase 2 evaluation and selection, it was anticipated that an initial order for 472 aircraft would be awarded in late 1978/early 1979. Hughes confidently predicted that its aircraft would have a flyaway cost of not more than $1.6 million, in 1972 dollars. Bell's YAH-63A drew heavily on its AH-1G experience and was essentially a scaled-up HueyCobra which retained Bell's trademark twin-bladed, 'teetering' rotor. Like the YAH-64 it was powered by a pair of 1,500-shp (1117-kW) General Electric YT700 turboshafts – an engine choice virtually dictated to the two manufacturers for commonality with the UTTAS (Utility Tactical Transport Aircraft System) helicopter. The YAH-64 followed the same configuration, though without the same

Hughes Helicopters responded to the AAH competiton with a design based on its egg-shaped OH-6. The 'Loach', a nickname derived from its LOH (Light Observation Helicopter) designation, was a Vietnam stalwart much respected by its crews. OH-6s were used as FACs and light gunships, and their losses were heavy – one wry saying at the time had it that 'the target is marked by the burning Loach'. However, Hughes's designers respected its structural integrity enough to use it as their starting point. All OH-6 developments soon turned out to be too small to make an effective AAH, so Hughes's engineers ultimately produced the Model 77. The mock-up (above) differed from the prototypes (top) in several respects, but is clearly the ancestor of the Apache. Note the original TOW missile pods on the mock-up.

Above: AV-02 (73-22248) was the first YAH-64 to fly. The first to be built (AV-01/73-22247) served its whole life as the GTV (Ground Test Vehicle). AV-02 is seen here soon after its first flight with the original T-tail configuration and mid-set rotor. Several tailplane configurations were tested, including reversing the 'arrowhead' tailplane and adding end-plate fins.

Top right: AV-03 (73-22249) is seen here with a revised tail configuration, featuring the low-set stabilator adopted for production AH-64s. For a period AV-05 flew with no horizontal stabiliser.

Above right: AV-02 flew with a (red) instrumentation boom on its earliest flights. It also carried a dummy gun under its nose, to maintain the YAH-64's centre of gravity.

Below: This photograph of dummy Hellfires fitted to AV-03 provides a clear view of the actuated trailing-edge flap originally fitted to the YAH-64's stub wings.

sleekness of form, sharing Bell's stepped tandem cockpit, widely-spaced podded engines, stub wings, narrow tailboom and nose-mounted sensors. It differed through its tailwheel undercarriage arrangement (versus a tricycle one), four-bladed main rotor and unfaired gun installation set well back under the fuselage. The YAH-63's cannon was located above and in front of the sensor turret. In the Bell design the pilot sat in the front seat (the direct opposite of the AH-1G), but not so in the YAH-64. Hughes positioned its pilot aft on the principle that by sitting just 2 ft (60 cm) forward of the rotorshaft he would be more attuned to shifts in pitch and angle of rotation – a useful aid to ultra-low-level flight.

The definitive YAH-64 mock-up did not appear until late in 1973, and Hughes soon refined some elements of it still further. Chief among these was the addition of a

revolutionary new gun, the single-barrelled XM230A 30-mm Chain Gun® cannon designed by Hughes Aircraft Corporation. It is worth pointing out at this stage that the YAH-64's manufacturer – Hughes Helicopters – was by then a division of the Summa Corporation, while Hughes Aircraft Corp. (which had not built an aircraft for 20 years) was a separate entity, although both owed their existence to Howard Hughes. The YAH-63 was fitted with the three-barrelled General Electric XM188 30-mm cannon, which also was originally specified by Hughes. Ongoing research at Hughes convinced its AAH designers that the Chain Gun® concept offered sizeable advantages over previous aircraft guns, chiefly light weight and resistance to stoppages, and Hughes rushed its development in parallel with that of the YAH-64. Another change made to the mock-up by July 1975 was the revised canopy, which had previously been curved and less heavily framed. The revised canopy used flat-plate transparencies to reduce the problem of glint (curved transparencies will reflect light in a number of planes and for an increased length of time compared to a smaller flat surface). Framing of the canopy was also made more pronounced, dividing the cockpit glass into seven distinct sections.

The YAH-64 consortium

The Hughes AAH entry was widely perceived as a conservative one, avoiding the complicated design features and advanced material techniques that dogged the Cheyenne. Its lightweight aluminium, conventional skin-and-stringer airframe design, rugged straight-forward power train and simple rotor system were tailored to meet the Army's design-to-cost requirements. A team of 12 major sub-contractors was formed to provide expertise in areas where Hughes was lacking and to cut costs. All were allowed the freedom to develop the solution to problems in their particular area of expertise, while meeting Hughes' basic criteria. These firms included Bendix Corporation's Electric Fluid Power Division, responsible for design/fabrication of drive shafts, couplings, electrical power systems. Bertea Corporation: hydraulic systems. Garrett Corporation: design/fabrication of IR suppressors, integrated air systems. Hi-Shear Corporation: crew canopy/escape system. Litton Precision Gear Division: main transmission, engine nose gear boxes. Menasco Manufacturing Inc: landing gear. Solar Division, International Harvester Corporation: APU. Sperry Flight Systems Division: auto-stabilisation system. Teledyne Ryan Aeronautical Division: fabrication of airframe structure. Teledyne Systems: design assistance for fire control computer. Tool Research and Engineering Corporation, Advanced Structures Division: main/tail rotor. Precision Products Division, Western Gear: intermediate/tail rotor gear boxes. Of all the above probably the most significant contribution was made by Teledyne Ryan, which not only supplied major sections of the airframe but later facilitated the demanding initial production schedule that had a major effect on the early days of the Apache.

By June 1976 Hughes had begun ground tests with AV-01 (Air Vehicle), the prototype. This aircraft would be tasked with all the preliminary power tests, but AV-02 would be

the first to fly. In fact AV-01 never flew and served as Hughes's *de facto* Ground Test Vehicle. In contrast, Bell had already run a dedicated YAH-63 GTV in April of that year and its apparent lead in the programme forced Hughes to hurriedly accelerate its work. The first YAH-64 succeeded in beating the YAH-63 into the air by a single day, on 30 September 1975. Pilots for the YAH-64's 38-minute maiden flight (delayed for several hours after the port starter unit failed) were Robert G. Ferry and Raleigh E. Fletcher. It was then Bell's turn to suffer delays as the YAH-63 experienced gearbox problems induced by its high-speed transmission. Gene L. Colvin and Ronald G. Erhart's maiden flight in the YAH-63 had ended after only 2½ minutes, when the aircraft began to experience main rotor vibration. Two more flights were made on that day, totalling 10 minutes, but vibration problems persisted on later flights. Hughes launched AV-03 on its maiden flight on 22 November 1975 (by which time AV-02 had logged 35 flying hours), while Bell's second aircraft followed on 21 December. Pilots for the maiden flight of Hughes's AV-03 were Morrie Larsen and Jim Thompson. Hughes conducted all ground and air tests at Palomar Airport, Carlsbad, California. The flight test programme entailed 342.6 hours between September 1975 and 31 May 1976 before the AAH competitor was handed over to the Army's integrated flight evaluation programme at Edwards AFB. A further 125.5 hours of flying ensued in Army hands, from 16 June, plus 384.4 hours of associated ground tests. The Army's senior Apache test pilot, Colonel Robert L. Stuart, later became the first astronaut to spacewalk (from the Space Shuttle) without using a tether.

Bell's transition to service testing did not go smoothly. On 4 June 1976, while being flown by an Army pilot in the front seat and a Bell pilot in the rear – just prior to its scheduled handover on 16 June – the number two prototype YAH-63 crashed. The accident was traced to a tail rotor drive shaft failure during high-load, sideways flight. Both crew survived but the aircraft was destroyed, and so Bell desperately scrambled to make its GTV airworthy for the US Army.

Sensor systems and Hellfire

The Army test programme was not concerned merely with the AAH aircraft but also with the TADS/PNVS (Target Acquisition and Designation Sight/Pilot's Night-Vision Sensor) suite which was being developed for it. As in the AAH competition, there were two firms vying for this contract – Martin-Marietta and Northrop, which both submitted their proposals on 27 November 1976. Both systems were broadly similar, combining a FLIR and electro-optical sensors in a rotating ball turret mounted on the aircraft's nose. The Martin-Marietta system provided a

permanent FLIR for the pilot above the nose faring, but Northrop's design was retractable. TADS/PNVS evaluation would be an important part of the Phase 2 evaluation of the AAH winner.

Before revealing which of the two designs would be the winner, the Army announced a major change in the AAH specification, one which must have caused dismay to all concerned at the time but which set the seal on the Apache's future as the most lethal helicopter on the battlefield. In 1972 the requirement had been for an aircraft armed with eight basic TOW missiles that had a maximum range of 3000 m (9,843 ft), in day or night. By 1973 this had been modified to include the extended-range XRTOW with its 3750-m (12,303-ft) range. By 1975 the shortcomings of TOW were acknowledged and a replacement weapon was introduced for AAH. This was the Rockwell Hellfire (HELicopter-Launched, FIRE-and-forget), a laser-guided anti-tank missile which promised effective engagement ranges in excess of 6 km (3.7 miles). The unproved, and then unbuilt, Hellfire had a development history that stretched back to the early 1960s, but the risks inherent in its adoption were wisely seen to be less serious than allowing the AAH programme to proceed with inadequate weaponry. On 6 January 1976 the Army System Acquisition Review Board approved the adoption of Hellfire, and this decision was recommended to the Defence Systems Acquisition Review Council on 26 February. Hughes Aircraft Corporation and Rockwell International were both awarded contracts for Hellfire engineering development, with a single contract to be awarded as a result. The decision to integrate Hellfire added five months to the AAH RDT&E schedule, and $49.6 million. It was expected to add, in 1976 terms, $6,000 to the price of each AAH (a figure which later turned out to be impossibly low) but would provide a quantum leap in penetration capability compared to the TOW and Shilleleagh missiles then in service. On 8 October 1976 the Hellfire development contract was awarded to Rockwell International.

Above left and right: As the competition to build the AAH airframe progressed, so too did the competition to supply the TADS/PNVS primary mission sensor. The two rival designs, built by Martin Marietta (left) and Northrop (right), are seen here displayed in front of a YAH-64. Directly above is a view of the unsuccessful Northrop design, mounted on an a testbed aircraft. The chief difference between the Northrop design and its rival was the former's pop-up pilot's FLIR (PNVS) mounted above the nose. Northrop did not develop independent FLIR and DVO turrets in the TADS, but (perhaps unwisely) combined them in a single 'ball' mounting.

Top: All the early prototypes (this is AV-01) flew with representative FLIR housings. When the definitive TADS/PNVS was fitted, the cheek fairings were extended to accommodate the avionics. Note also the long grab handle beside the cockpit which was deleted on production AH-64s.

Phase 2 proposals were submitted in two parts: technical and management portions on 31 July 1976, and cost proposals on 16 August. Details were discussed, debated and disputed with the Army programme managers for four months before each manufacturer submitted its final Phase 2 proposal on 22 November. On 10 December 1976, having reviewed the evaluation results, the Secretary of the Army announced that the Hughes YAH-64 was the winner of the AAH competition. Factors which counted against the YAH-63 included doubts about the damage tolerance of its twin-bladed rotor and the small footprint of its tricycle landing gear, which left the aircraft unstable on the ground. Some claimed that Bell's existing production commitments had made it a likely second choice, as the US Army had no wish to interfere with ongoing AH-1 production. Hughes had met the Army's performance demands in all but one area. The YAH-64's maximum speed was 196 kt (362 km/h, 225 mph) compared to the ultimate goal of 204 kt (377 km/h, 234 mph). The rate of climb achieved by the prototypes was 800 ft/min (244 m/min), twice the original requirement, and the Phase 2 aircraft were expected to achieve 1,100 ft/min (335 m/min). Weapons demonstrations were conducted twice – 1,176 rounds were fired by the XM230 Chain Gun® during forward flight at angles up to 90°, and 184 2.75-in rockets were launched from the hover and at forward speeds of up to 130 kt (241 km/h, 150 mph). The streamlined TOW pods developed for the AAH were also test flown, but they subsequently were replaced by a yet-to-be designed Hellfire launcher. These weapon tests brought about a further success for Hughes – the Army's adoption of the M230 as the YAH-64's onboard gun.

Main rotor redesign

There had been some problems during the Phase 1 evaluation. Perhaps the most alarming of these was described by Hughes thus: "Apparently adequate rotor to canopy clearance was provided within this dimension (the requirement to limit vertical height to allow transportation by the C-141 airlifter), however, during flight testing it was found to be inadequate under sever manoeuvring conditions. In fact, under one extreme condition, it was possible to demonstrate an interference of the non-structural trailing edge of the blade with the corner of the canopy." In short, during negative-g (-0.5 g) pushovers the aircraft hit its own blades. The rotor masts on the two flying prototypes were lengthened by 9.5 in (24.3 cm) to allow safe operations up to -0.4 g, the first aircraft flying in this revised configuration on 9 February 1976. The rotor mast was subsequently lengthened by an additional 6 in (15.24 cm) for production aircraft to permit NoE flight to the design limit of -0.5 g, even in a 54-kt (100-km/h, 62-mph) headwind. On the other hand, during NoE evaluations one crew hit the tail wheel hard enough to burst the tyre, but no 'tailboom bounce' back into the main rotors occurred.

A build-up in blade vibrations as the rotor system entered the high-speed regime led to a redesign of the blade tips, which were swept back. The refined tip design reduced noise and increased the AH-64's maximum speed, exceeding the Army's goals. The flat-plate transparencies on the side of the cockpit were rounded, to add stiffness and reduce vibration-induced 'drumming' caused by the frequency of the rotor system.

Black Hole IR suppressors

The YAH-64 had a predicted primary mission weight of 13,200 lb (5988 kg) but the prototypes exceeded this by about 1,000 lb (454 kg). This figure was significantly reduced through the redesign of the all-important IR-suppression system. Hughes had originally developed an engine-driven cooling fan system which mixed surrounding air with exhaust efflux. This was replaced with Hughes-designed Black Hole IR-suppressors, using a

newly-developed material known as Low Q. The Low Q liner absorbs heat from the exhaust and radiates it slowly into the airflow surrounding the nacelle. Exhaust flow through each duct is used to draw ambient air into the dynamic section of the helicopter, cooling the transmission – via the oil heat exchangers – and the two engines. The fan system drew the equivalent of 50 hp (37 kW) from the 1,536-shp (1143-kW) T700-GE-700 turboshafts, so its removal, coupled with the addition of the lighter (and far less complex) Black Hole system, amounted to a saving of 400 lb (181 kg) in airframe weight. The bulk of the remaining weight saving came through changes in the tail design. This was achieved through a revision of the prototypes' T-tails (a process detailed elsewhere), but not their transformation to the low-set configuration intended for production aircraft. This lightweight tail, coupled with the extended rotor head, became known as the Mod 1 package.

Phase 2 proceeds

The $317.6 million Phase 2 contract called for the building of three production-standard AH-64s, conversion of the two prototypes and GTV to this standard also, and complete weapons and sensor system integration. The 50-month Phase 2 flying programme began on 28 November 1976, although an AH-64 production decision was not expected until May 1980. Notwithstanding, Hughes made the decision to commit to the massive expansion of its production facilities that would be needed to cater to the AAH. The Army's stated initial requirement now stood at 536 aircraft. Hughes began to issue long-lead materials contracts, recall laid-off staff and lease an additional 157,000 sq ft (14585 m²) of factory space. Its partners were faced with similar decisions. Hughes instigated a computerised management control system to its 'Team to the AAH' programme, one in which the Army was very interested. Flight tests continued to be conducted at the Palomar facility, using the gunnery range at the nearby MCAS Camp Pendleton. Full-scale weapons tests were conducted by the Army at the Yuma proving ground, while some Army flight test activity was carried out at Edwards AFB. Environmental testing was conducted at the indoor controlled climate facilities at Eglin AFB, Florida, and icing tests were conducted at Moses Lake, Washington.

All initial Phase 2 activity was limited to the AH-64 GTV, on which every design change was extensively tested.

As a result, only 21 months of the 56-month programme (financial hiccups had forced its extension) remained when the first flight of the modified AV-02, now in production configuration, took place on 28 November 1977. Pilots Bob Ferry (Hughes's chief experimental test pilot) and Morrie Larsen (dedicated AAH test pilot) logged 9.1 hours in 10 flights on that one day alone. After 50 hours of GTV Pre-Flight Approval Tests (PSAT) intended to check out the transmission and gear box systems, AV-04, the first true AH-64, was cleared to fly on 31 October 1979. Bob Ferry and Jack Ludwig were at the controls for the 18-minute maiden flight, which was the first made with a redesigned low-set all-moving tailplane, dubbed the stabilator.

Above: Phase II testing revealed problems with the AH-64's rotor tips. As a result, the blade tips were swept back, leading to a reduction in compression loads and overall noise signature.

The dramatic desert scenery around the Apache production plant at Mesa, Arizona, has provided a spectacular backdrop for many AH-64 photos. One of the pre-production aircraft is seen here skirting a nearby peak.

Opposite page, top: Early rocket tests were conducted with Mk 40 rockets, which have now been replaced in the inventory by Mk 66s, as seen here.

Opposite page, bottom: Hellfire testing began in 1980 and the problems encountered delayed actual missile production until 1982. Initial tests were undertaken in clear desert conditions and some doubts were expressed as to how the missiles would perform under European conditions. As a result, a trial was held in 1981 involving eight shots fired in fog, smoke, dust clouds and rain. Two missiles failed to hit their targets and the Army had to admit that under some conditions Hellfire would not be 100 per cent reliable.

Hellfire tests began in April 1979, initially from an AH-1 fitted with a trial Airborne Target Acquisition Fire Control System (ATAFCS). AH-64 tests were conducted at Camp Pendleton. Initially, missiles were fired (by AV-02) unguided from the critical upper inboard station on the left wing, This station was almost in direct line with the tail rotor so the possible effects of rocket plume and associated debris were a cause of concern, which proved groundless. While these early tests provided useful basic information, true weapons tests could not proceed without a complete onboard weapon guidance and fire control system. The two competing TADS/PNVS systems were installed on the AH-64 prototypes – AV-02 carried Martin-Marietta's system and AV-03 Northrop's. A competitive fly-off between the two sensor fits, at the Yuma Proving Ground, was scheduled for December 1979 after the preliminary guided missile test shots. The first of these autonomously-

guided Hellfire tests was made by AV-02 in October 1979. Within a month Hellfires were scoring self-guided bullseyes on 10-ft x 10-ft (3-m x 3-m) targets. TADS-guided Hellfire tests were part of the overall Armament and Fire Control Survey (A/FCS) test programme, during the early stages of which the AH-64 test fleet passed the 1,000 flying hours mark. The addition of the full-standard fire control system went hand-in-hand with the Mod 2 changes to the AH-64 which added to the prototypes the long cheek fairings of AV-04, and all subsequent aircraft.

In December 1979 AV-05 made its maiden flight, followed by the last of the Phase 2 batch of three aircraft, AV-06, on 16 March 1980. This final aircraft was the first to fly with the definitive stabilator design and extended (by 10 in/25 cm) tail rotor. By April 1981 the prototypes had amassed over 1,000 flying hours. Performance milestones included a new top speed for the AH-64 of 206 kt (381 km/h, 237 mph) achieved in a dive by AV-04 with a further refined tail rotor design, and manoeuvres of +3g. In April 1980 a crucial landmark in the AAH story was reached with the selection of the Martin-Marietta TADS/PNVS for production. A two-month fly-off comprising day and night firings against autonomously-designated and ground-designated targets resulted in Martin-Marietta achieving a three-hits-from-three-firings record and winning a $45.6 million contract for a further 26-month development programme. Phase 2 concluded with a three-month Operational Test programme, from June to August 1980, during which three aircraft flew representative combat missions against simulated enemy armour, ADA and opposing aircraft. Sadly, 1980 ended on a tragic note. On 20 November 1980 AV-04 departed on a routine tail incidence/drag test, accompanied by a T-28D photo chase plane. Flying in close formation, the two collided, and only the pilot of the T-28 survived.

US Army test phase

In May 1981 AV-02/-03/-06 were handed over to the US Army, in preparation for the AH-64's final Operational Test II (OTII) evaluation at Ft Hunter-Liggett. This marked the first time the AH-64 had flown in service hands since the original 1976 fly-off. Under the eye of Army AAH Project Manager Major General Edward M. Browne (one of the strongest supporters of the AAH since before its inception), 2,500 hours were accumulated in advance of a major exercise with the 7th Infantry Division, in August. The AH-64 was deployed for 400 flying hours in difficult desert conditions where temperatures reached 110°F

(43°C). One of the most impressive performances of OPII was turned in by the Martin-Marietta PNVS, which had always been superior to its rival. The same was not true of its associated TADS. Design changes incorporated after Martin-Marietta had won the system fly-off forced a delay of six months in its development, and so defects remained to be corrected. Production go-ahead for the first batch of 13 TADS/PNVS systems was not obtained until 30 April 1982.

AH-64 for the Corps

In September 1981 the US Marine Corps conducted a limited (two-week) assessment of the AH-64's suitability for Marine operations, including shipboard compatibility tests. The Corps had a requirement for 120 AH-64s, for delivery in 1985, and so joined a list of other customers beginning to express an interest in the aircraft. These included Saudi Arabia and West Germany, which had then launched its PAH-2 attack helicopter requirement. Also in September 1981, the first photographs of Soviet Mi-24 'Hinds' operating in Afghanistan were released. Soviet armed helicopter philosophy was quite different to the West's, particularly the doctrine being developed for the AAH, and so the Mi-24 was a very different beast to the AH-64. Nevertheless, the 'Hind' menace became yet another worry for NATO generals already horrified (in public at least) by Soviet armoured superiority in Europe. It also remained the most obvious 'Red' parallel to the AH-64. It was then, during the final stages of AAH Phase 2 testing, late in 1981, that the name Apache was first applied to the AH-64.

The deadline for an AH-64 production decision, known as DSARC III (Defense Systems Acquisition Review Council), was fixed for 10 December 1981. Funding for the first 14 aircraft (Lot 1) had already been included in the 1982 budget, which would, hopefully, see deliveries begin in November 1983 and IOC in October 1984. However, delays in assimilating the results of OPII delayed this decision until March 1982. It was not until 15 April 1982 that full-scale go-ahead for Apache production was finally given. There then followed a complicated delay in funding, not helped by the rising costs of the programme which had been steadily increasing since the oil crisis and recession of the mid-1970s. The $365 million that had been requested for FY82 was increased to $444.4 million, but now this would buy only 11 helicopters. As a result the next (Lot 2) batch of 48 AH-64s was put on hold until a new deal could be hammered out between the DoD and its contractors.

Below: This is the ill-fated AV-04 (79-23257) which crashed on 28 November 1980. Before its loss, AV-04 was instrumental in proving the new tail design.

By autumn 1979 both prototypes had flown over 1,000 hours with the T-tail configuration. This had underlined Hughes original mistrust in that configuration, for the fatigue penalties incurred through rotor downwash were severe. As a result, a low-set, all-moving stabilator design was incorporated on AV-04, which solved the fatigue problems and also expanded the AH-64's flight envelope, with the trade-off of some engineering complications caused by its more complex design. The new vertical tail was extended by 3 in (7.6 cm) and the tail rotor repositioned 30 in (76 cm) higher to clear the new stabilator position. Some contractor delays set back AV-04's maiden flight, first scheduled for August, to 31 October 1979. During its first months of flight test activity, AV-04 trialled several differing designs of stabilator leading to the definitive, smaller production design which was flown in March 1980. These changes were well in hand by the time AV-03 undertook brief naval trials with the US Marine Corps in 1981. This view of AV-03 also clearly shows the new blade tips adopted as a result of OPII testing. The shipboard element of the 1981 USMC evaluation was conducted with the USS Pelelieu (LHA-5).

Another element of fall-out from OPII was the decision to move to an uprated version of the T700 engine, the T700-GE-701, rated at 1,690 shp (1259 kW). The -701 engine had already been run on the SH-60B Seahawk (as the T700-401) and the improved performance it promised would greatly benefit the Apache in 'hot-and-high' conditions. On 15 January 1982 AV-05 made its maiden flight with the new turboshaft which would become the definitive production engine for the Apache. Testing was completed by August.

Price wars

While the Apache embarked on a European sales tour in 1982 and completed advanced environmental testing in the US, disputes over its affordability continued. Hughes submitted its production proposals for Lot 2 while AV-02 was amazing the crowds at the Army Air 82 show, held at Middle Wallop – the home of British army flying – and the subsequent Farnborough air show. The US Army had increased its Apache requirement to 536 aircraft, but was then forced to cut this back to 446. On this basis Hughes estimated the total programme cost would be $5,994 million. The US Army had always accepted that the unit cost would creep up from $1.6 million (in 1972 dollars) but was now faced with a price per aircraft of over $13 million (rising to $16.2 million later that year). The AAH was faced with serious political opposition from proponents of a lower-cost Cobra-based aircraft, one which might be far more attractive to other customers such as Germany. (Germany conducted an evaluation of the AH-64 from 25 June to 16 July.) However, the Apache had powerful

friends. A letter dated 22 July 1982, from General Bernard C. Rogers NATO C-in-C Europe to the Apache's chief detractors in the Senate, spelled out the threat to Europe posed by the Warsaw Pact, and the urgent need for a counter. It ended with the words "we need the AH-64 in Europe now and cannot afford the luxury of another trip to the drawing board."

A reassessment on all sides led to the conclusion of the Lot 2 production agreement in November 1982. Hughes agreed to supply 48 aircraft under the terms of three phased contracts, each worth $105.6 million. The US Army, in turn, increased its intended buy of Apaches to 515. Work continued apace at Hughes's huge newly-developed Mesa, Arizona facility, which had 240,000 sq ft (22300 m²) of floor space. Hughes had committed to build the facility in July 1981, as the November 1983 delivery date for the first Apache had remained constant throughout all the wrangling and uncertainty. Mesa acted as the assembly point for components sourced from 36 states, including the major airframe assembly supplied by Teledyne Ryan Aeronautical in San Diego. It was here that the first production Apache, PV-01, began to take shape in spring 1982. The first production TADS/PNVS set was delivered in July 1983. As the first three production aircraft progressed down the line at Mesa a welcome FY84 purchase of 112 aircraft was approved, bringing the total to 171 to date.

Apache handover

The first Apache for the United States Army was rolled out in a ceremony held at Mesa, ahead of schedule, on 30 September 1983 – eight years to the day of the first flight and just 18 months after ground had been broken at Mesa. The aircraft was accompanied by an Apache warrior, brandishing a rifle and riding a white horse, beneath a massive Stars and Stripes. The stated price of the aircraft, its 'over the fence' cost according to the then-Project Manager Brigadier Charles Drenz, was $7.8 million in 1984 terms or $9 million in real-year terms. This equated to a unit cost of approximately $14 million when development costs were included. Hughes planned to accelerate production to a peak of 12 per month by 1986, with purchases of 144 AH-64s in FY85 followed by 144 (FY86) and 56 in (FY 87) in prospect.

PV-01 made its 30-minute maiden flight on 9 January 1984, flown by chief test pilot Steve Hanvey and Ron Mosely. By then the prototype fleet had logged over 4,500 hours in the air. This noteworthy event was obscured in

the headlines by the announcement on 6 January 1984 that Hughes Helicopters was about to become a subsidiary of McDonnell Douglas. Under an agreement signed by Jack G. Real, President of Hughes Helicopters, Sanford N. McDonnell, Chairman of McDonnell Douglas, and William R. Lummis, administrator of the estate of Howard Hughes, McDonnell Douglas agreed to purchase 100 per cent of Hughes Helicopters' stock for $470 million (and to pay off debts owed to the estate) – a very reasonable price. The reasons for the sale of Hughes Helicopters for such a seemingly bargain basement price were not readily apparent. Certainly, after the death of Howard Hughes in 1976, the huge and complex industrial monster he left behind was labyrinthine and inefficient. Hughes Helicopters should have been in a healthy position, with a secure future and large order book, but Summa Corporation had incurred major debts to the estate of the late Howard Hughes and Hughes Helicopters itself, apparently, had not made a profit in 30 years. Although Hughes initially was allowed to operate under its original identity, its new ownership spelled immediate change. Aircraft production ceased at Culver City and the workforce there dropped from 5,000 to 1,800. It was Hughes Helicopters' 50th anniversary year.

Buy-out negotiations with McDonnell Douglas had been finalised on 16 December 1983, but prior to that Hughes attracted attention from 15 other interested buyers. A possible influencing factor in Summa Corporation's decision to dispose of Hughes Helicopters was revealed in 1985 when the US Army launched an investigation into McDonnell Douglas's accounting methods. Payments were suspended while Army Under-Secretary James R. Ambrose was ordered to investigate "serious charges of accounting irregularity." Major errors dating back to 1983, and beyond, were discovered. McDonnell Douglas defended itself, claiming that these problems predated its total assimilation of Hughes, but the Army disputed these claims, too. In the midst of these negotiations Hughes Helicopters finally disappeared, on 27 August 1985, to become the McDonnell Douglas Helicopter Company. The dispute between the Army and McDonnell Douglas did not directly involve the cost of the Apache, the price of which fell slightly as production continued. In FY86 terms the unit cost of an AH-64 was down to $7.03 million, or $13.9 million if procurement, acquisition (type R&D and development expenses) and Hellfire development costs were included.

The first handover of an Apache to the US Army took place on 26 January 1984, although this was only a formality since the heavily-instrumented aircraft concerned, PV-01, would remain with Hughes/McDonnell Douglas along with PV-02. PV-03, handed over in May, was the

first aircraft to be truly built to production standards, but initially it, too, remained in use with the manufacturer. PV-04 and PV-05 were the first examples to be handed over to the Army, in July 1984, and, along with four of their successors, operated from Mesa and the Yuma Proving Ground as part of the Initial Key Personnel Training (IKPT) programme. PV-08 and PV-10 were tasked with operational trials alongside the subject of the Army's Advanced Helicopter Improvement Program (AHIP) – the OH-58D Kiowa Warrior. These trials were conducted at Hunter-Liggett. It was not until the delivery of PV-13 that an Army crew could fly an Apache away and call it their own.

Air-to-air Apache

In 1984 the prospect of sales to the USMC was resurrected by the display of an aircraft at the annual Marine Corps League convention in Washington, DC. This was remarkable for the fact that the Apache was fitted with two AIM-9H Sidewinders, bolted on to the end of the stub wings. McDonnell Douglas also offered an air-to-air Stinger and anti-radiation Sidearm missile fit, for delivery to the Marines in 1988. The USMC has always wanted to acquire

Above: The AH-64's rotor blades feature a high (21-in/55-cm) constant camber and an additional fixed trailing-edge tab. This upturned tab positions the blades' centre of pressure for best aerodynamic performance (to 27° rather than the usual 25°), cancelling the nose-down pitching associated with a cambered airfoil. The airfoil section was named HH-02 and is based on the NASA 6400 airfoil. Each blade has five stainless steel spars to reduce the effect of a direct hit, coupled with separate skin plates to prevent cracks propagating. Approximately 60 per cent of each blade is load-bearing (stainless steel) structure. The rest of the blade comprises composite Nomex honeycomb and a fibre-glass skin. Each blade has a leading edge of 040-gauge AM355 stainless steel and a submerged de-icing blanket to provide resistance to abrasion. The US Army requirement for resistance to sand erosion specified 450 hours of hovering over sand before replacement.

Above left: This 1989 view of the Mesa plant shows AH-64A production in full swing. The Mesa facility was purpose-built by Hughes Helicopters, which was bought out by McDonnell Douglas in 1984 and became the McDonnell Douglas Helicopter Company in 1985. The plant was expanded, in 1986, from 570,000 sq ft (52950 m²) to an immense 1,904,500 sq ft (176930 m²).

Above: The AIM-9 Sidewinder missile was first introduced to the AH-64A as a result of USMC interest in the aircraft. Tests were also undertaken, in 1988, with the Sidewinder-based AGM-122A Sidearm anti-radiation missile.

Right and below: Both Apache crew can use the Honeywell IHADSS helmet-mounted display as their primary flight information display and weapons controller. The helmet's monocle sight can be slaved to the Chain Gun® cannon to follow the crew member's line of sight (below).

Apaches (and has also placed a stronger emphasis on helicopter air-to-air operations that the US Army) but the Apache's price tag has kept it off the Corps' shopping list to this day.

First deliveries, first problems

Initial deliveries were made to US Army Training and Doctrine Command (TRADOC) bases at Ft Eustis, Virginia (home of the Army logistics school), and Ft Rucker, Alabama (the Army's centre of flying training). Qualified pilots transferred from Ft Rucker to Ft Hood, Texas, where units were trained at a battalion level. By the mid-1980s the free-spending Reagan years were in full swing, and in autumn 1984 Defense Secretary Casper Weinberger authorised the acquisition of an additional 160 Apaches (at an FY85 cost of $1.6 billion), bringing the total on order for the Army to 675. This was subsequently increased yet again to 807 aircraft, a number which surprised even the Army. With an eye on the ever-rising costs of the Apache the Army suggested that 48 AH-64s of the FY85 acquisition be delayed, but this was rejected by Congress on the grounds that it would actually add $1.2 million to the unit cost by lengthening the production schedule. Apache acquisition was ultimately amended as follows: 138 (FY85), 116 (FY86), 101 (FY87), 77 (FY88), 54 (FY89), 154 (FY90) and a follow-on batch of 10 (FY95), for a grand total of 827 AH-64A Apaches. The unevenness in these numbers is a reflection of the troubles that hindered Apache production throughout those years. The acceleration to the 12 aircraft per month target did not go smoothly, and neither did Hellfire or TADS/PNVS development/production. Then the investigation by the Defense Contract Auditing Agency (as mentioned above)

intervened and by June 1985 the US government was withholding funds amounting to $3,500 million from McDonnell Douglas.

By January 1986, 68 aircraft had been handed over when suddenly a new and more serious problem reared its head. On 15 January routine maintenance discovered a crack in a rotor blade, a component that had a 4,500-hour service life but had in fact only accumulated 330 hours. Another 12 cracks were found across the inventory. On 27 January 1986 the Apache was grounded, and the US Army refused to accept any more deliveries. Hughes/McDonnell Douglas had been proud of the survivability tests the rotor system had passed, and photographs of the blades intact after hits from 23-mm shells were the centrepiece of every company presentation. The outcome of a rapid and intensive investigation was an immense relief to all concerned: the fault lay not with the design or materials or manufacturing process but with a defective tool that creased the trailing edge of the blade. Later that year a second fault arose when a flight critical bolt failed in the flight control system. The hardened bolt, supposedly proof against a 12.7-mm round strike, had suffered hydrogen embrittlement and sheered off. Although these bolts were replaced with a revised material, the example that broke was found to be the only one so affected.

Into the field

The first unit to convert to the Apache was the 7th Battalion, 17th Cavalry Brigade at Ft Hood, which began its 90-day battalion-level conversion in April 1986. The 7-17th was followed by the 1st and 2nd Battalions, 6th Cavalry Regiment, 6th Cavalry Brigade. These two units departed the United States in September 1987 for the Apache's first deployment to Europe. Their 38 AH-64s were part of Reforger '87 (REturn of FOrces to GERmany), flying 725 hours in large-scale exercises in night and bad weather to achieve a mission-capable rate of 90 per cent. Upon completion, the aircraft of the 1-6th remained at Illesheim to became the first Apache unit to be based in Europe, while its sister battalion returned to Ft Hood. By 1990 Germany had became home to eight AH-64 battalions, with over 160 aircraft. As early as 1987 Apaches were replacing Cobras in Army National Guard units. The first was D Company, 28th Aviation Regiment, North Carolina ANG. By 1991 nine regular Army units were active in the USA and, by 1994, 33 of 35 battalions (including seven Army National Guard and two Army Reserve battalions) were combat ready. By 1 September 1989 McDonnell Douglas had handed over 500 Apaches. The 700th delivery was made in December 1992 and the 800th AH-64 was delivered in July 1993. ARI (Army Restructure Initiative) 'downsizing' cut back the number of intended/deployed Apache units and changed their composition. However, although units were withdrawn from Germany, the first Apaches arrived in Korea in March 1994 with the 17th Aviation Brigade (5-501st AVN). The last of 821 AH-64As destined for the US Army (excluding prototypes) was delivered on 30 April 1996. This was the 915th production Apache.

Over 200 AH-64s have been ordered by export customers. The first of these was Israel, in 1990, followed by Saudi Arabia, United Arab Emirates, Egypt, Greece, the Netherlands and the United Kingdom. Details of these users and other prospective Apache customers can be found in the AH-64 operators section that follows. Confirmed Apache production, in early 1997, stood at 1,040 aircraft for delivery by the year 2000.

HARS (heading and attitude reference system) is the Apache's inertial navigation system which uses a Doppler radar altimeter and stabilised gyros to provide the pilot with attitude signals for pitch, roll, yaw and heading, along with velocities and acceleration. On engine start-up the HARS requires six to nine minutes to spin up and align itself, although a hasty and less accurate start can be made within four to six minutes. Of course, if the helicopter has not moved since the HARS was last shut down, realignment can be accomplished in 90 to 120 seconds. The Apache's reliance on Doppler is one of its greatest shortcomings. Doppler errors are easily induced, particularly over water, so a strap-on GPS kit is essential mission equipment (though it is not approved as a primary flight instrument). This situation will change with the arrival of the AH-64D and its embedded GPS.

for fighting in the dark. For Apache crews, night-time operations are perhaps even more crucial, as the AH-64's vulnerability to infantry SAMs and gun fire is immeasurably increased on the daytime battlefield. The AH-64 crew can conduct NoE operations at night, locate, identify and destroy targets and then find their way home again – thanks to the Apache's TADS/PNVS.

TADS/PNVS and IHADSS

Design of the TADS/PNVS system and the AAH went hand-in-glove. The system chosen for the AH-64 was built by Martin-Marietta (now Lockheed Martin Orlando) and approved for production in February 1982. As its awkward acronym implies, the system is divided into two parts – the AAQ-11 Mk III PNVS and AN/ASQ-170 TADS – which are independent of each other. The system comprises a dual FLIR for pilot and gunner with additional optical sensors and a Litton Laser Range-Finder/Designator (LRF/D). The steerable PNVS (Pilot's Night Vision System) is mounted above the Apache's nose and provides wide-angle (40° horizontal x 30° vertical field of view/FoV) FLIR imagery for the pilot. The PNVS can be slewed up to 90° off the aircraft's centreline and +20°/-45° in elevation. When not in use the sensor housing can be rotated through 180° to protect its optics. FLIR imagery can be displayed on the pilot's console 5.5-in x 5.5-in (14-cm x 14-cm) CRT Video Display Unit (VDU). The VDU is used typically as a back-up system, because the Apache is flown, and fought, using the Honeywell IHADSS (Integrated Helmet and Display Sight System).

The huge IHADSS helmet, which incorporates standard visors (including laser protective visors) and radio, has a helmet-mounted sight for the right eye, which uses a bulky side arm to mount a small combiner glass in front of the eye. This is the HDU (Helmet Display Unit), or 'hudu'. The pilot's PNVS imagery can be displayed on the HDU, with flight information overlaid, in the same fashion as a conventional aircraft HUD. The PNVS FLIR produces a one-for-one image – it has no magnification – so the (two-dimensional) image the pilot sees in the HDU should correspond with the view outside the cockpit. The PNVS and IHADSS can be slaved so that the FLIR follows the pilot's head and looks where he is looking. An IR head tracking system mounted behind each Apache crew member's head will slew the PNVS at a maximum rate of 120°/sec in azimuth and 93°/sec in elevation, and it can be used to cue the gunner's TADS FLIR.

The TADS (Target Acquisition and Designation System) is more complex, and boasts slightly better FLIR imagery. The TADS system is housed below the PNVS using two roughly hemispherical turrets mounted side-by-side yet capable of independent movement. The complete TADS system can be slewed through 120° and from +30°/-60° in elevation, and is divided into 'day' and 'night' sides. To starboard is the massive 23-cm (9-in) aperture FLIR which is equivalent to the PNVS FLIR. The CPG's (Co-Pilot/

Above: TADS that have been upgraded to OI (optically improved) configuration – that is, most in service – have been modified with a series of optical filters to protect the CPG from laser energy. They will also protect the FLIR from video 'bloom' caused by lasers. Four filter setting are available: normal (clear, no protection), S (Short, provides protection against short-wavelength lasers), L (Long, protects against long-wavelength lasers) and MAX (combined L and S filters). The DVO system has filters applied to fixed optics which are thus always in place.

After a long and somewhat troubled development, the Apache began to establish itself as the world's premier battlefield helicopter. The Apache's sophistication brought with it the ability to conduct regimental-sized operations, at night, in the European theatre. The key to its success was its TADS/PNVS sensor system, which for many years had no rival, and the Hellfire missile which has always solidly maintained its claim to be able to destroy any target on the battlefield. Allied with this was the US Army's comprehensive training and exercise system which has evolved to such a degree that the full-scale air/land manoeuvre battles now fought at the US Army's National Training Center are accomplished as a matter of routine. The US Army trains to fight at night. It has poured money into giving all its combat forces – air and land – the ability to manoeuvre and fight around the clock. Desert Storm experience underlined how effective this capability is against an enemy unprepared

Right: The Apache's fixed rotor mast allows the transmission and gear box to be removed without interfering with the main rotors. The rotor mast is fixed to the fuselage at eight points and, as the rotor drive shaft runs through it, no flight loads are imposed upon the drive shaft itself. This greatly aids the Apache's agility.

Gunner) FLIR differs from the pilot's in having selectable fields of vision: 50°, 10°, 3.1° and 1.6°. Target tracking can be achieved manually, with the image auto-tracker or the laser spot tracker. The spot tracker facilitates target handover from another laser designator. The image auto-tracker has the capability to offset-track one target while automatically tracking another. Automatic linear motion compensation aids in the tracking of moving targets. All TADS imagery can be relayed to the CPG's 'hudu', or the 'ort'. The ORT (Optical Relay Tube) is a small monochrome display in the front cockpit, positioned in the middle of the 'T-bar' of weapons/laser controls that dominates the CPG's station. From here the co-pilot can control all the Apache's weapons and sensors.

Finding and marking targets is the job of the TADS, and on the port side of the nose are the rest of the systems required to do this. Here the TADS has three windows, arranged like traffic lights, behind a vertical, two-facet optical screen. The uppermost of these sensors is the DVO (Direct View Optics) – an optical telescope with a x4 magnification capability at an 18° FoV or x16 magnification at 4° FoV. Beneath this is a near-IR TV system which offers up to x127 magnification with a much-reduced FoV (as little as 0.45°). The third station houses the Apache's laser rangefinder and target marker. All the TADS/PNVS have filters to protect the crew from the potentially devastating effects of battlefield lasers. The Apache's own neodymium laser is definitely not eye-safe and has an effective range of up to 20 km (12 miles). All Apache training ranges must have a large (21 km/13 miles wide) laser backstop.

FLIR pros and cons

The TADS/PNVS system was once without equal and there is still nothing better in service. However, it was over 10 years in development and it has been over 10 years since it was fielded, so, needless to say, technology has moved on significantly. Perhaps the biggest flaw in the TADS/PNVS system was incurred at the very beginning of the AAH design. Mounting the sensors on the nose of the aircraft, just about the lowest point on the Apache apart from the gun and the wheels, forces the AH-64 to unmask completely from terrain to find/designate targets. Keeping the optics stabilised and remote from airframe vibration was a major concern, so a mast-mounted solution was rejected from the start. At the time it was seen as too great a technical challenge. A roof-mounted sight was not included on any AAH design, either, so the Apache was built around a nose-mounted sensor fit. The TADS/PNVS uses two sets of gimbals – a 'coarse' outer set and a 'fine' inner set – coupled with rate-integrated gyros to keep the sensor turrets aligned and stable. Apache maintainers know that the system is not

perfect and will admit that the bulk of the aircraft's regular down-time is caused by vibration-induced malfunctions – as one said, "90 per cent of my problems are in that nose." Apache crews know that the one rule for TADS/PNVS operations is to "boresight, boresight and boresight", to ensure that the system is always up and running correctly.

Ironically for a helicopter designed to fly and fight on the Central European Front, typical central European cold wet weather causes the biggest problems for the AH-64 FLIR. All FLIRs are subject to IR crossover, a phenomenon encountered when humidity and ambient temperature conspire to turn target and terrain the same cold, flat temperature, and the AH-64A FLIR offers no discrimination between either. In situations where target discrimination is not completely clear the CPG can change the polarity on the targeting FLIR, switching from 'white hot' to 'black hot'. The system also has selectable, infinite gain (contrast). Acknowledged limitations in FLIR performance are an important reason why the Apache has a combined FLIR/TV system.

The Apache has a video-recording system linked to the TADS/PNVS. Although now outdated and bulky (and incompatible with any other outside video system), the tactical benefits of such an onboard system are immense. Having reached its battle position under cover, the Apache will pop up, quickly view the target, record the scene and then remask to watch the tape. This allows the crew the luxury of assessing the enemy at length without endangering themselves. Over the tactical radio net, the Apache teams will then make the final engagement decisions, allocate targets, fine-tune the shooter/designator pairs, and wait for the word to go. A new 'Hi-8'-based video system is currently in flight-test for the AH-64A. Developed by TEAC and Merlin, the new recorder uses an industry-

The Apache is fitted with the AN/APR-39(V)1 or APR-39A(V)1 radar warning receivers. The RWR cockpit display produces a radial strobe showing a line of bearing to the detected radar. An audio signal is emitted from the RW control panel and in the crews' headphones. The alarm's frequency represents the strength of the threat signal. A missile alert lamp is also illuminated. The RWR can be set to alert the crew to specific signals or all emissions in the area. AN/APR-39A(V)1 is more advanced and uses an onboard threat library to identify radars and display appropriate symbology. APR-39A(V)1 also has a more sophisticated aural warning. If a threat is detected a synthetic voice will announce, "SA, SA-8 12 o'clock tracking." A second mode provides a more terse warning: "missile, missile 12 o'clock tracking." Twin RWR antennas are located on the rear of the fin cap and forward on cheek fairings. A single antenna is found under the tailboom.

Apache weapons and walk-round

Left and above: The M230E1 30-mm Chain Gun® has a void space above it, to fold into in the event of a crash, protecting the crew. The Chain Gun's 'chain' can be seen above, at the point where it interfaces with the ammunition flatpack. The chain carries rounds to the right to feed the gun

Above: 30-mm rounds are loaded using the motorised uploader/downloader which propels shells up a flex chute, along the port side of the fuselage and into the flatpack or 'ammo can'.

Above and left: All AGM-114 Hellfires are painted black, with olive drab markings. Yellow (3 x 3-in) square markings on the front of the missile denote an HE warhead. Brown squares to the rear signify a solid propellant motor. Inert handling training rounds are designated M34; training rounds with functional seeker heads (above) are M36s.

Above and left: US Apaches use 2.75-in Hydra 70 rockets, typically fired from 19-round M261 pods. Rockets are packed with their fins taped up, prior to loading. Blue warheads denote training rounds. Live rockets are olive drab with yellow warheads.

Right: The Shorts Starstreak/Helstreak air-to-air missile will most likely be carried by the UK's WAH-64Ds in a two-round wingtip canister, as seen here. The three darts of the missile's warhead are plainly visible on this model.

Right: The MATRA Mistral has been carried for 'form and fit' tests on the AH-64, but no test firings have ever been made. Air-to-air Mistral is already operational on French army Gazelles.

Left: The 30-round M130 chaff launcher is located on the tailboom. Apaches do not routinely use flares – they are ineffective at low-level, tend to hit the tail rotor and can set surrounding vegetation on fire.

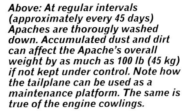

Above: At regular intervals (approximately every 45 days) Apaches are thoroughly washed down. Accumulated dust and dirt can affect the Apache's overall weight by as much as 100 lb (45 kg) if not kept under control. Note how the tailplane can be used as a maintenance platform. The same is true of the engine cowlings.

Left: A T700-GE-701 turboshaft fitted to an AH-64A. The engines are built in Lynn, Massachusetts.

Above: Visible above the TADS optical and laser turret (right) is the LRU-28 transmitting antenna for the Apache's ALQ-136 radar jammer. The Apache's laser – the lower-most of the three components in the turret – is a neodymium-yttrium aluminium garnet (Nd-YAG) laser. The glass panels of the TADS turrets are heated to protect against icing. Note the wire deflector between the turrets and the cutter above them, in front of the PNVS.

Left: The AH-64's video recorder is housed in an avionics bay, in the starboard fuselage, below and behind the engines.

Left: The three secondary nozzles (vents) of the Black Hole infra-red suppressive system are seen from above.

Right: This view of the port cheek fairing shows LRUs (line replaceable units) for the TADS and laser systems (top row), dimmer controller, IHADSS symbol generator and fire control computer (bottom row).

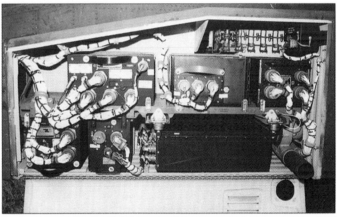

Above: The Apache's rotor head is fully articulated, allowing the blades to 'hunt' (lead or lag) individually. The flexible elastomeric bearings, which regulate this effect, are the large rectangular blocks seen at the end of each blade.

Left: The Sperry-built air data sensor, positioned above the rotor head, is referred to as the 'Pacer System'. It monitors air velocity, temperature and pressure, and is vital for the flight instruments and weapons fire control system.

Right: The AH-64D's Longbow MMW radar.

Above: The Apache's rotor blades are each attached to a delta-hinged hub. The whip FM/AM antenna above the fin is not found on all AH-64As. Two AN/APR-39 RWR antennas are located to the rear of the fin cap.

flight to 1,000 m (3,280 ft) is two seconds, and 12.2 seconds to 3000 m (39,843 ft). The Chain Gun® is accurate, but is used primarily as an area weapon for suppressive fire 'to keep heads down'.

One extra item of equipment that crews would have liked during Desert Storm was a laser tracker to follow rounds 'down range'. The Apache does not carry tracer rounds, so, if firing at night, the gunner can only see his fall of shot if rounds are actually impacting on the target at which he is looking. If the gunner is 'head-down' using the TADS and the gun is not correctly aligned, the gunner may have to zoom back out from the target to redirect his fire, possibly losing the target in the process.

Conventional M230E1 ammunition is the M789 HE dual-purpose (HEDP) round. Each shell has a 0.76-oz (21.5-g) explosive charge and a shaped charge liner that collapses, upon impact, into an armour-piercing molten metal jet. The projectile body also fragments up to a range of 4 m (13 ft). In tests, Chain Gun®-fired rounds penetrated more than 2 in (5 cm) of rolled homogenous armour at 2500 m (8,202 ft), but, during Desert Storm, Apaches destroyed T-55 tanks with the Gun alone. For fire training purposes inert M788 rounds are used, while dummy M848 rounds are used for function checks of the gun mechanism.

Rockets – the area weapons system

The Apache's primary area weapons system is its 2.75-in rockets. The rockets in use today are known as the Hydra 70 family, a name which applies to any warhead fitted to the Mk 66 rocket motor. The Mk 66 has replaced the earlier Mk 40 motor and has a longer tube, improved double-base solid propellant and a different nozzle/fin assembly. Increased velocity and spin improve trajectory stability for better accuracy, though its smoke trail and launch signature remain the same as the Mk 40's. Mk 66 rockets were developed by the Army's Redstone Arsenal and are carried in a 19-round pod, although a seven-round pod is also available. The pods are inexpensive enough to be disposable, but are sturdy enough to be reused. Rocket warheads come in several forms. The most basic of these is the M151 HE warhead, traditionally referred to as the '10-pounder'. The M151 is an anti-personnel, anti-material warhead with a burst radius of 10 m (33 ft). Fragments are lethal up to 50 m (164 ft). The M274 Smoke Signature (training) round is a ballistic match for the M151. It carries a potassium perchlorate/aluminium powder charge to provide 'flash, bang and smoke' for training.

The M229 HE warhead is referred to as the '17-pounder' and uses 4.8 lb (2.17 kg) of B4 high-explosive, the same as in the M151. The M247 HE warhead is no longer in production but is held in reserve stocks. It uses a small shaped-charge warhead of composition B explosive.

The 13.6-lb (6.16-kg) M261 HE multi-purpose submunition (MPSM) warhead can be used against light armour and vehicles. It adds an M439 fuse, programmable to detonate between 550 m (1,640 ft) and 7000 m (22,966 ft), along with nine M73 submunitions. The M73s are dispensed approximately 150 m (492 ft) above the target. Each

standard format that offers sharply increased horizontal line resolution, with output at 525-line standard (the existing Apache system uses a non-standard 875-line resolution).

M230E1 Chain Gun® cannon

The Apache's weapons are divided into two (tactical) categories: area weapons and point weapons. Starting at the front of the aircraft, the M230 Chain Gun® cannon is the Apache's secondary area weapon (due to its relatively short range). The Chain Gun® was a unique invention, pioneered by Hughes as an integral part of the AH-64's development. The concept behind the Chain Gun® is straightforward. The name derives from its ammunition feed mechanism, which uses a one-piece metal chain to feed linkless shells from a central magazine. Hughes had already done substantial research on 7.62-mm and 20-mm chain gun concepts and scaled up their designs to produce the 30-mm M230. Using aluminium-cased ammunition (half the weight of brass), the Apache can carry approximately 1,200 rounds (the AAH requirement was for 320) – 1,100 in the magazine and 90 in place on the chain feed to the gun. The gun's feed mechanism is a continuous, flat rectangular 'loop' driven by a 6.5-hp (4.84-kW) motor. The chain loads ammunition (along the starboard side of the aircraft) into the breech and seals it until the gun is fired – a simple system resistant to dirt and wear. The M230 fires a 'loosely NATO-standard' round, compatible with the UK's ADEN and French DEFA 30-mm shells. The gun fitted to production Apaches is the M230E1, which can trace its lineage back to the XM230A, first test fired in April 1973. It has a maximum rate of fire of 600-650 rounds per minute (60 per second) and 'spools up' to this rate in just 0.2 seconds. Time of

bomblet has a steel body and a 3.2-oz (91-g) shaped charge to penetrate armour. The submunition then explodes into approximately 195 fragments, each travelling at 5000 m/sec (16,404 ft/sec). At 1000 m (3,280 ft) a single M261 warhead will cover an oval area of 56 x 17 m (184 x 56 ft), decreasing to 22 x 13 m (72 x 43 ft) at 5000 m (16,404 ft). Each M73 can penetrate up to 4 in (10.16 cm) of armour. The M267 Smoke Signature (training) round uses three M75 practice submunitions with small pyrotechnic charges. The M267 fulfils the same training role as the M274.

The M255E1 flechette warhead contains 1,180 60-grain hardened steel flechettes and is primarily an anti-personnel/ soft target weapon, although it does have a limited air-to-air application. M156 White Phosphorous (smoke) rounds are used for target marking and incendiary purposes. The M156 has a 2.2-lb (1-kg) WP filler with a small HE bursting charge. The M257 Illumination warhead provides one million candlepower over an area of 1 km² (10,764 sq ft) for at least 100 seconds (descending on a parachute at 4.5 m/sec; 15 ft/sec).

Close-in tactics

Rocket and gun attacks can be made from the hover, as running fire or as diving fire. Before any attack, it is crucial to remember to check the 'four Ts' – Target (verify azimuth, and that target is correct), Torque (select the correct torque required to maintain altitude and do not change it), Trim (horizontal and vertical) and Target (check it again). When firing in the hover the AH-64 pilot may not be able to see directly over the aircraft's nose and will have to use other reference points to maintain position. When engaging a target with running fire the Apache crew will select an IP 8 to 10 km (5 to 6.2 miles) from the target, then depart the IP flying NoE to mask the helicopter's approach. At 6 km (3.7 miles) the Apache will pop up just enough to reacquire the target visually, then level out. Rocket engagements can begin at 5000 m, cannon at 1500 m, and the aircraft will enter a shallow (3° to 5°) 100-kt (184-km/h, 115-mph) dive before opening fire. The pilot should disengage at 3000 m (using rockets) or 1000 m (using guns) to break for terrain cover. The helicopter should never overfly the target.

Diving attacks are used only in circumstances where there is minimal ADA (air defence artillery) and LoS to the target is obstructed, or a high concentration of firepower is needed at a precise point, or weight/temperature restrictions prevent hover fire. From approximately 3000 ft AGL the Apache will dive at 10° to 15° (30° for a steep dive) and engage the target before breaking away above 1000 ft AGL. Dive recovery has to be planned in time to avoid the controls 'mushing' from an abrupt recovery at high airspeed.

Of course the key to the Apache's success as a tank-killer is its point target weapons system – the Rockwell AGM-114 Hellfire missile. Each Hellfire is just 7 in (17.8 cm) in diameter, 64 in (162.5 cm) in length and weighs 99.5 lb (45 kg), except for the AGM-114F which is slightly longer and heavier. The basic weapon, the AGM-114A, is no longer in production and stocks are being used in live-fire training. The AGM-114B is a version for naval use with HERO (Hazard of Electronic Radiation to Ordnance) safeguards. The AGM-114C is the baseline model in current Army

The altitude from which rockets are fired, and the range to target, determine the angle of impact and fragmentation pattern. Rockets fired with a high angle of impact produce fragmentation patterns that are close together. A rocket fired at NoE altitudes produces an elongated pattern.

AH-64 Apache and Longbow Apache

Above: An AH-64A manoeuvres hard with a load of Hellfire training rounds and Hydra 70 rocket pods. Note how the TADS sensors have been rotated inwards to protect their optics in flight, while the PNVS is exposed.

Right: The Apache's Hydra 70 rockets can be fitted with M433 multi-option fuses. Impact fusing allows surface and subsurface warhead bursts. Targets in open terrain will be engaged with superquick fuses that detonate upon contact. Targets with overhead protection, such as heavy tree cover or in fortified emplacements, will be engaged with a delay/forest penetration setting. Timed fuses produce airbursts and are most effective against targets with no overhead protection. Flechette, smoke and illumination warheads incorporate timed fuses, which are controlled by motor burnout. MPSM warheads can use M439 fuses, remotely set from the aircraft with range (time) to target information. Once fired, the forward motion of the rocket initiates fuse countdown. At a point slightly above and before the target, the submunitions are ejected and their ram air decelerators inflate. This arms the submunitions and places them in a near-vertical descent over the target.

service. It has a semi-active laser seeker and an improved low-visibility detection capability, compared to the A model. The AGM-114C also flies a flatter trajectory to the target with a low-smoke motor. The AGM-114F (sometimes referred to as interim Hellfire) has a tandem warhead for use against reactive armour.

The next version was developed as a result of Gulf War experience and began life as the Hellfire Optimised Missiles System (HOMS), now referred to as the AGM-114K Hellfire II. The AGM-114K has been totally redesigned and features improved tandem warheads, electro-optical countermeasures hardening, a semi-active seeker head and a programmable autopilot for trajectory shaping. This new autopilot works by regulating launch speed from 300 kt to Mach 1.1, allowing a steeper terminal dive. The AGM-114K's seeker has been improved to overcome backscatter interference (as discussed later). All previous models of Hellfire used an 8-kg (17.6-lb) conical shaped charge warhead with a copper liner cone. The HE charge shapes the liner into a supersonic jet of molten metal that is effective against every armour technology known today. In the Hellfire II the copper liner has been replaced by molybdenum steel with a larger precursor charge. Hellfire II is believed to have a maximum range in excess of the 8000-m (26,247-ft) range quoted for earlier versions. Hellfire has been extensively tested on US ranges against Soviet (and modern US) armour and on the battlefield during Operation Desert Storm. When used against the Iraqi army the striking power of Hellfire was absolute – a single Hellfire strike

would destroy any target, except perhaps at the edges of the engagement envelope. Prior to the war US intelligence reported that Iraqi T-72s were being fitted with armoured fences set 18 ft (5.5 m) away from the tanks to defeat tandem, shaped-charge warheads. A T-72 was set up in this configuration in the US and shot, and destroyed, with a single Hellfire. Longbow Apache will use a version of the Hellfire based on AGM-114K, the AGM-114L. This version will be laser- or MMW radar-guided.

Hellfire employment

When a Hellfire leaves the rail it accelerates at 10g and reaches Mach 1.3 within six seconds in a g-bias climb (i.e., the missile climbs sharply on a defined parabola to a predetermined altitude, to begin searching for the laser spot). Depending on the type of missile, range to target, launch altitude and designation mode, the missile climbs to between 500 ft (152 m) and 1,500 ft (457 m) for a terminal dive on the target. The minimum range for a Hellfire engagement is 500 m (1,640 ft) and textbook maximum range is 8000 m (26,248 ft). Because the missile needs to climb to engage a target, a low cloud ceiling will hamper Hellfire operations as the missile can lose lock-on. This is one realm where the radar-guided AGM-114K will transform Apache operations.

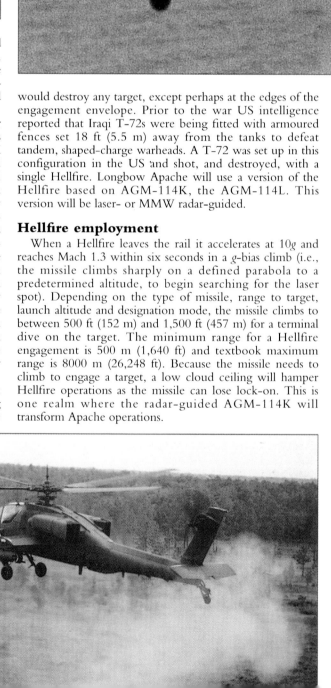

Hellfire can be launched in two designation modes: Lock-On Before Launch (LOBL) in which the AH-64 self-designates, and Lock-On After Launch (LOAL) in which the target is designated by another laser, on the ground or in the air. The Apache can designate its own targets up to ±10° off-boresight. If another Apache is designating for the 'shooter' (indirect designating) the maximum angle between the laser LoS (Line of Sight) and shooter LoS must be ±60° for the designator to remain visible. The Hellfire's trajectory shaping and seeker scan-pattern force minimum engagement ranges to increase, in LOAL mode, if launch altitude increases above target altitude. As launch altitude increases the missile's ability to see the target at shorter ranges decreases. With an AGM-114F, minimum LOAL range is 2000 m (6,561 ft) if the launch aircraft is 50 ft (15.24 m) above the target (800 m/2,625 ft for AGM-114C). In LOBL mode, minimum range decreases to 1400 m (4,593 ft) for an AGM-114F and 800 m (2,625 ft) for an AGM-114C. During the early stages of Desert Shield Apache crews were afflicted with 'dirt diver' Hellfires that came off the rails and plunged straight into the desert. The problem was one of laser backscatter, wherein the beam was diffracted by dust and sand in the air and reflected back at the designator. This problem is not unique to a desert and can be caused by fog, snow or haze. If the missile seeker is tracking backscatter the seeker head LoS and designator LoS should differ (by more than 2°) and this should alert the CPG that he needs to re-acquire the target. In the desert the backscatter was caused by the Apache's own dust cloud so the solution was to launch a missile and wait several seconds before firing the laser to allow the missile to get clear.

Laser technique

A target must remain illuminated by the laser 'sparkle' once the Hellfire is in terminal phase; once the seeker is tracking, the laser cannot be turned off. To achieve 90 per cent Pk (probability of kill) the target must be illuminated for eight to 10 seconds. The CPG has to be conscious of illumination faults such as boresight error, spot jitter (caused through motion of the designator), beam divergence (the further the laser is from the target, the wider the spot will be on the target), attenuation (the beam will be scattered by obscurants or bad weather), overspill (placing the spot too high on the target so it 'slips' over onto the terrain behind) and underspill (placing the spot too low on the target so that false targets are created in the foreground).

'Servicing' the target

To fire a Hellfire the CPG must consider four elements – mode, code, quantity and type. The mode will be LOBL or LOAL (with LOAL-LO and LOAL-HI options depending on the desired trajectory of the missile). The code is a NATO-standard four-digit code that matches the missile seeker head to the pulsed frequency of the laser. Missile codes are issued in blocks, at a unit level, and then allocated at a company level. Each Apache will have its own code, but can also store up to eight codes (A to H) to designate for other aircraft if required. Codes are entered via the Apache's data entry keyboard. Since laser codes are allocated to individual aircraft, knowing which 'chalk' has been allocated which codes is an essential element of the mission brief. The CPG selects the number of missiles he wishes to allocate to a code, then selects 'type', which will always be laser-guided in the AH-64A. A maximum of two codes can be used at the same time, referred to as upper and lower channels. Normal procedure is to allocate the upper channel to the Apache's own code and the lower channel to a remote designator. It is possible to allocate both channels to remote designators, so that the shooter can remain hidden while firing missiles at two separately designated targets.

The laser rangefinder provides distance to target and LoS provides azimuth. For an LOBL engagement the missiles seeking the first selected code will lock-on if they are within the laser spot LoS. A solid box appears on the HDU target display, indicating that the laser return is valid. The CPG verifies that the range to the target is within limits and that the laser has a firm hold on the target. Missiles can be fired with the laser on or off, but the laser must be engaged

The accuracy and effectiveness of any weapons launch from a helicopter is dictated by the aircraft's flight conditions. Hellfires, for example, are not always silver bullets. Rotor downwash acts on any projectile, causing its trajectory to change. A noticeable change in trajectory will occur when the Apache is operating below effective transitional lift. This distortion is most pronounced with rockets, but will also trouble guided missiles, especially if they are fired at short range. If the Apache is hovering in ground effect, air flowing down through the rotor system causes the missile to pitch up as it leaves the rail. When the missile passes beyond the rotor disc, air flowing upwards (bouncing off the ground) causes the missile to wobble and can induce lateral (azimuth) and linear (range) errors. When the Apache is hovering out of ground effect, the downwash strikes the missile only once. However, the increase in velocity of this downwash (increased because of the additional power needed to maintain the hover out of ground effect) may further worsen linear dispersion.

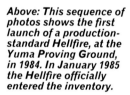

Above: This sequence of photos shows the first launch of a production-standard Hellfire, at the Yuma Proving Ground, in 1984. In January 1985 the Hellfire officially entered the inventory.

Above right: Positive threat ID with the FLIR system is acknowledged to be difficult. While the crew can easily detect the heat signature of a potential target, determining whether the 'blob' is friend or foe is less straightforward. The phenomenon of IR crossover – caused at night when targets have cooled to the same temperature as the surrounding terrain – can make even acquisition impossible. IR crossover occurs most often when the environment is wet, as moisture in the air creates a buffer in the emissivity of objects. The PNVS FLIR lacks the magnification of the TADS and so cannot reliably detect wires or other small objects.

for terminal guidance. It takes an eight-second (approximate) 'sparkle' to ensure the missile will find the target. For an engagement at maximum range an AH-64A may have to remain exposed for 45 seconds (including acquisition time and 37 seconds of flight). For a remote LOAL engagement the shooter's wingman will lase the target and provide the range and azimuth information. The shooter points at the target and can fire with, or without, a solid lock. Upon firing, the shooter calls the time of flight for the missile and calls for 'laser on' from the designating aircraft. In a LOAL engagement the shooter can remain permanently masked, and out of harm's way.

If the engagement is autonomous (self-designating) or remote (designated from another source), with all missiles on the same code, a proficient crew could reasonably expect to have two or possibly three Hellfires in flight simultaneously. Crews generally train to fire (depending on range) with an eight-second separation to allow adequate time to transition from one target to another. If the LOAL engagement is a 'ripple' (missiles on two separate codes), a good crew could have four missiles (two autonomously- and two remotely-guided) in the air at once. Launch separation times between an autonomous missile and a remote missile can be as little as two seconds.

JAAT – co-operative tactics

In 1986 a new form of combined Army/Air Force operations was pioneered by 7-17 Cavalry, 6th Cavalry Brigade, almost by accident. A phone call from the AFRes's A-10-equipped 917th TFG, requesting the use of the AH-64's weapons range at Ft Hood, led to a deal. The 'Hogs' could

come and drop their bombs if the 7-17 Cav could try out their laser designator with the A-10's Pave Penny marked target seeker. When the A-10s hit the target first time using the Apache's laser, both teams realised that a small revolution was in prospect. This early exercise lead to formal AJAAT (Advanced Joint Air Attack Teams) trials at Nellis AFB. The Ft Hood Apaches (which had become the 3-6 Cavalry) joined with the USAF's 422nd TES in 1987 to conduct operations in high- and low-threat environments on the Nellis ranges. Phase II saw the team moving to Ft Hood in December for night-time/bad-weather operations, and in Phase III the AJAAT trials moved to Ft Still, to work out against an unfamiliar target array. The success of the 300 missions flown paved the way for today's JAAT tactics. To the Army, JAAT becomes AJAAT when an 'Advanced' helicopter, such as the Apache, is designating rather than troops on the ground (for example).

The AH-64's optics allow it to find and identify targets at ranges unavailable to A-10s. This in turn translates to safer stand-off ranges for the A-10s, whose Pave Penny trackers can see the Apache's lasers at ranges in excess of 8000 m (26,246 ft). A-10 pilots could, for example, make blind firing passes at targets hidden in tree lines that they never saw, simply by following the HUD cues. Although the A-10's GAU-8 cannon has a well-deserved reputation for destruction, the 'Hog' has to close to a range of 2,000 ft (610 m) for it to be guaranteed effective. The longer-ranged IR Maverick is the A-10's preferred weapon, but its seeker head has a magnification capability of just x6 compared to the Apache's x127 system. This alone underlines the value of the Apache to the JAAT mission.

Apache FACs and scouts

JAAT also brought about the birth of two-ship Apache scout teams. During the early trials traditional scout helicopters were too slow to keep up with the JAAT teams, so the 3-6 Cav started to use three two-ship Apache sections in favour of traditional scout/gun combinations. The role of the Apache scout is crucial. The scout conducts the target brief and relays it to the Air Force aircraft, if there is no FAC. This is the 'nine-line' FAC-to-fighter brief, which specifies IP, heading to target, target elevation, target description, target co-ordinates, target marks (laser code), friendly forces, egress direction plus any necessary remarks (hazards, restrictions, threats or abort code).

If no FAC is available the scout will also hand over the incoming aircraft to the designating AH-64s. The scout maintains communications to higher headquarters and acts as 'traffic cop' to marshall the next troop of AH-64s entering the area. The Apaches should not be fighting an engagement alone but should be calling up artillery support to drive the enemy into the kill zone, break off comms antennas and button up the tanks. The squadron Fire Support Officer (FSO) is the link between the aviators and the gunners, and it is he who must have pre-planned the artillery engagement to the flanks or the rear of the kill zone. The artillery unit's Forward Observer (FO) should be airborne with the scouts, to best integrate his battery's fire.

The A-10s fly in four-ship formations which permit pairs of aircraft to make independent attacks. If both pairs are needed for a single attack, they will be controlled by two Apaches simultaneously. When conducting this type of four-ship attack, each A-10 section is given its own laser code. A single AH-64 works a four-ship section by putting all the A-10s on a single code for a sequential attack.

The Apaches do not remain passive on the battlefield. While designating for an A-10 an AH-64 can also be shooting a target that has been coded and designated by its wingman. It can also cover the A-10 coming off its attack.

The A-10's Pave Penny seeker has a laser-to-target offset of 60° (similar to the Apache's own limit), and although attacks can be made outside that range they are undependable. Ingressing to the target, the A-10s may make a recce 'bump' at their IP to find the Apache's laser then remask to maintain terrain cover en route. The laser is detectable at ranges up to 20 km (12.4 miles). At the IP the A-10s will expect the initial brief from the scout commander on the common UHF frequency (which is a Have Quick secure radio). FM radios are used to talk to the ground forces, while the Apaches use an internal VHF net.

Running the attack

Once handed over to the designating AH-64, the A-10s receive the specific target brief. This comprises target location (a six/eight-digit map UTM), target description (e.g., 'northernmost tanks'), elevation (derived from the AH-64's fire-control system and input to the A-10's sight), laser code (chosen to deconflict with the Hellfire codes in use and entered to the Pave Penny through cockpit switches – a typical training code would be 1668), laser-to-target line (ensures that the A-10 is within the parameters to see the laser and also allows the A-10 pilot to calculate the AH-64's position by drawing a back azimuth from the target),

The Apache/Kiowa 'gun' and 'scout' team has fallen into disuse. This is largely due to the US Army's massive ARI restructuring which has forced aviation units to do more with less. Though the number of Apaches deployed by each attack helicopter battalion has increased, so too have the demands made of them, and Apaches must now undertake their own scout and security missions. It is also true that the AH-64 outclasses the available scout helicopter, the OH-58C Kiowa. With the advent of the OH-58D, the scout/cavalry community now has a far more capable mount, arguably more capable than the AH-64 in some respects.

Left: The front (CPG's) cockpit of the AH-64A is dominated by the ORT and its 'T-bar' handgrip. On the front console the CPG has a fire control panel (left) and a set of basic flight instruments (right). On the port side-console (from front to back) can be seen the Hellfire missile control panel, data entry keyboard, anti-icing controls, power lever quadrant, fuel control panel, interior lighting controls and circuit breakers. The starboard side-panel contains the communications system control panel, AN/ARC-186 radio controls, Doppler control panel and a blank area (with provision for KY-58 secure voice control) used for map storage. The pilot and CPG have identical collective controls, but slightly different cyclic grips. The CPG cyclic (centre stick) is folded to the floor in this photograph.

Above: The ORT (Optical Relay Tube) is the primary station where the CPG can monitor TADS/PNVS imagery, then select, designate and shoot targets. Its bulky construction is also the greatest threat to the CPG's well-being in the event of a crash. The hooded monocle display at the top can be used head-down, while the screen below allows the CPG to remain 'head-up'. Beneath the open screen are video-source (TADS or PNVS) and filter selection switches. Flanking the open screen are gain, brightness, grey-scale and FoV adjustment switches. On the left-hand grip can be found the sensor select switch (FLIR, DVO, DTV), weapons action switch (gun, rocket, missile), weapons trigger, primary FoV (wide, medium, narrow, zoom) controls and image autotracking controls. On the right side of the 'T-bar' grip can be found the laser spot tracker controls, manual turret slew controls, FLIR polarity switch (black/white), video recording switch, main laser trigger and boresighting controls.

AH-64D Longbow Apache

1 Pilot's Night Vision Sensor (PNVS)
2 Rotating PNVS turret
3 Target Designation Sight unit (TADS)
4 Night vision sensor (FLIR)
5 Direct Vision Optics (DVO)
6 EW antenna
7 Chain Gun® cannon muzzle
8 Environmental Control System (ECS) evaporator and fan
9 Co-pilot/gunner's rudder pedals and cyclic pitch controls
10 Signal data converter
11 Armament control panel
12 Sight viewer
13 Gunner's windscreen panel
14 Starboard side cockpit entry hatch
15 Pilot's windscreen panel
16 IR head position sensors for IHADSS system
17 Co-pilot/gunner's armoured seat
18 Collective pitch and engine condition controls
19 Side console panel
20 Avionics equipment bay, port and starboard
21 Link return chute, ammunition
22 Mainwheel shock absorber mount
23 Pilot's instrument console
24 Blast screen between cockpits
25 Cockpit hatch balance strut
26 Starboard stub wing weapons carriage
27 Cable cutter
28 Pilot's armoured seat
29 Collective pitch lever
30 Engine condition levers
31 ECS compressor
32 Boarding steps

33 Stowage bay
34 Avionics equipment
35 Forward fuel cell
36 Flight control system mechanical linkages
37 Rotor head hydraulic actuators (three)
38 Cooling air intake
39 EW antenna
40 Temperature sensor
41 Rotor blade root attachment points
42 Composite main rotor blades with stainless steel spars
43 Mast-mounted Longbow MMW radar radome
44 Longbow radar avionics
45 Articulated radar scanner
46 Omnidirectional airspeed sensor

47 Rotor blade lead-lag friction dampers
48 AN/ALQ-144 'disco light' infra-red jammer
49 Rotor head swash plate mechanism
50 Laser warning receiver
51 Gearbox mounting frame
52 Main gearbox
53 Generator
54 Ammunition bay and feed drive
55 Stub wing attachment joints
56 Port engine intake
57 Engine transmission right-angle gearbox
58 Gearbox input shaft
59 Tail rotor output shaft
60 Engine accessory equipment gearbox
61 Intake particle separator air duct
62 General Electric T700-GE-701C turboshaft
63 Environmental control system

64 Auxiliary Power Unit (APU)
65 APU exhaust
66 'Black Hole' infra-red suppression exhaust ducts
67 Hydraulic reservoir
68 Central maintainance walkway
69 Electro-luminescent lighting strip
70 Tail rotor transmission shaft
71 Shaft bearings
72 Tail rotor control rod
73 Intermediate gearbox
74 Tail rotor final drive shaft
75 Swept main rotor blade tip

76 Final drive right-angle gearbox
77 Tail rotor pitch control servo actuator
78 VHF/FM antenna
79 Electro-luminescent formation lighting strip
80 GPS antenna
81 Rear radar warning antennas
82 Tail navigation light
83 Dual twin-bladed teetering tail rotor
84 All-moving tailplane
85 Tailplane hydraulic actuator
86 Castoring tailwheel
87 Cable deflector
88 Chaff/flare launcher
89 ADF antenna
90 Rolls Royce/Turboméca RTM 322 alternative engine for British army aircraft
91 IFF antenna
92 ADF loop antenna

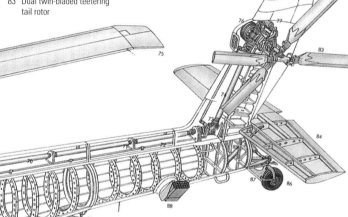

93 Doppler antenna fairing
94 Survival packs, port and starboard
95 Anti-collision strobe light
96 Port navigation light
97 Ground equipment stowage bay, battery bay to starboard
98 VHF antenna
99 Rear fuel cell
100 ECS condenser
101 Port stub wing
102 Electro-luminescent formation lighting strip
103 Weapons pylons with articulated carrier/ launchers
104 Articulated carrier hydraulic actuator
105 Four-round missile launcher
106 Hellfire anti-armour missiles, maximum load 16
107 19-round 70-mm rocket launcher
108 2.75-in Hydra 70 rocket
109 Dual ATAS Stinger launcher, for wingtip mounting
110 (FIM-92) Stinger air-to-air self-defence missile
111 Chain Gun® ammunition magazine,1,200 rounds
112 Port mainwheel
113 Boarding step
114 Cable cutter
115 Swivelling ventral gun turret mounting
116 Ammunition feed and link return chutes
117 Gun elevation hydraulic actuator
118 Articulated gun mounting frame
119 Cable deflector framework
120 M230 Chain Gun® 30-mm cannon

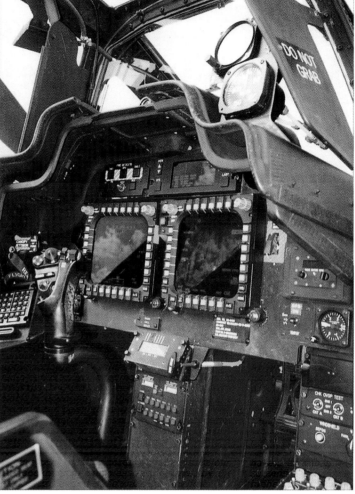

Above left: The rear (pilot's) cockpit on the AH-64A has an instantly more spacious feel to it than the CPG's. The screen in the console centre is the video display unit (VDU) and beneath it are the horizontal situation indicator (HSI) and smaller, hydraulic systems gauges. To the left are the airspeed indicator (ASI) and standby ASI. Further left are the strip indicators for the Apache's engine torque, turbine gas temperature, engine gas generator, oil and fuel levels. Below and beside them, on an 'L-shaped' panel, are the fire control switches. The black and yellow canopy jettison handle is clearly marked. On the right side of the console are the radar altimeter, radio-call placard, encoding barometric altimeter, RWR display, vertical speed indicator (VSI), clock, HARS controls and accelerometer. To the far right can be seen the (red and yellow) icing severity meter, radar/IR countermeasures panel, chaff dispenser control and RWR control panel. Below them is a bank of caution/warning lights. The circular lens above the coaming on each Apache cockpit is the boresight reticle unit. The rear cockpit side-consoles are dominated by a bank of radio (and some weapons) controls.

Above and below: Both cockpits in the AH-64D have been transformed by the addition of twin Bendix King MFDs, while still retaining some of their 'old-style' feel. The 6 x 6-in (15 x 15-cm) screens were monochrome on development AH-64Ds, but will be full-colour in production aircraft. The first colour displays were delivered to McDonnell Douglas in late 1996. Note how instruments have been raised above the coaming in the pilot's cockpit.

AH-64 Apache and Longbow Apache

This Apache is loaded with a varied air-to-air missle armament. On the port pylon is an AIM-9M Sidewinder AAM, with a FIM-92 Stinger to starboard. The Air-To-Air Stinger (ATAS) is the weapon with which the US Army has conducted the most extensive trials (note the cameras on the wingtips to film separation tests). Its small size allowed two missiles to be carried on each station – at the expense of fuel, rockets or Hellfires. A wingtip-mounted twin-launcher has been developed as a result. Opponents of an air-to-air role for the Apache believed that adding AAMs might distract crews from their primary mission. However, the arrival of the AH-64D Longbow Apache will undoubtedly bring with it an expanded air-to-air role for the Apache.

restrictions (an optional call, perhaps to keep the A-10s from overflying impacting artillery) and remarks (requesting the A-10s to call when departing the IP so the designator is ready). Every Apache within the AJAAT team must be capable of making this brief and designating targets. This vital task is notionally the responsibility of the aviation commander, but he will frequently have to delegate.

Co-ordination between A-10s and Apaches of the 2-22nd AVN during the 101st Airborne Division's assault on Objective Toad, in Iraq, on 20 February 1991 was cited as a perfect example of JAAT in action. Two teams of A-10s working with the Apache's Air Liaison Officer and Air Battle Captain attacked Iraqi bunkers with Mk 82 bombs and CBUs. Only the lack of any Iraqi armour prevented the use of the A-10's Mavericks. With the A-10 no longer dominant in the close-air support role, the AH-64 is capable of working equally well with the LANTIRN-equipped F-16. The F-16 brings with it the added dimension of being able to operate at night, which was never the A-10's forte.

Air-to-air weapons

The US Army does not yet anticipate a major air-to-air combat role for the Apache or the Longbow Apache, which is more suited to the task. US Army units do not train for this mission, unlike US Marine Corps attack helicopter pilots. As a result, a dedicated air-to-air weapon for the Apache has been frequently discussed but never deployed. Initial US trials were conducted with AIM-9 Sidewinders, at the White Sands Missile Range in November 1987. Although further Sidewinder trials were undertaken, serious attention moved to a modified version of the FIM-92A, the AIM-28 Air-to-Air Stinger (ATAS). ATAS trials also began in 1987 and by 1989 test firings had been undertaken at the Yuma Proving Ground. The Stinger could be carried in a two-missile box housing on the ends of the AH-64's stub wings. Only a single (larger) Sidewinder could be carried on a specially-developed rail. Trials were also undertaken with the anti-radar Sidearm, a modified RF-homing AIM-9 developed as a small and affordable anti-radiation missile. Successful Sidearm trials were conducted at China Lake Naval Weapons Center in

April 1988. Captive carry trials of the Shorts-developed Helstreak/Starstreak anti-aircraft missile began in 1990, followed by six live firings at the Yuma Proving ground in 1991. The Helstreak is the main contender for the UK's air-to-air weapon and is also being regarded with some seriousness by the US Army. The first of the US Army Starstreak trials resulted in access panels on the AH-64 being jarred open by the missile's shockwave. This problem was quickly solved and the firing programme encountered no debris damage from the missile plume – one of the major concerns regarding the high-velocity Starstreak.

In early 1997 the US Army drafted a Mission Need Statement calling for an improved air-to-air armament for the AH-64. Limitations of the Stinger were acknowledged, including its lengthy engagement 'time-lines' – during which the Apache is exposed to enemy fire. The US DoD now anticipates a further two-year trial of what it dubs the Air-to-Air Starstreak (ATASK) under the supervision of Army Aviation's Applied Technology Directorate, Ft Eustis. A series of 20 firings will be made against drone targets during this phase. As a result, the UK decision to acquire Starstreak/Helstreak, once expected in 1997, will be delayed perhaps until 1999. The BAe/MATRA Mistral AAM is also an outside contender for the UK requirement.

Standard Apache weapons have a limited air-to-air application. In fixed gun mode the M230E1 has a round impact set at 1575 m (5,157 ft) with a time of flight of 3.9 seconds. Hydra 70 rockets with M255E1 flechette warheads are perhaps the AH-64's best anti-helicopter weapon. Upon detonation the flechettes are deployed at a 12° angle, and the flechette cloud becomes cylindrical in shape after 150 m (492 ft) of travel, over 15.7 m (49.7 ft) in diameter. Test firings indicate that at ranges of 2000-2500 m (6,562-8,202 ft) three pairs of rockets will have a 75 to 82 per cent chance of scoring a hit. Hellfire can be used to engage

targets at up 8000 m (26,247 ft). The preferred employ-ment method is to designate the target indirectly, allowing the Apache to fire from cover.

Ft Rucker - where it all begins

Before any Apache pilot can come to grips with the AH-64's technical sophistication and tactical employment he, or she, must be fully conversant with the aircraft's basic qualities. All flying training for the US Army begins in the pleasant surroundings of Ft Rucker, Alabama, home to the network of airfields, training areas and 500 helicopters of the US Army Aviation Center. The 1st Aviation Training Brigade handles the huge amount of flying conducted at Ft Rucker. Basic flying training for helicopter pilots is increas-ingly undertaken on the Bell TH-67A Creeks of the 1-212 AVN (Training). Once students have become IFR qualified with the TH-67As of 1-223 AVN, those destined for the Apache move to the 1-14 AVN at Hanchey AAF. 1-14 AVN conducts all Apache flying at Ft Rucker (with 48 AH-64As at its disposal) and AH-64D training will begin in 1997.

New students, arriving with 'bars and wings', are faced with three stages of AH-64 training. The complete AH-64 qualification course takes 62 training days. Five days of introductory academics are followed by the Contact Phase (Day 6-15). This is literally the students' first contact with the aircraft, comprising seven days in the CWEPT (Cockpit, Weapons, Engine Procedure Trainer). For many

Above: The first launch of a Sidewinder (AIM-9M) was made by an Apache at the White Sands missile range, New Mexico, in November 1987. Several factors led to the adoption of the Stinger missile in favour of the Sidewinder, but one of the most significant of these was the Sidewinder's dramatic launch signature.

Left: This photograph shows the first launch of an Air-To-Air Stinger (ATAS) at the Yuma Proving Ground in 1989. Like the aircraft above, this Apache is fitted with cameras above the stub wings and on the rear fuselage to record the launch. ATAS capability was one of the primary elements planned for the AH-64A+/AH-64B upgrades, using a newly-developed two-round box launcher, but this never progressed beyond the trials stage. There is now a good possibility that the US Army might adopt the Shorts Starstreak/Helstreak AAM, which is undergoing joint US/UK trials for Britain's Army Air Corps.

All US Army, and a great deal of non-national, Apache training is conducted at Ft Rucker. The full conversion course lasts for 12 weeks and two days. Apache flying at Ft Rucker is based at Hanchey AAF, home to the 1-14 AVN ATB. 'D' Company is 1-14's active AH-64 unit. It has seven flight platoons, which in order (first to seventh) are – Apache, Loco, Cochise, Geronimo, Natchez, Mescalero and Apache (again). The names derive, in the most part, after famous Apache warriors or Apache tribes.

Right: This is the 'bag' – the screened-off rear cockpit of an Apache from where the student pilot must fly the aircraft using the FLIR alone. 'Bag' training is conducted by day and by night and is the most strenuous element of the Apache flying training course. Note the grey outline around the canopy. This is detonating chord to blow off the canopy in the event of an emergency rescue.

Right: This student is attempting one of the most demanding elements of flying training at Ech (pronounced 'Ek') Field, one of Hanchey's busy satellite airfields. Ech is the scene of slope training, where students learn to land the aircraft safely on an incline. This Apache is positioning for a slope landing in the 'bag'. The pilot cannot see the ground behind and around him and forward vision is provided by the FLIR alone.

students this will be their introduction to twin-engined helicopter operations and they will learn basic operational procedures (start-up, shut-down, emergency routines) from both seats. This portion of the training also involves a sizeable amount of classroom learning 'by rote', aided by large animated schematics of onboard systems such as the hydraulic, fuel, electric systems. Flying training follows, alternating with returns to the classroom for half-day periods. One Instructor Pilot (IP) will be allocated to two students for their first 12.4 hours of contact flying in the AH-64. They will undertake basic take-off and landing training, emergency procedures (engine failures at altitude or in the hover) and flying in mission configurations (using rolling take-offs to simulate a full weapons load, for example).

The second phase (days 16-36) of training is the most demanding, and perhaps the most demanding flying training requirement anywhere. The student must master flight using only the PNVS, at day and night, flying in the 'bag'. The 'bag' is a shrouded Apache rear cockpit, where all light is blocked out to simulate night-time operations. Students fly with only the PNVS and Helmet-Mounted Display (HMD). Basic flight information is superimposed over the FLIR imagery in the HMD monocle, so with just one eye, in the dark, the student pilot must learn to handle the Apache as if it were the most routine of afternoon trips. PNVS day training (all in the 'bag') comprises 18 flight hours followed by 7.2 hours of actual night operations. Throughout this demanding stage the IPs of 1-14 AVN are not trying to fail pilots, and those students who experience difficulty will be allowed a recheck. However, for some the stress of flying with just a 1 x 1-in black-and-white TV 'window' is just too much.

The third phase, the Gunnery Phase (days 37-55), is the students' introduction to the Apache's weapons system and its tactical employment. It involves a substantial amount of simulator training and live-fire experience. After 10.5 hours of simulator training the Apaches go to the ranges for four live firing days, which still have to interleave with training in the classroom. The student will fire all Apache weapons, spending one day in the front seat, then one day in back, then repeating that sequence at night, culminating with a check ride. Having learned how to fly the aircraft, by day or night, and used all of its systems, the student then returns to the simulator complex for Combat Skills training and the final evaluation (days 56-62). This is where the attack mission is taught – deep attack tactics, mass engagements, zone/route reconnaissance tactics, BDA, gunnery fire correction. In the words of one senior IP, "(we teach) everything, which seems to be our mission of late."

Apache and the US Army today

The Apache force, and the US Army with it, is currently in some doctrinal confusion about the exact role of the AH-64 on the battlefield. Not so long ago, the situation was clear: the US Army had two combat helicopter missions – Attack and Scout/Cavalry. Attack units flew Apaches to destroy enemy (armoured) forces or leveraged targets. The Scout/Cavalry mission was more diverse. While it included scouting for the attack force, the OH-58s and AH-1s of the 'Cav' undertook guard and screening missions for their own armoured units, route and logistics site reconnaissance, and still maintained the capability to engage in (limited) shooting matches of their own.

Once the Apache was operational in Europe the division between these two roles disintegrated, not least because the AH-64 had better sensor systems than its scouts, which in any case were not fast enough to keep up with the Apaches. While the OH-58C/AH-1F team in Cavalry units continued to work well (and just how well has long been a cause of friction between Apache and Cobra

communities), both of these ageing types are about to disappear from the inventory in favour of the OH-58D Kiowa Warrior (see *World Air Power Journal*, Volume 15). This will transform the scout role in the US Army and should pave the way for the reintroduction of workable Scout/Attack teams once more.

The Army's ARI (Army Restructure Initiative) has reinvented many aspects of Army aviation by virtue of the inventory cuts and budget restrictions inherent in it. Under ARI, surviving Apache battalions were boosted from 18 to 24 aircraft, because the Apache must now act as its own scout. (Previously, battalions had operated with a mix of 18 AH-64As and 13 OH-58Cs.) The Hellfire-capable and Mast Mounted Sight-equipped OH-58Ds will not routinely scout for Apaches because, as one Apache pilot put it, "they'll be too busy with their own things to do"; what's more, there will not be enough to go around. Today, the Apache is firmly its own scout. ARI diluted the Apache's role from 'classic, pure attack' to one of security. Now the Apache, expressly designed to kill tanks in the Fulda Gap, and its crews, must undertake the screen, guard and other missions that were never its forte. Obviously, the Apache has many strengths that lend themselves to this mission, but attack crews have their misgivings. Some question the wisdom of placing the Army's most capable and expensive asset so consistently in harm's way – in a role, after all, that the OH-58 once fulfilled. However, it is inevitable that as Army doctrine increasingly coalesces around 'Stability and Support Operations' (the emerging tenet replacing the cumbersome Operations Other Than War/OOTW concept) the Apache will find itself on unfamiliar ground, and one need look no further than Bosnia to see the truth in that.

Attack helicopter units

Each divisional commander will employ his attack helicopters as he sees fit. Under ARI two (Apache) attack helicopter battalions (ATKHBs) are attached to heavy divisions and one to light divisions. The few AH-1Fs that survived into 1997 with these units are being replaced by OH-58Ds. Each Apache ATKHB has 24 aircraft divided into three companies (ATKHC), plus a headquarters/head-quarters company (HHC) and aviation unit maintenance (AVUM). The AVUM provides unit-level maintenance for the battalion. The three ATKHCs provide an offensive capability against armour, personnel and infrastructure/

logistics targets. Each company has its own headquarters section, a scout platoon (three AH-64s) and an attack platoon (five AH-64s). The expected fully mission-capable (FMC) rate is 75 per cent – six aircraft. A two-ship 'lead/wingman' team (platoon) is the basic operational grouping, as its offers a high degree of flexibility and mutual support between teams. Each team will have a platoon leader, while the company commander will fly as a member

Apaches at Hanchey: the uppermost aircraft is exiting a tiny forest clearing after let-down and departure practice, while the aircraft above is engaged in the long sequence of slope training.

During normal peacetime operations US Army Apache crews fly, approximately, 70 hours every six months. This annual figure of 140 flying hours might seem very low – and is one reason why there is a certain amount of resistance from other US Army aviation helicopter crews to joining the AH-64 community. It is not, however, an unusual total in the military helicopter community as a whole. System reliability for the Apache itself (originally specified as 2.8 hours MTBF) has improved from 3.83 hours to 4.15 as the aircraft became mature.

The OH-58C Kiowa scout was a successful partner to the AH-1 Cobra, but far less so for the AH-64. The Kiowa has none of the sensors and equipment of the Apache, nor the performance to keep up with the larger helicopter in the field. Kiowa crews rely on their aircraft's small size and NoE flying to survive, but can be forced to operate within lethal range of enemy ADA to carry out their missions. As the OH-58D Kiowa Warrior enters wider service, remaining OH-58C units are preparing to trade in their Kiowas for Warriors. (To US Army crews a 'D' is never an AH-64D but always an OH-58D. The AH-64D is always the 'Longbow'.)

A masked Apache presents a small target but its nose-mounted sensors are also hidden from the target. This is where the crew must make maximum use of their aircraft's agility to pop up, acquire the target and remask. The AH-64 autopilot even has a 'bob-up' mode to facilitate this. The Apache's noise signature is negligble beyond 1 km (3,270 ft) – 75 per cent of that noise is caused by the tail rotor.

of the third team, positioning himself as required. An Air Assault Division, such as the 101st, follows the same aviation battalion organisation, while an Airborne Division (such as the 82nd) will have a single OH-58D ATKHB.

Attack helicopter tactics

The ATKHB is an instrument of precise firepower, with the manoeuvrability to mass combat power at a decisive time, yet one which should always work as part of a combined arms team. The Apache is tasked with nine primary missions: to attack massed armour or light forma-tions, to attack in depth to extend the influence of its own land forces, to dominate avenues of approach, to reinforce ground forces by fire, to defeat enemy penetrations, to protect the flanks of a friendly force – be it on the move or static, to provide security for the movement and passage of lines by ground forces, to conduct reconnaissance and, finally, to conduct search and attack missions.

The Apache's role in offensive missions is categorised in several ways. The first of these is a 'movement to contact' – to gain or re-establish contact with the enemy, though not necessarily to engage it. Engagements from a manoeuvre to contact should be against targets of opportunity, or through chance rather than design. The primary function of a movement to contact is to place the Apache battalion in a secure position to conduct its pre-planned attack.

Attacks are sub-divided into two categories, 'hasty' and 'deliberate'. A hasty attack takes advantage of an enemy's weakness or sustains the momentum of the main attacking force. A deliberate attack is conducted against an enemy that is well-organised and cannot be turned or bypassed. It will be pre-planned and briefed using all the intelligence, and time, available. After a successful attack comes 'exploitation', to prevent the enemy from regrouping or withdrawing. The ATKHB will still be operating as part of a larger force and will attempt to strike the flank and rear of the enemy force. Then comes the 'pursuit', in which the Apache ATKHB will leave flank and contact engagement to the ground forces and instead reach deep to cut off the retreating enemy force and block any relieving forces. This calls for precise and well-planned C^2 co-ordination between friendly forces.

There are two forms of defensive operations which concern the ATKHB, 'area' and 'mobile'. ATKHBs conduct area defence in terrain where the enemy has a mobility advantage and must be denied avenues of approach or specific areas. A mobile defence allows the enemy to advance to a point where it is vulnerable to attack

AH-64A anti-armour deep attack

This series of diagrams describes a typical AH-64 deep attack mission – an attack directed against enemy forces not currently engaged but which could influence division or corps operations within the next 24 to 72 hours. This particular mission could also be termed an interdiction against a moving force. Deep attacks are made against high-risk/high-payoff targets, but the attack helicopter battalion (ATKHB) itself is a high-value target and this must always be born in mind before committing it. Deep attacks by corps ATKHBs help the corps commander to shape the battlefield and set the terms for close operations.

❶ Right: *The arrow indicates the direction of movement of an enemy armoured column. The engagement area (EA), a valley, will have been scouted by other aircraft from the aviation unit, or determined from map terrain analysis or overhead imagery. A 15-km (9.3-mile) bracket has been choosen, though this will vary in relation to the size of the unit, terrain and avenues of approach. The red cross marks the 'trigger point' where the armoured column will be directly in the centre of the engagement area and where maximum firepower can be brought to bear. Attack helicopters use terrain for masking and concealment. They may be behind terrain fetaures, but also among terrain features concealed by intervening folds in the hill 'mass' or by vegetation.*

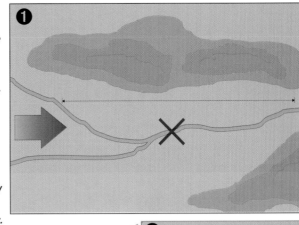

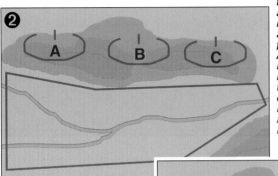

❷ Above: *Company-sized battle positions (BPs) are established – A, B and C. BPs are selected to provide good fields of fire, cover, conceslaed routes of entry and exit, range and relationship to targets. BPs must allow the attacking units to cover their own rear and flanks.*

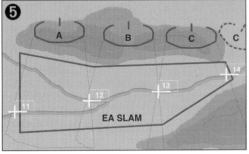

❸ Left: *The EA must have recognisable boundaries, 'channelisation' of moving enemy elements and limited escape routes. Fields of fire are established, taking into account the need to prevent overkill while covering all the targets.*

❹ Above: *Target reference points (TRPs) for supporting artillery fire are set up by the fire support officer.*

❺ Above: *The engagement area is always given a name ('slam' is a generic title). TRPs (yellow crosses) are used as aiming points or references for quickly shifting fire (left, right, add, drop). The placement of these RPs at the intersections of sector boundries would allow them to be used for smoke markers to define those boundries during the battle. Alternative BPs are set up, for use if the primary BPs become unusable, threatened or if the engagement has to be repositioned to continue the attack.*

❻ Right: *Each battle position (A, B, C) will be occupied by three two-ship Apache teams. Phase lines (PLs) are used to mark and control areas, and trigger actions. Like EAs, they are always named. The vertical PL 'Trigger' serves as a 'trip wire' to initiate the engagement. PL 'Red' is a 'no-penetration' line. If enemy forces reach this point the Apaches will have to shift to alternate BPs. Range markers are set up to define the theoretical maximum range of the Hellfire (8 km) and enemy ADA fire (6 km). Red crosses serve as range markers for individual battle positions.*

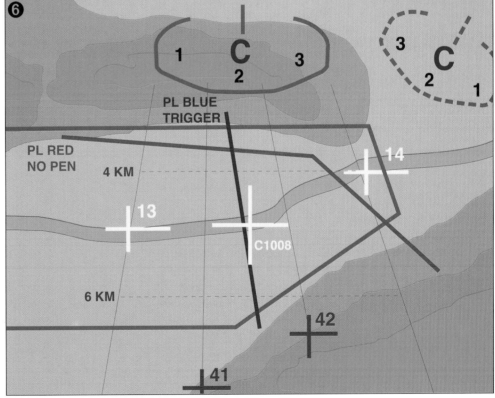

by two sub-divided units, one to contain the advancing force and one to destroy it.

Task Force Normandy was a classic example of an ATKHB 'deep' operation, an attack mission directed against forces not currently engaged but one which will shape the outcome of future events. Deep operations are high-risk, high-payoff missions.

Traditional scout missions are now part of the Apache crew's repertoire. Such missions fall into two broad categories, reconnaissance and security. Reconnaissance missions may be conducted for a zone (covering all routes, obstacle and terrain in a defined area), an area (gaining

detailed information on a specific area such as a ridge line or woods), a route (alone which ground units may be preparing to travel) or as a reconnaissance in force to provoke the enemy into revealing itself. Security missions can be categorised as screen (to provide early warning), cover (operating independently of the main force to distract the enemy), guard (keeping the enemy out of range of the main force), area (securing a specific area such as a convoy route) and air assault security (protecting an LZ).

The defined capabilities of the Apache ATKHB include mobility, speed, range and versatility. Mobility: the ability to rapidly move the force to the decisive place at the

optimum time. The area of operations for the ATKHB will be the entire corps or divisional sector. Speed: attack helicopters move across the battlefield at speeds in excess of 3 km (1.86 miles) per minute. Planning airspeeds are 100-120 kt during daytime and 80-100 kt at night. Range: targets can be attacked up 150 km/93 miles across the FLOT, without additional fuel. Versatility: no longer are there specific airframe-based mission responsibilities. The AH-64 can carry 16 Hellfires, which allow the battalion to engage 384 enemy targets at ranges up to (and beyond) 8 km (5 miles).

The specific limitations imposed on the Apache ATKHB include the weather and Combat Service Support/CSS. With a 500-ft (152-m) cloud ceiling the Hellfire's engagement profile forces the Apache to get too close to the target and exposes it to enemy ADA. The same is true if visibility is reduced to >3 km (1.86 miles). For CSS, an ATKHB will normally require two established FARPs, one for a specific mission and one for future operations, stocked with fuel, ammunition and spares. Each FARP will typically have four rearm/refuel points, allowing the entire battalion to be turned around in two hours, or less.

AH-64 at NTC

Since 1982 the US Army has been training with battalion-sized exercises at the National Training Center (NTC), located in the desert at Ft Irwin, California. These exercises entail an entire battalion deploying to the NTC for a period of several weeks to train in air and ground manoeuvres against the Army's OPFOR (OPposing FORces) units, which use Soviet equipment and tactics. Sessions at the NTC are conducted semi-annually, perhaps

every 18 months, and involve up to six weeks in the field. Before deploying, units form hard crews who will fly together consistently. Apache units do not fly uniformly during peacetime with hard crews, in order to spread experience around the unit and avoid crews becoming complacent with each other. In time of war, this practice would cease and hard crews would be flown constantly. Pre-NTC training will be undertaken for several months without distraction, before the battalion deploys.

Train the way you fight

The first week at NTC is given over to outfitting every aircraft with the Loral MILES (Multiple Integrated Laser Engagement System) laser simulation system and transponders essential for accurate scoring on the ranges, followed by a work-up flying period. The second and third weeks are spent in the 'box' (the NTC manoeuvre area) deployed in the field, living with aircraft and following the OPFOR engagement syllabus. Conditions in the NTC are demanding. The Santa Ana winds can blow at up to 30 kt (55 km/h; 34 mph) and the high ambient temperatures make it easier to over-torque rotors. All operations are conducted under the supervision of the central 'Star Wars building' centre which runs the exercise, backed up by Operational Controllers deployed in the field. Missions begin on day one of the war against the 'Krasnovian' forces who have invaded Mojave from the east. Blue forces start west and work east. The Apaches fly screening missions looking for forward security elements of the invading forces. Operating in pairs for the scouting mission, the Apaches fly 'at the same altitude as the tanks' in front of the advance Bradley IFVs of their own ground forces, operating

on a common radio net. Apaches operating in the traditional deep attack role will go deep to attack Krasnovian installations and armour, through weak points in the defences.

The mission planning imperative

All Apache missions begin with an in-depth mission brief, no matter what the objective or the urgency of the mission. A typical mission analysis begins when the unit commander, operations officer (S3), intelligence officer (S2) and fire support officer (FSO) receive the tasking from higher command. The mission analysis team assembled as a result will include the above personnel and their assistants, plus the unit adjutant (S1), supply officer (S4), liaison officer (LNO), individual company planners (as many as are attached to the regiment), EWO, safety officer and senior IP. This team will spend as much time as it can (up to 90 minutes) on its mission analysis, even under the most extreme circumstances. The S2 will update the IPB (intelligence preparation of the battlefield) and conduct the terrain analysis. This utilises the OCOKA procedure (Observation and fields of fire, Cover and concealment, Obstacles and movement, Key terrain and Avenue of approach). The S2 also conducts weather analysis and threat evaluation to produce the 'illustration of the enemy', which is a situational map and enemy course of action (COA) sketch. The assistant S3 integrates the brigade's mission with other operations in the area. He ensures that the practical details for the mission – battlefield calculus, battle position/engagement area graphics, communications cards – are ready. The FSO will co-ordinate required field artillery support, determining what units are available, where they are deployed, types of ammunition and available stocks, and target priorities. If NBC operations (including smoke) are anticipated, then substantial additional planning is required. An assessment of the enemy ADA capabilities is essential – their available weapons, their employment parameters and how they are integrated with the primary target. The battalion S4 identifies the logistics required for the missions and the constraints on them and comes up with the battalion combat power assessment. The S1 determines medevac and casevac procedures. The XO (executive officer) has the

ultimate responsibility of analysing the level of risk inherent in the mission and whether or not it is acceptable. Finally, the battalion commander reviews the mission intent, adds his own guidance, and approves the course of action.

The results of this mission analysis will include draft route and communication cards, mission graphics, an assessment of friendly forces in the operational area, the mission statement, the commander's intent, the enemy assessment and course of action sketch. A battlefield matrix will have been developed that combines seven defined elements: artillery, C^2, intelligence, manoeuvre forces (infantry, armour and aviation assets), mobility/counter-mobility (engineering support), combat service support and deployed AAA/ADA.

Above and top: Apache units deploy to the National Training Center every 18 months or so and are well-versed in desert operations as a result. Conditions in the Mojave are demanding and can stretch the capabilities of men and machines. However, the frequent complaint of many flyers – lack of power, particularly in hot-and-high conditions – is not one heard from Apache crews.

AH-64 Battle Drills

US Army Aviation battle drills are essential, basic 'collective actions' used by aviation units that have suddenly encountered a threat. They are learned by every crew through exhaustive, repetitive training, so that they become second nature in combat situations. They should require little or no orders to execute and are generally applied to platoon-sized or smaller units. Battle drills are initiated by the first element of the platoon in response to a specific threat from a given direction. The primary objective is to warn the other crews, then initiate a reaction. Battle drills for air threats or ground threats can be categorised in four ways – break, dig, split or static drills.

A **break drill** allows aircraft to respond to a threat from the flank. In a break the AH-64s will turn to orientate on the threat while manoeuvring to avoid, threaten or engage it.

A **dig drill** is designed for an air threat approaching from ±15° to the Apache formation's direction of flight. The objective is to separate friendly elements to avoid the threat or distract the threat while other AH-64s manoeuvre against it.

A **split drill** is carried out in response to a threat from the rear and (almost by definition) the aircraft will be responding from a disadvantageous position.

A **static drill** is designed for friendly aircraft operating from a static position, such as a BP (Battle Position) or during slow forward flight (such as a screening operation).

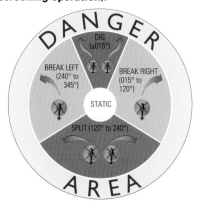

Battle Drill Templates

Battle drills are run on the assumption that a two-ship element (of the platoon) is the basic and most efficient manoeuvring element. This battle drill template (left) shows the appropriate response to a threat (dig, break or split) depending on how it is encountered. If a threat encroaches upon the Danger Area there will hopefully be enough time for one aircraft to make the essential alert call and initiate the appropriate drill.

ALERT CALLS *are the most critical element of the battle drill. The call consists of key words and phrases and initiates a specific response. The first crew to observe the threat must* **ACT** *to manoeuvre on the target and maintain visual contact. Secondly it must* **DETERMINE THREAT STATUS** *– known or unknown, 'bandit', 'bogey' or 'target'. Then this crew must* **TELL** *the rest of the formation – stating its own callsign, threat status, distance to threat, required drill and any other essential information. The rest of the formation must act immediately to perform the drill or mask, or to continue, as required. If there are* **FOLLOW-ON ELEMENTS** *behind this formation they will support the engaged platoon if required, bypass the engagement or mask to avoid the threat.*

The **FORM OF AN ALERT CALL** *is tightly defined, and will follow the pattern of : "Gun 2, target tanks, 300 metres, break right, engage" or "Gun 1 targets, 360, 5000 metres, dig."*

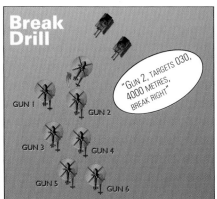

Break Drill

Gun 2 of the lead platoon sees attacking targets at bearing 030° to the formation.

He acts (orientates on the threat) and determine's its intentions.

As Gun 2 manoeuvres to cover the tanks he alerts the rest of his platoon and the follow-on Apache platoon.

Gun 1 acts (manoeuvres to a vantage position and engages the threat to cover Gun 2).

Gun 2 tells Gun 1, and the remainder of the company, that he sees the threat and is engaging.

The second platoon leader hears Gun 2's alert call. He executes a hook right to place his platoon in a position to support the first platoon.

From this position the engagement is extensively wargamed in an attempt to predict every possible enemy action and the Apaches' counter to it. It is a major task, but an essential one for every AH-64 mission. Each wargame is run with a strict timeline. The S2 plays the enemy, the S3 plays friendly forces. The FSO supports the S3, and any NBC operations are also included. The S4 organises support measures, such as FARPs, while the S1 runs medevac. The company commanders manoeuvre their units on the imaginary battlefield and the 'games' are run and rerun until time expires; there are no real answers, only potential ones. The US Army has a mission planning system called Terrabase, which is similar to the USAF's Elvira system. Terrabase uses US military mapping information to generate a three-dimensional, computer-based model of the engagement area. This is of crucial importance when it comes to working out the battle positions of each Apache team. A 3-D model allows the wargames to see the actual fields of fire and identify the 'dead space' where Apaches cannot be seen or cannot see the target.

The final 'production of order' will reunite the planning team to produce all the mission-relevant information for the entire battalion. This will include area of operations maps and sketches, holding area maps, engagement area maps, order of battle, ADA threat, communications frequencies, en route/navigational information, fire support graphics, FARP plan, medevac locations and a mass of other details, which must be digested by every crew.

The entire planning process can take up to six hours with an experienced team, or up to eight hours with new staff. During an NTC deployment, for example, this is exactly what each unit will strive to achieve for maximum training benefit. In time of emergency, such as when planning for a hasty attack, the planners will have to go straight to the wargame phase, leaving the S2 to catch up as best he and his team can. Before the mission (approximately 90 minutes prior to launch), the battalion will ideally conduct a rehearsal, but the most important element remains the mission analysis procedure. This intense planning requirement obviously affects the operational tempo of the unit. Although 'sortie' levels depend on the mission, an attack battalion will, hopefully, be allocated just one deep attack mission per night as a function of planning.

Mission launch

Once inside the aircraft, the crew run through the pre-start checklist: batteries on, APU on-line, cool the TADS/PNVS, boresight, HARS (Heading and Attitude Reference System) position input, then engine start. Once the engines are running the rest of the onboard systems come on line. The AH-64 handles well, but nothing is 'hands off' in the Apache and the pilot has to maintain control input for every second the aircraft is in the air. The pilot flies with the PNVS if required, but can also use the TADS FLIR in an emergency. The pilot may also be allocated control of the rockets while the gunners uses the 30-mm cannon. Once in the air the CPG runs through his SWRM ('swarm') procedure: Sight (select HDU or TADS, day or night), Weapons (activate, select appropriate type and fusing), Range (manual – set at 3 km/1.8 miles as an *en route* 'battlesight' – or automatic, using the laser rangefinder) and Messages (who has control of which weapons, and when). There is a third ranging system, dubbed 'automatic', that uses a flat-earth, line-of-sight/slope-to-target calculation combined with the Apache's radar altimeter. It is little used but, like the manual setting, has the advantage of not requiring the laser – making the Apache that much more undetectable.

The lead/wingman team offers maximum operational flexibility, since it enables proper look-out techniques, aggressive manoeuvring, rapid weapons employment and good mutual support. There are two basic tactical formations: combat cruise and combat spread. In a combat cruise

Left: Night operations are generally undertaken using the onboard FLIR systems, and not NVGs (though it is noteworthy that TF Normandy used both systems). The PNVS is superior to NVGs as it combines FLIR imagery with overlaid flight symbology on the HDU or cockpit displays, allowing the pilot to fly 'head-up and eyes-out'.

Below: The AH-64A has g limits of +3g/-2g. The Apache has operational pitch limts of ±30° and roll limits of ±60°. The Apache has been rolled, but finding someone who will admit to doing so is another matter.

spread the wingman positions himself to best cover the lead, offset to the lead's right side by 10° to 45°. This is also the basic night-flying formation. The combat cruise keeps aircraft staggered, passing through hostile areas with the minimum footprint. Aircraft should avoid flying in trail; if the enemy is alerted by the first aircraft, it is a simple task to shoot at those following in a straight line behind. However, combat trail formations are used when speed is required, or when transiting through defiles or close terrain. The combat spread formation allows both aircraft to cover each other as the two Apaches fly roughly parallel by ±10°. The team must be scanning the terrain, ready to spot incoming fire, and at no time should both crews be looking in the same direction.

Attacks can be made from a variety of attack patterns, dictated by the number of Apaches involved and the type of target, weapons capabilities (enemy and AH-64), disposition of friendly forces and the need to reattack. The cloverleaf pattern allows a team in combat cruise to attack a small target from several differing directions, firing on the inbound leg of each 'leaf'. The 'L' pattern uses a four-ship to attack from two different directions (at 90° to each other) and places maximum firepower on a point for a short duration. In an 'L', the fire of one team should cross the line of the other, forcing the enemy to attempt to engage in two directions at once. The 'inverted V' is a disengagement pattern from combat cruise if the team suddenly takes fire. Lead engages with cannon and breaks away covered by his wingman, firing rockets. Continuous fire can be directed from 'racetrack' or 'wagon-wheel' patterns, particularly used to cover air assault landings and pick-ups.

Panamanian debut

In 1989, eager to flex the Apache's muscles in combat, 11 aircraft from 'B' Company, 1st Battalion, 82nd Airborne Division were deployed by C-5A to Fort Armador, Panama, in advance of Operation Just Cause (the US military ousting of Panama's President Manuel Noriega). The

Apache's first taste of combat was brief and indecisive. Operating as Task Force Wolf, the Apaches undertook combat missions in conjunction with AH-1Es and OH-58Cs, from the early hours of 20 December 1989 until the ceasefire was declared on 9 January. This was the first combat use of NVGs by US Army aviation units, and also the combat debut of the Hellfire. During the assault on General Noriega's headquarters, two Hellfires were fired through selected windows in the building from a distance of 4 km (2.5 miles). Apaches chalked up 247 combat hours during Operation Just Cause, and several aircraft were hit by ground fire, including one aircraft which was hit 23 times and survived. In all, the Apaches of TF Wolf achieved an 81 per cent mission-capable rate.

It was in Iraq that the Apache finally won its true battle honours, during Operation Desert Storm. Army aviation units did not have the experience of the 39-day air war, before troops moved into Kuwait and Iraq, but the AH-64 had an essential part to play in the success of the air campaign. Three Iraqi radar sites close to the Saudi border had to be destroyed to allow the first wave of coalition

Below left and below: As the armoured build-up in Saudi Arabia accelerated in Operation Desert Shield, the AH-64 became even more in demand. Despite the hectic pace of training during the months leading up to G-Day, only a single AH-64A was lost (on 20 January 1991), and its crew survived.

Above: Much has been made of the Apache's supposedly poor serviceability during Operation Desert Storm, but criticisms of the aircraft's record do not bear up to the facts. One 1st Cav veteran of the war in Iraq remembers that of the 18 AH-64s attached to his battalion only one ever needed an engine change. In contrast, each of the OH-58Cs attached to his unit needed to have engines changed and one UH-60 lost three in succession.

Above right: FARPs (Forward Air Refuelling Points) were established by UH-60s and CH-47s that carried fuel and supplies into Iraq, ahead of armoured units. This allowed the Apaches to jump far into Iraq, scouting for and engaging enemy units.

Opposite top: Apaches came to Saudi Arabia by sea. For example, the aircraft of the 4th Brigade, 1st Armoured Division self-deployed from their base at Katterbach, Germany, to Valkenburg AFB, Holland, on 29 November 1990. From there they were loaded onto ships at Rotterdam. It took seven days to get from Katterbach to Rotterdam, but a further three weeks before all 124 helicopters were on board and underway to the Kuwaiti theatre of operations. They arrived in Saudi Arabia on 2 January 1991.

Opposite centre: These aircraft are seen deployed at a forward airstrip, 50 km (31 miles) south of the Kuwaiti border, just prior to Desert Storm.

Opposite bottom: It is almost impossible to discern the Apache in this photograph, which dramatically illustrates the 'brown-out' dust-storms that so hamper desert operations. The key to surviving this sudden loss of visibility is to expect it and keep the aircraft level while climbing away or executing a rolling landing.

attack aircraft safely into western Iraq to attack the Iraqi 'Scud' sites that threatened the political fabric of the coalition forces.

Task Force Normandy

CENTCOM planners decided that the mission could be accomplished in one of three ways: inserting SOF troops to destroy the sites, inserting SOF troops to laser designate for AH-64s, or allowing Air Force aircraft to attacks the sites. Using SOF personnel always entailed an element of risk if the troops were compromised before reaching their target. USAF aircraft could attack the radar sites but could not guarantee that they had been 100 per cent destroyed – the crucial requirement which General Schwarzkopf repeated again and again. Only the AH-64s could bring enough fire-power to bear on the targets and undertake the BDA required to confirm that they had been destroyed. The obvious choice for the mission was the AH-64As of the 1st Battalion, 101st Aviation Brigade, which was one of the US Army aviation units most experienced in night operations. The 1-101st teamed up with the USAF's 1st SOW, whose GPS/INS-equipped MH-53Js would lead the attack force into Iraq. The operation was codenamed Eager Anvil, but Lieutenant Colonel Richard A. Cody named the task force Normandy, in honour of the troops of the 101st who parachuted behind enemy lines into Normandy in advance of H-Hour on D-Day.

Training for the mission began on 26 September 1990 when Lieutenant Colonel Cody's Apaches began to train at night with MH-53Js of the 20th SOS in the FOB Bastogne area. (FOB Bastogne was a Forward Operations Base established to defend the 101st's massive Area of Operations, AO Normandy, 85 km/53 miles south of the Kuwaiti border. It was named after the Belgian town of Bastogne where the 101st Airborne famously held out against besieging German forces during the Battle of the Bulge in 1944.)

The team's helicopters flew the same mission profile that would be required of them on the night – 50 ft (15.24 m) AHO (above highest obstacle) at 120 kt (110 mph; 177 km/h) – and engaged their target with Hellfires and rockets. The route was never flown for real, to ensure their mission was never revealed. Three teams had been organised for the three targets – Red, White and Blue – each with three Apaches plus Pave Low IIIs. It was later determined that the northwestern-most radar site was not linked to the others, so it was dropped from the target list. As a result, the Blue Team was integrated with the others and the mission was flown by four AH-64s, with one spare. On 14 January 1991 the two teams made their way from the 101st's tent-city home of Camp Eagle II (CEII) over 220 nm

(407 km, 253 miles) to King Khalid Military City. The helicopters arrived radio-silent, refuelled, and departed for Al Jouf, doing their best to look like just another training flight. Al Jouf was a small single-runway staging strip, northeast of Tabuk, that was the closest Saudi airfield to the Iraqi border. Only on 15 January did Cody and his S2 (intelligence officer) reveal details of the mission and its target to the rest of the task force. At around 14.00 the following day, word arrived that H-Hour would be 03.00, 17 January 1991.

The first mission of the war

At 00.56 on 17 January 1991 Lieutenant Colonel Cody lead the White team of two MH-53Js and four AH-64As out of Al Jouf. The Red team, led by Captain Newman Shufflebarger, departed 12 minutes later. In all there was a total of nine AH-64As, two MH-53Js and one UH-60 in the air. One Apache acted as a back-up and the Blackhawk was a SAR aircraft, which waited at the border. The Apache crews flew with their FLIRs and ANVIS-6 NVGs. Formation was kept tight, with just three rotor spans between aircraft, and no external lighting. The Pave Lows dropped chemical lights at specific GPS reference points which the AH-64s used to update their onboard Doppler navigation systems. The flight to the target area would take 90 minutes and the round trip back to CEII would be 900 nm (1667 km, 1,036 miles). Even though Al Jouf was

'close' to the border, it was still far enough away to require the Apaches to refuel en route. Ordinarily a FARP would have been established in northern Saudi Arabia, but the danger this would cause in exposing the task force called for a another solution. Lieutenant Tim DeVito came up with the 'single tank option', fitting just one 230-US gal (870-litre) fuel tank to the right inboard pylon and giving the aircraft a 440-nm (815-km, 506-mile) range while still carrying eight Hellfires, 19 Hydra 70 rockets and 1,100 rounds of 30-mm ammunition.

TF Normandy was fired at twice over Iraq, by ground forces alerted by the sound of their passing, but no-one was hit. At 20 km (32 miles) south of the target the MH-53Js delivered their last position update and then peeled off to orbit at their RV. The Apaches approached the radar sites at 60 kt (111 km/h, 69 mph), then each team split into two two-ship groups positioned 500 m (1,640 ft) apart. The two radar sites were close to the Iraqi/Saudi border – the furthest of the pair was only 7 miles (11 km) behind the border – but approximately 69 miles (111 km) lay between them. Each radar site had a combination of Spoon Rest, Squateye and Flatface dish radar antennas, a tropo-scatter radar, generators, EW vans, barracks and ZPU-4 AAA. At 02.37 both teams were in position and marked their targets with the laser spot tracker from 12 km (19 miles) out. At 02.37.50 came Tom Drew's "party in 10" call, followed 10 seconds later by "get some." At a distance of 6 km (3.7 miles) each Apache fired two Hellfires at its primary target, an element of the radar system. The ZPU-4 guns did not come under fire until the radar sites were seen to be destroyed. Some aircraft got as close as 800 m (2,624 ft) to attack targets with their Chain Gun® cannons. The raid was over in 4½ minutes. The Pave Lows were waiting for confirmation of the mission, to relay it to Riyadh. Codeword 'Charlie' meant minimal destruction, 'Bravo' partial and 'Alpha' total. 'Alpha, Alpha' meant no friendly casualties. The Red team had been allocated objective 'Nebraska' and White team objective 'Oklahoma'. From his Apache, named *Rigor Mortis*, Lieutenant Colonel Cody transmitted the phrase, "White Six, Oklahoma, Alpha, Alpha."

A 20-mile (32-km) wide strip had been opened in the Iraqi radar network and SF troops were inserted by MH-47 to place 11 radar reflectors marking the safe corridor for coalition aircraft. As the Apaches turned south to regroup they flew at 100 ft (30.5 m) and 140 kt (259 km/h, 161 mph). Minutes after the firing had begun, the first wave of F-15Es and EF-111s swept overhead at 400 ft (122 m) to knock out fixed 'Scud' sites near H2/H3 airfields. The

Apache crews could see them coming through their NVGs until the jets extinguished their external lights 20 miles (32 km) from the border. At 02:51 F-117s knocked out the air defence control centre for the region, completing the job. TF Normandy returned to Al Jouf at 04.30 to debrief. Early the next morning they flew back to KKMC, rearmed with Hellfires and returned to CEII – only 15 hours after the attack – ready to face any potential Iraqi counter-attack against the 101st.

Apache in Operation Desert Storm

The three-day, 100-hour ground war that commenced at 04.00 (local) on 24 February 1991, G-Day, was accomplished with lightning speed thanks to the mobility of the coalition armoured divisions. US Army aviation's chief contribution to the victory came through its airlift and airmobility assets. The Army deployed 1,193 helicopters in support of Desert Shield/Storm, and only 277 of these were Apaches. On G-Day, an entire brigade of the 101st Airborne Division was moved into Iraq, by air, to Forward Operating Base Cobra, 35 km (22 miles) southeast of As Salman. Apaches were always in the air running screen and security missions for their own ground forces. Their importance to the ground forces was summed up by the words of Major General Griffith, commander of the 1st Armored Division, who said, "I don't want another minute to go by without Apaches out in front of this division."

Apart from TF Normandy the first Apaches into Iraq were 18 aircraft from 2-6th Cav, based at Illesheim, ('Fighting Sixth'), which crossed the border to attack Iraqi communications and surveillance facilities on 16 February 1991. Ten days later 2-6th led the 3rd Armored Division into Iraq and the unit claimed 211 Iraqi armoured vehicles

The AH-64 was one of the success stories of Operation Desert Storm. Yet, despite the amount of literature generated by that brief war, the Apache's achievements go largely unrecorded. One senior commander from a Europe-based attack battalion remembered events thus: "As an aviator who had fought Cobras in Vietnam, (in) my mind's eye (I) expected to see a period of rapid improvement from the initial combat missions. This did not happen. From the first mission on, each aircrew and unit functioned in full synchronization. I attribute this to peacetime training and the great stand-off range of the Apache. The Apache crews very quickly and methodically killed enemy formations in order of priority – tanks with Hellfires, BMPs with rockets and 30-mm, and wheeled vehicles with 30-mm...a great measure of our success (in Desert Storm) can be attributed to the Aviation Branch."

Right: Throughout Desert Storm and subsequent regional operations Apaches retained their dark-green (IR-suppressant) finish.

Below: The Operation Provide Comfort deployment to Turkey was frustrating for all those invoved, as political restrictions prevented them from defending the Kurdish refugees they were supposed to be protecting.

The Apache is fitted with the RT-1296/APX-100(V)1 and RT-1557/APX-100(V) IFF system. APX-100 operates on Modes 1, 2, 3/A, 3/C and 4, transmitting specially coded identification of position or emergency signals as required. Each mode offers progressively more code combinations and ease of use. Mode 4 is the classified operational mode for security identification. IFF antennas are installed on top of the fuselage aft of the canopy, and under the fuselage as an integral part of the UHF-AM antenna. Some Apaches have an IFF antenna located on the work platform forward of the main rotor mast and aft of the tailboom jack pad. IFF transmission from the upper antenna can cause the PNVS to malfunction and slew to the centreline before returning to the pilot's LoS. If this occurs, the transponder must be disengaged or rerouted to the lower antenna.

destroyed in the space of just 45 minutes. Elements of the 3-227th Aviation Brigade ('Spearhead Attack') are credited with pushing further into Iraqi territory than any other US unit. The 3-227th deployed from Hanau in September 1990 and, during one deep attack mission, it advanced 400 km (249 miles) to attack tanks in the Euphrates valley. The 2-227th Aviation Regiment, also based at Hanau, deployed in December 1990 and by the end of the war had flown over 3,200 hours. The unit is credited with destroying 200 Republican Guard vehicles and maintaining a 100 per cent mission-availablity rate during combat. The 1-82nd Aviation Brigade ('Wolfpack') deployed from Ft Bragg in August 1990 and flew 1,893 hours until April 1991. The 3-1st Aviation Regiment ('Night Eagles') deployed from Katterbach and over a three-day period flew 280 combat hours. Its Apaches flew deep attacks against

Al Busayyay, destroyed two Iraqi divisions and over 200 tanks/APCs, and captured 248 Iraqi troops. Apaches from the Ft Rucker-based 2-229th Attack Helicopter Regiment ('Flying Tigers') flew 5,900 incident-free hours to the end of Desert Storm. The unit was involved in the destruction of Iraqi forces along the A-Hammar causeway bridge and the Basrah highway. Apaches from 2-1st Aviation Regiment ('Strike Eagles') flew 235 combat hours and all of its missions were 'cross-FLOT' (Forward Line Of Troops), in day and night. The 2-1st engaged targets of opportunity up to 60 km (37 miles) behind enemy lines, destroyed 35 tanks and took the surrender of over 400 prisioners. The Ft Hood-based 1-3rd Aviation Regiment, (now the 2-101st 'Death Angels' based at Ft Campbell) flew 750 combat hours, including the destruction of Iraqi fire trenches. The 1-3rd was credited with one of the highest direct-fire tank kill totals of the war. Weisbaden-based 5-6th Cavalry Regiment ('Knight Raiders') conducted operations across its corps' sector, including deep attacks and armed reconnaissance. At the time of the ceasefire it was preparing to attack elements of the Republican Guard.

A significant contribution

Singled out for special mention among all the Desert Storm Apache units was the 4-229th Attack Helicopter Regiment ('Flying Tigers'). Deploying from Illesheim, and logging 1,478 hours from January to April 1991, the 4-227th destroyed 100 armoured vehicles in the US Army's first night 'cross-FLOT' and deep attack mission of the war. The 4-229th then made an unprecedented reattack of Iraqi armoured targets, through intense enemy fire, to destroy a brigade-sized element and block reinforcement of the Iraqi frontline. For this achievement the 4-229th was awarded the Army's Valoros Unit Award.

AH-64s flew around the clock, ahead of the advance, engaging Iraqi units as they found them, until it almost became routine. Of all the gun camera/FLIR imagery seen during the war, a team of AH-64s brought back one of the most chilling sequences. Through the TADS of one aircraft a column of Iraqi AFVs could been seen, stationary on a road where their crews believed themselves to be hidden by the smoke from Kuwait's burning oil fields and immune from attack. From a distance of 5 km (3.1 miles) the Apaches could see clearly through the smoke and engaged the column with Hellfires. The silent TADS video showed the lead and trail vehicles destroyed first, to cut off any escape route, and then, methodically but in less than a minute, the dozen or so remaining APCs were wiped out. The Iraqi crews who had been standing in groups, smoking, had no warning and no way out.

Apache ascendant

Any targets that were found were destroyed – over 800 tanks and tracked vehicles, 500 other military vehicles, 60 bunkers/radar sites, 14 helicopters, 10 combat aircraft plus innumerable artillery and AAA positions were claimed by Apaches. A total of 2,876 Hellfires was fired by AH-64s. One Apache was shot-down, by an RPG round fired point-blank from a surrendering Iraqi position. The Apache was hit in the rotor system and crashed, but both crew walked away. All aircraft damaged during fighting returned to base. The overall mission-capable rate for the AH-64 in the desert was over 85 per cent. One unit flew its 36 aircraft constantly for four days, with limited maintenance support, and all remained fully mission-capable. One AH-64 killed two tanks with the same Hellfire. During the appalling weather of 25/26 February, Apaches were the only Army aviation asset to remain operational. During Desert Storm, Apaches did not fly definable 'sorties', for they were active and moving almost constantly. In seven days of operations one AH-64 pilot logged 70 combat

hours, which was by no means unusual. The bulk of missions flown were movement to contact and hasty attacks. The war in Iraq was the ultimate 'fluid environment'. Typically, two-ship teams operated, with the lead Apache carrying rockets for area security and the wingman in 'heavy Hellfire' (16 missiles) configuration. Many pilots in action in Iraq had never fired a live Hellfire before and many remember the (standard) two-second delay after trigger-pull, encountered for the first time, with a mixture of terror and amusement. When the Iraqi surrender was accepted at Safwan it was six Apaches (from 4-229th AVN and 2-6th Cav) that escorted the C-in-C's Blackhawk to the meeting. Even then the Apache's mission in Iraq was not quite over.

The last action of a brief war

On 2 March 1991, after the ceasefire of 28 February, AH-64As from 1-24th Attack Battalion (24th ID) were patrolling the Euphrates valley when the 'battle of the Rumaylah oil fields' broke out. Elements of the Republican Guard's Hammurabi Division were attempting to escape further north, but began shooting at US troops. The US responded with withering MLRS and tank fire, backed up by three companies of AH-64As from the 1-24th. The Apaches fired 107 Hellfires (for 102 hits), 100 70-mm rockets and 2,000 rounds of 30-mm ammunition to destroy 32 tanks and 100 vehicles over the course of an hour. Successful Hellfire engagements began at 6700 m (21,982 ft) – a remarkable distance – and the shooting continued until 15.00. A single US soldier was wounded. One M1A1 tank was damaged and another desroyed, both by secondary explosions from Iraqi vehicles.

After the ceasefire came Operation Provide Comfort and Operation Haven, a hastily prepared humanitarian mission to protect the Kurds in northern Iraq. Iraq's Kurdish population immediately came under attack from the Iraqi army after their uprising against Saddam Hussein failed when the

The Apache training system

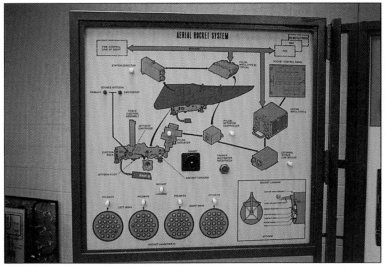

All aviators who come to Ft Rucker for Apache training begin their studies in the classrooms of the Goodhand Simulator complex, learning about the basic systems of the AH-64. This elementary, but essential, phase involves a series of animated 'billboards' and a lot of 'book learning'.

More sophisticated systems training is undertaken on the TSDT – TADS Selective Task Trainer. Ft Rucker has eight TSDTs (including two on the flight line at Hanchey AAF),which use Silicon Graphics computers to generate FLIR imagery and symbology, and teach basic cockpit 'switchology'.

Left: The third stage in Apache training sees students progressing onto the CWEPT (Cockpit, Weapons and Engine Procedure Trainer). Students start in the back (pilot's) seat to learn engine start/shut-down procedures. This is often their first encounter with twin-engined helicopter operations. In 1996 Ft Rucker trained 275 Apache fliers, 75 of whom were for the US Army.

Below: This is the control desk for the unique Apache Crew Trainer, from where missions are monitored and controlled.

Above: A single Apache Crew Trainer (ACT) has been built from a modified CWEPT, to which has been added wrap-round screens plus an Evans and Sutherland 3-D graphics system. The ACT allows crews to fly realistic missions (using a complete graphical terrain database of Ft Rucker), while integrating FLIR and HDU flying. A developed version of this system, for the AH-64D, will allow missions to be 'flown' and linked to other participants, via satellite – a revolutionary mission planning aid.

Right: Ft Rucker's AH-64A full-motion simulator was developed at a time when computer graphics technology did not have the capability to accommodate two crew in one station, so pilot and CPG sit separately while 'flying' the same aircraft.

Wire strike protection system
Unlike some other helicopters, the Apache's wire strike protection system (WSPS) is discreet and not immediately apparent. The WSPS has six cutter assemblies and 11 deflectors. The deflectors are mounted along the canopy hinges, windscreen wipers under the tail and tail wheel, and around the TADS/PNVS and gun assembly. Cutters are located above the TADS/PNVS, below the rotor hub, in front of the gun and on both main landing gear legs.

Weapons pylons
The Apache's external stores subsystem (ESS) consists of a stores controller and up to four pylon assemblies. The stores pylons are articulated to provide the desired elevation for various fire control modes and for aerodynamic/handling purposes. When an Apache lands, or is on the ground, the pylons automatically translate to ground stow mode so that they are parallel with level terrain. In flight stow mode the pylons tilt to present minimum flat plate drag area in forward flight. The pylons remain in flight stow until missiles or rockets are activated, when they then come under fire control computer (FCC) control. The FCC can command the pylons through a range of +4.9° to -15°, but only at airspeeds below 100 kt (185 km/h, 115 mph).

IDF/AF AH-64A markings
Unlike any of its other combat helicopters, the IDF/AF's Apaches are painted in an (IR-suppressive) olive drab finish. Squadron badges (in the case of No. 113 Sqn at least) are regularly seen. For operations in southern Lebanon aircraft carry an IR-reflective 'V' identification marking on the rear fuselage.

Black Hole IR suppressors
The Black Hole system developed by Hughes was originally dubbed the 'Black Hole Ocarina'. (An ocarina is an obscure musical instrument, a small whistle, shaped like a sweet potato. Apaches have a distinctive whistling noise, some more than others.)

Main landing gear
The Apache's main landing gear has shock struts to absorb impact and a kneeling facility to allow air transportation. Each main landing gear utilises a trailing arm and a nitrogen/oil shock strut. The trailing arms transfer landing and static loads to the airframe, while the shock struts absorb vertical loads. The upper end of each trailing arm attaches to a cross strut that passes through the airframe and is supported by fuselage-anchored pivot bearings. In addition to its normal energy-absorbing function, each shock strut has a one-time high-impact absorbing capability, using shear rings and rupture disks to permit a controlled collapse of the strut.

Audio warning system
In addition to visual cues, critical threat warnings and aircraft malfunctions are relayed as aural warnings through the crew's headsets. Engine out, low rotor RPM, stabilator failure, IFF signals, missile launch warning and radar warning alert all have their own distinct tones. The crew also has a tonal signal to indicate that they are transmitting in secure radio mode.

AH-64A Apache
No. 113 Sqn, IDF/AF

Israel became an Apache operator in September 1990 and in the intervening years its AH-64As have seen combat on Israel's front-line of southern Lebanon. For example, on 16 February 1992 a pair of AH-64As carried out the ambush on the convoy carrying Hizbollah's Secretary-General Abbas Musawi along the mountinous road from Jibchit to Sidon. The precision of the Apache's Hellfire system is greatly valued for attacks on small terrorist targets which are often surrounded by other buildings or civilians.

Mk 66 rocket
The Mk 66 is 41.7 in (106 cm) long without a warhead. It weighs 13.6 lb (6.16 kg).After launch. the Mk 66 reaches a maximum velocity of 2,425 ft/sec (739 m/sec) before the motor burns out 1,280 ft (397 m) from the launch aircraft. Rockets spin at nine to ten revolutions per second. Its maximum range is 10425 m (34,203 ft) compared with 8080 m (26,509 ft) for the previous Mk 40 rocket.

Rotor system
The Apache's four-bladed main rotor is fully articulated, allowing each blade to flap, feather, lead or lag independently of the others. The main rotor hub is a steel and aluminium assembly, driven by the main rotor shaft which routes through the static mast that supports the rotor assembly. The Apache's rotor system gives the AH-64 an unprecedented degree of agility and makes it a star performer at air shows.

Chaff/flare fit
The Apache can carry removable 30-round M130 chaff dispensers on a mounting on the rear of the tail boom, to starboard. The M130 can fire M1 chaff cartridges to defeat radar-guided weapons.

The ocean-going Apaches

Hughes and McDonnell Douglas made several attempts to adapt the AH-64A for a dedicated naval role. The first of these 'marinised' versions came in 1984. An Apache equipped with Harpoon or Penguin anti-ship missiles, Sidewinders for self-defence, TOW missiles and a mast-mounted radar was proposed for both USMC and USN use. In USMC service the proposed 'sea Apache' could operate in support of amphibious operations from LHAs or LHDs to protect the assault force at sea and on the beach-head. USN aircraft could be based on frigates to provide distant protection for battle groups from surface threats. The 'sea Apache' would have had a combat radius of 142 miles (228 km) and a mission endurance of 2.8 hours

These ideas matured into a more developed 'Naval Apache' concept which was unveiled in 1987. This aircraft was radically modified through the addition of a completely redefined forward fuselage (plus IFR probe) with the avionics shifted to a ventral housing, increasing the fuel load. TADS/PNVS sensors and cannon were replaced by a Hughes AN/APG-65 radar. Redesigned stub wing/undercarriage sponsons could mount Sidewinder missiles and the 'Naval Apache' retained its Harpoon anti-ship missile capability. Hopes for over 100 sales proved to be premature.

Below right: The US Army maintains a large fleet of Apaches for test and trials duties. This is one of the aircraft attached to the Airworthiness Qualification Test Directorate, now based at Ft Rucker. Until 1996 AQTD was based at Edwards AFB as the Aviation Engineering Test Activity (AETA).

Right: Seen here is AV-05, in use with McDonnell Douglas Helicopters as a technology demonstrator for the US Army's LHX programme. McDonnell Douglas and Bell Helicopter Textron joined forces as the 'Superteam' to bid for LHX. The competition was eventually won by the 'First Team' combination of Boeing/Sikorsky with the RAH-66A Comanche. The YAH-64 was dubbed the ACE (Advanced Cockpit Evaluator) and (over the course of several incarnations) was fitted with fly-by-wire controls, a sidestick controller and advanced cockpit avionics. It joined a dedicated trials group of helicopters which included a Bell 222 with the high-agility 680 tail rotor system and a NOTAR MD500.

US refused to actively back them. In April/May 1991, Apaches were deployed to Turkey and provided 24-hour armed support for the fleet of transport helicopters supplying the Kurdish refugee camps in the mountains. The aircraft involved were from the 6th Squadron, 6th Cavalry Regiment and self-deployed from Illesheim on 24 April 1991 for the 23-flight hour, 3,000-mile (4828-km) journey to Turkey – a unique achievement. The Apaches of the 'Sixshooters' operated with four Hellfires, 38 rockets and a full load of Chain Gun® cannon ammunition in temperatures of over 100°F (37.7°C). Their night-fighting capability was particularly useful against Iraqi units operating under cover of darkness.

Lessons of Desert Storm

During Operation Desert Storm some operational problems were encountered, of varying degrees of seriousness. Sand ingestion led to beter filtration. Ingestion problems in the air turbine starters and fuel boost pump were caused chiefly by the dust clouds spun up by aircraft landing and taking off alongside each other, and not by routine flight. Abrasion of the Hellfire seeker heads was encountered, and the 'dirt diver' missile problem was another minor irritant. For the

pilot, the greatest hazard (true of any desert operations) was 'brownout' – losing contact with the ground in the dust cloud created by the rotor. When taking off the pilot simply had to anticipate the problem and ensure that the aircraft remained straight and level until out of the 'dust storm'. When landing, the technique was to roll ahead of the cloud until safely on the ground – an option not available to a helicopter with skids. The Apache's dust cloud can also betray its position to the enemy. NTC experience has shown that the AH-64's dust signature can be seen up to 10 km (6.2 miles) away, so the pilots must choose their operating conditions with care.

The most important lesson of Operation Desert Storm, learned with tragic effect, was that the Apache can kill at distances that far exceed its ability to identify the target. At night, FLIR contrast was negligible and aircraft needed to get within 2 km (3.2 miles) of a target before making a positive ID, which placed the Apache well within any ADA envelope. This also opened up the possibility of blue-on-blue kills, or 'friendly fire', which, as it turned out, was the greatest threat to coalition forces. On 17 February 1991 the lead pilot in a formation of three Apaches, in error of his actual position and inaccurate in his vehicle ID, fired on a US Army Bradley and M113, destroying both with Hellfires. Before deploying to Iraq some units had undergone a hasty exercise at Ft Riley where every type of Iraqi combat vehicle likely to be encountered in the desert was paraded for the crews to give them some additional recognition practice. The Apache crews found they could not positively ID the targets as hostile beyond 3 km (4.8 miles). Since then, major R&D effort has been expended on developing an effective battlefield IFF system for the US Army. A visual 'threat library' of IR imagery is under development for the Apache and other aircraft, but remains a long-term project. What is needed is an improved battlefield sensor system, one that retains the benefits of the AH-64A's optics with an added level of sophistication and discrimination. That solution, along with many others, will be found in the AH-64D Longbow Apache.

Apache improvements

Since the earliest days of AH-64A operations there have been attempts to upgrade the aircraft. In the mid-1980s McDonnell Douglas began studies of the Advanced Apache/Apache Plus, which was later referred to, unofficially, as the 'AH-64B'. The AH-64B would have had a revised, updated cockpit with a new fire control system, Stinger air-to-air missiles, a redesigned Chain Gun® and a fin-mounted video camera. AH-64B was aimed at the US Army, but a similar AH-64G was proposed for the German anti-tank helicopter requirement, now filled by the Eurocopter Tiger. In 1988 funding was released for an AH-64 Multi-Stage Improvement Program (MSIP) to improve the Apache's sensor and weapons suites while integrating new digital databus and communications systems. The MSIP was abandoned before it reached the hardware stage. The

reason was that new technologies, which had always been 'earmarked' for application to the Apache, were finally becoming real – and with them came the possibility for transforming the already formidable Apache into something even better. A series of upgrades was proposed after Operation Desert Storm, the so-called AH-64A+/Desert Storm fixes. These included VHF/FM NoE communications improvements (a long-recognised Apache problem), a desert filtration kit, ground-proximity warning system, TADS/PNVS and Chain Gun® accuracy improvements, GPS, new HF radio, SINCGARS secure radio, improved IFF and flight control computer upgrade. Like the proposed MSIP these changes were abandoned in favour of a far-reaching and highly integrated transformation of the AH-64A, through the addition of a revolutionary new radar system and completely revised onboard systems.

Millimetre-wave (MMW) radar guidance had always been an option for Hellfire guidance, but was rejected for the AH-64A as the technology was not mature enough. In the Airborne Adverse Weather Weapon System (AAWWS), Westinghouse, in collaboration with Martin-Marietta (now Lockheed Martin Orlando), developed the Longbow MMW radar. Longbow is now being integrated into the US Army's Apache fleet, transforming existing aircraft into AH-64D Longbow Apaches. MMW technology overcomes the existing limitations in the Apache's targeting optics/laser combination. At present, the AH-64A can simultaneously engage two targets using its own designator, at a range of up to 8000 m (26,247 ft), day or night. However, the laser and FLIR are constrained by atmospheric conditions and the Hellfire's range is limited if the cloud ceiling is less than 400 ft (122 m) AGL. To make a self-designated kill at maximum range, the AH-64A must unmask for 37 seconds.

Longbow – the next generation

The Longbow radar is largely impervious to atmospheric interference, allows the Apache to fire-and-forget all 16 AGM-114Ls in rapid succession, and gives the aircraft a new lethal SEAD capability. The Longbow system comprises the mast-mounted fire control radar (FCR), a programmable signal processor and the Longbow Hellfire missile. The Longbow radar can scan a 50-km^2 (19.3 sq-mile) swathe of territory and detect up to 1,024 potential targets. Of these, 128 can be classified and displayed simultaneously, and software improvements will increase this to 156. The system will prioritise 16 targets depending on the desired engagement criteria and the target characteristics (wheeled,

tracked, airborne, moving, static etc.). Longbow programme officials are keen to point out that while the radar can 'classify' a target, it does not 'identify' it. It can, however, determine if a contact is a wheeled vehicle or a tank or an air-defence system. The FCR has a detection range of 8000 m (26,247 ft) against moving targets and 6000 m (19,685 ft) against static ones. The Longbow's SEAD capability is provided by its radar frequency interferometer (RFI), a sophisticated RWR that can identify and target any emitting (ADU/air defence unit) system on the battlefield. The RFI has 360° coverage – 'fine' in its 180° forward hemisphere, and 'coarse' in the rear 180°. The system will provide an azimuth to target, although not a range. The Longbow radar also gives the AH-64D an effective air-to-air targeting capability. Longbow's MIL-STD 1760 databus will accept ATAS on its wingtip stations, but Stinger integration is not a priority purely on cost terms.

Digital warrior

The AH-64D has a totally new digital databus/systems fit, which is at the heart of the Longbow. Although the AH-64D is based on the AH-64A, the modification process involves reducing each Apache to a shell before the new equipment is added. The first item to be stripped out is the AH-64A's old wiring, to be replaced by four dual-channel MIL-STD 1553B data buses and lightweight wiring. The

Above: Greece was the first European customer for the Apache and was subsequently followed by the Netherlands and the UK – who both opted for the AH-64D. There are still several small batches of Apaches to be sold in Europe, but Boeing/McDonnell Douglas is now looking further east for the next round of substantial sales.

Top: In 1990 Israel became the first export customer for the AH-64A. In Israeli service the Apache is known as the Peten (Cobra) and the Israel Defence Force/Air Force is believed to operate three squadrons of the AH-64As. Israel is an obvious potential customer for the AH-64D Longbow Apache.

Apache over Bosnia

United States Army ground forces were committed to NATO's peacekeeping effort in Bosnia-Herzegovina in December 1995 after the Dayton peace accords brought the country's three-year civil war to an end. Spearheading the US Implementation Force (IFOR) contingent was the 1st Armoured Division under the command of Major General William Nash. The deployment of the division from its bases in Germany was a major logistical task, and its AH-64A Apache attack helicopters played a key role in ensuring that US forces were able to successfully deploy into Bosnia.

At the start of the deployment the division's aviation component, its 4th Brigade, was based at Hanau, near Frankfurt. It contained two Apache-equipped units – the 2-227th and 3-227th Attack Helicopter Battalions. The 7th Combat Aviation Battalion provided logistic support with Sikorsky UH-60 Blackhawks, and the 1st Squadron, 1st Cavalry had OH-58Ds for scout and target-marking work. Getting the brigade to Bosnia was difficult due to snow storms in central Europe that delayed its self-deployment to US staging areas around Taszar air base in southern Hungary. By the end of December 1995 advanced elements of the brigade had leapfrogged from Taszar to a forward operating base in Croatia, near Zupanje, to provide close air support for US Army engineers building a huge pontoon bridge over the River Sava for the main tank units of the division. Boeing CH-47 Chinooks were used to airlift the pontoon sections and the Apaches flew security patrols around the site to prevent interference with the bridging operation.

It took another month for all of the US division to be established in its bases around IFOR's North East Sector, and for the 4th Brigade to set up its main operating base at Tuzla air base alongside the USAF's 4100th Air Base Group. The old Yugoslav air force base proved an ideal location because of its runways and old hardened aircraft shelters. As US troops – along with Russian, Nordic, Polish and Turkish troops – began to separate the

warring factions in the northeast of Bosnia, the Apaches were regularly tasked to fly patrols along the Zone of Separation to deter infringements. Helicopters had to fly in pairs due to US concerns about hostile attacks on their forces, and when VIPs were airborne in helicopters two Apaches were always tasked to 'fly shotgun'. Twenty four AH-64As have been deployed to Bosnia, some with improved systems fit to enhance their operational capabilities. Six aircraft have a real-time datalink to allow them to send FLIR/DVO video imagery to local command units. Three of these have an additional SATCOM capability to allow direct transmission to national command authorities in the USA.

The Apaches were called upon during February and March 1996 to support IFOR operations in Sarajevo. They flew security missions around the city on 3 September when US Secretary of State Warren Christopher came to visit.

By the summer of 1996, the IFOR mission was all but complete, with the warring factions so impressed by its firepower – particularly the heavily armed Apache – that they had been all but confined to barracks. The two US Apache battalions continued their patrols but also began to carry out live firing training on the large British run ranges at Glamoc, firing their cannon, rockets and Hellfire missiles in a series of very impressive firepower demonstrations. They also participated in joint firing exercises with allied air and ground forces. In December 1996 IFOR began to withdraw and the 4th Brigade started to deploy back to Germany, handing over its duties to aviation elements of the 1st Infantry Division, the US ground component in NATO's new Stabilisation Force (SFOR) for peacekeeping into 1997. The Apache's deadly reputation played a major part in ensuring Bosnia's warring factions were not tempted to take on IFOR. Peace through superior firepower.

Tim Ripley

An IFOR Apache lands in typical winter weather at Taszar, in Hungary.

new databus is allied with totally integrated 6-32 bit processors and coupled with an uprated onboard electrical system which can cope with peak loads of 90 kVA (the Improved Electrical Power Management System/IEPMS). This digital architecture empowers the Longbow's 'manprint' (manpower integration) cockpit layout. Gone are the dials and 1,200 switches of the AH-64A, to be replaced by a Litton Canada upfront display, two AlliedSignal Aerospace 15-cm x 15-cm (6-in x 6-in) colour (initially monochrome) CRT displays and just 200 switches. The CRT displays and helmet-mounted displays use improved Honeywell raster-generated symbology to combine the DVO, FLIR and radar sensor data. The display processors (which 'drive' the screens) are capable of handling a digital colour moving-map, when such a system becomes available. An improved Plessey AN/ASN-157 Doppler navigation system and Honeywell AN/APN-209 radar altimeter have also been incorporated. AH-64D will have a dual embedded GPS and inertial navigation (EGI) fit plus AN/ARC-201D VHF/FM radios. EGI is being developed as a tri-service project. The improved navigation fit for the AH-64D gives it near all-weather capability compared to the adverse weather-capable AH-64A. Hamilton Standard has also developed an advanced lightweight FCS computer to take advantage of the 32-bit processor system. The larger volume of avionics in the AH-64D has forced the expansion of the Apache's cheek fairings, to become EFABs (Enhanced Forward Avionics Bays)

Communications revolution

Mission planning will be greatly eased by the AH-64D's data transfer module (DTM). The DTM allows key mission data such as flight routings (waypoints/hazards, FARP location, FLOT location), enemy/friendly forces dispositions, unit sectors, battle positions, priority fire zones and communications (callsigns, frequencies, secure codes) to be input directly to the AH-64D's mission computer on a single cartridge. The DTM will ease the battalion mission planning load, but the AH-64D's Improved Data Modem (IDM) will revolutionise the way the AH-64D flies and fights. The high-speed (16 KB/sec) IDM uses the newly developed variable message format (VMF) based on the 18820 protocol, which allows an AH-64D not only to talk to other AH-64Ds, OH-58Ds and RAH-66s but also to Rivet Joint (RC-135), J/STARS (E-8), airborne A^2C^2S (UH-60C 'C+CHawk'), the battalion TOC (Tactical Operations Center) and armoured manoeuvre units. IDM uses a communications standard that is tri-service (and still expanding in scope), digital, multi-channel, secure (using Have Quick and SINCGARS systems) and applicable to virtually any radio. The MMW/RFI system provides the Longbow commander with a digital picture of the battle-field where all targets are classified and prioritised using clear symbology. Targets can be classified as tracked,

wheeled, air defence, helicopter or fixed-wing aircraft. Once the radar has scanned the engagement area, automatic target handover to the fire control system takes place "faster than it takes to read this sentence", according to one Longbow programme official. The Longbow TADS/PNVS can be slaved to the MMW radar for visual ID, but in most cases the radar exceeds the FLIR's target recognition capability. In the words of a Longbow project officer, "The AH-64A finds the target and asks you what it is; the AH-64D finds it, then tells you." Target sort and handover can be accomplished with a few keystrokes.

More importantly, the engagement parameters can be changed with as little effort. Longbow Apache divides the battlefield using information transmitted in real-time to all the other members of the attack team. The prioritisation system allows targets to be clearly marked as 'shoot first', 'shoot second' or 'already shot at'. This minimises overkill and allows the battalion/company to make maximum use of its missiles. The Longbow can also minimise fratricide by setting up a 'no-fire zone' where it is impossible to engage targets, without man-in-the-loop override. The AH-64A is terrain-dependent, which limits the engagement areas and battle positions available to the attack force. AH-64As have to operate in relatively close formation to maintain LoS communications and station-keeping. The Longbow's C^3 capability allows it to conduct on-the-spot target handovers, without any of the intensive pre-briefing of the AH-64A mission – then find and kill virtually any targets regardless of conditions. The AH-64D has greater stand-off range and its digital communications fit enables aircraft to disperse widely. The rapid-fire, fire-and-forget AGM-114L can bring massive firepower to bear in a short time, during which the AH-64D is not exposed to enemy ADA fire.

Power for the AH-64D

The Apache's existing General Electric GE T700-GE-701 turboshafts are to be completely replaced by uprated 1,723-shp (1,285-kW) T700-GE-701C engines. The -701C has already been fitted to existing AH-64As from the 604th production aircraft (delivered in 1990). When the Longbow programme was initiated, the US Army planned to field a dual standard of upgrade. The full-upgrade AH-64Ds would be complemented by AH-64Cs which would not have the MMW radar or -701C engines. This designation was abandoned in 1993 with the decision to rebuild all aircraft to AH-64D standard, even though not all would be equipped with the Longbow radar. The AH-64C designation was an unnecessary complication (not least for the US Army's logistics system) and no longer exists. Apaches without the MMW radar will now be known simply as AH-64D Apaches while radar-equipped aircraft will be AH-64D Longbow Apaches.

The advent of the AH-64D will transform the composition of Army aviation battlefield units. However, the

Longbow is not being fielded in isolation and is ultimately expected to work with the RAH-66A Comanche stealthy advanced scout. After intense uncertainty about the future of the Comanche, including its virtual cancellation, the RAH-66A now has a proposed first unit equipped (FUE) date of 2005. Current Army attack helicopter battalions comprise 24 AH-64s, divided among three companies, each with three AH-64A scouts and six attack-dedicated AH-64As. With the introduction of the AH-64D, battalions will graduate to nine Longbow aircraft and 15 baseline (AH-64D) aircraft. The objective for future battalions is to again have 24 aircraft, but divided between 15 Longbow AH-64Ds and nine Longbow-equipped RAH-66As.

The US Defense Acquisition Board authorised a 51-month AH-64D developmental programme in August 1990. In December this was extended to 70 months to incorporate AGM-114L missile development. On 11 March 1991 an AH-64A (82-23356) made its maiden flight as an aerodynamic testbed with a mast-mounted radar housing. The first of six actual AH-64D prototypes (89-0192) flew on 15 April 1992. A total of 232 full-standard Longbow Apaches will be fielded from a total of 758 examples in the current inventory. In June 1994 the Army demonstrated that is was capable of converting an AH-64D to Longbow AH-64D standard in four hours, as required. This involved the transfer of -701C engines, the Longbow radar and associated equipment from the first prototype AH-64D to the sixth, which was then flown for 30 minutes.

Full-scale production authorised by US Under-Secretary of Defense Paul Kaminsky on 13 October 1995 for 232

Opposite page above: The US Army has abandoned plans to field a dual-standard AH-64C/D, which originally called for the conversion of 308 AH-64Cs and 227 AH-64Ds. Now all 758 Apaches will be rebuilt to the full AH-64D standard. However, not all will be routinely equipped with the Longbow radar.

Above: Initial MMW-guided Hellfire tests have been completed and proved to be largely successful. As in the original tests, some problems emerged, but they were far less serious.

Top: The first US Army unit to transition to the Longbow Apache will be 1-227 AVN, based at Ft Hood, Texas. Instructor pilots from 1-227 will begin their training in July 1997 and the AH-64D will be active with the unit by December of that year.

McDonnell Douglas AH-64D Longbow Apache

The first 'AH-64D' to fly was an AH-64A with a dummy radome. The six pre-production aircraft that followed were full-standard AH-64D conversions – though the last two of these were not equipped with the Longbow MMW radar. This aircraft is the fourth AH-64D development aircraft (90-0423), which first flew on 4 October 1993. The Longbow flight test programme was between Mesa, Arizona, and Ft Hood, Texas – in the charge of the US Army Material Command's Apache Attack Helicopter Project Manager's Office.

Crew protection and crashworthiness

The Army specified that the Apache crew must survive a vertical descent of 42 ft/sec (12.8 m/sec) applied to the landing gear. Such an impact translates to a 37-*g* load on the crew. The Apache's sliding seats attenuate that load to a highly unpleasant, but survivable, 13-*g* load. During early flight tests after a catastrophic engine failure one of the Apache prototypes dropped 300 ft (91.4 m) straight down. The crew walked away. All Apache crews have unshakeable faith in their aircraft, provided it does not come down sideways. The crew's seats provide ballistic armour protection through blast/fragmentation shields, around and between the two seats. In October 1995 Phoenix-based Simula Inc. was awarded a contract to install and test a system of airbags for the AH-64A. Head and torso injuries account for more than half of the crew injuries sustained during otherwise survivable crashes, and the Army has determined that such injuries could be cut by 50 per cent using airbags. A series of 30 drop tests conducted during 1993 confirmed the suitability of air bags for an attack helicopter. The Apache air bag modification kits were fielded in 1997. Air bags are located to the side and in front of each crew member. In a series of simulator tests held at Ft Rucker, crews were subjected to three 'inadvertent' air bag deployments which reportedly did not interrupt the mission or compromise the aircraft. The Apache's air bags are designed not to obscure critical flight instruments.

Hellfire launch

In a LOAL (Lock-On After Launch) engagement the AGM-114K Hellfire II can be fired in three pre-launch programmed trajectories. Two launch modes are available – normal (sometimes referred to as 'rapid') and ripple. In normal mode only missiles coded on the priority (autonomous guidance) channel can be fired. In ripple engagements priority and alternate (remotely designated) channel missiles are fired, alternately.

Self-protection fit

Behind the Apache's rotor mast is the AN/ALQ-144(V) IR countermeasures set – the 'disco light' jammer. ALQ-144 transmits modulated radiation at high and low frequencies using an electrically heated source, to confuse IR-guided SAMs. The Apache also has an onboard radar jammer, the AN/ALQ-136, to defend it from ground-based fire control radars. The ALQ-136's signals induce range and angle errors in the hostile tracking radar. The transmit antenna for the ALQ-136 is located on the TADS housing, between the FLIR and DVO turrets. The receive antenna is situated above the fuselage, behind the pilot's canopy.

Longbow Hellfire

Martin-Marietta (now Lockheed Martin Orlando) and Westinghouse won a two-year $30.5 million US Army contract for initial production of the AGM-114L Longbow Hellfire II in January 1995. Up to that point Rockwell had been the Army's sole supplier of Hellfires. Allied with the initial $31 million production funding contract for the fire control contract, the contract provided a major boost for the two firms at a time when the RAH-66 had been officially shelved (it was later resurrected, then cancelled again in February 2004). In June 1995 Lockheed Martin and Rockwell formed a joint company to manufacture the AGM-114L. This ended fierce competition between the two for production batches of the AGM-114L. Belfast-based Shorts Missile Systems is the prime contractor for the UK's acquisition of Hellfire II and Longbow Hellfire missiles.

Laser-guided rockets

Although a Hellfire missile is the Apache's most accurate weapon, it is also the most expensive (the unit cost of a basic Hellfire is in excess of $35,000). In an attempt to provide the AH-64, and other helicopters, with a precision weapon that does not cost more than some of its targets, Texas Instruments has unveiled the APKWS – a laser guidance package for 2.75-in rockets such as the Hydra 70 or CRV7. The system uses an adapted Paveway seeker head with small thruster ports arranged around the forward section of the projectile for manoeuvre control. Thus modified, the cost of individual rockets is estimated at between $10,000 and $12,000.

Main rotor head

When it came to designing the Apache rotor system, Hughes did not forget its Vietnam experience. Even though the OH-6 was worlds apart from the YAH-64, it had a profound effect on the latter's design. This was most obvious in the YAH-64's fully-articulated rotor head, which was essentially a scaled-up version of that of the OH-6A. A series of 22 redundant laminated straps are used to fix the blades to the fully-articulated rotor head. These straps are flexible enough to permit blade flapping and feathering, and fatigue tests have shown that up to 10 can fail and the Apache will still remain flyable. The blade retaining bolts are expandable, a design feature first incorporated on the OH-6, to permit easy blade folding for transportation. The main rotor mast is a static, non-rotating design. It houses an inertia-welded Nitralloy drive shaft which, like all elements of the main rotor system, has a fatigue life of +4,500 hours. Even if the drive shaft were to fail, the mast carries much of the rotor loads and controls would not be affected for an autorotation. The mast is bolted directly to the fuselage and will sustain an impact of 20g before collapsing. Like the OH-6 before it, there has never been a recorded case of the AH-64 suffering a mast failure in flight or in a survivable crash.

Apache powerplant

The basic AH-64A was powered by the General Electric 1,696-shp (1265-kW) T700-GE-701 turboshaft, which was downrated to provide reserve power in 'red-line' combat/emergency situations. From the 604th production aircraft these engines were uprated to 1,890-shp (1409-kW) T700-GE-701C standard. All AH-64Ds will be fitted with the more powerful -701C engine. The UK's Longbow Apaches are fitted with the Rolls-Royce Turboméca International (RRTI) RTM322 turboshaft, an engine designed from the outset to compete with the T700 while offering greater power. The RTM322 is rated at 2,100 shp (1566 kW) and has already been flown on the Sikorsky S-70C/UH-60, EH101 and NH90. The RTM322-powered Longbow Apaches have a newly-developed FADEC (Full-Authority Digital Engine Control), modified from that fitted to the EH101. Although this existing FADEC system has been altered to cope with the Apache's dynamic characteristics, it has the hidden advantage of being immune to electronic interference during shipborne operations – a potentially important future UK Apache role.

Swept blade tips

Results from the flight test portion of Phase 2 testing forced a revision in the blade tip design of the AH-64. The original straight tips were cambered, and a constant-thickness and constant-chord section were added. Coupled with a 20° sweep applied to the final 20 in (51 cm) of the blade, and tip weights inside the blade, this new design delayed the onset of drag divergence as tip speeds approached Mach 1, the so-called 'Mach truck' effect (the build-up of a large shock wave in front of the blades was likened to the 'bow wave' of America's giant Mac trucks). The new tips also provide a useful dynamic twist by using the upload on the retreating tip to decrease the angle of attack. The blade tips are designed to be replaced every 1,000 to 2,000 flying hours but are susceptible to abrasion faster than the rest of the blade.

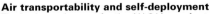

Air transportability and self-deployment

The basic requirement for the AH-64A was for two aircraft to be carried in the C-141B and six in the C-5A. Fitting two Apaches into the StarLifter was a complicated task, requiring the removal of the entire rotor head, folding the vertical tail and stub wings, plus kneeling the landing gear to allow the aircraft to 'scrape' in. On a Galaxy the rotors and wings simply had to be folded back, but the tail and rotorhead remained untouched. The Apache was granted its air transportation certificate in November 1981 when Hughes loaded two aircraft onto a C-141B in 80 per cent of the allotted time. With rotors, stub wings and other components removed (transport configuration), three AH-64As can be carried by the C-17, along with two cargo pallets and 50 personnel. If the Apaches remain in tactical configuration (wings and major components in place) two aircraft can be accommodated by C-17, along with four cargo pallets and 38 personnel. AH-64D loads are similar, with the added need to remove the mast-mounted radar. recently, some US Army Apaches have been fitted with a blade-folding system which allows them to be made ready for deployment, and then made ready for combat, in a very short time. The AAH requirement also called for self-deployment ability of an 800-nm (1481-km, 920-miles) ferry range with a 20-kt (37-km/h, 23-mph) headwind and a 45-minute reserve. This permitted a wartime Reforger deployment from the US to Germany via Goose Bay (Canada), Frobisher Bay – now known as Iqaluit – on Baffin Island (Canada), Sondrestrom (Greenland), Reykjavik (Iceland) and Prestwick (Scotland).

Tail section and rotor

The Apache features a semi-rigid, teetering, twin-bladed tail rotor mounted at offset degrees of 60° and 120° rather than 90°. Each pair of blades has one stainless steel spar and two aluminium spars and is fastened to its own delta-hinged hub. The airfoil is a NASA 63-414 section. This unusual design has provoked some disagreement, not least within the Apache community, as to why it was implemented. The accepted answer has always been for reasons of noise reduction. Certainly, the tail rotor's low rotation speed of 634 ft/sec (193 m/sec) cuts back on aircraft noise, but the offset position was also definitely a function of the T-tail and the need to accommodate the Apache in a C-141B. The teetering twin-blade approach is unique, to date, and did away with the need for conventional centrifugally-loaded oscillating bearings. However, the resultant Coriolis loads (whirling blades deforming into a cone shape rather than a flat disc) during operation called for a high-strength titanium rotor fork. The original AAH mock-up had featured a folding tail, a design feature that was retained by AV-01 and AV-02. However, field tests proved that by careful positioning two AH-64s could be accommodated in the hold of a C-141B (the dimensions of which had been the constant limiting factor for AAH designers) without removing the tails. This allowed Hughes to dispense with the heavy and fatigue-sensitive structure.

Right: In May 1995, Joint Project Optic Cobra '95 (JPOC '95) was integrated as an element of the regular Roving Sands joint air defence exercise, held at Ft Bliss/White Sands missile range. JPOC '95 was a Theatre Missile Defence (TMD) exercise that integrated US Army, Navy, Air Force and Marine Corps (plus Dutch and German) units in the hunt for surface-to-surface missile threats during a regional conflict against Iran ('Dahib'). Responding to the 'Dahabian' invasion of 'Sabira' (New Mexico), in the 'West Gulfacia' region, allied forces had to defend the strategic port city of El Paso against attacks that included the use of SS-2 'Scud-B' and SS-21 SSMs. AH-64As from the 3rd Battalion, 6th Cavalry were integrated into both sides, but the Apaches allocated to the allied (blue) forces were used on 'Scud'-hunting missions in conjunction with F-15Es. Future operations of this kind will increasingly involve unprecedented integration of sensor data from airborne, naval and ground-based systems. Optic Cobra '95, and other similar exercises, have paved the way for such complex military operations. The digital AH-64D will be ideally placed to act in unison with other systems in the hunt for small, mobile targets such as missile TELs.

Below: This AH-64D Longbow Apache in UK AAC configuration has (dummy) Starstreak box launchers on the wingtips.

aircraft. The complete US Army AH-64D contract also calls for 13,311 AGM-114L missiles, 227 fire control radars and 3,296 launchers. AH-64D remanufacture began at Mesa in November 1995, in advance of the December 1995 contract for the remanufacture of the first batch of 24 aircraft. The first production AH-64D flew on 17 March 1977. From start to finish it takes 15 months to convert an AH-64A into an AH-64D. The maximum remanufacture rate of eight per month will be reached in the last quarter of 2001. The first operational unit will be equipped by July 1998 and deliveries will continue until 2008.

The Longbow received spectacular validation in a series of field tests. Between 30 January and 9 February 1995, at China Lake, a team of AH-64As and AH-64Ds conducted preliminary gunnery trials against moving and static T-72s and static ZSU 23-4s. Eight gunnery 'events' were flown, half by day and half by night, and targets were protected by smoke (including IR obscurant smoke), decoys and camouflage netting. These Phase 1 trials paved the way for the 'all-out' force-on-force IOT&E (Initial Operational Test & Evaluation) trials, held at Ft Hunter-Liggett, California, between 6 and 31 March 1995. Two units ('A' Company and 'B' Company, 2-229th AVN) from Ft Rucker conducted a series of paired trials, AH-64A ('B' Co./eight aircraft) versus AH-64D ('A' Co./six aircraft). Twelve missions were flown at night – seven close attack and five deep attack – along with three daytime close attack missions. The Apaches were hunting an integrated threat force of US/Russian armour and mostly Russian ADA systems comprising 20 M1A1 MBTs, 10 M2/3 Bradley IFVs, six 2S6 Tunguskas, two SA-8B 'Geckos' (9K33 Osa), one SA-11 'Gadfly' (9M38 Buk), three SA-13 'Gophers' (9M37 Strela-10), one SA-15 'Gauntlet' (9M330 Tor), 10 SA-18s (9K38 Igla) and a Swedish-built Ericsson Giraffe radar. This 'red' force used smoke, RF/IR blankets, conformal RAM camouflage netting, decoys, corner reflectors and active jammers to further defend itself. No external SEAD, artillery support, or area weapons (rockets) were available to the Apaches. The tanks involved were advanced US Army M1A1 Abrams, with sophisticated reactive armour, active countermeasures and an anti-helicopter capability of their own. The parameters of the test were designed to isolate the attack helicopters and confront them with a 21st Century threat. The AH-64Ds flew in a 'heavy Hellfire' configuration, with 12 AGM-114Ls

Apache exports

Two important AH-64D customers are the Netherlands (left) and Singapore (above).

Egypt
Egypt was initially offered 12 AH-64As in December 1994, but in March 1995 this was raised to 24. This first batch of 24 was delivered from 1995, and was followed by 12 more from late 1996. They were allocated to two squadrons within an attack helicopter brigade at Abu Hammad. An upgrade for the 35 survivors to AH-64D standard was approved in September 2000 and signed on 3 December 2001. Longbow radar is not included in this deal.

Greece
On 24 December 1991 the Elliniki Aeroporia Stratou (Hellenic army aviation) signed a Letter of Acceptance covering the purchase of 12 AH-64As, plus options for a further eight (subsequently exercised). The first six helicopters arrived by sea in June 1995 and were delivered to 1 TEEP (Tagma Epithetikon Elikopteron – Attack Helicopter Regiment) at Stefanovikio. While waiting for the advanced AH-64D, Greece opted to procure a further four AH-64As in 2000 to complete the equipment of the 1 TEEP, which is sub-divided into three companies.

On 28 August 2003 Greece placed an order for 12 AH-64Ds, plus options on a further four, to equip a second TEEP. Deliveries are due to begin in early 2007.

Israel
The IDF/AF's first AH-64 (locally named Peten – python) order was placed in 1990 and was delivered from September. In the aftermath of Desert Storm, 24 AH-64As were transferred from the US Army in 1993. They were initially allocated to Nos 113 (Ramon), 127 (Palmachim) and 190 (Ramat David) Squadrons. Initially armed with early Hellfires, the AGM-114K was added in 1998.

In the late 1990s Israel looked to acquire the AH-64D. A purchase of 24 AH-64Ds was shelved in 1999 and replaced by an upgrade of 12 AH-64As to D standard, plus an option to upgrade 12 more. The deal then was reduced to cover nine AH-64Ds (eight new plus one rebuild), which were ordered through FMS in 2001. On 31 May 2002 three more rebuilds were added, for a total of 12. Israeli AH-64Ds incorporate some local equipment, and the first was delivered in June 2003 for development trials by the US Army. The D, which will be fielded in 2005, is named Sharaf (serpent) in IDF/AF service.

Japan
In August 2001 the Japan Ground Self Defence Force announced that it had selected the AH-64D to meet its AH-X requirement, intended to eventually replace the Fuji-Bell AH-1S Cobra. Negotiations then began concerning an initial 10-aircraft batch to be built entirely by Boeing, followed by procurement of a further 50 or so helicopters, with some component manufacture and final assembly being undertaken by Fuji Heavy Industries. Japan's first eight AH-64Ds will be assigned to the Kuchu Kido Ryodan (Air Mobility Brigade, AMB), a new unit which the JGSDF is forming.

Kuwait
Kuwait submitted an FMS request in 1997 for 16 AH-64Ds plus four spare engines, 384 AGM-114A Hellfires, 19,918 Hydra-70 rockets and related spares and support equipment. The Letter of Acceptance was allowed to lapse, but was renewed in 2001, resulting in a revised order which includes 16 helicopters, eight Longbow radars, four spare engines, 288 AGM-114Ks and 96 AGM-114Ls. Kuwaiti Apaches will also be fitted with the advanced BAE Systems HIDAS (helicopter integrated defensive aids system). The deal was finalised on 31 August 2002 for first deliveries in early 2005.

Netherlands
In the early 1990s the Netherlands set about the creation of a new airmobile force – the Taktische Helikopter Groep – and examined various attack helicopters. On 24 May 1995 the AH-64D was announced the winner and 30 were ordered, without Longbow radar. In the interim, 12 AH-64As were leased from the US Army to allow training and operational development to begin. They were handed over to the Koninklijke Luchtmacht on 13 November 1996 to equip 301 Squadron at Gilze-Rijen. The first of the 30 AH-64Ds flew on 13 May 1998 and 301 Squadron began re-equipment. Six of the AH-64As were returned to the US Army in September 2000 followed by the remaining six in February 2001. The

second squadron – 302 – received its first Ds on 13 July 1999. The last was accepted on 10 June 2002. Each squadron has 11 aircraft assigned, the remaining eight being allocated to the Netherlands Apache Training Detachment at Fort Hood. Under force cuts six are to be mothballed, but the released funds may allow the purchase of Longbow radars.

KLu Apaches have been active on international peacekeeping missions. Between June 1998 and September 1999 two were deployed to Tuzla in Bosnia, and between February and June 2001 four operated in Djibouti in support of UN policing operations along the Eritrea/Ethiopia border. In March 2004 six AH-64Ds were sent to Kabul Airport for a six-month deployment to assist the International Security Assistance Force in Afghanistan.

Saudi Arabia
In 1993 12 AH-64As were delivered to the newly formed Army Aviation Command of the Royal Saudi Land Forces, to be based at King Khalid Military City. In 2002 the US supplied pricing details covering the upgrade of the 12 aircraft to AH-64D standard, plus details of 12 new AH-64Ds in which the RSLF have an interest in acquiring. Both options are under review but are currently without funding.

Singapore
Under Peace Vanguard Singapore placed an order for eight AH-64Ds (plus two spare engines, 216 Hellfires and 9,120 Hydra-70s) in March 2000. The deal included 12 options (taken up in August 2001) towards a total requirement of 32. The aircraft were initially to be delivered without Longbow, but this was reinstated following US agreement to release the equipment for sale to this region. The first aircraft was handed over at Mesa on 17 May 2002. Training of RSAF Apache crews officially began at Marana, Arizona, on 9 April 2002, the detachment having been established in October 2001 with assistance from the Arizona Army National Guard. After conversion at Marana, aircrew then go on to Fort Hood for advanced training. Technicians are trained at Fort Eustis. The first AH-64D arrived at Marana on 17 May 2002 and all 20 are to be based there initially. The aircraft are due to be deployed to Singapore in 2006, to be based at Sembawang for operations with 123 Squadron.

United Arab Emirates
The UAE Air Force reached agreement with McDonnell Douglas Helicopters in December 1991 covering the purchase of 20 AH-64As. The first was handed over on 3 October 1993. Deliveries continued

through 1994, after which an additional 10 aircraft were ordered. The Apaches serve with the Western Air Command and are based at Al Dhafra.

In early 2002 US congressional approval was granted covering the upgrade of the UAE's 30 AH-64As to AH-64D standard, complete with Longbow radar. Included in the deal were 240 AGM-114L Longbow Hellfires, plus 49 AGM-114M anti-ship missiles. This deal is currently under study, as is the procurement of new-build AH-64Ds.

United Kingdom
Following several years of examining the possibilities of replacing its Lynx helicopters in the attack role, the British Army issued invitations to tender in February 1993. After a hard-fought competition, the WAH-64D was chosen on 13 July 1995, an order for 67 aircraft being placed, all with Longbow radar. The WAH-64D is unique in being powered by the RTM332 engine, and apart from the first eight aircraft which were completed by Boeing at Mesa, is built by Westland at Yeovil using base fuselages supplied by Boeing.

The RTM332 testbed first flew on 29 May 1998, with the first production aircraft handed over to Westland on 28 September. Formal acceptance of the first aircraft by the Army occurred on 15 March 2000. The 67 aircraft are to be divided between QinetiQ (one for trials), 667 Squadron (one for development), 671 Squadron (eight for training) and six eight-aircraft front-line squadrons in 3, 4 and 9 Attack Regiments at Dishforth and Wattisham. The remaining nine aircraft form an attrition reserve. 9 Regiment at Dishforth will have a Royal Marines support tasking.

Above: The UAE has operated the Apache since 1993. It sent aircraft to Kosovo to join peacekeeping operations after Allied Force.

Below: Full brigade capability for the UK's WAH-64D force is expected in 2007, following the first regiment forming in early 2005.

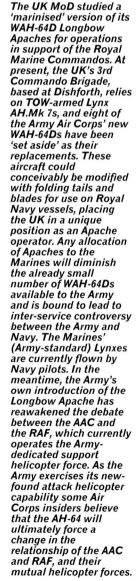

The UK MoD studied a 'marinised' version of its WAH-64D Longbow Apaches for operations in support of the Royal Marine Commandos. At present, the UK's 3rd Commando Brigade, based at Dishforth, relies on TOW-armed Lynx AH.Mk 7s, and eight of the Army Air Corps' new WAH-64Ds have been 'set aside' as their replacements. These aircraft could conceivably be modified with folding tails and blades for use on Royal Navy vessels, placing the UK in a unique position as an Apache operator. Any allocation of Apaches to the Marines will diminish the already small number of WAH-64Ds available to the Army and is bound to lead to inter-service controversy between the Army and Navy. The Marines' (Army-standard) Lynxes are currently flown by Navy pilots. In the meantime, the Army's own introduction of the Longbow Apache has reawakened the debate between the AAC and the RAF, which currently operates the Army-dedicated support helicopter force. As the Army exercises its new-found attack helicopter capability some Air Corps insiders believe that the AH-64 will ultimately force a change in the relationship of the AAC and RAF, and their mutual helicopter forces.

and four AGM-114Ks, plus 330 30-mm rounds. The AH-64As flew with an all-AGM-114K loadout.

The results of the test were staggering. The AH-64Ds achieved 300 confirmed kills, the AH-64As notched up just 75. Four AH-64Ds were shot down while the AH-64A force lost 28 aircraft. Most importantly, in the eyes of many, the Longbows failed to make a single blue-on-blue kill; the AH-64As made 34. One test official stated, "In all my years of testing, I have never seen a tested system so dominate the system it is intended to replace." An opposing 'red' force member paid a more succinct tribute when he said, "We always knew when it was the Longbow Apache attacking. Everybody died with no warning." In fact, so successful were the tests that the Pentagon's OT&E office cancelled the final two elements in the programme. According to the AAH Program Manager Colonel Robert Atwell, "In a very, very short time frame we figured out that the A model would be incapable of operating on what we consider the modern battlefield. It's time to move on to the next generation."

Some problems needed to be corrected, however. The AH-64D's communications fit is not perfect and the existing TADS/PNVS is now starting to show its age, particularly when used alongside the Longbow radar. Longbow itself has some difficulty in acquiring stationary targets, and AGM-114K's ability to deal with multiple countermeasures has not been 100 per cent proven. A US General Accounting Office report stated that after evaluation it became clear that there were instances where the radar failed to detect and identify targets. Some missile engagements failed against multiple countermeasures such as smoke/jammers. The pilot's greatest wish is for a radio system that is truly independent of terrain. The AH-64D's digital communications suite is far better than that of the AH-64A, but can still be improved.

In early March 1997 the US Army initiated its Task Force XXI exercise at the NTC, Ft Irwin, California. Two Longbow Apaches were integrated into this advanced warfighting skills/technology exercise. Task Force XXI represented the first operational fielding of the AH-64D's IDM in conjunction with the US Army's entire combat force. It also marked the US Army's continued advance into the digital battlefield.

In a ceremony at Fort Hood on 12 June 1998, the first AH-64D was accepted into US Army service. The 1st Battalion of the 227th Aviation Regiment was the first unit to get the new type, followed by the 3rd Battalion, 101st Aviation Regiment at Fort Campbell, Kentucky.

Universal Apache

The end of Desert Storm brought with it a clamour for the Apache from customers worldwide, but particularly in the Middle East. Countries that had been toying with the idea of acquiring the Apache began to sign on the dotted line, and many others, like the UK and Holland, at last drew up serious requirements for an attack helicopter. A flood of new orders was answered with deliveries to Saudi Arabia and a batch to the UAE in 1993. In 1994 Egypt took delivery of its first batch of AH-64As, and in the following year so did Greece. The second batch for the UAE was handed over in 1996 and Egypt's second batch was delivered in 1997. Dutch and British aircraft followed, as did orders from Singapore, Kuwait and Japan. The aircraft is also under consideration in Korea and Taiwan.

While McDonnell Douglas/Boeing's salesmen have been busy with the Apache, its crews were back in action again. In December 1995 USAREUR AH-64As were deployed to Bosnia as part of NATO's determined IFOR (Implementation FORce) contingent monitoring the Dayton peace agreement. It is a testament to the Apache's reputation that the AH-64 force was never fired upon.

In 1997, McDonnell Douglas was acquired by the Boeing Company in a $13.3 billion deal ($63 per share). As a result, Boeing inherited and expanded McDonnell Douglas's mantle as the world's leading producer of combat aircraft. Boeing-Vertol has substantial helicopter experience of its own, and the company held a 50 per cent stake in the Bell/Boeing V-22 Osprey and Boeing/Sikorsky RAH-66A Comanche programmes, the latter being subsequently axed in February 2004. With the acquisition of the Apache, only the AH-1W and UH-60 helicopters lie outside Boeing's sphere of influence in the United States. Boeing enjoys a respectable order book for the Apache, with more in prospect, coupled with the major AH-64D remanufacturing effort for the US Army.

Peacekeeping in Kosovo

Following its fine performance in Bosnia in 1995/97, the Apache returned to the Balkans in 1999, amid considerable controversy. NATO launched Operation Allied Force on 24 March 1999, following the refusal of Serbian President Slobodan Milosevic to withdraw forces and special police from the troubled province of Kosovo. With the fixed-wing air campaign in full swing, on 4 April General Wesley Clark requested the deployment of Apaches for deep strike attacks. Task Force Hawk was authorised, comprising 24 AH-64As drawn from 2-6 and 6-6 CAV, based in Germany, along with supporting UH-60s and CH-47s, and ground forces. They would deploy to Albania, but it was estimated that the force would need 115 C-17 'lifts' to get it in place. An additional 11 AH-64As were authorised for TF Hawk, drawn from the 229th Aviation but they were ultimately not deployed. The first Apaches arrived at Tirana-Rinas on 21 April and by 26 April all 24 were in place, although one was lost in a training accident the same day, and another on 4 May. The crashes added fuel to the growing criticism of the time taken to get TF Hawk into action, exacerbated by President Clinton's 18 May announcement that the AH-64 would not be used "any time soon", leaving close support duties to the A-10 and the RAF's Harriers. Clinton feared that the use of the AH-64 would spark a land war with the Serbs. The Apache, thus, played no part in Allied Force.

However, it was to spearhead Operation Joint Guardian, the NATO occupation of Kosovo following the withdrawal of Serbian forces. Twelve 6-6 CAV Apaches were redeployed from Tirana to Camp Able Sentry (Petrovec) in Macedonia as Task Force 12, and on 11 June two of the aircraft were first to cross the border, escorting five RAF Pumas. Apaches then escorted the main British force of Chinooks as it took the vital Kacanik gorge, and then pushed on to Pristina.

Operating from Camp Able Sentry, the Apaches were instrumental in the policing of Kosovo after the successful occupation. Just as in Bosnia, when the Apaches were airborne little happened on the ground, such was their deterrence value. They were especially useful at night, and in patrolling the northern Kosovo border with the remainder of Serbia. UAE Apaches were later deployed to operate alongside US Army machines.

On 12 July 2001 Boeing flew the first of an enhanced Longbow Apache version, which incorporates enhanced COTS (commercial off-the-shelf) systems which reduce costs and will allow the system to accept future improvements. The first flight also marked the beginning of the

second multi-year procurement contract, which adds 269 more conversions to raise the funded AH-64D total to 501. AH-64Ds from the first contract arrived in the crucial Korean theatre in October 2001, to serve with 1-2nd Aviation (Attack) at Camp Page, Chunchon. AH-64Ds arrived in Europe (with the 6-6 CAV) in July 2002. In early 2003 the first aircraft flew equipped with an improved sight (M-TADS) and pilot night vision system (M-PNVS), collectively known as the Arrowhead system. Arrowhead is being installed as a retrofit to some in-service aircraft, and to all production Block II aircraft from 2005.

Boeing also equipped an AH-64D with a newly designed main rotor blade-fold system. The Army approached the

Above and below: The advent of the AH-64D Longbow Apache heralds the rejuvenation of the Apache and has sparked new life into the order book. The most recent customers for the aircraft have all opted for the AH-64D and there is no obvious rival for the Longbow in the market. It does, however, come at a price, forcing some potential customers to look at alternatives.

contractor with a request to develop this system in November 2002 in an attempt to reduce the time required to reassemble an aircraft after it is removed from a transport. The new system allows the main rotor blades to be folded rather than being removed. It also allows the Longbow's radar dome to be stored on the aircraft aft of the rotor hub during transport. Boeing delivered the first 24 units in March 2003. The first demonstration took place at Lackland AFB, Texas, in May 2003, when six Apaches were prepared for deployment, loaded aboard a USAF C-5 transport, unloaded, reassembled and flown. The demonstration verified that the Apaches could be deployed from Fort Hood, Texas, to the Middle East and placed in operation in as little as 66 hours.

Apache in Afghanistan

Operation Enduring Freedom was the initial US response to the terrorist outrages of 11 September 2001, and involved the removal of the Taliban regime in Afghanistan and the clearance of al-Qaeda terrorists who operated freely iunder Taliban patronage. Apaches were not involved in the initial air campaign, but seven from Alpha Company, 3rd Battalion, 101st Aviation Regiment were deployed to support US forces involved in mopping up operations. The best known of these was Operation Anaconda, a major campaign by the 101st Airborne Division to surround and destroy a sizeable force of al-Qaeda fighters which had regrouped in the Shah-i-Kot valley.

Anaconda was launched on 2 March 2002 and ran into stiff resistance. Seven Apaches were deployed on the first day, and all took hits (27 of the 28 main rotor blades had bullet damage). Damage to one was so bad that the aircraft had to land under fire, be filled with emergency oil and then flown back to the FARP under the very real danger of the engines seizing. However, the Apaches saved the day and had restored the type's reputation after the Kosovo fiasco. In the wake of the first day of Anaconda, 16 more Apaches were rushed to Afghanistan, arriving two days later to assist with mopping up and policing duties.

Operation Iraqi Freedom

For the invasion of Iraq which was launched on 21 March 2003, the US Army deployed a sizeable number of AH-64As and Ds, comprising three D battalions and one A unit with the 101st Airborne Division, and one D unit supporting the 3rd Infantry Division. The opening shots were fired by AH-64Ds of the 1-3 AVN 'Vipers' who undertook the first combat firings of the AGM-114L Longbow RF-guided Hellfire in attacks against observation posts along the Kuwaiti border. On the next day AGM-114L was used for the first time against an armoured target, in this case a T-54. All appeared to be going well.

However, on the night of 23/24 March a deep strike mission was organised against elements of the Medina division of the Republican Guard near Karbala. A total of 32 AH-64Ds (from 2-6 CAV, 6-6 CAV and 1-227 AVN) was dispatched from a forward operating base at Najaf, operating on its own without any ground support. In a rare example of good tactics, the Iraqi force, warned of the Apaches' approach by observers equipped with cell phones, was quickly dispersed and camouflaged, while the defences put up withering fire from small arms and RPGs. The result was something of a bloody nose for the Apaches – only four or five tanks were destroyed, along with a few APCs. In return, 31 of the 32 Apaches were hit to some degree, and one was forced down. It appeared all over the world's media the next day as Kalashnikov-armed Iraqis danced on it. An attempt to destroy it with an MRLS rocket strike failed, and an airstrike by F-14s was thwarted by weather, and it was not found and destroyed until two days later, the Iraqis having moved it in the interim to a location near Baghdad airport. Another Apache returned to Najaf with one engine shot away.

Equipped to survive on the battlefield of the 21st Century, the Apache has had a checkered career in its first two conflicts of the new millennium. In Operation Anaconda in Afghanistan it performed excellently, and despite the small force being hit on numerous occasions, the Apache is widely credited with 'saving the day' for the 101st Airborne troops who were facing defeat in the Shah-i-Kot valley. By contrast, operations in Iraq highlighted deficiencies in the aircraft and the way in which it is operated. The Apache proved vulnerable to small-arms fire, although this was accentuated by the hover tactics employed by the Army, while the FLIR was found to be inadequate for long-range identification. Another lesson from Iraq was that for deep strike missions the AH-64 is most effective when fully integrated with ground-based artillery, in turn requiring better communications. These deficiencies are being attended to in the Block III upgrade.

Following the Karbala fiasco, the Army was forced to rethink its Apache operations, resulting in the force largely reverting to close support and escort missions, in which the aircraft proved more adept than the much-vaunted deep-strike missions and for which the crews were better prepared. Deep strike missions did continue, sparingly, but were integrated with long-range artillery or ATACMS long-range missile strikes. Identified as one of the reasons for the number of hits sustained was the tactic of hovering while firing. The USMC's less sophisticated Cobra fleet, by contrast, suffered far less than the Apaches during Operation Iraqi Freedom, largely because they never stayed still for a minute, shooting Hellfires and TOWs while on the move. Another Apache was lost on 31 March in an accident sustained while attempting to land in 'brown-out' conditions.

In the aftermath of the main campaign, Apaches were heavily involved in policing operations. A second shoot-down occurred on 12 June near Tikrit, when an Apache was forced down by small-arms fire. The AH-64 has remained an essential part of the coalition's policing of Iraq in the months since the end of the main campaign to oust Saddam Hussein.

Block III Apache

In 2003 Boeing and the US Army began planning for a new variant of the AH-64D Apache Longbow – the Block III. Production of this advanced model, which is based upon the Block I AH-64D, could begin in 2007 and includes 284 upgrades through 2012. The Block III aircraft will be completely equipped with digital avionics and linked to ground, air and space communications, and intelligence systems via links that include the joint tactical radio system (JTRS) and the cognitive decision aiding system (CDAS). The modifications will allow the electronic transmission of position and target information to and from the Apache. Open system architecture will enhance the ability to upgrade internal systems, and the aircraft could also be equipped with an upgraded main rotor and drive system. The AH-64A model has no digital capability, while the current AH-64Ds have limited digital communications. Block III Apaches will also be capable of controlling UAVs. Further improvements associated with Block III will simplify systems and reduce weight and costs, and include survivability improvements.

In February 2004 the US Army announced it was cancelling the Boeing/Sikorsky RAH-66 Comanche stealthy scout helicopter programme, throwing further emphasis on to the Block III Apache upgrade and ensuring more funds for AH-64 modernisation. While Block III, on paper at least, represents the same capability as the Comanche with the exception of stealth, it is likely that some newer items developed for the RAH-66 will find their way into the Block III. Beyond this step, a notional Block IV is being discussed for the 2010-2012 period, probably with new engines.

The Block III Apache will be a very different beast from the AH-64A which entered service in 1986. However, for the troops who fly and maintain it, the job remains essentially the same. One senior IP spoke for many when asked what the most important things were for him when it came to flying the Apache. He replied, "to serve my country, and kill tanks."

Robert Hewson; additional material by David Donald

Not only does the Longbow Apache own the night, it can also use its millimetre-wave radar to detect targets that otherwise remain invisible. The Longbow system allows the launch of RF Hellfires (below), and gives the lead Apache crew the opportunity to 'battle-manage' by presenting an overall tactical display of the battlefield. Targets can be assigned to and designated for other Apaches equipped with a suitable modem link, enhancing their effectiveness.

Bell
AH-1

It can be a 'Snake' or a 'Viper' or a 'Skid' or a 'Whiskey'. Soon it will be a 'Zulu'. Bell's near-immortal AH-1 Cobra family has had many names and many forms. It was born in haste during the Vietnam War and was only ever supposed to be a stop-gap aircraft. Many of its intended replacements have come and gone, while the Cobra stays fighting. Operators around the world still fly the single-engined AH-1S Cobra, while others have the twin-engined AH-1W SuperCobra to call on. The US Marine Corps has just taken its AH-1Ws to war in Iraq, for the second time – and now the Marines are looking to the latest AH-1Z, almost a new aircraft, to take their aviators well into the 21st Century.

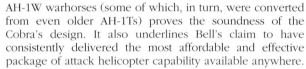

AH-1W warhorses (some of which, in turn, were converted from even older AH-1Ts) proves the soundness of the Cobra's design. It also underlines Bell's claim to have consistently delivered the most affordable and effective package of attack helicopter capability available anywhere.

The Cobra has never been a perfect aircraft. With each new variant the problems of the preceding versions have been tackled and solved, to some degree – but the Cobra has still been a clever compromise. The current benchmark service version, the AH-1W SuperCobra, is light years away from the original AH-1G – although still very recognisable as the same basic aircraft.

The early years

The pre-history of the AH-1 begins in Korea where helicopters found themselves truly at war for the very first time. Korea was not really the birthplace of the armed helicopter, however. There are stories of how US Army OH-13s (Bell Model 47 Sioux) were rigged to carry weapons on the front-line – some Army Aviation legends talk about bazookas strapped to the skids of these fragile machines – but there is no hard documentary evidence that this ever happened. Most helicopter historians agree that helicopters began to shoot back at the enemy during the French conflicts in Algeria that flared into life from 1954 onwards. There, the French forces did arm their Bell 47Gs and H-21C Shawnees, fitting them with machine-guns and 20-mm cannon for use against the rebel forces of the Armée de Libération Nationale, dug into mountain strongholds.

Armed helicopters in the 1950s were not combat helicopters in the modern sense – they had weapons for self-defence. They did show that the helicopter could be a major battlefield asset and, in the United States, work progressed on arming Army helicopters. Early work with the OH-13 was led by Colonel Jay Vanderpool, who championed the Aerial Combat Reconnaissance platoon concept (known to some as 'Vanderpool's Fools'). The OH-13 was always too small to be of practical use, but the ACR philosophy was tested with Sikorsky H-19s, H-34s and Vertol H-21s. By the early 1960s, H-34s had even fired Bullpup air-to-surface missiles and the birth of the attack helicopter was just around the corner.

Hand-in-hand with the development of the Bell AH-1 is the story of Bell's UH-1 – 'grandaddy' of the modern helicopter (and helicopter industry), engineering marvel, Vietnam icon and still one of the most numerically important helicopter types in service today. Bell's XH-40 prototype flew on 22 October 1956 and it entered production in 1959 as the HU-1A for the US Army. It was the 'HU' designation that spawned the eternal 'Huey' nickname, although

ell's AH-1 Cobra was born in war. Like so many of the best aircraft designs, it was conceived to answer an urgent operational requirement. It was also the first of a whole new class of aircraft. The AH-1 was the first true combat helicopter, the first real gunship. Today, Cobras remain in service in the United States, Bahrain, Pakistan, Iran, Israel, Japan, Jordan, Taiwan, Thailand and Turkey. With some of these operators it is coming close to the end of its operational career, but with others the AH-1 is about to embark on a whole new lease of life. The US Marine Corps is gearing up to take its next-generation AH-1Z SuperCobras into service later this decade. The AH-1Z re-invents the Cobra design and is sure to find a home with other export users. The fact that the Marines' 180 AH-1Zs are being rebuilt from their 20-year old fleet of the re-alignment of US service designations in 1962 transformed it into the more familiar UH-1. The UH-1 made the theory of air mobile warfare practical. The new tactics for 'air cavalry' called for US forces to be highly mobile across a wide area. They would not stand and fight pitched battles, and they would not stay and hold static positions. Instead, troops would range across the countryside, carried by fleets of Hueys, to fight the enemy at times and places of their own choosing. They would win with overwhelming firepower and then fly out again to secure areas. That, at least, was the plan.

It immediately became clear that the unarmed UH-1 troop transports – the 'Slicks' – were not able to make unopposed troop drops in the landing zones (LZs). Some heavy firepower was needed to clear the Viet Cong and NVA enemy out of the way first. By 1962 a handful of armed HU-1As (soon to be UH-1As) were escorting H-21 (CH-21) troop transports in and out of the LZs (strict rules of engagement at the time meant that the gunships could not fire until fired upon, which did little for their combat effectiveness). By November 1962 UH-1B gunships had arrived in Vietnam, factory-fitted with four 7.62-mm M60 machine-guns mounted on pylons outboard of the main cabin. The US was sliding deeper and deeper into the pages of history in Vietnam, and the massive expansion of the American military presence there ushered in a whole new era of war from the air. Helicopters were the linchpin of US Army tactics and the protection of those helicopters became a new and vital role.

Birth of the Cobra

By December 1962 Bell had stepped in with a company-funded venture to provide a purpose-built gunship to fight in Vietnam. The role of this new helicopter would be to protect the troopships, but also to wield a fully-fledged combat capability of its own. Strangely, Bell's first design was built around the Model 47 (albeit a much modified one) leading to the small and sleek Model 207 Sioux Scout that first took to the air in July 1963. As the Sioux Scout was being put through its paces, Army Aviation was still refining its concept of helicopter operations. The Army was not clear on what its next steps needed to be, and it was certainly not clear that there was any requirement (or any budget) to support the kind of dedicated armed helicopter that Bell was proposing.

A glance back at the Sioux Scout design shows how prescient it was. All the key features of a modern combat helicopter were there – a tandem cockpit, stub wings for

weapons and a chin-mounted gun turret. Beginning in January 1964, the Sioux Scout was evaluated by the 11th Air Assault Division, and it shone. The Army was impressed by what it saw but equally it believed that the Sioux Scout was too small, too underpowered, too unsophisticated and too fragile to be of real practical use. Unfortunately for the Army, its solution to this 'problem' was to launch the Advanced Aerial Fire Support System (AAFSS) competition.

It was the AAFSS requirement that would give birth to the infamous Lockheed AH-56 Cheyenne – a heavyweight battlefield helicopter that would prove to be over-ambitious, over-complex and massively over-budget before being cancelled in 1972. The 10-year Cheyenne programme was a splendid failure. It developed some fascinating technology and demonstrated some impressive performance, but it was never made to work as a functional combat helicopter. The Cheyenne experience did serve to underline the one unbreakable rule of the combat helicopter – survival on the battlefield would be ensured only by the right mix of speed, agility and weapons.

Meanwhile, despite the Army's preference for the AAFSS (for which Bell Helicopter was not selected to compete), Bell had the vision and perseverance to stick with its own smaller, lighter gunship ideas. In January 1956, it stumped up $1 million to proceed with its next-generation Model 209 design. It would prove to be a very wise investment.

Taking the proven elements of the UH-1 (transmission, rotor system, T53 turboshaft) and mating them with the design philosophy of the Sioux Scout, Bell's engineers (headed by J. R. Duppstadt) produced a design classic. The slender, sharp-nosed Model 209 looked every inch a thoroughbred – an aircraft built for fighting. In Vietnam, events were also conspiring in the Model 209's favour. Vietnamese attacks on US forces were increasing, and by 1965 the US response had escalated into the Rolling Thunder bombing campaign. By the end of June 1965 there were 50,000 US

In 2001 the US Army retired the AH-1F from service, although numbers remain available for onward sale to export customers or use by other government agencies such as the Forest Service. Conversion of active-duty units to the sophisticated AH-64 Apache and the OH-58D Kiowa Warrior took over 10 years, with the last Cobras leaving Europe in 1996 and Korea in 1997. Cobras saw out their last days of service with the National Guard. In 1990 the Army still flew over 1,000 Cobras, but by 2000 the force was down to 346 (many of which were unflyable), operating with Army National Guard units like California's 1-18 Cav (below). Under the US Army's force modernisation roadmap, most of the Cobra units were scheduled for eventual conversion to the AH-64 Apache and (now cancelled) RAH-66 Comanche, but in the interim converted to the OH-58A Kiowa, itself slated for retirement by October 2004. A massed flypast over New York was planned for the AH-1F's retirement at the end of September 2001, but the events of the 11th of the month put an end to that.

This view of an AH-1F highlights the M197 cannon which was introduced by the Up-Gun AH-1S. This aircraft was allocated to 1-7 Cav at Fort Hood, one of the last active-duty squadrons. The final active-duty user of the AH-1F was the 1st Battalion, 25th Infantry Division, based at Wheeler Army Airfield, Hawaii, which retired its last aircraft on 15 March 1999. When the AH-1F was retired from Army National Guard service in 2001, all survivors were gathered together at Fort Drum, New York, for storage in the first of a three-phase retirement plan. In the second phase aircraft were released for export sale, use by other government agencies (including the USMC which took some for spares recovery), or donation to museums and schools. The final phase covers the destruction of remaining aircraft at the end of FY04.

ground troops in Vietnam. 1965 was also supposed to be the deadline for AAFSS selection, but the programme was mired in technical difficulties and political in-fighting. Suddenly, the US Army needed an interim gunship to carry the load in Vietnam and it asked five companies to provide a rapid solution. Submissions came in for armed variants of the Boeing-Vertol CH-47A, Kaman UH-2, Piasecki 16H Pathfinder, Sikorsky S-61 and the Bell 209. While the others were noble attempts at delivering a 'fast-track' capability, none of these offers came near the level of capability promised by the Model 209.

On 3 September 1965 Bell rolled out its prototype Model 209. Four days later, on 7 September, it made its first flight. It had taken just eight months from go-ahead to maiden flight. The Army was not persuaded out-of-hand. Bell still had to face up to an evaluation of all the rival helicopters, but the 209 waltzed through the competitive fly-off held in November-December. By April 1966 the US Army had signed the first production contract for 110 aircraft.

The first AH-1G HueyCobras were delivered in June 1967. Originally, the Army designated the aircraft as the UH-1H, seeing it as an offshoot of the existing Huey family. However the 'A' for attack designation was soon adopted, and when the improved UH-1D became the UH-1H, the HueyCobra became the AH-1G. Between 1967 and 1973 Bell built 1,116 AH-1Gs for the US Army. The aircraft gave sterling service in Vietnam, where they had a rapid baptism of fire and chalked up something like one million opera-

tional flying hours. The basic AH-1G weapons fit featured an undernose Emerson M28 turret fitted with an M134 7.62-mm Minigun and an M129 40-mm grenade launcher. The stub wings could carry additional 7.62-mm gun pods and 2.75-in rocket pods. The M28 turret could also be fitted with twin M134s or twin M129s.

Cobras for the Corps

As it turned out, the real future of the Cobra would not remain in US Army hands. Army Cobras would stay in service with regular aviation units until 1999 – and even longer with the Army National Guard – while equivalent aircraft still fly with several export operators. However, it was the twin-engined, upgunned SeaCobras fielded by the Marine Corps that would fully exploit the potential of the AH-1 design. It is Marine Cobras that make up today's US front-line AH-1 fleet, and it is their new aircraft that will be in service for many years to come.

When the US Marine Corps came to assess the AH-1 in 1967 it recognised that the helicopter would be much more effective and reliable with two engines. This was an essential requirement for over-water operations. The Corps also saw that the basic gun armament fit was too light and lacked range. As thoughts turned to a twin-engined Cobra there was an obvious solution already in place. Pratt & Whitney Canada had developed its PT6T Twin Pac configuration, under a jointly funded US/Canada programme for the Model 212 Twin Huey (UH-1N). It was a logical step to swap out the AH-1G's single Lycoming T53L-13 and replace it with the PT6T-3. However, the Marines' ambitions were not matched by their wallets. The Corps did not have the funding to adopt and support an entirely new engine, so it was forced to retain the T53 in its single-engined AH-1Js.

Like the HueyCobra before it, the navalised AH-1J SeaCobra was thrown in at the deep end in Vietnam. In 1968 the Tet Offensive took US forces by complete surprise and the requirement for the AH-1J (set at a modest 28 aircraft in the FY68 budget) soared. More importantly, it was decided to dump the compromise T53 configuration and go for the full-spec twin-engined layout. The new AH-1J was also armed with the much more effective three-barrelled M197 cannon. On 10 October 1969 the first SeaCobra was rolled out at Fort Worth. By early 1971 the first aircraft were undergoing combat evaluation in Vietnam.

At this stage it was becoming very clear that the AH-56 Cheyenne was a failed project and that there would be no immediate replacement for the 'interim' AH-1. The Cheyenne programme had essentially died in 1969 and survived only as a research project, but with no future. Bell saw this as a good time to introduce a developed version of the AH-1, the twin-engined Model 309 KingCobra. This was a scaled up AH-1 with a more advanced set of mission systems than the AH-1G (drawing heavily on equipment developed for the Cheyenne) that would be a true day/night-capable combat helicopter. The KingCobra would prove to be a dead-end (two prototypes were built), but it did point to what the basic AH-1 design was capable of, and underlined the superiority of the twin-engined layout.

All Cobras up to this stage had been daytime-only aircraft, with very limited navigational aids and simple optical sights. American attention would soon turn away from Vietnam and refocus on the Soviet threat in Europe, where it was becoming clear that the ability to fight at night would be crucial for NATO forces. This would be especially true for combat helicopters, which were now taking on a whole new role with a whole new weapon. The Cheyenne and the KingCobra were designed to use the Hughes BGM-71 TOW (Tube-launched, Optically-tracked, Wire-guided) missile, now a product of Raytheon Missile Systems. For the first time, TOW gave helicopters the ability to kill armoured vehicles, up to and including main battle tanks, to a distance of 3750 m (4,100 yards). The French had demonstrated the first air-to-surface missiles on helicopters many years previously with SS.10- and SS.11-armed Alouettes, but the TOW was a next-generation weapon that was more effective – and more practical – than anything that had come before it. As the Cheyenne and KingCobra were smothered by the post-Vietnam draw-down, the AH-1 once again stepped up to take on the job of the US military's *de facto* battlefield attack helicopter.

Work on integrating the TOW with a handful of UH-1B test beds began in 1972, to pave the way for its adoption on dedicated combat helicopters. When North Vietnamese forces slashed across the DMZ and into the South's Quang Tri province in March 1972, they fielded heavy armour for the first time in the war. The NVA was operating out-dated but still effective Soviet vehicles, including T-34 and T-54 tanks, plus the PT-76 light tank. Six days after the order to deploy, on 14 April, TOW-armed Hueys fitted with the experimental XM26 launch system arrived in Vietnam. In the right place at the right time, they played an important part in pushing back the NVA forces, particularly in the fighting around Kontum. The first combat use of a TOW fired from an Army helicopter came on 2 May 1972 (this was also the first ever launch of an American-made guided missile by American troops).

Missile-armed HueyCobras did not fight in Vietnam, but by 1973 the Improved Cobra Armament Program (ICAP) was delivering TOW-capable AH-1Gs to the US Army. By January 1974 Bell was delivering the follow-on AH-1Q, designed from the outset to carry eight TOWs. It had the (now production standard) Hughes M65 optical sight in a nose turret, known as the telescopic sight unit (TSU), and uprated 1,800-hp (1343-kW) Lycoming (now AlliedSignal) T53-L-703 engines. All service AH-1Qs were rebuilt from existing AH-1Gs. This was the first purpose-built TOW-armed variant for the US Army but, despite its better engine, the AH-1Q was still lacking in performance and aircraft rarely carried the maximum load of eight missiles (anything between two and six being common).

AAH competition

The AH-1's shortcomings were recognised and by 1972 the US Army had already begun the search for another new attack helicopter. Out of the ashes of the Cheyenne programme (finally cancelled in August 1972) came the new Advanced Attack Helicopter (AAH) requirement. The AAH competition would prove to be almost as controversial as the AAFSS, but it did finally deliver the Hughes (later McDonnell Douglas, now Boeing) AH-64A Apache. The operational driver behind the AAH (and ultimately the Apache) was the ability to fight at night on the threat-heavy European battlefield of the future. At the same time, the US Army had a substantial fleet of well over 600 valuable

AH-1s (becoming AH-1Qs) that could not just be thrown away. In 1976 a new modernisation effort for the AH-1Q was launched, the ECAP (Enhanced Cobra Armament Program). The product of the ECAP was the AH-1S, a fully TOW-armed aircraft with a more powerful engine, an uprated transmission and a higher gross operating weight.

There were several standards of AH-1S as new modifications were made to progressive production blocks of aircraft. The initial Production standard (known as the Step 1) introduced the trademark seven-pane flat-plate canopy, improved main rotor blades, AN/APR-39 radar warning system and a curved, semi-circular exhaust suppressor. The first examples entered service with the 82nd Airborne in August 1977.

Over-water safety was the prime driver behind the USMC's requirement for a twin-engined Cobra, which initially resulted in the Pratt & Whitney Canada PT6T (T400)-powered AH-1J SeaCobra. The AH-1T had an uprated T400, whereas the current AH-1W has two General Electric T700s.

Marine helicopter units routinely practise operations from austere locations.

Four Middle East countries fly the Cobra, including Jordan, which received 24 AH-1Ss in 1985 (plus a top-up batch in 2000/01). The aircraft fly with two squadrons based at Al Matar, near the capital Amman. The other Cobra users in the region are Bahrain, Iran and Israel.

Thailand had ambitious plans to establish an attack helicopter force equipped with the Cobra. Four AH-1Fs were acquired in 1990 to form an evaluation cadre, around which it was planned to create a force of at least squadron size. At various points in the 1990s further procurement was planned of either new-build AH-1Ws or ex-US Army AH-1Fs. As Thailand's 'tiger' economy suffered dramatically in the late 1990s, and the defence budget was prioritised towards more pressing needs, so plans for any further attack helicopters expired. One of the quartet was lost in a crash, but the remaining three continue to serve with the army aviation centre at Lop Buri.

Beginning in 1978 the Production AH-1S standard gave way to the Up-Gun AH-1S (AH-1S Step 2). On these aircraft, the outdated M28 turret was replaced by an M197 20-mm cannon mounted in the General Electric-designed M97A1 Universal Turret that had already been adopted by Marine Corps Cobras. The M128 helmet sight system (HSS) was another feature of these aircraft. Linked to the Universal Turret, it allowed crew-members to point the gun at a target just by looking at it.

The final standard was the 'Modernized AH-1S' (AH-1S Step 3). Produced between 1979 and 1981, these aircraft were fitted with the M143 air data sensor (located on the forward fuselage, starboard side) that fed information to the new M26 fire control system. Rocket-firing capability, not available to the previous AH-1S models, was returned on the Step 3 aircraft with the inclusion of the M147 rocket management system (RMS). A laser rangefinder was added to the M65 sight and an AN/AAS-32 laser tracker was fitted in a bullet fairing in front of the rotor housing. The crew was also provided with the improved M136 HSS.

Better self-defence measures included the AN/ALQ-144 infra-red jammer (mounted above the rear engine housing), along with a new upwards-angled tubular exhaust shroud. The cockpit was fitted out with the M76 HUD, a new Doppler navigation system, the APX-100 IFF and KY-58 secure radios. NVG-compatible instruments were also added for the first time. These aircraft were much easier and safer to fly at low-level (thanks largely to the HUD), thus making them more survivable. The layout of the cockpit was rearranged to make key instruments and switches more accessible (although the Cobra cockpit was far from being a masterpiece of man-machine interface design). The AH-1S upgrade programme was completed by 1985. A total of 530 aircraft was fielded (387 AH-1G upgrades and 143 new-build).

Further enhancements were made to several hundred late-model aircraft, including the integration of the Cobra Night Vision (C-Nite) system that turned the AH-1 into a night-capable aircraft for the first time, and the improved TOW 2 missile. In 1988 the US Army redesignated all of its Cobra variants – leaving a trail of confusion that has inhabited the AH-1 story ever since. The Step 1 (Production standard) AH-1S became the AH-1P. The Step 2 (Up-Gun) AH-1S became the AH-1E. The Step 3 (Modernized) AH-1S became the AH-1F.

From the late 1980s onwards, the spread of AH-64s into Army Aviation saw the withdrawal of the AH-1 from front-line units and into the hands of the Army National Guard (ArNG). The AH-1s that remained in use with regular units shifted into scout/gun teams flying alongside OH-58C Kiowas, often operating for Cavalry units. Both types were largely replaced in that role by the OH-58D(I) Kiowa Warrior. The last AH-1Fs in the regular US Army were retired in March 1999. On 15 March, eight AH-1Fs of the 1st Battalion, 25th Aviation Regiment (Attack), 25th Infantry Division (Light) launched for a ceremonial flypast from their base at Wheeler Army Airfield, Hawaii, to close the book on 32 years of front-line Cobra flying. The unit would become the last Army Aviation battalion to transition to the OH-58D(I), in May 2000.

On 4 April 2000 the Army released its Aviation Force Modernization Plan, which specified that the AH-1F would be retired by 30 September 2000. This date was subsequently extended to 16 December, and then again to 30 September 2001, the Army coming under pressure from Adjutant Generals in the affected state ArNGs who were concerned about the readiness of their forces. On 3 May 2001 the US Army Aviation Logistics School graduated its last class of Cobra armament technicians, and on 30 September the AH-1F was formally retired. A number were passed on to existing overseas customers and the Forest Service.

Marine developments

The Cobra story is certainly not over for the Marine Corps. The development of the Cobra with the Marines has followed a much different path. In the mid-1970s the Marines jumped from the twin-engined AH-1J to the AH-1T Improved SeaCobra. This version had an extended fuselage and tail boom, and could operate at even higher weights than the J model (a sizeable jump to a 14,000-lb/6350-kg maximum take off weight). The new weight limits meant the AH-1T was also far better able to operate with a full TOW load. In 1979 another step forward came when Bell began fitting General Electric T700 turboshafts to an AH-1T. A demonstrator aircraft flew in April 1980 and represented a highly attractive proposal because it offered powerplant commonality with the bulk of the modern twin-engined US helicopter fleet (AH-64, UH-60, SH-60). The improved Cobra was offered to the Marines as the AH-1T Plus (AH-1T+), and by 1982 attrition in the Marines' Cobra fleet made the purchase of new aircraft almost inevitable.

Bell made a cut-price offer to build the first batch of 44 AH-1T Plus aircraft at $15.2 million dollars each (unit cost), equivalent to a 'flyaway' price of $7.1 million. A deal was done and the new Cobras were ordered for delivery from March 1986 onwards. A definitive T700-GE-401-powered prototype flew on 16 November 1983 and the new up-engined and fully marinised aircraft became the AH-1W.

The AH-1W SuperCobra, often referred to as the Whiskey Cobra, is the most powerful, well-armed and best equipped evolution of the Cobra family to enter service. The first aircraft began operations with the US Marine Corps in 1986 – at around the same time that the AH-1S started to give way to the Apache in the US Army's inventory (the first Apaches were deployed to Europe in 1987). The USMC acquired a mix of converted (from AH-1T) and new-build AH-1W airframes.

AH-1Ws are fitted with the Night Targeting System (NTS) – a modification of the original M65 – that was developed from 1987 by Kollsman, in the US, from an Israeli design

produced by IAI's Tamam Division. The NTS comprises a FLIR and CCD TV sensors (with a video recording function), a laser designator/rangefinder and automatic target-tracking capability. Its introduction gave the Marines a significant leap forward in capability over the outdated M65. As part of the NTS integration effort, the AH-1W received the canopy cockpit modification (CCM) that replaced all the existing canopy, nose section and the front cockpit (co-pilot/gunner) instrument panel. Along with the NTS came a new tactical navigation system (TNS) that, from 1996, incorporated the AN/ASN-163 GPS/INS.

For improved self-defence the AH-1W received the ECP-1674 electronic warfare suite. This integrated the AN/AAR-47 missile warning system with the AN/ALE-39 countermeasures dispenser. The AAR-47 is an optical sensor that gives the crew an aural warning when it detects the plume from a surface-to-air missile launch. The launch direction is shown on a cockpit display and chaff/flares are automatically deployed by the ALE-39. During Operation Iraqi Freedom Cobra crews found that the AAR-47 was responsive enough to alert them to rocket-propelled grenades (RPGs) being fired at their aircraft. The AH-1W is also fitted with the AN/AVR-2 laser warning receiver that detects and warns if any pulsed laser energy (such as laser rangefinders or weapons designators) are being aimed at the aircraft. The AVR-2 is even sensitive enough to detect office laser pointers. Finally, the AN/APR-39A(V)2 radar warning receiver monitors ground and airborne radars and alerts the crew if any become threatening by tracking or locking on to the aircraft.

Cobra weapons

The basic weapons set of all AH-1s in service today comprises the M197 20-mm cannon, the BGM-71 TOW and 2.75-in (70-mm) rockets – typically in LAU-61 or LAU-68 pods. This is the weapons fit first fielded on the AH-1J and Up-Gun AH-1S. The M197 cannon can carry a maximum load of 750 20-mm shells and has a maximum rate of fire of 650 rounds per minute. The gun is normally fired in nine-second, 100-round bursts. For years now, the M197 has been acknowledged to be prone to jamming and this problem came to the fore again during the 2003 war in Iraq. The gun still remains a vital weapon and the gunners

Japan is the only country so far to build the Cobra under licence, Fuji Heavy Industries being responsible for building 89 AH-1S Step 3 aircraft (similar to the US Army's AH-1F) following the delivery of two Step 2 (AH-1E) aircraft from the US. The later production machines were fitted with the C-Nite system, adding night capability. Japan's Cobras serve in five front-line attack helicopter units, each of two squadrons, plus a single training squadron. The front-line units also operate OH-6D/OH-1 scouts. Production was originally to have included a number for attrition, but no Cobras were lost during the first years of service and the eight-aircraft batch was cancelled. In February 2004 the JGSDF suffered its first AH-1S losses when two aircraft collided during a training mission. Thankfully all four crew survived.

air-to-air missile, in the shape of the AIM-9 Sidewinder. The Marines qualified the AGM-122 Sidearm, an anti-radiation missile based on the Sidewinder airframe (and using the common LAU-7 launcher), for their Cobras too.

While the AIM-9 was a useful capability to possess, it was a compromise weapon that is too large and too unwieldy to be used effectively on the AH-1W. While the Corps has always been mindful of the air-to-air role for its attack helicopters, it has been unable to spend much money on developing more suitable weapons. The AH-1W has never adopted the air-to-air Stinger (ATAS), as found on US Army Kiowa Warriors, and recent US Army Apache trials with the British-built Helstreak (Starstreak) AAM have passed the AH-1W by. The AIM-9 remains an option for the AH-1W (the AIM-122 is now out of the inventory) and Marine pilots still do some air-to-air training, but the Sidewinder is no longer seen as a practical weapon. One big disincentive for carrying Sidewinder is that it precludes the loading of any other stores on the remaining wing station.

Over the years Marine aviators have gazed across at the Army's Apaches and wished they could afford them. Several attempts have been made to introduce the Apache into USMC service but, always the branch of the US military that has had to do the most with the least, the Marines have never been able to fund an Apache purchase. Paying for a marinised Apache variant would not come cheap and the USMC was likely to be the sole customer. This is why the AH-1W (and soon the AH-1Z) remains the core combat helicopter for the Corps. While this has often been viewed as a second-best situation for the USMC, much of the Apache's gloss has worn off in recent years, and today the Marines actually find themselves with what the numbers show to be the most survivable combat helicopter in US service.

Hellfire for the Cobra

What the Cobra has always lacked was hitting power, hence the Hellfire for the AH-1W. The Marines knew that if their SuperCobras were going to have to fight their way off the beaches against serious opposition, they would need some serious additional firepower. The TOW's 3750-m (12,300-ft) range is insufficient to out-reach current battle-field air defence systems. Neither can its warhead defeat the most modern tank armour. These deficiencies were already recognised during the mid-1970s when (what was then) Rockwell International was contracted to develop the

Although the IDF/AF now operates a sizeable fleet of Petens (AH-64s), the Zefa (AH-1) remains an important part of the Israeli military machine, seeing widespread action throughout its career. In recent times it has been spotted regularly during news footage of attacks on targets within the Palestine Authority, and some analysts suggest that it is preferred over the Peten for attacks where pinpoint accuracy is essential, such as missile strikes against individual houses where terrorist subjects are believed to be hiding and where collateral damage has to be kept to the absolute minimum. The use of Spike has been reported in such attacks, although there is no official confirmation.

Right: A 'Southern Squadron' Zefa flies at typically low altitude during a training sortie. Israeli Cobras are very well protected, this aircraft being fitted with radar/missile warning receivers, infra-red countermeasures turret and large flare dispensers.

have learned how to manipulate the ammunition feed, keeping pressure on and off the ammunition belt, to minimise the risk of jams.

The AH-1W went a step further than any previous AH-1 variant, adding the laser-guided AGM-114 Hellfire missile that was developed originally for the AH-64A Apache. In order to provide some air cover for troops 'on the beach', the AH-1W also became the first US helicopter to field an

AGM-114 Hellfire. This new laser-guided missile was far more flexible than the TOW (offering lock-on before launch or lock on after launch guidance modes), had a warhead capable of wiping out anything in its path and came with an effective range of more than 8000 m (26,247 ft). Hellfires can be fired from either seat in the AH-1W but the controls for the laser are in the front cockpit only.

When the Marines went to war in Iraq in 2003 they brought the latest version of the laser-guided Hellfire II (AGM-114K), the newly-developed blast/fragmentation variant (AGM-114M) and the (hitherto) completely unknown AGM-114N missile with its thermobaric warhead. Thermobaric weapons (from the Greek *therme*, meaning heat and *baros*, meaning pressure) use intense heat and blast pressure to destroy targets. They are often equated to fuel air explosives (FAE) but modern thermobaric (TB) explosives have a far more concentrated and direct effect. The Marine Corps has led the development of TB weapons in the US, with an eye on the considerable range of operational systems already tested and fielded in Russia (and elsewhere).

In late 2001, spurred on by the terrorist atrocities of 11 September, the Indian Head weapons facility began serious work on new TB weapons, drawing on its existing development efforts with the BLU-118/B TB bomb for the USAF. The Marines wanted an equivalent weapon to use for fighting in caves and mountains. It was decided to adopt the Hellfire, and replace the PBX-109 explosive fill of the AGM-114N with a new TB compound, PBX N-12. By mid-2002 the development team was getting ready for the first live fire tests from a helicopter. The aim was to produce a weapon capable of completely destroying, for example, six rooms inside a building over a penetration range of 60 ft (18.3 m). Two AGM-114Ns had been successfully fired before the Iraqi conflict and a development batch of 60 missiles was rebuilt from existing AGM-114Ks.

During Operation Iraqi Freedom Marine Cobras typically flew with a mix of Hellfires, TOWs and rockets, which meant that they were always operating at or beyond their maximum weight limits. One pilot who fought in Iraq recalled, "the Cobra has a NATOPS limit of 14,750 lb [6691 kg] all-up weight but we always flew above that – because it was war. You'd be carrying four TOWs, four Hellfires, seven HE rockets and seven flechette rockets, plus 300 rounds for the gun and you'd be operating at over 15,000 lb [6804 kg], always." The AH-1W can carry a maximum ordnance load of 1,500 lb (680 kg).

Israeli Zefa

In Israel, the AH-1 has a special role to play within the ranks of the Israel Defense Force/Air Force (IDF/AF). Israel has been a Cobra operator since the late 1980s and currently operates an uncertain number of around 50

Left: Wearing the badge of the 'Northern Squadron', an IDF/AF AH-1F fires a Spike-LR missile during tests for the Polish army. This weapon uses fibre-optics relaying seeker imagery directly back to the Cobra, resulting in very high accuracy. It is believed that the Spike has been used operationally by the IDF/AF in pinpoint attacks against urban targets.

Above and above left: A Zefa fires a BGM-71 TOW at a target during a firepower demonstration. The TOW uses a wire link between the missile and the aircraft, through which guidance commands are relayed.

The IDF/AF's two Zefa units regularly practise operating from deployed locations, like these 'Northern Squadron' AH-1Fs.

AH-1S (AH-1F) aircraft, known locally as Zefas (vipers). When the Cobras entered service they formed part of a high/low mix together with the IDF/AF's TOW-armed Hughes 500MD Defenders. The AH-1s were Israel's sophisticated attack helicopters while the 500MDs were the affordable force multipliers. As the Defenders were retired from use and the AH-64A began to enter IDF service in increasing numbers, the status of the Cobra force was reversed, but they remained invaluable.

Operated by Nos 160 and 161 Sqns, Israel's Cobras were armed with a range of TOW variants including the BGM-71A TOW (P'teel, chord), BGM-71C I-TOW (Peeg'yon, dagger), BGM-71D TOW 2 (Pit'yon, bait) and the subse-

quent TOW 2A and TOW 2B variants. Israel also developed its own second-generation anti-tank guided missiles, including the TAAS (later IMI) MAPATS, which seems to have been based on the TOW, but is improved and refined.

During the 1990s the wraps came off a new fibre optic-guided missile system developed by Rafael. The Spike series of weapons was developed as the NT family (Neged Tank, anti-tank) and three variants were produced under the codenames Gill, Spike and Dandy (NT-G, NT-S, NT-D). In 2002 Rafael gathered all these weapons under the Spike banner. The original Spike variant (now known as Spike-

ER) was the first helicopter-launched version to be developed. It was a 13-kg (28.6-lb) missile with a range of around 4000 m (13,123 ft). This was followed by the much larger Dandy (now known as Spike-LR) which had an 8000-m (26,247-ft) range.

All of these missiles use an innovative (and so far unique) man-in-the-loop guidance system. After launch, the fibre-optic cable that connects the missile to the launch platform relays seeker imagery back to the operator, who can see exactly where the missile is going and correct its course accordingly. This makes the Spike a very accurate

weapon, more accurate than any laser-guided missile, for example. The Spike also has an autotracking fire-and-forget capability and the combination of these two very different control modes makes it a unique weapon. The Spike has been integrated on Israel's Cobras – in fact, they are thought to be the only operational Spike platforms in service. The weapon gives IDF/AF Cobras an unparalleled precision attack capability. There have been persistent rumours that Spike, or a modified version of the missile with a smaller warhead (for lower collateral damage), has been used on Israel's targeted 'assassination' air strikes during 2003 and 2004.

IAI has developed another air-launched weapon that is probably also in service on IDF/AF Cobras. This is the LAHAT, known as the SkyBow in its air-launched form. SkyBow is a small laser-guided missile, originally designed to be fired from tanks or self-propelled guns. It is therefore a very compact and lightweight weapon suitable for use on small helicopters or even UAVs. IAI is now offering the LAHAT/SkyBow for export – usually (although not always) a sign that the system is already in Israeli service. There has been a suggestion from some Israeli sources that this missile, claimed to be accurate to within 72 cm (2.4 ft), has been used in the anti-personnel strikes in the Occupied Territories.

Cobras at war

Post-Vietnam, Israel's Cobras were the first to be used in combat. Press reports place their operational debut in May 1979, when TOWs were fired at targets in the Halil refugee camp, near Tyre. Their first major combat experience was during the 1982 invasion of Lebanon (Operation Peace for Galilee). This does not appear to have been an unqualified success, as the terrain and tactics used did not suit the aircraft. At least two Cobras are believed to have been shot down by Syrian air defences, while several others were damaged. However, the Cobras were used to engage Syrian armour and fired over 100 TOWs, claiming kills on T-72 tanks (later hotly disputed by other branches of the Israeli military who also claimed credit).

While Israel's Cobras were on the front line through the 1980s, Iran's substantial force of AH-1Js fought long and hard against Iraqi forces during the first Gulf War of 1980 to 1988. The Islamic Republic of Iran Army made very effective use of its 'International' AH-1Js, which fought Iraqi ground and air forces over the course of the conflict. There is good evidence to support several reported air-to-air kills against Iraqi helicopters using both TOW and the M197 gun. Iranian sources even claim three air-to-air kills of Iraqi

MiG-21s by IRIAA Cobras. At the same time Iranian helicopter losses were high and only about half the original fleet of 202 AH-1Js remained available at the end of the war.

The Cobras fought in several key offensive and defensive engagements, supporting advances through the Iraqi front lines in 1982, 1984 and 1986, while fending off the Iraqi offensive of 1988 and claiming kills on T-72 tanks. Not all of Iran's Cobras were TOW-capable and, towards the end of the conflict, Iranian technicians began to integrate alternative weapons on the AH-1Js (several such efforts were undertaken, including attempts to fit Hawk and Standard SAMs on F-14s and F-4s). A few Iranian Cobras were armed with AGM-65 Mavericks and the small supply of available missiles was reportedly used with success against static positions. The IRIAA also tried to arm its Cobras with Sidewinders, but this project failed.

In the early hours of 20 December 1989, US forces invaded Panama to overthrow the regime of General Manuel Noriega. Operation Just Cause was launched from the existing American bases in the Canal Zone and was supported by additional troops flown in from the United States. Helicopters played a key role in the brief – but bloody – action, which saw the first combat missions undertaken by female US Army pilots (piloting UH-60 Blackhawks). Five US Army Task Forces were deployed against various targets in Panama, and AH-1s delivered fire support for these operations. This included Task Force Bayonet's capture of Fort Amador, the air assault of El Renacer prison, and the crucial H-hour battle for the Cerro Tigre army barracks. The fighting around Cerro Tigre saw the first combat use of NVGs by US Army aviators.

Guns and rockets remain essential arrows in the Cobra's quiver. Marine AH-1s operate very closely with the ground forces, and they may be regularly called upon to clear small pockets of resistance being faced by the infantry. At close quarters the 2.75-in rocket and 20-mm cannon remain highly effective means of countering 'soft' targets, while the carriage of TOW and Hellfire allows the Cobra to handle 'hard' targets such as tanks and bunkers at greater ranges. Here a pair of AH-1Ws from the USMCR squadron HMLA-775 fire rockets on the range at Camp Pendleton, California.

Short-range MANPADS (man-portable air defence systems – shoulder-launched weapons) are one of the main threats to the attack helicopter, and a sophisticated and fast-reacting defensive suite is required. Here an HMLA-775 Cobra releases flares while firing 'on the run'.

During the 1990s Turkey's Cobras were used to fight a high-intensity but low-profile war against Kurdish insurgents along the southern border region with Iraq. In 2004 Pakistan's AH-1S force found itself fighting a similar action as part of the March campaign to hunt down suspected al-Qaeda figures hiding out in the border regions of South Waziristan. Between 5,000 and 7,500 troops were involved in fighting with perhaps 400 armed tribesmen.

Operation Desert Storm

Both US Army and US Marine Corps AH-1s went to war in Iraq during 1991, but the 100-hour ground campaign of Operation Desert Storm gave the crews relatively little operational exposure. Army Apaches grabbed the headlines when Task Force Normandy made the first strike across the Iraqi border in the early hours of 17 January. Eight AH-64As of the 101st Airborne Division fired the first shots of the war in an attack that destroyed key Iraqi radar positions. According to the official record the US Army took 145 AH-1s (and 277 AH-64As) to war in Iraq. The Cobras played a supporting role to the Apaches – in what was to be the high-point of the AH-64's operational career. While the Apaches took on the deep strike mission, the Cobras flew constant security and reconnaissance missions, providing over-watch and flank security for the advancing Army units.

The Marines deployed 48 AH-1Ws for the first war in Iraq, or about 20 per cent of the available attack helicopter

force. Yet these aircraft flew more than 50 per cent of the total attack force flight hours. The AH-1Ws also turned in a mission readiness rate of 92 per cent. The Marine Cobras were heavily involved in the fighting around the Saudi town of Khafji, between 29 January and 2 February, which was subject of an Iraqi incursion before being retaken by Saudi and US troops. After the ground war had begun, Marine Cobras operated in their classic roles of armed reconnaissance, escort and close air support. The speed of the Allied advance, the bad weather and smoke from burning oil fields made life hard for the helicopter crews. The AH-1Ws operated in direct support of the 1st Marine Division, and as part of the Task Force Cunningham manoeuvre element (alongside AV-8B Harriers).

On G Day +2 (26 January) Marine Corps Cobras, flying with a single UH-1N, supported Task Force Ripper in its battle with the Iraqi 3rd Armoured Division. Along with Task Force Papa Bear, TF Ripper was one of the two main assault forces of the 1st Marine Division into Iraq. Fitted with a more modern FLIR system than the AH-1s, the UH-1N led units through the smoke and under power lines into battle positions where they could engage Iraqi tanks with Hellfires. The Huey even designated targets for the Cobras' Hellfires. The Cobras were also very active with the two flanking elements (TFs Grizzly and Taro).

In the years that followed the liberation of Kuwait, Marine Corps Cobras supported expeditionary deployments around the world and saw active service in Somalia, Bosnia, Haiti and Liberia. The AH-1W is a key component of the Marine Expeditionary Unit (Special Operations Capable), or MEU(SOC), concept.

When the Cobra went back to war against Iraq in 2003, this time the Marines' AH-1Ws were on their own – the Army had only Apaches. The aircraft that the crews flew in 2003 were essentially unchanged from those of 12 years previously, but the nature of the war was dramatically different. In 1991 Marine Corps troops had pushed almost as far as Baghdad in about four days but were not attempting to take over the country. This time US forces would cross virtually all of Iraq and, while the combat phase of the campaign was relatively brief, the scale and ferocity of the fighting bore no resemblance to that of Desert Storm.

Operation Iraqi Freedom

The experience of HML/A-269 (REIN) in Operation Iraqi Freedom (OIF) was typical. During peacetime, Marine Light Attack Helicopter Squadron 269 (HML/A-269) 'Gunrunners' is one of two AH-1W squadrons based at MCAS New River, North Carolina. New River is itself attached to the huge

Camp Lejeune facility, home to many thousands of Marines. The squadron operates as part of Marine Air Group 29 (MAG-29), which is commanded by the 2nd Marine Aircraft Wing (2 MAW).

In October 2002 the squadron's commanding officer, Lt Colonel Jeffrey Hewlett, was told to prepare his unit for combat operations in Iraq. In preparation for deployment the squadron was expanded, or reinforced (hence the 'REIN' suffix) with additional AH-1Ws and UH-1Ns from HML/A-167 'Warriors', its sister unit at New River, plus others taken from the 22 MEU (Marine Expeditionary Unit). This gave HML/A-269 (REIN) control of 18 AH-1Ws and nine UH-1Ns. The squadron got its deployment orders on 12 January 2004 and over 13 and 14 January it flew its aircraft onto the USS *Saipan* (LHA 2) and USS *Ponce* (LPD 15) for onward shipment. HML/A-269 was part of MAG-29 which, in turn, was just one element of the 2nd Marine Expeditionary Brigade (II MEB), along with ground troops (2nd Marines) and combat support units. The force called itself TF Tarawa and it sailed on 18 January with some 7,000 Marines aboard seven LHAs, LHDs and LSDs (as Amphibious Task Force East). Four of these seven ships carried MAG-29 aircraft. To the Marine aviators this was the II MEB ACE (aviation combat element) – a total of 26 AV-8Bs, 12 CH-53Es, 12 CH-46Es (plus four dedicated SAR aircraft), 11 AH-1Ws, nine UH-1Ns and two SAR H-60s.

It took 10 days to make the Translant passage. During that time the embarked aircraft flew day and night deck landing operations, although these were hampered by bad weather. There was a fear of terrorist attack at the various maritime 'choke points' through which ATF East had to pass. The first of these was the Straits of Gibraltar (or STROG in Marine-speak). During these sensitive transits there were usually six fully-armed AH-1Ws flying as outriders to protect the ships. Once the ATF had emerged from the Suez Canal, aircraft flew to Djibouti for a brief live-fire exercises with other elements of II MEB. The last airborne alert by the AH-1Ws was flown on 13 February, when the Task Force passed through the Straits of Hormuz. Once the ATF reached the Gulf the ACE was reconfigured and all the AH-1Ws were collected aboard the USS *Saipan* before flying off to Kuwait to provide some deck space. On 14 February the ACE was 'chopped' to the command of the 3rd Marine Air Wing (3 MAW).

The Cobras arrive

When MAG-29 (the 'War Eagles') arrived in the Iraqi theatre of operations it became one of 3 MAW's five flying groups; along with MAG-11 (F/A-18, KC-130), MAG-13 (AV-8B), MAG-16 (CH-46E, CH-53E) and MAG-39 (AH-1W, UH-1N, CH-53E). The 3rd MAW was headquartered at Al Jaber airbase, in Kuwait. Just to give some idea of the scale

of Marine Corps air power deployed for Operation Iraqi Freedom, the commander of 3 MAW could call on five EA-6Bs, 60 F/A-18s, 68 AV-8Bs, 54 AH-1Ws, 27 UH-1Ns, 48 CH-53Es, 54 CH-46Es and 18 KC-130s. Between MAG-29 and MAG-39 the Marines deployed three numbered AH-1W squadrons to Iraq, although these 'squadrons' (with 27 AH-1Ws and UH-1Ns) were far larger than regular units, and bore no resemblance to the typical HML/A detachment for a typical Marine Expeditionary Unit cruise which usually numbers about six AH-1Ws. HML/A-269, the single East Coast squadron, brought 18 AH-1Ws and nine UH-1Ns to Iraq, with 22 aircraft forward-deployed.

Marine Cobras were involved during the latter stages of Operation Enduring Freedom, the campaign to remove the Taliban regime from Afghanistan and to hunt down al-Qaeda terrorists. On 25 November 2001 Cobras from the 15th MEU(SOC) aboard USS Peleliu (LHA 5, above) and the 26th MEU(SOC) aboard USS Bataan (LHD 5) escorted CH-53Es moving Marines ashore to Camp Rhino, a forward base set up at the remote Dolangi airfield to the west of Kandahar. Able to take KC-130s and (later) C-17s, Camp Rhino provided a base from which Marine ground elements could move out into the surrounding areas, under cover of Cobras and fixed-wing aircraft. On their third day ashore the Marines were threatened by a Taliban vehicle convoy moving towards Dolangi, Cobras joining US Navy F-14s and F/A-18s in the ensuing action. In early December the 15th MEU moved to Kandahar airport.

Left and above left: Two views show AH-1Ws assigned to HMM-165 departing from USS Bonhomme Richard (LHD 6) on 4 March 2002. At the time the 13th MEU(SOC)'s Aviation Combat Element was undertaking missions in support of Operation Anaconda, the major US effort to round up and eliminate a major pocket of Taliban/al-Qaeda resistance in the Shah-i-Kot Valley in eastern Afghanistan. Between 4 and 26 March, HMM-165's five Cobras fired 28 TOWs, 42 Hellfires, 450 rockets and 9,300 20-mm rounds in the course of 217 Anaconda missions.

While an SH-60 approaches in the background, three AH-1Ws from HML/A-269 are seen after landing on USS *Saipan* (LHA 2) on 13 January 2003 while the vessel sailed off the North Carolina coast. At the time *Saipan* was embarking elements of the II MEB ACE in preparation for the voyage to the Persian Gulf for operations against Iraq, a journey which began on 18 January. Task Force Tarawa passed through the Straits of Hormuz and into the war zone on 14 February.

AH-1Ws from HML/A-269 prepare to depart from *Saipan* on 18 March 2003. On this day the squadron sent a detachment of Cobras to a forward operating base (TAA Coyote) in Kuwait, in preparation for the opening of the ground assault on Iraq (G-Day). AH-1Ws were involved from the very start of the war, supporting Marines as they forged into the Rumaylah oilfields, encountering resistance from the start. As well as operations from the tactical assembly area, AH-1s flew from the assault carriers, transiting to the forward operating base at Jalibah (codenamed Riverfront). The second and third days saw the Cobras supporting British forces around Basrah, and the Marines as they pushed up towards An Nasiriyah.

On 18 March HML/A-269 detached 10 AH-1Ws and two UH-1Ns to TAA (tactical assembly area) Coyote, a point in Kuwait about 35 km (22 miles) south of the Iraqi border. The days leading up to the war were lived in fear of an Iraqi missile attack. Months later, back in the US, one pilot recalled watching a CSS-3 missile fly "right over our heads." Another remembered, "the Patriots hit a missile right above us, you could follow the trail of used Atropine injectors to the bunkers."

The squadron was preparing for its first mission, an attack on Iraqi forward reconnaissance positions at Safwan. The plan was to use the AH-1Ws to support the insertion of Marines in CH-46Es onto high ground known as Safwan Hill, following an air strike by Marine Hornets and Harriers. The raid was planned for the evening of 20 March but it did not go as expected. The F/A-18 attacks, using 20 JDAMs, obliterated the Iraqi positions and there was so much smoke and flying debris that it proved impossible to fast-rope in the troops as intended – the CH-46Es 'browned out' in the dirt and sand on four successive attempts. The cue for the troop assault was to have been a napalm strike by the Harriers, but in the end there was nothing left for the Harriers to drop on. Nine hours later the troops were inserted, covered by four AH-1Ws.

However, combat operations by AH-1Ws on 20/21 March 2003 did see one very notable achievement for the Cobras – the first combat launch of the first AGM-114N thermobaric Hellfire. The missiles were fired by an HML/A-269 crew and the squadron was able to get its

hands on the brand-new (and hitherto classified) missiles because its CO, Lt Col Hewlett, was one of the few people who knew that they even existed. Just prior to taking charge of the 'Gunrunners', Hewlett had held a senior post in Marine weapons development and had been closely involved with the work on the new thermobaric warhead. Hewlett knew that the AGM-114N Advanced Technology Demonstration programme had produced 60 'residual' weapons, all sitting in a storage facility and ready for use.

Among all the soldiers in Iraq was a very real fear that combat would descend into street-by-street and house-by-house fighting. The thermobaric (TB) Hellfire had been designed precisely for this kind of warfare. The Marines already realised that standard Hellfire warheads could go in through the front of a building and straight out through the back without scratching enemy troops standing on the other side of the room. They were also discovering that the new blast/fragmentation warhead of the AGM-114M variant was not sufficient to "kill buildings dead", as one AH-1W pilot put it.

The US Navy would not ship the AGM-114Ns to Iraq because they had not been certified for carriage by ship. Instead, the Marines turned to the US Air Force, which flew the missiles in straight away. HML/A-269's plan had been to keep the precious few TB Hellfires for the final show-down in Baghdad, but they also wanted something on film to prove that the missiles worked. The Secretary of Defense himself was known to be taking a personal interest in the efficacy of the TB Hellfire and the Safwan attacks showed that it worked right out of the box.

During the course of the war about 10 or 15 AGM-114Ns were used, and HMLA-267 did shoot some against targets in Baghdad. One Cobra guy recalled, "there was sniper fire coming from a building, a big building. We shot it and the damn thing just collapsed." The HML/A-269 pilot who fired the first AGM-114N in combat noted, "most of the targets we hit demanded a blast/frag warhead because they were buildings or structures of some kind – unconventional Hellfire targets. But what we found was that if you fired a Hellfire at a brick or clay building you could see something happen inside, but we wanted to take the whole thing down. Rockets and TOW had pretty much the same effect, so we really needed the AGM-114N. It would have been good to have at An Nasiriyah."

Push into Iraq

On G-Day, 21 March, three US armoured formations pushed into Iraq. The Army's 3rd Infantry Division (3 ID) took the western route following Route 8, the combined 5th and 7th Marine Divisions took the central route using Route 1 and the 1st Marine Division went east along Route 7. Aviation operations were supported from a main joint forward operating base at Jalibah, known as FARP (forward air refuelling point) Riverfront, about 135 nm (250 km) from the AH-1W's jumping off point aboard the USS *Saipan*. JFOB Jalibah was home to the Marines' 'expeditionary maintenance' teams. HML/A-269's Cobras managed to maintain an 80 per cent operational readiness thanks to the unceasing work of their ground crew. All of the work was conducted outdoors, with zero facilities. Eight engines were changed in the field using just forklifts and tool boxes. Other major component exchanges included turrets, main rotor blades and rotor hubs.

A vital early objective was the capture of the southern Rumaylah oil fields. Colonel Hewlett says his aircraft went "hell bent for election across the border on G-Day to take the strategic oil fields." HML/A-269 flew 31 AH-1W sorties (and 21 UH-1N sorties) in support of Marine ground units on the first day of the war. From the opening hours of the fighting Cobra crews say they encountered Iraqi troops who would hold up their hands in surrender and then fire on the helicopters as soon as they had passed. The Rules of Engagement (RoE) at the outset of the campaign were very strict when it came to the destruction of Iraqi military vehicles and equipment – all were to be spared for use by the reconstituted Iraqi armed forces after the war. Lt Col Hewlett remembers, "we found that to be a bad idea. The RoEs said 'don't hit abandoned materiel', but you'd fly past a ZPU-4 AA position and then a few clicks later there'd be tracer coming up at you. After three of four days we began working with the ground FACs (forward air controllers) to destroy pretty much everything we saw."

While the Army's 3 ID sped north in the western desert, moving unopposed for six days, the Marines found themselves fighting all the way from the moment they crossed the border. On 22 March AH-1Ws were detached to support British forces in the capture of Basrah airport. HML/A-269 flew 91 Cobra missions that day alone.

The fight for An Nasiriyah

The first black day for the Marines in Iraq came on 23 March, when the lead units reached An Nasiriyah. The town sat between two waterways and stood as a potentially lethal bottleneck across the route north. The Marines of Task Force Tarawa planned to sweep east, avoiding most of the built-up areas and bypassing any possible resistance. Instead, the Marines met with heavy and determined fire that had not been anticipated. Capturing the two vital bridges became critical and AH-1Ws and armed UH-1Ns were cycled relentlessly through close air support (CAS) missions all day long as the Marines suffered Iraqi fire and started to take more and more casualties.

HML/A-269 flew 138 AH-1W sorties that day and eight of its aircraft were damaged by small arms, AAA (anti aircraft artillery) and MANPADS fire (man-portable air defence systems – shoulder-launched SAMs). That was not all the troops had to contend with. First a Marine Amtrak was hit by Iraqi RPG fire and then one of the USAF A-10s that were closely engaged in the battle fired on a company of Marines, causing 23 casualties. It was the most costly blue-on-blue incident of the war, and another desperate lesson in the perils of CAS.

Lt Col Hewlett remembers 23 March as a day like no other, "When we reached An Nasiriyah and attempted to cross the Saddam Canal we found that the ground had

been flooded with sewage, four tanks got stuck, then the Amtraks all got stuck. We spent the whole day cycling Cobra two-ships in and out to protect those guys. We were flying combat air patrols for the stuck company. Then Charlie Company took friendly fire from the A-10s, that cost 23 Marines. All the time the Cobras are taking heavy 37-mm and 57-mm fire. Several of the guys called MANPADS shots, but maybe they were RPGs.

"What we did learn is that the AAR-47 is a champ, it really works. Only seven out of 18 Cobras had it fitted but it was reassuring to hear it go 'bip, bip, bip' and then see the expendables come off. All the time you are looking at buildings and the windows are blinking at you. Constant gunfire. When we flew back to the FOB we'd land and check for holes and then go back. We'd been up since 5 am." The toughness of the Cobra airframe was proven once more when an aircraft took a 23-mm round straight through one of its rotor blades. The shell left a hole the size of a cricket ball in the leading edge, but the crew stayed on station for another four hours before flying 40 nm (74 km) back to the FOB.

Marine Corps Cobras spent virtually all of Operation Iraqi Freedom in the air and under fire – yet this is not reflected in any loss statistics. Marine Corps sources state that of the 54 AH-1Ws deployed by two Marine Air Groups (MAG-29 and MAG-39), 44 aircraft sustained battle damage of some kind. Ten of HML/A-269's 27 deployed aircraft were damaged, but only one of these was not returned to the front-line within 24 hours. The East Coast squadrons had a better war than their West Coast brothers, who lost two UH-1Ns and two AH-1Ws, along with other aircraft that were forced down during operations. But the Cobras never suffered anything like the bloody nose inflicted on the Army's much-vaunted AH-64D Longbow Apaches during the now infamous Karbala engagement of 23/24 March. There, an attempted deep strike mission by 32 AH-64Ds was battered into submission by clever Iraqi tactics and the same kind of unexpected enemy fire that the Marines met at An Nasiriyah. Of the 32 Apaches involved, 31 suffered battle damage of some kind or another. One Longbow was

An AH-1W ('Fear the Reaper') from HML/A-269 prepares to take off for another close air support mission during the taking of Basrah airport by British forces on 22 March. The aircraft carries a typical mixed load of four Hellfires on the starboard wing, four TOWs on the port wing and a pair of LAU-68 seven-round rocket pods on the inboard pylons.

Another HML/A-269 Cobra is seen at a well-established refuelling point, probably FARP Riverfront at Jalibah, at an early stage in the Iraqi war. It has a 19-round rocket pod on the starboard wing, meaning that only three Hellfires can be carried. A major factor of desert operations was the effect on visibility caused by dust and sandstorms – for two days (25 and 26 March) virtually all helicopters were grounded by severe 'brown-out' conditions.

Red-shirted ordnancemen check the four AGM-114 Hellfires and seven-round LAU-68 rocket pod on an AH-1W aboard Saipan prior to the helicopter departing for the action on 27 March. This was the day the advance was resumed after two days of blinding sandstorms halted tanks in their tracks and kept most aircraft firmly on the ground. This, and the days that followed, also represented the most intensive operations of the campaign as the Marines closed on Baghdad from the southeast, heading towards what was expected to be a major setpiece battle with the Republican Guard at Al Kut. In the event, this battle never materialised, but local resistance remained fierce and the Cobras were worked extremely hard throughout the approach phase.

shot down while another was destroyed in a crash on landing. None of the crews was seriously hurt but the Army does not appear to have deployed its Apaches in a major operation for the rest of the conflict.

This experience stands in contrast to the Marines', flying an aircraft that is older and far less capable than the AH-64D. The Marine Cobras were used intensively in the close support role, against targets in built-up areas, in what was always a high-risk environment at the edge of the coalition advance. While one Marine Cobra did manage to attack a Marine tank in the early days of the fighting, no aircraft were lost to enemy action and they were highly praised by the US and British Commanders that tasked them. The Cobras never stayed still over Iraq – in fact they speeded up. Pilots went into combat believing it would be too difficult for a gunner on the ground to track a helicopter flying at about 70 kt (130 km/h), so they briefed to keep moving at this speed at all times. Combat proved even this estimate to be insufficient – more speed was needed to stay safe – and the Marines revised their tactics and flew ever faster when over exposed terrain. The US Army's OH-58D Kiowa Warriors had a similar approach. As one experienced OH-58D pilot put it, "it's all about training and adapting to your environment. You'll never catch me hovering. If you want to stay alive, you've got to keep moving."

The Marines are reluctant to point the finger at AH-64 pilots, but there is a general acknowledgement that bad tactics and inflexible battle drills are part of an Apache 'mindset' that contributed to the Karbala fiasco – poor intelligence and restrictive RoEs did not help either. Lt Col

Hewlett reflected, "We made a decision before we went to war that we were never going to hover. Ever. We went back to the lessons learned in Vietnam, where they said start at 60 kt [111 km/h] and then get faster. You have to go. Get situational awareness. Run in. Once, then out. Reattack from a different direction." Despite the huge number of sorties they were generating and the amount of hostile fire aimed at them, HML/A-269 Cobras suffered battle damage on only 15 missions – and, as noted above, only 10 aircraft were ever actually hit. All 10 aircraft were able to remain on station to complete their assigned missions. The Cobras absorbed and survived 7.62-mm, 12.7-mm and 23-mm rounds – in all a total of 27 separate hits. It is not surprising that Marine Cobra flyers have confidence in their tactics and faith in their aircraft.

Sitting out the storm

The huge storms of 25 and 26 March brought a welcome 'operational pause' for the troops, especially the exhausted Marines. The USS *Saipan*, sitting 40 miles (64 km) offshore, was covered in sand. After a week spent flying 12 or 14 hours a day, suddenly everyone in the squadron was corralled on the FOB's tiny hard stand, a space measuring 100 m x 300 m. No-one could leave the area because of the real danger of never finding their way back. Visibility was down to 5 m (16 ft), at best. There was also the risk of mines or of meeting irregular Iraqi forces. The only flying was done by two emergency Medevac UH-1Ns and one of those was lost in an accident during the diabolical weather of 26 March. The aircraft suffered an engine failure and landed in a minefield. It was badly damaged by the crash. Its crew was rescued by the second Medevac aircraft, which continued to fly Casevacs for the Division at the height of the storm. The crashed aircraft was recovered later, after it had been completely stripped by locals.

When the weather lifted the Cobras were quickly back in the air to support the push north, from 27 to 31 March. This would be the first 'big' fight for the Marines as they approached the Republican Guard Division, south of Baghdad. The Marines also encountered the remnants of the Iraqi 14th Infantry Division pulling back from An Nasiriyah. By now the tempo of operations was becoming gruelling. One senior officer described flying during those days, "We conducted armed reconnaissance 2 km in front of the lead trace. You'd find a FAC in an M1 telling you to go and have a look at a target 6 km over there, and we'd say 'no thanks'. He's sitting in a 70-tonne tank while I'm in 14,000 lb of aluminium. Something that's 6 km away is out of the box, it's no threat to us. Forget it.

"Typically we'd fly four two-ships every day, from 06:30 to 18:30. Then three two-ships at night, from about 17:00

Cobras at An Nasiriyah

Major Craig Streeter, one of HML/A-269's Cobra pilots, was at An Nasiriyah on 23 March 2003. He had been ready to launch with two other Cobras and they knew the situation around the town was getting worse. However, events forced Streeter's aircraft to transit as a singleton.

"A bad, bad thing, you never want to do that. Anyway, as soon as I came into the fight the FAC gave me the friendly/enemy sitrep – 'the enemy is everywhere' he said. I told him I was a Cobra – and he needed help. The West Coast helos had been working there all day but they'd gone by now and I ended up controlling an F/A-18 strike as a FACA (airborne FAC).

"I am FACA-qualified – the FAC on the ground (call-sign HAWK) said 'I've got two F-18s with LGBs but I can't control them. I said 'I can' and I called 'NAIL 53 and 54 I have targets for you in the tree line'. It was a tank that I had already shot at with a Hellfire, but the boresight was off so I missed. HAWK gave us the talk on. I set a laser code for the bombs, quad 1, called laser on, good spot, the bombs went in the basket and the Hornets put two LGBs on the tank position. Now, my Dash 2 and Dash 3 [the other two Cobras] showed up with fuel, and I had none. They started fighting as a section. Then the CO and another Cobra showed up and 45 minutes later I'm back too. I jumped into the CO's section, and there we were all shooting at the tree-line. Five Snakes in action together, all before lunch.

"We were routinely shooting TOWs inside 500 m [1,640 ft], then it was down to 150 m [492 ft] and then out to 3750 m [12,300 ft]. I had shot a Hellfire earlier because the TOW wasn't working, and when the boresight is off you've just got to

sit there and recycle the laser boresighting system, that takes anywhere between one and three minutes. There was a MANPADS call 'SAM in the air, flares, flares, flares'. There were five Cobras racetracking and every single one had flares going, all at once.

"For 'round three' at An Nasiriyah, from about 13:00 onwards, we were flying two-hour missions, then getting gas for 45 minutes, then back to the fight. There wasn't so much

shooting this time, we were doing a lot of visual reconnaissance, but we were prepared to run and shoot if called. The FACs were down with the ground units, they were the guys giving out the trade. You'd show up, call 'MOUTH this is DEADLY 41', tell him what fuel you had and then he'd tell you to go and check out that building, then maybe you'd jump across to escort some 'Frogs' (CH-46s), then do a recce, then CAS, then escort, then radio relay." Squadron CO Lt Col Hewlett said with a laugh, "We never had a nine-line brief once."

to 06:30. The nights were long, and you can't recover on goggles [the Marines flew with ANVIS-9 night vision goggles]. Dusk and dawn were the worst times for NVGs, when it was too dark to see but too light to use the goggles effectively. We made tremendous use of the approved performance-maintaining drugs [Dexadrine, Restoril], for the first time by helicopter pilots. A 5-mg dose was extremely effective and we had a set limit of three per day."

Maximum intensity operations

The daily routine in this phase of the war seemed unbearable. "For the advance," says another Cobra pilot, "we were flying four sections by day and three by night. We had aircraft that stayed running for 48 hours non-stop. All we did was put new pilots, more fuel and more weapons in them. You'd fly two days on and one day off, but it was not unusual to spend 24 hours in an aircraft over a two-day period. You could have a nine or 10-hour day spent fighting from 3 or 4 in the morning. Then you'd get back, debrief, sleep – but by 11 am it's already 100° so you're not sleeping. Then at 14:00 or 15:00 you're up, brief and then go again." There were no crew rest facilities or even tents to sleep in. Most crews slept in hammocks strung between the skids and the stub wings. After the war, another AH-1W flyer recalled. "I flew 140 hours in 30 days and 100 of those were under goggles. We probably couldn't have kept it up much longer. We were at maximum sustain rate. We were worn out."

Even getting in and out of the Cobra – never an easy task – was complicated by the war. The forward fuselage is only 3 ft (1 m) wide so the small cockpit is a very tight fit. Major Craig Streeter, a pilot with HML/A-269, recalled how having to fight in the Cobra made 'putting it on' each time much more difficult. "We flew with so much gear, and in the Cobra there's really only room to slide a map down between you and the side of the cockpit. But for each mission we had to cope with body armour, NVGs, back-up NVGs, NBC kit, our 'hit-and-run' survival bag … we had to have packing drills to figure out how to get the maximum amount of stuff in with us."

Since 22 March 15 AH-1Ws had been based at JFOB Jalibah (Riverfront). As the US forces moved further and further north the lines of communication to Riverfront became stretched and it was necessary to set up new FARPs closer to the action. At locations anywhere between 100

The provision of FARPs (forward air refuelling points) was vital to the ability of the Cobras to rearm and refuel rapidly, and thereby maintain almost continuous close air support coverage for the ground forces. These two views show an AH-1W rearming on 14 April at a FARP established by MWSS (Marine Wing Support Squadron)-373 near Tikrit, on the day that Task Force Tripoli took Saddam Hussein's home town.

Below: On their way home from the warzone, HML/A-269 Cobras aboard Kearsarge provided back-up for President Bush's visits to Egypt and Jordan.

and 120 miles (160 and 193 km) further in-country, new FARPs were established – all named after baseball parks (like Fenway, Camden and Wrigley). It was a simple equation – without the FARPS there were no helicopters. The Marines who ran the FARPS worked far harder than any air

Two AH-1Ws assigned to HMM-264 'Black Knights' operate with dummy AIM-9 Sidewinder missiles in March 2003 during the deployment to the Arabian Sea to support Enduring Freedom operations in Afghanistan. HMM-264 was based aboard the US Navy's newest amphibious assault vessel, USS Iwo Jima (LHD 7), which was undertaking its maiden deployment.

The attack on the USS Cole in Yemen demonstrated a new threat to US Navy vessels: attacks by terrorists in small boats. As a counter, armed Cobras are put on alert when ships transit through choke points, such as this AH-1W aboard USS Kearsarge as the ship transits the Strait of Gibraltar on its return from Iraq.

crew and provided everything from bullets to water to a place to sleep, all the time working under enemy fire.

HML/A-269's Lt Col Hewlett had nothing but praise for the FARP teams, "they would leapfrog in front of us, by as much as 80 miles [130 km], set up and they'd always be where they'd told us they'd be. In a Cobra you can be 'Winchester' (out of ammunition) in 10 minutes but still have two hours of fuel on board. Without the FARPs we'd have spent a lot of time out of the fight. The Cobras like to use JP-5, but we can burn anything. You'd see the C-130s from VMGR-234 that were delivering the fuel landing at night under NVGs, all blacked up and then reversing 5,000 or 6,000 ft along roads with tracer rounds being shot at them. Hasty FARPs were essential too. Even when prepared sites weren't ready we could radio down to a convoy and have them set up a hasty FARP so that we could land right beside the fuel trucks."

By 1 April the Marines had reached Al Kut, but the expected battle with the Republican Guard failed to materialise. "There was nothing left of them when we got there," remarked Hewlett. Between 1 and 3 April the 1st Marine Division (1 MARDIV) finished off what was left of the Iraqi forces and pushed on through An Numiniyah towards Baghdad. The Cobras flew 146 sorties over those three days. As had happened before, however, things

suddenly changed the next day. On 4 April 1 MARDIV encountered greatly increased resistance from irregular and paramilitary forces along Route 6 into the capital city. Both the AH-1Ws and UH-1Ns flew a mass of CAS sorties (101 and 53, respectively) to clear the way forward for ground troops. In the course of the fighting eight AH-1Ws were hit and damaged by enemy fire, two were forced down and one HML/A-267 aircraft (FAZER 43) was destroyed in a collision with a pylon – both its crew were killed. The Cobra crews describe the event as a planned ambush in treacherous flying conditions caused by smoke from the burning oil trenches around Baghdad, the nearby oil refinery and concealed wires and towers.

Storming Baghdad

The 'battle for Baghdad' lasted four days from 8 to 12 April. The US Army's 3 ID took Baghdad International Airport on 9 April and then launched its 'thunder run' into the heart of the city. Meanwhile, 1 MARDIV encircled the capital and entered from the east. The supporting helicopters encountered intense small arms and AAA fire and gave stand-off fire support because of the threat. Once it became clear that Baghdad was not going to become another Stalingrad, as everyone had feared, the Marines repositioned their aviation forces to make the jump further north to Tikrit. Beginning on 11 April, MAG-26 redeployed to Salman Pak East airbase, near Baghdad (known as Yankee FARP). HML/A-269 deployed 10 AH-1Ws and four UH-1Ns and got ready to support the next phase of the campaign – the advance along Route 2. The Marines established a new manoeuvre unit, Task Force Tripoli, to take on the job of tackling Saddam Hussein's home town. The squadron's AH-1Ws flew 258 sorties over the next 11 days.

"It was supposed to be an Army mission," said Lt Col Hewlett, "but they said they couldn't do it for another two weeks, so Task Force Tripoli went to Tikrit. We headed down that four-lane highway with the AH-1Ws capping overhead a Marine force of LAVs. The Cobras would call incoming vehicles for the ground troops and the LAVs would try and skip 7.62-mm rounds in front of the vehicles so that the guys inside would stop and get out. In one incident the LAVs were shooting at Iraqis that were shooting back, and they called up to the Cobras 'did we get them?' 'No' said our guys, and five seconds later they started taking rounds through the cockpit.

"On another occasion we were flying at night when we spotted two pickups driving at high speed with no lights, but following each other at a distance of about 20 ft. That was our Task Force 20 [special operations] guys driving with NVGs."

The mechanised units of TF Tripoli arrived at Tikrit on 13 April and within 24 hours the town had been taken by US forces. HML/A-269 flyers recall that on the first day they were taking heavy fire from Iraqi positions on Tikrit South airfield, but by 14 April they held the airfield which had been turned into an operational FARP, named for pilot Ben Sammis who had been killed on 4 April. The Cobra crews were particularly pleased with the footage of their aircraft, dripping with Hellfires, that appeared on CNN's coverage of the 'Taking of Tikrit'.

One final event that several crews all remember was the discovery and destruction of a huge ammunition dump near Tikrit. One pilot described the scene, "We found this expanse of camouflage netting and we thought 'what the hell's under there?' – because those dudes didn't camouflage jack. I pushed the rotor blades towards and under the netting, to blow it all back, and we found about 350 or 400 Roland missiles, all just sitting there. That was the last target to be attacked in Iraq. We took seven aircraft and fired about 100 PGMs into that place, plus it was hit by 25 or 30 fixed-wing aircraft too. On NVGs it was like *Die Hard 3*. There were huge explosions reaching up to 12,000 and 15,000 ft."

By 20 April the fighting was done and units had already begun to pull out of the Jalibah FOB (Riverfront) to the USS *Saipan*. MAG-29 helicopter assets, including six AH-1Ws, moved to Blair Field, at Al Kut (a FARP named for a Marine killed in action near An Nasiriyah). The Cobras and other helicopters flew security patrols over the areas still occupied by TF Tarawa until 15 May. On 29 May the first batch of HML/A-269's AH-1Ws embarked aboard the USS *Kearsarge* to begin the return journey home. Unfortunately for the Marines the squadron was then reassigned to support operations in Liberia, where civil strife had broken out. Eventually, the Cobra crews got home in June.

During the war HML/A-269's Cobras – it took 18 to Iraq in total – fired 334 Hellfires, 345 TOWs, 5,665 2.75-in rockets and 64,106 rounds of 20-mm ammunition. The squadron's nine UH-1Ns disposed of 107,787 0.50-cal bullets and 119,891 7.62-mm rounds. The squadron claimed 697 tactical targets destroyed, including 47 T-55s, nine T-62s and 34 T-72s, 77 APCs, 47 S-69 AA guns, 65 ZU/ZPU AA guns, 25 missile positions (SAMs), 82 artillery positions, 20 mortar sites, 156 cars/trucks/'technicals', plus buildings, bunkers and storage sites. About 30 or 40 per cent of those targets were manned, says Hewlett. "While

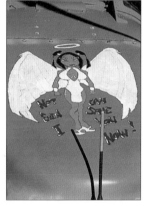

we were out there we were duelling with 37-mm SPAAGs (self-propelled anti-aircraft guns), we killed FROGS and Ababils (short-range surface-to-surface missiles), we hit SA-2s and SA-3s and nailed a couple of helicopters on the deck. I spotted an Su-25 on the ground at Tikrit but when I went back for it, it had gone. The Iraqi air force was hiding in the streets of northern Baghdad. We saw at least four MiG-29s under cover, but we were not allowed to engage them."

Cobra tactics

Marine Cobra tactics were to fly in two-ship formations (sections) or four-ships (divisions). Typically the East Coast crews flew sections while the West Coasters flew divisions. Hewlett's view was, "I didn't see any targets that required four Cobras. It's a bad use of (scarce) assets, and if we go away (to rearm and refuel) we'll only be gone an hour. We didn't have to cover the entire country, we were only needed where the fighting was, so we conquered Iraq within 200 m (650 ft) of the MSRs (main supply routes)." From 20 March to 13 May HML/A-269's 18 AH-1Ws flew a total of 1,957 combat hours, while the nine UH-1Ns flew 951 hours. The squadron always had a minimum of 12 AH-1Ws and six UH-1Ns available throughout the conflict (an 80 percent mission capable rate). The Cobras averaged 36 flight hours per day. Throughout all that time the unit had no personnel losses to enemy action or mishaps.

Each day that they went out, the Cobra crews had to load up weapons with their best guess of what the threat would be. Major Streeter explained, "TOW gives you a

As has become traditional in wartime, many AH-1Ws committed to operations in Iraqi Freedom sprouted nose art, as displayed by these HML/A-269 aircraft. The squadron was one of the principal participants in the operation, dispatching 18 aircraft (out of a total Cobra force of 54). During the operation three AH-1s were lost, but these losses were lighter than could be expected given the type of operations in which the Cobras were involved, and compared favourably with the US Army's experience with its better equipped AH-64s. The answer, it would appear, lay in the tactics involved, the Marines attacking their targets while moving at speed. In a battlefield where guns and even RPGs represented as big a threat as SAMs, hovering was off the agenda as far as the Marines were concerned.

And yet, the AH-1W had a good war. The aircraft and crews gave exemplary service and always fulfilled their mission of flying and fighting with their troops on the ground. One pilot commented, "The Cobra is great to fly and so durable. If a target needs shooting, you can shoot it in a Cobra. The whole air/ground thing works so well in the Marines. We are so close to the grunts, we understand fire support. We live, eat and breathe it." The Cobras were often called on to fly ISR (intelligence, security and reconnaissance) missions – in other words, scout flying – but this did not always prove to be a good idea. Although it is a classic Cobra role, in Iraq the crews knew that if their helicopters were pushed too far forward of the lead ground elements they became vulnerable to hostile fire.

Maintaining the bubble

Lt Col Hewlett had no doubts about what the Cobras needed to do, "Our job was to maintain a 2-km bubble around the troops as they headed up the MSRs. Outside that it was Indian country. Don't go there. I should stress that that was true for the day only. At night things were much better and we didn't need to fly down low where it gets dangerous." Pilots knew never to fly in a straight line, never to follow linear features and never fly predicable routings. Because of the pace at which CAS missions were being flown, hot-reloading skills became essential and the Cobras will now spend more time practising this at home than ever before. New skills in urban CAS planning have to be developed and new tactics to work out the split between Section and Division flying will have to be considered.

The war in Iraq also highlighted the deficiencies that everyone knows exist in the AH-1W, and that everyone is waiting to be fixed in the AH-1Z. Chief among these are the aircraft's archaic sensor fit and its compromised payload/range capability. Even when conditions are at their best it can take valuable time and some real operator skill to locate and identify targets using the Cobra's NTS sight. Also, because of the gross weight limitations on the AH-1W, pilots are frustrated by their inability to carry all the weapons that they should, in theory, be able to hang on their helicopters.

Lt Col Hewlett explained, "Our number one problem is the (FLIR) sensor in the nose. Right now we have to close to small arms range to visually ID a BMP, theirs, or a LAV, ours. With the Zulu we will have an 8- to 10-km stand-off range instead of the 800- to 1000-m that we have now. In Iraq a vast amount of the ID work we did was visual, using NVGs. You'd look with the goggles, mark the position and then try with the FLIR again. If it's a nice night then maybe you can break out an image by 800 m [2,625 ft]. By day the TV camera is fine. I can look out to 6 or 7 km and ID things. But at night it's no good. When the Zulu enters service we'll have a lot more fuel and a third-generation FLIR. At the moment an AH-1W can carry enough fuel to stay airborne for 1.8 hours. With the Zulu that will climb to 2.7 hours. All the wing stations have a universal interface, the Whiskey only has two stations for PGMs (the outboard hardpoints, Nos 1 and 4). With the Zulu we'll be able to carry 16 Hellfires, although you'd probably never want to."

Above: Nearly 40 years after it entered service with the USMC the AH-1 Cobra is still a highly potent vehicle, as displayed by its 'star' appearance in Iraqi Freedom. The conflict represented an ideal environment for the current warfighting doctrine of the Marines in general, and the Cobra in particular: a fast and fluid battlefield with a mix of 'hard' and fleeting 'soft' targets, many of which would pop up unexpectedly to threaten the advancing forces, requiring immediate action from the escorting helicopters.

Above right: For several years Marine AH-1Ws have had a meaningful anti-aircraft capability thanks to the AIM-9 Sidewinder, although no other ordnance can be carried on the wing when it is fitted. The missile is carried on an LAU-7 launch rail which could also launch the AGM-122 Sidearm anti-radiation derivative when it was still in the inventory.

close-in warm and fuzzy feeling, but Hellfire gives you stand-off. In practice we always kept the TOWs and Hellfires on there because it's too much trouble to reboresight the stations. Ninety-nine per cent of the time the debate was over rockets – do you carry HE, or flechettes or both? We fired more PGMs as the war progressed. In the early days we shot more from the hip – rocket, rocket, shoot, run. The gun has reliability issues. In my experience it jammed about 35 per cent of the time, which is not good. In fact, the more you shoot the gun the more problems it has. We had problems with the rockets too – just one of those things I guess. The ground guys would always fix it, but it took a lot of trouble-shooting. It was very rare to go out with everything working. I had a go/no go line – if 80 per cent of my helicopter was working I was still in the fight. "

The threat of NBC (nuclear, biological, chemical) warfare was a constant for all the deployed coalition forces. The Cobra crews were not always happy about their ability to cope with an NBC battlefield. The directives on NBC posture were widely felt to be confusing and the effect of wearing protective gear in the desert environment had dangerous heat and fatigue implications. Pilots were already carrying a large amount of equipment into the cramped cockpits of the Cobras, and to this had to be added NBC protective gear for the air and for the ground. If the Cobras did find themselves flying through contaminated areas no-one quite knew what the effect of bringing a 'dirty' aircraft into a 'clean' FARP might be – and everyone knew that the NBC detection equipment available to them was substandard.

Another OIF veteran agreed, "Right now we have 1980s technology and a borderline Gen II FLIR. At night, on a good night, you might be able to see a tank at 5 km, but those perfect conditions just don't exist and in Iraq we were lucky if we could see things at 2 km. We would fix the FLIR to look straight ahead, set the rad alt [radar altimeter] at 300 ft and just go."

Cobra pilots are also looking to the Zulu to fix the cockpit interface problems that have built up in the AH-1W over the years. One pilot spoke for them all, saying "It has very poor human engineering, you have to toggle too many switches and really be a contortionist to get ready for the fight. For example, you can't actually see the switch for the defensive aids system. You have to reach over and feel for it. Forget to flip another switch and that's it – no weapons. There are too many black boxes in the back seat. There's the AIM-9 controls, the RWR, the HUD – it all blocks your view. The forward visibility is also impaired, so instead of flying anywhere nose on, you have to weave so that you can see to get there." While every AH-1W pilot loves their aircraft, all are waiting for the AH-1Z and it can't come too soon.

AH-1Z: the 'Zulu Cobra'

For an aircraft that entered service as an 'interim solution', the AH-1 still has a big future ahead of it. Built-up from the current baseline twin-engined AH-1W configuration but incorporating a host of new technology, the AH-1Z – the Zulu – is the Cobra for the 21st Century. The AH-1Z is at the heart of the US Marine Corps' aviation rotary-winged modernisation plans (along with the similarly upgraded UH-1Y) and it is also on offer to several prospective export customers, including Turkey and Taiwan. Despite the radical differences between it and its predecessors, the Zulu will share the same name as the AH-1W. To the Marine Corps it will be the AH-1Z SuperCobra.

Colonel Doug Isleb, the Marine Corps H-1 Upgrade Program Manager, described his new helicopter thus, "It will be a much more effective warfighting platform. We will do all the same missions, but we'll do them better. With the sensor, we are going from one of the worst fielded to what is probably the best. We can carry more weapons and payload so we can find the opposition, identify them from further away and shoot more of them. The biggest problem with the AH-1W is the cockpit, there's too much management and not enough fighting. With the Zulu's digital integrated systems and helmet-mounted sight, day or night the crew is going to be heads-up and fighting."

Designs for an improved aircraft that embodied many of the features of today's AH-1Z have been around for a long time, and have had many names. Back in December 1979 Bell flew its Model 249 – essentially an AH-1S airframe fitted with the four-bladed rotor system that had been developed for the Model 412. This aircraft, the Cobra II demonstrator, made its international debut at the 1980 Farnborough air show. The Cobra II would have offered full Hellfire capability with a new targeting system and improved engines. Bell suggested that the changes could be incorporated in the ongoing AH-1S upgrade programme but the Army decided instead to invest its resources in the LHX competition that spawned the RAH-66 Comanche. The Cobra II was then offered for the Advanced Scout Helicopter requirement but was beaten by the OH-58D.

There was also a Cobra 2000 proposal that had some key elements of the Zulu design, such as T700 engines and the four-bladed rotor. The Marine Corps was attracted by the performance offered by a four-bladed Cobra, but again there was no funding to support the programme. Bell persevered and offered the Cobra to Germany as a rival to the PAH-2 design that eventually gave birth to the Eurocopter Tiger. The Model 249 remained in service as a test aircraft only, but plans for a four-bladed Cobra never went away.

In 1993 the UK's Army Air Corps issued a tender for a new attack helicopter. Bell, together with UK prime contractor GEC-Marconi Avionics (now BAE Systems), offered the British an aircraft very similar to what became the AH-1Z – the CobraVenom. Based on the AH-1W airframe, the CobraVenom would have been a fully modernised, twin-engined, new-build aircraft. It had redesigned stub wings with four 'smart' pylons that were

At present the gun of the AH-1Z remains the same A/A49E-7(V4) system with M197 20-mm cannon, despite its acknowledged jamming problems. The weapon can be operated in three modes: in the fixed mode the gun fires directly ahead, aimed by the pilot manoeuvring the helicopter; in IHSS mode the gun is slaved to the helmet-mounted sight; and in TS/Gun mode the gun is slaved to the sight's auto-tracking system. The gun fires at 650 rounds per minute, and can fire a maximum of 450 rounds in a single burst, after which it must cool for six minutes.

Right: The third NAH-1Z poses with its maximum missile load of 16 AGM-114 Hellfires plus two AIM-9 Sidewinders.

Below: Designated NAH-1Z, the no. 1 Zulu is seen in the hangar at Patuxent River. This aircraft lacks the avionics suite. Note the test air data probe in front and temporary low-speed air data boom.

each capable of carrying Hellfires or TOWs, along with the Brimstone anti-armour missile. It was hoped that the new fully-integrated digital avionics suite designed by GMAv would also be adopted by the US Marines, as part of an integrated weapons system upgrade then being contemplated for the AH-1W. In June 1995 the CobraVenom design was revised to include the four-bladed rotor system, but in July the AH-64D was announced as the winner of the UK competition. The CobraVenom proposal had many fans within the AAC and the work done on that design translated directly into the AH-1Z programme, which was officially launched in 1996.

The Marines had long been looking at how they could field a credible battlefield helicopter fleet into the 2010 timeframe and beyond. The answer lay in a joint upgrade path for both the AH-1W and the UH-1N. On 15 November 1996 the USMC signed the contract with Bell Helicopter that launched its H-1 Upgrade Program. The aim was to remanufacture the existing fleet of AH-1Ws and UH-1Ns into 180 AH-1Zs and 100 UH-1Ys. The USMC inventory, circa 2001, included 194 AH-1Ws and 96 UH-1Ns. The USMC will get 'zero-time' airframes (good for 10,000 hours), with integrated avionics systems and glass cockpits, along with four-bladed rotors and upgraded drive trains that are common to both aircraft. The AH-1Z (and UH-1Y) is expected to deliver dramatic performance improvements, including increased range, payload and speed, plus increased ballistic tolerance and crash survivability. The two upgraded aircraft are expected to have 84 per cent identical major components (said to be identical down to the part numbers), including their T700-GE-401/C engines and transmission, tail unit, composite main rotor system, hydraulic and fuel system, integrated avionics and software, and crashworthy seats.

Looked at in the round, most people would describe the AH-1Z as virtually a new aircraft. Identifiable components taken from existing AH-1Ws include the (modified) tail section, engine doors and cowling, (modified) combining gearbox and the (modified) forward fuselage. Items that are found on the Whiskey but which have been newly built for the Zulu include its tail fin (plus elevators and tail stinger), a redesigned 90° offset gearbox and magnesium-free gearbox casting, improved crashworthy landing gear (capable of withstanding a 12 ft/3.6-m per second impact), the uprated rotor driveshafts, the revised upper fuselage cowling and redesigned stub wings. Neither does this list include the completely new equipment such as the rotor system and cockpits.

Key Performance Parameters (AH-1Z/UH-1Y)

KPP	Threshold	Objective
Payload (lb)	2500/2800	3500/4500
Cruise Speed (kt)	140/140	165/165
Mission Radius (nm)	110/110	200/200
Manoeuvrability (g)		
AH-1Z	-0.5 to +2.5	-0.5 to +2.5
UH-1Y	-0.5 to +2.5	-0.5 to +2.5

By the end of 2003 the AH-1Z had demonstrated a maximum airspeed of 222 kt (411 km/h) and 160 kt (296 km/h) in the cruise, while the UH-1Y had reached a maximum of 190 kt (352 km/h) and was cruising at 166 kt (307 km/h).

There are five development aircraft in NAVAIR's joint test flight programme, underway at NAS Patuxent River.

Airframe	MSN	Reissued BuNo.	Former BuNo.	First Flight
AH-1Z (Z1)	59001	166477	162549	7 December 2000
AH-1Z (Z2)	59002	166478	163933	4 October 2002
AH-1Z (Z3)	59003	166479	162532	26 August 2002

Aircraft Z3 was the first production AH-1W

UH-1Y (Y1)	55001	166475	160446	7 July 2002
UH-1Y (Y2)	55002	166476	159193	20 September 2002

From 1996 to 2003 the AH-1Z programme was essentially a research and development effort. The first aircraft to fly (Z1, at Fort Worth) had the airframe and drive train of a Zulu, but none of the advanced avionics. The programme's early years were hit with problems and delays that brought cost overruns and schedule slippages. Difficulties encountered by the H-1 team included cracking in the vertical stabiliser and issues with the main rotor blade, yoke, hydraulic system, manufacturing tooling and the integrated avionics systems. Bell also had to re-assess the amount of material that would be reused in each rebuild, while still trying to keep to the target per helicopter. The original plan called for an LRIP start in FY03 (meaning before October

2003) with aircraft in operational service by FY06. By May 2001 the low-rate initial production date had been pushed back by a year. Then, the number of aircraft in the EMD (engineering manufacturing and development) phase was cut by three to try and balance the budget. To smooth things along all five aircraft moved from Bell facilities to NAVAIR's home at NAS Patuxent River, Maryland, where the test effort is being supported by a combined contractor and government team.

By the second half of 2003, the programme was in a 'design reconfiguration' phase. Only one example (Zulu 1) was in flight test, at that time evaluating a new moving stabiliser. The two additional test AH-1Zs and UH-1Ys had been stripped down to be fitted with the new avionics suites. The OT-IIA and OT-IIB operational assessment phases, to include live-fire trials, were set for completion in time for operational evaluation in late 2004. On 23 October 2003 the Defense Acquisition Board approved Lot 1 low-rate initial production (LRIP) for the H-1 Upgrade Programme. This was a major triumph for the project (worth about $6.2 billion in its entirety) which had come close to cancellation on several occasions. The DAB gave the go-ahead for the remanufacture of three AH-1Ws to AH-1Z standard during FY04, along with six UH-1Ys. The Lot 2 LRIP batch, another three AH-1Zs and six UH-1Ys, should enter production in FY05. Full rate production is expected to commence with the subsequent Lot 3 order.

Service entry schedule

The Marines hope to begin training operations with the first batch of upgraded H-1 aircraft in 2006 using LRIP aircraft delivered to HMT-303 at MCAF Camp Pendleton, California. Initial operating capability (IOC), defined as the first group of six AH-1Zs and three UH-1Ys capable of independent operational deployment, is hoped for 2008/09. Those aircraft will be based either at Camp Pendleton, or MCAS New River, North Carolina. Peak production rate requires 24 AH-1Ws to be upgraded annually, with final deliveries in FY14 for a goal of continued operations beyond 2020. Any export deliveries could begin around 2005.

The AH-1Z is built by Bell at Fort Worth, Texas, using new airframe assemblies that come from the company's Amarillo plant and teardown kits that have been produced from disassembled helicopters at the Cherry Point NAD. The most obvious difference between the AH-1W and the

AH-1Z is the new four-bladed main rotor. This uses all-composite blades with an elastomeric bearingless (no lubricated components) rotor head that incorporates a semi-automatic folding system. The composite head assembly takes up all the normal lead/lag and feathering functions of a helicopter rotor system, and is ballistically tolerant to a 23-mm shell impact.

The General Electric T700-GE-401 engines that power the AH-1W are retained, but they are coupled to an entirely new main transmission (and a higher output tail rotor system) that can cope with and deliver increased power levels. One Whiskey pilot describes the experience of flying his current aircraft thus, "the aircraft has power but you have to treat it gently. The engines will perform but the transmission can't handle them. You have to be very careful not to torque it out. You end up flying with an invisible hand that holds the collective down." The Zulu should solve these problems. It will also come with a new Hamilton Sundstrand APU that has its own independent gearbox. The Zulu offers an empty weight of 11,900 lb

BuNo. 162549 was the first remanufactured AH-1Z, and is seen here flying near the test centre at 'Pax' River.

The main sensor of the AH-1Z is the AAQ-30 Hawkeye Target Sighting System (TSS) turret, which completely replaces the M65/NTS of the AH-1W. This combines the very latest in FLIR technology with eye-safe lasers and a colour low-light TV, and incorporates a highly accurate auto-tracker. It can be controlled by hand grip or by the helmet-mounted sight. It can provide seeker cues for AIM-9 seeker heads.

The AH-1Z can carry the current range of Cobra ordnance, but the wingtip stations allow it to carry Sidewinders as well as other stores.

Developed by Thales, the TopOwl helmet-mounted display can project FLIR imagery as well as flight information.

'Zulu 1' prepares for a flight on 14 June 2001 with deputy commandant for Marine Aviation Lieutenant General Fred McCorkle in the front cockpit.

(5398 kg) and a maximum gross weight of 18,500 lb (8392 kg). Simply expressed, on any given mission it will offer crews either twice the range or twice the payload of the AH-1W. The AH-1W has a combat radius (out and back range) of only 70.5 km (43.8 miles).

The airframe uses a mix of conventional metal assemblies (aluminium, steel and titanium) with some composites. The tail unit is taken directly from the AH-1W, but fitted with a new 'stinger' and some structural modifications to cope with the higher loads and sink-rates that the Zulu will experience. The test programme has suffered several problems with the tail, not least the tendency for the (deflected) exhaust stream to heat-damage it. A similar problem has been faced by the Eurocopter design team. The engines are able to consistently deliver an extra 500-600 lb (2.22-2.67 kN) extra thrust, thanks to the new transmission, and this has forced the AH-1Z test team to scab on a doubler to thicken the tail skin. For the longer term an exhaust redesign is under consideration to divert the hot air flow away from the sensitive areas.

The Zulu's new longer span wing stubs look simple but are very different to those on the AH-1W. Each of the AH-1Z's pylons has a 'smart' interface (MIL-STD 1760 bus) and each wing also carries 50 US gal (189 litres) of internal fuel. The new wing assembly weighs the same as the old unit, but the centre-section airframe has been reinforced to cope with the increased loads that will be hung on the wing.

The Zulu cockpit is a radical shift away from anything that Cobra pilots have known before. Thirteen Marine pilots and an aircrew system advisory panel worked for 18 months in simulators and mock-ups to create an efficient man-machine interface. Development of the integrated avionic system (IAS) is now in the hands of Northrop Grumman, ever since NG took over the original system developer Litton. Several delays to the H-1 upgrade programme were due to problems with this very advanced mission fit, which was common to Australia's SH-2G(A) SuperSeasprites – and caused similar difficulties for that programme. The IAS operates on a MIL-STD 1553 databus, linked to a central mission computer and all the communications, navigation and mission systems. The two crew stations are dominated by a pair of 6 x 8-in (15 x 20-cm) high-resolution (640 x 480 pixel) colour liquid crystal MFDs (multi-function displays), each with a digital moving map capability. The MFDs are backed up by a smaller (4.2 x 4.2-in/10.6 x 10.6-cm) dual function display (DFD). The DFD also serves as the standby flight display if the main avionics system should fail.

TopOwl helmet

The Zulu comes with a Honeywell dual embedded GPS/INS navigation fit and a brand new helmet-mounted sight (HMS) in the shape of the French-built Thales Avionics TopOwl system. The TopOwl is a modular HMS that integrates day and night sensors. It uses an electro-magnetic head-tracking system that requires a magnetic 'map' to be produced for each aircraft cockpit so that the position of the crewmember's head can be accurately plotted. The system is already in operational service and is being fielded on at least four helicopter types (Tiger, NH-90, Rooivalk and AH-1Z) in more than 10 countries.

The basic protective helmet incorporates radio communications systems, while an add-on display module projects sensor imagery onto the visor, using integrated night vision sensors (image intensifier tubes) or aircraft FLIR, video and/or synthetic symbology. The Marines are integrating a 'virtual HUD' function on their helmets which will display flight symbology to the pilots when they are facing straight ahead, but which will 'declutter' when their heads move from side-to-side. A pointer on the display indicates where the other crewmember is looking at any given time.

At the moment the Marines have decided not to display sensor imagery on the helmet visor, seeing it as a possible safety issue. Instead they will use the helmet's own 'plug in' night vision system and keep sensor imagery on the MFDs. The HMS is also slaved to the gun and the TSS. The HMS is binocular with a 40° field of view (FoV). It is lightweight (2.2 kg/4.8 lb) and its own integral image intensifying system (that replaces conventional NVGs) provides a valuable dual-sensor capability for night flying. Thales delivered a pre-production batch of 16 TopOwls to the Marines in 2002/03 and production of the full batch of 560 helmets to support both the AH-1Z and UH-1Y began in 2004. The first flight with a TopOwl was made by a UH-1Y on 9 October 2003.

Unlike the Whiskey, the Zulu can be flown and fought from either cockpit – only the position of a few circuit breakers sets the two crew stations apart. The slick new design will come as a relief to one experienced HML/A-269 flyer who noted, "as the years have passed the ergonomics (in the AH-1W) have become very bad. The systems are not well integrated and so much stuff has been stuck in, over time, that the cockpit is packed out with all this bulky kit and there's just no room." The flight controls are now fully hands-on-collective-and-stick (HOCAS) configured, and there are no longer any switches located behind the crew members. The aircraft is mush easier to fly thanks to a four-axis automatic flight control system, which has functions such as hover hold and height hold that all reduce crew workload.

Every pilot who flew in Iraq said they needed a better sensor on the aircraft. There was praise for the embedded

GPS/INS fitted to the AH-1W, which was a great targeting aid. Pilots could 'lase' a target and then send its co-ordinates (accurate to a 10-digit grid) over the secure radio net. However, the existing NTS sight system badly needs replacing. On the AH-1Z the primary mission sensor is the Lockheed Martin Missile and Fire Control-built target sight system (TSS), the AN/AAQ-30 Hawkeye. Gone are the direct view optics of Cobras past, replaced by a three-chip colour TV and FLIR system. The AAQ-30 incorporates several off-the-shelf components, housed in the same L-3/Wescam Model 20 turret fitted to US Navy P-3Cs. The Hawkeye TSS also uses elements of the USAF's AN/AAQ-33 Sniper XR targeting pod, and even the electro-optical targeting system now under development for the Joint Strike Fighter. The Hawkeye has a FLIR sensor, CCD colour TV camera, laser rangefinder/designator (LRFD), inertial measurement unit (IMU), boresight module and electronics unit. Each sensor is auto-boresighted to the others and to the AH-1Z's dual-embedded GPS/INS. The third generation (Gen 3) FLIR has a relatively large (81/2-in/21.5-cm) aperture, and uses a 640 x 512 staring array (indium antimonide) that operates in the mid-range IR spectrum (3 to 5 µm). The FLIR has already demonstrated its ability to pick up targets with "TV quality" at ranges of 13 miles (21 km). The integrated avionics system can direct the FLIR (or any of the sensors) to look at or look ahead to any designated point on the digital map.

A Sony-built TV camera covers the visible and near-IR wavebands with three CCD detector arrays. The camera is fitted with a x2.5 extender lens and provides continuous zoom up to x18 magnification. Two TV FoVs are matched to two of the four offered by the FLIR, permitting easy switching between either system. The LRFD has been adopted from the AN/AAQ-14 LANTIRN targeting pod, with a selectable eye-safe function. It is the same system fitted to US Navy SH-60s, giving them Hellfire capability too. The TV system is capable of tracking 13 targets simultaneously, with three held in the current FoV and another 10 previously selected targets being tracked by the sight's own IMU. The operator has just to cycle between the different target sets to keep them updated and tracked. The system is capable of launching Hellfires to engage these targets every eight seconds. The weapons system is augmented by a new air data sensor, developed by BAE Systems (formerly GEC-Marconi) and fitted to a Marine Cobra for the first time. The TSS EMD phase was completed by March 2003 and the first TSS-equipped AH-1Z was scheduled to enter Operational Evaluation in October 2004.

Longbow radar

In 2001 it was announced that Longbow International had teamed with Bell to develop the Cobra Radar System (CRS), consisting of a pod-based millimetre wave radar (as used on the AH-64D Apache Longbow) that could be

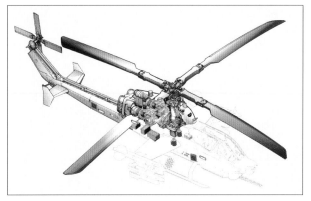

mounted on a wingtip or stores position of the AH-1Z. This would give the AH-1Z access to the RF-guided AGM-114L Longbow Hellfire missile that currently equips only the Longbow Apache. The USMC has not made any decision on whether or not to acquire the CRS and it remains largely an export option. Marine operators say that you cannot rely on a radar alone to deliver positive IDs on the battlefield, and a visual sensor is also needed, but they view the Longbow 'enhancement' as desirable when it comes to target classification or the ability to cue the FLIR to unseen targets.

The AH-1Z retains the AH-1W's ability to carry the AIM-9 Sidewinder and not just on the wingtip stations, but on any of the hardpoints. The Zulu's higher operating weights make the missile a more viable weapon than it is on the Whiskey. The M197 cannon also has an air-to-air role and can fire M50-series rounds designed specifically for anti-

Above: The wider wings and taller rotor mast fairing are readily apparent in this view of an NAH-1Z. The main rotor can be semi-automatically folded, with one blade folding forwards and another backwards so that the aircraft takes up a similar amount of space as the two-bladed AH-1W. The Zulu continues the Cobra's tradition of presenting a low visual signature, especially when viewed from the front. The canopy presents little glint, and the paint is an IR suppressant. The four-bladed rotors have a much lower noise signature than the familiar 'slap' of the two-bladed Cobras.

Above left: This cutaway highlights (the shaded portions) the main airframe/powerplant elements of the AH-1Z that are common with the UH-1Y Yankee that will serve alongside the Zulu in HMLA squadrons. Other elements, such as portions of the avionics system, are also common, combining to greatly ease the logistic supply lines and maintenance requirements for the two types.

Reserialled as BuNo. 166477, NAH-1Z no. 1 hover taxis at Patuxent River with four dummy Hellfire missiles carried on the outboard pylon. Zulu trials are being overseen by HX-21, the US Navy's rotary-wing test squadron. The aircraft is fitted with a new moving tailplane which lacks the endplate fins on the tailplanes originally installed on the prototypes.

By late 2003 only the no. 1 NAH-1Z aircraft was flying while the other two 'prototypes' had new avionics installed. In October the go-ahead was given for six LRIP aircraft to be converted, these machines being earmarked for service with the training unit (HMT-303) at Camp Pendleton from 2006. Full production is currently slated to cover 180 aircraft, all conversions of existing AH-1Ws, to be delivered by 2014/15.

Right: Currently an option for the AH-1Z is the Longbow millimetre-wave radar, as employed in a mast-mounted position on the AH-64D. In the Zulu the radar would be mounted in a wingtip station, as illustrated by this mock-up, or possibly in an underwing pod. The radar can detect targets that would otherwise remain unseen by the FLIR, and can be used to cue other sensors. The radar would allow the support of AGM-114L Hellfire missiles.

Below: Fitted with Hawkeye turret, an NAH-1Z taxis along the HX-21 ramp at 'Pax'. In the background is a prototype of the UH-1Y, which shares many of the features of the Zulu. The bulk of avionics test work is to be undertaken by Zulus 2 and 3, leading to an operational evaluation in late 2004.

aircraft use. The Zulu team is also trying to address gun reliability problems with the M197, which is unchanged on the new aircraft. A new linkless feed system has been considered but at the moment this remains an "unfounded deficiency" in the words of one programme official.

The Zulu comes with a big boost in its self-defence capabilities. Four ALE-47 countermeasures dispensers are now fitted (compared to the AH-1W's two ALE-39s). The APR-39B(V)2 radar warning system has been improved, and integrated on an individual databus to read out on the cockpit MFDs. The AAR-47(V)2 combined optical warning system has now taken on the role of the earlier AVR-2 laser warning system. One item that is missing from the current AH-1Z EMD plan is the AN/ALQ-144 infra-red jammer found on the AH-1W. The ALQ-144 is seen as old technology by many, and is only effective against uncooled IR seekers, but the Marines are still pushing to have the ALQ-144 reinstated. The Zulu uses its inherent design and specialised exhaust shrouds to minimise its IR signature but the crews, especially those who have been shot at recently, are not convinced. Says one "Are you nuts?! Put that thing

on my aircraft." The Zulu was supposed to have been fitted with an active countermeasures system like DIRCM, but this has not yet been funded.

There are more misgivings about other items of equipment that will be left off the AH-1Z, under current plans. The most significant of these, in the eyes of many, is the loss of the TOW missile. As a 'legacy' weapon the TOW has no place on the all-digital Zulu, but combat experience in Iraq proved that the TOW – or a weapon like it – was invaluable. Because the TOW is directly controlled by an operator, using wire guidance, it can be flown at a target in a number of different ways. A TOW does not have the range and the killing power of a Hellfire, but because Hellfire is a top attack weapon only, a TOW can reach targets that Hellfires cannot. The most common examples of this encountered in Iraq were armoured vehicles hidden under bridges, overpasses or any kind of top cover. TOWs could be flown under or around the cover, to hit the target. "We need a trajectory shaping missile," says one OIF veteran "we need TOW on the Zulu. It looks like they are going to give us APKWS, which will be a flat trajectory weapon and useful, but Hellfire just can't kill the tank hidden under an underpass. We're going to get the Joint Common Missile (JCM) too – well OK, but that's going to be expensive."

Another OIF pilot agreed, "there will be no replacement for TOW and that's bad. In Iraq we shot more TOWs than Hellfires because TOW is much more easily employable in urban environments." A member of the AH-1Z test team concedes, "There will be no TOW and we have not demonstrated Zunis (rockets). We want the APKWS to take care of the TOW 'issues' and there's always the JCM, but that is an expensive way to blow up tanks."

APKWS and JCM

The APKWS (Advanced Precision Kill Weapons System) – also known as LCPK (Low Cost Precision Kill) – is a new laser-guided 70-mm (Hydra 70) rocket system that the US is developing to give its helicopters (primarily) a new affordable precision-guided weapon capability. The weapon is being developed by General Dynamics and BAE Systems, and the development programme was launched in February 2003. APKWS will fill the large capability gap between the Army's 2.75-in (70-mm) rockets and the AGM-114 Hellfire. The Marines are also very interested in the system and the Zulu will be one of the first types to be equipped with the APKWS.

The Joint Common Missile (JCM, formerly known as the Common Modular Missile) is another 'big ticket' future weapons programme that is intended to replace the AGM-65 Maverick and AGM-114 Hellfire on a range of rotary- and fixed-wing platforms across the US Army, Navy Air Force and Marines. Three competing bids from Boeing/Northrop Grumman, Lockheed Martin and Raytheon answered the JCM request for proposals in September 2003 and a decision on which to take forward is expected before the end of 2004. The JCM is slated to enter service in 2009 on the AH-1Z, which has been designated as the 'pilot platform' for the missile. The JCM is supposed to incorporate a direct fire mode, to replace the TOW capability that Cobra crews crave.

AH-1Ws pilots are supremely enthusiastic about the AH-1Z but they still retain an element of professional cynicism. As one pilot put it, "Well, we look at the Hornets and their experience. Only now, with the E/F, are they doing everything they promised for the A/B. They tell us that the Zulu will do everything. We'll wait and see."

With a positive LRIP decision secured for the Marines, Bell Helicopter's attention has now firmly switched to potential export customers for the AH-1Z. It was one of the bidders for the Australian Army's Air 97 requirement, that was won by the Eurocopter Tiger. Bell offered a variant dubbed the 'Viper' that was essentially identical to the Marines' AH-1Z. It became embroiled in a legal challenge to the Australian selection process when it failed to make

the shortlist in 1999. The following year Bell was allowed to resubmit its bid but it was ultimately unsuccessful.

Bad news in Australia was offset by some good news in Turkey where Bell was selected to supply up to 145 new attack helicopters worth up to $4 billion. A variant of the AH-1Z, the AH-1Z KingCobra, was chosen by the Turkish Army to meet its ATAK combat helicopter requirement. Turkey was already a satisfied customer for the AH-1S and AH-1W. The plan for the KingCobra, in July 2000, called for three production batches to be built in Turkey by Tusas Aerospace Industries (TAI), beginning in November 2003 (delayed from an the intended date of 2002). Since then, the Turkish deal has been mired in controversy and dispute – most concerning pricing and industrial co-operation issues – and it seems to have largely disintegrated. Hopes that the deal would get back on track following the 2003 DAB approval of the AH-1Z programme in the US proved to be over-optimistic.

While Bell will make little comment on the saga of the renegotiation of the renegotiations, the latest press reports in March 2004 suggest that the whole programme will now be cancelled (along with others in Turkey) as a result of budgetary restrictions. If this happens it would leave Taiwan as the only near-term prospect for the AH-1Z.

Taiwan is already an AH-1W customer, but beginning in mid-2003 it evaluated both the AH-64D Longbow Apache and the AH-1Z as possible future attack helicopters. Taiwan had hoped to launch its procurement plan by the end of that year, leaving the AH-64D as the only available candidate, but this schedule has now slipped well into 2004. No funding has yet been reserved for the programme. There is a requirement for up to 75 new helicopters to equip three aviation brigades in Taiwan, although most observers expect an initial order of around 25 helicopters to equip just one unit and perhaps a final buy of only 45. A decision in Taiwan is now expected to emerge in mid-2004. Bell's chances may be improved by the prospect of a deal with Taiwan's AIDC (rather than TAI) to supply tail boom assemblies for the US AH-1Z programme. If the AH-1Z is selected by Taiwan, Bell and AIDC may also strike a local production deal for the whole aircraft. There is also the possibility that Bell could find a role in Korea's still emerging Korean Multi-role Helicopter (KMH) project.

Robert Hewson

Bell has been trying to sell its AH-1Z to Turkey for some years, and despite being chosen as the winner of the ATAK competition in 2000, a conclusion to the deal seems as far away as ever in early 2004. Turkey currently operates both single- and twin-engined Cobra variants (AH-1W above). The AH-1Z KingCobra on offer for the ATAK requirement has been illustrated with a wheeled undercarriage (below), an option for AH-1Z customers.

As the chance of selling new Cobras to Turkey wanes, Taiwan – which already operates the AH-1W (illustrated) – has become the brightest hope for an export order for the AH-1Z. Export capacity theoretically becomes available in 2005, fitting well with Taiwan's nascent plans. Bell is also dangling the 'carrot' of sub-contract work on the USMC's AH-1Z programme, and also the possibility of licence production if Taiwan chooses the AH-1Z over the rival Boeing AH-64.

AH-1 Cobra operators

BAHRAIN

The Bahrain Amiri Air Force, which was established in 1976 as a small paramilitary air wing, was expanded considerably in capacity from the mid-1980s. In the aftermath of the Iraqi invasion of Kuwait in August 1990, Bahrain was offered eight AH-64A Apaches plus 450 associated AGM-114 Hellfire missiles in October, but this offer was rejected in favour of a cheaper option. This covered eight AH-1E Cobras and six TAH-1P combat trainers. The Cobras were delivered from 1994. Another batch of 16 AH-1Es followed, deliveries of which ran until July 1997. The Cobras were allocated to Nos 8 and 10 Squadrons at Rifa'a. It is thought that 12 of the AH-1Es remain in service, and all of the TAH-1Ps. In 2001 Bahrain announced its intention to upgrade the aircraft. However, the BAAF is now looking at a batch of 17 ex-US Army AH-1Fs, of which 14 would be made operational with the remainder acting as spares sources.

IRAN

Between 1975 and 1978 202 specially-developed twin-engined AH-1J 'Internationals' were delivered to the Shah's Imperial Iranian Army Aviation corps, in both TOW-capable and non-TOW versions. Flying with the post-revolutionary Islamic Republic of Iran Army, the Cobra won a solid combat reputation during the war against Iraq in 1980-1988. Both the armed forces and the Iranian Revolutionary Guard Corps have expressed a keen interest in keeping the AH-1 fleet in active service, and improving the aircraft where

Iran has kept a sizeable number of its AH-1Js operational by the reverse-engineering of spare parts. The type serves with both regular army aviation (IRIAA) and the Revolutionary Guards aviation (IRGC).

possible. About half of Iran's Cobra fleet was destroyed in the war with Iraq. The number of currently operationally available Cobras is unclear, but is probably in the region of 50 or 60, if not more.

The Tehran-based Iran Helicopter Support & Renewal Company (IHSRC) is the primary overhaul source for civil and military helicopters in Iran. With such a diverse helicopter fleet in Iranian military service, the IHSRC has developed a wide range of expertise on types from the JetRanger and the Mi-17, to the Chinook and RH-53. However, Iran's large number of pre-revolutionary aircraft is ageing, and hit by international embargoes on parts supply. As a result, an innovative series of helicopter upgrade and reverse-engineering projects have sprung up in Iran.

Overhaul and maintenance support for the AH-1 force is undertaken by the IHSRC and by the country's primary aviation umbrella organisation, HESA (the Iran Aircraft Manufacturing Industry Co.). HESA has exhibited an upgrade for the AH-1 that is understood to be flying on at least five AH-1Js. During the Iran Air Show of 2002 the fourth Cobra upgrade prototype, painted as 'HESA P4', participated in both the static and flying displays. This aircraft had been fitted with a range of new avionics systems, although other items such as the engines and weapons are believed to remain unchanged. The aircraft did, however, sport new flat-pane glazing, similar to that fitted to the AH-1F.

In the forward (gunner's) cockpit a new rectangular MFD screen with soft-touch controls has been fitted in the main panel. This screen was demonstrated during the show to display flight-related data – including engine status (torque, temperature etc.) and basic navigational and positional information. The new MFD completely dominates the space in the cockpit previously given over to the TOW targeting system for the nose-mounted M65 sight, and so it must be assumed that the MFD is directly linked to the TOW weapons system. Mention was made by one HESA spokesman of a new FLIR system for the AH-1, which was not fitted to this aircraft (the M65 sight is a daytime-only system). A Garmin GPS receiver has also been fitted on top of the front coaming of the forward cockpit, with the relevant satellite antenna fitted above the Cobra's nose. Below the aircraft a new radome corresponding to a radar altimeter has been fitted.

The upgraded Cobra has also been equipped with a new RWR system, with four receiver antennas mounted on the nose and tail to provide 360° coverage. The operator's panel for this system is located in the rear cockpit.

Robert Hewson

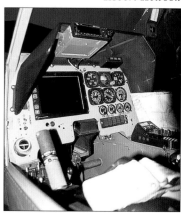

Above and below: Under 'Project 2091' Iran's HESA has upgraded at least five AH-1Js with flat-pane canopies and a new front cockpit.

ISRAEL

Israeli interest in the attack helicopter concept was accelerated by lessons from the Yom Kippur War. The fundamental issue was how to compensate for an initial 10:1 imbalance of force between the regular armies of Israel and its surrounding Arab nations until such time as Israel's reserves could be mobilised and deployed to the front. Until the October 1973 Yom Kippur War, Israeli generals were sure that any sign of Arab aggression could be detected in time to mobilise the Israeli reserves, but the surprise Egyptian and Syrian attack on 6 October 1973 shattered that belief. Moreover, it became apparent that the Israel Defence Force/Air Force (IDF/AF) was unable to fill the void, for four main reasons:

■ during the first 24 to 48 hours of a war the IDF/AF was committed to the air superiority battle, and could only spare a meagre force of less capable fighters to support the hard-pressed regular ground forces during that critical period.

■ the air superiority battle which opened the Yom Kippur War was a complete disaster for the IDF/AF, which failed to destroy the Egyptian and Syrian Air Defence Force (ADF) and consequently had to operate within hostile ADF-protected areas, in turn restricting the ability of the IDF/AF's fighter-bombers to properly support the ground forces.

■ lack of accuracy or precision strike capability.

The IDF/AF's first Cobra unit formed at Tel Nof with AH-1Qs. It subsequently standardised on the AH-1S, moved to Palmachim and became known as the 'Northern Squadron'.

■ lack of real-time intelligence.
Interestingly, NATO was facing similar a scenario in the event of a surprise Soviet attack in Europe. The US answer was to modify the attack helicopter concept, which had gained momentum in Vietnam as a suppressive fire platform in heliborne operations, into a Main Battle Tank (MBT) hunter. The attack helicopter promised to cure the four shortcomings in IDF/AF Close Air Support (CAS) during the first 24 to 48 hours of a war:

■ the attack helicopter force mission would be CAS, therefore these helicopters would not participate in the air superiority battle and would be dedicated to the support of IDF troops.

■ operating around the flanks and using Nap Of Earth (NOE) flying, it was hoped that the attack helicopters would be able to operate within ADF-defended zones.

■ compared with 1970s fighter-bomber technology, the attack helicopter armed with Anti-Tank Guided Missile (ATGM) was a true pinpoint attack platform.

■ as the attack helicopters would

operate in direct contact with brigade-level forces, the problem of lack of real-time intelligence would be eliminated.

Initially, Israel purchased six Bell AH-1G Cobra helicopters, essentially still heliborne assault escorts without any ATGM capability. The Cobra was allocated the Hebrew name Zefa (Viper), initiating the IDF/AF tradition of naming its attack helicopters after snakes. An evaluation unit was formed at Tel Nof air base during 1975, staffed by a mix of helicopter pilots, fighter pilots and fighter navigators. Less than a year after the arrival of the six AH-1Gs in April 1975, the decision was made to upgrade the flight to squadron status, to convert the AH-1Gs to AH-1Q standard (which was capable of launching TOW ATGMs), and to purchase additional helicopters.

The six AH-1Gs were shipped to the US in May 1977, the flight was disbanded and a squadron was formed. The return of the six AH-1Qs in August 1978 prompted an extensive campaign of co-operation exercises with IDF armoured brigades. The drill was to allocate a formation of attack helicopters to a certain brigade, and it was up to the brigade commander to decide how to utilise the re-enforcement. The most common variations were to allocate an individual sector to the attack helicopters – usually on the flanks of the

brigade's sector where the helicopters enjoyed freedom of operation, or to co-ordinate the attack helicopters with a regiment's sector, where they would work closely with the MBT crews.

As tactics were refined the concept of scouts was also introduced, at first using Bell 206s and then Hughes 500M-Ds. During 1979 the squadron added six Zefa helicopters to its inventory and moved from Tel Nof to Palmachim. The new Zefa helicopters were to AH-1S ECAS standard, with 20-mm cannon and flat-pane canopy to reduce sun reflections that revealed the presence of the attack helicopters to hostile forces. Thus, with 11 Zefa helicopters and four 500M-D scouts, the squadron was tested during the June 1982 Lebanon War. The scenario was not quite like the one for which the attack helicopters were purchased, as in this case Israel was on the offensive. The squadron flew 62 sorties, launched 72 TOW ATGMs, claimed the destruction of 51 targets including T-62 and T-72 MBTs, and lost two helicopters.

The first of 30 AH-1S Modernized Cobras were delivered to Israel in 1983, the new variant being equipped with an improved weapon-aiming system including a laser range-finder, composite rotor blades, and a large black nozzle to cool the hot air emission rather than just pointing it upwards, as in earlier Cobra

Israel's first Cobras were six AH-1Gs, which served with the Cobra Evaluation Flight (badge left) at Tel Nof between 1975 and 1977.

The 'Southern Squadron' also has a snake motif as part of its badge, as well as a fuselage marking. It is co-located with the 'Northern' unit at Palmachim.

variants. In 1985 a second Zefa squadron was formed, with the first unit becoming known as 'The Northern Squadron' while the new unit became 'The Southern Squadron' to reflect the respective location of the two units within Palmachim air base.

Following the service entry of the McDonnell Douglas AH-64A Peten (Python) in 1990, the IDF/AF turned its attention to a 'night-time operational capability gap closure' programme, aimed at giving the Zefa fleet the option to operate at night with much the same capability as the Peten. The primary elements of this programme were the Elbit Yarchon (Journal) Night Vision Goggles/Head Up Display (NVG/HUD) system that was introduced in 1992, and the replacement of the original daytime targeting system with the IAI Tamam Night Targeting System (NTS), a system identical to the NTS installed in the US Marine Corps AH-1W Super

Cobra and known in IDF/AF service as Reshafim (Flashes). Deliveries commenced in 1992, with a formal service entry date in June 1993. This resulted in a vastly expanded operational envelope, as well as certain operational changes. The use of air-to-ground rocket pods was stopped in 1993 as a result of the shift towards precision strike with minimal collateral damage, while the installation of a small Multi-Function Display (MFD) in the front cockpit just above the NTS sight caused a change in the gunner's working methods. Instead of placing the gunner's head close to the sight and virtually ignoring the outside world during the launch of a TOW missile, the MFD (displaying either a daytime TV image or night-time Forward Looking Infra Red/FLIR image), offers the gunner the option to retain situational awareness even when launching a TOW. The original sight has been retained, however, and pre-NTS era gunners tend to use it as they did in the old days. However, all of the younger gunners use the MFD.

Once Zefa crews got accustomed to the Yarchon NVG/HUD system they demanded the introduction of a similar daytime system. The El-Op Zaharon (Noon) – basically a helmet-mounted HUD – entered service in 1994. Further improvements included a Data Transfer Equipment (DTE) system to ease the loading of the navigation system, GPS receiver, missile launch debrief system and a self-protection system. The most recent addition in the ongoing modernisation of the Zefa fleet is the installation of the Elbit Nadiv (Generous) D-Map digital map display, while Zefa aircrews hope that the introduction of the digital map will be followed by the installation of a data link that will allow them, for example, to receive an image of their designated target in real-time for an Unmanned Air Vehicle (UAV).

The Zefa is currently the IDF/AF 'entry-level' attack helicopter platform. The delivery of 14 AH-1Es in 1996 enabled the IDF/AF to introduce the Zefa as the IDF/AF Academy's attack helicopter pilot trainer, while a further 15 US Army surplus Cobras delivered in 2003 are a source of spare parts. A capable platform, the Zefa is also elderly and, as such, is an obvious candidate for an upgrade project. IAI has proposed a General Electric T700 re-engining

project, while Bell is promoting the AH-1Z, including the demonstration of a cockpit in Israel in December 2002. However, the IDF/AF is currently committed to an AH-64D purchase programme so attack helicopter force funding is tight at the present. Furthermore, there is an opinion that the operational gap that the attack helicopter was created to fill no longer exists. Combat aircraft field Precision Guided Munitions (PGM), the ADF no longer poses such a threat as it did during the 1970s and a battlefield littered with MBTs is a vision of the past. Reflecting this attitude, a committee headed by former IDF/AF commander (1996-2000) Eitan Ben-Eliyahu recommended in December 2003 to cut the number of IDF/AF attack helicopters by 20 per cent.

Though Soviet MBTs flooding Europe or Syrian MBTs flooding the Golan Heights may be a vision of the past, the attack helicopter has diversified considerably in its operational repertoire since the 1970s, when it was viewed primarily as an MBT hunter. It is fair to assume that the familiar sound of the AH-1's two-bladed rotor will continue to be heard over Israel for at least another decade.

Shlomo Aloni

IDF/AF gunship crews learn their trade on the AH-1Es of the IDF Academy (badge above) attack helicopter training squadron. Although the aircraft have NTS, and some have IR suppressing nozzles, they do not have IRCM or chaff/flare dispensers.

JAPAN

In the late 1970s the Rikujo Jiei-tai (Japan Ground Self Defence Force, JGSDF) began to study the potential of attack helicopters seriously. Shortly before this, some JGSDF UH-1B/Hs had been equipped with rockets and tested during some exercises, but they were ineffective against heavily armoured vehicles such as main battle tanks, and also inaccurate. Furthermore, they had no sophisticated sighting systems. In 1977, the JGSDF decided to purchase a dedicated attack helicopter to fully evaluate this capability, and the Bell AH-1S was selected as a matter of course. The AH-1S was the only such aircraft in existence at that time.

The first two AH-1Ss (s/n 73401 and 73402) were imported from the US, and were in the Step 2 configuration. In the US this was redesignated as the AH-1E but the JGSDF continued to use the name of AH-1S. The two aircraft were assigned to the Kyoiku Shien Hiko-tai (School Support Squadron, SSS) at Akeno AAB in 1979. The main role of the SSS was to establish the standards of education and training for aircrew, but they also flew the aircraft on research, development, test and evaluation tasks. The evaluation period for the AH-1S took almost three years, after which the JGSDF confirmed the firepower effectiveness that the dedicated attack helicopter would bring. A plan to establish the Tai Sensha Herikoputa-tai (Anti-Tank Helicopter Unit, ATH) was settled in 1982 and procurement of the AH-1S was authorised.

Fuji Heavy Industries (FHI) had a long relationship with Bell Helicopters through maintenance and modification programmes, and had manufactured Model 204s and 205s under the license. Therefore, FHI was named as the licence-manufacturer of the AH-1S. In the initial plan, enough helicopters for 5½ squadrons were to be produced. The regular complement of a squadron is 16 aircraft, so 5½ squadrons equated to 88 AH-1Ss. A further eight aircraft were to be manufactured to cover for attrition, for a total of 96. In the event, the plan was revised to 90 AH-1Ss due to the lack of attrition, and finally cut to 89. In the late 1990s the JGSDF embarked on a follow-on attack helicopter programme (AH-X), ending procurement of the AH-1S. The final order for the 89th aircraft (73492) was made in FY1998 and delivered to the JGSDF on 14 December 2000.

These licence-built AH-1Ss were all in the Step 3 version, which subsequently became the AH-1F in US Army parlance. However, again the JGSDF elected to retain the AH-1S designation for its aircraft.

AH-1S in service

Five front-line ATHs have been formed since 1986. The JGSDF divided Japan into five Homen-tai (Regional Army) by geographic areas. They are Hokubu Homen-tai (Northern Army), Tohoku Homen-tai (Northeastern Army), Tobu Homen-tai (Eastern Army), Chubu Homen-tai (Central Army) and Seibu Homen-tai (Western Army). Each Regional Army has a Homen Koku-tai (Regional Army Air Group, for example Hokubu Homen-tai has Hokubu Homen Koku-tai = Northern Army Air Group) and one ATH was assigned to the control of each Regional Army Air Group. Each ATH consists of two squadrons called Dai 1 Hiko-tai (1st Squadron) and Dai 2 Hiko-tai (2nd Squadron), and each squadron was

equipped with eight AH-1Ss and two OH-6Ds for scout duties (in recent years, conversion to the Kawasaki OH-1 from the OH-6D has been under way).

Dai 1 Tai Sensha Herikoputa-tai (1st ATH): the 1st ATH was formed on 25 March 1986 at Obihiro AAB in Hokkaido as the first ATH in the JGSDF. The 1st ATH started to receive the AH-1S on 30 September 1985. 1st ATH is assigned to Northern Army Air Group.

Dai 2 Tai Sensha Herikoputa-tai (2nd ATH): the 2nd ATH was formed at Hachinohe AAB on 25 March 1989. The unit received its first AH-1S on 25 March 1988. 2nd ATH is under the control of Northeastern Army Air Group.

Dai 3 Tai Sensha Herikoputa-tai (3rd ATH): the 3rd ATH was formed at Metabaru AAB on 29 March 1990 and is assigned to Western Army Air Group.

Dai 4 Tai Sensha Herikoputa-tai (4th ATH): the 4th ATH was formed at Kisarazu AAB on 31 March 1992 and is assigned to Eastern Army Air Group. The first two AH-1Ss which were imported were eventually assigned to this unit although they were withdrawn from use in 2001.

Dai 5 Tai Sensha Herikoputa-tai (5th ATH): the 5th ATH was formed at Akeno AAB as the final ATH in the JGSDF on 28 March 1994. Because of procurement budget restrictions, the 5th ATH was established with only half of its strength with only one squadron initially assigned. When the final AH-1S was delivered to the JGSDF, the 5th ATH reached full strength. The 5th ATH is under the control of Central Army Air Group.

Koku Gakko Honko (Headquarters School): this unit at Akeno AAB handles training with a strength of eight aircraft.

Japan's AH-1S aircraft are essentially the same as those of the US Army. After the two earliest aircraft (73401

These AH-1Ss are from the 5th ATH (right) at Akeno and the 4th ATH (below) at Kisarazu. Akeno was the first JGSDF base to host Cobras during the evaluation phase, and today houses the Cobra training school.

and 73402) were retired, all of the JGSDF's AH-1 fleet were to the same standard as the AH-1F. Standard weapons consist of eight BGM-71 TOWs and two M261 rocket pods (each containing 19 2.75-in/70-mm FFARs). It is possible to switch M261 and TOW launchers, so alternate configurations are 16 TOWs or four M261 pods. An M197 three-barrelled 20-mm cannon is fitted under the nose. In the extreme nose is an M65 telescopic sight unit for the TOW.

After the 73rd aircraft (73473, including the two imported AH-1Ss), the C-Nite FLIR system for night operations was introduced. In the JGSDF's C-Nite aircraft the transmitter for the radar jammer was moved to forward of the front cockpit, while the same system's receiver was moved to the main rotor mast fairing. A pair of wire-cutters was added to the top and bottom of the forward fuselage. These are also being retrofitted to the existing aircraft but the work is proceeding slowly.

Not all of Japan's AH-1s have yet been fitted with wire-cutters, but the work to fit them fleet-wide continues. The Cobras wear their unit assignment in black letters behind the pilot's cockpit, in this case 'IIIATH' for the 3rd ATH at Metabaru.

At present, the JGSDF is to reorganise and to form a new unit called the Kuchu Kido Ryodan (Air Mobility Brigade, AMB). This unit will be a mixed aviation force comprising eight heavy transport helicopters (CH-47JA), eight utility helicopters (UH-60JA), five observation helicopters (OH-1) and eight attack helicopters. The attack helicopter for the AMB is the AH-X, for which the Boeing AH-64D Apache Longbow has been selected. Initially, there will be no effect on the current AH-1S fleet and the five ATH units, but when procurement of the AH-64D is half-complete, at least one ATH is due to disband.

Yoshitomo Aoki

JORDAN

The Royal Jordanian Air Force identified a requirement for an anti-armour helicopter in the late 1970s. Initially the HOT-armed Aérospatiale SA 342 Gazelle was considered, but this was rejected after the US offered a batch of 24 AH-1S Cobras with BGM-71 TOWs in 1981. A contract worth US$196 million was signed in September 1982, and the aircraft were delivered between January and December 1985, equipping Nos 10 and 12 Squadrons at Al Jafr (serialled 1001 to 1012 and 1201 to 1212). The Cobras were delivered in AH-1S Modernised configuration with heat-shields on the exhausts but lacking IRCM turrets. They were subsequently redesignated as AH-1Fs.

The two Cobra squadrons subsequently moved to Al Matar Air Base near Amman/Marka, from where they continue to operate the survivors (believed to number 20). In 2000/01 nine ex-US Army AH-1Fs were delivered to augment the fleet.

Jordan's Cobras are operated by No. 10 (top left) and No. 12 (top right) Squadrons, both based at Al Matar Air Base.

REPUBLIC OF KOREA

In 1978 the Republic of Korea Army Aviation received eight TOW-armed, twin-engined AH-1J Internationals. Experience with these led to the later adoption of the single-engined AH-1S as its principal attack helicopter. An initial order, for 21 TOW-armed AH-1Ss, was placed in 1985 with a value of US$178 million, including spares and support. By 1987 the contract had been expanded to cover 42 aircraft at a cost of US$260 million, to be purchased through regular commercial channels.

The first of them was delivered in 1988, and deliveries were maintained at around three per month. In 1990 an additional 20 were ordered through FMS (part of an option for 28), the sale being approved by the US Congress in November. The helicopters were delivered as Modernised AH-1S equipped with C-Nite, subsequently becoming AH-1Fs.

Augmentation and replacement of the RoKAA Cobra fleet has been a long saga, beginning in July 1992 when the service ordered 37 AH-64A Apaches (and 775 Hellfires) through FMS channels but did not complete the purchase. The requirement was revived in 1996, and in March 2000 Requests for Proposal for a new attack helicopter were issued to seven companies, including Bell. The competition was subsequently whittled down to the AH-1Z, AH-64D and Kamov Ka-52K. An initial order for 36 aircraft was expected, with an eventual requirement of around 60. Funding problems continue to postpone the final decision, and it is likely that the requirement will be rolled into a requirement for a smaller multi-purpose attack scout helicopter, for which the indigenous KMH is front-runner.

This AH-1S belongs to the RoKAA's 107th/1st Aviation Brigade.

PAKISTAN

Pakistan's Army Aviation Corps underwent a considerable expansion from the mid-1970s. An attack helicopter requirement resulted in competition between the Hughes 500MD and the Bell AH-1S, resulting in an order for the Cobra. Twenty were ordered (with an option for a further 20) and the first batch of 10 was delivered in late 1984. They officially entered service in March 1985. The second batch of 10 was delivered in early 1986. A revised US$89 million option for 10 more through FMS was due to be exercised, and formal notification was given in Washington in January 1990. However, the subsequent arms embargo placed by the US later that year over Pakistan's nuclear weapons programme ended any further deliveries. In late 1995 Washington was prepared to resume arms sales, resulting in the delivery of 18 C-Nite night targeting sets, 135 TOW 2 launchers and 16,720 2.75-in rockets for the 19 remaining Cobras.

Pakistan's Cobras (serialled 786-001 to 786-020, now designated AH-1F) were placed in service with Nos 31 and 32 Squadron at Multan, from where the survivors continue to operate. Both squadrons also operate a few Bell 206B JetRangers for communications and training. Serviceability of the Cobras was hampered by the arms embargo, but it is believed that 18 of the 20 are still in use.

In 2004 Pakistan was expecting to receive a large batch of ex-US Army AH-1Fs, thought to number 40 aircraft.

Pakistan has two squadrons of AH-1Fs at Multan. Since the end of Operation Enduring Freedom the fleet has seen sporadic action against Taliban/al-Qaeda insurgents operating in the mountains along the Afghan border.

TAIWAN

Taiwan issued an initial requirement for attack helicopters in 1984, evaluating the MBB BO 105 and Hughes 500. Following the ironing out of export difficulties, by early 1992 the requirement had crystallised into a firm order for 42 Bell AH-1Ws. The aircraft were completed to Integrated Weapons System (Phase 1) specification, including the Tamam/Kollsman NTSF-65 night targeting system, compatible with the AGM-114A Hellfire missile. As part of the same package 12 Hellfire-capable OH-58D Kiowa Warriors were also ordered (with 14 options, later

The RoCAA's AH-1Ws are a powerful counter to any aggression from the mainland.

exercised). In May 1997 Taiwan placed an order for a further 21 AH-1Ws as part of a US$479 million contract.

Taiwan's 'Whiskeys' were built in six production lots, the first (serialled 501) being delivered in March 1993. Deliveries of the first batch of 42 ran until 1997. The aircraft are distributed between the Army Aviation Training Centre at Kuejien-Tainan and two Attack Helicopter Wings within the Republic of China Army Aviation. Each wing has two squadrons: No. 1 Attack Helicopter Wing (also known as the 601st Aviation

Brigade) at Lungtan-Tao Yuan parents Nos 1 and 2 Attack Helicopter Squadrons, while No. 2 Attack Helicopter Wing (602nd Aviation Brigade) at Hsinshe includes Nos 3 and 4 Attack Helicopter Squadrons. The AH-1Ws work closely with the OH-58D force, which is divided into two helicopter Reconnaissance Squadrons,

one of which is allocated to each wing.

In mid-2003 the RoCAA opened an evaluation for a new attack helicopter, for which the Bell AH-1Z and Boeing AH-64D are competitors. A decision to proceed with this requirement had not been taken by early 2004, but might be expected to result in an order for up to 75 aircraft.

THAILAND

Thailand's army aviation gained independence from the air force in 1952, and was established as the Kongbin Tha Han Bo – Royal Thai Army Aviation Division. The RTAAD was primarily equipped with transport types such as the UH-1H, but in the mid-1980s decided to add an attack helicopter capability.

In mid-1986 four Bell AH-1S Cobras were ordered to form an attack flight. They were delivered in 1990 as AH-1Fs (serialled 9996 to 9999), and were intended to form an operational cadre pending procurement of larger numbers of surplus US Army aircraft. However, plans for further procurement of AH-1Ws or more AH-1Fs have been shelved due to budgetary restraints in the light of Thailand's economic problems of the late 1990s. A minor upgrade for the three existing aircraft has been funded, 9999 having been written off in an accident on 23 July 2001.

TURKEY

The Türk Kara Kuvvetleri (Turkish army aviation) sought attack helicopters from the late 1970s. The TKK was offered six AH-1Ss through FMS in late 1983, the deal being worth US$50 million, including BGM-71 TOW missiles, but this deal lapsed. However, in July 1990 five AH-1Ws were delivered, diverted from Lot III production for the US Marine Corps. Another five were delivered in 1993, this time from Lot IV production. At the time it was planned that another 42 would be assembled locally. Attempts to purchase a further 10 AH-1Ws for US$145 million foundered in 1996 due to Turkey's

disputes with Greece and over its continued use of attack helicopters against Kurdish insurgents.

The 10 AH-1Ws were delivered to a newly established Taaruz Helikopteri Taburu (attack helicopter battalion) at Ankara-Güvercinlik. The aircraft were subsequently augmented by 32 ex-US Army AH-1P/S aircraft delivered between 1993 and 1995. Included in this batch were four TAH-1P trainers. AH-1Ws serve with 1nci Filo, while the AH-1P/Ss are divided between 2nci and 3nci Filos.

The AH-1P/Ss were subsequently upgraded to a similar standard to the AH-1F, with GPS, three-barrelled 20-mm M197 cannon in place of the original 7.62-mm Minigun, radar warning

receiver and night targeting system. One AH-1W was shot down by Kurdish guerrillas on 18 May 1997 during operations in northern Iraq.

In May 1997 the TKK requested proposals from Agusta, Bell, Boeing, Denel, Eurocopter, McDonnell Douglas Helicopters, Mil and Sikorsky for a new attack helicopter, outlining a US$3.5 billion requirement for an initial batch plus ensuing licence production for a total of 145. A last-minute proposal was also received from the MiG group, representing Kamov's Ka-50. The programme was repeatedly delayed by political changes and continuing international hostility to Turkey's handling of the Kurdish independence question. Eventually, in August 2000 the

Bell AH-1Z King Cobra was selected, although continued wrangling over financing has resulted in further delays. Kamov's Ka-50-2 Erdogan with Israeli avionics technically remains in the running until a Bell deal can be concluded. The original 145-aircraft requirement is now considered too expensive, and current plans suggest 50 machines, with the first seven to be built at Fort Worth. However, in 2004 it was also considered likely that the whole attack helicopter requirement would be cancelled.

Based at Güvercinlik, the Taaruz Helikopteri Taburu has three squadrons of Cobras: one with AH-1Ws (below) and two with AH-1P/Ss (below left).

UNITED STATES MARINE CORPS

The US Marine Corps has operated the world's largest fleet of Cobras since 2001, when the US Army National Guard retired the AH-1F. Since receiving its first AH-1G HueyCobras in 1968 the USMC has operated four distinct variants of the Cobra, SeaCobra and SuperCobra that include the AH-1J, AH-1T and AH-1W. Although 186 AH-1Ws are currently in the inventory, Bell delivered 225 examples to the Marines between 1986 and July 1998. Production comprised a single prototype, and 180 new-build AH-1Ws. Additionally, 44 earlier AH-1Ts were updated to the later configuration and delivered between 1989 and 1992.

Whereas Marine Attack Helicopter Squadrons (HMA) originally operated the aircraft, today the AH-1W is in service with eight Marine Light Attack Helicopter Squadrons (HMLA) and a single Marine Helicopter Training Squadron (HMT). Six of the HMLA squadrons are assigned to the active component while the remaining two are components of the Marine Corps Reserve Force. Although the number of aircraft operated by the individual squadrons varies, each is nominally assigned 18 AH-1Ws and nine UH-1Ns. The reserve units are unique in being broken down into the parent squadron and a geographically separate detachment. While each of the parent squadrons is nominally assigned 12 AH-1Ws and six UH-1Ns, the detachments are equipped with six AH-1Ws and four UH-1Ns.

Super Cobras are also operated by three US Navy squadrons in support of test and operational evaluation efforts. The test pilots and support personnel within these squadrons include sailors and Marines.

Tom Kaminski

MCAS New River is 'home' to two Cobra/Huey units, HML/A-167 'Warriors' (above) and HML/A-269 'Gunrunners' (right). The New River-based squadrons officially retain the '/' in their unit designations, although it is deleted by West Coast squadrons.

2nd Marine Air Wing (MAW) – MCAS Cherry Point, North Carolina

HML/A-167 'Warriors' – 'TV'
Activated as Marine Light Helicopter Squadron One Six Seven (HML-167) on 15 March 1968, the 'Warriors' were equipped with the UH-1E. HML-167 was the last Marine helicopter squadron to operate in Vietnam and its final pair of helicopters departed on 15 June 1971. The squadron transitioned to the UH-1N in April 1972 and in January 1984 accepted its first AH-1Ts. Redesignated as HML/A-167 on 1 April 1986, the squadron transitioned to the AH-1W beginning on 11 August 1989. HML/A-167 is a component of Marine Air Group MAG-26 and is stationed at MCAS New River, North Carolina.

HML/A-269 'Gunrunners' – 'HF'
Initially equipped with the AH-1J, the 'Gunrunners' were activated as HMA-269 on 1 July 1971. Beginning in December 1977, the squadron transitioned to the AH-1T. It began operating the UH-1N alongside the Sea Cobra in 1983 and received its current designation on 1 April 1986. In 1990 the 'Gunrunners' exchanged the AH-1T for the AH-1W. HML/A-269 is assigned to MAG-29 and is stationed at MCAS New River, North Carolina.

3rd MAW Marine Air Wing (MAW) – MCAS Miramar, California

HMLA-169 'Vipers' – 'SN'
When activated as HMA-169 on 30 September 1971, the 'Vipers' were equipped with the AH-1G. The unit transitioned to the AH-1J in 1975 and the AH-1T followed in May 1978. On 1 October 1986 the squadron received its current designation and just 10 days later took delivery of its first AH-1W. HMLA-169 is stationed at MCAS Camp Pendleton, California, as a component of MAG-39.

HMLA-267 'Stingers' – 'UV'
The 'Stingers' were activated as Marine Observation Squadron VMO-5 on 15 December 1966 and were equipped with the OV-10A and UH-1E. Redesignated HML-267 on 15 March 1968, the unit operated both types until November 1971 when the Broncos were reassigned. The 'Stingers' took delivery of the first UH-1N in March 1976 and added the AH-1J in May 1983. The squadron received its current designation on 1 March 1987 and began its transition to the AH-1T later that same month. HMLA-267, which is assigned to MAG-39 and stationed at MCAS Camp Pendleton, California, took delivery of its first AH-1W in 1989

HMT-303 'Atlas' – 'QT'
Activated on 30 April 1982, Marine Helicopter Training Squadron HMT-303 is the fleet readiness squadron (FRS) for both the AH-1W and the UH/HH-1N. The squadron is a component of MAG-39 and is based at MCAS Camp Pendleton, California.

HMLA-367 'Scarface' – 'VT'
Stationed at Camp Pendleton, California, HMLA-367 is a component of MAG-39. Activated as VMO-3 on 1 August 1966 and equipped with the UH-1E, the unit was redesignated as HML-367 on 24 March 1968. It transitioned to the AH-1G in 1969 but later exchanged its Cobras for UH-1Es in 1971. In January 1976 the unit transitioned to the UH-1N, however a detachment of AH-1Js was added to the organisation in 1977. The first AH-1Ts arrived in 1985 and the

Above: HMLA-169 'Vipers'   *Below: HMLA-267 'Stingers'*

Above: HMLA-367 'Scarface'   *Right: HMLA-369 'Gunfighters'*

squadron received its current designation on 1 January 1988. It took

delivery of its initial AH-1W on 11 August 1989.

HMT-303 'Atlas' acts as the training squadron for both the AH-1W Cobra and the UH/HH-1N Huey.

HMLA-369 'Gunfighters' – 'SM'
When activated on 1 April 1972, HMA-369 was equipped with the AH-1J. However, the squadron received a small number of UH-1Ns during 1984. The

Hueys were permanently assigned in 1987 and the unit was redesignated as HMLA-369 on 15 September 1987. The squadron's first AH-1W was assigned on 30 October 1987 and the last AH-1J departed on 1 May 1988. HMLA-369 is currently stationed at MCAS Camp Pendleton, California, as a component of MAG-39.

4th Marine Air Wing (MAW) – NSA New Orleans, Louisiana

HMLA-773(-) 'Red Dogs' – 'MP'
Activated as HMA-773 on 1 September 1971, the 'Red Dogs' were initially equipped with the AH-1G but transitioned to the AH-1J in late 1978. HMA-773 accepted its first AH-1W on 8 October 1992 and the first UH-1N arrived in November 1993. The squadron, which is assigned to MAG-42 and stationed at NAS Atlanta, Georgia, received its current designation on 1 October 1994.

HMLA-773, Det. A 'Red Dogs' – 'MM'
On 1 October 1994 HML-767 was redesignated as HMLA-775 Detachment A, at NAS New Orleans, Louisiana. The unit, which was then a component of HMLA-775 at MCAS Camp Pendleton, was equipped with the AH-1W and UH-1N. During 2000 the unit was reassigned to HMLA-773 at NAS Atlanta, Georgia, and assumed its current identity.

HMLA-775(-) 'Coyotes' – 'WR'
Activated as HMA-775 on 7 January 1989, the 'Coyotes' were equipped with the AH-1J. The squadron received its first AH-1W in May 1992 and added the UH-1N to its inventory in June 1994. It received its current designation in October 1994. HMLA-775(-) is a component of MAG-46 and is stationed at MCAS Camp Pendleton, California.

Below left: HMLA-773. Below: HMLA-775

HMLA-775 Det. A 'Coyotes' – 'WG'
Originally established as HMLA-773 Detachment A, at NAS JRB Willow Grove, Pennsylvania, on 10 September 1997, this unit was equipped with AH-1W and UH-1N from the outset. During 2000 the unit was reassigned to HMLA-775 at MCAS Camp Pendleton, California, and assumed its current identity. On 3 March 2001 the detachment relocated to Johnstown-Cambria County Airport, Pennsylvania.

United States Navy

Commander Naval Air Systems Command (COMNAVAIRSYSCOM)

HX-21 'Rotary Wing'
Stationed at NAS Patuxent River, Maryland, HX-21 operates three AH-1Ws in support of research, development test and evaluation (RDT&E) associated with the AH-1W. Based at NAS Patuxent River, Maryland, and assigned to the Naval Air Warfare Center Aircraft Division (NAWC-AD), the squadron also supports the H-1 Upgrades programme.

VX-31 'Dust Devils'
VX-31 is tasked with conducting RDT&E in support of AH-1W weapons programmes. The squadron, which is

based at NAWS China Lake, California, and is a component of the Naval Air Warfare Center Weapons Division (NAWC-WD), operates a single AH-1W.

Commander Operational Test & Evaluation Force (COMOPTEVFOR) – NS Norfolk, Virginia

VX-9 'Vampires' – 'XE'
Stationed at NAWS China Lake, California, the 'Vampires' operate three AH-1Ws in support of operational testing (OT) and tactics development efforts.

Trials and development work for the Cobra fleet is undertaken at the US Navy's two main test sites: China Lake and Patuxent River. Weapons and tactics trials are undertaken at the former by VX-31 and VX-9 (left). Systems evaluation is undertaken at 'Pax' by HX-21, which operates some AH-1Ws (right). The Zulu upgrade evaluation is also undertaken at 'Pax', using NAH-1Zs (above right).

Firefighting Cobras

The US Department of Agriculture Forest Service will soon begin testing a modified AH-1F as an aerial firefighting supervision platform. Known as the 'Firewatch Cobra', the aircraft is one of 25 retired AH-1Fs acquired by the Forest Service via the US Army's excess property programme in early 2003. The modified aircraft will initially

be assigned to the Redding Air Attack Base in California during the 2004 fire season. In addition to serving as a lead plane and as an airborne command and control platform, the 'Firewatch Cobra' is capable of providing video and infrared mapping and downlinking the data to a receiver on the ground in real time. Although equipped with an EO/IR turret, the aircraft is not capable of carrying cargo or delivering retardant.

Three former US Army AH-1Ps that are operated by the Florida Division of Forestry Aircraft Operations Division are, however, capable of conducting firefighting operations. The helicopters can carry a 320-US gal (1211-litre) bucket, or a foam/retardant insertion system can be installed in the Cobra's forward ammunition bay. The system is equipped with a 360-US gal (1363-litre) fixed tank capable of delivering

water/retardant or foam. Developed by Garlick helicopters Inc., the aircraft are known as B-209 'Firesnakes'.

AH-1F	N109Z	69-16422	USDA Forest Service
AH-1P	N130FC	76-22694	Florida Division of Forestry Aircraft Operations division
AH-1P	N131FC	76-22570	Florida Division of Forestry Aircraft Operations division
AH-1P	N132FC	77-22747	Florida Division of Forestry Aircraft Operations division

Sukhoi 'Frogfoot'
Su-25, Su-28 and Su-39
Sukhoi's Jet Shturmovik

The concept of the *Shturmovik* is a uniquely Russian one, born even before the dark days of the Great Patriotic War. The *Bronironanyi Shturmovik* – literally an armoured attacker – was intended to support the troops on the ground from the air, yet survive punishing ground fire itself. In the years that followed the end of the war in Europe, several jet *Shturmovik* designs evolved. After bitter battles between rival design bureaux, Sukhoi's Su-25 won through. Inspired by experiences in Vietnam and the Middle East, and blooded in Afghanistan, the unflatteringly named 'Frogfoot' is now a proven combat aircraft – one which the Sukhoi bureau still hopes to improve.

P. Sukhoi Design Bureau

Su 25

Sukhoi Su-25, Su-28 and Su-39 'Frogfoot'

Standing beside the original wooden mock-up of the Sukhoi T8 army attack aircraft is Oleg Samoylovich. He was the chief designer for the project from August 1972 until October 1974, when he moved to the T10 (Su-27 'Flanker') design team. The T8 design seen here is recognisable as the antecedent of the Su-25 but is obviously a long way from becoming the rugged ground attack aircraft that we know today. Indeed, inherent fragility in the final Su-25 design did not truly become apparent until the aircraft saw real combat in Afghanistan.

This sharkmouthed Slovak air force Su-25K is one of the 11 'Frogfoots' acquired by the newly-established Slovak Republic in 1993. Czechoslovakia had been the first export customer for the Su-25, and it was from Czech sources that the West received its first clear public views of the Su-25. Even before the partition of the two countries, the Su-25 force had a reputation for decorative unit markings. Sharkmouths were seen on several aircraft of the former Ceskoslovenske Letectvo and this tradition was carried on in Slovakia.

The Su-25 has often been assumed to be a Soviet clone of the USAF's AX COIN aircraft, based on the losing Northrop A-9 (rather than the winning A-10), and less agile and less armoured more as a result of Soviet incompetence than by deliberate design. The USAF's Vietnam War-inspired AX requirement was for the close air support of troops in contact and for counter-insurgency, which assumed a degree of air superiority or at least a low level of air and SAM threats. By contrast, the Russian aircraft was designed to meet a slightly later and very different requirement which stressed anti-armour and fighter-bomber capabilities over the modern battlefield. Combat proven in Afghan skies, the Su-25 is considerably more versatile than were its American counterparts, and is a remarkably efficient and cost-effective fighter-bomber.

Its export success has been limited by its lack of air-to-air fighter capability and by its lack of supersonic performance, since prejudice against the very idea of a subsonic combat aircraft remains strong. This can be gauged by the fact that even in the former USSR the aircraft was never procured in large numbers, while arguably less effective fighter-bombers (like the early Su-17s and MiG-27s) poured off the production lines in huge numbers. Overseas, sales of the Su-25 were further diminished by the ready availability of cheaper alternatives, many of which are retired and reroled fighters. Those customers willing to overlook the aircraft's

lack of speed have found it to be a remarkably potent weapon – perhaps unsuitable for independence day parades, but remarkably useful in its intended role once the bullets start flying. Combat experience pointed the way towards some obvious improvements and refinements, many of which were incorporated during production; more major changes resulted in an extensive redesign to produce a second-generation 'Frogfoot'. This aircraft emerged as the Cold War was ending, and it has proved almost impossible to win orders for the new variant either at home or overseas.

Shturmovik origins

During the Great Patriotic War (the approved Soviet term for the struggle against German invaders, which began in 1941) Russia pursued the design, manufacture and tactical use of dedicated ground attack and close support aircraft known generically as *Shturmoviks*, following the German lead set with aircraft like the Henschel Hs 123 and Hs 129. Britain and America preferred to use aircraft retired or switched from fighter or bomber duties (like the countless Spitfires, Hurricanes and Thunderbolts), or aircraft which had proved unsuitable for their design role (like the Hawker Typhoon). This Western approach set the pattern for the post-war world, with redundant or second-best jet fighters being hastily armed with bombs and rockets and pressed into service in the ground attack role.

Having successfully built up a family of dedicated ground attack and close support aircraft during the war, the USSR threw away its lead and followed Western practice afterwards. Successive generations of MiG-15s, MiG-17s and MiG-19s were pressed into service as fighter-bombers as soon as they were replaced in the fighter and interceptor roles.

The Ilyushin Design Bureau, previously responsible for the Il-2 and Il-10, attempted to produce a jet-powered *Shturmovik* in the shape of its Il-40, responding to a 1948 order. The aircraft was a jet *Shturmovik*, powered by twin AM-9 engines. It had a rear gunner and internal bomb bays in the wings, although it also drew heavily on the OKB's Il-28 twin-jet bomber. The Il-40 featured a quadruple package of NR-23 23-mm cannon, which could be traversed from the horizontal almost down to the vertical. It was also planned to use the new 'Groza' missile system. The prototype made its maiden flight on 7 March 1953 and the type was recommended for production in March 1954,

although it had problems with gun gas ingestion. A modified second prototype flew in October 1955 and passed its state acceptance tests in March 1956. This had extended air intakes stretching forward to the nose, which were inevitably nicknamed 'nostrils'. Three sub-variants were planned: the basic cannon-armed Ilyushin Il-40P, the Il-40R (Il-40ARK) reconnaissance and fire correction platform, and the Il-40UT trainer. The project was cancelled soon afterwards on 18 April 1956, apparently at the personal orders of Nikita Krushchev, who felt that it was an unnecessary diversion from the serious business of missile procurement. Records relating to the decision have reportedly disappeared from the official archives (see *World Air Power Journal* Volume 17 for more information on the Il-40 and Ilyushin's revived Il-102 design).

Five completed airframes at Rostov were destroyed, as well as one of the prototypes and the production tooling. This effectively killed off the concept of a jet *Shturmovik* until well into the 1960s, when USAF experience in Vietnam seemed to point out the weaknesses and inadequacies of the converted jet fighters used in the ground attack role, and the usefulness of ageing and slow propeller-driven strike aircraft like the Douglas Skyraider.

Revival of the concept

The USAF launched its own AX requirement with a request for proposals on 6 March 1967. This step, and those leading to it, were studied with great interest in the USSR. Existing fighter-bombers were studied with particular interest during the Warsaw Pact's major Dniepr '67 exercise: to everyone's surprise, the elderly MiG-17s and MiG-15s proved more effective than the faster but less agile MiG-21s and Su-7s. During the Six Day War, the devastating effectiveness of 30-mm cannon-equipped Israeli fighters (including obsolete Ouregans and Mystères) against ground targets (including tanks) provided further food for thought, and prompted Colonel General M. N. Mishuk to call for immediate production of the ancient Il-40. General I. P. Pavlovskii, commander of the Red Army, strongly supported those of his officers who argued for a new ground attack aircraft, and momentum began to build.

Deputy commander of the VVS, General Alexander Yefimov, was another powerful supporter, seeing a need for an aircraft like the Il-2s which he had flown during the Great Patriotic War.

While the Ministries of Defence and of the Aviation Industry considered the evidence and requests which were steadily accumulating, Sukhoi took matters into its own hands and in March 1968 began the design of a jet-engined *Shturmovik*. Ilyushin dusted off its drawings of the old Il-40 and revised it to become the Il-42.

Sukhoi's *Shturmovik* was designed by a loose group of senior personnel, including Oleg Samolovich, D. N. Gorbachev, Y. V. Ivashetchkin, V. M. Lebedyev and A. Monachev, who based the design on a configuration produced by I. V. Savchenko, commander of the air force air academy. It was known as the SPB project. The aircraft was designed around a pair of 17.2-kN (3,865-lb st) Ivchenko/Lotarev AI-25T engines. It was estimated that these would give the aircraft (which had an MTOW of 8000 kg/17,635 lb) a maximum speed of between 920 and

Above: This is a later mock-up of the T8 design than that seen on the page opposite. Note the changes that have been made to the cockpit and the three widely-spaced underwing pylons. Even at this early stage the outermost pylon was reserved for AAM carriage; however, the Su-25 was never fitted with such extravagant triple racks.

Top: In recent years Czech and Slovak Su-25s have appeared in increasingly outrageous colour schemes. The most extreme of these was undoubtedly this 'Frogfoot'-inspired monster.

Above, from left to right: These very basic models of the Mikoyan MiG-21Sh, MiG-27Sh and MiG-27II illustrate some of the completely different, almost random, approaches made by the Russian design bureaux to the 1969 LSSh 'Shturmovik' requirement.

Right: This early, and rare, photograph of the T8-1 prototype in flight (taken in 1975) clearly shows some of the important differences between it and subsequent aircraft. They included its ventral gun pack, smaller rudder and wing and lack of wingtip pods.

Ilyushin's contribution to the history of the jet Shturmovik is substantial. Ilyushin had already turned the Shturmovik concept into reality, in the shape of the piston-engined Il-2 and Il-10. On 7 March 1953 Ilyushin flew the prototype of its Il-40 'Brawny' (Il-40-I) design, powered by two small AM-5F axial turbojets. The Il-40-I (below right) inherited its tail section from the Il-28 'Beagle' bomber and its rear gunner's position (equipped with twin NR-23 cannon) from its wartime experience. Political antagonism and military antipathy meant that the Il-40-I never really passed beyond its prototype stage. However, before Krushchev cancelled the programme, some or all of a five-ship pre-production batch were completed; the first of them, the Il-40-II, is seen here (far right). Problems with the first prototype, most notably gun gas ingestion, led to the radical modification of the Il-40-II's engine intakes – though from the wing leading-edge backwards it was essentially the same aircraft. It is unclear if Ilyushin secretly saved one of the Il-40s it was ordered to destroy, from which the Il-42/-102 may have been built.

1,475 kt (500 and 800 km/h; 310 and 500 mph) and a range of 1,390 nm (750 km; 465 miles) with its 2500-kg (5,510-lb) warload, which included an internal cannon. Sukhoi stressed 'closer, lower and quieter' as its key words, rather than the contemporary VVS slogan of 'higher, faster, further'. Programme goals were to design an aircraft with very high battle damage resistance and tolerance, which would be economic and simple to produce, operate and maintain, which would have unmatched performance and agility at very low level, and which could operate fully laden from a semi-prepared 120-m (390-ft) airstrip. Officialdom caught up with the two bureaux in March 1969, when an official LSSh 'Shturmovik' request for proposals was issued by the Ministry of the Aircraft Industry.

The launch of the competition did not represent a complete change of heart, however, since development of the swing-wing Su-17 and ground attack variants of the new MiG-23 continued apace. There was no guarantee that any design produced as a result of the competition would ever enter production, and if an aircraft type were to be manufactured it seemed likely that it would be in only small numbers, for further evaluation of the concept.

The jet *Shturmovik* competitors

Nevertheless, the new requirement was important enough for four experimental design bureaux to work on competing designs. Sukhoi continued with its T8, while Ilyushin continued with the Il-42. Yakovlev designed a version of its Yak-28 'Brewer' bomber as the Yak-25LSh, and Mikoyan worked on a pair of designs under the provisional designation MiG-27, although neither bore any

resemblance to the MiG-27 we know today. The MiG-27Sh was based on the MiG-21 airframe, but with side-mounted intakes and a broad-chord, modestly swept wing like that fitted to the Hawker Hunter and a heavily framed canopy incorporating great slabs of armoured glass. The cockpit was moved forward. The MiG-27II was more revolutionary, a supersonic *Shturmovik* with a similar armoured cockpit and canopy and with similar fuselage and intakes, but with the ogival delta wing of the A-144 Analog. The aircraft was powered by a pair of unspecified engines installed side-by-side in the rear fuselage, and was intended to carry a warload of up to 3000 kg (6,610 lb). A rewinged MiG-21LSh design was considered, but most of the attention was focused on the MiG-27 derivatives.

The Sukhoi T8 was redesigned under the guidance of bureau chief P. O. Sukhoi before it was formally submitted in response to the LSSh requirement. The most important of the changes suggested by Sukhoi was the addition of a pair of 29.5-kN (6,630-lb) (or 27 kN/6,070 lb, according to some sources) Mikulin RD-9B engines, non-afterburning versions of the MiG-19's turbojet powerplant.

Sukhoi takes the day

These changes were enough to allow the Ministry of the Aviation Industry to select the Sukhoi design as the winner of the competition, much to the annoyance of the Ilyushin OKB, which felt that their aircraft was superior and that their history and experience made them the natural choice to design a jet *Shturmovik*. They suspected that their aircraft had been rejected for the wrong reasons, conjecturing that the motive for selecting the T8 could be found in its single-

seat configuration, which did not require the training of a new generation of dedicated gunners. To Ilyushin this was an expensive heresy, for they believed that operational experience had shown that a rear gunner was absolutely essential in a slow-moving *Shturmovik*. They were also amazed that their turbofan-engined aircraft (powered by a pair of non-afterburning derivatives of the MiG-29's RD-33) had been beaten by an aircraft powered by thirsty and old-fashioned turbojets, which necessitated the carriage of a larger explosive and inflammable fuel load, and which the OKB also believed were more prone to battle damage.

The Ilyushin Design Bureau was now officially out of the picture, but it continued work on its aircraft privately, describing it as an aerodynamic research aircraft and later moving the prototype to a Byelorussian airfield to avoid attention. Much later, following criticism of the Su-25 after its initial combat experience in Afghanistan, the Ilyushin aircraft re-entered the 'Frogfoot' story, as will be described.

With the T8 declared as the winner of the design competition, approval was given for further development. Prototype drawings, and production tools and jigs were prepared at Factory No. 153 at Novosibirsk, a plant traditionally associated with Sukhoi aircraft. Production of the first prototype was scheduled to begin in June 1970, but was delayed until August 1971 when air force officers increased the required warload to 4000 kg (6,435 lb), and tried to force an increase in low-level maximum speed to 1200 km/h (745 mph). Sukhoi argued strongly that supersonic speed was unnecessary and would impose unacceptable penalties, but some air force officers, conditioned by their experience with Su-7s and MiG-21s, simply could not conceive that any aircraft could survive without supersonic capability. Sukhoi compromised on Mach 0.82 (having originally favoured Mach 0.7). The aircraft was redesigned to meet the amended requirement (becoming the LVSSh) with larger fuel tanks, bigger overall dimensions and a revised MTOW of 10530 kg (6,540 lb).

The T8 team

Mikhail Simonov was appointed as project manager, with Oleg Samolovich remaining as chief designer on the aircraft from August 1972 until 9 October 1974, when he moved to the T10 (Su-27) and Y. V. Ivashetchkin took over. This was one month before the redesign was complete, in September 1972. Ivashetchkin had been Samolovich's deputy from 25 December 1972. Under Ivashetchkin was Vladimir Babak, who supervised a design team consisting of Yuri Rybishkin (detail airframe design), Alexander Blinov (durability), Pietr Lyrshchikov (combat

survivability) and Alexei Ryzhov (engine integration). The production supervisor was Valerii Nikolskii, and the chief of testing was Colonel Stanislav Nazarenko.

At around this time, the Sukhoi designers got their first glimpse of the US Fairchild A-10, and this caused something of a crisis. Several members of the team were keen to follow the US example of mounting the engines in pods above the fuselage, but this was felt to impose an unacceptable drag penalty; anyway, it was already too late for such a fundamental change.

The T8 mock-up was presented to the authorities at Khodinka, near Moscow, but an official order for prototypes was not placed. Two prototypes (T8-1 and T8-2) were in fact already under construction, Sukhoi having authorised the start of work after approving the preliminary design on 6 June 1972. The reason that the prototypes were not officially ordered became clear at a meeting between the OKB and the Minister of the Aviation

Top: Despite the problems that affected the T8, and the bitter combat experience of early-model Su-25s after they entered service, the Su-25 ultimately became a formidable attack aircraft.

Above centre: Another view of the T8-1 prototype.

Above: The Il-40 'Brawny' design reappeared – astonishingly, but once more unsuccessfully – in the early 1990s, in the shape of the Il-102. The Il-102, originally designated Il-42, might even be a rebuilt Il-40.

Sukhoi Su-25, Su-28 and Su-39 'Frogfoot'

Right: Sukhoi rebuilt the T8-1 to become the T8-1D. This aircraft was re-engined with R-95Sh turbojets and also gained the revised engine nacelles and inlets, armoured cockpit, larger wing (with leading-edge slats), larger fin and rudder, and the extended nose and tail adopted for production-standard Su-25s. The T8-1D first flew on 21 July 1978.

Below: Sukhoi used the T8-3 airframe for damage resistance testing. Sections of the cockpit were specially armoured and then fired at, from close range.

Below: T8-4 was the second production-standard aircraft and is seen here at the Tbilisi plant – the badge on the nose is believed to be the factory emblem. This aircraft is carrying FAB-250 bombs and B-8M1 rocket pods. T8-4 made its maiden flight in September 1979. By then the Sukhoi design had already been catalogued as 'Ram-J' by Western intelligence agencies.

Industry, P. V. Dementiev, when the aircraft's MTOW was again revised upwards, to 12220 kg (5,540 lb), and warload was increased to 5000 kg (3,110 lb) (although this was later relaxed back to 4000 kg/2,485 lb). A maximum *g* limit of 6.5 was specified, and the important systems were to be protected against damage by shells of up to 20-mm calibre.

P. O. Sukhoi lived long enough to see the mock-up of the aircraft for which he had fought, but died in 1973 before the prototypes were formally commissioned. The order to complete two T8 prototypes (one, T8-0, to be a static test airframe) was finally issued on 6 May 1974. This order was a tactical-technical requirement, which funded prototype aircraft and a limited flight test programme, but

held out no promise of production funding. Sukhoi realised that the aircraft would have to be produced on a shoestring budget, and that existing equipment, avionics and systems would have to be used wherever practical.

The T8-0 was delivered for static testing on 12 September 1974. The T8-1 prototype was completed with a modified version of the nav/attack suite fitted to the Su-17M2 'Fitter' and had a modified version of the SPPU-22 cannon pod mounted internally as the VPU-22 gun station. This contained a GSh-23 twin-barrelled 23-mm cannon with barrels which could be depressed for strafing. It was almost certainly only ever intended as an interim gun for the Su-25, whose concept had stressed the advantages of heavier calibre 30-mm weapons. The aircraft's avionics included the FON-1400 laser rangefinder, DISS-7 Doppler, and KN-23 navigation computer (designed for the MiG-23B series fighter-bombers). The flying prototype was delivered to the LII Gromov Flight Research Centre's Zhukhovskii airfield for testing in early December 1974. The Sukhoi bureau's chief test pilot, General Vladimir Ilyushin, was nominated as the initial project pilot and made the first high-speed taxi runs on 25 December 1975. The first taxi runs with the nosewheel raised off the runway took place on 3 January 1975. On 11 January, two days before the scheduled date for the maiden flight, one of the RD-9 engines (which had actually been scavenged from a redundant MiG-19, according to legend) suffered a turbine bearing failure, and several blades separated, causing major damage. The first flight was finally made on 22 February 1975.

Engine shortfalls

These problems with the RD-9 engine represented a particularly bitter pill for Sukhoi to swallow, since it had already been decided that a more powerful engine would be needed to cope with the aircraft's planned increased weight, and since the Minister for Aircraft Production, P. V. Dementiev, had already refused to authorise production of the Su-25 with the 'obsolete' RD-9. This was found in the shape of the Tumanskii R-95Sh, which was essentially the MiG-21's R-13F-300 with its afterburner removed. The new engine was again based on an afterburning turbojet, and not on a more modern, more suitable, and more economical turbofan. For the rest of its life, the Su-25 was handicapped by its primitive powerplant, and from time to time proposals were made that the aircraft should be re-engined with RD-33s (without afterburners). The answer was always the same: the necessary structural changes were too extensive to make re-engining worthwhile.

Although it was undeniably primitive, the R-95Sh was extremely robust and reliable. The powerplant was a twin-spool turbojet, with an axial compressor, a three-stage low-pressure section and a five-stage high-pressure section. The axial turbine was of two stages. The engine also had a

10-chamber annular combustor, with twin igniters. Auxiliary gearboxes were mounted on the bottom of each engine, driving the DC starter and generator, the AC generator, and the hydraulic, fuel and oil pumps. The R-95Sh was also designed to be able to run using different fuels, although this was only possible for four hours when using non-standard fuels such as vehicle diesel fuel. While the new engine was being developed, the aircraft continued to fly, and continued to experience difficulties. The aileron control system proved to have inadequate power, and eventually (from about 1984) BU-45 hydraulic boosters had to be fitted.

Despite the problems, the aircraft was transferred to Akhtubinsk in June 1975, where it undertook a variety of live weapons firing trials. These were concluded in August, military pilots noting that the aircraft's control forces were unacceptably high (even by Soviet standards, where higher stick forces are accepted as the norm), and that the cockpit was inadequately ventilated. The RD-9 engine had also proved prone to stalling when the cannon or rockets were fired, and was considered to be deficient in thrust.

In its original configuration, the first T8 looked quite different to all subsequent Su-25s. It had a shorter fin, with a small, single-piece rudder, and the wing was of shorter span and lacked the later Su-25's distinctive wingtip airbrake pods. The wings may have been slightly more swept, but this cannot be confirmed. The VPU-22 gun station took the form of a streamlined constant-section tube semi-submerged into the lower forward fuselage, with a fore-and-aft aperture in the front for the depressing gun barrels. The nosewheel was mounted 210 mm (8.3 in) to the left of the centreline.

The 'all new' T8D

The problems suffered by the first T8 prompted the eventual decision to entirely rebuild the aircraft with a host of modifications and improvements, completely changing its appearance and capabilities. It was rolled out after a two-year lay-up on 26 April 1978, just in time to take part in the state acceptance trials which began on 21 July 1978, for which the aircraft flew under the revised designation T8D (D for *Dvigyatel*, or engine). The second prototype had already joined the flight test programme, making its maiden flight on 26 December 1975. This aircraft was the first with a production-representative titanium cockpit bathtub, the first aircraft having had steel armour of the same weight. The T8-2 was also the first prototype which actually looked like a real Su-25, with long-span wings and a tall tailfin. The long-span wings included longer span (and thus increased area) ailerons, servotabs and a leading-edge dogtooth discontinuity. The aircraft was re-engined with R95Sh engines to become the T8-2D in March 1976 (before the first prototype was re-engined). The new engines had a new thrust line, and the tailplanes were modified in consequence, going from 5° anhedral to 5° dihedral. This was achieved by simply swapping the tailplanes from one side to the other and turning them upside down.

When it emerged from its rebuild, the T8D closely resembled the second aircraft in appearance, with a dihedral tailplane, taller fin, long-span wings and ailerons, and wingtip pods. The wingtip pods first fitted to the T8-2 contained a retractable landing light forward, and had a horizontally split rear section, with upper and lower halves which split apart to act as airbrakes. It was originally intended that the split airbrakes could be operated together to act as speedbrakes, or individually (in conjunction with appropriate rudder input) to generate side force. This capability was found not to be tactically significant, and the physiological effects on pilots were unpleasant. The T8-1 was originally built without airbrakes at all, and before it gained its wingtip pods the T8-2 had petal-type airbrakes mounted on the back of the engine nacelle sides.

'Ram-J' is revealed

The original VPU-22 gun station had been removed and replaced by an AO-17 30-mm twin-barrelled cannon mounted in the lower port forward fuselage. This necessitated moving the nosewheel again, to a position to the right

Top: This view of T8-2 shows the aircraft after it had been rebuilt as the T8-2D, in 1976. T8-2 was the first of the two initial prototypes to be re-engined and rebuilt (T8-1 followed in 1977/78).

Above: T8-5 is seen here at Kubinka air base, where much of the trials programme was hosted. T8-5 was lost in a crash in June 1980, soon after its maiden flight.

Below: With surprising speed – almost as soon as T8 development gave way to Su-25 production – export 'Frogfoots' were delivered to Czechoslovakia.

Right: This view of T8-9 shows the aircraft fitted with the TL-70 Kometa podded winch and towed target system. In fact, T8-9 was revised, rebuilt and repainted to serve as the Su-25BM (Bukshir Mishenyei) prototype – a dedicated target-tug variant. Work on the Su-25BM project began in 1986 and aerial trials commenced in 1989. A total of 50 Su-25BMs was eventually built for the VVS. Operationally, a single pod was always carried on the centre wing pylon, counterbalanced by another store (such as the FAB-500 bomb seen here) on the opposite wing.

Above: T8-12 rapidly drew attention to itself when it appeared on public display. It had been modified – reportedly for radar cross-section reduction – with what appeared to be radar-absorbent material on the nose and a faired-over gun port. However, as its air data probes, IFF antenna and other protuberances had not been removed, the true purpose of the changes to this Su-25 remain a mystery.

Below: This Su-25 is seen at Akhtubinsk in CFE verification photo-calibration markings.

of the aircraft's centreline. The change of cannon finally fulfilled Soviet air staff demands for a larger calibre gun packing a heavier punch. The T8 was eventually 'spotted' at Zhukhovskii by a Western intelligence satellite during 1977, and the aircraft was allocated the provisional Ramenskoye-series (the nearest town to the then anonymous test and trials airfield) reporting name 'Ram-J'.

Avionics improvements

Underneath the skin, even more important changes had been made. The navigation and attack suite of the Su-17M-2 was replaced by the upgraded and enhanced avionics of the Su-17M-3. The Fone laser rangefinder was replaced by a Klen-PS laser ranging unit, while the aircraft also received a KN-23 navigation computer, a DISS-7 Doppler, an RV-5M radar altimeter and an ASP-17BC-8 gunsight. This equipment suite was fitted to the T8-3 and subsequent pre-production aircraft from the start. The net effect of the many equipment changes was to enhance the accuracy of both navigation and weapon aiming. The KN-23 navigation

computer, the DISS-7 Doppler, and the ASP-17BC-8 gunsight were retained in the production avionics suite.

So little priority was accorded to the T8 that production of the aircraft had to be moved from Novosibirsk after the construction of only the first two prototypes to make way for more important work on the Su-24 'Fencer' and Su-27 'Flanker'. Even the factories at Smolensk and Irkutsk were busy with Su-24 and Su-27 work, and Sukhoi was forced to look elsewhere. Licence-production in Poland was seriously considered, before the OKB eventually took the project to the under-utilised Factory No. 31 at Tbilisi in Georgia. The T8-3 and T8-4 were built at Tbilisi to the revised configuration, making their maiden flights on 18 June 1979 and during September 1979, respectively.

T8 trials in Afghanistan

The Su-25 has been associated with the Soviet intervention in Afghanistan since the start of its career. From 16 April until 5 June 1980 (50 days), the first and third T8 prototypes were sent to Afghanistan to participate in a portion of the state acceptance trials which were to be 'conducted under as near real battlefield conditions as possible'. These trials, undertaken under the codename Romb-1, were not operational trials, although the pilots were warned that they might be asked to undertake missions by local divisional commanders. The two aircraft operated from a semi-prepared strip at an Afghan tank base near Shindand. They made 100 combat sorties in Afghanistan, 30 of which counted towards the state acceptance trials. They flew real missions, tasked by ground force commanders, who quickly found the agile T8s especially well-suited for attacking inaccessible targets in ravines and steep valleys. A pair of AV-MF Yak-38s participated in Romb-1 in Afghanistan at much the same time. The Su-25s were seen and photographed by Western journalists accompanying Mujahideen guerrillas, and though taken from very long range the photos were distinct enough to allow Western intelligence officers to see that the aircraft they knew as 'Ram-J' was flying operations. The full ASCC reporting name 'Frogfoot' was allocated soon afterwards.

The fourth Su-25 prototype (T8-4) was left to complete state acceptance tests at Mary in Turkmenistan until March 1981, when production was finally recommended. One of the loudest voices arguing in favour of this step was that of General Alexander Yefimov, deputy commander of the VVS and himself a distinguished former *Shturmovik* pilot during the Great Patriotic War. While this marked a successful step in the T8's career, the step forward was accompanied by two steps back. The test fleet was already depleted by the planned use of the T8-3 for battle damage resistance tests, in which weapons of increasing calibre and

velocity were fired at the airframe, but was due to be further reduced. The fifth T8 prototype (T8-5, which had joined the test programme during early 1980) had already been destroyed on 23 June 1980. It disintegrated at only 7.5 *g*, killing the test pilot, Y. A. Yegerov, and in January 1981 the Afghan veteran T8-1 disintegrated in a dive from which A. Ivanov ejected safely.

T8 trials developments

Additional T8 airframes soon joined the flight test programme. The T8-6 was used for gun-firing trials, while the T8-9 was used for aerodynamic and spinning trials. Rough field and external warload trials were undertaken by T8-10, including trials of backward-firing rocket projectiles from a heavily modified B8M pod (which still appeared to face forward). The T8-11 was the first aircraft with boosted ailerons. It later tested the new W-section four-part airbrakes. The next prototype finished its test-flying life trialling a special radar-absorbent ('stealthy') skin, and reportedly undertook compatibility trials with at least one type of tactical nuclear weapon. This laid the groundwork for the Su-25's later secondary (and little known) nuclear role. Su-25s have been associated with the IAB-500 'shape' that is believed to be the training weapon associated with the RN-61 nuclear bomb carried by various Frontal Aviation fighter-bomber types. With its 'stealthy' coating, the T8-12 had its laser window and gun port covered over, and at the end of these trials was retired to the museum at

Khodinka. This was an accidental breach of the security surrounding the new coating (which may have been under test for a more advanced aircraft type, possibly the MiG 1-42) and, when it was noticed, the aircraft was quickly withdrawn and replaced by a less sensitive Su-25. The aircraft is now believed to be in the Central Museum of the Great Patriotic War in Bralev Fonchenkou in Moscow.

The T10-14 and T10-15 were eventually used as R-195 engine testbeds, after extensive service as development mules. The T10-15's career included combat service in Afghanistan. The T8-7, T8-8 and T8-13 designations were not used by flying prototypes, and may have been static test and battle damage airframes, or may have become the Su-25UB and Su-25T prototypes.

Su-25 into production and for export

The first production Su-25s rolled off the line at Tbilisi and were delivered to the 200th OShAE at Sital Chai in Azerbaijan during April 1981. Universal export success was destined to elude the Su-25 – only two of Russia's Warsaw Pact allies ever bought the aircraft – but the type was exported (albeit in modest numbers) from quite an early stage in its career. The export version of the little fighter-bomber was designated as the Su-25K, and was externally identical to the version delivered to Frontal Aviation *Shturmovik* regiments. The first Su-25Ks were delivered to Czechoslovakia in April 1984, and the first good quality photos of the Su-25 started to appear in Czech aviation

T8-15 had an important early career as an engine testbed, trialling the R-195 engine. The extended (IR-suppressant) jetpipes and extra air cooling scoops (above the rear cowling) required by the new engine are obvious in this view. This aircraft has also been fitted with an additional bank of ASO-2V chaff/flare dispensers above the engine. The R-195 was an improved version of the R-95Sh, but it was never fitted to many aircraft and the Su-25 remained hampered by its ancient engine technology. The R-195 did find an application in the improved T8M (Su-25T) series, however. Remarkably, T8-15 is alleged to have gone on to see combat service in Afghanistan. Following this, the same aircraft was given a new identity, as 'Blue 301', and appeared at the Paris air show in 1991.

This anonymous Su-25 is wearing the original dark camouflage scheme tested on the Su-25, but soon abandoned. Throughout their entire service history Soviet/Russian Su-25s have worn a single camouflage scheme of two-tone brown and green, with light grey undersides.

magazines the following year. The deliveries to Czechoslovakia took place early in the Su-25's career, even before the type had reached the Group of Soviet Forces in Germany, and while only one of the 60th OShAP's squadrons was available for combat in Afghanistan. The Su-25Ks delivered to Czechoslovakia and Bulgaria differed little from the aircraft used by Soviet regiments during the same period, although they almost certainly had slightly downgraded defensive avionics equipment and were not compatible with nuclear weapons. Identically designated Su-25Ks delivered to other customers (e.g., North Korea and Iraq) were probably even more downgraded, although they displayed few external differences to the Soviet Su-25s.

Shopping for an Su-25

The costs of military aircraft are seldom revealed. Even when one is, it is hardly clear what level of spares support, ammunition, and ground support equipment has been included. Furthermore, prices actually differ according to political circumstances, the customer's 'status' (in relation to the supplier), and the extent to which the deal is being financed by the home government (as aid, as a genuine commercial deal, or in exchange for some commodity). Today, Russian aircraft manufacturers often find themselves supplying their aircraft as part of debt repayment packages. Prices can also differ according to whether the deal involves offsets, or according to the currency in which the customer will be paying. Finally, the exact specification of the aircraft being delivered will have an impact on price, as will the inclusion of any training within the USSR.

For all of these reasons, it is unusual for the price of a military aircraft to be openly released. The price offered to a long-standing customer or a close ally, paying with gold (or \$US) and not demanding complex offsets, will be very different to the price offered to a customer paying in palm oil and unlikely to make even those payments on time or in full. Surprisingly, quite detailed prices for the Su-25K emerged during the early 1990s. They gave an indication of the amount of equipment and weaponry supplied in a standard package (to equip a single squadron).

Above: Two-seat Su-25UBs operated alongside the front-line Su-25Ks in the East Germany-based units. This is one of the 'Frogfoot-Bs' attached to the 368th OShAP, formerly based at Demmin-Tütow.

Below: This is the T8UB-1 prototype, the first Su-25UB. Consideration was given to training Su-25 pilots on existing types, such as the MiG-15UTI but, wisely, the decision was made to develop a two-seater.

Weapons which could be supplied included 3,360 S-8KM unguided rockets (at $1,607 each), 840 S-13T rockets (at $5,110 each) and 840 S-13OF rockets (at $4,450 each). The larger S-24B (retailing at $5,210 apiece) were supplied in batches of 336, and 84 S-25-OFM-PUs were offered at $14,167 each.

For the built-in 30-mm cannon, 5,000 rounds of OFZ shells were offered at $26,364 per thousand, while similar OFZ shells for underwing 23-mm cannon retailed at $7,460 per thousand and were supplied in batches of 30,000. The 23-mm BZT round (supplied in the same quantity) cost $5,653 per thousand.

Missiles available included the Kh-25ML (168 of which constituted a standard batch, at $103,643 each) and the Kh-29L (84 for $175,241 each). Inert captive acquisition training rounds for both missiles were available in pairs, at $77,734 and $131,433 each, respectively.

Most types of bomb were supplied in quantities of 336, and unit prices included $1,445 for a FAB-250-270 fire bomb, $1,956 for a FAB-250M62, $8,705 for a BETAB-500, $10,195 for a FAB-500SHL, $12,054 for an ODAB-500PM, $13,728 for an RBK-500 AO-2 cluster bomb and $20,538 for a BETAB-500SHP. The RBK-500 PTAB-1 was the most expensive bomb offered, at $21,021 each. Smaller bombs were generally delivered in bigger batches, with the bargain basement $859 OFAB-100-120 coming in batches of 1,344 bombs. A handful of specialist stores were supplied in smaller quantities. A batch of 20 FOTAB-250T photoflashes retailed at $5,060 each, while 100 SAB-250-200 illuminators cost $4,821 each.

Technical description

The Su-25K's service life was given as 1,500 flying hours before a major overhaul, and the service interval as 700 hours. They obviously did not expect high utilisation, since the 700-hour interval was also given as a seven- to eight-year gap. The first production Su-25 hardly differed from the later prototypes, and a technical description of one would apply just as well to the other. In fact, all Su-25s up until the Su-25T/TM were structurally similar, with much the same systems. Only a handful of changes were made as a result of later combat experience in Afghanistan, and they were limited in scope, despite their impact and significance.

The Su-25 was of conventional configuration and construction, apart from the extensive use of armour plate. The aircraft was an all-metal monoplane with a high-set, high aspect-ratio wing which was modestly tapered and slightly swept on the leading edge, but not on the trailing edge. The wing incorporated 2°30' of anhedral. Engines were mounted to the fuselage sides in semi-conformal nacelles. Sixty per cent of the aircraft's structure was of

Twelve Su-25Ks, with a set of tools, spares and ground maintenance aids, were quoted at $132 million ($11 million each), plus two Su-25UBKs cost an additional $23.8 million ($11.9 million each) with the same tools, spares and equipment. Each aircraft was supplied with two SPPU-22-01 gun pods, eight BD-3-25 pylons, two PD-62-8 pylons, two APU-68-85E launchers, two APU-60-1MD launchers and three empty B8M rocket pods, while two BD-3-25AKU pylons and their associate two AKU-58E launchers were supplied with each group of four aircraft. These allowed the aircraft to carry the Kh-58 (AS-11 'Kilter') anti-radiation missile. A conversion training course was costed at $1.596 million, and a KTS-18 simulator at $5.35 million. Four spare R-195 engines were priced at $4.72 million ($1.18 million each).

The Su-25UB retains all the combat capability of the single-seat Su-25. This aircraft is unlikely ever to see any dangerous action, however, as it is the sole Su-25UB in the possession of the Slovak air force. The Czech air force also operates a single Su-25UB. All Slovak 'Frogfoots' are based at Malacky-Kuchyna air base, north of the capital city of Bratislava. Interestingly, Slovak Su-25s have retained the original white horse badge – the Ostrava coat of arms – which was worn by the aircraft when they were all in Czechoslovakian service, and is still worn by Su-25s in today's independent Czech air force.

Above: The second Su-25T prototype is seen here carrying pairs of R-60 (AA-8 'Aphid') AAMs, B-13L 122-mm rocket pods, FAB-500M-62 HE bombs, 9M120M Vikhr anti-tank missiles (16), one KAB-500L LGB and one Kh-29T (AS-14 'Kedge') TV-guided missile.

Below: A detailed view shows the seeker heads of the Kh-29T and the semi-active laser-homing Vikhr M missiles.

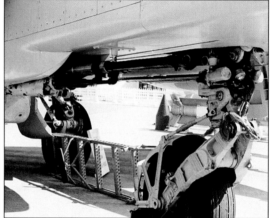

This Su-25K (above) has the late-model single-piece muzzle for its GSh-2-30 30-mm cannon. On the Su-25T (left) and Su-25TM the same gun has been moved to a ventral housing (designated NPPU-8M). Below can be seen the sideways feeding ammunition train for the GSh-2-30's VPU gun assembly. Up to 250 30-mm rounds can be carried.

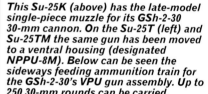

Below: Seen here under the wing of an Su-25T is a (red-nosed) Kh-25ML (AS-10 'Karen') semi-active laser-guided missile. Kh-25ML has a range of 20 km (12.5 miles) and a 90-kg (198-lb) warhead. Beside it is a B-13L 122-mm rocket pod. The B-13L is a five-round pod that can fire rockets with a range of warheads. A dummy R-60 is also carried.

Right: This Su-25TM is carrying a grey MPS-410 Omul ECM pod alongside an (extremely fanciful) Vympel R-77 (AA-12 'Adder') medium-range AAM – the so-called 'AMRAAMski'. No Su-25 yet has the capability to use such a weapon.

Below: This eight FAB-100s bombload on this Guards Regiment Su-25 is more representative of the capabilities of the 'Frogfoot' than some of the other loadouts seen here. The Su-25 excels as a 'bombtruck', as proved in Afghanistan and other more recent conflicts.

Below right: The greatest lesson learned by the Soviets in Afghanistan was the need for much improved self-defence measures. Twin banks of ASO-2V dispensers are now fitted to the Su-25.

Left and below: The nose avionics bay of the Su-25UB and Su-25 (below) are similar, despite the lack of the Klen-PS system in the former. Visible here are the modules for the RSBN-6 beacon tracking system. Weapons-related systems are housed to port.

Left: The Su-25 has a neat integral access ladder, while the Su-25UB has a less heavily framed design.

Right: This is the housing for the Su-25's twin drag chutes. Both chutes are held in a single tidy package until required. Above the chute housing is an RSBN antenna.

Above and below: The front cockpit of the Su-25UB (or UBK) trainer is largely identical to that of the Su-25, but the rear cockpit has the weapons sight replaced by an additional stores control panel, which replicates the functions of the same panel in the front seat. The heavy framing around the second cockpit substantially limits the vision of its occupant, to an even greater degree than that of the frontseater.

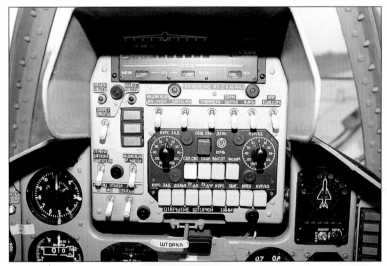

Above: The Su-25 (seen here) has a Klen-PS laser rangefinder, while the Su-25TM is fitted with the advanced Prichal system. The aircraft's nosecone hinges down for access.

Below: The Su-25 has five underwing pylons, on each wing. The four inner pylons are stressed to carry up to 500 kg (1,102 lb). The outer pylon is reserved for lightweight AAMs only.

Right: Like most front-line Russian-built combat aircraft, the Su-25 is fitted with the extremely reliable Zvezda K-36L zero/zero ejection seat. The firing handles for the seat are between the pilot's legs. This view of a K-36L shows the 'windshield' fitted above the seat (in the 'Frogfoot') and the two tubular housings for the seat's unique stabilising drogue parachutes.

Sukhoi Su-25, Su-28 and Su-39 'Frogfoot'

conventional Duralumin construction, with 13.5 per cent titanium alloys, 19 per cent steel, 2 per cent magnesium alloys and 5.5 per cent fibre-glass and other materials. Virtually no use was made of carbon-fibre composites or advanced aluminium lithium alloys.

Electrical power was supplied by a single 28.5-volt DC circuit, and by three 36-volt/400-Hz and one 115-volt/400-Hz AC circuits. The DC circuit consisted of a transformer, voltage regulator, and circuit breakers. Power was generated by a pair of engine-driven GSR-ST-12/400 generators, with two 25 Aph NiCad batteries available as an emergency power source.

Fuel system

The Su-25's fuel system delivers fuel to the engines from four pressurised main tanks, and from any external tanks (up to four of which can be carried underwing). The system incorporated DCN-44S-DT supply pumps, ECN-91B centrifugal delivery pumps and SN-6 ejector pumps, together with an NR-54 regulator, filters, cleaners, and dump valves, and with flow-meters, pressure and contents sensors. The internal tanks are pressurised using bleed air from the compressor's eighth stage. The No. 1 and No. 2 tanks are located in the fuselage, with the No. 2 (rear) tank sub-divided into two and acting as a collector tank. The fuselage tanks contained a total of 2386 litres (525 Imp gal) and had armoured bottoms and sides, beside

being self-sealing and lined with reticulated foam. The wing tanks contained a total of 1274 litres (280 Imp gal). The tanks could be filled manually, through gravity filler caps, or using a single pressure-refuelling point in the No. 1 tank. The engines can run using five types of aviation kerosene (PL-4, PL-6, T-1, TS-1 and RT) or in emergency can run for a limited time on diesel.

The Su-25 has independent twin hydraulic systems, each powered by an engine-driven NP-34-1M supply pump and each using 18 litres (4 Imp gal) of AMG-10 hydraulic fluid, pressurised to between 20 and 23 MPa using nitrogen. The port engine drove the system designated as the primary hydraulic system (PGS), which powered the nosewheel steering unit, the initial chambers of the aileron boosters, the airbrakes, the slats, the flaps and the tailplane, and could be used for emergency undercarriage extension. The starboard engine drove the secondary (VGS) system, which was used for undercarriage extension and retraction, main-wheel braking, and the yaw damper, and for the second chambers of the aileron boosters.

The semi-monocoque fuselage consisted of four sections (nose, forward fuselage, centre section and rear fuselage) and was built up around 35 bulkheads, longerons, auxiliary bulkheads, stringers and a stressed skin. The foremost nose section extended from the first to the fourth bulkhead, to which were attached the twin air data booms with their pitot-static sensors. The nose incorporated a downward-

opening forward fairing, whose chiselled front edge included the Klen PS laser rangefinder window, and which swung down to give access to the Klen equipment. The unpressurised navigation and auxiliary avionics bay behind this incorporated four upward-opening access doors.

The nosewheel bay contained the rearward-retracting nose oleo, which incorporated a twin-chamber hydro-pneumatic shock absorber (containing nitrogen and AMG-10 hydraulic fluid) with a maximum stroke of 340 mm (13.4 in). The nosewheel was hydraulically steerable through 60°, and was covered by a large mudguard/debris deflector. The nosewheel bay was covered by tandem twin doors, the long, thin rear door closing again after undercarriage extension. The undercarriage doors were linked to the oleo by rods. Retraction and extension was controlled hydraulically, usually by the secondary hydraulic system, but by the primary system in emergency.

Armour plated

A key feature in ensuring survivability over the battlefield was the provision of an armoured cockpit to protect the aircraft's most vulnerable component: the pilot. This took up most of the forward fuselage section, back to Bulkhead No. 11, together with the nosewheel bay, the gun bay and the main avionics bay. The cannon bay lay between bulkheads 4 and 7 in the lower left 'corner' of the fuselage and accommodated a single AO-17A twin-barrelled 30-mm cannon (also known as the GSh-30-2, or as the 9A623) with its 250-round ammunition box. This weapon had a rate of fire of 3,000 rpm and a muzzle velocity of 870 m (2,855 ft) per second.

The Sukhoi OKB originally planned a steel-armoured cockpit 'bathtub' that would come up to the pilot's shoulders. It was designed to use two layers of hard and soft

steel. Welding such a structure meant losing some of the armoured properties, but using rivets or bolts risked these fasteners becoming secondary projectiles when hit. It was finally decided that the pilot's cockpit 'bathtub' would be of welded titanium plates, each between 10 and 24 mm (0.4 and 0.9 in) thick. This was an expensive but highly efficient solution to the problem, and resulted in the pilot sitting in a box of armour which was reportedly capable of withstanding hits by up to 50 20-mm or 23-mm rounds. The titanium cockpit was not ready for installation in the first prototype, so steel plates machined to be the same weight as the 24-mm titanium sheets were used.

Protecting the pilot

The pilot sat as low as possible in the cockpit, and, because this restricted his ability to maintain a good all-round lookout, he was provided with a rear-facing periscope set into the top of the canopy, and with rear-view mirrors mounted on the windscreen arch. By necessity, the pilot's head projected a certain amount above the cockpit rails where it was vulnerable to ground fire. To protect his head, the pilot looked out through a windscreen of armoured glass, and a massive plate of armour sat above the ejection seat headrest, protecting the pilot from rounds coming from above and behind.

It was not only the pilot that was protected by armour. Virtually all vital systems and components were protected by armour, or duplicated, or both. The main engine oil tank, housed in the starboard nacelle, was protected by armour plate, and the main fuel lines leading from the main fuel tank to the engines were armoured and routed so that they could not spray fuel onto the engines if severed. The fuel tanks themselves were self-sealing and filled with reticulated foam to prevent explosions if breached.

The single Su-28 (which has also been referred to as the Su-25M or Su-25UT) was painted in a red, white and blue display scheme and wore DOSAAF titles on the tail. The paramilitary DOSAAF was the 'private flying' organisation of the former Soviet Union that provided basic flying training for students – most of whom would end up in the armed forces or other state aviation bodies. The Su-28 was mooted as a replacement for the DOSAAF's huge number of Czech-built Aero L-29 and L-39 jet trainers which were becoming increasingly difficult to support, even before the fall of the Warsaw Pact. In truth, the ungainly Su-28 was ill-suited to such a task, but it did make a few brief appearances at Western air shows in this guise. After a Paris debut in 1989, it travelled to Dubai (as seen here, in 1991) and later to the Philippines.

The control surfaces were actuated via titanium control rods each 40 mm (1.5 in) thick, proved against damage by small-calibre (up to 12.7-mm) machine-gun fire. Unlike cables, these could be distorted or nicked and still continue to function. The elevator control rods were duplicated. It has been suggested that pitch controls were better protected than roll and yaw controls so that the pilot would have the maximum chance of being able to pull up to eject if he suffered catastrophic damage while at low level.

Cockpit systems

The pilot sat on a Severin K-36L ejection seat. The K-36L was a simplified version of the K-36D or K-36DM used by aircraft like the MiG-29 and Su-27. Surprisingly, the seat was not capable of zero-zero operation; instead, it was cleared for operation at ground level, at speeds of over 55 kt (100 km/h; 65 mph). The seat was able to cope with inverted ejections at heights of 150 m (490 ft) or above, and 90° ejections from heights of 50 m (165 ft) and above. The cockpit also incorporated an air conditioning system, though this was intended more to maintain a degree of overpressure (between 3 and 5 kPa) in the cockpit, to prevent NBC contamination, than to maintain pilot comfort. The air conditioning system also supplied air to the pilot's anti-*g* suit and ventilated the windscreen and canopy, while also providing cooling air for the avionics compartments. Air for the system was bled from the eighth (final) compressor stage, and then passed through two heat exchangers and a turbocooler.

The separate oxygen system supplied a mix of air and pure oxygen to the pilot at altitudes in excess of 2000 m (6,560 ft), with pure oxygen above 7000 m (23,000 ft). The oxygen/air mix was produced in a KP-52M mixer unit. The oxygen was drawn from four 5-litre (15-MPa) bottles housed in the nosewheel bay. A BKO-3VZ emergency oxygen system was housed in the ejection seat, primarily for use during an ejection at high altitude, and gave a three-minute supply.

The cockpit was as conventional in layout as the aircraft was conventional in configuration: ergonomically laid out, but with rows of conventional analog instruments, switches and selectors, and without any electronic 'glass' display screens. The overall effect was old-fashioned and cramped, and the layout would have felt familiar to a late-generation MiG-21 pilot, or to pilots accustomed to the MiG-23 or Su-17. The panel was painted in a blue-grey colour slightly less vivid than the near-turquoise once used in Soviet combat. The cockpit incorporated many typically Soviet features, from the painted white vertical line on the lower

Above: 'Blue 08' was the prototype Su-25UTG carrier trainer and made its first landing aboard the carrier **Tbilisi** *(which became the* **Admiral Kuznetsov***) in November 1989. The Su-25UTG was intended to train Soviet/Russian pilots in basic carrier operations, but they were never conducted at a proper operational tempo. The Soviets' headlong rush into carrierborne aviation was defeated by lack of funding, before the terrible problems caused by moving straight into full-blown fast-jet operations at sea became manifest.*

Above right: The prototype Su-28 (T8UTG-1) is seen here making its first ski-jump at the Saki naval training airfield.

Right: 'Blue 08', and the production UTGs, have a modified rear fuselage structure to cope with the loads imposed by arrested landings. The Su-25UTG has an (arrested) landing distance of 90 m (295 ft) and is stressed for a load of 5g on landing.

panel which showed the pilot the stick central position (useful when recovering from a spin or departure) to the rail-mounted throttles and chunky-topped control column.

The throttles were mounted on a pair of parallel rods on the port cockpit wall, below the canopy rail. The port console mounted external stores, weapons selectors and jettison controls, as well as trimmers, drag chute, oxygen and air conditioning controls. The starboard side console and cockpit wall contained navigation system, radio, transponder, lighting and chaff/flare dispenser controls, plus the engine start panel and generator controls.

The rear cockpit of the two-seat Su-25UB was broadly similar to the single-seat or front cockpit. It lacked the gunsight and instead had a control panel for a system which allowed the instructor to simulate emergencies in the front cockpit, or to generate synthetic symbology in the front-seat sight. Full dual controls were fitted.

Su-25 avionics

The Su-25 was well equipped, with superb equipment and aids for precise navigation, accurate weapons delivery and self-defence. Even before details of the exact equipment fit became known, Western analysts were able to make some fairly accurate estimates of what types of equipment were fitted from the plethora of antennas, fairings, bumps and protrusions which littered the airframe from nose to tail. The nose culminated in an angular 'chisel', whose sloping face was transparent, behind which was the Klen-PS laser rangefinder. Immediately above the tip of the nose was a pair of parallel instrumentation booms, serving as pitot-static sources for the instruments and the weapons aiming system. The main (port) PVD-18G-3M probe is always thought to have carried sideslip and AoA sensor vanes, and a cruciform RSBN-6S antenna, whereas the tandem cruci-form finlets all seem to have been fixed antennas for the RSBN, and not pivoting vanes. The starboard (secondary) PVD-7 probe is a simple pitot. The RSBN-6 system is used in conjunction with RSBN-2N or RSBN-4N ground beacons for navigation, or with PRMG-4 for instrument

landing approaches. This allows approaches down to 60 m (200 ft) above the runway. The DUA-3 AoA vanes were actually mounted low on the forward fuselage sides, roughly in line with the forward edge of the windscreen. A single DUA-3M yaw vane was mounted below the nose, on the centreline, just ahead of the gun muzzle. The nose

Ukraine's Su-25UTGs were obtained from former Soviet forces, left behind when Ukraine split from the USSR/CIS. The aircraft adopted Ukrainian markings (left) over their existing camouflage and squadron badges. Today, some if not all of Ukraine's Su-25UTGs are operated by the International Fighter Pilot's Academy (above), which flies from Kirovskye air force base in the Crimea.

After the Kuznetsov made its IFOR deployment to the Adriatic in 1996, it made a port visit to Malta with this Su-25UTG on board.

ejection seat survival pack. The wingtip pods mounted dielectric leading edges which covered SPO-15 (L-006LE) Sirena RHAWS antennas, and some later Su-25 variants had a square antenna projecting from the side of the pod. This served the Gardeniya active jammer.

Under the rear fuselage were a short 'towel rail'-type antenna serving the R-828 'Eucalyptus' radio. The 20-W R-828 radio is used for communicating with army units on the ground. Further aft on the rear fuselage was a blade antenna for the MRP-56P radio beacon receiver, and a flush disc-shaped antenna serving the RV-15 (A-031) radio altimeter. Further aft (behind the towel-rail), there was sometimes a tripole antenna below the rear fuselage, similar to that above the nose, this serving the SRZ/SRO IFF system. The sharp spike-like fairing projecting aft above the tailcone housed an RSBN antenna in the tip, with scabbed-on SRZ/SRO antennas on the sides.

The pilot entered the cockpit using a three-rung retractable boarding ladder, which is telescopic and which then folds upwards into a well incorporating two footholds. From the top foothold, the pilot steps across forward to a fold-down step, from which he can reach the cockpit itself. Grab handles are mounted behind the canopy and further aft on the side of the spine. The two-seater was fitted with a simpler entry ladder, which consisted of a simple telescopic pole to which were attached folding footsteps. This freed the pilot from reliance on ground support equipment ladders. Surprisingly, in view of this advantage, many late Su-25UBs seem to have been built without an integral boarding ladder.

Internal fuel tankage

The centre fuselage incorporates the wing centre-section and two integral fuel tanks, and runs between bulkheads 11B and 21. The No. 1 fuel tank (between bulkheads 11B and 28) contained 1128 litres (250 Imp gal), and the No. 2 tank (between bulkheads 18 and 21) contained an additional 1250 litres (275 Imp gal). The top of the centre fuselage section contained a duct through which ran the control rods, fuel lines and other hydraulic, air conditioning and wiring runs. In the bottom of the centre fuselage, between bulkheads 12 and 18, were the mainwheel bays. The main oleos, which incorporated 400-mm (16-in) stroke twin-chamber hydro-pneumatic shock absorbers, retracted forwards. The mainwheels braked automatically during retraction, and were each covered by tandem doors. The forward doors were hinged outboard, and closed inward again after undercarriage extension.

The engine nacelles and intake ducts were attached to

contours were broadly similar to those of the similarly equipped MiG-23B and MiG-27 fighter-bombers.

Below the 'roots' of the instrumentation booms, well in front of the AoA vanes, were two small spherical antennas serving the SRO RWR, and two broadly rectangular dielectric fairings which covered the SO-69 transponder. Under the nose, just behind the yaw vane, was a small blade antenna which served the SO-69 transponder.

Further aft, the tandem antennas for the DISS-7 Doppler were housed under a flush dielectric panel immediately ahead of the gun bay access door. A similar panel on the fuselage spine covers the ARK-15M radio compass, while a slightly-swept T antenna further forward serves the R-862 radio. The 30-W R-862 VHF/UHF radio is used for routine air-to-air and air-to-ground communications in the 100-149.975 MHz and 220-399.975 MHz ranges. A 10-W R-855 emergency radio (20-59.975 MHz) is housed in the

the sides of the centre fuselage. They were constructed from bulkheads, longerons and double skin, and stood 60 mm (2.4 in) from the fuselage sides, leaving a slot for the extraction of boundary layer air. The intake lips were raked forward by 7°, giving slightly better air flow at higher angles of attack.

Rear fuselage assembly

The rear fuselage ran back from bulkhead 21, and incorporated the engine mounts (at auxiliary bulkheads 20 and 27) and the tailplane attachment points. The brake chute compartment and its upwards-hinging cover were mounted on the last bulkhead, No. 35. The compartment contained a pair of cruciform PTK-25 brake chutes, each of 25 m² (270 sq ft) area, which were deployed using springs and small drogue chutes. The three-spar fixed tailfin was attached to three points above the rear fuselage, and incorporated a cooling inlet at the root for the electrical generator.

A Tester UZ flight recorder was buried inside the fin structure, which also served as the mounting point for the antenna (below a dielectric fin cap), and for SPO-15 RHAWS and R-862 UHF/VHF radio antennas on the trailing edge. The trailing-edge rudder was divided into upper and lower sections, with the upper section independently controlled through the SBU-8 oscillation damper and an RM-130 hydraulic actuator.

Above the brake chute compartment, behind the fin leading edge, four upward-firing chaff/flare dispensers were recessed into the top of the rear fuselage decking, each containing 32 cartridges. Between the side-by-side pairs of chaff/flare dispensers on each side of the centreline was a slender tubular fairing projecting aft and culminating in a sharp dielectric spike. This housed an antenna for the RSBN TACAN, and had antennas for the SRO IFF system scabbed onto its sides.

The horizontal tailplane had a swept leading edge

This view of an Su-25T shows the redesigned chaff/flare housing above the brake chute fairing. For the 'Super Frogfoot', Sukhoi expanded even more on the Su-25's already substantial self-defence fit. The Su-25T's UV-26 countermeasures dispenser can carry a mixture of 192 PPI-26 IR decoys and PPR-26 chaff cartridges.

The Su-25TK is the export-dedicated version of the Su-25T – though whether its equipment fit is equivalent to the Su-25T or Su25TM remains unclear. Any actual systems fit can probably be dictated by the customer, but this confusion is a reflection of the lack of information about the Su-25T/Su-25TM family in general. For example, this is the aircraft displayed at the Farnborough air show of 1992 as an Su-25TK, yet 'Blue 10' was probably built to Su-25TM standard, from a converted Su-25T. Russian sources have labelled this aircraft as the T8M-10, Su-25T and Su-25TK.

Sukhoi Su-25 'Frogfoot'

Sukhoi Su-25 'Frogfoot-A'

1 Pitot head
2 Secondary dynamic pressure probe
3 RSBN ILS antennas
4 Klen-PS laser ranger and marked target seeker
5 Gun camera
6 SO-69 transponder antenna
7 SRO RWR antenna
8 Yaw vane
9 Cannon muzzle aperture
10 DISS-7 Doppler navigation antennas, offset to starboard
11 Nose avionics equipment bays, access port and starboard
12 SRZ IFF antenna
13 Armoured glass windscreen panels
14 ASP-17BC-8 weapons sight and recording camera
15 Instrument panel shroud
16 Control column
17 Rudder pedals
18 Ammunition magazine, 250 rounds
19 Cartridge case collector
20 Incidence transmitter
21 GSh 30-2 (AO-17A) twin-barrelled 30-mm cannon
22 Levered suspension nosewheel leg strut, hydraulically steerable
23 Single nosewheel with mudguard, aft-retracting
24 Nose undercarriage pivot mounting and hydraulic retraction jack
25 Fold-out cockpit step
26 Slide-mounted engine throttle levers
27 Pilot's K-36L ejection seat
28 Cockpit canopy, hinged to starboard
29 Rear view periscope mirror
30 Cockpit head armour
31 Welded titanium box structure armoured cockpit pressure section
32 Centre fuselage avionics equipment bay
33 Boarding steps
34 Nosewheel housing, hinged for avionics bay access
35 5-litre oxygen bottles (4)
36 Telescopic boarding ladder
37 Port engine air intake

38 No. 1 forward fuselage fuel tank, armoured and filled with fire-suppressant foam; total internal fuel capacity, 3660 litres (805 Imp gal)
39 Control runs, damage-tolerant duplicated system
40 Dorsal avionics equipment compartment
41 Starboard engine intake duct
42 Fuselage tank gravity fuel filler
43 R-862 UHF/VHF antenna
44 Starboard wing integral fuel tank
45 Wing tank fuel filler

46 Leading-edge slat guide rails and operating linkage
47 Stores pylons, five per side
48 1150-litre (252-Imp gal) ferry tank, maximum of four
49 S-250FM unguided rockets
50 Outboard pylon with R-60M (AA-8 'Aphid') air-to-air self-defence missile
51 Starboard five-segment leading-edge slats
52 Landing light glare shield
53 Retractable landing light

54 Forward and starboard oblique SPO-15 RHAW antenna
55 Starboard navigation light
56 Starboard 'crocodile' airbrake, open
57 Starboard aileron
58 Aileron geared tab
59 Trim tab, starboard only
60 Aileron hinge control linkage
61 Starboard two-segment double-slotted flap
62 Ferry tank tail fins
63 Exhaust duct cooling air intake
64 ARK-19 DF antenna
65 ASO-2V 32-round chaff/flare launchers (8)
66 Dual generator cooling air intake
67 Rudder control linkage
68 Starboard trimming tailplane
69 Yaw damping upper rudder segment hydraulic actuator
70 Fin-tip VHF antenna

71 Rear SPO-15 RHAW receiving antenna
72 Tail navigation light
73 Upper rudder segment
74 Manually operated lower rudder segment
75 Rudder geared tab
76 Trim tab
77 Rear chaff/flare launchers
78 Rear SRO RWR antennas, port and starboard
79 Rear RSBN ILS antenna
80 Parachute door
81 Dual brake parachute stowage
82 Elevator geared tab, additional trim tab to starboard
83 Port manually operated elevator
84 Port trimming tailplane
85 Lower SRZ IFF antenna
86 Three-position trimming tailplane hydraulic actuator
87 Tailplane hinge mounting
88 R-828 HF antenna
89 RV-15 (A-031) radar altimeter antenna
90 Port engine duct chaff/flare launchers
91 Exhaust stream cooling air injector plug (infra-red suppression)

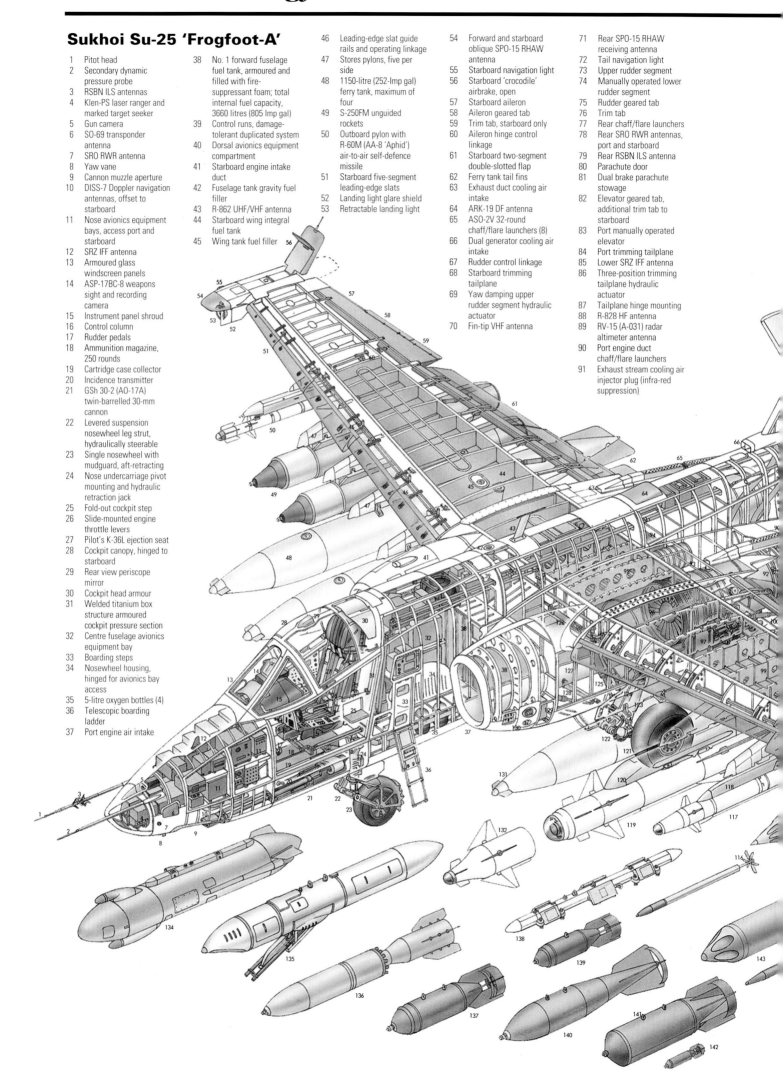

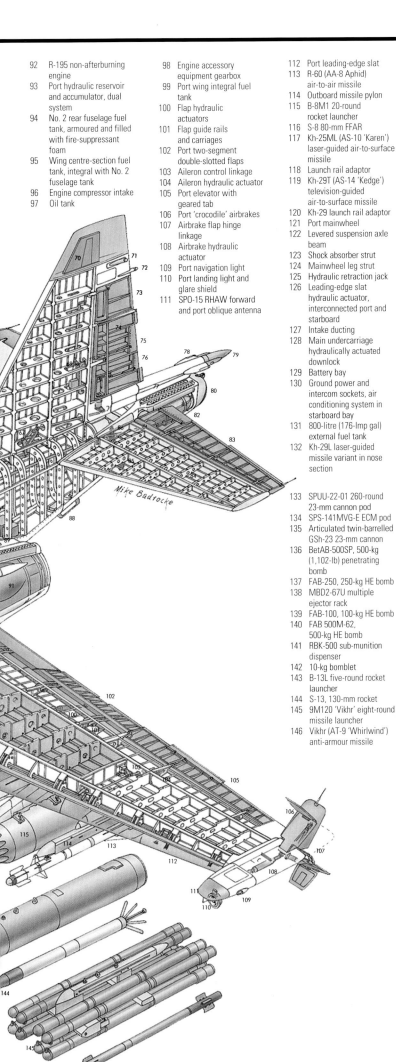

92 R-195 non-afterburning engine
93 Port hydraulic reservoir and accumulator, dual system
94 No. 2 rear fuselage fuel tank, armoured and filled with fire-suppressant foam
95 Wing centre-section fuel tank, integral with No. 2 fuselage tank
96 Engine compressor intake
97 Oil tank
98 Engine accessory equipment gearbox
99 Port wing integral fuel tank
100 Flap hydraulic actuators
101 Flap guide rails and carriages
102 Flap two-segment double-slotted flaps
103 Aileron control linkage
104 Aileron hydraulic actuator
105 Port elevator with geared tab
106 Port 'crocodile' airbrakes
107 Airbrake flap hinge linkage
108 Airbrake hydraulic actuator
109 Port navigation light
110 Port landing light and glare shield
111 SPO-15 RHAW forward and port oblique antenna
112 Port leading-edge slat
113 R-60 (AA-8 Aphid) air-to-air missile
114 Outboard missile pylon
115 B-8M1 20-round rocket launcher
116 S-8 80-mm FFAR
117 Kh-25ML (AS-10 'Karen') laser-guided air-to-surface missile
118 Launch rail adaptor
119 Kh-29T (AS-14 'Kedge') television-guided air-to-surface missile
120 Kh-29 launch rail adaptor
121 Port mainwheel
122 Levered suspension axle beam
123 Shock absorber strut
124 Mainwheel leg strut
125 Hydraulic retraction jack
126 Leading-edge slat hydraulic actuator, interconnected port and starboard
127 Intake ducting
128 Main undercarriage hydraulically actuated downlock
129 Battery bay
130 Ground power and intercom sockets, air conditioning system in starboard bay
131 800-litre (176-Imp gal) external fuel tank
132 Kh-29L laser-guided missile variant in nose section

133 SPUU-22-01 260-round 23-mm cannon pod
134 SPS-141MVG-E ECM pod
135 Articulated twin-barrelled GSh-23 23-mm cannon
136 BetAB-500SP, 500-kg (1,102-lb) penetrating bomb
137 FAB-250, 250-kg HE bomb
138 MBD2-67U multiple ejector rack
139 FAB-100, 100-kg HE bomb
140 FAB 500M-62, 500-kg HE bomb
141 RBK-500 sub-munition dispenser
142 10-kg bomblet
143 B-13L five-round rocket launcher
144 S-13, 130-mm rocket
145 9M120 'Vikhr' eight-round missile launcher
146 Vikhr (AT-9 'Whirlwind') anti-armour missile

Above and below: In the cockpit of the Su-25, primary flight instruments (KUS-2 airspeed indicator, UV-75-15-PV altimeter, A-031-4 radar altimeter, PPD-2 VOR/DME, KPP-K1 artificial horizon, NPP-MK navigation/heading indicator, DA-200P VSI and turn gauge, clock, fuel gauges and other systems gauges) are flanked to the left by the main weapons panel, and to the right by the SPO-15 RHAW display, master warning lights, RHAW controls, brake and hydraulic controls. The left side-panel houses jettison switches, radios, drag-chute release, environmental and oxygen controls. The POM throttle assembly is mounted above this panel. The right side-panel (below) contains the RSBN and ARK-2 controls, transponder and radio switches, interior lighting, engine start switches and chaff/flare panel.

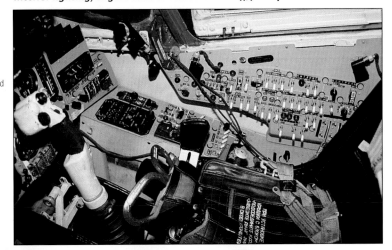

Left: The Su-25 has nothing as sophisticated as a HUD in the cockpit. Instead, the main instrument panel is dominated by the ASP-17 BC-8 electro-optical weapons sight. The black pipe-shaped object mounted in front of the sight's reflecting flat glass panel is the AKS-5-75os 'gun camera', which films directly through the sight.

Sukhoi Su-25, Su-28 and Su-39 'Frogfoot'

Top: Until the arrival of the Su-25T the only 'Frogfoots' to be fitted with uprated engines were the handful of Su-25BM target-tugs. Their improved R-195 engines fit neatly into the existing engine bays and only small clues betray their presence. Chief among them are the extended jet-pipes that protrude from the engine efflux cowlings. If the Su-25BM were not carrying the TL-70 target-towing system, it could still be identified by the missing intake at the base of the fin.

Above: Experience in Chechnya, when bad weather grounded the VVS Su-25 force, underlined the need for the all-weather Su-25T/TM. This Su-25TM is seen at Zhukovskii carrying the Kopyo-25 radar pod.

(slightly more swept than the wing) and a forward-swept trailing edge. It was built around two spars in two halves, and was then joined by a centre-section which ran through the rear fuselage. The tailplanes incorporated some dihedral to keep them clear of the jet wash from the engines, and to keep them out of the turbulent air coming off the wing. The tailplane was hydraulically adjustable to any one of three positions, one used for take-off and landing, one for normal flight, and one for dive attacks. The elevators were joined to the trailing edge of each tailplane by three hinges and were aerodynamically and mass balanced. They could deflect to 14° upward and to 23° downward. An elevator trim tab was fitted to the starboard elevator.

Wing design

The wing, like the tailplane, was built in two halves, and each section was constructed around a central box-section spar with ribs, longerons and stringers. The area between the first and 10th ribs on each side was sealed to form an integral 637-litre (140-Imp gal) fuel tank. Control rods (including those for the aileron) and wiring was buried in the leading edge, with slat actuator hinges mounted on load-bearing ribs. The trailing-edge section contained fuel and hydraulic lines, and mounted the flap and aileron hinges and boosters.

Moving control surfaces extended across virtually the

entire span of the leading and trailing edge. Two-section double-slotted flaps occupied the inboard part of the trailing edge, with conventional ailerons outboard. The flaps could be extended to 20° for manoeuvring, or to 35° (inboard sections) and to 40° (outboard sections) for take-off or landing. The ailerons deflected to 18° upward or 18° downward. The leading edge of each wing was occupied by an interconnected five-section slat (each section with two hinges). A leading-edge dogtooth discontinuity began at the root rib of the third flap section. The slats could be deployed through 6° for manoeuvring, or to 12° for take-off and landing.

Broad flat pods were attached to the wingtips. They consisted of a dielectric antenna for the SPO-15 RHAWS forward, with a pop-down PRF-4M landing light in the underside (usually with a fixed vertical anti-glare shield inboard), and with the appropriate red or green navigation light on the outboard edge. The trailing edge of each pod was split into upper and lower sections which opened as airbrakes. The wingtip pods also incorporated connectors for the SPU-9 pilot-to-ground crew intercom system.

Weapons hardpoints

The wing also served as the mounting point for the Su-25's external warload, which was carried on 10 underwing hardpoints. The four inboard hardpoints under each wing were fitted with universal BD3-25 pylons, and the outboard hardpoint a PD-62-8 pylon. The latter are believed to mount only APU-60-1MD missile launch rails, compatible with the R-60 or R-60M (AA-8 'Aphid') IR-homing dogfight missiles, carried for self-defence. There is no reason why the R-73 (AA-11 'Archer') AAM should not be carried with the appropriate pylon adaptor.

The inboard underwing pylons could be fitted with a range of adaptors, allowing the carriage of a wide variety of stores. The pylons closest to the wingroot, and next but one outboard, were 'plumbed' for the carriage of PTB-800 800-litre (175-Imp gal) or PTB-1150 1150-litre (253-Imp gal) external auxiliary fuel tanks. These outboard 'tank-capable' hardpoints (the middle station of the five under each wing) can also be used for the TL-70 Kometa target winch system on the Su-25BM, and for the carriage of an SPS-141MVG-E ECM pod on aircraft assigned to the anti-radar role. These hardpoints may be the ones used for

the carriage of nuclear weapons.

The BD3-25 pylons were stressed for the carriage of a wide variety of stores weighing up to 500 kg (1,100 lb) per pylon, up to the maximum load of 4340 kg (9,570 lb). The eight main pylons were seldom used simultaneously, for the Su-25 normally carries much smaller warloads on only a portion of its available hardpoints, since the carriage of a full load imposes range, performance, agility and take-off penalties.

The 'man pod'

Arguably the most unusual stores which can be carried underwing are the pods which constitute the AMK-8 mobile maintenance unit. The Su-25 is optimised for operation from primitive forward airstrips, and can ferry its own vital ground support equipment in underwing pods modelled on the airframe of the PTB-800 external fuel tank. There are four standard types of pod. The K-1E houses electrical power units, with a compressor and tools for maintenance and field repairs. The K-2D contains refuelling equipment (a pump and rubberised cells). The K-3SNO has maintenance tools and intake blanks, chocks, and camouflage netting, while the K4-KPA has diagnostic and checking equipment, and equipment for radio and avionics maintenance. A final, slightly reshaped AMK-8 pod is available (but is understood not to have been deployed at unit level). This is designed to transport a ground crew member, albeit in some discomfort.

The Su-25's orthodox and conventional configuration,

systems and construction were accompanied by predictable and benign handling characteristics. Transitioning to the Su-25 was thus not a major step for even fairly inexperienced pilots, since the aircraft enjoyed relatively simple and uncomplicated handling procedures. It was possible to conduct most training solo, with an instructor flying chase, and it was felt that the MiG-15UTI and Aero L-39 would be adequate for instrument training and check rides, although the air force did issue a draft requirement for an Su-25UB as early as 1975. The preliminary design for the two-seat Su-25 was completed in 1977, but the project was not accorded a high priority, since many felt that the

Above: The basic Su-25 still has an inventory of largely 'dumb' ordnance, such as the 57-mm FFAR rocket.

Top: 'Yellow 25' is now the dedicated Su-25TK demonstrator. The greatest sales effort for this version has been directed at Persian Gulf states and the Su-25TK has visited the IDEX show in Dubai.

Su-25 'Frogfoot' in Afghanistan

The USSR invaded Afghanistan in December 1979. The Su-25's involvement in that war was initiated with a combat trials deployment for the T8, but began in earnest when early-production Su-25s were delivered to Shindand in 1982. These photographs were largely taken around Bagram air base, near Kabul, in 1988, the last full year of Soviet involvement. By February 1989 Russian forces had left completely, after an unsuccessful 10-year war of attrition.

MiG-15UTI was adequate for the conversion and continuation training of Su-25 pilots.

The two-seat Su-25UB

Even after the decision was made to produce a two-seat trainer, the project was always subject to interruption, delay and the diversion of resources. The first export successes of the Su-25 in 1984 added impetus to the development of the trainer, and the first example of an Su-25 (designated T8UB-1 and coded 'Red 201'), finally made its maiden flight on 10 August 1985. An original Su-25UB prototype had been started in 1981, but the incomplete airframe, and two more, were actually completed as the T8M-1 and T8M-2 prototypes (and as the T8M-0 for static testing) of the advanced Su-25T. This variant of the aircraft is described in detail later. Work on the Su-25UB was delayed, and finally passed to the Production Plant No. 99 at Ulan-Ude, where a second, new T8UB-1 prototype was built, which had that plant's distinctive bear badge on its nose. The same insignia was worn by the second Su-25UB built at Ulan-Ude, 'Red 202', which acted as the second prototype. Further Su-25UBs had a similar bear, slightly smaller, on a tilted rectangular shield. The two-seater retains full combat capability and is said to be universally known as the 'Sparka' in Russian and Soviet air forces service.

In order to reduce development time to a minimum, airframe changes were avoided wherever possible. Instead of lengthening the fuselage to accommodate a second cockpit (which would have involved other airframe modifications simply to compensate), the instructor's cockpit replaced a fuselage fuel tank, with a new pair of heavily framed cockpit canopies fairing into a bulged spine. The second cockpit was raised by 0.44 m (1.44 ft), giving the instructor a 7° sight-line down over the nose. This gave the two-seater a considerable increase in keel area forward, and the tailfin was enlarged to compensate. The horizontal tail was increased in area, and was of revised profile. The Su-25's usual retractable folding ladder was replaced by a simpler telescopic tubular strut supporting three narrow footrests. The Su-25UB's heavily stepped cockpits gave the backseater a better view forward than was obtainable in most Soviet two-seat trainers, and this made provision of the almost-traditional periscope less essential. It was offered as a customer option on the Su-25UBK, the export version of the two-seater, but was seldom requested. The prototypes and early Su-25UBKs did not have the periscope fitted, but many Soviet UBs were so equipped.

Some reports suggest that Sukhoi made plans for a three-seat trainer (with all three cockpits 'in tandem') but the reasons for such an aircraft remain unclear, unless it was expected to serve as a high-speed liaison aircraft. Develop-

Above and below: Some Su-25s based in East Germany wore distinctive disruptive camouflage schemes that Western observers dubbed 'Afghanistan camouflage'. Two contradictory stories emerged from Soviet ground crew to explain the unusual paint schemes. Some said that the colours had been worn in-theatre in Afghanistan, and had been retained when the aircraft returned to Europe. Others said that the schemes had been painted on only in Germany, but as a direct result of their experience in Afghanistan, to better camouflage the aircraft in European conditions. To date no photographic evidence has emerged of aircraft in Afghanistan wearing anything other than the standard three-tone scheme.

Sukhoi Su-25, Su-28 and Su-39 'Frogfoot'

Two VVS Su-25 units
were based in East
Germany as part of the
16th Air Army (Group of
Soviet Forces in
Germany). They were
the 357th Otdelnyi
Shturmovoi
Aviatsionnaya Polk
(OShAP/Independent
Shturmovik Aviation
Regiment) based at
Brandis, and the 368th
OShAP based at
Demmin-Tütow. The
357th arrived with its
aircraft in October 1985,
while the 368th arrived in
December 1988, directly
from Afghanistan.
Aircraft from the two
regiments were largely
indistinguishable as
both used individual red
codes with white
outlines. This is an
Su-25 of the 368th
OShAP, seen landing at
Tütow.

The other major
European operator of the
Su-25 was the
Czechoslovak air force
(the Su-25 is also in
service in Bulgaria).
Czechoslovakia was the
first export customer for
the 'Frogfoot', gaining its
aircraft even in advance
of Soviet units engaged
in Afghanistan. Initial
deliveries were made, by
Soviet pilots, to Hradec
Králové air base in April
1984 (by June, Czech
pilots were undertaking
these flights). These
aircraft are seen at
Pardubice, in 1993,
following the split of the
Czech and Slovak
Republics. Czech aircraft
were delivered with
black, stencilled four-
digit codes, which later
became solid numerals
with white outlines
(mid-1980s) and finally
all-white, by the early
1990s, as seen here.

ment was reportedly abandoned soon after it began in 1991. The aircraft was allegedly referred to within the OKB as the Su-25U3.

Trainer family

The Su-25UB combat trainer formed the basis of the stillborn Su-25UT (later redesignated Su-28). This aircraft was intended as a dedicated advanced trainer to replace the Aero L-29 and Aero L-39, both with the Soviet air forces and with the paramilitary DOSAAF. It was a simplified, unarmed two-seater, with no combat capability, no gunsight, no laser rangefinder, no RHAWS, no chaff/flare dispensers, and no internal cannon. Weight was reduced by 2000 kg (4,400 lb). Fuel tank linings were removed, and provision was made for just four underwing pylons, for the carriage of external fuel tanks only. The prototype was produced by conversion of the T8U-1, and first flew in its new guise on 6 August 1985. The Su-25UT introduced a revised wing leading-edge planform, with the dogtooth discontinuity between inboard and outboard leading-edge sections replaced by a short length of leading edge of reduced sweep, giving a gentle step in the leading-edge profile. The Su-25UT prototype was painted in a predomi-nantly white colour scheme, with red and blue trim, and initially with DOSAAF tail markings and the code 'Red 07'. The aircraft took part in the 1988 DOSAAF aerobatic championships, and in the hands of Yevgeni Frolov seized a

creditable third place. It was later recoded with the Paris air show code 'Blue 302' for the 1989 Paris Air Salon, by which time it also wore the revised Su-28 designation on its intakes. Only a single prototype of the Su-25UT was completed, and no orders were forthcoming. Reports that the Su-25UT prototype was subsequently converted to become the Su-25UTG are entirely without foundation, and the aircraft remains in use with the OKB's test fleet at Zhukhovskii.

Su-25UTG for the navy

Another derivative of the Su-25UB was the navalised Su-25UTG. This had many of the same modifications as the Su-25UT/Su-28, but was especially strengthened to withstand the stresses of a carrier landing and was fitted with a retractable arrester hook, a revised undercarriage and a carrier landing system. The hook resulted in the new variant's change in designation (the Russian for hook being Gak). Sukhoi had hopes that a carrierborne single-seat Su-25 might be selected as a carrierborne attack aircraft for the Tbilisi (now Kuznetsov) and its sister ships (all later scrapped or cancelled). The T8-4 was tested on the dummy deck at Saki in 1984 at the same time as were the T10-24, T10-25 and the MiG-29KVP. The selection of the multi-role MiG-29K for the new carrier air wings led to these hopes being frustrated, although it was clear that the Su-25 could form the basis of a cheap and simple land-based but

carrier-capable trainer for teaching carrier landings. It was anticipated that the aircraft would primarily be used for teaching experienced MiG-29 and Su-27 pilots the rudiments of carrier landing, mainly using dummy carrier decks like the one at Saki. The majority of actual carrier landing training would be conducted after pilots had converted to their operational type (the Su-27K or MiG-29K), perhaps after a familiarisation flight or two in the Su-25UTG. Since the Su-25UTG would not actually be based aboard carriers, but would instead fly to and from a carrier from its shore base, it was decided that wing folding would not be required.

The varied career of the Su-25UTG

The Su-25UTG prototype (designated T8-UTG1 and coded 'Blue 08') made its maiden flight in September 1988. The aircraft was flown onto *Tbilisi* on 21 November 1989 by Sukhoi project pilot Igor Votintsev and LII pilot Alexander Krutov, landing after the Su-27K and MiG-29K. The Su-25UTG may have been converted from an Su-25UB in the OKB's own workshops. The aircraft certainly wore a Sukhoi logo on its nose, instead of the Ulan-Ude factory bear badge applied to most two-seaters (though, interestingly, never to export Su-25UBKs). The single prototype was followed by a batch of 10 new production Su-25UTGs. Five aircraft (coded 'Red 04', '06', '07', '10' and '11') were sent to Severomorsk, home to the Kuznetsov's air wing and to an AV-MF Su-25 regiment. Five more (coded 'Red 60', '61', '62', '63' and '64') were left behind at Saki where they became part of the Ukrainian

forces. 'Red 60' is believed to have been written off in an inadvertent wheels-up landing, while 'Red 07' suffered a fatal accident near Murmansk on 11 November 1992.

Even though only one carrier entered service, the four Su-25UTGs in service with the unit at Severomorsk were considered to be inadequate for the training task which faced them. Accordingly, Sukhoi was asked to produce 10 similar aircraft by conversion of existing Su-25UBs under the designation Su-25UBP. They were to have the same airframe strengthening and naval features as the Su-25UTG, but were also to be fitted with a retractable inflight-refuelling probe. There have been reports that the Su-25UBP programme has been halted, but it is unclear whether this situation is temporary. The Sukhoi OKB has not given up its quest to produce an operational carrier-borne Su-25 derivative, and reports suggest that the bureau may still be working on a single-seat, carrier-capable, probe-equipped Su-25TP based on the advanced Su-25T airframe, equipped with Kh-31 and Kh-35 ASMs.

The true combat debut

Following the successful combat evaluation of the Su-25 in Afghanistan, it became inevitable that production examples of the type would be used in the conflict when they became available. Twelve of the first Su-25s equipped the 200th Independent *Shturmovik* Squadron (often erroneously described as a Guards unit, and as being either a regiment, or alternatively a flight) at Shindand. This unit later transferred to Kabul (probably during 1982) and expanded to 24 aircraft (with 80 pilots) to become the 60th OShAP (some-

Czech Su-25s were briefly based at Hradec Králové, in Eastern Bohemia, between 1984 and 1985. Their unit, the 30th 'Ostravsky' Fighter-Bomber Air Regiment, then moved to Pardubice in June 1985, becoming the 30th Ground Attack Air Regiment later that year. The Communist party collapsed in Czechoslovakia in November/December 1989, following the 'peaceful Revolution', and occupying Russian forces were ordered to leave. The military structure of the Warsaw Pact was disbanded on 31 March 1991 and the last Russian forces departed in June 1991. Both Czech and Slovak Republics began to move towards independence in the early 1990s, and the armed forces were reorganised in anticipation. By 1992 the division of the Su-25 force into two had begun.

Sukhoi Su-25, Su-28 and Su-39 'Frogfoot'

These aircraft and personnel of the 368th OShAP in Germany are seen preparing to depart for one of their final training missions, in 1993. By this time Russian forces were unwelcome guests who had outstayed their welcome in the reunited Germany. The 357th OShAP had already left Brandis in April 1992 and the 368th would follow in June 1993 – one of the last GSFG units to do so.

times described as the 80th OShAP). The regiment's commander was given special dispensation to conscript reinforcement aircraft and aircrew from Su-25 units in neighbouring republics, notably Turkmenistan. The 60th OShAP finally withdrew to Sital Chai in Azerbaijan in 1988.

Another long-term Su-25 unit in Afghanistan was the 378th OShAP, in action from 1984. A third Su-25 regiment served in Afghanistan between October 1986 and November 1987. This was the 368th OShAP, which transferred to Afghanistan from Uzbekistan, and moved to Demmin-Tütow in East Germany following its combat tour, during which it was based at Bagram and Kandahar. The unit may have been one of several which made brief deployments to Afghanistan.

While the Su-25 demonstrated great accuracy and good battle damage tolerance from the very start of its involvement in Afghanistan (especially by comparison with other aircraft in use in the theatre), it was equally clear that there was considerable scope for improvement. The threat posed by Blowpipe, Stinger and Redeye SAMs prompted the installation of four ASO-2V chaff/flare dispensers in the upper surfaces of the rear fuselage, on each side of the fin trailing edge. These usually contain up to 30 PPI-26 IR decoy flares, giving a total of 120 flares.

The effect of the Stinger

The advantage of having two engines was fully exploited in the Su-25, in which the powerplants are mounted so close together that damage to one engine could cause collateral damage to the other. This became abundantly clear following the 1984 introduction of the Redeye SAM by the Mujahideen, and by the October 1986 delivery of General Dynamics FIM-82A Stinger SAMs. The introduction of Redeye was followed by the loss of two Su-25s in very quick succession, these aircraft having proved unable to decoy the SAMs away using flares. Flare capacity was increased from 128 to 256, by the addition of four 32-round dispensers scabbed onto the top of the engine nacelles. When the Mujahideen started using Stinger, the effect was even more dramatic. Four Su-25s were destroyed in three days, with two pilots lost. The Stingers tended to detonate close to the engine exhaust nozzles, piercing the rear fuel tanks with shrapnel and causing fires which could burn through control runs, or causing damage to the far engine. In order to prevent damage to one engine from taking out the other, a 5-mm armour plate was added between the two engines (acting as a giant shield and firewall), about 1.5 m (5 ft) long.

A new inert gas (Freon) SSP-2I/UBSh-4-2 fire extinguisher system was provided. This consisted of six UTBG sensors in the engine nacelles, which were connected to cockpit displays. The pilot had four push-buttons to actuate the extinguisher's first and second stages for each section of the engine. The Freon was stored in spherical 4-litre (0.87-Imp gal) bottles, each containing 5.64 kg (12 lb) of gas pressurised at 6.9 to 14.2 MPa.

These modifications proved a great success, dramatically reducing the Su-25's loss rate. No Su-25 equipped with the inter-engine armour was lost to a Stinger, although many were hit. The modifications were quickly incorporated on the production line, and were retrofitted to existing Su-25s.

Additional improvements were added during the period in which Su-25s were fighting in Afghanistan. On aircraft from the 10th production series, for example, the aileron control rod was fully faired in and the aileron trim tab was deleted. Elevator pivots were more effectively faired. Tenth

Above and right: The GSFG Su-25 units each had Su-25UBs which routinely operated alongside their Su-25s. The 357th OShAP was allocated two two-seaters, and one of its aircraft is seen above. The 368th OShAP had five aircraft (right). Most front-line units in Germany operated two-seat versions of their aircraft, largely to make up for their lack of simulation facilities. This task was less important to the 'good weather only' Su-25 regiments, who had little need for instrument training. The Su-25UBs did, however, make excellent liaison aircraft and base 'hacks'.

series Su-25s also gained a second external APU/GPU socket. Other features appeared gradually, and cannot yet be pinpointed to a particular production series. The nose-wheel was changed, from one which accepted a tubeless KN-21-1 tyre to one which took a tubed K-2106 tyre. The single long fuel tank access panel on the top surface of each wing was replaced by three shorter access panels, side by side. Small fins were added to the inboard faces of the bottom of each wingtip fairing, acting as glare shields when the PRF-4M pop-down landing lights were deployed. At the trailing edge of these pods, the airbrakes themselves were modified. Previously simply splitting 50° up and 50° down to give a > shape with the point forwards, they gained auxiliary segments which hinged upwards through another 90° at their trailing edges to give a shape reminiscent of a W turned on its side, with the central point pointing forwards. During production of the ninth production series the cannon muzzle was redesigned, with the ends of the twin barrels covered by a single muzzle shield. Many late production Su-25s had their distinctive SRZ and SRO 'Odd Rod' antennas replaced by simple blade antennas, similar to the SRO antennas fitted to later MiG-29s (which retained the traditional tripole SRZ antennas above their noses). The revised antennas may have combined interrogator and responder functions.

The 'Frogfoot' becomes the 'rook'

The Su-25 proved extraordinarily successful in Afghanistan, enjoying greater accuracy and a lower loss rate than the MiG-27s, MiG-21s, MiG-23s and Su-17s used there. The Mujahideen dubbed the Su-25 the 'German product', believing that its prowess and effectiveness marked it out from the other Soviet aircraft operating in-theatre, and indicating that it must have come from elsewhere. Combat experience in Afghanistan also generated a Russian nickname for the aircraft: 'Grach' (Rook). Publicists and official historians credit the nickname to ground troops, who reportedly appreciated the aircraft's close support capability which they likened to the mother rook's habit of covering her young with her wings when faced with danger. Other sources suggest that the 'Grach' nickname was first applied by the pilots of the 200th

The comparatively small number of Su-25s based in east Germany is somewhat surprising. It is a reflection of the fact that Soviet Shturmovik theory had largely been applied to the attack helicopter and that the Su-25 was a useful adjunct to this, instead of the primary exponent. There is little doubt, however, that the existing regiments would have been extensively reinforced in time of war. This aircraft is seen landing at Gross Dölln (Templin), north of Berlin, which was home to the Su-17M-4s of the 20th APIB. Like the Su-25, there were two 'Fitter' regiments based in East Germany.

Though unit markings and badges were not common throughout the GSFG, the Su-25 units were perhaps the least colourful of all. Only the grach badge, carried on some aircraft, broke the monotony of their camouflage. Soviet/Russian military aviation units do have an intense pride in their history and traditions, but this is rarely expressed through special colour schemes or badges, as in the West. Most of the bases in East Germany had gate guards of historic aircraft, including Il-2s, which the units brought with them when they moved from the Soviet Union and took away again when they returned.

Sukhoi Su-25 'Frogfoot'
378 OShAP/378 OSAP
VVS-SSR

This 'Frogfoot', 'Red 29', was one of those based at Bagram in Afghanistan during the late 1980s, and is seen here in the markings it wore in 1988. It was during this period that Soviet operations in Afghanistan were at their peak – a fact reflected by the number of incursions made by VVS combat aircraft over the Pakistani border. In August 1988 an Su-25 was shot down by a Pakistani air force F-16. This particular aircraft is carrying an unusually heavy warload for an Afghan combatant. Standard loadouts usually comprised a small number of very large calibre rockets.

The *grach*
It was in Afghanistan that the *grach* (rook) marking, which has become synonymous with the Su-25 in Soviet (and Russian) service, first appeared. The origins of the cartoon bird are unclear, but it was soon worn by virtually all of the aircraft that served in Afghanistan. When some of these units returned to their bases in East Germany the black *grach* artwork returned with them.

Sukhoi Su-25 specification
Dimensions: fuselage length including probe 15.530 m (50 ft 11½ in) (15.36 m/50 ft 5 in for Su-25UB); fuselage length excluding probe 14.59 m (47 ft 10½ in); span 14.36 m (47 ft 1 in); area 30.1 m² (324 sq ft); tailplane span 4.65 m (15 ft 3 in); tailplane area 6.47 m² (69.7 sq ft); overall height 4.8 m (15 ft 9 in) (5.2 m/17 ft 1 in for Su-25UB); wheel track 2.5 m (8 ft 2 in); wheelbase 3.58 m (11 ft 9 in)
Powerplant: two Soyuz/Gavrilov R-95Sh turbojets each rated at 40.21 kN (9,039 lb st) thrust
Weights: empty operating weight 9185 kg (20,250 lb); normal take-off weight (early aircraft) 14250 kg (31,415 lb); normal take-off weight (late aircraft, after 1984) 14530 kg (32,025 lb); maximum take-off weight (early aircraft) 17350 kg (38,250 lb); maximum take-off weight (late aircraft, after 1984) 17530 kg (38,645 lb); normal landing weight 10800 kg (23,810 lb); maximum landing weight 13300 kg (29,320 lb)
Fuel and load: internal fuel 3000 kg (6,614 lb) or 3600 litres (790 Imp gal); normal weapon load 1340 kg (2,954 lb); maximum weapon load 4340 kg (9,568 lb)
g limits: +6.5 to -3 at basic design gross weight
Performance: maximum level speed 'clean' at sea level 1000 km/h (620 mph); limiting Mach No. 0.71 (early aircraft) or 0.82 (late aircraft, after 1984); service ceiling 7000 m (22,950 ft); range with underwing tanks 1950 km (1,053 nm; 1,212 miles) (1850 km/999 nm/1,450 miles for early aircraft, manufactured before 1984); range with 3000 kg (6,615 lb) of fuel 500 km (270 nm; 310 miles); take-off run 500-900 m (1,640-2,953 ft); landing roll 600-800 m (1,969-2,625 ft); take-off speed 240-270 km/h (130-135 kt; 149-155 mph); landing speed 225-260 km/h (121-124 kt; 225-230mph)

Sukhoi Su-25TK specification
Dimensions: fuselage length including probe 15.33 m (50 ft 4 in); span 14.52 m (47 ft 8 in); overall height 5.2 m (17 ft 1 in)
Powerplant: two Soyuz R-195 turbojets each rated at 44.13 kN (9,921 lb st) thrust
Weights: maximum take-off weight 19500 kg (42,990 lb)
Fuel and load: internal fuel 3840 kg (8,465 lb); normal weapon load up to 4360 kg (9,610 lb) air-to-ground
g limits: + 6.5 at maximum design gross weight
Performance: maximum level speed 950 km/h (513 kt; 590 mph); limiting Mach No. 0.82; service ceiling 10000 m (32,810 ft); ferry range 2500 km (1,350 nm; 1,550 miles); low-level radius of action 400 km (215 nm; 250 miles) with 2000 kg (4,410 lb) of weapons; high-level radius of action 700 km (380 nm; 435 miles) with 2000 kg (4,410 lb) of weapons

Wingtip airbrakes
Early-production Su-25s had a straightforward two-section, clamshell airbrake. It was subsequently modified and two smaller 'petals' added, resulting in an enlarged, four-section, staggered, articulated airbrake.

The Ulan-Ude bear
While Su-25s have adopted the 'unofficial' rook badge, two-seat Su-25UBs all wear the factory badge of their home, the Ulan-Ude Aviation Plant (Joint-Stock Company), situated in the Buryat Republic.

Warload
This aircraft is seen carrying a load of four FAB-250-270 250-kg bombs and four UV-32M rocket pods. FAB- (*fugasnaya avia-bomba/*'aerial demolition bomb') series bombs have been in production since the 1950s and are unsophisticated high-drag weapons, filled with high explosive. The Su-25 can carry a maximum load of eight FAB-250s – the outermost pylons on each wing are not stressed to carry that weight. The UV-32 rocket pod can carry up to 32 S-5KP 57-mm rockets. The Su-25 can carry a maximum load of eight pods. Aircraft serving in Afghanistan often carried a lighter load of two or four S-24 240-mm rockets on the outer pylons, with (small) bombs inboard.

Undercarriage
The nose gear of the Su-25 is offset to port and fitted with a mudguard, to lessen the risk of debris ingestion to the engines. The main undercarriage uses levered suspension legs, an oleo-pneumatic shock absorber and low-pressure tyres to enhance rough-field performance.

Variation on the *grach* badge

Brake chute
All (land-based) Su-25s have a pair of brake chutes housed in the extended tail fairing, hidden behind a neat 'flip-up' cover. The chutes themselves are cruciform PTK-25 brake chutes, each of 25 m² (270 sq ft) area, which are deployed on landing, using springs and smaller drogue chutes.

Armoured cockpit
The Su-25 pilots sits on a K-36L ejection seat surrounded by 24 mm (0.94 in) of welded titanium, under an armoured canopy – which opens to starboard. Above the canopy is a small mirror to compensate for the pronounced lack of rearward visibility. The canopy transparency is curved, apart from the reinforced (flat) front panel.

Su-25 antenna fit
The large blade aerial behind the cockpit of this Su-25 is the R-862 UHF/VHF radio aerial. Above the nose the three SRO-2 'Odd Rod' IFF aerials have been replaced by the single blade antenna of a newer system. The small dielectric panel on the side of the nose serves the SO-69 transponder. The small circular antennas for the SRO radar warning receiver were later added to the nose of Su-25s, in front of the SO-69 fairing. Jutting ahead of the nose are the main (starboard) and auxiliary pitot probes – the first of them also carries antennas for the RSBN navigation system. Inside its 'chisel' 'nose, the Su-25 carries the Klen-PS laser rangefinder and marked target seeker. Underneath the nose is a pitch vane, and some aircraft have an additional IFF antenna immediately behind this. On the side of the fuselage, below the cockpit, is the Su-25's angle-of-attack sensor. On the front of each of the wingtip fairings are antennas for the SPO-15 RHAW system. Formation lights and pop-out landing lights are located on the side of, and underneath, the tip fairings, respectively. Not visible here are the RV-15 radar altimeter and MRP-56P beacon tracking antennas, located between the engines on the underfuselage. Behind the engine outlets is a second RV-15 antenna and the large 'towel-rail' antenna for the R-828 radio. Another IFF aerial is located under the fin and on the extended tail 'sting', which itself is tipped by a second RSBN antenna.

Variations on the *grach* badge

*This 368th OShAP
Su-25 is armed with
B-8M1 20-round rocket
pods. Standard 'Frogfoot'
loadouts with the B-8M1
seem to involve only two
pods, whereas either four
or eight UV-32-57 pods
were often carried. The
B-8M1 fires the 80-mm
S-8 FFAR rocket. The
B-8M1 is the streamlined
80-mm pod developed for
use on fast jet aircraft
(helicopters, for which
the system was
originally developed, use
the B-8V20A pod). The
S-8 rocket comes fitted
with a HEAT anti-armour
warhead, an 'anti-shelter'
demolition warhead, a
fuel/air explosive
warhead or as a 2-million
candlepower
illumination round.*

*Most Soviet/Russian
flying operations are
routinely conducted in
the open, from the flight
line. Both Brandis and
Tütow had a large
number of revetments
for their Su-25s, but no
hardened shelters.*

OShAE, many of whom were former MiG-21 pilots, who likened the slow and ungainly Su-25 to a rook, by comparison with their fast and graceful Falcons. Whoever invented the name, cartoon rook badges soon started to appear on Su-25s flown in Afghanistan. This rook badge has become a widely accepted insignia for Soviet Su-25s, and was applied to many of the aircraft used in East Germany. There have been unconfirmed suggestions that the badge is worn only by Su-25s that flew in Afghanistan.

Bringing back the pilots

The aircraft were often hit by ground fire and SAMs, habitually after they had overflown the target and were egressing. The damaged Su-25s usually limped home (even after a direct Stinger hit), often too badly damaged to fly again but generally saving the precious pilot. The aircraft were even sometimes repairable and were always at least a good source of spare parts. The Su-25 was effectively invulnerable to cannon fire; it took 80 20-mm hits to down an Su-25, compared with only 15 for a MiG-21 or Su-17.

Colonel Alexander Rutskoi, later briefly President of the Russian Federation, flew as an Su-25 pilot in Afghanistan while serving on the staff of the Commander of the 40th Air Army, and became the war's most highly decorated pilot. Some reports suggest that the T8-15 ('Blue 15') was one of the aircraft flown by Rutskoi in Afghanistan, and one which was severely damaged while being flown by him on two separate occasions, once by ground fire and once by two AIM-9s fired by a Pakistani F-16. Rutskoi was unluckier in April 1986 when he was downed by a SAM, ejecting inverted at only 100 m (330 ft) altitude. He was forced to eject again during his second tour of duty in Afghanistan, on 4 August 1988, when he was once more

engaged by a Pakistani F-16. Hit by an AIM-9, Rutskoi was forced to eject from his crippled aircraft ('Red 03') and was captured, being released after two weeks. The remains of his aircraft were put on display at Kamra. Some reports suggest that Rutskoi commanded a unit (perhaps an element of the 378th OShAP) which conducted sustained night operations before being disbanded and split up between other units in-theatre.

Afghanistan weapons

The Su-25 used a wide variety of weapons during the long involvement in Afghanistan. In order to maximise performance and agility, the Su-25s were seldom fully laden, often carrying weapons on only two or four underwing pylons. A common loadout was two or four S-24 240-mm unguided rockets, or a similar number of shaped-charge S-25 OFMs. Underwing fuel tanks were sometimes carried, either on the innermost hardpoints or on the third pylons out from the root. Various 250-kg or 500-kg (550-lb or 1,100-lb) bombs were also used in Afghanistan, and unguided small calibre rockets were carried in UB-32-57 (32 unguided 57-mm rockets per pod) or B8M (20 unguided 80-mm rockets per pod) pods. Towards the end of the Soviet involvement in Afghanistan, Su-25s started to be seen carrying guided weapons, including the S-25L laser-guided, tube-launched 250-mm rocket, the Kh-25ML and the Kh-29L laser-guided ASMs. According to the OKB, 139 laser-guided missiles were launched by Su-25s in Afghanistan, and 137 of them scored direct hits.

Another commonly seen Su-25 weapon which may have been used in Afghanistan is the SPPU-22-01 cannon pod. The Su-25 can carry up to four of these pods, usually on its innermost pylons. Each pod contains a single twin-barrelled

This admittedly poor photograph does provide evidence of Su-25s in the markings of the AV-MF (Russian navy). This aircraft, 'Red 15', is seen at Panevezys in April 1993, where several other 'Frogfoots' were also based. Substantial numbers of VVS aircraft were transferred to the AV-MF in the early 1990s to circumvent CFE treaty restrictions on Russian military aircraft 'west of the Urals'.

23-mm NR-23 cannon, with 260 rounds of ammunition, and with barrels which can be depressed through 30° up, allowing the aircraft to strafe a target simply by overflying it in level flight. This is especially effective against line targets (e.g., vehicles on a road). The pod may be mounted backwards, with the barrels elevated through 23° up, allowing the aircraft to fire backwards after overflying the target. It is common practice to pair a forward-firing and rearward-firing pod. Each pod had a rate of fire between 3,000 and 4,000 rounds per minute.

Afghanistan combat report

Twenty-three Su-25s were lost in action in Afghanistan; more were destroyed on the ground, including eight at Kabul in a single rocket attack on 23 June 1988. The aircraft shot down represented about 10 per cent of Soviet fixed-wing losses in Afghanistan, with a reported loss rate of one per 2,800 flying hours. The type made 60,000 operational sorties. Interestingly, the cockpit armour of the Su-25 proved particularly successful, and no Su-25 pilot was killed by projectiles or shrapnel. Several Su-25 pilots received the Soviet Union's highest honour, the Hero of the Soviet Union. Lieutenant Colonel Pietr V. Ruban was given a posthumous award, and a second was awarded to a Captain Dyakov. Other well known Hero of the Soviet Union awards were made to Captain Vladislav Gontcharienko, who flew 415 combat missions, and to Senior Lieutenant Konstantin G. Paliukov, who destroyed two Stingers launched against his formation leader, using gunfire and unguided rockets, during a December 1986 mission. He was killed on 21 January 1987, ejecting after being hit by another Stinger. He held off the Mujahideen for an hour before killing himself (and several of his tormentors) with a hand grenade.

According to official reports, only one type enjoyed a lower loss rate in Afghanistan than the Su-25, and that was the obsolete Il-28. Their tail gunners tended to discourage Mujahideen gunners from popping out of cover to fire as the ancient bombers egressed, and were also able to call out rear hemisphere threat warnings. Encouraged by this, Ilyushin again promoted its aircraft (as the Il-102) as an Su-25 replacement, but the aircraft was again rejected and the air force preferred to concentrate on Sukhoi's own extensively modified Su-25 derivative, the Su-25T.

War in the former republics

Afghanistan was not the only war from which the designers of the Su-25 could draw lessons based on real combat experience. Azeri forces used Su-25s in their war against Armenia during 1992, while from late 1992 the Georgians used Su-25s against Abkhazian forces fighting for independence, who were themselves supported by Russian forces, which included Su-25s. Among the earliest incidents of this brief but bloody conflict (which lasted until the end of 1993) was an engagement on 27 October 1992,

involving two Georgian Su-25s and two Russian Su-25s which were escorting Mi-8s delivering humanitarian relief. None of the aircraft were shot down. Six Georgian Su-25s (then virtually the entire Georgian Su-25 fleet) were shot down later in the war, together with a Russian Su-25 and one of the Su-25s handed over by Russia for operation by Abkhazian forces. Following the secession of Abkhazia, the last Georgian Su-25 was shot down on 5 November while conducting operations against rebel Zviadist forces who supported former President Zviad Gamsakhurdia. Georgian Su-25s wore standard Russian camouflage and red star markings, and this may have been the origin of the Russian tricolour tailfin badges applied to some Russian Su-25s.

While development of the extensively redesigned Su-25T progressed slowly, Sukhoi introduced some final improvements to the baseline single-seat Su-25 and

Bulgaria is an often forgotten European operator of the Su-25, and until recently little was known regarding the status of the Su-25 in the Bulgarski Voennvazdushi Sily (Bulgarian air force). The BVVS took delivery of 36 Su-25Ks, 35 of which survive and two of which are seen below. Both are carrying UV-32-57 pods.

two-seat Su-25UB. The most important of these was the
adoption of the R-195 engine, a derivative of the R-95
which offered increased thrust and a lower IR signature.
The powerplant had been intended primarily for the heavyweight Su-25T, but its availability came as a blessing to
Sukhoi, which saw it as a welcome means of improving
Su-25 and Su-25UBK performance, even though only a
relatively small number of aircraft remained to be built. The
new engine was first flown in the T8M-1 prototype, while
the T8-14 and T8-15 were re-engined to enable the engine
trials to be completed more swiftly.

The T8-15 (c/n 10192, already used for combat trials in
Afghanistan, and badly damaged while being flown by
Alexander Rutskoi) was used to make the Su-25's Western
public debut at the 1989 Paris Air Salon at Le Bourget.
Some sources suggest that the aircraft was again re-engined
with its original R-95s to preserve secrecy, but this seems
unlikely. It is more probable that the Sukhoi OKB merely
failed to remark on the change of engine.

The installation of the new engine necessitated some
changes to the engine nacelles and to the rear fuselage.
Auxiliary intakes were added below the rear part of the

nacelle, and additional auxiliary intakes were added above
the nacelle. The small intake at the base of the tailfin was
removed. A tubular pipe projected from the centre of the
jet pipe of the R-195, mixing cool bypass air into the
middle of the jet efflux to reduce the engine's IR signature.
The R-195 had a designated service life of 1,500 flying
hours or seven years, with a 500-hour TBO. Following its
participation in the Paris Air Salon, the T8-15 was used for
a variety of trials, including some maximum weight
weapons tests. It was finally retired to the Central Air and
Space Museum at Khodinka airfield on Leningradsky
Prospekt in Moscow.

The Su-25BM target tug

There is some confusion regarding the designation of the
R-195-powered single-seat Su-25s. Some have suggested
that the only single-seaters powered by the new engine
were the batch of 50 Su-25BM (Bukshir Mishenyei)
dual-role fighter-bomber/target tugs. Others suggest that
more Su-25s were built or retrofitted with the R-195
engine, and only a proportion of these should be referred to
as Su-25BMs. Confusingly, some authorities have even
suggested that certain Su-25BMs were powered by the
R-95 engine. The re-engined aircraft does retain the same
ASCC 'Frogfoot-A' reporting name.

Work on the Su-25 target tug began in 1986, and the
OKB looked at the possibility of producing either a single-
seat or two-seat version. As far as is known, a decision was
made to concentrate on producing a target-towing derivative
of the R-195-powered single-seater, under the designation
Su-25BM. This was always intended to be a 'convertible'
which could be reconfigured for full combat duties at
squadron level. When operating in the target-towing role,
the aircraft carried a TL-70 winch unit with a Kometa
towed target below the port wing, and an inert FAB-250
or FAB-500 bomb below the starboard wing to counter the
asymmetry in weight and drag. The TL-70 winch could
wind out 2300-3000 m (7,545-9,845 ft) depending on the
type of target. A new TL-70 target control unit panel
replaced the gunsight and gunsight control panel, and an
unidentified fairing, with a long, shallow knife-blade

antenna, was carried on the centreline. This may have served the Planyer-M system, which could detect target miss-distances and display them in the cockpit, and simultaneously transmit them to a suitably equipped ground station. As an alternative to towed targets, the Su-25BM could carry four rocket-powered free-flying PM-6 targets, or four M-6 parachute targets.

As far as can be ascertained, the R-195-engined Su-25BM has attachment points for the Vyuga datalink pod, used in conjunction with the Kh-58U/E (AS-11) anti-radiation missile. This latent capability may have been the reason for the reported transfer of Su-25BM target tugs from the 16th Air Army's target facilities unit at Damgarten to the 368th OShAP at Demmin-Tütow. Certainly, the 368th OShAP did include 12 R-195-engined aircraft, but it cannot be confirmed that they were the ex-Damgarten target tugs, nor that they were designated as Su-25BMs. Su-25BM target tugs probably equipped a number of squadron-sized specialised target-towing units, but were doubtless also attached to other units in ones and twos.

The Su-25BMK designation is theoretically applied to export versions of the Su-25BM, but, as far as is known, none have been delivered to any overseas customer, and the R-195 engine was once rumoured not to have been cleared for export.

Su-25T: the second generation

The main application of the R-195 engine was for the advanced 'Frogfoot' in all of its T8M forms – the Su-25T, Su-25TM, Su-34 and Su-39. These designations covered similar sub-variants of an advanced single-seat attack aircraft, based on the airframe of the two-seat Su-25UB, but with the former instructor's cockpit space occupied by advanced avionics and some restored internal fuel tankage in new No. 3 and 4 fuel tanks. Total internal fuel capacity increased to 3840 kg (8,466 lb) from the Su-25UB's 2725 kg (6,008 lb) and the original single-seater's 3000 kg (6,614 lb). The T8M retained the profile of the Su-25UB, but with metal skinning replacing the rear cockpit canopy. This gave the aircraft a distinctively humped appearance.

Bulgaria's Su-25Ks and Su-25UBKs are operated by the 22nd Iztrebitelno-Bombardirovachen Aviopolk/Fighter-Bomber Regiment (22 IBAP), based at Bezmer air base. The 'Frogfoots' are divided between two squadrons.

The Su-25K is just one element in the BVVS inventory of attack/strike aircraft. Bulgaria also operates Su-22M-4 'Fitter-Ks', MiG-23BN 'Flogger-Hs' and MiG-21MF 'Fishbed-Ks'. In addition, the BVVS has Mi-24D/V 'Hind-D/E' assault helicopters.

Work on a 'super Frogfoot' began in 1981, just as the results of the combat evaluation of the original T8 prototypes were being evaluated, and as recommendations were being made that this original aircraft should be put into production. The new variant would be a heavier aircraft, with even better resistance to ground fire and battle damage, and with more advanced sensors and systems optimised for the night and all-weather attack roles. Vladimir Babak was given leadership of the project, which was accorded a high priority.

T8M changes

Such was the importance attached to the new T8M that the partially complete T8U prototype airframes (and a T8U static test airframe) were taken over to form the basis of the new version. Work on these airframes began in 1983. Internal volume was exploited wherever possible, allowing the increased internal fuel already referred to, and making it possible to find space for many new avionics systems. These included a new Voskhod navigation system, with twin digital navigation computers. Armour was increased and improved, with the avionics bay, fuel feed tank and fuel

pipes all gaining extra protection. Fuselage compartments adjacent to the fuel tanks were filled with a porous elastic filler, intended to prevent impulse splashing of the fuel if hit by a bullet or shrapnel fragment. The OKB estimated that survivability had been enhanced by a factor of between four and six.

In order to provide extra internal volume, the original cannon bay was deleted, and it was decided to carry the gun externally, below the belly. At first it was hoped that the T8M (soon given the air force designation Su-25T) would be armed with a new 45-mm cannon, with depressing barrels for ground strafing. In the event, the Su-25T used the same AO-17A (GSh-30-2, 9A623) 30-mm cannon as the basic Su-25, but carried below the fuselage as the NPPU-8M, offset to starboard by 270 mm (10.5 in). This necessitated moving the nosewheel another 220 mm (8.6 in) to port.

Improved sensor system

The nosecone was lengthened slightly, and tapered less sharply in plan view. The nose window was enlarged to allow it to serve the Krasnogorsk OMZ I-251 Shkval (squall) optical-TV system, which combined high-resolution television, a Prichal laser rangefinder and target designator, and a Vikhr laser guidance system. The Shkval could present a wide-angle (36° x 27°) picture for target search, or a 23-times magnified (1° x 0.7°) picture for tracking. The sight-line could be steered through 70° horizontally, and from 15° above the centreline to 80° below. A moving armoured target could be tracked to an accuracy of 0.6 m (2 ft) at ranges of up to 8 km (5 miles). The laser designator illuminated a 5 x 5-m (16.4 x 16.4-ft) box, and transmitted steering commands directly to the laser sensors mounted at the rear of the 9M120 Vikhr laser-guided tube-launched missiles. The system was essentially the same as that fitted to the Ka-50 'Hokum', and made the Su-25T fully compatible with a wide range of laser-/TV-guided bombs and missiles.

For night and all-weather missions, the Su-25T could carry a Mercury LLTV pod under the fuselage. The image from this conventional TV camera could be electronically enhanced, and offered an 18.2° x 13.7° field of view for search and a 7.3° x 5.5° field of view for tracking. This allowed a tracking range of 3 km (1.9 miles) for a tank-sized target. Narrow FoV pictures were displayed on a CRT display, while wide FoV imagery was displayed on the new wide-angle HUD. Surprisingly, this was one of the few new features within the cockpit, since, unlike second-generation versions of the MiG-29 and Su-27, the Su-25T's cockpit was not subjected to a major redesign or modernisation. A new IT-23 hooded display screen for the I-251 Shkval was added to the top part of the right-hand side of the panel, but there were no CRT or LCD display screens.

The Su-25T was given a much improved Irtysh ECM and defensive avionics system, with a Gardeniya active ECM jammer, an SPO-15 Beryoza RHAWS, and SPO-32

Pastel RWR. RHAWS coverage is through a full 360° in azimuth, and 30° in elevation, going from 1.2-18 GHz. The system can be used for cueing Kh-58 ARMs. From the third prototype an L-166S1 Sukogruz IR jammer (based on a powerful 6-kW Cesium lamp) was installed in a cylindrical fairing at the base of the tailfin, alongside the UV-26 chaff/flare dispensers flush-mounted in the rear fuselage. They contained a total of 192 PPI-26 IRCM or PPR-26 chaff cartridges. The airframe of the T8M was otherwise almost unchanged, although it gained BU-45A hydraulic boosters (as used by the MiG-21) for the elevator controls.

The T8M-1 prototype made its maiden flight at Zhukhovskii on 17 August 1984, in the hands of A. N. Isakov. This aircraft (apparently coded 'Red 02') had a glazed rear canopy painted onto the spine. Subsequent aircraft did not hide the fact that they merely had metal skinning which followed the same contours as the two-seater's cockpit. Two more prototypes joined the test programme in 1985 and 1986, although A. Gontcharov was forced to eject from the T8M-2 during trials. Two more non-flying airframes were used for static (damage to airframe) and fatigue tests.

Su-25TK for export

The new variant was offered for export under the designation Su-25TK (with the T8M-3 serving as prototype/demonstrator, after slight changes to the avionics), until an entirely new designation was applied by the OKB. The Su-25TK was redesignated Su-34 in an effort to attract funding, and to give the impression that it was a new design. The designation was not recognised by the air force, and was eventually reassigned to the production version of the Su-27IB, although again it remained unrecognised by the air force. One of the Su-25Ts made its debut as the export Su-25TK demonstrator at Dubai in 1991. The aircraft was fitted with a BA-58 Vyuga datalink pod under

Slovak air force aircraft all wear the air force insignia of a shield bearing the Slovak cross (cross of Lorraine). This shield is also the centrepiece of the national flag. Slovakia gained its independence from its larger and better developed Czech neighbour in 1993 – though the move towards independence was politically inspired by the leaders of the day and was not a desire strongly shared by the bulk of the citizens. Assets of the Czechoslovakian air force were mostly split on a 2:1 basis and so 11 Su-25Ks and one Su-25UBK were handed over to the Slovak air force, from late 1992 onwards. These aircraft now make up the 3rd Flight of the 33rd Air Base, at Malacky-Kuchyna. They had previously been based at Piestany and Trencin air bases (as the 1st Flight of the 2nd Mixed Regiment).

This aircraft, from the 10th Su-25 production batch, is one of the 24 Su-25Ks that remain in service with the Czech air force. Sharkmouths have also been seen on some Russian Su-25s, noticeably on aircraft of the 186th (Instructors) ShAP, at Buturlinovka air base.

Sukhoi Su-25, Su-28 and Su-39 'Frogfoot'

the fuselage, for compatibility with the Kh-58 (AS-11 'Kilter'). The streamlined fairing at the base of the rudder was clearly empty on this aircraft, lacking the IR jammer in its trailing edge, and instead having flush-fitting twin chaff/flare dispensers let into the sides.

The end of the Su-25?

An initial production series of eight Su-25Ts was produced at Tbilisi, the first flying in July 1990. By then, work was already well advanced on the further improved T8TM, or Su-25TM, which combined radar and imaging infra-red sensors to maximise night/all-weather capability. Unfortunately, once Georgia gained its independence it was decided that all further Su-25 production would have to be undertaken at Ulan-Ude. This effectively brought production to a complete halt for months, or perhaps even years. The step was essential, however, since production of the baseline Su-25 in war-torn Georgia ground to a halt almost immediately, and has not recommenced. Any nation wishing to buy a new single-seat Su-25 or Su-25K would probably have to persuade the factory at Ulan-Ude to tool up for production of the type. This would be by no means straightforward, since the plant has hitherto built only Su-25 variants based on the hump-backed two-seat airframe. It is probably safe to say that the first-generation Su-25 is effectively dead in its single-seat form.

The Su-25TM differs very little from the Su-25T/TK in external appearance. Its principal advantage lies in its ability to carry new pods under the fuselage centreline. The first of these was the Kinzhal (Dagger) 8-mm MMW (Millimetre Wave) radar pod, and the second was the Khod (Motion) FLIR or IIR pod, which used virtually the same pod airframe. The Leninets Kinzhal pod was dropped after development problems, mainly because it had been sourced from the Ukraine, and the OKB understandably wanted all equipment to come from a single republic, after the difficulties it had experienced having a production plant in Georgia. Leninets is based in St Petersburg, and estimated that it would take at least two years to build a new version using Russian-supplied components. Babak himself estimated that four years would be required, including the writing of new software.

Kopyo-25 radar for the Su-25TM

The aircraft can also carry a centreline Kopyo-25 radar pod. The Phazotron Kopyo radar is a close relation to the same company's Zhuk, but with a somewhat smaller antenna. It has some air-to-ground radar modes but is usually thought of as an air-to-air radar, and was developed primarily for use in MiG-21 upgrades. Of four test sets produced, one was used for ground and airborne rig testing, two were provided to Mikoyan for the MiG-21-93, and one was podded for trials with the Su-25TM. To the Su-25TM, the Kopyo pod brought a degree of terrain-avoidance capability, as well as various types of Doppler beam sharpening, radar mapping, target designation and missile guidance function.

The Kopyo-25-equipped Su-25TM is described as being compatible with the BVR-capable R-27 (AA-10 'Alamo') and R-77 (AA-12 'Adder') air-to-air missiles. Such a capability did not come anywhere close to transforming the sluggish and slow Su-25TM into a fighter, but it did introduce some useful versatility, and a healthy self-defence proficiency. More importantly, the new radar allows the Su-25TM to carry weapons like the Kh-31A (AS-17 'Krypton') and Kh-35 (AS-X-20 'Kayak').

The first Su-25T prototype (T8M-1) served as the Su-25TM prototype, redesignated as the T8TM-1. It was followed by two more prototypes (T8TM-2 and T8TM-3, 'Blue 09' and 'Blue 10'), which may have been converted from Su-25Ts (perhaps T8M-9 and T8M-10), or which may have been newly built. The second Su-25TM made the type's public debut at the massive display mounted for CIS leaders at Minsk Maschulische in February 1992. The Su-25TM is designated Su-39 internally, by the OKB, but this designation remains entirely unofficial.

Development of a navalised version of the Su-25TM (known as the Su-25TP) – which combined features of the Su-25TM with the specific naval features of the Su-25UTG – may have been halted, suspended or abandoned. No prototype has yet been flown. During 1995 and 1996, the Sukhoi OKB appeared to have lost some of its political influence, and other aerospace organisations, including the MiG/MAPO/Kamov grouping, seemed to be winning back some of the influence they had lost. The fulfilment of Russian air forces' requirements became more open to competition, and Sukhoi could no longer expect orders for all of its products. In this new environment, the Su-25TM has failed to win a production order, and its future must be open to question. An offer of licence-production in Poland failed to generate an order from the Polish air force, and only the UAE and Bulgaria have seriously looked at the type. Bulgaria and Slovakia would reportedly be interested in acquiring a handful of Su-25TMs to act as pathfinders for their respective air forces' existing fleet of baseline Su-25s. Negotiations began in late 1993 and 1995 for the lease of small numbers of Su-25TMs to both nations.

An uncertain future

The Sukhoi Su-25 has proved the validity of its original concept, but has also demonstrated a need for more effective night-attack sensors and systems, and for improved armour and self-protection systems. Unfortunately for Sukhoi, just as these were finally developed for the advanced Su-25T and Su-25TM, the end of the Cold War resulted in a massive decrease in defence spending. The Su-25TM is probably still too revolutionary to be a core programme, and to attract a share of much more scarce funding. Money is far more likely to be allocated to advanced versions of the MiG-29 and Su-27, which have been designed to be compatible with advanced precision-guided air-to-surface weapons, and which offer greater versatility. In a time of economic cutbacks, such multi-role aircraft are almost certainly more likely to prosper than less flexible single-role aircraft, even if the latter are superior. The future of the Su-25 and its advanced derivatives will depend on their ability to attract export orders. Unfortunately, overseas customers have so far proved to be no more far-sighted than the superpowers in being able to order such a specialised attack aircraft, and such a superficially unimpressive performer. America has allowed the A-10 to wither and die, and Russia looks set to do exactly the same with the Sukhoi Su-25. **Jon Lake**

An Su-25UTG lands on Kuznetsov, under the gaze of an Su-27K. Prestige projects such as the Su-27/35 'Flanker' have pushed the Su-25 into the background at Sukhoi and this, coupled with production and funding problems, may sharply curtail any plans for future 'Frogfoots'.

Su-25TM (T8-M10)
Sukhoi OKB Flight Test Department
Detached to 929th GLITs (State Flight Test Centre)
Akhtubinsk, Russia

Akhtubinsk houses the front-line fast-jet and offensive elements of the Air Forces' Scientific and Technical Institute (NII-VVS). Primarily responsible for service clearance and acceptance of new aircraft types, systems and weapons, the centre is also used for trials by some of the aircraft design and production companies, who use the base's infrastructure and the adjacent ranges. No Russian air forces order has been placed for the Su-25T or TM but the type has been evaluated and tested at Akhtubinsk, although the aircraft operate primarily from the Sukhoi facility within the LII airfield at Zhukhovskiy. 'Blue 10' was probably the 10th T8-M, and probably the third Su-25TM (T8-TM). The aircraft was also almost certainly the first built to Su-25TM standards from the start. It has been used for demonstration flights overseas, and as such has sometimes been referred to as an Su-25K. It has led a busy life as a weapons/weapons system workhorse, testing different elements of the Su-25TM's weapons system, including both Mercury LLTV and Khod FLIR pods. The aircraft wears the standard Su-25 brown and green camouflage, unlike some Su-25TM and Su-25Ts which were painted in experimental grey/blue colour schemes. Some reports suggest that the aircraft was converted to serve as the carrier-capable Su-25TP prototype, but this cannot be confirmed. In the austere funding environment following the end of the Cold War, the advanced Su-25TM has so far been unable to win a vital launch order, though there were reports of orders from Slovakia, Georgia, Bulgaria and a number of other customers, most of whom were already operators of the baseline Su-25.

Cockpit

The Su-25TM's retention of the Su-25UB airframe gives it a uniquely hump-backed profile, with what was once the rear cockpit fixed in place and 'skinned over'. The canopy, based as it is on the front canopy of the two-seater, is longer than that fitted to the baseline Su-25, and more heavily framed. Unlike the basic single-seat model, the Su-25TM's canopy incorporates no overhead rear-view mirror, instead having provision for rear-view mirrors around the canopy arch. Inside the cockpit, there is little change from the instrument layout of the original Su-25, though a CRT screen is provided for the display of LLTV or FLIR imagery. The aircraft also features a new head-up display, which looks similar to that fitted to the MiG-29, in place of the original Su-25's simple gunsight. Production versions of the Su-25TM might incorporate new cockpit displays, perhaps similar to those flying in the Su-27M.

Nose window
The Su-25T and Su-25TM had a recontoured nose with an enlarged hexagonal forward oblique window covering the collimated optics for the Prichal laser rangefinder and target designator, and for the I-251 Shkval LLTV missile guidance system. Shkval is not used as a low-level night flying aid, for which a Mercury LLTV pod can be carried.

Structure and construction
The Su-25TM was based on the airframe of the basic Su-25UB trainer, with no real change in construction techniques or materials, and with no appreciable increase in the use of new materials or advanced alloys. Thus the airframe remains primarily of Duralumin (60 per cent), with significant amounts of steel (19 per cent) and titanium alloys (13 per cent), and comparatively little use of magnesium alloys (2 per cent), composites and plastics (5.5 per cent). This makes manufacture fairly simple and economical, and gives scope for licence assembly or component manufacture if required. The relatively extensive use of steel and titanium bestows good battle damage tolerance and considerable airframe strength. The fuselage is a conventional semi-monocoque, constructed from bulkheads, longerons, stringers and a stressed skin. Unusual features include the welded titanium cockpit 'bathtub', and the huge 'keel' between the two engines. Simple, double-skinned, oval-shaped fixed intakes are attached to the fuselage sides extending back into the engine nacelles and jetpipes. The engines drop down for removal or replacement, and are covered by massive doors. Access for routine servicing is superb. The fuselage incorporates the centre-section of the wing, with two integral fuel tanks, to which the wings themselves are attached. The wings are constructed around a central box spar, to which the leading and trailing edges are attached. Generally the aircraft is simply designed and well engineered, useful virtues in an aircraft intended to operate from austere forward airfields and in the high-threat environment over the battlefield.

Nose pitots
Like early Su-25s, the Su-25TM retained a pair of PVD pitot probes projecting from each side of the upper surface of the nose. The main probe, offset to starboard, incorporated antennas for the RSBN-6S tactical navigation system, based on a system of RSMN-2N and RSBN-4N ground beacons and used in conjunction with INS, and Doppler. The navigation system of the Su-25TM allowed more turning points and targets to be entered than did the navigation system of the baseline Su-25, but still lacks the flexibility of modern Western systems. Teaming with a Western avionics manufacturer might give the aircraft a great deal more appeal to potential customers.

Cannon
In the second-generation Su-25T and Su-25TM, the original GSh-30-2 (AO-17A/(A623) cannon in its internal VPU-17A carriage was originally to have been replaced by an internally-mounted elevating 45-mm cannon, but this weapon was abandoned before development was complete, and the original cannon bay was soon filled with avionics modules for the Shkval (Squall) system. With the new variant's night-attack capabilities and increasingly sophisticated PGM capability, some consideration was reportedly given to dropping the cannon altogether, marking a complete shift from CAS to BAI duties, but this met fierce resistance. When the GSh-30-2 cannon was reinstated it was fitted in an externally mounted, partially-faired NPPU-8M gun carriage, mounted further aft and offset 270 mm (10.7 in) to starboard. The nosewheel and nosewheel bay had to be relocated 220 mm (8.6 in) to port to compensate. Ammunition capacity was reduced from 250 to 200 rounds.

Underfuselage pods
Although the space once occupied by the rear cockpit provided additional internal volume for avionics and increased fuel capacity, the Su-25TM was always intended to carry some of its mission-specific sensors in external pods, on the centreline. Pods available include the Merkuriy (Mercury) LLTV (Low-Light TV), the Khod FLIR (Forward-Looking Infra-Red), and podded versions of the Khinzhal MMW radar or the Kopyo radar. The Khod and Khinzhal pods are understood to use a common airframe, shown in this view of the T8-M10. When carrying Khod, the front of the pod incorporates a sensor window, protected by articulated upward/downward-opening doors. Khod and Merkuriy are both primarily intended as aids to low-level navigation at night, the Shkval LLTV in the aircraft nose being for weapons guidance. The LLTV or FLIR picture may be displayed on a small CRT display high on the right-hand side of the panel, next to the HUD's up-front controller. This screen may also be used to show the Shkval picture. It is not known whether the HUD itself can display a FLIR (or LLTV) picture. The Khinzhal millimetre wave radar is associated with guidance of the Vikhr ATGM. Kopyo is a pulse-Doppler radar (also used in a number of MiG-21 upgrade applications) and is a more versatile multi-mode radar with attack, mapping and other modes. The Kopyo radar pod would be especially useful in the carrierborne, maritime attack Su-25TP. The Su-25TM's centreline pylon may be able to carry a number of weapons instead of the sensor pods listed above, though such loads have never been photographed. There have been suggestions that SPPU-22-01 gun pods, Kh-35, Kh-31, or Kh-58 ASMs may have been cleared for carriage on the centreline.

Powerplant

The Su-25T and Su-25TM are powered by the 44.1-kN (9,913-lb) R-195 engines used by late-series Su-25s and Su-25Ks, rather than the original 40.2-kN (9,036-lb) R-95Sh engines fitted to early aircraft. The newer, higher-thrust engine can be distinguished externally, even installed in its nacelle, by the unorthodox mixer tube which projects from the centre of the jet pipe, and which mixes bypass and core efflux to reduce IR signature. Both the R-95 and the R-195 are non-afterburning derivatives of the Tumanskii R-13F-300, and are of broadly similar configuration and layout. The engine has a twin-spool, axial-flow compressor, with a three-stage LP compressor, five-stage HP compressor and a two-stage turbine. The annular combustor consists of 10 chambers, with two igniters.

Underwing hardpoints

Apart from the lightly-stressed PD-62-8 pylons furthest outboard, all of the pylons fitted to the Su-25 are of the heavy-duty universal BD3-25 type, with the inboard and centre pylons being 'plumbed' for the carriage of external fuel tanks. Two types of fuel tank are available: the 800-litre (175-Imp gal) PTB-800 and the lengthened PTB-1150, which holds up to 1150 litres (252 Imp gal). The BD3-25 pylon can accommodate any current Russian air-to-ground bomb up to a maximum weight of 500 kg (1,102 lb), and with adaptor rails to allow the carriage of a wide range of air-to-air and air-to-ground missiles. The centre pylons on each side are wired to allow the carriage of SPS-141MVG-E Gvozdika ECM jammer pods. This aircraft carries an atypical 'air show'-type loadout, with a Kh-29T (AS-14 'Kedge') TV-guided ASM just launched from the innermost pylon; eight 9M120 Vikhr ATGMs next; an S-25L laser-guided high-calibre (250-mm) tube-launched rocket next; and a B-13L pod on the outermost BD3-25.

Fuel system

The basic Su-25 had internal fuel totalling 3660 litres (805 Imp gal). This comprised 2386 litres (525 Imp gal) in the fuselage and 1274 litres (280 Imp gal) in the wings. The Su-25T and Su-25TM had increased total capacity of 4890 litres (1076 Imp gal), thanks to the new nos 3 and 4 tanks in the space once occupied by the instructor's cockpit. The tanks can be gravity refuelled individually, or pressure refuelled from a single point in the no. 1 fuselage tank. The bottoms and side walls of each tank were armoured, and reticulated foam, self sealing linings and inert gas pressurisation are all available for production Su-25TMs to maximise battle damage tolerance. The engines can run on five types of aviation fuel (PL-4, PL-6, T-1, TS-1 and RT), or even, in emergency and for up to six hours, on ordinary diesel. Internal fuel tankage can be augmented by the carriage of up to four underwing tanks, each of 800- or 1150-litre (176- or 253-Imp gal) capacity.

Tail unit

The second-generation Su-25 variants retained the tail unit of the Su-25UB trainer, with the taller, increased-area vertical fin, increased-area tailplane and reversed profile. Below the rudder, the fixed part of the fin trailing edge was replaced by a cylindrical fairing housing the Irtysh ECM system, with an aft-facing Sukhogruz IR jammer in the flat-ended tip, and later with two ASO-2V 32-round chaff/flare dispensers, firing PPI-26 IR decoy flares. The horizontal tailplane can be trimmed to one of three positions: for take-off and landing, for normal flight, and for attack manoeuvres. The starboard elevator is fitted with a trim tab for elevator trimming. The Tester UZ flight data recorder is mounted in the vertical fin. The small intake at the base of the tailfin serves to cool the main generators. On the Su-25T and Su-25TM, BU-45A boosters are added to the elevator control circuit.

Hydraulic systems

In the original Su-25, only the tailplane trim, slats, flaps, ailerons and upper section of the rudder were hydraulically boosted, whereas the Su-25T and Su-25TM have hydraulically actuated elevators as well. The primary and secondary hydraulic systems are also used for nosewheel steering, undercarriage retraction and braking and for yaw damping. The hydraulic systems of the Su-25 are exceptionally well protected against battle damage.

Self-defence

Like the basic Su-25, the outermost underwing pylons (PD-62-8 pylons) can be used for the carriage of IR-homing air-to-air missiles. They are almost inevitably R-60M (AA-8 'Aphid') AAMs; reports suggest that the aircraft may also carry the R-73 (AA-11 'Archer'), but no photos have been seen showing this missile on a flying Su-25 of any sub-type. Many believe that the Su-25TM would be more likely to carry at least one MSP-410 Omul ECM pod (an improved, podded version of Gardeniya) on the outermost pylons, perhaps with S-13ALC decoys to be fired from B-13L five-round rocket launchers, as seen on the pylon next inboard from the outermost hardpoint. These pods can also be used to fire a variety of rocket-propelled weapons, of course.

Wing

The wing of the Su-25TM incorporates 2° 30' of anhedral (negative dihedral or droop) with modest sweep on the leading edge and a straight trailing edge. The wing box spars are built up around top and bottom flanges, with front and rear walls and a network of ribs and stringers. The area between the first and 10th ribs is sealed to form an integral fuel tank. The leading edge is built up around ribs and a skin, and incorporates the aileron control rods, wiring for the lighting, wingtip antennas and pylons. They also mount the five-section leading-edge slats, each section of which is connected to the leading edge using two hinges. The slats extend to 12° for take-off and landing and to 6° for combat manoeuvring. There is a dogtooth leading-edge discontinuity at the root of the third slat section, reducing induced drag by generating a powerful vortex across the wing. The trailing edge of the wing incorporates a two-section flap inboard, with ailerons outboard. The flaps deploy to 20° for combat manoeuvring and differentially (35° inboard and 40° outboard) for take off and landing. The boosted ailerons (deflecting to ±18°) are actuated via a BU-45A booster unit.

Wingtip pods

Most examples of the Su-25TM were fitted with redesigned wingtip pods incorporating extra RWR and ECM antennas. On the port wingtip, they included a box-like dielectric antenna on the upper surface of the pod, and Pastel RWR antennas on the sides of each pod, forcing the navigation lights to be relocated further aft. Each pod incorporated a glare-shield inboard of the PRF-4M pop-down landing light, with the later 'double-jointed' four-section airbrakes forming the rear part.

Su-25 'Frogfoot' family
Developments and upgrades

Ugly, sturdy and hard-hitting, the Su-25 emerged in the 1990s as arguably Russia's most important combat aircraft. This situation was created by a variety of factors, most notably the collapse of funding for the armed forces, which severely restricted the procurement and operation of more sophisticated systems. At the same time, the Russian air force rapidly switched from its Cold War posture to one of internal policing, faced with growing unrest around the fringes of the former Soviet Union.

Left: It is uncertain how many Su-25UBs were built, although the number is probably around 60/65. This example, posing with an Mi-17 built at the same plant, wears the bear badge of the Ulan Ude factory which built all the two-seaters.

Right: The hump-backed Su-25T programme greatly increased the aircraft's abilities, but it foundered with the break-up of the Soviet Union. This is one of the service test batch, seen over the Volga during a test flight from Akhtubinsk.

Below: In its original guise the Su-25 was designed to fly short-range close air support missions, and it remains a powerful weapon in this role, despite its austere avionics fit. With five hardpoints available under each wing, it can carry an impressive rocket and bomb load.

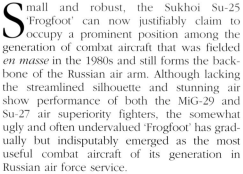

Small and robust, the Sukhoi Su-25 'Frogfoot' can now justifiably claim to occupy a prominent position among the generation of combat aircraft that was fielded *en masse* in the 1980s and still forms the backbone of the Russian air arm. Although lacking the streamlined silhouette and stunning air show performance of both the MiG-29 and Su-27 air superiority fighters, the somewhat ugly and often undervalued 'Frogfoot' has gradually but indisputably emerged as the most useful combat aircraft of its generation in Russian air force service.

In the 1990s, the ubiquitous jet attack aircraft saw active use in numerous local conflicts that erupted over the territory of what is now known as the Commonwealth of Independent States (CIS), and on at least six occasions was used in anger by foreign operators.

Recent developments of the Su-25 core programme, especially the two newly-promoted upgrade packages – Russian and Israeli/Georgian ones – as well as the latest series of export successes between 1998 and 2001, have refuted to some degree the conclusion of some analysts who maintained that the first-generation Su-25 is effectively dead in its single-seat form. In fact, the basic 'Frogfoot-A' has proved yet again that – like its American counterpart, the A-10 – the type can be considered a fairly successful and long-lasting programme.

Luckless Su-25T/TM

In the early and mid-1990s, the Su-25T (design bureau internal designation T8M) was built as a specialised anti-tank aircraft for the Central European war theatre. Equipped with

the highly-automated SUV-25T Voskhod (Rise) navigation/attack suite, the aircraft's prime anti-tank weapon was the then-new 9M120 Vikhr tube-launched laser-guided anti-tank missile. A total of 16 Vikhr missiles, able to penetrate armour up 900 mm (35 in) thick, could be carried on two eight-round underwing launchers, in addition to all 1980s-vintage Soviet laser- and TV-guided missiles and bombs. The T8M-1 prototype was flown for the first time in September 1984, and was soon followed by two more prototypes and eight Tbilisi-built pre-production aircraft to be used in the flight test programme; another airframe was used for ground static testing. The protracted development programme, especially the trials of the complex nav/attack suite, held back the type's introduction into regular squadron service prior to the collapse of the Soviet Union.

In short, the very promising Su-25T had the bad luck to approach the completion of its flight test programme at the wrong time, i.e., just as the Soviet Union and its mighty aviation industry and air force suddenly collapsed in 1991. To make matters worse, it originally had been planned to build the new aircraft in a factory outside Russia, which was politically unsuitable. And finally, some analysts argue that there was no urgent need for such a highly-specialised, rather expensive and somewhat over-sophisticated new combat aircraft to enter service with the violently downsized and poorly financed VVS (Voenno-Vozdushnye Sily – Russian air force); in fact, only six pre-production Su-25Ts are known to have been taken on strength by the VVS in the early 1990s.

Not surprisingly, in the early and mid-1990s, the Su-25T programme reported disappointingly slow progress. The first machine of the 12-aircraft operational trials batch to be built in the Tbilisi, Georgia-based factory (formerly known as Factory No. 31 and now as Tbilisi Aerospace Manufacturing – TAM) was flight-tested in June 1990. A total of eight aircraft was used in a flight test programme that comprised over 3,000 flights and no fewer than 40 Vikhr live launches. The type's state trials were reported to have been completed in September 1993.

In the early 1990s, in the wake of the dissolution of the USSR, some 18 fully- or partially-completed Su-25T airframes of the pre-production batch were left in the Tbilisi-based factory, along with about three dozen basic Su-25s in various states of assembly.

The new type received its baptism of fire during the second Chechen war. Between late 1999 and mid-2000, two Su-25Ts drawn from the Lipetsk-based 4th TsPLSiBP (Aircrew Conversion and Combat Training Centre) were deployed to Mozdok in nearby Dagestan and were used to destroy a number of high-value targets in Chechnya, such as a satellite communications facility, radio relay station, the fortified house of well-known Chechen field commander Shamil Bassaev, a hangar housing defence equipment and, curiously, an An-2 light transport on the ground, suspected to be ferrying weapons from nearby Georgia. Kh-29L (AS-14 'Kedge') and Kh-25ML (AS-10 'Kegler') laser-guided missiles were the main types of weapons employed in Chechnya, but KAB-500 laser-guided and ODAB-500 1,102-lb (500-kg) free-fall fuel-air bombs were occasionally used to destroy underground shelters and weapons storage facilities.

As well as the Su-25UB/UBK combat trainer, the Ulan Ude factory built 12 hooked Su-25UTG carrier trainers for the AVMF. For some time it was thought that a carrier-capable single-seater would provide an anti-ship element in the AVMF's carrier air wing, using Kh-31 and Kh-35 missiles.

In the late 1990s, reports surfaced that the Georgian air arm had ordered as many as 50 Su-25Ts. These can be considered entirely erroneous, as that cash-strapped air arm cannot currently afford even a few more basic Su-25s.

'Frogfoot' for Ethiopia

Two Su-25Ts (TKs), drawn from the Lipetsk-based Aircrew Conversion and Combat Training Centre, and two Su-25UBKs (drawn from VVS regular units) were delivered to the Ethiopian air force in March 2000. The Su-25UBKs were refurbished by the VVS-controlled 121st ARZ (Overhaul Facility) based at Kubinka, and the Su-25Ts were prepared for

An Su-25T is seen with a wide array of weapons, from standard FAB bombs in the foreground to Kh-29L missiles on the inboard pylons. The aircraft also carries the five-round B-13L 122-mm rocket pod and KAB-500 laser-guided bombs.

Lessons from Afghanistan saw defences on Su-25s added and improved. The Su-25T introduced a redesigned tail area with a new cylindrical fairing housing ECM and IR jammers, and two 32-round ASO-2V chaff/flare launchers.

export by Lipetsk's own technical service, rather than passing through costly and protracted overhaul. One of the Su-25UBKs was reported to have been written off in a landing accident in April or May 2000, probably at Debre Zeit air base near the Ethiopian capital of Addis Ababa.

Piloted by Ethiopian aircrew, the three surviving aircraft took part in the closing stage of the war against Eritrea, which ended on 10 June 2000. One Kh-29T TV-guided and two Kh-29L laser-guided missiles were reportedly used, in addition to a large number of S-24 240-mm (9.5-in) rockets. A total of 17 combat sorties was flown in three weeks of fighting as the aircraft operated from Debre Zeit and Mercele airfields.

This instance of successful Su-25T export after a decade of fruitless marketing efforts was eventually revealed by the Sukhoi Shturmoviks company president and designer general, Vladimir P. Babak. In an article written for the Russian defence magazine *Voyennyi Parad* (*Military Parade*) in June 2000, he alluded that Su-25TK pilots from a hot-climate export operator (not identified by Babak but believed to be the Ethiopian air arm) had mastered the employment of laser-guided missiles and successfully used them in combat.

In 2000, six to 10 ex-Russian Su-25s (including a pair of second-hand two-seaters) were acquired by Eritrea, and probably used in anger in the closing stage of the war against Ethiopia.

In the early 1990s, Russian aircraft industry authorities had decided to transfer Su-25T production to the Ulan Ude-based factory (formerly known as Factory No. 99 and now as Ulan Ude Aviation Plant – UUAP), which is located in the Russian Republic of Buryatiya near Lake Baikal. This factory had previously been intended to act as the sole manufacturer

of the two-seat Su-25UB conversion and continuation trainer and Su-25UTG carrier-based trainer (about 50 and 12, respectively, built until the late 1990s). From the start, the Su-25T's production rate at UUAP was extraordinarily slow due to the lack of proper funding; announcements appearing throughout the mid-1990s indicated that the VVS was no longer interested in supporting the Su-25T project. Supporters of this view still maintain that the anti-tank role can be handed over entirely to army aviation, which began to acquire the new Kamov Ka-50 attack helicopter, also armed with the Vikhr anti-tank missile.

Attempts to sell or lease to Bulgaria and Slovakia a small number of Su-25Ts – up to eight, probably the aircraft taken from the uncompleted pre-production batch at TAM – also proved unsuccessful.

Eventually, the Su-25T programme was salvaged, thanks to funding provided by the Sukhoi Shturmoviks company (the authority responsible for the Su-25's design, upgrades, after-sales support and marketing) and some of the subcontractors.

All-weather Su-25TM

It is of note that the development programme for a further upgraded 'Super Frogfoot' commenced as early as 1986. It was a night-capable, all-weather Su-25T derivative, designated Su-25TM (bureau designation T8M). This variant was to be equipped with pod-mounted Kinzhal (Dagger) millimetric wave radar and/or the Khod (Motion) FLIR. However, radar and FLIR trials revealed that the systems had lower-than-expected performance and reliability and, eventually, the Phazotron-NIIR Kopyo (Spear) 3-cm radar was chosen. New equipment also included the two-pod Omul ECM system, and the T8TM was able to use a wide variety of new precision-guided air-to-surface and air-to-air weapons.

Two Su-25Ts were upgraded in the early 1990s to be used as Su-25TM development platforms. These were the T8M-1, redesignated T8TM-1; and the T8M-4, redesignated T8TM-2. The former made its maiden flight in its new guise on 4 February 1991, and undertook testing and evaluation of the Khod FLIR and the new EW system. The T8TM-2 was used in development trials of the Kinzhal system, and

Between 1991 and 1994 the Khod imaging infra-red pod was tested by the Su-25T. This aircraft is shown with a Kh-31P anti-radar missile, along with Vikhrs.

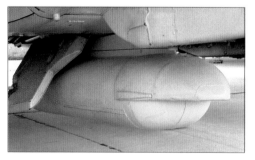

Another Su-25T pod is the Merkuriy LLLTV, which allows the pilot to see a bridge from a distance of up to 8 km (5 miles), or a tank from 3 km (1.9 miles).

On the inboard pylon of this Su-25T is the Kh-29T missile, the TV-guided version. This weapon is easily distinguished from the laser-guided version by having a much larger seeker head.

The twin-barrelled 30-mm GSh-302 cannon of the Su-25T is mounted externally in the NPPU-8M installation, with 200 rounds. The standard Su-25 has a similar weapon installed internally in the VPU-17A system, with 250 rounds. Su-25Ts have Pastel RWR and other EW antennas in the wingtip fairings.

later for the enhanced Shkval-M development, as well as for the new SUO-39 weapons control system. In late 1994, the T8TM-2 was fitted with a dummy Kopyo pod on the centreline hardpoint, and in August 1995 it was displayed at the MAKS-1995 exhibition.

The first 'Super Frogfoot' (T8TM-3) to be assembled at UUAP, serialled 'Bort 20', took to the air on 15 August 1995, followed by the second (T8TM-4) on 15 March 1998. The former was used in aerodynamic trials with the Kopyo pod, whereas the latter featured the full-standard SUO-39 fire control system and was used for trials of the radar and the new two-pod MSP EW system. The T8TM-4 was displayed for the first time at MAKS-99 wearing the serial 'White 20'.

A total of seven Su-25TM airframes was laid down on UUAP's production line, but only five have been delivered to the VVS, and the current programme status is unclear. According to often over-optimistic Sukhoi Shturmoviks press releases, the Su-25TM's state trials were to have been completed by the end of 2001, but, given the perpetual delays and scarce funding, it would be realistic to predict that the new type will be cleared for regular VVS service no earlier than the end of 2003.

It was reported that UUAP is capable of building up to 12 Su-25TMs annually, should proper programme funding materialise. A plan for the procurement of as many as 24 Su-25TMs to equip a number of regional rapid-reaction aircraft groups (using a mixture of Su-25TMs and Su-25s) was briefly announced in 1999, but it is now considered impossible for such a plan to be pursued, due to lack of funding.

Yet again, however, this does not mark the end of the Su-25TM programme. A number of reports in late 2000 and early 2001 mentioned that the assembly of aircraft numbers four and five has been completed, thanks to funds generated by the Ethiopian sale.

The Su-25T's export price is now quoted as being between US$8.5 and $10 million per unit, depending on the weapons, spare parts, training and support equipment package; the more sophisticated Su-25TM is being offered for around US$12 million, including the pod-mounted Kopyo-25 radar. Newly-built Su-25s are now being offered by TAM for up to US$6 million, with refurbished ex-VVS aircraft going for US$3 to $5 million.

VVS upgrade efforts

Considerable delays in the Su-25T/TM programme had left the Russian air force in a rather uncomfortable situation by the early 1990s, as the service began to experience a notable shortage of cost-effective precision strike aircraft. The basic Su-25 was originally designed as an affordable single-role aircraft, being optimised for clear-weather co-ordinated close air support of advancing ground forces. It was intended to operate only up to 54 nm (100 km) behind the forward edge of battle. In the event of large-scale conventional war in Central Europe or the Far East in the 1980s, the jet Shturmovik's main task would have been to complement more sophisticated types such as the Su-17M4 and MiG-27M/K.

Left: The Su-25T was based on the airframe of the Su-25UB, utilising the space of the second seat to house additional avionics for the SUV-25T Voskhod nav/attack suite. The space was also used to increase fuel capacity from the UB's 2725 kg (6,008 lb) to 3840 kg (8,466 lb) – more than the standard single-seater.

Su-25 'Frogfoot', 4th Air Army

Su-25s from the 4th Air Army bore the brunt of attack operations during both Chechen wars. During wartime missions the Su-25s were mainly used to deliver a variety of unguided bombs and rockets, as well as undertaking strafing attacks. Two Su-25Ts were deployed in an operational evaluation programme which involved several launches of Kh-25 and Kh-29 laser-guided weapons.

The Su-25TM built on the advances made by the Su-25T, and added true night/all-weather capability. This came courtesy of a podded Kopyo radar carried on the centreline and FLIR. After trials with two converted Tbilisi-built Su-25Ts, the first Ulan Ude-built Su-25TM flew in August 1995, but progress with the programme has been slow, and only around five are believed to have been completed. The first aircraft is shown here (left) with the wing-mounted Omul ECM pod. Another aircraft (below) carries R-73, Vikhr, Kh-29T TV-guided missile and a Kh-58 anti-radiation missile.

Both Su-25T and TM have a wider nose housing the Shkval-M system (similar to that used by the Ka-50), comprising a high-resolution TV, Vikhr laser guidance system and the Prichal laser rangefinder/designator.

However, the situation changed entirely in the mid- and late 1990s: following the end of the Cold War, such a front-line fleet composition was considered prohibitively expensive and unnecessarily complex. Moreover, the subsequent sharp reductions in the Russian defence budget led to some abrupt air force inventory rationalisation moves.

In the early and mid-1990s, the entire Su-17M3/M4, MiG-23MLD and MiG-27M/D/K fleets (a total, in round numbers, of nearly 1,500 aircraft) were withdrawn from use. Significant reductions in the number of active Su-24Ms and MiG-29s also took place. And finally, all development and test programmes for new-generation multi-role tactical fighters and dedicated strike aircraft were either notably slowed or scrapped entirely.

In 1990, the mighty Soviet air force had an inventory of 385 Su-25s based in East Germany and the European part of the Soviet Union, with 40 more operated in the Far East; no fewer than 80 examples were in service with naval aviation. As many as 60 per cent of the 'Frogfoots' (between 280 and 300 airframes, including up to eight serviceable Su-25Ts) were retained in Russian air force and naval aviation service following the Soviet Union's collapse. By the late 1990s, the Russian air arm had an active inventory of around 200 to 220 'Frogfoots'; Belarus inherited 99 and Ukraine about 80; and a dozen or slightly more Su-25s went to other CIS republics such as Armenia and Azerbaijan. In the mid-1990s, a small number of ex-VVS Su-25s had been redistributed to the air arms of CIS republics such as Turkmenistan (at least five aircraft noted in regular service in 2000) and Uzbekistan.

Meanwhile, the role of the Russian air force's tactical fighter fleet changed considerably as emphasis shifted to the capability of participating in local rather than in global armed conflicts; inevitably, this led to the definition of a number of new requirements. The Su-25 fleet has escaped reductions on as large as scale as those suffered by the MiG-29 and Su-24M fleets, and only a small number of airframes produced prior to 1985 have been either grounded for use as spare part sources or offered for export.

Eventually, the faithful 'Frogfoot' emerged as the most cost-effective Russian air force aircraft to cope with the challenges of the low-intensity wars that erupted in various corners of the former Soviet empire.

'Frogfoot' in action

Major conflicts in which the VVS Su-25 fleet was used in anger in the post-Soviet era were those between Georgia and Abkhasia in 1993 and 1994, and also in 1994 during the Russian offensive against Moslem fundamentalists near the Tajikistan-Afghanistan border. Very soon afterwards, the 'Frogfoot' saw extensive use in the bloody Chechen wars as VVS Su-25s flew more than 6,000 missions in both campaigns there. Three aircraft were lost to enemy air defences in the first Chechen war (1993-1994), and another five or six were lost either to rebel AAA or in collisions with mountains in the second campaign (1999-2001). During the latter war, the 'Frogfoot' fleet was used mainly in the 'bomb-truck'/'rocket battery' role, leaving the complex guided weapons and bad weather missions to the Su-24Ms and two Su-25Ts.

As expected, the simple and robust 'Frogfoot' lived up to VVS expectations in these encounters, demonstrating yet again fairly good reliability and mission availability, given the primitive Afghanistan-like operating conditions and scant field maintenance. This is particularly true for the airframe and powerplant.

The type's mission avionics are no longer considered modern, as it has unimpressive capability and low precision for some complex types of missions such as would be required in future low-intensity conflicts. Ten years ago these taskings would have been assigned to the now-defunct Su-17M4 and MiG-27M/K fleets. Obviously, most – if not all – of these missions are within the Su-25T/TM's capability, but this new, potent, rather expensive and still-

This Kopyo-equipped Su-25TM carries the Kh-35 (AS-20 'Kayak') anti-ship missile. Note also the downward-firing chaff/flare launcher fitted to the lower fuselage below the engine intake.

One of two Su-25SMs initially upgraded by the 121st ARZ at Kubinka was displayed at the MAKS exhibition at Zhukovskiy in 2001. The new variant did not begin flight-testing until March 2002, and conversion of further examples has proceeded slowly.

unproven type will not enter mass squadron service for at least three to five years (and it is still unclear if the new type will ever enter squadron service, due to the competition posed by a number of higher-priority programmes). Thus, it was decided in early 1998 to upgrade part of the existing VVS 'Frogfoot' inventory.

Initially, it was intended that the majority of the existing VVS 'Frogfoots' would undergo such an upgrade, but eventually the percentage of aircraft to be upgraded fell to the more modest 40 per cent; in numerical terms, this accounts for about 80 aircraft, which should be sufficient to equip five or six first-line squadrons. However, some senior Sukhoi officials interviewed at the ILA 2002 exhibition in Berlin maintained that the VVS has expressed a desire to upgrade most, and perhaps all, of its currently active Su-25s and Su-25UBs.

Su-25SM/UBM – Russian upgrade

Preliminary design work on the 'Frogfoot' upgrade started at Sukhoi Shturmoviks in mid-1998, and the concept was announced publicly later that year. A highly sophisticated – and hence rather expensive – upgrade standard was initially offered for both the single- and twin-seat VVS Su-25s. This comprised the Pantera (Panther) nav/attack suite, nose-mounted Kopyo-25SM radar and pod-mounted electronic warfare suite, as well as a number of measures for improving the type's survivability and maintainability, and extending airframe and engine service life, thus reducing life-cycle costs by 30 per cent. Introduction of radar-absorbent coatings and a new type of paint, in order to reduce the probability of radar and visual detection, were also on offer. Range extension would be possible from additional external tanks on twin-carriage pylons. Most of the components were already proven, or were planned for use in the Su-25TM.

The first Su-25SM conversion is seen on display with laser-guided Kh-29L (foreground) and Kh-25ML missiles. The SM has a single LCD display in the cockpit on to which imagery from EO-guided weapons can be displayed, along with navigation and flight data.

By early 2000, VVS and Sukhoi Shturmoviks officials announced that they would go ahead with a far cheaper and less extensive upgrade standard for the single-seaters, priced at between US$500,000 and $1 million per unit. This comprises a downgraded version of the Pantera nav/attack suite, and perhaps a new EW suite for some of the aircraft. The upgraded 'Frogfoot' was redesignated Su-25SM (*stroyevoy modernizirovannnyi* – Line Upgrade, indicating that all work is to be carried out at the VVS's own maintenance facilities).

Depending on funding available beyond 2002, it would be possible for a small number of Su-25UBs to be upgraded to the definitive standard that included the Kopyo-25SM radar. These aircraft would be designated Su-25UBM and would possess genuine anti-ship and beyond visual range (BVR) air-to-air capability. The former capability would come from the integration of the Kh-31A (AS-17 'Krypton') and Kh-35 (AS-20 'Kayak') anti-ship missiles, while BVR air-to-air capability would be possible via the active radar-homing R-77 (AA-12 'Adder') air-to-air missile. In order to minimise the necessary airframe structural re-work, the Kopyo-25SM would be pod-mounted under the fuselage (as on the Su-25TM) instead of in the nose, as originally planed.

However, the Russian air arm currently has a limited number of Su-25UBs – no more than two dozen are on hand – most, if not all, of which are being heavily utilised in conversion

This model shows the initial Su-25SM configuration, with Kopyo-25SM radar in a neat nose radome. This proposal was dropped as being too expensive and the current Su-25SM upgrade has no radar.

A nose-mounted radar was also part of the original Su-25UBM proposal. The Kopyo-25SM radar may be retained in the revised concept, but only as a pod-mounted unit. Note the provision of radar-guided AAMs, including the R-77, and Kh-58 ARM.

Two views show the Scorpion demonstrator's cockpit. New to the Su-25 is a head-up display – earlier aircraft had a simple sight. The HUD, upfront controller, two large MFDs and HOTAS provide a more modern feel to the cockpit although some old instruments are retained. Cockpit instrumentation is a mixture of Russian and English.

and advanced training roles; small numbers have seen action in Chechnya. The acquisition of 10 to 15 newly-built Su-25UBs, to be upgraded on the production line or later to the Su-25UBM standard, is a possibility.

The Su-25SM's Pantera nav/attack suite is built around a new digital computer, borrowed from the Su-25TM. All the analog components of the existing KN-23-1 nav/attack suite, which have poor reliability and are maintenance-intensive, will be replaced by mostly digital ones. Aircraft navigation accuracy will be improved tenfold thanks to the A-737 satellite navigation receiver integrated into the existing ICV gyro reference platform (the receiver can use signals from satellites of both the Russian GLONASS and the US NAVSTAR Global Positioning System). This will bring the Su-25SM closer in line with the Su-25T/TM's remarkable navigation accuracy of about 0.2 per cent deviation from track on a typical route. Navigation (non-visual) bombing in bad weather and at night against fixed targets that have a precisely known position, using data from the upgraded navigation system, is also becoming possible.

TV and laser weapons

The Su-25SM's guided weapons suite was enriched with the Kh-29T TV-guided air-to-surface missile and the KAB-500Kr TV-guided bomb (both 1980s-vintage, but still considered to be very effective lock-on before launch weapons). The upgraded aircraft is to be capable of dropping and firing several types of weapons in a single attack pass, and also to use the highly agile R-73 air-to-air missile, an extremely effective weapon for slow-speed

target intercepts over the battlefield, especially when integrated with a helmet-mounted sight.

Some of the existing nav/attack system components that have demonstrated good performance and reliability – such as the Klyon-PS laser rangefinder/target marker and the ASP-17BTz-8 electro-optical sight – were retained.

According to reports from the Sukhoi Shturmoviks company, the Su-25SM's cockpit had undergone a redesign in order to improve the ergonomics, thus reducing pilot workload during complex attack missions. One LCD colour display was installed on the instrument panel (two LCDs would probably be employed in the front and rear cockpits of the Kopyo-25SM-equipped two-seat aircraft, in addition to a new HUD), and possibly a Russian interpretation of the HOTAS controls concept was adopted, at least partially, by the Su-25SM/UBM. There is (or will be added at a later stage) provision for the integration of new-generation Russian FLIR/laser designation pods, such as the UOMZ Sapsan, to enable day/night laser-guided bomb employment. An ECM system comprising the two-pod Omul jammer covering the frequency band between

7 and 10 GHz, which can operate in co-operation with the Pastel radar warning/emitter locator system, is probably also being planned to equip some of the upgraded Su-25SMs.

The majority of the VVS Su-25s originally slated to serve until about 2010 are now thought to be under-utilised, falling well below the half-way point of their 2,500-hour limit. Airframe life extension to a total of 40 years and 4,000 hours is being offered as part of the Su-25SM upgrade package (in such a case, TBO is 2,000 hours); it may also be adopted for the rest of the VVS Su-25s, and is known to have been offered to foreign operators.

The Su-25SM is set to retain the tried Gavrilov R-95Sh turbojets. Although often described as old-tech and rather uneconomical, the 1960s-vintage R-95 is still readily available in large numbers. Remarkably reliable and fairly cheap to maintain, it features a total life of 1,500 hours, with overhauls required every 500 hours. Engine life extensions up to 2,000 or even 2,500 hours are options.

Rework begins

In March 2001, the first two VVS Su-25s were sent for upgrade to the VVS 121st ARZ (Overhaul Facility) at Kubinka near Moscow. One of these, serialled 'Bort 33', was displayed on the static line at the MAKS-01 exhibition in August that year, in what was reported as being an upgraded configuration (cockpit photos were prohibited), although it still awaited the commencement of flight testing. By early March, reliable information was still lacking about whether the Su-25SM had begun its flight test programme, leading to the conclusion that the programme still suffered from chronic lack of funding. Eventually, the first upgraded

Elbit's Scorpion demonstrator, resplendent in Georgian Air Force markings, has made high-profile appearances at the Paris and Farnborough air shows, including impressive flying displays by Yehuda Shafir, Elbit's chief test pilot.

Although it lacks radar, the Su-25KM is a far more capable upgrade package than the Su-25SM, due to its modern avionics architecture which allows the integration of modern precision weapons and man/machine interface, including helmet-mounted sight.

Su-25SM made its first test flight in its new guise on 5 March 2002. Tests were expected to have been completed by August 2002, and production upgrades started in spring 2002 (a total of five Su-25s, including one two-seater, was reported to have been upgraded by the Kubinka-based 121st Overhaul Facility).

Su-25KM Scorpion

The most radical Su-25 upgrade package yet announced is that offered by Elbit Systems, an acknowledged leader in ex-Soviet platform upgrades that has established successful co-operation with the original manufacturer TAM. The joint venture's aim is to produce a 'digitalised' 'Frogfoot' derivative; the Elbit/TAM upgrade package, known as Scorpion, was developed in late 2000 and early 2001. The technology demonstrator aircraft, wearing Georgian air force insignia and the serial '01', was flown for the first time by Yehuda Shafir on 18 April 2001. He later successfully demonstrated the Scorpion, known also as the Su-25KM (KM standing for *kommercheskiy*, Modernised), at the Le Bourget air show in June that year. In 2002, the Su-25KM was demonstrated at the Farnborough air show.

For Elbit Systems, the Su-25KM is yet another Russian combat platform to be upgraded using proven and fairly modern digital avionics, a process that considerably improves the type's overall combat capability. Main improvements are to the nav/attack system and man-machine interface/situational awareness, with the introduction of all-weather day/night capability and advanced debriefing facilities.

The Su-25KM's new avionics suite, featuring an all-new 'glass' cockpit, was developed around Elbit's Multi-Role Modular Computer

(MMRC) controlling dual Mil-Std 1553 data-buses – one responsible for navigation, the other for the weapons delivery system. The 'glass' cockpit is dominated by an El-Op Head-Up Display (HUD), up-front control panel, two 6 x 8-in (15 x 20-cm) LCD colour displays, and solid-state backup instruments. Precise navigation capability is provided by a laser-gyro INS/GPS hydride system. NATO- and ICAO-compatible navaids – VOR/ILS and DME (TACAN optional) – are added, as are two new radios (one UHF and one VHF).

Elbit's Display And Sight Helmet (DASH) is offered, significantly improving the pilot's situation awareness. The DASH is reported to have been integrated into both the R-73 air-to-air missile and the new navigation system, for marking points of interest on the ground during strike or reconnaissance missions. Complete mission pre-plan capability is also included in the core package. Some of the original Russian-made instruments are retained, such as the SPO-15LM radar warning receiver (RWR), RV-15 radar altimeter, AoA indicator, engine RPM and fuel meter. New weapons that the Su-25KM can

employ include the above-mentioned R-73 air-to-air missile (also manufactured by TAM), as well as Elbit's infra-red-guided Opher and laser-guided Lizard bombs.

The Scorpion package is thought to be more advanced and flexible, to some degree, than the competing Su-25SM export derivative. More importantly, unlike the Elbit-upgraded MiG-21 Lancer and MiG-29 Sniper, the Scorpion is being strongly backed by the original manufacturer, which has legal rights to the type's design and in-service documentation, and possesses the required expertise and experience to introduce major changes to the aircraft's structure and avionics suite, as well as to offer logistic support and depot-level maintenance.

An aggressive marketing campaign, initiated by Elbit in 2001 and continued in 2002, is aimed at a number of current European and Third World 'Frogfoot' operators. However, at

Weapon options introduced by the Su-25KM Scorpion include the R-73 air-to-air missile (carried on the centre pylon) to augment the existing R-60 (outboard), and the Elbit Opher infra-red guided bomb. The Lizard laser-guided bomb is also available.

Most Su-25s are powered by the 40.2-kN (9,036-lb) Soyuz/Gavrilov R-95Sh, and the engine is retained in the Su-25SM upgrade, rather than being replaced by the more powerful (44.1-kN/9,913-lb) R-195 fitted to a few late-production Su-25s and the Su-25T/TM.

By Soviet standards of the 1970s, the Su-25's cockpit was well laid out, and was praised by pilots. The panel is topped by an ASP-17BTz-8 reflector sight, complete with a canopy strut-mounted gun camera.

the time of writing (October 2002), there were no signs that any upgrade contracts were being seriously negotiated or awarded to the Israeli-Georgian team.

Upgrade market

Russian and some foreign military aviation observers estimated in 2001 that the overall Su-25 upgrade market may be as huge as 400 airframes; however, that is now viewed as a notably inflated figure. As might be supposed, the main reason for the lack of strong interest in both the Su-25KM and Su-25SM upgrades is that the full-standard Scorpion package is too expensive and, sometimes, over-sophisticated for most, if not all, of the existing Su-25K operators. These operators are subject to tight budgets and are much more concerned about maintaining fleet airworthiness than undertaking costly upgrades. They are likely to be interested only in introducing low-cost upgrades to improve navigation accuracy and maintainability (through extension of the airframe and engine time between overhauls), and in some cases in integrating a limited range of guided weapons. The Su-25K's direct operating costs in Eastern Europe are quoted at around US$5,000 per flying hour, which is roughly 60 per cent of those of the Su-22M4 and 80 per cent of those of the MiG-23MF/BN.

SEAD-capable two-seat 'Frogfoots'

The only upgrade package known to have been ordered by an export customer is the Suppression of Enemy Air Defence (SEAD) package. It has been introduced to some,

perhaps all, of the eight Fuerza Aérea del Peru (FAP – Peruvian air force) Su-25UB two-seaters, as well as to a limited number of Belarussian air force Su-25s. These aircraft received the L150 Pastel radar warning receiver/emitter locator system housed in an underfuselage KRK-UP pod (the same size and shape as that used to house the Su-25T/TM's Khod and Kinzhal systems), alongside the launch control equipment for the Kh-58U/E ARM. The Kh-58U/E is the most widely used Russian anti-radar missile; it weighs 1,411 lb (640 kg) including the 328-lb (149-kg) warhead, and can be launched at distances of 4.3 to 54 nm (8 and 100 km).

The rear cockpit's instrument panel of the SEAD-capable Su-25UB received a new IM-3M-14 monochrome CRT display, onto which the target information derived from the Pastel can be displayed. Data (in the form of range, bearing and probable type information) for up to six enemy radars in frequencies between 1.2 and 18 GHz can be displayed, and radar emissions can be detected at a range nearly 20 per cent greater than the radar's own detection range.

The upgrade of the eight or so Peruvian and an unknown number of Belarussian Su-25UBs is known to have been carried out by the Baranovichi-based 558 ARZ facility in Belarus, in close co-operation with the Sukhoi Shturmoviks company. It is likely that some of the Russian two-seat 'Frogfoots' will also receive such a capability in the near future (complementing, and perhaps partially replacing, the MiG-25BMs and Su-24Ms in the dangerous SEAD role), instead of being converted to the much more expensive Su-25UBM standard.

One innovative role of the FAP Su-25 fleet is anti-drug intercept operations. In 1999 and 2000, FAP 'Frogfoots' were rushed into action to reinforce the nation's anti-drug campaign. Due

to its remarkable low-speed manoeuvrability, the straight-winged and heavily armoured jet, featuring an impressive thrust-to-weight ratio, can successfully be used to intercept single- and twin-engined general aviation aircraft smuggling raw cocaine and cocaine paste from the Upper Hullanga Valley in Peru to neighbouring Colombia. In some cases, the Su-25 pilots who intercepted and identified suspected drug-carrying aircraft were ordered to shoot them down, for which they used R-60 air-to-air missiles and the powerful GSh-302 built-in 30-mm gun.

European small-scale upgrade effort

In 1999, two Czech air force Su-25Ks underwent a so-called 'small-scale' upgrade (more precisely, it should be called adaptation) of their communication, navigation and identification equipment to ensure limited NATO and ICAO compatibility and to improve navigation capability in operational missions. This involved the use of affordable and proven Western commercial hardware, the work being carried out by the local CLS company, based at Prague-Kbely. Trimble 2101 I/O Approach Plus commercial GPS receivers, as well as VOR/ILS and DME receivers (TACAN optional), were added to the aircraft's existing nav/attack system, and the new navigation components were integrated via an interface unit developed by CLS. The navigation suite upgrade is designed in such a way that information from the new navigation components can be displayed on the existing 'clockwork' HIS navigation indicator. Anti-collision lights and an additional radio were also installed. However, plans for the type's withdrawal from use in late 2000 prevented the fleet-wide upgrade of the Czech air force Su-25Ks.

It is likely that similar packages may soon be adopted by other under-funded European air arms, such as those of Bulgaria and Macedonia, whose Su-25s are set to soldier on for some years. East European operators are reportedly set to implement some measures for NATO/ICAO interoperability and life-cycle costs reductions.

The newly established air force of Macedonia turned to the Ukraine for its initial equipment, receiving four Su-25s to provide a cost-effective yet hard-hitting attack force. They were thrown straight into action in the fight with Albanian rebel forces.

The second seat makes the Su-25UB a sought-after commodity, especially as it is more adaptable than the single-seater to missions requiring sophisticated systems. However, it is also in high demand for training. Russian Su-25s are expected to serve until around 2020.

The Macedonian air arm is the latest European Su-25 operator, receiving four ex-Ukrainian Su-25s (including one two-seater) in June 2001. They feature the full set of self-protection aids, including scabbed-on flare dispensers. The newly-acquired aircraft were used in anger immediately following their delivery, attacking ethnic Albanian rebels who occupied the villages of Arachinovo and Radusha. There, the Macedonian Su-25s were reported to have used powerful FAB-500M62 1,100-lb (500-kg) high-explosive bombs (mostly due to the great psychological effect of the powerful blast, rather than their destructive power), as well as 57-mm and 80-mm rockets. They also carried out a number of visual reconnaissance and 'force projection' missions over the occupied villages.

In addition to their main role of ground attack, Macedonian Su-25s, armed with R-60 air-to-air missiles, are employed as fighter-interceptors – because they are the only jet aircraft in the air arm's inventory. There were a number of reports in early 2002 that Macedonia was considering the acquisition of at least two more ex-Ukrainian Su-25s, and imminent low-cost upgrades of their nav/attack systems cannot be ruled out.

Future exports prospects

Between 1992 and 1998, some 12 to 15 newly-manufactured Su-25s at TAM were taken on strength by the newly-born Georgian air force. Up to six of these aircraft were later reported to have been lost during the conflict in Abkhasia in 1993 and 1994. Another Georgian air force example was shot down during operations against rebel groups in the republic. Currently, the Georgian air arm has an inventory of six to eight single-seaters and one or two two-seaters. Interestingly, in the mid-1990s,

TAM began production of a five-unit Su-25UB batch (TAM designated these two-seaters Su-25U) originally ordered by the Georgian air arm, but lack of funding meant only two aircraft were delivered. The only known TAM Su-25 export deal following the Soviet Union collapse involved 10 single-seaters acquired by Congo in 1999 and 2000.

Between 1979 and 1999, TAM built more than 820 Su-25s (825, according to unconfirmed information) in four main variants: the basic single-seater and two-seater, target-towing Su-25BM single-seater, and anti-tank Su-25T. These were distributed as follows: 582 basic Su-25s for the Soviet/CIS and Georgian air arms, 50 Su-25BM target tugs, between 180 and 185 Su-25Ks, and up to 22 Su-25Ts (some partially completed and still stored at TAM), as well as one to three Su-25U two-seaters built at TAM using uncompleted Su-25T airframes fitted with two-seat nose fuselages supplied by UUAP. Ulan Ude Aviation Plant produced 150 to 200 two-seat Su-25UBs and Su-25UBKs, and three or four Su-25TMs.

By the mid-1990s, 'Frogfoot' export sales amounted to 201 aircraft (185 single-seaters and 16 two-seaters), sold to five states: Bulgaria – 40, Czechoslovakia – 38, Iraq – 73, Angola – 12, and North Korea – 36. Another 46 (35 being second-hand aircraft) were sold between 1998

and 2001 to five other non-CIS states: Peru (18), Ethiopia (four), Eritrea (up to 10), Congo (10) and Macedonia (four).

Regarding the Su-25's future sales prospects, it can be noted that newly-built Su-25Ks and more modern Scorpions, the latter priced at about US$12 million per unit, are viewed as being highly competitive with modern attack aircraft such as the BAE Systems Hawk 200 and Alenia/EMBRAER AMX. The Su-25 is still being offered as a low-cost replacement of the older ground attack types (AT-37, F-6, F-7, MiG-21, MiG-23 and Su-20/22) used by a number of Third World states. UUAP and TAM are active in this combat aircraft market, and the former has offered a number of Southeast Asian states its fully combat-capable Su-25UBK in basic or upgraded form, at a price of about US$10 million.

It would be reasonable to predict that a renewal of the type's export success will take place in the early 2000s, most likely in traditional Soviet/Russian customers such as Syria, Libya, Algeria and Vietnam, whose air arms have to replace their inventories of aged Su-20/22s, MiG-21M/MFs and MiG-23BNs. Existing African and Asian customers – Ethiopia, Eritrea, Iran and Iraq – have air arms that may also opt to acquire more Su-25s. Thus, in the forthcoming decade, 'Frogfoot' exports of both newly-built and second-hand machines may number as high as 60 aircraft.

A similar number of Su-25s belonging to the air arms of some ex-Soviet republics may be upgraded, to greater or lesser extent, and the market for life extension and maintenance rationalisations may be as large as 100 aircraft. Su-25TM low-rate production at UUAP and TAM is likely to continue for some years to come, though it is probable that the new type will have only limited service in Russia and, at best, will enjoy only limited export success.

Alexander Mladenov

Above: In Europe, Bulgaria and Macedonia are the last remaining 'Frogfoot' operators. Bulgaria has a fleet of 39 Su-25K/UBKs, and around half are expected to serve on until 2010/2014. Six Su-25Ks and two Su-25UBKs will undergo a minor upgrade for NATO/ICAO interoperability in early 2003.

Left: Slovakia operated 10 Su-25Ks and a single Su-25UBK (left) until early 2002, but they are now grounded and are to be formally withdrawn in late 2002.

Mil Mi-24 'Hind'
Combat Crocodile

Mikhail Leontyevich Mil's Mi-24 design was a revolutionary one, a 'flying IFV' that combined heavy firepower with the ability to carry squads of fully-equipped troops to the front of the battlefield. There has never been a combat helicopter quite like the 'Hind', and it is still feared and respected. The Mi-24 earned the nickname 'devil's chariot' from the Mujahideen, in Afghanistan – though to its Soviet crews it was always the 'krokodil'. Since then the Mi-24 has gone on to see more combat worldwide than virtually any other military aircraft in service today.

Mil Mi-24 'Hind'

Above and right: The appropriately coded Mil V-24 mock-up bore a striking resemblance to the Bell 'Huey', but also incorporated all the basic elements of Mil's 'flying IFV' concept – cabin space for troops and onboard weapons with which to protect them. The V-24 was clearly far too small and fragile to be a practicable assault helicopter and Mil's subsequent 10.5-tonne, twin-engined 'Hind' designs bore no resemblance to this early contraption. The wooden V-24 model is seen here outside the OKB's experimental workshop at Panki. Features of note include the split folding cabin doors, the GSh-23L cannon attached to the starboard skid and dummy missiles canted at an angle that seems sure to fire straight through the main rotor disc. When Mil was ready to take its final Mi-24 design forward for approval, it faced competition from the rival design bureau led by Nikolay Il'yich Kamov, the Soviet Union's other major helicopter designer. Kamov suggested a cheaper solution – an army CAS version of the proven Ka-25 Hormone ASW helicopter with two FFAR pods on outrigger pylons, which was actually built and tested. This later evolved into the Ka-25F (frontovoy – tactical) project of 1966 featuring a totally redesigned streamlined fuselage with two double doors on each side, a GSh-23 cannon in a chin barbette and skid landing gear. Mil's idea to build an all-new, heavily-armed assault helicopter prevailed and Kamov's low-cost option was dropped.

The father of the Mi-24 and the man who brought about a revolution in Soviet battlefield tactics was General Designer Mikhail Leontyevich Mil. As Soviet forces became more mechanised during the 1960s, Mil saw that the next logical step would be to create 'flying IFVs' (infantry fighting vehicles) which could deliver a squad of troops and provide close air support (CAS). The first tangible form of Mil's concept came in 1966 when the full-scale mock-up of a new combat helicopter designated V-24 (V, *vertolyot* = helicopter) was rolled out at the experimental shop at the Ministry of Aircraft Industry's factory No. 329 in Panki, a suburb of Moscow. This factory is now known as MVZ (*Moskovskiy vertolyotnii zavod* = the Moscow Helicopter Plant named after M. L. Mil).

Outwardly, the original mock-up had nothing in common with the prototype which took to the air several years later; in fact, it looked strikingly similar to the Bell 204 (UH-1A Huey). Yet, it incorporated all the main features of the helicopter which was to gain fame (and notoriety) as the Mi-24 'Hind'. It had two crew – a pilot and the weapons systems operator (WSO) – and accommodation for seven or eight fully-armed troops. The armament comprised a Gryazev/Shipunov GSh-23 double-barrelled 23-mm (0.90-in) cannon, four or six anti-tank guided missiles (ATGMs) and two or four UB-16-57 rocket pods, each holding 16 57-mm (2.24-in) S-5 folding-fin aircraft rockets (FFARs). (UB, *unifitseerovannii blok* = standardised [FFAR] pod, and the designation UV-16-57 sometimes found in Western literature is wrong; S, *snaryad* = in this case, unguided rocket.) The cockpit, troop cabin and vital systems had armour protection.

Mikhail L. Mil proposed his 'flying IFV' to the leaders of the Soviet Armed Forces. He won the support of some young strategists, but many high-ranking MoD officials, notably the then-Defence Minister Marshal Roman Yakovlevich Malinovskiy, opposed the idea.

Luckily, by 1967 Mil persuaded the minister's first deputy, Marshal A. A. Grechko, who was always in favour of assault helicopters, to establish a special expert panel and look deeper into the matter. The opinions of military experts ranged from open support to blunt rejection, but

the supporters won and Mil received a go-ahead. On 29 March 1967 the Defence Industry Commission of the Soviet Council of Ministers issued what might be called a request for proposals – a directive ordering the Mil OKB to prepare and submit its plans for a battlefield support helicopter.

The engineers soon had two preliminary design (PD) projects ready. One envisaged a 7-tonne (15,430-lb) helicopter powered by a single 1,700-eshp (1268-kW) Isotov TV3-117A turboshaft, the other was a 10.5-tonne (23,150-lb) helicopter powered by two TV3-117As. The OKB's experimental shop completed three different mock-ups plus five versions of the helicopter's forward fuselage so that the best placement of pilot and WSO could be chosen.

The twin-engined PD project was accepted, but the military demanded that the fixed cannon be replaced by a fast-firing heavy machine-gun in a powered chin turret. Importantly, they also specified the 9M114 Shturm-V (Assault) ATGM (known to NATO as the AT-6 'Spiral'), which was still under development at the time. The helicopter was to have a new weapons control system comprising a stabilised WSO's sight, an automatic pilot's sight and a laser rangefinder. Advanced day/night targeting systems and defensive electronics were to be incorporated as they came along.

Mi-24 'Hind-B' (Izdelye 240)

Work on the advanced development project (ADP) of the future Mi-24 began immediately after the Central Committee of the Communist Party and the Council of Ministers issued a joint directive to this effect on 6 May 1968. The Mi-24 programme progressed under the overall supervision of General Designer Mikhail L. Mil (succeeded after his death in 1970 by Marat Nikolayevich Tischchenko). The design effort was led by chief project engineer V. A. Kuznetsov, Tischchenko's deputy, and the team included project engineer V. M. Olshevets, and V. D. Zernov and B. V. Smyslov who were in charge of the flight test programme, etc.

Detail design work commenced in August. Appropriately coded '24 White', the full-scale mock-up passed the so-called mock-up inspection commission of the VVS (Voyenno-vozdushniie seely = [Soviet] Air Force) in February 1969. Prototype construction got under way soon after and progressed quickly, the first prototype being completed in June 1969.

The pace of development and construction was increased by Mil's decision to borrow the main dynamic components (engines, main and tail rotors, swashplate and parts of the power train) from the proven Mi-8 − or, rather, its naval derivative, the Mi-14, which was undergoing trials at the time. Its main rotor was not identical to that of the Mi-8, being somewhat smaller (17.3 m/56 ft 9.1 in versus 21.3 m/69 ft 10.58 in). The new TV3-117 turboshaft of the Mi-14 was then one of the world's best helicopter engines. It had a nominal rating of 1,700 eshp (1268 kW) and a take-off/contingency rating of 2,200 eshp (1641 kW); if one engine failed, the other automatically went to full take-off power. The Mi-24's engines were started pneumatically by an Ivchenko AI-9V APU located dorsally behind the main gearbox. The oft-repeated notion that early versions of the Mi-24 were powered by the Mi-8's 1,500-eshp (1119-kW) Isotov TV2-117As is wrong. Firstly, the TV2-117A has electric starting and does not need an APU (as shown by the first-generation Mi-8), whereas all Mi-24s and the second-generation Mi-8MT have an APU. Secondly, the TV2-117 has a circular-section jetpipe with several thin pipes running along it; the 'Hind' has clean oval-section jetpipes characteristic of the TV3-117.

Design features

The Mi-24, or Izdelye 240 as it was known in-house, employed the classic layout, featuring a five-bladed main rotor and a three-bladed tail rotor. Here, the similarity to the 'Hip' ended. The relatively slender fuselage was carefully streamlined and the tricycle landing gear was fully retractable. All three units retracted aft into the fuselage, the main units turning so that the wheels remained vertical but at 90° to the direction of flight. The relatively narrow aft fuselage meant that the fat low-pressure mainwheels could not be stowed completely, resulting in characteristically bulged gear doors.

The small stub wings with marked incidence (19°), which were one of the helicopter's main recognition features, not only carried weapons pylons but reduced rotor disc loading in forward flight by 19 to 25 per cent, depending on speed; the Mil OKB had clearly benefited from its experience with the Mi-6. On the original Mi-24 the wings had zero anhedral and two BD3-57Kr-V (BD, *bahlochnii derzhahtelí* = beam-type [weapons] rack; Kr, *krylíyevoy* = wing-mounted; V, *vertolyotnii* = for helicopters) pylons each side for FFAR pods and bombs; the ATGMs were carried in pairs on detachable racks on the lower fuselage sides ahead of the wings. To offload the tail rotor in forward flight, the tailboom, which was faired into the fuselage, had a relatively large area and the large tail rotor pylon had an asymmetrical cross-section.

The crew sat in tandem under a common angular 'greenhouse' canopy with optically-flat glass panels. The pilot sat behind the WSO, offset to port. The WSO detected and identified the targets, fired and guided the anti-tank missiles, worked the chin turret and dropped bombs. The pilot could fire unguided rockets (FFARs) or podded guns on the wing stations and the machine-gun, providing the latter was pointing in the direction of flight. In service, a third crew member, the aircraft's technician, was also carried. The cockpit was accessed via a forward-opening car-type door for the pilot and a large upward-opening window for the WSO on the port side.

The centre fuselage was occupied by a troop/cargo cabin accommodating up to eight fully armed troops back to back and accessed via horizontally-split doors on either side. The upper and lower halves of each door opened simultaneously by means of mechanical linkages, and the lower half incorporated boarding steps. The cabin windows could be

This (inset) is how the US DoD presented the Mi-24 'threat' in the 1986 edition of Soviet Military Power – the great Reagan-era bible of the 'Red Menace'. The Mi-24 was rightly seen as a major asset to Warsaw Pact theatre forces in Europe, and one which would lead an anticipated chemical warfare assault against NATO. This artist's impression shows a pair of 'Hinds' spraying chemical agents on a European battlefield – a deadly task that the 'Hind' had already fulfilled in Afghanistan. Today, the 'Hind' is much less of a threat to a modern army and no longer such a mystery. The US Army now has its own Mi-24s (above) – three aircraft quietly acquired through friends and allies. They are used to play the part of OPFOR 'Red Air' in US military exercises, to train units in threat recognition and to develop new air defence systems.

The A-10 – Mil's record breaker

In 1975 the Mil OKB modified one of the uncoded 'Hind-Bs' built in 1970 (c/n 0200204, possibly the last-but-one pre-production aircraft) for an attempt on the Class E (helicopters) world speed and time-to-height records. In keeping with the usual Soviet practice of allocating untrue designations to military aircraft used for such record attempts, the helicopter was called A-10 in the documents submitted to the International Aeronautical Federation.

Every possible step had been taken to cut weight. The stub wings were removed and their mountings covered by shallow fairings to reduce drag. The main rotor head featured inertia-type vibration dampers later fitted to some Mi-8s (notably passenger and VIP versions). For some reason the rearmost cabin window on each side was faired over. Like most 'Hind-Bs',

the A-10 had no tactical code.

On 16 July 1975 a female crew consisting of pilot Galina Rastorguyeva and navigator Lyudmila Polyanskaya reached 341 km/h (184.3 kt) on a 15/25-km (9.3/15.5-mile) course. Interestingly, both crew members were civilian, representing the Central Aero Club named after Valeriy P. Chkalov (Tushino airfield, Moscow). Two days later, flown by the same crew, the A-10

attained 334 km/h (180.54 kt) over a 100-km (62.11-mile) course. On 1 August 1975 the helicopter clocked 331 km/h (178.9 kt) over a 500-km (310.55-mile) course with Lyudmila Polyanskaya in the driver's seat. A week later the A-10 reached 3000 m (9,843 ft) in 2 minutes 3⅝ seconds. On 13 August, defying superstition, Rastorguyeva set another speed record, reaching 333 km/h (180.0 kt) over a 1000-km (621.12-mile) course. Another time-to-height record was set on 26 August – 6000 m (19,685 ft) in 7 minutes 43 seconds. All of these records stand as of early 1999.

On 21 September 1978 company test pilot Gourguen R. Karapetyan set an absolute world helicopter speed record of 368.4 km/h (228.82 mph/199.13 kt). This stood until 1986 when it was broken by a Westland Lynx with the then-experimental BERP main rotor.

Above: This is the second V-24 prototype, seen on an early test flight. It has not yet been fitted with ATGM launch rails and the nose turret is lacking its gun. The two initial prototypes were built with straight (no anhedral) stub wings. Also of note is the original position of the tail rotor, to starboard.

Right: This is the V-24 prototype, seen before its first flight. The V-24 mock-up was coded 'Yellow 24', but the real aircraft appears to have gone unmarked.

Right: This mixed-up aircraft is either one of the V-24 prototypes, or one of the 10 pre-production 'Hind-B' 'dogships'. It has straight stub wings but the production standard lengthened nose and a port-side tail rotor. The white stripes on the fin are probably for icing detection tests.

opened and featured flexible mounts for the troopers' assault rifles. The cabin could also carry four casualties or up to 1500 kg (3,306 lb) of cargo. Outsized loads weighing up to 2000 kg (4,409 lb) could be carried externally slung.

Much attention had been given to survivability and crew protection. The cockpit and cabin were combined into a single pressurised cell to prevent chemical or biological agents getting in. The cockpit had a bullet-proof windscreen and armoured pilot's seat; the sides of the cockpit and cabin were armour-plated, as were the engine cowlings.

The aft fuselage incorporated an electrics and avionics bay. The avionics suite comprised the SAU-V24 automatic control system (SAU, *sistema avtomateecheskovo upravleniya*) including the VUAP-1 autopilot (VUAP, *vertolyotnii unifit-seerovanny avtopeelot* = standardised helicopter autopilot), a compact gyro and automatic approach system, a DISS-15 Doppler speed and drift indicator (DISS, *dopplerovskiy izmereetel skorosti i snosa*), an automatic navigation map, a short-range radio navigation system etc.

Fuel was carried in five self-sealing bladder tanks holding 2130 litres (469 Imp gal). Two cylindrical metal tanks holding 1630 litres (359 Imp gal) could be installed in the cabin for ferry flights. The control system featured four hydraulic boosters mounted on a massive plate attached to the main gearbox; stabiliser incidence was adjusted in concert with collective pitch. The Mi-24 had three separate hydraulic systems – main, back-up and auxiliary.

Interim weapons fit for the Mi-24

The Mi-24 was completed well ahead of its intended armament and, thus, Mil had to make do with what was available at the moment. He opted for the K-4V weapons system (or 'armament complex' in Soviet parlance) which had achieved a good service record on the Mi-4AV and Mi-8TV. It included four 9M17M Falanga-M (AT-2 'Swatter') ATGMs. The missiles were carried in pairs on removable launchers and manually guided by the WSO, using radio control and a sight originating from a tank.

The nose incorporated a 12.7-mm (0.50-in) Afanasyev A-12.7 (TKB-481) single-barrelled machine-gun on an NUV-1 flexible mount borrowed from the Mi-4AV (NUV, *nosovaya ustanovka vertolyotnaya* = nose-mounted helicopter [gun] installation). The pilot could fire it using a primitive PKV collimator gunsight. However, it was not until the first production version appeared that the gun was fitted. The wing pylons carried four UB-32 pods with 32 S-5 rockets each or four 100-kg (221-lb) and 250-kg (551-lb) bombs. Two 500-kg (1,102-lb) bombs or napalm tanks could also be carried.

Flight tests began on 15 September 1969, when the first tethered hover was made. Four days later the uncoded prototype made its first free flight with G. V. Alfyorov at the

controls. The second prototype joined the test programme soon after, followed by a pre-production batch of 10 helicopters, five of which were built at MVZ (plant No. 329) and the rest at the Progress Aircraft Factory (plant No. 116) in Arsenyev in the Far East. These aircraft were the workhorses of the manufacturer's trials programme, later finding extensive use in testing the improvements introduced on later versions of the Mi-24. Other pilots involved in the trials included G. R. Karapetyan and M. A. Materialnii.

Trials and troubles

State acceptance trials began in June 1970, proceeded intensively for the next 18 months, and showed that the new helicopter generally met project specifications. Mil engineers had successfully addressed the Mi-24's structural strength and fatigue life problems and designed excessive vibration out of the helicopter. Vibration levels were comparable to the Mi-8, despite a higher cruising speed.

However, some trouble areas requiring major structural changes were discovered. In turbulent conditions the helicopter was prone to Dutch roll at speeds in excess of 200 km/h (108 kt) IAS with the autopilot disengaged, forcing the pilot to take constant corrective action. To improve lateral stability the engineers introduced 12° anhedral on the stub wings; this was not associated with the 'unfavourable interaction of the main rotor downwash with the wings', as some Western authors claimed.

Immediately, another problem arose: the removable ATGM launchers on the lower fuselage sides were incompatible with the FFAR pods on the stub wing pylons, as the rockets coming out of the pods could strike the missiles. Additionally, the launchers were located in line with the cabin doors, which meant the latter could not be opened when the launchers were fitted. Therefore, the detachable launchers were deleted and downward-angled vertical endplates were added to the stub wings, terminating in horizontal frames with 2P32M (K-4V) missile launch rails inboard and outboard of the endplate. The Mi-24 received its unmistakable wing/pylon arrangement.

NATO got wind of the Mi-24's existence in 1972, shortly after the helicopter had entered service with the VVS, and allocated it the ASCC codename 'Hind'. Curiously, the pre-production version with no wing anhedral became known in the West after the first production version, the Mi-24A; thus, the Mi-24A was codenamed 'Hind-A' and the pre-production Mi-24 became the 'Hind-B'.

Mi-24A 'Hind-A' (Izdelye 245)

More changes were required before the helicopter was cleared for full-scale production. Flight tests showed that the forward fuselage of the 'Hind-B' was too cramped to accommodate the Raduga-F (Rainbow) semi-automatic command line of sight (SACLOS) guidance system for the anti-tank missiles and the fast-firing machine-gun installation. The two prototypes were converted at Mil's experimental shop in Panki by cutting off the cockpit section and grafting on a new forward fuselage. While being basically

similar to the original version, the new nose was slightly longer and had a more pointed profile, with more sharply raked upper windshield segments to reduce drag. The car-type pilot's door was replaced by a sliding bubble window to give the pilot some downward vision (incidentally, the Mi-8 had undergone the same evolution earlier when the flight deck doors of the V-8 prototypes were replaced by sliding windows and a common flight deck/cabin port-side entry door), and the A-12,7 machine-gun was fitted.

Another external recognition feature was the small teardrop fairing of the command link transmitter antenna immediately forward of the nose gear. Other changes included rudimentary flight controls for the WSO (cyclic and collective pitch and pedals) so that he could fly the helicopter home should the pilot be disabled.

In this form (with extended nose, anhedral wings, and modified controls and mission avionics), the helicopter entered production in Arsenyev in 1970 as the Mi-24A (Izdelye 245). Attaining initial operational capability the next year, the 'Hind-A' was officially accepted into the VVS inventory in 1972 after passing its State acceptance trials. Initially, the Mi-24A was operated by independent helicopter regiments within mechanised infantry or tank armies and air assault brigades. Later, the helicopter equipped independent combat control helicopter regiments; when the Army Aviation was formed within the Soviet armed forces, Mi-24s equipped independent helicopter squadrons within mechanised infantry divisions.

Early operational experience

Mi-24A deliveries to the Soviet Air Force commenced in 1970. The Voronezh detachment of the 4th TsBPiPLS (Tsentr boyevoy podgotovki i pereuchivaniya lyotnovo sostahva = Combat and Conversion Training Centre), the main facility of which is in Lipetsk, was the first to master the new helicopter. It was soon followed by VVS units located in Chernigovka (Far East Defence District), Brody (Carpathian DD), Parchim and Stendal (Group of Soviet Forces in Germany, later renamed Western Group of Forces). Later, the Mi-24 equipped units based in Prouzhany (Belorussian DD), Mogocha (Transbaikalian DD), Raukhovka (Odessa DD), Berdichev (Carpathian DD), etc.

One of the Mi-24A's major deficiencies was its propensity to rotate uncontrollably around the vertical axis when hovering in a crosswind. Often, this uncommanded rotation could not be countered even by applying full opposite 'rudder' because of insufficient tail rotor authority, and resulted in accidents. Early-production Mi-24As had the tail rotor on the starboard side, as on the Mi-8; the rotor turned clockwise when seen from the hub so that the forward blade went with the main rotor downwash. However, the helicopter had poor directional control in some flight modes, and service pilots were quick to point this out. In 1972 the tail rotor was relocated to port,

Above left: This view of 'Red 77', an early production Mi-24A 'Hind-A', shows the 'Hind' looking far more warlike – as its designers intended. The stub wings have been remodelled with 19° anhedral, giving the aircraft its distinctive hunched look. Launchers for the Falanga-M (AT-2 'Swatter') ATGMs have been fitted and the gunner's position is armed with an Afanasyev A-12,7 machine-gun. Confusion and a lack of information on the part of NATO intelligence operatives led to the follow-on model Mi-24A receiving the 'Hind-A' codename.

Above: This alternative view of 'Red 77' clearly shows its starboard tail rotor, which would soon be changed. The pilots of early 'Hind-As' were generally pleased with the type's handling and agility, which was surprising for a helicopter of this size and weight: the Mi-24A could climb at up to 50° Alpha, make turns at over 60° bank, and perform stall turns and other vigorous manoeuvres. Nonetheless, the Mi-24 had its fair share of teething troubles. The TV3-117 engines were the chief source of annoyance, as their service life initially was only 50 hours. Poor visibility from the driver's seat was another problem area; to make matters worse, the optically-flat glazing panels reflected lights on the ground during low-level night flying, which could cause pilot disorientation.

Mi-24 museum pieces

Above: 'Red 50' (2201201) was an Mi-24A used to test the revised tail rotor configuration. Today it is part of the Monino museum collection.

Left: This strangely camouflaged Mi-24A is preserved at the Akhtubinsk test centre museum.

Left: 'Red 33' (3201902), a late-model Mi-24A, is preserved at Khodynka, alongside an Mi-24V, 'White 60'.

Right: This freshly repainted and uncoded late-model Mi-24A (3202109) is preserved at the Armed Forces Museum, in Moscow.

Above and left: This Mi-24A is on display at the Vietnamese People's Air Force Museum, in Hanoi. Vietnam's 'Hind-As' entered service in the mid-1980s and saw combat in Cambodia.

As the Mi-24A became operational, the VVS began demonstrating it to various VIPs. One of the first displays was at Kubinka air base west of Moscow, where 4th TsBPP pilots put on a show of force for the defence ministers of Warsaw Pact nations, impressing them with the agility of the 'Hind'. Later, the helicopter was demonstrated to the then-Defence Minister Marshal Gheorghiy M. Grechko at the Alabino range near Naro-Fominsk, southwest of Moscow. A flight of Mi-24As, again flown by 4th TsBPP crews, spectacularly destroyed the targets with 'Swatter' ATGMs, S-5 FFARs, 100-kg (220-lb) bombs and machine-gun fire. The demonstration was a success – not least because the organisers had strategically placed fuel drums beside the tanks and APCs used as targets to create huge fireballs, adding to the effect of the show. When the explosions had subsided the marshal said with satisfaction, addressing his retinue: "The enemy will sure have to keep their heads down on a battlefield like this!"

switching from pusher to tractor configuration, as on the Mi-14 and Mi-8MT/Mi-17 'Hip-H'. The rotor still turned clockwise, so that now the forward blade went against the main rotor downwash; this increased tail rotor efficiency dramatically. According to OKB sources, the new arrangement was introduced on production 'Hinds' in 1974; however, there are several known Mi-24As built in 1973 with the port-side tail rotor.

About the same time, seven reinforcement ribs were added on the port fuselage side aft of the wings, the APU exhaust was extended and angled downwards to prevent rain from getting in, and the characteristic triple aerial of the SRO-2M Khrom (Chromium)/'Odd Rods' IFF transponder (SRO, *samolyotnii rahdiolokatseeonnii otvetchik* = aircraft (-mounted) radar [IFF] responder) were moved from the canopy frame to the oil cooler atop the engine intakes.

The armament, borrowed directly from the Mi-4AV, rendered the helicopter ineffective in its intended CAS role. The early manually-guided 9M17M (AT-2 'Swatter') missiles had an appallingly low hit ratio of 30 per cent. This improved radically to over 80 per cent when the 9M17P with semi-automatic guidance and the Raduga-F guidance system were introduced on the Mi-24D; the Mi-24V's 9M114 (AT-6 'Spiral') has a kill ratio in excess of 92 per cent.

More than 240 Mi-24As had rolled off the line in Arsenyev by the time production ended in 1974. Once again, the seemingly illogical Soviet practice of launching full-scale production even before an aircraft had been officially phased-in (as had been the case with the Mi-4, for example) had paid off, allowing flight and ground crews to familiarise themselves with the helicopter by the time approval came from the Air Force.

Getting the 'Hind' up to scratch took some time, and the learning curve was steep; it was not until the Mi-24V entered service that the Soviet Army Aviation got a dependable tank-buster. Over the years, engine life and reliability were much improved. There have been cases

when the TV3-117 turboshaft has continued to run normally after major bird strikes or ingesting foliage. During the Schchit-79 (Shield 79) WarPac exercise, one Mi-24 crew mistimed its arrival and popped up late over the target, by which time the range was already being pounded by heavy artillery. As the pilot turned the aircraft around to exit the area, one of the engines was hit by several shell fragments. On the way back to base the crew could hear that the engine had developed some knocking, but it showed no signs of catastrophic failure.

The helicopter could land in autorotation mode in the event of a double engine failure. "Test pilots in Minsk showed us what the helicopter could do," Colonel V. N. Kvashevich recalled. "The pilot shut down both engines over the runway at 250 or 280 km/h and about 30 to 50 m, then made a U-turn and landed safely."

Mi-24B 'Hind-A' (Izdelye 241)

As the Mi-24A entered production, the Mil OKB continued improving the helicopter's armament. The Mi-24B, or Izdelye 241, as the next version was designated, featured a USPU-24 powered chin turret (USPU, *universahl'naya s'yomnaya pulemyotnaya ustanovka* = versatile detachable machine-gun installation) with a 12.7-mm Yakoushev/Borzov YakB-12,7 four-barrelled Gatling-type machine-gun (also referred to as TKB-063 and 9A624 in some sources) traversable through +20°/-40° in elevation and ±60° in azimuth. This was slaved to a KPS-53AV sighting system which made corrections for the helicopter's movement. The system featured an analog computer receiving input from the helicopter's air data sensors.

The manually-guided 9M17M Falanga-M anti-tank missiles of the Mi-24A gave way to an upgraded version, the 9M17P Falanga-P (P, *poluavtomateecheskoye navedeniye* = semi-automatic guidance). The missiles were controlled by the Raduga-F SACLOS guidance system which increased kill probability three to four times. The targeting part of the

system comprised low-light-level television (LLLTV) and forward-looking infra-red (FLIR) sensors in a slab-sided ventral housing offset to starboard ahead of the nose gear, with twin protective metal doors covering the sensor window. The system was gyro-stabilised, enabling the helicopter to manoeuvre vigorously to avoid ground fire while targeting. The guidance command link antenna was located in a small egg-shaped fairing offset to port which could traverse as the missile manoeuvred, since the antenna dish was fixed. The Mi-24B successfully passed the manufacturer's trials in 1971-72, but was abandoned, becoming a stepping stone towards an even more radical redesign – the Mi-24V and Mi-24D.

Mi-24D/Mi-25 'Hind-D' (Izdelye 246)

Experience with the Mi-24A showed that cockpit visibility was surprisingly poor, the spacious cockpit and the relative placement of the crew creating large blind zones. The WSO obscured the right front quadrant for the pilot, who in turn impaired the WSO's visibility in the left rear quadrant. The flat glazing generated annoying reflections, and the heavy windscreen framework did not help.

This led the Mil OKB to radically redesign the forward fuselage in early 1971 – "making an already ugly helicopter truly hideous in the process," as one Western writer put it. The crew sat in separate cockpits in a stepped-tandem arrangement, the pilot sitting above and behind the WSO. The narrow cockpits had extensive armour protection and bubble canopies with large optically-flat bullet-proof windscreens which gave far better all-round visibility. The pilot entered via a rearward-opening car-type door on the starboard side, and the port half of the WSO's cockpit canopy hinged open to starboard. A long air data boom with DUAS-V pitch and yaw vanes (DUAS, *dahtchik uglah atahki i snosa* = AoA and drift sensor) was offset to starboard and the IFF aerials were mounted on the WSO's canopy frame.

The redesign improved visibility not only for the crew but also for the Raduga-F LLLTV/FLIR sensors, and enhanced operating conditions for the missile guidance antenna. However, this in turn called for more changes. To ensure adequate ground clearance for the LLLTV/FLIR sensor fairing, the nose gear unit was lengthened, giving the helicopter a pronounced nose-up attitude on the ground (unlike earlier versions). The nosewheels were semi-exposed when retracted, so the bulged twin nosewheel doors of the Mi-24A gave way to single door linked to the oleo strut. Changes were made to the fuel system: the wing pylons were 'wet', permitting the carriage of 500-litre (110-Imp gal) drop tanks and leaving the cabin free.

The up-gunned Mi-24B 'Hind-A' was an interim version that bridged the gap between the glass-nosed 'Hind-As' and the definitive Mi-24D/V. This is one of the Mi-24B prototypes (above) with its signature four-barrelled Yakoushev/Borzov YakB-12,7 machine-gun, housed in a USPU-24 chin turret. Before the real Mi-24Bs first flew, a full-scale mock-up was produced (left). This is believed to have been rebuilt from the original 'Hind-B' mock-up, since it had no wing anhedral and featured the tested-but-failed detachable missile launchers on the fuselage sides (ahead of the main gear). The real prototypes were converted from several early-production Mi-24As with starboard-side tail rotors.

The dual-cockpit version was allocated the designation Mi-24V (this is the third letter of the Cyrillic alphabet). Unfortunately, however, its intended armament of Shturm-V ATGMs was still unavailable, forcing the Mil OKB to do the next best thing and develop a hybrid – a combination of the new airframe with the 'old' armament system as fitted to the experimental Mi-24B. This stopgap version was designated Mi-24D or Izdelye 246. Note that the fifth letter of the Cyrillic alphabet was used instead of the fourth (G); there was never an Mi-24G – possibly because G could be deciphered as *gavno* (shit).

Above and right (two): The two Mi-24D 'Hind-D' prototypes were converted from early 'Hind-As' and so came with the starboard-mounted tail rotor. For their initial flight tests the helicopters were fitted with additional pitot booms on the standard air data boom and immediately ahead of the port cabin door, and the ATGM launch rails were removed. The wing-mounted strike camera was fitted inboard of the weapons pylons (on the port side). The camera remained in this position on early-model 'Hind-Ds' but it was soon moved outboard, as the plumes from the rockets obscured its view.

The 'Hind-D' was a major step forward as it not only added new weapons and better sensors to the airframe but offered the crew far better protection in their heavily-armoured individual cockpits. This is one of the earliest Mi-24Ds delivered to Poland (actually the third aircraft, which arrived in 1978). Today it is still in service with 3 Eskadra 'Scorpions', 49 PSB (49th combat helicopter regiment), based at Pruszcz-Gdanski.

Warsaw Pact nations and the Soviet Union's Third World allies. The ASCC codename for the Mi-24D and Mi-25 was 'Hind-D'.

Mi-24V/Mi-35 'Hind-E' (Izdelye 242)

The 9K113 weapons system based on the 9M114 Shturm-V (AT-6 'Spiral') supersonic ATGM specified by the Air Force's operational requirement finally became available in 1972, marking the appearance of the Mi-24V (Izdelye 242). This version has sometimes been referred to as Mi-24W in the Western press, a misconception caused by the German and Polish spelling of the designation (in the latter case because there is no letter V in Polish).

The new missile was not only faster than the 'Swatter' but had greater accuracy and longer range. It was also more compact thanks to folding fins, coming in a neat disposable tubular launcher/container. Like its predecessor, the 'Spiral' employed SACLOS guidance; the command link antenna 'egg' was slightly larger than the Mi-24D's and had a more rounded front end with a large dielectric dome. The new antenna was fully articulated and the pod did not need to rotate. Trials of the missile were completed in 1974.

The Mi-24V prototype was converted from an early-production Mi-24D in 1973. Apart from the 'canned missiles' replacing the rather untidy wingtip launch rails of the D, the Mi-24V differed in having TV3-117V engines (V, *vysotnii* = 'for high altitudes', i.e., for 'hot-and-high' conditions) uprated to 2,225 eshp (1660 kW) and an ASP-17V automatic gunsight for the pilot. On production Mi-24Vs the protective doors of the Raduga-F LLLTV/FLIR pod moved aft on a system of linkages to lie flat against the sides of the pod; this arrangement created less drag. A second (non-retractable) landing light was added on the port side of the nose.

New communications equipment was fitted, as indicated by two new aerials on the tailboom: a dorsal blade aerial for the R-863 VHF radio and a ventral 'towel rail' aerial for the R-828 radio used for communication with ground troops. The SRO-2M Khrom IFF was replaced by the SRO-1P Parol ('Password') transponder, aka Izdelye 62-01, with characteristic triangular blade aerials. (Some late-production Mi-24Ds also had the new avionics.)

'Hind-E' trials and improvements

The 'Hind-E', as the helicopter was codenamed by NATO, completed its State acceptance trials about a year later than the Mi-24D; however, both models were formally included in the VVS inventory by a single government directive on 29 March 1976. By then, some 400 Mi-24As and Ds had been delivered. The Mi-24V entered production in 1976, and more than 1,000 had been built in Arsenyev and Rostov by 1986. An export version with downgraded avionics was designated Mi-35.

Late Mi-24Vs received an L-006 Beryoza (Birch) radar homing and warning system (RHAWS), aka SPO-15, with characteristic protuberances on the forward fuselage sides and the tail rotor pylon's trailing edge to give 360° coverage. The forward 'horns' were usually fitted aft of the rear cockpit, but some aircraft (e.g., Polish and Hungarian Mi-35s) had them located between the two cockpits. Four ASO-2V-02 infra-red countermeasures (IRCM) flare launchers with 32 flares apiece were mounted under the tailboom for protection against heat-seeking missiles, later giving way to six identical units on the aft fuselage sides, and an L-166V-11E active IRCM jammer, aka SOEP-V1A Lipa (Linden; NATO 'Hot Brick'), was installed aft of the main rotor head. The jammer was a thimble-shaped fairing enclosing a powerful xenon lamp with a rotating reflector, in the fashion of the flashing blue light on a police car. It emitted a pulsed IR signal which darted erratically, disappearing and reappearing, causing the missile to lose track of the target. They were also fitted to some late Mi-24Ds which have sometimes been referred to as 'Hind-D Mod'.

The two Mi-24D prototypes were converted in June 1972 (probably from early-production Mi-24As) and thus were unique in having a starboard-side tail rotor. State acceptance trials began the next year, continuing well into 1974, and the helicopter passed them with flying colours. In 1973 the Mi-24D entered production at the Progress Aircraft Factory and the Rostov Helicopter Factory (plant No. 168, now called Rostvertol Production Association); some 350 had been built when production ended in 1977.

The Mi-24A featured an S-13 strike camera at the port wing/inboard pylon junction. However, the smoke trail left by the FFARs streaking towards the target made recording the attack results a chancy affair, so the camera was soon moved to the port wingtip/endplate junction on the Mi-24D. An export version with slightly downgraded mission avionics, designated Mi-25, was developed for

Triple-lobe air/exhaust mixers called EVU (*ezhektorno-vykhlopnoye ustroystvo* = ejector exhaust device) could be fitted to reduce the helicopter's IR signature. After mixing the exhaust with cool outside air they directed it upwards into the main rotor downwash, reducing exhaust gas temperature by 350° to 400°C (662° to 752°F). However, the mixers could only be fitted to aircraft built from about 1984 onwards, as they had downward-angled jetpipes.

The Mi-24V is known to have carried eight 9M114 ATGMs (on the endplate racks and the outboard wing pylons), at least during trials. Multiple missile racks increasing the number of ATGMs to 16 were tested successfully in 1986. The 'Hind-E' also evolved into several experimental versions and avionics or weapons testbeds in the 1980s (Mi-24M, Mi-24N, Mi-24F, etc.), details of which are not available.

Mi-24P/Mi-35P 'Hind-F' (Izdelye 243)

Mil engineers had obviously never been happy about the Air Force's demand to substitute the Mi-24's projected cannon armament with a machine-gun. Accordingly, in 1975 the OKB commenced trials of a more heavily armed derivative of the Mi-24V designated Mi-24P, or Izdelye 243; the P stood for *pushechnii* = cannon-equipped.

The USPU-24 barbette was deleted, resulting in a smooth nose. A 30-mm (1.18-in) Gryazev/Shipunov GSh-30K double-barrelled rapid-firing cannon (also referred to as GSh-2-30) was fitted; the cannon had passed its State acceptance trials in 1976 and was fitted to the Sukhoi Su-25. The cannon was much too heavy and its recoil was too violent for it to be installed in a chin barbette, so it had to be scabbed on to the starboard side of the forward fuselage in an elongated fairing under the pilot's cockpit. The pilot was to aim the cannon by turning the whole helicopter.

The Mi-24P entered production in 1981, and more than 620 had been built when production ended in 1989. The 'big gun' 'Hind' was also offered for export as the Mi-35P; the uncoded Mi-35P prototype is said to have had construction number 3532431723858. Mi-24 construction numbers (manufacturer's serial numbers) follow several systems. Until 1973, Mi-24As had seven-digit c/ns, e.g., 3201902. The first digit denotes the year of manufacture (1973), the second is presumably an in-house product code at the Arsenyev factory (not the Mil OKB!), 019 is the batch number and 02 the number of the helicopter in the batch, with five (later 10) to a batch. The NATO codename was 'Hind-F'.

The responsibilities of the 'Hind' were fully defined after the helicopter had been officially phased in as being cover and close air support for ground forces and assault groups airlifted by Mi-8T/TVs and Mi-6s. The YakB-12,7 machine-gun or GSh-30K cannon, UPK-23-250 gun pods and 'iron' bombs of up to 500 kg (1,102 lb) were fairly effective in this role. The GUV gun pods, on the other hand, proved disappointing in both machine-gun and grenade launcher configuration. Afghan war experience showed that the 57-mm S-5 FFARs were ineffective, and they were gradually supplanted by 80-mm S-8 FFARs.

'Hind' v Cobra

Destruction of low- and slow-flying aerial targets, notably other helicopters, was another role filled by the Mi-24. Until the advent of the AH-64 Apache, the most dangerous rotary-wing adversary of the 'Hind' was the AH-1 HueyCobra. In an encounter with the HueyCobra, the Mi-24's strengths were its higher speed and rate of climb, while its main weakness was its relatively poor horizontal manoeuvrability, especially at low speed. This was important, as numerous trials had established that in a duel between two helicopters the one which could out-turn the enemy at low speeds had a better chance of making a kill.

VVS 'Hinds' met the HueyCobra when operating in the air defence role in the former East Germany. Usually, such encounters were peaceful enough – the two helicopters flew side by side along the border between East and West Germany as the crews studied each other intently. One occasion in the early 1980s, however, ended in disaster. An

Above: The 9M17 Falanga ATGM (also referred to as the Skorpion) – as fitted to the Mi-24D – was originally designed for use on light armoured vehicles. It was a short-ranged and relatively inaccurate second-generation weapon that relied on a radio guidance system prone to interference and failure. The 9M17M missile was replaced by the improved 9M17P which extended its range from 3000 m (9,842 ft) to 4000 m (13,123 ft).

Top: This late model Hungarian Mi-24D has gained the distinctive 'horned' antennas of the L-006 Beryoza radar warning system on its forward fuselage. This aircraft is also carrying a full load of live 9M17P Falanga-P missiles (with the associated Raduga-F SACLOS guidance system undernose) as it prepares to depart its base at Szabadja for a live-fire exercise.

Mi-24 based in the southern part of East Germany scrambled
to 'intercept' an AH-1G which manoeuvred a few hundred
yards from the wire mesh fence running along the border.
Russian sources described the Cobra pilot as 'a real pro',
who would follow the border at low level, repeatedly
accelerate and then pitch up sharply, to bleed off speed.
The Mi-24 had a tough time staying on the Cobra's tail,
yet the Soviet crew did not give up. Again the AH-1 put
on a burst of speed and then pitched up, stopping short
within seconds. Determined to stay with the Cobra, the
Soviet pilot hauled back on the stick but the big, heavy
'Hind' started to tumble. The pilot did the only thing
possible and pushed the stick forward sharply, putting the
helicopter into a dive to gain forward speed, but he was too
low and had to pull back on the stick just as sharply to
avoid hitting the ground. Seconds later the main rotor
blades struck the tailboom and the helicopter crashed,
killing the crew.

Mi-24VP (Izdelye 258)

Experience with the Mi-24P proved that cannon were
the way to go, yet the fixed cannon of the 'Hind-F' and
the need to aim it by pointing the helicopter was a liability.
The 30-mm cannon was also too much firepower in some
circumstances when a smaller and lighter 23-mm cannon
would have done the job. A new version designated Mi-24VP
(V, *pushechnii* = 'cannon-equipped Mi-24V'), Izdelye 258,

was developed in 1985. It differed from the 'Hind-E' in
having the USPU-24 barbette and YakB-12,7 machine-gun
replaced by a new NPPU-24 barbette with a GSh-23
cannon (NPPU, *nes'yomnaya podveezhnaya pushechnaya
ustanovka* = non-detachable movable cannon installation).
The Mi-24 finally received the armament which Mikhail L.
Mil had wanted it to have all along. State acceptance trials
began in 1985 and dragged on for four years. The Mi-24VP
entered production in 1989 but, unfortunately, only 25
were completed before 'Hind' production was 'terminally
terminated' same year.

Weapons development

New weapons options were developed for the various
versions of the 'Hind' in the late 1970s. The first of these
was the massive GUV gun pod (*gondola universahl'naya
vertolyotnaya* = versatile [gun] pod for helicopters), aka
9A669. It could be configured with either a YakB-12,7
four-barrelled machine-gun flanked by two 7.62-mm
(0.30-in) TKB-621 four-barrelled Gatling machine-guns or
a 30-mm (1.18-in) AGS-17 Plamya (Flame) automatic
grenade launcher. Next came the UPK-23-250 pod (*unifitseerovannii pushechnii konteyner* = standardised gun pod)
containing a GSh-23 gun with 250 rounds.

The UB-32-57 and UB-32A FFAR pods with 57-mm
S-5 rockets were supplanted by B-8V20 pods with 20 80-mm
(3.15-in) S-8 rockets apiece, B-13 pods with five 122-mm

(4.8-in) S-13 rockets apiece and single 250-mm (9.84-in) S-24 rockets. Other stores included illumination flare packs for night operations, KMGU sub-munitions pods (*konteyner dlya malogabaritnykh gruzov universahl'nii* = versatile small items container, typically loaded with anti-tank or anti-personnel mines) and various free-fall bombs weighing up to 500 kg (1,102 lb).

Air-to-air role

The Mil OKB experimented with giving the 'Hind' counter-air capability as well, to which end R-60 (AA-8 'Aphid'), R-73 (AA-11 'Archer') and 9M39 Igla-V ('Needle') air-to-air missiles were tested on the Mi-24. Even though the results were not particularly encouraging, a few Mi-24Vs were retrofitted in service with launchers for R-60 AAMs in the late 1980s. One of the units involved in testing the R-60 installation was the 1038th TsPLS (Tsentr pereuchivaniya lyotnovo sostahva = conversion training centre) in the Turkestan Defence District which undertook much test work to investigate the helicopter's capabilities.

The pilot aimed the R-60s by means of the ASP-17V gunsight, turning the helicopter until he got a lock-on from the missiles' IR seekers. During early tests the missiles were fired against flare bombs, with considerable success. However, in mock combat with helicopters fitted with IR-suppression exhaust mixers (when the pilot did everything short of actually firing a missile), target acquisition

range was no more than 600 m (1,968 ft), and less against piston-engined targets. The climate of Central Asia did not help, either, as ground temperature reached 60°C (140°F) and confused the missiles' seeker heads during NoE flying. As a result, the R-60 was not widely used on the Mi-24, but a few 'Hind' squadrons, including some stationed in East Germany, had their helicopters equipped with AAMs.

The Soviet Air Force's interest in the Mi-24 as an air defence weapon against slow-flying targets grew considerably following Matthias Rust's notorious landing in Moscow's Red Square, on 29 May 1987. Consequently, several Mi-24 squadrons were transferred to the Air Defence Force's fighter arm, IA PVO (istrebeetel'naya aviahtsiya protivovozdushnoy oborony). The 'fighter' 'Hinds' saw real action against intruders into Soviet airspace, notably in the Kaliningrad PVO District where Mi-24s often had to deal with wayward aircraft – and forced them down on Soviet airfields in several instances.

On the other hand, it has to be said that Mikhail L. Mil's 'flying IFV' concept, which was the core of the Mi-24's design philosophy, was seldom put into practice. The 'Hind' was only sporadically used as a troopship, mostly for inserting and extracting search and destroy groups. For example, during the Zapad-81 (West-81) exercise, two Mi-24 squadrons from Prouzhany AB, Belarus dropped off Spetsnaz groups tasked with seizing bridges and the opposing force's air base command centres. Each helicopter

Above: This low-flying Czech Mi-24D is seen in service with the 51st Helicopter Regiment, based at Prostejov in 1992. The strap-on ASO-2V chaff and flare dispensers under the rear tailboom can carry 32 expendables and are usually fitted in blocks of three.

Inset: This classic head-on view of a Hungarian Mi-24D shows the 'Hind' at its most predatory. The cluttered cockpit of the WSO contrasts with that of the pilot sitting behind him. Also of note are the downward-sloping exhausts, a feature of late-model 'Hind-Ds' and all subsequent versions.

Three colour schemes are used on Bulgaria's Mi-24s. The oldest is an equally-spaced light and dark green camouflage – the original ex-Soviet colours in which they were delivered. An overall dark green scheme, with vertical stripes of even darker green, was applied on a number of helicopters that underwent major overhauls at the Sofia-based TEREM Letetz repair facility in 1993-1994. A third 'lizard camouflage' (equally-spaced green and brown stripes) was applied to Mi-24s after overhaul in Hungary in 1994-1996. BVVS 'Hinds' wear no squadron markings, with exception of three of the six Mi-24Vs.

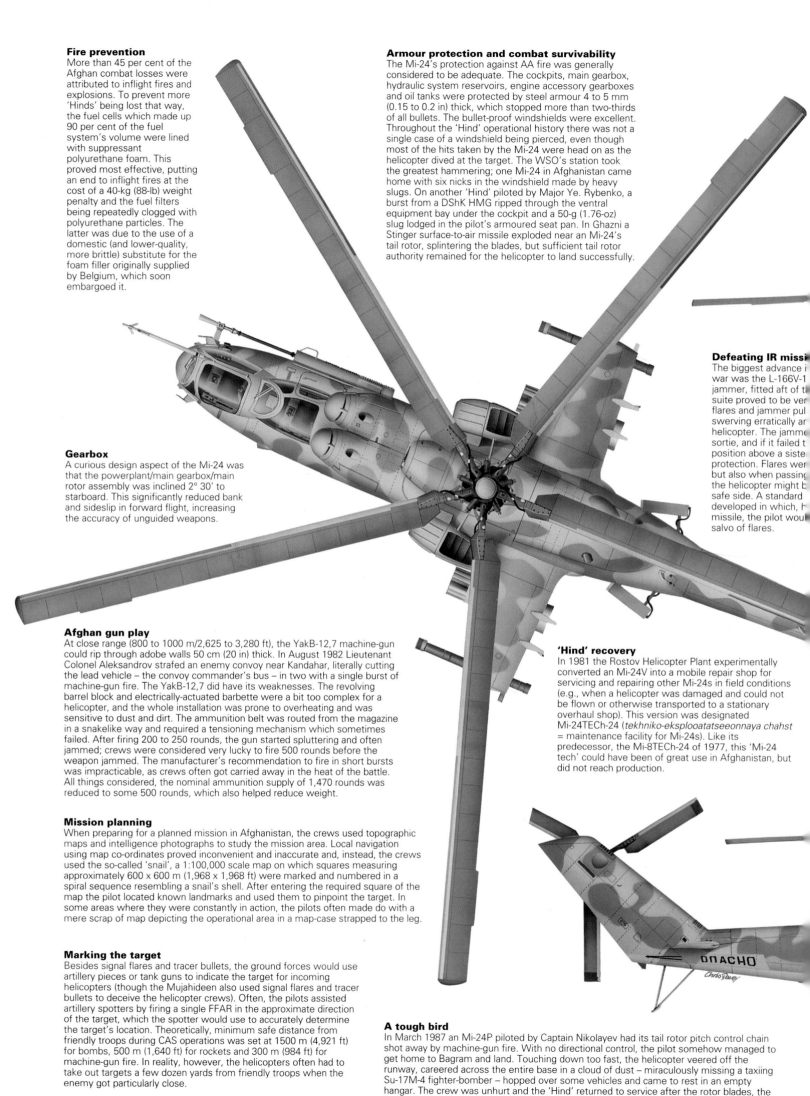

Fire prevention

More than 45 per cent of the Afghan combat losses were attributed to inflight fires and explosions. To prevent more 'Hinds' being lost that way, the fuel cells which made up 90 per cent of the fuel system's volume were lined with suppressant polyurethane foam. This proved most effective, putting an end to inflight fires at the cost of a 40-kg (88-lb) weight penalty and the fuel filters being repeatedly clogged with polyurethane particles. The latter was due to the use of a domestic (and lower-quality, more brittle) substitute for the foam filler originally supplied by Belgium, which soon embargoed it.

Gearbox

A curious design aspect of the Mi-24 was that the powerplant/main gearbox/main rotor assembly was inclined 2° 30' to starboard. This significantly reduced bank and sideslip in forward flight, increasing the accuracy of unguided weapons.

Afghan gun play

At close range (800 to 1000 m/2,625 to 3,280 ft), the YakB-12,7 machine-gun could rip through adobe walls 50 cm (20 in) thick. In August 1982 Lieutenant Colonel Aleksandrov strafed an enemy convoy near Kandahar, literally cutting the lead vehicle – the convoy commander's bus – in two with a single burst of machine-gun fire. The YakB-12,7 did have its weaknesses. The revolving barrel block and electrically-actuated barbette were a bit too complex for a helicopter, and the whole installation was prone to overheating and was sensitive to dust and dirt. The ammunition belt was routed from the magazine in a snakelike way and required a tensioning mechanism which sometimes failed. After firing 200 to 250 rounds, the gun started spluttering and often jammed; crews were considered very lucky to fire 500 rounds before the weapon jammed. The manufacturer's recommendation to fire in short bursts was impracticable, as crews often got carried away in the heat of the battle. All things considered, the nominal ammunition supply of 1,470 rounds was reduced to some 500 rounds, which also helped reduce weight.

Mission planning

When preparing for a planned mission in Afghanistan, the crews used topographic maps and intelligence photographs to study the mission area. Local navigation using map co-ordinates proved inconvenient and inaccurate and, instead, the crews used the so-called 'snail', a 1:100,000 scale map on which squares measuring approximately 600 x 600 m (1,968 x 1,968 ft) were marked and numbered in a spiral sequence resembling a snail's shell. After entering the required square of the map the pilot located known landmarks and used them to pinpoint the target. In some areas where they were constantly in action, the pilots often made do with a mere scrap of map depicting the operational area in a map-case strapped to the leg.

Marking the target

Besides signal flares and tracer bullets, the ground forces would use artillery pieces or tank guns to indicate the target for incoming helicopters (though the Mujahideen also used signal flares and tracer bullets to deceive the helicopter crews). Often, the pilots assisted artillery spotters by firing a single FFAR in the approximate direction of the target, which the spotter would use to accurately determine the target's location. Theoretically, minimum safe distance from friendly troops during CAS operations was set at 1500 m (4,921 ft) for bombs, 500 m (1,640 ft) for rockets and 300 m (984 ft) for machine-gun fire. In reality, however, the helicopters often had to take out targets a few dozen yards from friendly troops when the enemy got particularly close.

Armour protection and combat survivability

The Mi-24's protection against AA fire was generally considered to be adequate. The cockpits, main gearbox, hydraulic system reservoirs, engine accessory gearboxes and oil tanks were protected by steel armour 4 to 5 mm (0.15 to 0.2 in) thick, which stopped more than two-thirds of all bullets. The bullet-proof windshields were excellent. Throughout the 'Hind' operational history there was not a single case of a windshield being pierced, even though most of the hits taken by the Mi-24 were head on as the helicopter dived at the target. The WSO's station took the greatest hammering; one Mi-24 in Afghanistan came home with six nicks in the windshield made by heavy slugs. On another 'Hind' piloted by Major Ye. Rybenko, a burst from a DShK HMG ripped through the ventral equipment bay under the cockpit and a 50-g (1.76-oz) slug lodged in the pilot's armoured seat pan. In Ghazni a Stinger surface-to-air missile exploded near an Mi-24's tail rotor, splintering the blades, but sufficient tail rotor authority remained for the helicopter to land successfully.

Defeating IR missi

The biggest advance i war was the L-166V-1 jammer, fitted aft of t suite proved to be ver flares and jammer pul swerving erratically ar helicopter. The jamme sortie, and if it failed t position above a siste protection. Flares wer but also when passing the helicopter might b safe side. A standard developed in which, h missile, the pilot wou salvo of flares.

'Hind' recovery

In 1981 the Rostov Helicopter Plant experimentally converted an Mi-24V into a mobile repair shop for servicing and repairing other Mi-24s in field conditions (e.g., when a helicopter was damaged and could not be flown or otherwise transported to a stationary overhaul shop). This version was designated Mi-24TECh-24 (*tekhniko-eksplooatatseeonnaya chahst* = maintenance facility for Mi-24s). Like its predecessor, the Mi-8TECh-24 of 1977, this 'Mi-24 tech' could have been of great use in Afghanistan, but did not reach production.

A tough bird

In March 1987 an Mi-24P piloted by Captain Nikolayev had its tail rotor pitch control chain shot away by machine-gun fire. With no directional control, the pilot somehow managed to get home to Bagram and land. Touching down too fast, the helicopter veered off the runway, careered across the entire base in a cloud of dust – miraculously missing a taxiing Su-17M-4 fighter-bomber – hopped over some vehicles and came to rest in an empty hangar. The crew was unhurt and the 'Hind' returned to service after the rotor blades, the cannon (which had been wrenched loose) and the crushed nose fairing had been replaced.

Maritime 'Hinds'

The Mi-24's high power-to-weight ratio and spacious cabin gave it ample development potential. A multi-role naval version designated Mi-24M (*morskoy* = naval) or Izdelye 247 was developed in 1970. However, Mikhail L. Mil shelved the project so as not to undermine the position of the Kamov OKB, which was the Soviet Navy's traditional supplier of maritime helicopters. Mil came back to the idea of navalising the Mi-24 in 1973, at the demand of the Soviet government which urgently wanted a mine countermeasures (MCM) helicopter. To this end, an Mi-24A was extensively modified as the prototype of an MCM version designated Mi-24BMT (*buksirovschchik minnovo trahla* = mine-clearing sled tug). The Mi-24BMT lacked stub wings, armament and armour plating. The landing gear was fixed. The aft fuselage incorporated a winch and stowage for the mine-clearing sled, and an extra fuel tank was installed to increase endurance. The Mi-24BMT remained in prototype form, this time because the Mi-8BT developed in 1974 for clearing mines in the Suez Canal was found to be more efficient in the MCM role, as was the later Mi-14BT 'Haze-B'.

Mil Mi-24P 'Hind-F'
Soviet Army Aviation, Afghanistan

The 'Hind-F' was the penultimate production version of the Mi-24, but boasted the last word in heavy helicopter armament. The addition of the twin Gryazev/Shipunov GSh-30K 30-mm cannon gave it immense firepower which proved invaluable in Afghanistan. This aircraft is carrying a light load of just two 9M114 Shturm (AT-6 'Spiral') tubes and two B8V20 80-mm rocket launchers. The weight of the cannon affected the overall warload of the Mi-24P, and 'Hinds' in Afghanistan always tended to operate with less then the optimum combat load due to the 'hot-and-high' conditions.

elf-defence of the Afghan
SOEP-V1A Lipa) active IRCM
main rotor head. The IRCM
ffective. Distracted by the
the missile would start
xplode a long way from the
tayed on throughout the
Hind' would manoeuvre into
ip, using its jammer for
red not only during an attack
er dangerous spots where
red upon, just to be on the
-SAM manoeuvre was
g spotted an incoming
ake a sharp turn and fire a

Indestructible 'Crocodiles'

In Afghanistan, hopelessly damaged aircraft were destroyed on the spot to prevent them from falling into enemy hands. This was no small task, as the Mi-24 could not be set alight by incendiary bullets and would not explode even when hit by FFARs, which merely pierced the structure, going clean through. A specially developed manual required the crew to "put all remaining S-5 FFARs in the troop cabin and cockpit(s), place the bombs beneath the fuselage, rupture fuel and hydraulic lines in the lower fuselage, lay tarpaulins soaked in jet fuel to make a fuse at least 20 m long so as to allow the crew to take cover."

Employing rockets

Rockets were one of the principal weapons of the Afghan war. However, until recently, the 130-mm S-13 FFARs and 250-mm S-24 heavy unguided rockets (both common weapons of the Su-25) were not widely used by the Mi-24 because its targeting system was ill-suited for these weapons and accuracy was poor; this was not helped by the type's higher vibration level compared to the 'Frogfoot'. Additionally, there was considerable risk of engine surge after ingesting rocket exhaust gases. However, during the Chechen war Russian Air Force Mi-24 pilots developed a technique of firing S-24s after pitching up the helicopter into a climb, and made more than 200 successful launches in this fashion.

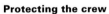

Protecting the crew

Analysis of Afghan combat losses led to the obvious conclusion that crew protection was the first priority, for unless the crew was incapacitated, it could usually bring home a crippled helicopter. However, a head-on approach to the problem by fitting bullet-proof side windows inside the cockpits dismally failed, as the 35-kg (77-lb) glass panels impaired visibility and made the cockpits so cramped that the crew literally had no room to turn their heads. The specially-developed protective suit proposed in 1980 was a failure too, looking and weighing like a medieval knight's suit of armour. Bullet-proof vests were rarely used (and then mostly in winter, more for the sake of warmth than protection). The ZSh-3B helmets were criticised for their weight, the 3-kg (6.6-lb) helmet severely straining neck muscles during high-*g* turns, but things improved when the lightweight ZSh-5B titanium helmet became available.

Mil Mi-24 'Hind'

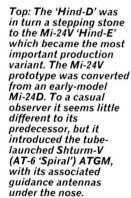

Top: The 'Hind-D' was in turn a stepping stone to the Mi-24V 'Hind-E' which became the most important production variant. The Mi-24V prototype was converted from an early-model Mi-24D. To a casual observer it seems little different to its predecessor, but it introduced the tube-launched Shturm-V (AT-6 'Spiral') ATGM, with its associated guidance antennas under the nose.

Above: Production Mi-24Vs had several small changes compared to the prototypes – differences which also set them apart from the similar-looking Mi-24D. The doors over the undernose optical sight (starboard) had a revised twin-arm hydraulic actuator while the (fixed) egg-shaped radio antenna for the missiles was rounder than the Mi-24D's, with a black dielectric nose.

carried six commandos which disembarked while the 'Hind' was moving at a couple of dozen feet and 50 km/h (31 mph). Despite its under-use as a troopship, the 'Hind' could well qualify for the title of the most battle-proven helicopter in the world: in less than 20 years, it has participated in some 30 wars and regional conflicts on three continents.

'Hind' combat debut

The Mi-24 received its baptism of fire in early 1978 when Somalia's leader, General Siad Barré, sent his troops into neighbouring Ethiopia, trying to capture provinces which Somalia regarded as its own. Flown by Cuban pilots, Ethiopian Mi-24As raided Somalian positions with virtual impunity, knocking out armoured vehicles and artillery.

Hostilities did not end when General Barré's troops were forced out of the country. Ethiopia was soon torn apart by a prolonged civil war in which the Addis Ababa government fought to quell separatism in the northern province of Eritrea. Once again, more than 40 'Hind-As' were thrown into battle against the Eritrean Liberation Front guerrillas. The helicopters were used in the CAS role, their main armament being S-5 FFARs. None is known to have been shot down, but several were destroyed on the ground by Eritrean separatists which overran Asmara air base on the night of 21 May 1984.

Soviet military advisors and technicians assisted the government forces in training 'Hind' crews and maintaining the helicopters. "Mi-35s were delivered from the USSR in 1988," Major S. A. Melnichenko, one of the advisors,

recalled. "The graduates of the local flying school flew them successfully. Besides flying the usual missions of the Mi-24, they had to seek and destroy separatist gunboats in the Red Sea. These fast craft were the scourge of shipping in the area, appearing out of nowhere, attacking ships moored in the harbours and disappearing just as quickly. After the helicopters had sunk eight of these boats, the enemy gave up using them. In February 1989 UPK-23-250 gun pods were used with great success against tanks. An armoured convoy moving along a canyon was attacked by two groups of Mi-35s which took turns strafing it, destroying eight tanks."

As the conflict escalated, the separatists managed to shoot down several 'Hind-As'. No 'Hind-Es' were lost to enemy action until early 1990, but one Mi-35 was damaged beyond repair in a wheels-up landing. When spares supplies from the Soviet Union dried up, most of the Ethiopian Air Force's helicopters became unserviceable. A few 'Hinds' were flown to the rebels by Ethiopian defectors and used against the government forces until 1991, when Eritrea became a sovereign state.

War in Afghanistan

The most famous conflict in which the Mi-24 participated was undoubtedly the Afghan war. The type was introduced into Afghanistan in April 1979 when the Afghan air force took delivery of its first Mi-24As and Mi-25s. The helicopters were immediately pressed into action against the Mujahideen guerrillas of Burhanuddin Rabbani and Gulbuddin Hekmatyar, or 'the irreconcilable opposition', as they were referred to in the Soviet press. The Afghan pilots had been well trained and put the 'Hind' to good use. Still, it was not long before the Mujahideen air defences, weak as they were at the time, claimed their first victim. The first Mi-24 was shot down near Khost on 30 May 1979, crashing into a mountain slope after being hit by ground fire. The Kabul government kept urging the Soviet leaders to supply 20 or 25 more 'Hinds', but it was not before the Soviet Union put troops into Afghanistan on 25 December 1979 that a new batch was delivered.

The Kremlin strategists assessing the situation in the Democratic Republic of Afghanistan did not seem to realise that the country was, in effect, already in the throes of a civil war. The sporadic character of the war, and the ambush and hit-and-run tactics favoured by the Mujahideen, demanded quick and accurate response to enemy action. Thus, air support was of prime importance –

all the more so because, in Afghanistan's mountainous terrain, he who had the high ground was in control of the situation. In a nutshell, it looked like this was going to be a 'helicopter war', and the Mi-24 was to prove its worth in it.

Afghan tactics

After the first encounters with the enemy and the first shoot-downs, the helicopters began working in pairs, at the very least, so that if one went down the other could provide cover for the downed crew. Usually, however, the Mi-24s operated in flights of four or in groups of eight; this made for maximum strike effectiveness in areas providing ample natural cover for the enemy. The Mujahideen were well armed and returned fire whenever possible, so having strength in numbers allowed the helicopter crews to utilise many tactics which a pair might have found it impossible to use. These included the 'wheel of death' (introduced by Ilyushin Il-2s during World War II) during which the helicopters circled the target, spraying it with fire; the *konveyer* ('assembly line', or rather 'disassembly line') technique in which the helicopters approached in echelon formation and the wingmen consecutively turned head on to the target; and the innocuous-sounding 'daisy', whereby the helicopters fanned out in all directions in a manner reminiscent of the bomb burst aerobatic manoeuvre to intermittently pound the target from all directions at minimum intervals. To avoid AA fire, pairs of helicopters would zigzag or fly in a scissor pattern, alternately climbing and descending to complicate aiming for Mujahideen gunners; the higher-flying pair would provide protection for the attacking one.

Mi-24 crews did everything to maximise the effect of their fire, sometimes to the detriment of flight safety, and there were cases when the flight leader who had just finished a firing pass found his wingman's rockets whizzing past him on either side before he had time to get out of the way! Flexibility in tactics and mission planning was all-important, as following a rigid routine immediately led to blows; even following the same avenue of approach twice could lead to an ambush. On the way to and from the target and on combat air patrol (CAP) missions, the helicopters in a pair kept a distance of 1200 to 1500 m (3,937 to 4,921 ft) to avoid being hit by the same burst of ground fire; this gave the crews time to react, either taking evasive action or taking out the enemy right away.

The 'Hind' was fast but its high speed had a price – rotor disc loading was 50 per cent greater than the Mi-8's, which significantly impaired controllability in Afghanistan's extreme conditions ('hot-and-high', plus dusty). Worse still, the ingrained piloting techniques for normal conditions were often useless and could even cause accidents. The overly high rotor disc loading meant that sharp stick (cyclic) movements would cause the helicopter to sag; the pilot would then pull collective, trying to keep the helicopter airborne, but engines weakened by the 'hot-and-high' conditions could not accelerate quickly enough and the result would be an unceremonious landing.

At low speed or low altitude, where the frequent ground winds came into play, the 'Hind' would start acting up. Due to its inadequate directional control, the tail rotor would try to pull the helicopter into an uncommanded left turn and, at worst, could cause it to flip into a spin, with almost certainly disastrous results. The main rotor blades stalled during high-*g* manoeuvres at high speed and high Alpha, causing the Mi-24 to pitch up uncontrollably and fall through sharply. This phenomenon, known as *podkhvaht* ('pick-up'), often resulted in a hard landing on the wing endplates and FFAR pods. A 'pick-up' could be avoided by sticking to the book (in other words, taking it nice and slow), but this was hardly possible in combat.

Self-inflicted injuries

As a result of the 'pick-up' phenomenon or during recovery from a high-*g* dive, the main rotor blades could strike the tailboom. One such incident was recorded in August 1980 when two 'Hinds' flown by Squadron Leader Major Kozovoy and his deputy Major Alatortsev came back from a sortie with holes torn in their tailbooms caused by blade strikes. Both helicopters were repaired, but in its post-repair check-out flight Major Kozovoy's Mi-24 was hit by ground fire. A burst of a 12.7-mm DShK fire took one of the tail rotor blades right off, causing violent vibration; the hastily repaired tailboom broke and the helicopter crashed out of control, killing the crew.

Pulling out of a 20° dive at 250 km/h (155 mph), the Mi-24 could lose up to 200 m (656 ft). At low altitude and during all-out manoeuvring there was no room for error, and manoeuvre speed and co-ordination became all-important. There was a macabre joke among 'Hind' crews that flying in this fashion was 'just as easy as walking a tightrope'. The unit stationed in Kunduz learned it the hard way, losing six Mi-24Ds in the first year of the war, in accidents. Some of the helicopters collided with mountains due to fog or wind shear, and others were written off in unsuccessful landings on slopes or in cramped landing zones.

Development of the Mi-24V 'Hind-E' was driven largely by experience in Afghanistan, where the original TV3-117 engine of the Mi-24D was found to be wanting, especially when the helicopters were heavily loaded in 'hot-and-high' conditions. Though the 'Hind-E' also introduced an improved weapons and sensor fit, arguably the most important change was under its skin. Mil fitted the more powerful TV3-117V turboshaft, rated at 2,225 shp (1660 kW) compared to the 1,640 shp (1111 kW) of the TV3-117. 'Hind' engines are set at a slight angle of 4.5° and are interchangeable (left to right) once the exhaust has been rotated through 180°. This Czech Mi-24V wears the pale grey and dark grey/green camouflage scheme applied to all Czech 'Hind-Es'. The Mi-24Ds were delivered in a three-tone grey-green camouflage, but many were repainted with a green and brown scheme after overhaul in Hungary. Czech 'Hinds' have now started appearing in an all-new two-tone grey and dark green scheme.

Above: The cowlings of the Mi-24's TV-3 engine were purposefully designed to be used as a maintenance platform in the field. This aircraft is also carrying PTB-450 drop tanks. Like all the earlier Mi-24 versions, the Mi-24V was introduced with conventional engine air intakes. However, the 'Hind' would inevitably kick up a local dust storm when operating from dirt pads – this became a serious problem in Afghanistan. To prevent excessive engine wear and foreign object damage (FOD), vortex-type intake filters called PZU (piilezaschchitnoye ustroystvo = anti-dust device) were developed and introduced on production 'Hind-Es' in 1981. These proved extremely effective and were fitted as standard to later versions of the Mi-24 (and retrofitted to many 'Hind-Ds' and some 'Hind-As').

Right: These Mi-24Vs, not yet fitted with the PZU filters, operated from a forward airfield in winter during early service trials of the 'Hind-E'. The tactical codes applied to the forward fuselage (over the butterfly camouflage pattern) are noteworthy.

In April 1980 General Designer Marat N. Tischchenko visited several Mi-24 units in Afghanistan and the 'aerial hooligans', as the pilots were wryly referred to by the army top brass, demonstrated some of the officially banned manoeuvres to him, taking the helicopter to its limits. After watching a session of 'aerobatics' featuring ultra-steep climbs, spectacular spins and even the allegedly impossible (for a 'Hind') barrel roll performed by Major V. Kharitonov, the amazed OKB boss exclaimed, "I thought I knew what my helicopters could do, now I'm not so sure!"

The daredevil demonstration created a lasting impression, and the positive after-effect followed very soon when, in the summer of 1980, the Mil OKB began working on an upgrade package for the Mi-24. This included readjustment of the engines' automatic fuel controls to reduce power loss in 'hot-and-high' conditions (made *in situ* by the manufacturer's technical teams) and a contingency increase in

turbine temperature for the duration of the war, as the crews preferred to risk having a turbine casing burn through than to suffer from lack of power when they needed it most.

The engine air intakes were fitted with vortex-type dust filters which extracted 70 to 75 per cent of the dust and sand ingested by the engines, reducing compressor blade wear 2.5 to 3 times. The Mi-24 received the filters before the Mi-8 – even though the 'Hip' operated from unprepared landing zones (LZs) more often than the 'Hind' – because its TV3-117 turboshafts had higher idling rpm and mass flow than the Mi-8's TV2-117As and thus ingested sand more readily, making the engine wear problem more acute. (It has to be said that very few 'first-generation' Mi-8s have been retrofitted with these filters; conversely, they are standard on the 'second-generation' Mi-8MT/Mi-17 'Hip-F' and its versions, both civil and military.)

Mi-24Vs began arriving in Afghanistan in 1981, with TV3-117V engines giving 15 to 20 per cent more power in 'hot-and-high' conditions. Earlier Mi-24Ds were retrofitted with the new engines during overhauls.

Hitting the target

By the end of 1980 the helicopter element of the 40th army had been doubled to 200 aircraft. The combat helicopters made both planned sorties and extra sorties as requested by the ground forces if a pocket of resistance was encountered. Army aviation accounted for 33 per cent of all planned strike missions; by contrast, its share in real CAS missions was 75 per cent. By then there were three levels of ground force operations – army ops, unit ops and the so-called implementation (performed at division, brigade and battalion level, respectively). Each type invariably involved helicopter support, and the 'Hind' with its comprehensive weapons range was used as an armoured fist.

If a mix of bombs and rocket pods was carried, the pilot would let loose a salvo of FFARs at 1200 to 1500 m (3,937 to 4,921 ft) range and then hose down the area with machine-gun fire, allowing the WSO to aim and drop the bombs accurately. For such pinpoint strikes, which were made at high speed and low altitude, the bomb detonators were set with a delay of up to 32 seconds (as on attack aircraft) so that the aircraft was not hit by the bombs' fragments. This did not always work, as when, for example, in the summer of 1985 an Mi-24 operating from Ghazni in central Afghanistan came home with 18 fragments of its flight leader's bombs in its fuselage. Fully loaded, the 'Hind' could take up to 10 100-kg (220-lb) bombs on MBD2-67u multiple racks (MBD, *mnogozamkovii bomboderzhahtel'* = multiple bomb rack). In a simultaneous drop, accuracy was rather low, but this technique worked well against area targets such as Mujahideen camps.

Bombed-up Mi-24s often spearheaded assault groups, demolishing the thick adobe walls of Afghan houses which became death traps for Mujahideen gunners. Another favourite weapon for these missions was the UPK-23-250 gun pod. The GSh-23L cannon had a high muzzle velocity and proved far more effective against such structures than S-5 FFARs, for the shells pierced the walls to explode inside.

The Mi-24 could also carry large-calibre HE bombs, such as four 250-kg (551-lb) FAB-250s or two 500-kg (1,102-lb) FAB-500s (FAB, *foogahsnaya aviabomba* = high-explosive bomb). These bombs were used against ancient fortresses, which were abundant in Afghanistan and made convenient bases for the rebels, being strategically located on insurmountable cliffs, protecting settlements and road junctions, and had stone or adobe walls 3 m (10 ft) thick which were impervious to S-5s. In June 1980 eight Mi-24Ds toting big bombs played a vital role in the capture of Mt Sanghi-Douzdan, the famous Mountain of Thieves near Faozabad which Alexander the Great had failed to capture in his time. The mountain was riddled with caves

and passages and had sheltered local bandits from time immemorial, hence the name, and had become a major Mujahideen base. Truck-mounted BM-21 Grad ('Hail') multiple-launcher rocket systems pounded the mountain without respite, paving the way for the ground troops. The 'Hinds' joined in at night, flying sortie after sortie without a WSO, so that the helicopter could take more bombs.

Fuel/air explosives

August 1980 was probably the first time Mi-24Ds used fuel/air bombs against a Mujahideen ambush in the Faozabad canyon. Knowing that trials had shown lower-than-average reliability of these munitions, the pilots of two 'Hinds' covering the lead pair immediately fired a salvo of rockets into the resulting cloud of fuel mist for good measure. The bombs had been dropped at 300 m (984 ft), which was higher than usual, yet the blast wave caught up with the helicopters. As the pilots themselves put it, "The first thing we knew was our teeth snapping." Reliability problems with fuel/air bombs persisted throughout the war. Their efficiency was affected by many factors, including drop speed, altitude and 'hot-and-high' conditions; some sources claim that only 15 to 20 per cent of these bombs detonated properly. Hence, fuel/air bombs were used sporadically, and then usually in combination with HE or incendiary bombs. When they did work properly they were

a terrifying weapon, and not for nothing have been called 'the poor man's atomic bomb'. Buildings were flattened completely, and troops arriving on the scene would find charred bodies and a few deaf and blind survivors.

Mi-24 strike groups were sometimes accompanied by an Mi-8 fire director helicopter with a spotter on board. The latter was usually a local from the HAD (the Afghan secret service) who helped tell friend from foe in the vegetation below and identify the right house in a village, i.e., the one in which the enemy had hidden. Intelligence came from prisoners, friendly villagers, undercover agents in Mujahideen gangs or paid informers. The latter source was the least reliable as, all too often, an informer, having sold information on enemy positions, immediately went to the Mujahideen to warn of an impending air raid and get paid by them as well. Another pair of 'Hips' always tagged along as SAR helicopters. They also photographed the attack results and, in the case of heavily protected high-priority targets, undertook post-attack reconnaissance which helped assess possible enemy retaliatory action.

In March 1982 a squadron of 'Hinds' was tasked with eliminating a gathering of opposition leaders in Asadabad. A flight of Mi-24s was to keep the Mujahideen air defences busy while another secured the perimeter of the city block to stop anyone getting in or out. The Afghan spotter identified the building where the target was and the entire squadron

This Mi-24V of the 337th OVP (Independent Helicopter Regiment) was one of the 'Hind-Es', based at Mahlwinkel, in the former East Germany. It is seen here tucking up its gear at its German base for the last time, on 16 July 1994, when the unit finally returned to Russia. The 337th OVP had always been an important forward-deployed assault helicopter unit, latterly supporting the 8th Guards Infantry Army. The unit accepted its first Mi-24Ds in the mid-1980s before transitioning to the more capable Mi-24V. The 337th OVP also operated Mi-24Ps alongside Mi-8 'Hips'.

Another Mi-24V operator attached to the Group of Soviet Forces in Germany was the 439th OVP, based at Damm (known to NATO as Parchim). Like most other Russian 'Hind' units in East Germany, it operated a mix of Mi-24Vs and Mi-24Ps (with Mi-8 troopships), but its aircraft were unusual in carrying 'nose-art' – the badge of Soviet Army Aviation. This aircraft is also carrying B8V20A 20-round 80-mm rocket pods.

267

Above: The cannon-armed Mi-24P 'Hind-F' transformed the type into the ultimate helicopter gunship. Trials of the twin-barrelled Gryazev/Shipunov GSh-30K 30-mm cannon began as early as 1976. The 'Hind-F' was not widely exported but one customer was the former East Germany, which acquired 12 from 1986 onwards. These aircraft were fitted out to the highest specification and were eagerly flown and evaluated by the Luftwaffe (and other agencies) following German reunification.

Right, and below right: An early Mi-24D, with no intake filters, was converted into the Mi-24P prototype. 'Red 70', seen here, is an Mi-24P pre-production aircraft. Originally, the cannon had short barrels which terminated almost level with the end of the LLLTV/FLIR pod. This proved to be less than optimal, as the violent vibration generated by the cannon shook the avionics to pieces. A lengthy redesign and trials programme followed, and in the definitive version the barrels were nearly twice as long, extending beyond the nose and terminating in large funnel-shaped flame dampers that did not 'blind' the missile guidance sensors. This configuration was tested on the second prototype, a converted late-production Mi-24D or Mi-24V.

Right: These 'Hind-Es' are attached to the 248th OVE of the Belarussian air force, based at Minsk-Slepyanka. Belarus has retained the old-style Soviet red star marking and operates about 80 'Hinds', mostly Mi-24V/Ps.

came in, obliterating it. The spotter fled as soon as the helicopters returned to base, and it transpired that the house he had indicated belonged to a local 'big shot' and a long-time enemy of his; he simply saw the opportunity to take his revenge. Another tragi-comical incident which happened in Kandahar was a classic case of crew miscommunication. The spotter pointed to a house below which was promptly attacked; it turned out that the poor devil, who spoke no Russian at all, had merely wanted to show them his own home!

Bombing and shooting accuracy was affected by wind turbulence from the mountains, which could cause the bombs and rockets to drift far off course. Mi-24V pilots had been taught by experience to rely more on their eyes and good judgement than on the ASP-17V automatic gunsight and VSB-24 ballistic shooting and bombing computer (VSB, *vychisleetel' strel'bii i bombometahniya*). Sniper Pilot (a grade reflecting expertise) Nikolay Malyshev made no secret of his way to success: "It's all about hitting the target, not about taking aim." WSO Ivan Manenok operating from Jalalabad became something of a local legend for his ability to lob bombs squarely on top of Mujahideen fortresses and machine-gun emplacements. During operations against villages he could place HE bombs at right angles precisely at the base of a wall. In an attempt to hide from Soviet raids the Mujahideen began setting up shelters and AAA positions behind rocky outcrops. The 'Hinds' would get them even there, using the lob-bombing technique.

Some Mi-24s were armed with S-24 heavy unguided rockets with 123-kg (271-lb) warheads which could be launched at a range of up to 2 km (1.24 miles) without taking the helicopter within range of the enemy's air defences. A 'Hind' unit commanded by Colonel Gorshkov made 50 successful launches. The S-24 could be used successfully only by experienced crews and so did not find wide use, the reason being that the heavy missile produced an extensive smoke trail which enveloped the helicopter, causing considerable risk of engine surge.

ATGMs were used successfully not only against vehicles but against bunkers and gun emplacements if their positions were known in advance. At 1.5 to 2 km (0.93 to 1.24 mile) range, a WSO with good aim could place a 35-kg (77-lb) rocket squarely in an embrasure or the mouth of a cave. The 9M114 Shturm-V ATGM was especially effective for this if equipped with a fuel/air warhead which blew the bunkers apart from within. When fired at Mujahideen vehicle convoys, the Shturm-V had a kill rate of 75 to 80 per cent; pilots even complained there were 'too few suitable targets' for these weapons.

As noted earlier, the 'flying IFV' concept did not prove feasible in combat. The crews were reluctant to fly a 'battlebus' full of 'passengers' firing out the windows, as the Mi-24 was decidedly overweight and sluggish with a full payload, so armour plating and troop seats in the cabin were often removed to save weight. For the same reason, the payload was often limited to two FFAR pods or bombs (enough for most missions) and the fuel tanks were rarely filled more than two-thirds. Only 16 per cent of the sorties were flown fully loaded, and then for short distances only.

Day and night hunter teams

'Hinds' were often used as 'hunters' to patrol areas of interest and destroy targets of opportunity. The missions, known officially as 'reconnaissance/strike operations' (i.e., armed reconnaissance), were usually flown by pairs or flights of Mi-24s. The softer-skinned and less heavily armed Mi-8TVs ('Hip-C/Es') and Mi-8MTV-2s ('Hip-Hs') were rarely used alone for these dangerous missions but could provide welcome support for the 'crocodiles'. The normal weapons fit comprised two FFAR pods, two anti-tank missiles and 500 to 700 machine-gun rounds.

The helicopters assumed echelon formation angled at 15 to 20° with intervals of 600 to 800 m (1,968 to 2,624 ft) and patrolled the area at 1500 to 1700 m (4,921 to 5,577 ft), which gave everyone good visibility and freedom of manoeuvre. Having located a convoy, they would fire warning shots across its path, forcing it to stop and keeping it in check until the inspection group arrived in several Mi-8s. However, increasingly often the convoys included 'trap-mobiles' with heavy machine-guns hidden under tarpaulins,

so soon the hunters began simply shooting suspicious convoys, leaving the inspection group little to do except collect the booty and burn what trucks were left (if any).

At night, when the enemy moved about more freely under cover of the darkness, the hunters patrolled roads and mountain paths in pairs, keeping a difference in altitude of 80 to 100 m (262 to 328 ft) for safety's sake. Having located vehicle headlights or camp fires and received confirmation that there were no friendlies in the area, the group attacked immediately; quick reaction was crucial to prevent the Mujahideen from vanishing into the night. Usually, all lights on the ground were promptly extinguished when the helicopters put in an appearance, but the 'Hinds' fired special S-5-O (*osvetitel'nii*) illumination FFARs to 'pin down' the target, then dropped flare bombs and dived below them to attack. This tactic was later refined, so that the helicopters attacked from above the 'chandeliers' (as the flare bombs were called in Air Force slang), staying invisible to the enemy.

Night hunter operations required extensive training, but were extremely effective. On one occasion in April 1986, a Soviet tactical reconnaissance group reported a Mujahideen convoy approaching Gharkalay village near Kandahar and a flight of 'Hinds' took off to intercept. A single firing pass sent the Mujahideen scattering, abandoning six trucks full of weapons. In December 1986 the Mi-24 tested 'blinding bombs' near Bagram. These munitions were modified flare bombs which produced a tremendous flash, putting enemy personnel within a radius of 30 to 50 m (98 to 164 ft) out of action for several hours but not causing permanent blindness.

From the spring of 1980, the lean, predatory silhouette of the Mi-24 became an increasingly familiar sight in Afghan skies, and before long the mottled green 'crocodile' was a true symbol of the war. The 'Hinds' flew 'lower, slower and over shorter distances than anyone else', as their crews put it (paraphrasing a Soviet slogan of the 1930s, 'fly higher, faster and farther than everyone else'), but were far more effective in the strike role than supersonic fighters and fighter-bombers which streaked over the target without having time to do any real damage – those aircraft earned the disdainful generic nickname of svistok (whistle).

The 'Hind-F' brought with it much needed firepower, though the slower firing rate of its heavy cannon meant they were a less effective area weapon at short range.

'Hind' Trainers

Mi-24U 'Hind-C' (Izdelye 244)

A trainer derivative of the Mi-24A designated Mi-24U (Uchebnii = training *(attrib.)*), or Izdelye 244, was built in small numbers. Outwardly it differed from the 'Hind-A' in lacking the nose-mounted A-12,7 machine-gun, the wingtip ATGM launch rails and associated guidance system fairing under the nose. The instructor sat in the former WSO's position in the extreme nose which featured additional navigation equipment and full dual controls. The trainer version was codenamed 'Hind-C'.

Mi-24DU/Mi-25U 'Hind-D' (Izdelye 249)

A trainer version of the Mi-24D appeared in 1980. Designated Mi-24DU (D-uchebnii) or Izdelye 249, it differed from the standard 'Hind-D' in having a smoothly faired nose (instead of the USPU-24 gun barbette) and dual controls. The first prototype (coded 'Yellow 48') lacked the wingtip launchers for the Falanga-PV missiles and associated guidance equipment under the nose, but these were retained on later prototypes and production aircraft. The export version of the Mi-24DU was designated Mi-25U.

Mi-24V trainer version

A trainer version similar to the Mi-24DU was supplied to the Indian Air Force. Outwardly it differed from the Mi-24DU in having Mi-24V-style bearers for 9M114 Shturm ATGMs on the wing endplates instead of the earlier launch rails for 9M17P Falanga-P missiles and the associated restyled command link antenna pod. No separate designation is known. It should be noted that there never was a production 'Mi-24VU' for the Soviet Army, so the Indian trainers were probably custom-built.

Above right: 'Yellow 48', the Mi-24DU prototype, was the only Mi-24DU to lack the undernose Raduga-F system.

Right: India's 'Hind-E'-based Mi-24V trainers are unique in the world, and were built to order. All other active 'Hind' trainers are based on the 'Hind-D' airframe.

Above left: This is one of the original Mi-24U ('Hind-A' trainer) prototypes which had a smooth nose, devoid of its gun housing and also lacking missile rails and the ventral missile guidance fairing.

Above: The difference in expression between the instructor in the front seat of this Mi-24DU 'Hind-D' trainer, and the trainee in the back, is amusingly clear.

Opposite page, top: The GUV gun pods designed to boost Mi-24D/V firepower were not widely used. They were far too heavy, and crews agreed to fly with the 450-kg (992-lb) pods only when threatened by disciplinary action. As they rightly pointed out, the 4,350 rounds in each GUV was overkill – there were simply no targets in Afghanistan which could merit such a hail of fire. Soviet Army Aviation definitively lost interest in the GUV when the cannon-armed Mi-24P arrived. Identical in calibre to the pod's alternative 30-mm AGS-17 grenade launcher, the Mi-24P's GSh-30K cannon had twice the range and five times the weight of fire. Some 'Hind-Fs' were fitted with a laser rangefinder for increased accuracy. Recoil from the big cannon caused fatigue problems, and cracks and deformations appeared in the fuselage skin and frames after 1,500 to 2,000 rounds had been fired. This was alleviated by installing an external Duralumin reinforcement plate and two hefty L-section profiles, which extended the guaranteed life to 4,000 rounds.

One of the rotary-wing element's main roles in the war was vertical envelopment, i.e., insertion of troops in the vicinity of villages, roads and other points of importance held by the rebels. In these operations the Mi-24 acted as a steamroller, crushing enemy resistance with bombs and rockets to clear the way for incoming Mi-8s and Mi-6 'Hook-As'. One or two pairs of 'Hinds' escorted the transport helicopters (numbering as many as 60 at a time) all the way to the LZ, flying along the flanks and 200 to 400 m (656 to 1,312 ft) higher. The landing was preceded by artillery fire and strikes by attack aircraft, followed rapidly by one or two flights of Mi-24s. Before the confused enemy had time to collect his wits, the heliborne assault was coming in, covered by several pairs of helicopters which circled over the LZ at 1200 to 1800 m (3,937 to 5,905 ft), taking out any surviving enemy gunners. Another flight of Mi-24s stayed at the base on ready alert, replacing the ones which had expended their ammunition, if required.

Patrolling the roads

From the summer of 1980, the 'Hinds' were tasked with the important mission of escorting supply convoys, which accounted for 15 to 17 per cent of sorties. The 40th Army's daily needs amounted to hundreds of tons of fuel, ammunition, food, etc., and the convoys delivering them were perpetually ambushed by the rebels.

Several pairs of Mi-24s would take turns patrolling above the convoy, zigzagging at 150 to 170 km/h (81 to 92 kt). The crews checked the surroundings 2 to 3 km (1.24 to 1.86 miles) on each side of the road – this was the rebels' usual attack range – and 5 to 8 km (3 to 5 miles) ahead of the convoy. Having detected a Mujahideen ambush, the helicopters made a flank attack if possible, coming in along the road to avoid blue-on-blue incidents. *Ad hoc* helipads were built along the roads for refuelling and 'changing of the guard', as providing constant escort to convoys crawling along at 15 to 20 km/h (9 to 12 mph) would otherwise

have been impossible. The first stretch from Termez on the Soviet side of the border (Uzbekistan) to the infamous Salang pass was protected by 'Hinds' based in Kunduz, using helipads in Khairaton, Mazar-i-Sharif, Tashkurgan and Pul-i-Khumri. At the Salang pass, Mi-24s from Bagram took over, later passing on the convoys to crews from Jalalabad, Ghazni and other bases.

Still, losses were heavy; thousands of vehicles were lost each year and an army driver's profession was one of the most dangerous. In April 1983 a convoy of 180 trucks escorted by a tank battalion was ambushed in the Dori River valley not far from Kandahar. The place was crawling with Mujahideen, who opened fire from hideouts behind fences and in the jungle. When Mi-24s arrived on the scene, 20 fuel trucks and six tanks were ablaze on the road below. The helicopters fired 80-mm S-8 FFARs, marking the first operational use of this weapon; those on the ground mistook them for cannon fire of tremendous density and power. The rest of the convoy broke through, luckily for the Russians, for the fuel dump at Kandahar had only enough fuel for a couple more sorties.

The B-8V20 pods with 20 S-8 rockets apiece earned the highest praise in Afghanistan. The 3.6-kg (7.93-lb) warhead had considerable demolition effect and produced a large number of 3-g (0.1-oz) fragments with a kill radius of 10 to 12 m (33 to 39 ft). The new rockets began supplanting the S-5, yet the earlier model remained in use until the Soviet pullout from Afghanistan, despite pilots' complaints that the S-5s were only good for 'tickling the dookhi's [Mujahideen] heels' and fanned out 'like a tulip' when fired. To give credit where credit is due, the S-5 was still fairly effective in open spaces, it was simple and reliable, and the UB-32A pods were quickly and easily loaded, which was an undoubted asset during intensive operations with five or six sorties a day. Last but not least, huge stockpiles of S-5s had been built up at ammunition dumps and had to be expended to make room for new weapons.

As 'Hind' crews became more experienced and battle-hardened, tactics changed. Some 75 per cent of the sorties were flown in the early morning hours to escape the blistering mid-day heat. The first raid was made at dawn to get the Mujahideen in the open, when they were saying their morning prayers. Targets were distributed among crews in a strike group and the helicopters were armed accordingly; some crews would suppress the air defences and take out enemy personnel with FFARs and cluster bombs, while others destroyed buildings and other structures with HE bombs. Some 100-kg (220-lb) bombs were fitted with delayed-action fuses to act as mines, and explosions would continue for the next 24 hours, preventing survivors from getting out of the rubble. (However, there were cases when this method backfired; the Mujahideen would send some of their own men to disarm the bombs as punishment for transgressions and then use the bombs as land mines to mine roads ahead of Soviet convoys.) The last strike sortie of the day was flown late in the afternoon, again with a view to getting the Mujahideen in the open, since their religion required them to bury their dead before sunset.

Training for the war

Before being transferred to the Afghan Contingent, helicopter crews underwent special training at the mountain training range near Chirchik, Kazakhstan, and the desert range in the Kagana Desert near Bukhara, Uzbekistan, for 15 to 20 days to become accustomed to 'hot-and-high' conditions and operating in mountainous terrain. Upon arrival they were given a 'scenic tour' of the main areas of action in an Mi-8 by pilots who had completed their Afghan tour and were going home. Later, 12 to 15 per cent of the flying time was set aside for training, primarily combat manoeuvring and unconventional take-off and landing techniques.

The Flight Research Institute in Zhukhovskii near Moscow devised a radical take-off technique involving a precarious 10° to 12° tail-up run. Rolling along the tarmac on the nosewheels only, the helicopter accelerated quickly and became 'unstuck' after only 50 to 75 m (164 to 146 ft); another advantage was a 1000 to 1500-kg (2,204 to 3,306-lb) increase in MAUW. This technique, however, called for a lot of practice and a steady hand. On one occasion in November 1986, an Mi-24 pilot scrambling from Bagram began his take-off run directly from the flight line and over-rotated, the main rotor blades striking the tarmac. The helicopter became airborne and completed the mission, even though the blade tips were badly bent. The pilot, however, was too ashamed to come home with the damaged main rotor screaming like a banshee and so landed in a nearby field, waiting until the repair crew arrived.

Landing at unpaved LZs was fraught with danger, as the helicopter kicked up a dust storm and it was extremely easy to roll over after hitting an unseen pothole or stone. The solution was to land with a forward speed just high enough to keep the cockpit ahead of the dust cloud so that landing roll would be minimal. Roll was kept down to a few dozen feet by descending steeply with the engines at high rpm,

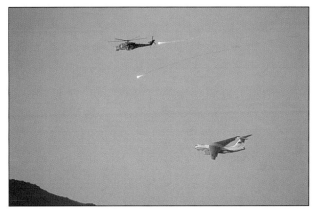

increasing collective pitch immediately before touch-down to avoid a hard landing, then immediately hauling back on the stick and standing on the brakes. This technique was hard on the tyres and brake discs, which were worn down to paper-thin condition in no time (this was known as 'Afghan wear'); in contrast, in normal conditions the brake discs lasted a year or more.

Afghan operations took an even heavier toll on the engines, which suffered from compressor blade erosion caused by sand ingestion and from combustion chamber and turbine casing failures (the higher turbine temperature was telling, after all). More than 50 per cent of the TV3-117 turboshafts had to be changed prematurely and, of them, 39 per cent were accounted for by compressor blade erosion and nearly 15 per cent by engine surge. Turbine blades failed extensively, causing loss of power, and, on one particular engine inspected in Bagram in the autumn of 1986, 17 of 51 turbine blades were missing!

Above: Vertical take-offs were all but impossible in the rarefied air where the helicopters had trouble keeping themselves up, never mind their payload. Thus, rolling take-offs were standard operational procedure, the helicopters becoming airborne after 100 to 150 m (328 to 492 ft).

Left: Mi-24s loaded with flares had to accompany all transport aircraft in and out of Kabul airport, to protect them against shoulder-launched SAMs. The 'Hinds' would routinely launch flares but, if they detected a Stinger launch, the helicopter pilots were ordered to meet the missile head-on, firing a salvo of flares and, if all else failed, present themselves as the target to save the transport. With typical macabre humour, the 'Hind' crews called themselves 'Matrosovs by order'. (Aleksandr Matrosov was a wartime hero who sacrificed himself by throwing his body across a German machine-gun emplacement to clear the way for a Soviet assault.)

Other than the problems caused by sand-ingestion and extreme operational wear-and-tear, the 'Hind' generally had a good reliability record in Afghanistan. This reliability and – even more importantly – the very high workload which kept the men at the airfields from the crack of dawn until darkness, led to the 'Hinds' being operated on a 'technical condition' basis – with maintenance undertaken only as required, rather than as prescribed by the manuals. Time-expired engines were allowed to amass up to 50 hours of 'life after death' before replacement, and some other equipment items were simply used until they packed up. This well-worn Mi-24P and its equally well-worn crew are seen just prior to departure for another operational mission.

All basic Mi-24 pilot training included combat manoeuvring, and this paid off in the war. Many new flying techniques invented in Afghanistan took the helicopter outside its normal flight envelope but allowed the crew to destroy the target more effectively, or saved them from being shot down. Apart from the customary turns and yo-yos, many skilled pilots practised NoE flying to the target, with a last-moment 3g zoom climb to fire the weapons and a 50° climb after the firing pass, followed by a sharp turn with bank angles exceeding 90° for an immediate second attack.

Dust would get into fuel tanks and congeal into a black slime which clogged fuel filters, pumps, etc., preventing engine start or putting the engine on a 'diet' at the worst possible moment (loss of power caused by clogged filters was known locally as 'quiet surge'). APU turbine casings often burned through, and many APUs were long since time-expired. Rotor blade leading-edge protective strips were eaten away completely by the sand, and when they came apart the remnants began flapping wildly, causing vibration and a high-pitched screech. Tail rotor pylons had to be replaced periodically due to fatigue cracks in the main ribs caused by high g loads during violent manoeuvring.

To avoid wasting time and service life on ferry flights, the 40th Army rotated only the crews; the helicopters were stuck there for the duration, or at best until they were due for a major overhaul. Not all Mi-24s were so lucky, as the Soviet contingent lost eight to 12 per cent of its helicopter component annually. Utilisation averaged 360 to 380 hours per year, being much higher in areas with especially bitter fighting. A pair of brand-new 'Hinds' delivered to the unit at Bagram in August 1986 clocked 1,000 hours (the limit set for the first overhaul) within a year.

Ground crews displayed, to put it in the words of Rudyard Kipling, infinite resource and sagacity, making field modifications and carrying out repairs which one would hardly think were possible in field conditions. Clogged filters were cleaned with compressed air. Helicopter batteries which perpetually boiled on hot days were cooled by immersing them in ditches with running water. Tanks and BMP-2 IFVs were used as ground power carts to fire up the APU (or the engines of 'Hip-C/Es'). Downed and recovered helicopters were cannibalised for spares for operational ones; in the autumn of 1982, having run out of spare engines, the technicians at Kandahar managed to assemble a usable TV3-117 from parts of three trashed engines.

Overall workload in Afghanistan may have doubled compared to normal conditions, but the weapons arming workload was 24 (!) times greater. Every available man had to handle bombs, load FFAR pods with rockets, cut open the zinc boxes of machine-gun ammunition and work the 'meat grinder' device which filled ammunition belts with bullets. Ammunition briefly was stocked next to the helicopters but this practice was soon discontinued because it split human resources and was plainly dangerous – a single well-aimed Mujahideen mortar could blow the entire flight line sky-high. Therefore, ammunition was prepared in advance in specially-designated areas and carted to the helicopters as soon as they came back from a sortie. Some units established an 'assembly line' routine, whereby the helicopters taxied to the arming area. The Mi-24's built-in weapons hoists were not very user-friendly and mobile bomb lifts were plagued by leaky hydraulics, so the ground crews often hooked up the heavy bombs with belts or crowbars, then the armourer would run around the helicopter adding and arming the detonators.

Heavy losses

For a long time the most potent adversaries of the 'Hinds' were the DShK HMGs and AA guns, which accounted for 42 per cent and 25 per cent of all Mi-24 losses, respectively. The engines and hydraulics were among the most frequently damaged items, surpassed only by the electrics and control runs which were all over the helicopter. Still, twin-engined reliability and systems duplication often allowed the Mi-24 to make it home. The engines had automatic power reserve, the good engine going to full power if the other one was hit. Even with main gearbox oil pressure down to zero, the helicopter could stay aloft for another 15 to 20 minutes, which was usually enough to get the crew out of immediate danger.

On 12 June 1982 a pair of Mi-24Vs piloted by Volkov and Lantsev spotted two Toyota Land Cruisers approaching a Mujahideen base near Kandahar and gave chase. Both jeeps were destroyed, but in the heat of the chase the attackers found themselves over the enemy camp and were shot up badly. The wingman was fired upon by three DShKs and, with hydraulic lines and wiring shot out, damaged rotor blades and dead instruments, he managed to limp back to base. There, the wounded technician had to open the cowling while the rotors were still turning and shut down one of the engines manually, as it would not shut down because of a damaged control rod.

The helicopter crews made up the majority of the aircrew fatalities in the Afghan Contingent. It was worse in the summer when the men were wearied by the heat and hard work, and the 'hot-and-high' conditions impaired aircraft performance, making them vulnerable. Sometimes, three or four crews would be lost per month. The dry formula 'injuries incompatible with life' found its way into the lexicon of military medics. Such injuries were usually sustained in crash-landings or inflight fires. Some 30 per cent of the fatalities were caused by head and spinal injuries, 55 per cent by extensive burns and 9 per cent by internal injuries. A helicopter pilot's death is an ugly one.

The once-popular lightweight blue flying suits were quickly discarded because they were made of a mixed fabric and, in a fire, the synthetic fibres melted, adhering firmly to the skin. Instead, camouflaged cotton field uniforms were introduced in 1984 (the helicopter crews were the first in the VVS to get them) and increased the chances of survival in a forced landing – as did the Kalashnikov AKS-74 5.45-mm collapsible-stock assault rifles with which crews were supplied; the more shrewd men strapped the AKS to their thigh or flank so as not to lose it when they bailed out. The standard-issue 9-mm Makarov PM pistols were exchanged for the more reliable Tokarev TT handguns, Stechkin APS automatic pistols or captured 20-round Berettas. The survival kit was 'revised' so that most of the food was omitted, leaving only the water flasks and a few chocolate bars, to make room for extra 30-round Kalashnikov clips and four RGD-5 hand grenades.

As noted earlier, Mi-24 pilots kept urging the Mil OKB to provide some protection for the rear hemisphere but the NSVT-12.7 Utyos machine-gun installation tested in 1985 proved disappointing. The 'Hind' had to make do with a technician who sat in the cabin and doubled as the tail gunner. To give him a bigger sector of fire, the cabin doors were modified so that the upper segment could be opened separately, the lower segment providing support for the gunner. The usual defensive armament was a 7.62-mm Kalashnikov PK general-purpose machine-gun (or the PKT vehicle-mounted version) which had earned respect for its range and accuracy. Sometimes two were carried to avoid wasting time transferring the MG to the other side of the cabin (which, incidentally, was dangerous; there was a case

in Kabul when the technician accidentally pulled the trigger while lugging the MG and shot up his own helicopter). Some crews used the lighter and more user-friendly infantry version, the RPK. When the Soviet high command ordered in the spring of 1986 that the technicians should stay on the ground 'to reduce unwarranted casualties', the crews objected, agreeing to fly without an extra gunner only if they chose to (i.e., when cutting weight was more important than extra protection).

Stopping the SAMs

Another 'Afghan upgrade package' introduced in the early 1980s was aimed at reducing the threat posed by shoulder-launched SAMs – FIM-43A Redeye and FIM-92A Stinger, Shorts Blowpipe and, ironically, captured Strela (Arrow)/SA-7 'Grail'. Large triple-lobe air/exhaust mixers were fitted to the engine jetpipes to reduce the IR signature; being draggy and inconvenient to use, they did not become obligatory until 1983, when SAMs became a distinct threat. Originally, two pairs of ASO-2V chaff/flare dispensers were strapped beneath the tailboom, but in 1987 they were replaced by triple ASO-2Vs on the fuselage sides immediately aft of the wings, angled forward for wider coverage and sometimes faired to cut drag. Finally, an L-166V-1E (SOEP-V1A Lipa) active IRCM jammer was fitted aft of the main rotor head.

Some of the proposed 'Afghan upgrades' (more powerful control actuators and the addition of vibration dampers) got stuck in bureaucratic red tape and were never introduced. Others created new problems as they eliminated old ones. For example, 'Hinds' and 'Hip-Hs' were fitted with a

The SAM threat to the Mi-24, and all Soviet tactical aircraft in Afghanistan, rose rapidly as Western intelligence agencies shipped increasingly sophisticated shoulder-launched weapons to the Afghan resistance. (Many of these weapons are now believed to be loose on the international arms market, ready to be used against their original suppliers.) To deal with the SAMs, the Mi-24s were fitted with boxy EVU infra-red suppressors over the exhaust stubs. These saved many aircraft, though they never completely prevented losses. Even though many Mi-24s were claimed by ground fire, the 'crocodile' was treated with respect by its enemies, as illustrated by an incident which took place near Toloukan in May 1983. Having run out of ammunition, Major Anatoliy Volkov continued to make mock attacks on a group of Mujahideen, scaring them off with just the sight and sound of the roaring, sinister-looking helicopter diving straight at them, thereby saving the lives of a company of troopers getting out of the bush. (Afghanistan is not all mountains, and some parts of the country are similar to the jungles of Vietnam.) This tactic earned him the nickname of 'proud falcon' (an allusion to the 1930s and 1940s when Soviet fighter pilots were referred to as 'Stalin's falcons'). On the subject of nicknames, the Mujahideen called the Mi-24 shaitan-arba ('devil's chariot').

Right: Technicians check out a battle-weary Mi-24V prior to its departure on an escort mission from a forward airstrip.

Far right: This Mi-24V, 'Red 28', is seen on patrol over Kabul city in the late 1980s.

Above: Flown by Captain G. Pavlov, this Mi-24P was one of those shot down in the summer of 1985. The crash site recovery team is already hard at work, removing any items from the aircraft that might be of use to the Mujahideen – including a Kalashnikov PK machine-gun from the cabin.

water/methanol injection system designed to compensate for the power loss caused by other modifications (the intake filters and the exhaust IR suppressors both removed 5 to 6 per cent of the total power output). However, when the system was switched on, power would increase explosively, which was hard to handle (in one case an Mi-24 lost control and rolled over during take-off in Kabul when the system kicked in). The system also required distilled water, which was unavailable in Afghanistan, and ordinary tap water quickly clogged the injector nozzles with sediment.

By 1987 the 40th Army's recovery and repair service was so well organised that 90 per cent of the damaged helicopters could be returned to service, compared with 70 per cent at the start of the campaign. To be able to fix a lightly damaged helicopter on the spot and get out of enemy territory, the crews trained in repair techniques and the 'Hinds' carried repair kits containing the most vital tools and spares. In the event of serious damage, a recovery team would be summoned to make hasty repairs so that the helicopter could be flown back to base. Such a team was usually composed of experienced and battle-hardened mechanics who could not only repair a helicopter quickly but fight back a Mujahideen attack, which they often had to do. There were cases when, arriving on the scene a couple of hours after the shoot-down, the recovery team found out the hard way that the helicopter had been booby-trapped by the Mujahideen.

Non-flyable helicopters were extracted by 'Hip-Hs' after being stripped down to 2500 kg (5,511 lb), the Mi-8MT's maximum payload. In the winter of 1986 an Mi-24 brought down near Ghazni landed on a dry lake-bed – not dry enough, as it turned out – and became firmly stuck in the mud. When all else failed the repair crew replaced the damaged engine and tail rotor, removed all non-essential items, literally chopped the helicopter free in the early morning hours when the mud had frozen, and Squadron Leader Shmelyov managed to pull the 'Hind' out 'by the hair', as they put it, and bring it home.

To boost their firepower 'Hinds' started carrying gunners in the main cabin, who had a wide field of view not covered by the Mi-24's main armament. Side gunners were particularly important in protecting the aircraft once on the ground. This crewman, Captain N. Goortovoy (above left), has a PKT machine-gun with a copious stock of 7.62-mm ammunition and the luxury of a swivelling seat, taken from a shot-down Mi-8. As in any war, the unsung heroes of Soviet 'Hind' operations in Afghanistan were the armourers and other ground crew – such as this one loading flare cartridges into ASO-2V dispensers scabbed onto the fuselage sides (above right). Other armourers are seen here removing jammed 30-mm shells from a GSh-2-30K cannon (right) and loading 12-kg (26-lb) S-8KO rockets into a B-8V20 pod (far right).

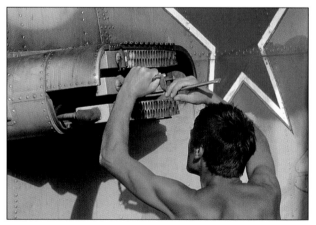

It finally became clear that the war was going nowhere and a political solution to the conflict would have to be found. An armistice was declared in early 1987 but proved of little use due to the general lack of good faith on both sides. The opposition continued to pressure the weak Kabul government, squeezing its troops out of the provinces. In mid-August 1987 a full-blown battle broke out for Bagram in which the local Soviet helicopter unit lost four aircraft and 10 men. In April 1988 one of the so-called contract gangs (operating under contract with the opposition) attacked government positions right outside Bagram air base. The entire Bagram wing had to be scrambled to fight back the bandits; for two days the aircraft spun an uninterrupted wheel of death, dropping bombs right next to the parking areas immediately after getting the wheels up. On another occasion the helicopter unit at Ghazni was fired upon by Afghan tanks which were supposed to protect it; it transpired that the tank crews had received a ration of sugar for every shot they fired, from the Mujahideen. Several Mi-24s were turned over to the Mujahideen by defectors. Two 'Hind-Ds' were flown to Pakistan in 1985 by defecting Afghan Air Force pilots who had been hired by the Pakistani intelligence service, and the ultimate fate of these helicopters is unknown.

Escape from Afghanistan

Of course, the Soviet command could not tolerate having the aircraft attacked and shot down over their own base, and preventive measures were taken. By 1987 the Soviet air bases were guarded by 25 army battalions, and as early as 1984 round-the-clock air cover and patrolling of the surrounding areas had been introduced. The helicopter crews spent virtually all their time on the flight line, sometimes relieving each other in the cockpits to maintain round-the-clock readiness.

Escorting Antonov An-12s and Ilyushin Il-76s carrying personnel out of the country became the highest priority. Each aircraft was escorted by a flight of 'Hinds'; one pair of helicopters searched the outskirts of the airfield while the other flew ahead or on the flanks, looking for a possible Mujahideen ambush. Sometimes a third pair followed close behind, firing IRCM flares until the steeply descending or climbing airlifter was out of range of a possible Stinger attack. Throughout the war, Kabul was still served by scheduled Aeroflot passenger jets which, of course, had no IRCM equipment (unlike the military transports), so the

local Mi-24s protecting them were fitted with double the usual number of ASO-2V flare packs.

Even liaison and SAR aircraft needed helicopter escort, as demonstrated by a tragic incident on 4 March 1987. Two Mi-8s took off to pick up the crew of a two-seat Su-17UM-3 who had ejected less than 2 miles (3.2 km) from Bagram. Unfortunately, the escorting Mi-24s were delayed, and when they arrived on the scene both pilots of the 'Fitter' had been killed and both 'Hips' shot down.

Disenchanted with the pointless war, the Soviet leadership realised it was time to pull out. In the concluding stages of the war the Soviets did not engage in major operations, keeping the Mujahideen in check by air strikes. Most sorties were planned ones against rebel camps and positions from which they shelled Soviet bases. For example, the helicopters regularly patrolled the areas around the villages of Gourdjay and Chakaray, which were good vantage points for shelling Kabul. These operations had limited success, as the Mujahideen made ever-increasing use of timer-actuated truck-mounted rocket launchers which disappeared immediately. As Colonel Aleksandr V. Rutskoy (a Su-25 pilot who later gained notoriety as one of the instigators of the failed 1993 coup) put it, "The air force flew just for the sake of flying and crushing stone."

Top: This rather bucolic scene, photographed during the Soviet disengagement from Afghanistan, shows a late-model Mi-24P (note RWR antennas on the nose) in standard camouflage, alongside two heavily-armed Mil Mi-8TV 'Hip-Hs' – both of which are fitted with the EVU IR-suppressors.

Above: One of the most important tasks for 'Hinds' in Afghanistan was to provide air cover for the resupply convoys that were the life blood of the Soviet garrisons in the field. This Afghan air force Mi-24V, carrying a full load of rockets, is escorting a convoy departing Kabul.

Most surviving Mi-24D 'Hind-Ds' are to be found in service with the former Warsaw Pact nations of Eastern Europe. Hungary's 87th 'Bakony' Combat Helicopter Regiment, based at Szentkirályszabadja, operates a mix of Mi-24Ds and Mi-24Vs. Under conditions of some secrecy, Hungary took delivery of 14 additional Mi-24Ds and six Mi-24Ps, all from ex-East German stocks, after Hungary's then-Minister of Defence György Keleti struck a deal with his German counterpart, Volker Rühe, in May 1995. Germany agreed to supply surplus military equipment – including (specifically) non-combat training aircraft. As a result, 20 Aero L-39ZOs were acquired, and so was the much larger batch of dedicated attack helicopters. The dismantled 'Hinds' were delivered to Hungary by rail, at night, and were soon hidden away in hangars. But no funds were made available to overhaul these aircraft or place them into service, and they have remained in a deteriorating condition ever since.

A village named Ada near Jalalabad, from where the air base was regularly shelled, was 'soup of the day' for the local helicopter pilots, who eventually levelled the luckless village. Many other villages near air bases met the same fate; caught in the perpetual crossfire between Afghan and Soviet forces, they were reduced to rubble and burnt-out fields.

Even the final months of the war were marked with losses. Two Mi-24s were shot down on 21 August and 30 September 1988, killing the crews. On the night of 2 February 1989, 50th OSAP CO Colonel A. Golovanov and his WSO S. Peshelhodko were killed in action while reconnoitring the pull-out route. Their helicopter was the last of 333 'Hinds' shot down in Afghanistan.

Iran-Iraq war

The Iran-Iraq war of 1980-1988 became another major chapter in the career of the 'Hind'. Iraqi Air Force Mi-24As and Mi-25s were used for a variety of tasks, including destruction of soft-skinned and armoured vehicles, personnel, artillery, emplacements and bridges, escorting heliborne assaults, providing CAS for armoured groups and commandos, minelaying, reconnaissance, artillery spotting and even chemical warfare.

In the course of the war there were 118 aircraft/helicopter engagements and 56 helicopter/helicopter engagements, including 10 between Iraqi 'Hinds' and Islamic Iranian Air Force AH-1J SeaCobras. The outcome of such engagements depended mainly on the situation and crew skill. If the SeaCobra pilots were lucky enough to spot the enemy first they tried to take him out with TOW anti-tank missiles at long range. If they missed, the AH-1J had no chances of outrunning the Mi-24 and would start turning sharply to prevent the 'Hind' crew taking accurate aim. In so doing, the Iranians would try to lure the pursuer within range of their air defences or would radio to Iranian fighters for help. If the Iraqis managed to catch the enemy off guard, they would climb to 1000 m (3,280 ft) and dive at the Cobra, trying to get it from behind.

The first air-to-air engagement involving a 'Hind' happened a few days before the Iran-Iraq war 'officially' began. On 7 September 1980 five Mi-24s crossed the border, attacking an Iranian border post; IRIAF fighters scrambled to intercept and shot down one of the attackers. The first helicopter duel in history took place in November 1980 near Dezful, Iran. Sneaking up unnoticed on a pair of Mi-24s, two SeaCobras attacked them with TOWs. One 'Hind' went down immediately, the other was damaged and crashed about 10 km (6 miles) away; the Iranians landed at the crash site and took a surviving Iraqi major prisoner. A second encounter between Mi-24s and AH-1Js happened on 24 April 1981 near Panjevin, and the scenario was repeated – the Iranians shot down both 'Hinds' with no losses themselves.

It was not until 14 September 1983 that the tables were turned, when an Mi-24 shot down a SeaCobra near Basra. On 5 February Iraq claimed the destruction of three more SeaCobras by Mi-24s. On 25 February 1984 a group of 'Hinds' attacked a group of AH-1Js, destroying three. Another SeaCobra fell victim to a 'Hind' on 13 February 1986, the Iranians also claiming one 'kill'. Three days later 'Khomeini's falcons' lost another AH-1J but took their revenge on 18 February, shooting down an Mi-24.

The last engagement between the two types was recorded on 22 May 1986 when Mi-24s attacked a pair of SeaCobras, destroying one of them. Thus, judging by the above data, the overall 'kill' ratio is 10:6 in favour of the 'Hind', although some Western experts claimed the opposite. Iraqi Mi-24s had encounters with other Iranian helicopters, as well: in May and June 1988 they shot down six AB 214s and one AB 212. By the end of the war Iraqi pilots flying Mi-8s, Mi-24As and Mi-25s and SA 342L Gazelles had destroyed 53 Iranian helicopters.

Iraqi 'Hinds' in the 1990s

One of the least known (and most shameful) pages in the operational history of the 'Hind' is the use of Mi-24s by Saddam Hussein to quell the Kurdish uprisings in northern Iraq. These operations, which deserve to be called genocide, included the use of chemical agents, though it is not clear whether the Mi-24 was the delivery vehicle. The type also participated in the Iraqi invasion of Kuwait in early August 1990, escorting Mi-8T and Mi-17 troopships, suppressing pockets of resistance and destroying a few Kuwaiti tanks. Fifteen Iraqi helicopters were lost to ground fire during the invasion, including a few 'Hinds'.

Conversely, Iraqi 'Hinds' were not used against the coalition during the Gulf War of 1991, and Saddam Hussein obviously wanted to save his combat helicopters for use

against 'the enemy within', i.e., the Kurds. Yet, losses were not altogether avoided. One Mi-25 was knocked out by an LGB dropped by a USAF F-15E, three more were destroyed on their hardstand by the vanguard of the US Army's 24th Infantry Division and a fifth was captured almost intact by the vanguard of the US Army's 28th Airborne Division at Basra.

After the coalition victory, 'No-Fly Zones' were established in northern and southern Iraq, but Iraqi air force aircraft regularly violated these zones, especially in the south where they were in action against Shiite rebels. 'Hinds' were used in these operations, which were finally terminated on 22 August 1992 when the USA threatened renewed strikes against Iraq. An Iraqi 'helicopter gunship' – almost certainly an Mi-25 – was destroyed along with several other military aircraft and an ammunition dump at Tikrit on the night of 26 May 1995. It is certain that the aircraft were sabotaged by oppositionary Iraqi National Congress forces.

Libyan 'Hinds'

Libyan Arab Republic Air Force (LARAF) Mi-25As and Mi-25s were actively used in the long and bloody civil war in Chad, supporting Goukouni Oueddi's pro-Libyan rebels who were fighting the regime of Hissen Habre backed by France and the US. In October 1980 LARAF 'Hinds' participated in the battles for the Chadian capital of N'djamena along with other Libyan aircraft, helping Oueddi to seize the city and win a temporary victory.

However, hostilities resumed a year later. In 1983 Libyan Mi-24As and Mi-25s saw action near Oum Chalouba, Abéché and Faya (Largeau), and raided Habre's bases in Sudan when the Kalat enclave was occupied by the Libyans. When luck turned against Oueddi in late 1986/early 1987, the 'Hinds' were used during the defence of Bardao, Zouar and Falah. One helicopter was shot down near the latter town on 3 January 1987.

In March 1987 Habre's troops began an offensive, seizing the LARAF base in Ouadi-Doum in northern Chad. The assorted aircraft captured there included three Mi-25s in reasonable condition. Habre turned them over to France, which, having thoroughly tested the helicopters, gave one 'Hind' to Great Britain and another to the US.

More frustration came on 8 August when Chadian forces overran Auzu, an LARAF base in the territory disputed by Chad and Libya, destroying one Mi-24 on the ground. From 17 to 23 August the Libyans launched a counter-offensive, to which the Chadians retaliated by shooting down nine LARAF aircraft (including an Mi-24 on the first day of the offensive) with captured Strela-2 (SA-7 'Grail')

Above and below: The Mi-24 has played a part in the ongoing and bitter civil war in Sri Lanka, between the Sinhalese-dominated government and the rebel Liberation Tigers of Tamil Eelam (LTTE). The LTTE, established in 1976, is conducting an armed struggle to gain independence for a separate Tamil state in the northern and eastern portions of Sri Lanka – a struggle which has claimed in excess of 40,000 lives since outright, open warfare began in 1983. In 1995 the Sri Lankan Air Force introduced its first six Mi-24Vs – three of which soon fell to hostile fire. Sri Lanka's 'Hind' force has since beeh quietly boosted to 13 aircraft, seven of which are now believed to remain in service.

shoulder-launched SAMs and vehicle-mounted S-175
Koob (SA-3 'Ganef') SAMs. Finally, on 5 September,
Chadian forces entered Libyan territory, raiding Maaten-as-
Sarah air base and knocking out two 'Hinds', one of which
was shot down while taking off, killing the crew.

The Western press often wrote that, owing to a shortage
of local personnel, Libyan military aircraft were flown by
Pakistani, North Korean, Syrian and Palestinian crews.
Quite possibly, Soviet personnel were also involved.

Syrian 'Hinds'

Syrian Air Force 'Hinds' made their debut in June 1982,
combating Israeli tanks in Lebanon during the fifth Arab-
Israeli war. Even though, generally, the Syrian Air Force
was no match for the Israelis during the June campaign,
Syrians helicopter operations can be deemed successful.
Together with SA 342L Gazelles, the Mi-24s made 93
sorties, scoring most of the 55 kills against Israeli tanks
claimed by the Syrian Air Force; they were especially
successful in an operation against an Israeli tank brigade
near the mountain village of Aon Zgalta. There were no
'Hind' losses during the summer campaign.

After the war, Syrian Mi-24s saw more action in
Lebanon – this time against paramilitary right-wing Christian
extremist groups. Their missions included blockading the
Lebanese coast in the areas controlled by the extremists. On
11 April 1989 a routine patrol mission ended in an incident

of mistaken identity when a pair of Syrian 'Hinds' attacked
two Soviet Navy support vessels (a tug and diver boat) 70 km
(44 miles) west of the port of Tar-toue, damaging them and
injuring seven sailors. Damascus acknowledged its fault and
presented an official apology.

Angolan 'Hinds'

In Angola the Mi-24V (Mi-35) was introduced in the
mid-1980s. Originally flown by Cuban and East German
crews, Angolan 'Hind-Ds' saw action against the UNITA
guerrillas led by Doctor Jonas Savimbi and supported by the
South African Defence Force (SADF). In addition to their
usual missions, they always escorted major supply convoys
which were a vulnerable and lucrative target. The Mi-25s
were much used against UNITA near Mavinga and
Cassinga, which were the scene of fierce fighting. Western
reports that by late 1985 all Angolan Air Force 'Hinds' had
been destroyed or rendered unserviceable gives some indication of the intensity of the fighting; e.g., an Mi-25 was
shot down on 3 June 1985 and another on 23 June.

The opposing forces admitted the high survivability of
the 'Hind', noting that weapons with a calibre of less than
23 mm were useless against it. Hence, both UNITA and the
SADF made wide use of Soviet-built air defence systems
captured from the Angolan Armed Forces – ZU-23-2 AA
guns, ZSU-23-4 quadruple self-propelled AA guns, Strela-1
SAM batteries and Strela-2/-2M and 9K38 Igla-1 (SA-18)
shoulder-launched SAMs. SADF units were also armed
with Bofors AA guns and Cactus SAM batteries. Angolan
helicopter pilots responded to this threat by inventing new
tactics. Flying at treetop level was one; the dense jungle
effectively muffled engine noise and rotor slap, and the
enemy could not detect the helicopter until it was on them.
Not to be outdone, UNITA soon began putting 'crocodile
hunters' armed with shoulder-launched SAMs in the tree-
tops to deprive the Angolans of this advantage.

A fresh batch of Mi-35s was delivered to the Angolan
Air Force in 1986 as attrition replacements. Between
October 1987 and early 1988 they were in action against
the SADF near Cuito Cuanavale, inflicting heavy losses in
both personnel and materiel. After the South African withdrawal from the conflict, UNITA had to deal with the
omnipresent 'crocodiles' on its own. At least three Mi-35s
were shot down on 27 September 1988, 22 August 1989
and 25 February 1990. Another 'Hind' was lost on 28
January 1990 when it crashed during a sand storm, killing
two of the seven occupants and injuring the other five.

When Soviet, Cuban and East German military advisors
left, the Angolan Air Force immediately faced huge problems maintaining equipment and skills. Today, only a
handful of Angolan 'Hinds' remains operational because
new equipment and spares supplies from Russia have been
reduced to a trickle or dried up completely. These few are
still in action against UNITA rebels.

Vietnamese 'Hinds'

The Vietnam People's Air Force (VPAF) took delivery
of its first Mi-24s in the mid-1980s, using them in
Vietnamese Army operations against the Khmer Rouge in
neighbouring Kampuchea. A few were also operated by the
Kampuchean (Cambodian) Air Force. The Vietnamese
were known to use the same tactic the US Army had used

against them in the Vietnam War. When a spotter aircraft – a Cessna O-1 or an Antonov An-2 – patrolling over the jungle located a target, the crew fired FFARs or dropped hand grenades filled with white phosphorus (the An-2s were locally modified with UB-16-57 FFAR pods). The burning phosphorus produced a dense white smoke that could be seen for miles, guiding the attack helicopters.

Indian 'Hinds'

The Indian Air Force (IAF) had a chance to evaluate the Mi-24 a few years before acquiring the type, and press reports indicated that groups of IAF pilots were in action in Afghanistan, practising and studying strike helicopter operations. Shortly after buying the first batch of Mi-25s in late 1984, India used them against the Pakistan Army when fighting broke out over the disputed Siachin Glacier in 1987.

The most celebrated action of the Indian 'crocodiles' was the Indian Peacekeeping Force operation in Sri Lanka in 1987-1989, an attempt to put an end to the prolonged civil war in that country (see *World Air Power Journal*, Volume 4). The Mi-25's first operation in that mission was the defence of Jaffna against the rebel Liberation Tigers of Tamil Eelam (LTTE) in October 1987. The 'Hinds' hunted and destroyed LTTE groups, escorted Mi-8T and Mi-17 transport and troopship helicopters of the IAF's 109th, 119th and 129th Squadrons during Operations Trishul and Viraat, cut the rebels' communications, and were used against LTTE boats carrying weapons and supplies across the Palk Strait. Other major actions were a battle with the Tigers in March 1989 which went on for several days (in which Mi-25s operating from Trincomalee and Vavuniya supported five Peacekeeping Force battalions) and Operation Checkmate held in the autumn of 1989 to prevent the LTTE from disrupting the municipal elections.

Throughout the peacekeeping mission, IAF Mi-25s and Mi-35s used only FFARs and machine-guns against LTTE targets. The ATGM launchers were removed, since there were no targets that merited a guided missile. There were no losses on the Indians' part, as the rebels' small arms fire was useless against the 'Hind'.

Sri Lankan 'Hinds'

In November 1995 the Sri Lankan Air Force acquired its own Mi-24Vs, using them with considerable success in a major air/land/sea assault called Operation Riverisa (Sunshine) and later in Riverisa II and Riverisa III. One 'Hind-E' (CH 614) was lost on 19 March 1997 when it exploded and crashed into the Bay of Bengal off Mullaittivu, killing the pilot. Since Mullaittivu is in the north of the island held by the LTTE, the helicopter was almost certainly shot down by the rebels who had obtained some shoulder-launched SAMs during the brief ceasefire of 1995.

Another was shot down near the same spot by a Stinger missile on 10 November 1997 while escorting SLAF Mi-17 troopship helicopters. The helicopter managed to deflect

the first Stinger with its IRCM equipment but was immediately hit by a second missile and crashed into the Kokilai lagoon. Two crew were killed and another two were rescued by Navy divers. The explosion also damaged one of the Mi-17s, which force-landed with no injuries to the occupants. Previously, on 12 September a third Mi-24V had been hit by AA fire near Puliyankulam during Operation Jaya Sikurui; this left the SLAF with just three serviceable 'Hinds'.

Nicaraguan 'Hinds'

A batch of Mi-25Ds was delivered to Nicaragua in 1983-1984 to help the Sandinista government of Daniel Ortega fight the Contras.

The 'Hind' was used both in the attack and counter-air roles, its high performance enabling it to intercept all types of aircraft used by the Contras. These were mostly light aircraft equipped for the COIN role, but sometimes the Mi-25s encountered more potent adversaries. For example, on 13 September 1985 as Fuerza Aérea Sandinista Mi-25s attacked enemy positions near Jalapa not far from the Honduran border, several F-86 Sabres and A-37 Dragonflies came to the rescue from across the border. One helicopter was damaged and force-landed, though it is not known whether the Contras or the Honduran Air Force was credited with this kill.

The biggest threat came from the Stinger and Redeye shoulder-launched SAMs used by the Contras, to which two 'Hind-Ds' were lost on 5 March and 19 June 1987. Another Mi-25 was lost in December 1988 when its pilot, Edwin Estrada Leiva, defected to Honduras – possibly lured by an ad in the *Soldier of Fortune* magazine offering US$10,000 to anyone who accomplished this 'feat'.

When the Contras won and the civil war ended in 1990, poverty-stricken Nicaragua could not afford to keep the Mi-25s and soon sold them to Peru. The latter nation was already a 'Hind' operator, having acquired 12 Mi-25s from

Opposite page and above: India acquired its first 'Hinds' in 1984, all Mi-25V 'Hind-Es' (along with the IAF's unique Mi-25V trainers). India's 'Hinds' have fought in border skirmishes against Pakistan, but received their true baptism of fire in 1987 during India's ultimately unsuccessful military actions in support of the Sri Lankan government, against the LTTE. The 'Hinds' flew sustained CAS missions, often armed with four 250-kg (551-lb) OFAB-250 bombs (opposite page), as the 'Hind' is an accurate dive-bomber. The Mi-25s also escorted Mi-8 troopships on airborne assault missions. The last Indian forces left Sri Lanka in 1990. As a result of their combat experience, India's Mi-25s were refitted with improved side-mounted ASO-2V chaff/flare dispensers. Also added were L-006 RAWS antennas (above).

'Hind-G1'

Mi-24R (Mi-24RKhR) 'Hind-G1' (Izdelye 2462)
Mil developed a dedicated NBC reconnaissance 'Hind' to replace the Mi-8VD of the mid-1970s. Service designation was Mi-24R (*[vertolyot-] razvedchik* = reconnaissance [helicopter]) or Mi-24RKhR (*dlya rahdiatseeonno-khimeecheskoy razvedki* = for NBC reconnaissance). The latter designation has been misrepresented as 'Mi-24RKR' or even 'Mi-24RCh' in Western publications. Mil's designation was Izdelye 2462, suggesting that it was based on the Mi-24D (Izdelye 246).

The Mi-24R would measure radiation and chemical/biological contamination levels and transmit this data to C³I centres by datalink. It had an air-sampling unit which breathed through a large protruding ventral intake offset to port aft of the nose gear, exhausting through a slit in the fuselage side above it (usually covered by wire mesh). The ATGM launchers on the wing endplates were replaced by unique remote-controlled claw-shaped devices for

The 'Hind-G1' was built because it was assumed that future wars would be fought in an NBC-contaminated environment. The Mi-24R's inboard pylons were usually occupied by drop tanks and the outboard pylons by additional mission equipment in small square-section pods, leaving the helicopter with only the nose-mounted machine-gun (or rockets, if required).

taking soil samples (called 'excavators' in OKB parlance), so the Raduga-F was deleted, as was the strike camera on the port wingtip.

The cabin, which accommodated mission equipment control consoles and two equipment operators, featured an enhanced life support and NBC protection system, yet the crew wore full NBC suits on operational missions. The two small windows in the upper segment of the port cabin door were replaced by a single elongated blister window to give one of the operators a degree of downward view. Finally, a triangular plate of unknown purpose (possibly a counterweight to balance the equipment in the nose) was mounted on the tailskid of production Mi-24Rs.

The uncoded prototype was converted in late 1978 from an early-production Mi-24V built in late 1977 (c/n 3532424708820). Production Mi-24Rs had

c/ns commencing with 353462. Curiously, the prototype lacked intake filters and had IRCM flare packs scabbed on outboard of the 'excavators'; in production these were carried as usual, under the tailboom or on the aft fuselage sides. Some 152 Mi-24Rs were built between 1983 and 1989.

Mi-24RA 'Hind-G1' (Izdelye 2462)
In 1989 some Mi-24Rs were equipped with an upgraded intelligence processing and communications suite and the crew was reduced to three (pilot, WSO and one equipment operator). 'Hind-G1s' thus modified were redesignated Mi-24RA. It is possible that these aircraft lacked the wingtip 'excavators', the port one being replaced by a small equipment pod, and had the standard strike camera. One such aircraft coded 'Yellow 46' was stationed in Germany.

'Hind-G2'

Mi-24K 'Hind-G2' (Izdelye 201)
In 1979 Mil rolled out the prototype of the Mi-24K (*korrekteerovschchik*) photo reconnaissance/artillery spotter version, aka Izdelye 201. Based on the Mi-24V, it was intended to replace the Mi-8TARK (Mi-8T *artillereeyskiy razvedchik-korrekteerovschchik* = artillery recce/spotter). Its mission was battlefield observation and tactical reconnaissance, spotting for artillery and missile units, and aerial photography.

The Raduga-F LLLTV/FLIR was replaced by an Iris wide-angle optical sensor system (possibly with other modes than optical) in a recontoured fairing with a characteristically curved upward-hinging protective cover over the sensor window; it featured a system of movable mirrors to increase the field of view. The cabin housed an AFA-100 oblique camera (*aerofotoapparaht* = aircraft camera) and a Ruta reconnaissance and spotting suite comprising an optical target identification system, a computer and a 'data processor' [*sic*, possibly meaning a data presentation system]. This necessitated major structural changes: the port-side cabin door was eliminated, leaving only the two rearmost windows, and a large rectangular camera window with optically-flat glass was added low on the fuselage side where the front end of the lower door half would have been. The starboard door was retained for access to the equipment.

The camera and optical sensors were operated by the WSO from the front cockpit. The Mi-24K had no provision for ATGMs (with no launch rails or guidance system fitted), but the machine-gun and rocket pods were retained.

The Mi-24K entered production in 1983, and 163 had been completed by 1989. Neither the Mi-24R nor the Mi-24K was exported, but both were stationed outside the Soviet Union (in former East Germany).

This Mi-24K 'Yellow 23' was based at Parchim with the 439th OVP. The reconfigured windows on the starboard side provided a field of view for the large onboard optics.

the Soviet Union in the early 1980s. Peruvian Mi-25s were used against the local drug cartels, the infamous Sendero Luminoso (Shining Path) Maoist terror organisation, and the equally radical Tupac Amaru Liberation Movement.

Sierra Leone 'Hinds'

In Sierra Leone the ill-trained government forces were steadily losing ground to the Revolutionary United Front (RUF), in effect a bunch of thugs led by Corporal Alfred Foday Sankoh with Libyan affiliations, anti-Western ideas and a determination to seize power. The tiny Sierra Leone Air Force, consisting of a single Mi-17-1V (Mi-

8MTV-2) gunship and a single Mi-24V (both flown by Belarussian contract crews and presumably acquired in Belarus), was used against the RUF on armed reconnaissance missions and, while greatly intimidating the rebels, had difficulty finding and attacking them in the dense jungle. Things got better only when the ruling military junta, the National Provisional Ruling Council (NPRC), hired Executive Outcomes (EO), a 'proactive security organisation' based in Pretoria, to conduct operations against the RUF and provide tactical planning and personnel training (see *World Air Power Journal*, Volume 28).

The 'Hind' was used mostly as a troopship and an escort aircraft, providing top cover for the 'Hip-H' gunship and EO's own Mi-17s,

US Army 'Hinds'

The US Army has at least two operational Mi-24s, with others held for spares support and testing. The flying 'Hinds' include this 'Hind-D' (above and right, new and old paint scheme) and an Mi-24P (below).

The Mi-24 'Hinds' of the US Army's Operational Test and Evaluation Command Threat Support Activity

Biggs Army Air Field is situated in southwest Texas near the border city of El Paso and is part of the Fort Bliss complex. At one time Biggs AAF was host to B-36s of Strategic Air Command. Now home to a variety of US Army rotary- and fixed-wing aircraft, the base is relatively quiet except for occasional exercises such as Roving Sands. The Biggs AAF flight line is bordered by hangars built in the 1940s and 1950s. One hangar, situated in the middle of the flight line, is surrounded by chain link fencing, itself covered with material that makes looking inside nearly impossible. The surrounding area is monitored by television cameras, and electric gates control entry and exit from the hangar. Additionally, access to the ramp from the hangar is controlled by electrically operated gates. The reason for this degree of security is the presence of the US Army's Operational Test and Evaluation Command Threat Support Activity (OTSA). This unique Army unit flies a variety of Russian aircraft including Mil Mi-2s, Mi-8s, Mi-17s, Mi-24s and Antonov An-2s.

In addition to supporting the joint Roving Sands exercises, OTSA aircraft contribute to USAF Red Flag and Green Flag exercises, held at Nellis ASFB, Nevada, and to the US Army's battalion-level training exercises held at the National Training Center, Fort Irwin, California. During an exercise such as Green Flag or Red Flag, Red force OTSA aircraft fly primarily in the interdiction role. Operating from the surface to a maximum of 200 ft (61 m), their role is to assault Blue (friendly) forces which enter their area of operations. This would include C-130s attempting to insert troops or materials. The OPTEC 'Hinds' would also interdict any BLUFOR helicopter operations such as SAR or long-range patrols. As a component of OPFOR – the US Army's 'Opposition Force' – OTSA maintains a presence at Fort Polk, Louisiana, home of the Joint Readiness Training Center. OTSA also provides threat simulation for the Apache and Comanche development programmes. Additionally, any Department of Defense agency can call on OTSA to test improvements to new US air defence systems and programmes anywhere in the world.

A select few US Army pilots and civilian technicians were first introduced to a captured Mi-24 'Hind' in the mid-1980s. The exact date is still classified and the sources and methods of acquisition of the remainder of the OTSA fleet of Russian-designed aircraft are also officially classified (see Mi-24 operators section for further details of the current aircraft). The OTSA fleet is kept airworthy by a staff of experienced maintainers drawn from the civilian/commercial rotary-wing field, as well as from the military.

OTSA operates three Mi-24/Mi-25 'Hinds' of different sub-types, all of which have been slightly modified (through the addition of the MILES laser training system) for their new-found training role. Two aircraft are believed to be former East German aircraft, acquired following German reunification in 1990: an Mi-24D named *Wild Thing* (with Tasmanian Devil nose-art) and an Mi-24P, *Patience*. The third aircraft, *Warlord* (?), is an Mi-25D captured from Iraqi forces in the aftermath of Operation Desert Storm (this aircraft was exhibited in full Iraqi camouflage and markings but its current status is unknown). It is likely that OPTEC had access to other aircraft in previous years, thanks largely to the French, who captured Libyan 'Hinds' in Chad during the mid-1980s. It is possible that one of the 'Hinds' which defected to Pakistan from Afghanistan in the early 1980s also found its way to the USA.

David F. Brown

which inserted and extracted search-and-destroy and mortar teams and carried supplies. CAS missions were also flown occasionally. The aircraft operated by EO were based at Freetown-Lungi airport, but purpose-built helipads were also established near Koidu.

The Mi-24's armament usually consisted of UB-32A FFAR pods and sometimes GUV gun pods in both machine-gun and grenade-launcher configurations. The nose-mounted YakB-12,7 machine-gun was described as 'deadly accurate' and the AGS-17 grenade launcher was found to be very effective against area targets. The Belarussians were Afghan veterans and used that experience to advantage, including the use of S-5S 'meat grinder' flechette rockets against RUF personnel. Drop tanks were rarely carried because they only left two wing stations free for weapons; the problem of limited range was solved by using the Mi-17s to carry fuel drums to helipads. The main problem with Mi-24 operations was that neither the Belarussians nor the South Africans spoke each other's language. Hence, a Sierra Leone officer who spoke Russian had to be carried as an interpreter, which complicated operations and increased the risk of 'friendly fire' casualties during CAS missions.

EO accomplished more in a week (not counting planning, training and preparation time) than the Republic of Sierra Leone Military Force had in four years of bush warfare. Soon EO and RSLMF personnel had recaptured the diamond-rich Kono district, and the first of the 30,000-odd inhabitants forced out of the area by the rebels' raids began to return. Eventually, the RUF was forced to call a ceasefire (though mainly in order to regroup and re-arm, as intelligence reports plainly indicated) and begin negotiations with the government.

UN 'Hinds' in Croatia

In the spring of 1996 the specially-formed 8th Combat Helicopter Squadron of the Ukrainian Army Aviation commanded by Colonel A. I. Lev was seconded to the United Nations Transitional Administration in Eastern Slavonia (UNTAES). UNTAES had been established in June 1996 to oversee the transition of this fertile and oil-rich enclave occupied by separatist Serbs since 1991 back to Croatian rule (the local Serb minority had raised a rebellion when Croatia declared independence from federal Yugoslavia).

On 10 April 1997 the squadron's six Mi-24P 'Hind-F' gunships and four Mi-24K 'Hind-G2' reconnaissance helicopters arrived at Klisa airport, located between Osijek and Vukovar. Only a few days earlier Klisa had been the scene of fierce fighting between Serbs and Croats. The helicopters were painted in the UN peacekeeping forces' white colour scheme with 'United Nation' titles. This was the first time that the Mi-24 – or the Ukraine – had participated in UN operations (see *World Air Power Journal*, Volume 30).

"We landed on an airstrip with Serb guns a mere 1.5 km [0.93 miles] away," Ukrainian Army Aviation Commander Colonel A. D. Korniyets recalled. "Now that peacekeeping operations are in progress, our pilots are patrolling the demilitarised zone, conducting reconnaissance and escorting Mi-8MT transport helicopters operated by a second Ukrainian squadron. Sorties are flown with full armament, including ATGMs; luckily, we haven't been forced to fire yet. In the first two months, 8th Sqn helicopters have logged 288 hours in 237 sorties and earned praise from the UNPF commander, the Belgian Major General Jozef Schoups. It should be noted that the UN pays the Ukraine US$2,900 for every hour of Mi-24 operations and the contract amount for the [first] six months in Eastern Slavonia is US$8 million."

The one-year UNTAES mandate was later extended for a second year and Ukrainian 'Hind' operations in Eastern Slavonia continued. The two Ukrainian squadrons were later combined into a single unit (17th Sqn) under Colonel Vladimir Pastukhov. It quickly turned out that the language barrier hampered operations, so translators were drafted in from the Ukrainian armed forces and tactical interpreters were carried for communication with NATO forces. By May 1997 UNTAES' 'Hip-Hs' and 'Hinds' had flown a total of 2,500 hours and carried some 7,000 passengers.

Croatian Mi-24Vs acquired in 1993-94 were used in the civil war in the former Yugoslavia, operating against the army of 'the current Yugoslavia' (Serbia and Montenegro). The 'Hinds' were acquired because neither the MiG-21bis nor the Mi-8TB could provide adequate battlefield support for the Croatian Army (and the slower 'Hips' were sometimes shot down on CAS missions). Armed with FAB-250 and -500 HE bombs, ZB-500GD napalm bombs (*zazhi-*

The introduction of Mi-24Ds to Nicaragua during 1983/84 (right) was perceived as a major destabilising move in the region by the USA. Nicaragua's Marxist Sandinista government was thought to be a major threat to neighbouring states, and the US waged a proxy war against the Nicaraguans through the Honduras-based Contra rebel forces. Overhead reconnaissance imagery of Sandino Airport, taken by USAF SR-71s or U-2s and showing several Mi-24s, and Mi-17s, was released by the US as evidence of the military build-up in Nicaragua. The 'Hinds' and 'Hips' (below) operated from Augusto César Sandino Airport (Managua), Punta Huete, Montelimar, Puerto Cabezas, Esteli, La Rosita, Bluefields and El Bluff.

Above: Nicaragua's Mi-24s did see combat, including air-to-air engagements with Honduran fighters. A peace deal was finally brokered between the two opposing sides, followed by elections in which Daniel Ortega's Sandinista government was removed from power. Much of Nicaragua's military was then dismantled, and the Mi-25s were sold to Peru.

gahtel'nii bahk ghidroreagheerouyouschchevo deystviya = literally 'water-reacting incendiary tank'), B8V-20 FFAR pods, 9M114 Shturm ATGMs and even Mk 44 auto-tracking torpedoes, the 'Hinds' operated from numerous agricultural fields in the war zone.

CIS conflict – Azerbaijan and Armenia

The Mi-24 has also seen quite a lot of action in its home country. Shortly before the break-up of the Soviet Union, a spate of bloody ethnic conflicts erupted in the southern republics. The first was the Nagornii Karabakh enclave, the subject of a long-standing territorial dispute between Armenia and Azerbaijan. As the Soviet Army was put into action to disengage the belligerents, Army Aviation 'Hinds'

patrolled over the front lines, escorted vehicle convoys and transport helicopters and suppressed artillery. Of course, both the Armenians and the Azeris fired at the helicopters with whatever weapons they had, from shotguns to 'anti-hail' guns (World War II-vintage AA guns firing special rounds filled with rainmaking compounds).

Mi-24s were among the heavy equipment used in a notorious riot control action in Baku. About the same time, a 'Hind' was seriously damaged by 'anti-hail' artillery near Gyandzha, making a forced landing. In July-August 1991 the press reported that Soviet Army Aviation helicopters were in action on the Azeris' side in Nagornii Karabakh. These operations were not altogether without incident, as when on 20 July 1991 three 'Hinds' were damaged by ground fire while attacking Armenian positions near Bouzlouk village in the Shaoumian region of the enclave and one crew member was wounded.

The conflict escalated still further after the break-up of the Soviet Union. The Azeris 'nationalised' a squadron of Mi-24s based at Sangachaly AB, as did the Armenians with the helicopters based near Yerevan.

Unfortunately, Russian Army units of the Transcaucasian Defence District also became involved in the hostilities. On 3 February 1992 Russian Army 'Hinds' escorting an Mi-26 'Halo' heavy transport helicopter carrying Armenian refugees were forced to drive off an unmarked Mi-8 which attempted an attack on the transport. However, the Mi-26 was downed by a shoulder-launched SAM and six people died in the ensuing crash. From 23 February to 7 March, the Mi-24s provided cover for Russian Air Force Mi-6s and Mi-26s airlifting 366th Mechanised Infantry Regiment personnel and equipment out of Stepanakert, Azerbaijan; one of the 'Hinds' was damaged and forced down by the Azeris. On 12 May several Russian 'Hinds' participated in the evacuation of the bodies of those killed in the 3 February shoot-down.

Azeri Mi-24s – piloted by ex-Soviet Air Force mercenary pilots hired by the Azeris – were first noted in Nagornii Karabakh on 19 February 1992 when they attacked Armenian positions near Karagaly village. The helicopters saw much action against Armenian tanks and fortifications. The Armenians claimed two Azeri 'Hinds' shot down in March 1992, another on 18 September that year and one more on 1 September 1993; not all of the crews lived.

In April 1992 the Armenians hijacked two Mi-24s operated by an independent squadron of the Russian Army's 7th GvVP (Gvardeyskiy vertolyotnii polk, Guards helicopter regiment) but returned them a few days later. The earliest confirmed reports of Armenian 'Hinds' date to August 1992. The Armenians used the type mostly for tactical reconnaissance and the 'Hinds' participated in most major operations against the Azeris, such as the Kelbojar operation. Losses included one Mi-24 shot down in September 1992 and another on 12 November. According to Western sources, by early 1993 Armenia and Azerbaijan had 11 and eight 'Hinds' on strength, respectively.

Civil war in Georgia

Even before the break-up of the Soviet Union, a prolonged civil war began in Georgia where South Osetia strove for independence. The South Osetian city of Tskhinvali was home to a Russian Army helicopter regiment flying Mi-8s and Mi-24s, which had orders to stay out of the conflict but frequently disobeyed them. On 12 February 1991 the 'Hinds' forced down a Georgian Civil Aviation Directorate Mi-8T which had violated the 'No-Fly Zone' over South Osetia and which, in addition to 'innocent civilians', was carrying weapons and ammunition. In June 1992, by when the Soviet Union was no more, the Mi-24s flew a sortie against Georgian APCs which habitually attacked the airfield with machine-gun fire. One of the APCs was put out of action; the enraged crew threatened to go in and murder the pilots but had no time to carry out

the threat, as the unit was disbanded in the same month and the helicopters were turned over to the Georgian army.

Less than two months later the new owners put the helicopters to good use when a new civil war broke out, this time in Abkhasia in the northwest of the republic. In addition to supporting Georgian troops which seized the Abkhasi capital of Sukhumi, the Mi-24s were used against Abkhasi armoured vehicles and boats, and filled the COIN role. On the night of 27 December 1992 they foiled an attempt to insert an Abkhasi sabotage group, damaging a gunboat. The first Georgian 'Hind' was shot down on 5 October 1992, and another was lost on 4 July 1993. There are reasons to believe that both helicopters fell victim to Strela-3 shoulder-launched SAMs.

It should be noted that, whether wilfully or by mistake, Georgian Mi-24 pilots frequently attacked Russian facilities in the area, ranging from a military seismic research laboratory to health and holiday resorts. At an early stage of the conflict, on 27 August 1992, a Georgian Mi-24 attacked the Russian Kometa-44 passenger hydrofoil in the Black Sea, killing one passenger and injuring 11 more. The Abkhasi war was followed by a new conflict in which the Georgian 'Hinds' were in action against armed groups loyal to the deposed President Zviad Gamsakhourdia.

Abkhasia, Tajikistan and Osetia

The Russian Army was dragged into the Abkhasi war as well. Russian Mi-24s flew primarily escort missions for transport helicopters and were fired upon by both Georgians and Abkhazis. Occasionally, however, they had to fire in anger when called upon to unblock Russian vehicle convoys. In October 1992 it was a case of 'crocodile eat crocodile', when an unmarked (probably Abkhasi) Mi-24 unsuccessfully attacked an Mi-8 carrying future Georgian President Eduard A. Shevardnadze to the conflict zone and was driven off by the escorting 'Hinds'.

In the same year, Tajikistan joined the list of places in the former Soviet Union where the 'Hind' was at war. Russian, Uzbek and Tajik Mi-24s were in action all over the republic against the armed Islamic opposition striving to topple the Dushanbe government. Starting in August 1992, they were tasked with destroying tanks which the Islamists had stolen from the Russian Army's 181st Armour Regiment/201st Mechanised Infantry Division in Kurgan-Tyube. In December the tri-national 'Hind' force participated in the defeat of the opposition forces near Kofirnihon, losing one helicopter to ground fire on 18 December. The next spring it helped to squeeze out of the Gharm region. Later, the main action moved south to the Afghan border; the Islamists' bases and training camps were located on Afghan territory, and sometimes the 'Hinds' would cross the border to get at them.

In the autumn of 1992 there was trouble again in Osetia, this time in North Osetia, which is part of the Russian Federation. A breach occurred between the Osetians and the Ingushes, and in November Russian federal troops (including helicopter units) were pulled into the conflict zone. The Mi-24s were tasked mainly with reconnaissance but sometimes flew strike sorties as well, as when on 4

November an 'unidentified' (as official reports phrased it, meaning suspicious) convoy consisting of two APCs and four trucks was destroyed.

A pair of Mi-24Vs overflew the Russian Federal Government building (known as the White House) during the failed hard-line Communist coup of October 1993.

Chechnya

In September 1994 the Mi-24 made its debut in Chechnya. Four well-used examples were flown by contract pilots hired by the Provisional Council of the Chechen Republic (PCCR) which opposed the government of General Dzhokhar Dudayev and his separatist tendencies. More 'Hinds' were acquired later and used with considerable success against government forces. On 30 September, 10 and 25 October and 25 November 1994, they raided airfields controlled by Dudayev, destroying or damaging several aircraft and helicopters.

On 23 November 1994 a joint strike group composed of Russian Air Force Su-25s and Chechen opposition 'Hinds' attacked a Chechen government armour regiment at its home base in Shali, destroying 21 tanks and 14 APCs, and killing 201 men. Three days later seven Mi-24s supported an unsuccessful armoured assault on the Chechen capital of Groznii in which Dudayev's forces claimed one helicopter shot down. In early December the Russian Federal Border Guards reported that PCCR Mi-24s had shot down an unidentified transport aircraft heading for Azerbaijan.

Meanwhile, as a result of Dudayev's separatism and the activities of illegal armed units, Chechnya was rapidly turning into a rogue state. Deciding it had had enough, Moscow issued an ultimatum demanding compliance with federal laws, which Groznii ignored. On 11 December 1994 the Russian federal armed forces began an all-arms offensive in Chechnya. It soon turned into a full-scale war which went on for 18 months until a ceasefire was signed in Khasavyurt on 30 August 1996. Even now, the situation in and around the republic is far from peaceful.

Right: Seen on 11 December 1994, this Mi-24V climbs away over the shattered remains of Groznii-Severnyy airport. The most widely publicised operations involving Russian Army 'Hinds' in Chechnya were the repeated attacks on Bamut village and the deactivated ICBM launch pad nearby, which the Chechens had turned into a fortress, and the (largely unsuccessful) liberation of hostages in Kizlyar.

Above: In the latter stages of the Chechen war, 'Hinds' were mainly used in the COIN, armed reconnaissance and convoy escort roles. FFARs and 9M114 Shturm ATGMs were the Mi-24's main weapons. The rockets were used strictly against area targets only, while the guided missiles were generally used against pre-set targets, such as ammunition dumps and Chechen tanks and IFVs.

Top: This typical scene across a Russian camp outside Groznii comes replete with bad weather and primitive facilities.

Two squadrons of Mi-24s were in action in Chechnya. Current Russian army aviation utilisation norms state that 65 to 70 per cent of the flight time in a combat situation should be allocated to actual combat operations, 15 per cent to transport operations and 5 to 10 per cent to 'special missions'. However, in the opening stage of the war (December 1994/January 1995) actual combat operations – mostly CAS and convoy escort – accounted for just 17 per cent of the flight time; this decreased still further from 6 January due to the seizure of Groznii by the ground forces. While the 'Hinds' were not used for troop support during street fighting in Groznii (presumably to avoid blue-on-blue incidents), they joined other helicopters in carrying troops, ammunition, wounded personnel and refugees. Mi-24s saw much action against the Chechen separatists in the south of the republic, each crew making five or six sorties (averaging 40 to 45 minutes) per day.

Generally, helicopter operations in the Chechen war were rather limited, due partly to the helicopters' inadequate navigation capabilities. Operations resembled World War II

in that CAS sorties were mostly flown in the daytime and in good visibility. The 'Hinds' flew only when visibility exceeded 1.5 km (0.93 miles) and the pilots were able to see the target clearly. Another factor limiting Mi-24 operations was that most 'Hinds' seconded to the federal forces in Chechnya had already served 15 years or more and, unbelievably, were not fitted with IRCM equipment for protection against the rebels' heat-seeking missiles. Finally, ammunition was in short supply and sorties were flown with the rocket pods and gun ammunition boxes half-full at best. Small wonder the pilots called themselves 'kamikazes'!

Planning and execution

Intelligence gathered by spotters on the forward edge of the battle area (FEBA) was processed by a special Russian Army unit at Khankala AB (once held by the rebels). The data were sorted in order of importance and sent to the higher HQ in Mozdok where the ultimate decisions as to the use of army and tactical aviation were made. Some of the spotters admitted that "the war in Chechnya was a rather strange one" and illogical decisions were often made. For example, having received information on concentrations of enemy forces or the whereabouts of Chechen tactical bases which absolutely needed to be taken out with an air strike, the HQ in Mozdok would often cancel sorties. Infuriatingly, the Chechens somehow would learn about it, and in such instances the Russians' forward positions would receive an especially vicious hammering.

The spotters believed that in all 'friendly fire' incidents involving helicopters the pilots were at fault. There are three main reasons for this. Firstly, the pilots had lost the touch of operating in a combat environment and were often not ready psychologically to fly in the forward area. If the pilots were sure that the Chechens had SAMs in the area they were supposed to attack, they would often fire the rockets hastily and exit without determining where the rockets went. Secondly, ordnance was sometimes defective. There were cases of uncommanded FFAR launches, and cases when the rocket motors failed immediately after launch. Finally, the commanders on the ground were reluctant to mark the FEBA, fearing that the Chechens might use the markers for their own purposes. However, the latter fact – and arguably the second one, too – renders the spotters' 'guilty on all counts' statement somewhat tenuous.

By early March 1995, Russian Army Aviation had lost two Mi-24s in the war. On 27 September 1994 an Mi-24 operating from Mozdok was hit by heavy machine-gun fire and made a forced landing, one of the crew being fatally wounded. On 30 April 1995 an Mi-24 was damaged by machine-gun fire near the township of Gilyany but made it back to base. A third 'Hind' was shot down on 24 May over Chechen-Aoul village and the three crewmen were killed. On 4 June another Mi-24 was downed near the township of Nozhay-Yourt 70 km (43 miles) southeast of Groznii and both pilots were killed. Thus, four 'Hinds' were lost in the first six months of the war.

Belarus retained the Mi-24s stationed on its territory after the break-up of the Soviet Union. While not being involved in any ethnic conflicts, Belarussian 'Hinds' gained a place in infamy on 12 September 1995 when an Mi-24 crew shot down a wayward hot-air balloon which had been participating in an international air rally, near the town of Byaroza in the Brest region. The two American balloonists were killed in the incident. The official story was that the 'Hind' crew misidentified the brightly coloured balloon as an unmanned reconnaissance balloon – but nevertheless fired warning shots at it before shooting it down. To add insult to injury, the crew were later decorated for their 'brave' actions.

Yefim Gordon and **Dmitriy Komissarov**

'Hinds' served in the Afghan region long after the Soviet withdrawal. Above a Russian aircraft flies near a mortar post on the Tajik/Afghan border in 1995, while below is an aircraft operated by the Taliban.

Mi-24 Testbeds

Fenestron

In 1975 an uncoded 'Hind-B' – one of the original prototypes or possibly one of the 10 pre-production aircraft – was fitted experimentally with a large-diameter eight-bladed fenestron replacing the standard tail rotor and pylon. The stub wings were removed, probably to save weight.

Rear protection

During the Afghan war Mi-24 pilots kept urging the Mil OKB to give the 'Hind' some protection for its rear. While the Mi-8, another Afghan war workhorse, had a hatch in the port half of its clamshell cargo doors where a Kalashnikov RPK machine-gun or equivalent could be mounted to cover the rear hemisphere, the Mi-24 had no such measures and was often shot up after making an attack. About 48 per cent of all damage from ground fire on the Mi-24 was in the rear hemisphere, compared to some 27 per cent on the Mi-8.

In 1985 an Mi-24V coded 'Red 43' was fitted experimentally with a 12.7-mm NSVT-12,7 Utyos (Cliff) machine-gun in a bulged enclosure replacing the aft avionics bay. The gunner's station was accessed from within via a crawlway passing through the rear fuel tank between the mainwheel wells. Trials promptly showed that the rear gunner's station was not a success. It caused a major shift in the helicopter's centre of gravity position and was always full of engine exhaust gases, making things almost unbearable for the gunner. The crunch came when the modified helicopter was demonstrated to VVS top brass and one of the portly generals got stuck in the narrow crawlway when he wanted to check the gunner's station, and the idea was abandoned. Instead, rear view mirrors were installed on operational 'Hinds' so that pilots could see they were being fired upon and take evasive action.

Mi-28 'Havoc'

A number of Mi-24s served as systems and avionics testbeds for the Mi-28 'Havoc'. One of them, possibly an uncoded early-production Mi-24A with starboard-side tail rotor, was used to test the new main rotor. The helicopter in question featured a large lattice-like boom with air data sensors on the fuselage nose (the machine-gun had to be removed, of course). There was also a similarly equipped Mi-24A without stub wings and missile director antenna, which quite possibly was the same aircraft at a later stage. Another 'Hind' served as a testbed for the Mi-28's squashed-X tail rotor.

Filters

A Mi-24D coded 'Red 74' was used to test an early model of the vortex-type intake filters which became standard on late 'Hinds'. Unlike the production model resembling partly deflated footballs, these looked like large buckets. The helicopter still sits derelict at the flight test facility in Lyubertsy.

PrPNK-28

Two Mi-24Vs coded 'Red 19' and 'Red 73' were converted into testbeds for the PrPNK-28 targeting/flight instrumentation/navigation system. The entire nose section of a 'Havoc' with the revolving laser rangefinder/LLLTV turret and thimble radome for the missile guidance system was grafted onto the nose of the 'Hind' in lieu of the usual excrescences, giving the helicopter a bizarre appearance.

'Red 73' is now withdrawn from use at the helicopter flight test facility in Lyubertsy (just outside the Moscow city limits) used by both Mil and Kamov bureaux.

Green 'Hind'

An Mi-24V (identity unknown) was converted by the Polyot (Flight) Scientific and Production Association into an environmental survey aircraft for detecting oil spills in bodies of water, monitoring air pollution, etc. The USPU-24 gun barbette was replaced by a flat fairing containing sensors, making the helicopter appear to be rudely sticking out its tongue; the LLLTV/FLIR pod and missile launchers were deleted, but the missile guidance antenna 'egg' was retained. Test instrumentation was carried in large slab-sided pods on the outer wing pylons, the inner ones being occupied by fuel tanks. The test engineer (operator) had the cabin all to himself. The demilitarised 'Hind' was one of the exhibits of the annual industry fair in Nizhny Novgorod in September 1991.

Above: Development of the Mi-24 fenestron was discontinued because the new system was found to be ill-suited for helicopters in the weight class of the 'Hind'.

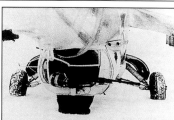

Right and below: The gunner could not be accommodated entirely and his legs stuck outside, scantily protected by rubberised fabric 'trousers'.

Above: This is the Mi-24D testbed used to develop new engine intake filters for the 'Hind'.

Right: This early-production 'Hind-A', outfitted with an air data test rig, may later have become an Mi-28 dynamic testbed.

Mi-24PS

A special troopship version designated Mi-24PS (in this case, *patrool'no-spasahtel'nii* = patrol/rescue (attrib.)) has been developed for the Russian Ministry of the Interior. Its missions are transportation and deployment of militia (police) search groups, support of police operations and SAR.

The Mi-24PS exists in two versions. The first prototype is a converted Mi-24P and retains the fixed 30-mm GSh-30K cannon. The LLLTV/FLIR fairing on the starboard side of the nose and the ATGM guidance antenna 'egg' on the port side are replaced by downward-pointing quadruple loudspeakers and an FPP-7 searchlight, respectively. The nose fairing is cut away to hold a gyrostabilised optical system in a neat ball turret and a weather radar.

The cabin accommodates an assault group of six policemen. Special brackets and handrails are mounted on the fuselage sides to ease disembarkation (up to four troopers can simultaneously rappel down lines dropped from the helicopter), and an LPG-4 hoist installed on the port side aft of the cabin door can lift up to 120 kg (264 lb) during SAR operations, etc. The Mi-24PS is equipped with satellite communications gear and a communications system as used by the Russian Army special forces (the famous Spetsnaz); the presence of additional communications equipment is revealed by two extra whip aerials on the tailboom.

The second prototype which was unveiled at the MAKS-95 air show is a converted Mi-24V; the c/n has been quoted as [353]2420338200 but this cannot be correct, as the quarter of manufacture appears to be zero (!) and the 'famous last five' digits are much too high. Unlike the first prototype, this helicopter is unarmed; the wing endplates and inboard pylons have been removed, leaving only the outboard pylons for drop tanks. There is no radar and the USPU-24 gun barbette is replaced by a thermal imager 'ball'. The rest of the equipment is identical to the first prototype. The helicopter is white overall with blue side flashes, Russian flag, Mil logos and Russian Militsiya titles but no civil registration, tactical code or visible c/n. A Mil representative said the Mi-24PS is similar in performance to the Mi-24V.

This is the second prototype of the decidedly unconventional Mi-24PS, which did not sport the 30-mm cannon of its predecessor.

The Mi-24PS carries a FLIR and loudhailer system (above), operated from the front cockpit (right).

Upgraded Mi-24M

On 4 March 1999 the prototype Mi-24M upgraded for the Russian army made its 25-minute official maiden flight (two brief and unofficial hops were made in February). The Mi-24M has a new main rotor system with composite blades and a redesigned tail rotor. The changes made to the 'Hind' increase its service ceiling from 2200 m (7,200 ft) to 3100 m (10,200 ft) in standard conditions, and from 1750 m (5,700 ft) to 2150 m (7,000 ft) in ISO +10° C. Climb rate has increased from 576 m/min to 744 m/min (1,890 ft/min to 2,440 ft/min). The new non-retractable gear inhibits cruising speed by 6 kt (11 km/h) to 167 kt (309 km/h, 192 mph).

The Mi-24M prototype has been converted from an Mi-24VP, the youngest variant in Russian service. Changes to note include the new tail rotor, fixed main gear and the much-modified stub wings.

Above: The rear (pilot's) cockpit of this Czech 'Hind-E' has been fitted with a new navigation display panel, but otherwise is completely standard.

Left: Two 9A669 GUV weapons pods are fitted with AGS-17 30-mm grenade launcher and TKB-621 7.62-mm machine-guns.

Weapons and systems of the Mi-24 'Hind'

Mi-24VP: The last 'Hind'

The Mi-24VP was the last production 'Hind' variant, and never gained a NATO codename. Based on the 'Hind-E' airframe it added a new NPPU-24 nose turret with a twin GSh-23 cannon. The Mi-24VP entered service in 1989, but only 25 were ever built.

The 9M17P Falanga missile (below left) was the first guided weapon to be fielded on the Mi-24. After launch it relies on radio guidance from the associated Raduga-F SACLOS (semi-automatic command line of sight) system undernose (below right).

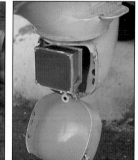

Above: The Mi-24P 'Hind-F' is armed with a Gryazev/Shipunov GSh-30K 30-mm cannon, the heaviest gun ever carried by an Mi-24.

Above: This Mi-24D 'Hind-D' is carrying a standard load of 9M17P Falanga (AT-2 'Swatter') missiles and UB-32A-24 rocket pods.

Above: The Mi-24V 'Hind-E' had revised endplate pylons allowing it to carry the tube-launched 9M114 Shturm (AT-6 'Spiral') anti-tank missile.

Upgrading the Mi-24/35 'Hind'

Still a feared weapon over the battlefield, Mil's 'Crocodile' serves in large numbers around the world. With no obvious replacement in sight, and with many of its operators facing severe budgetary restraints, the Mi-24/25/35 family is a prime candidate for modernisation. A number of companies are offering upgrade packages.

Above: A Ukrainian Mi-24V lets fly with rockets during a training flight. Combined with the nose gun and wing-mounted gun pods, rockets give the Mi-24 a powerful area attack capability.

Right: Rostvertol's Mi-35M demonstrator is currently the most sophisticated of the Russian upgrade proposals. It has a GOES-342 sensor turret, as also used in the Mi-24VM (VK-2) and PM (PK-2) upgrades for the VVS, and a GSh-23V cannon as well as airframe improvements.

The 21st century close air support/anti-armour and anti-insurgency focus of Russian army aviation, which since January 2003 has been under the control of the VVS (Voyenno-Vozdushniye Sily – Russian Air Forces), relies on the tried Mi-24V/P as its main workhorse. It is likely to soldier on with its principal operator for at least 15 more years – much longer than originally expected – due to the absence of credible successors.

It could be said that the Mi-24 is enjoying a prominent position simply because there is no real prospective, affordable replacement available in the required numbers, nor is there likely to be soon. The prospects of Mi-24 successors Ka-50/52 and Mi-28/28N entering large-scale production look rather bleak, because in 2000 the Russian Ministry of Defence redirected a significant proportion of the funds previously allocated for new hardware acquisitions to the launch of the Mi-8 and Mi-24 fleet-wide upgrade and life-cycle extension programmes. Apart from being considerably less costly, these upgrades were deemed much more urgent.

Today's 'Hind' still lacks any usable adverse weather and night operating capability and also, to some extent, weapons with useful stand-off range.

There is no credible and cost-effective alternative to an Mi-24 upgrade, and an array of options is now on offer in Russia and other parts of the world. Even the Central East European states which were granted NATO membership in 1999 now look committed to launching ambitious 'Hind' upgrade programmes; such investments are likely to turn the former Cold War combatant into a valuable NATO close air support/anti-armour (CAS/AA) asset. Non-European states such as India and Algeria have already elected to pump substantial finances into comprehensive operational capability enhancement programmes for their Mi-24 fleets, successfully carried out by non-Russian companies working as mission avionics/weapons system integrators.

Hybrid attack craft

Nicknamed 'Crocodile' in Russia and known as the 'Hind' in the West, the Mi-24 is considerably larger and heavier than its American cousin, the Bell AH-1 HueyCobra, as well as its projected successors the Mi-28 and Ka-50. It was originally designed in the late 1960s as an attack helicopter with a considerable assault transport capability, although the latter feature is very rarely used; moreover, the main cabin

imposes a significant weight penalty and limits manoeuvrability and agility, especially in 'hot-and-high' operating conditions.

Unlike the Western concept of anti-armour helicopter deployment, which calls for predominantly ambush tactics, the 'Hind' has been used by the Russian/CIS air arms and client states around the world much more like a modern-day equivalent of the famous World War II Ilyushin Il-2 Shturmovik low-level attack aircraft. Ingressing at a slightly slower speed over the battlefield , Mi-24 pilots are taught to use the same tactics as their World War II predecessors: approaching the target area at high speed and treetop altitude, attacking from different directions and, if threat level permits, circling over targets for additional firing passes in two-, four-, six- or eight-ship formations – the so-called 'wheel of death' attack pattern.

There are up to 700 Mi-24V/Ps (and several dozen Mi-24R/K specialised NBC reconnaissance/artillery fire correction and battlefield reconnaissance derivatives) in the Russian Air Forces inventory today, although fewer than 200 or so are believed to be serviceable at any time. The older Mi-24D 'Hind-D' was reported to have been formally withdrawn from use in Russia in 2000. The Ukrainian and Belarussian

air arms are other major Mi-24 operators among the CIS states, with inventories numbering around 200 and 75 'Hinds', respectively, although fewer than 60 and 35 are thought to have been in an airworthy condition in 2001/02.

Current airframe service life limits, authorised by Mil during the early/mid-1980s, call for 3,000 hours and/or 20 years, whichever is reached first. Time between overhauls (TBO) was initially set at seven to eight years, but later it was extended to 10 years, and in 2000 to 14 years for the Russian Air Forces fleet. TV3-117 engine TBO is set at 750 hours.

Most of the Mi-24 airframes in Russia, Ukraine and Belarus, as well as those with the air arms of Poland, Czech Republic, Slovakia, Hungary, Bulgaria and India, are well below the 2,000-hour mark. According to Mil Moscow Helicopter Plant (as the once-famous Mil Design Bureau is now officially known), if they are well maintained these airframes, all manufactured after 1980, could be good for 3,500 to 4,000 hours and 30 to 35 years of reliable service. Such significant activity would require extensive airframe structural wear points repair, rewiring and integrity/corrosion control efforts. By extrapolation, the life-extended 'Hinds' manufactured between 1980 and 1990 would be good – at least in theory – for use until 2010 to 2025, assuming that in the medium and long terms no troubles arise relating to unexpected airframe integrity, wiring and weapons/weapons control system reliability (due to ageing), and spare parts support.

Mi-24's apparent shortcomings

It is often claimed that the Mi-24's stressed-skin airframe structure, with extensive armour protection, can survive direct hits from small-calibre AAA projectiles. This is clearly an exaggeration: as real-world operations have shown, the Mi-24 (including powerplant, rotor system, transmission and systems) is vulnerable even to 12.7-mm (0.5-in) armour-piercing bullets, and some parts – especially the rear bottom fuselage and tailboom – to 7.62-mm (0.3-in) and 5.45-mm (0.2-in) bullets. Cockpit glazing is known to be a particularly weak point and is easily penetrated by small arms bullets. As well, the bladder fuel tanks, hydraulics and main gearbox oil system all demonstrated remarkably low resistance to combat damage in most local conflicts – especially those in Afghanistan (1979-1989) and Chechnya (1993-1995 and 1999-2000) – where Russian Army, Gendarmerie and Federal Border Service helicopters were involved in a great many combat and support operations.

Mi-24 fleets worldwide are known to suffer frequently from unreliable main rotor blades. Helicopters manufactured during the 1980s and early 1990s can be described as lacking any modern flight safety and combat survivability features such as further improved and refined armour protection, crash-resistant fuel systems, energy attenuating/armoured crew seats, self-defence aids and new digital avionics suites. Although the 'Hind' is, in general, considered to be an armoured platform, in today's typical threat environment its flight crews have to rely exclusively on good pre-mission planning and suitable tactics to keep out of harm's way.

It should be noted that, in complete contrast to the 1950s through 1970s, just 25 per cent of a modern attack helicopter's operational effectiveness comes from the airframe itself. Real battlefield effectiveness now comes from an integrated avionics suite for day/night operations, self-defence aids, and the man-machine interface.

Many flight safety problems during the most recent large-scale conflict for the Russian military, the 1999/2000 war in Chechnya, were caused by the Mi-24's poorly maintained and obsolete analog avionics suite. This was particularly true of the insecure communications gear (VHF/UHF and HF radios), radar altimeter and Doppler sensor. In addition, the unreliable main rotor blades essentially limited fleet availability. The basic Mi-24D/V/P is known to have only limited and somewhat untrustworthy autonomous navigation capability, something that is considered vital in any 21st Century operational environment. The original 'Hind' can use only Doppler navigation, which restricts a helicopter's usefulness in conditions of limited visibility, or when flying over featureless terrain or sea where map navigation could be difficult if not impossible.

As well, the Mi-24's vibration suppression is described as being particularly poor, with excessive pitch, roll and vertical vibrations generated by the far-from-perfect five-blade rotor system design at speeds below 80 km/h (43 kt) and above 300 km/h (162 kt), making weapons employment impossible when in the hover due to vibration-induced sighting problems. This particular inherent 'Hind' shortcoming does not allow Western-style tactics that rely on masking an attacker's presence behind

'Hinds' have been exported to over 30 nations and many remain in service. New-build aircraft are available from Rostvertol, the Rostov-on-Don factory which is closely allied with the Mil design bureau. This is an export Mi-35 'Hind-E', carrying 9M114 Shturm-V missile tubes, B-8V20 rocket pods and UPK-23-250 cannon pods.

available terrain and obstacles – so-called nap-of-earth (NoE) combat flying. To survive when operating *en masse* against targets with dense air defence cover, Mi-24 pilots are taught to use speed and surprise while approaching their targets at ultra-low altitude, thus limiting exposure to enemy air defences, then to execute a steep last-moment pop-up followed by a firing pass in a shallow dive.

The real-world experience gathered since 1979 clearly demonstrates that the Mi-24 often cannot absorb heavy punishment in combat and is particularly vulnerable to new-generation man-portable SAMs such as the Russian Igla and American FIM-92 Stinger. A usable stand-off engagement range was achieved only by introducing new sighting-observation systems, combined with the Mi-24V/P's existing 9M114 Shturm-V supersonic ATGM (anti-tank guided missile) or, better, with its considerably improved 9M120 Ataka derivative in the case of the Mi-35M. (The ATE-proposed 'Super Hind' Mk III upgrade would use the Kentron Ingwe,

Mi-24s serve with 11 VVS regiments/air bases and two independent squadrons, plus two test units. Well over half of the 700-strong fleet is in storage. This Mi-24P is being followed by an Mi-8MTKO, a night-capable 'Hip' version with GOES-321 FLIR turret that was rapidly fielded for target-spotting operations in Chechnya.

The standard 'Hind' cockpit is a mass of dials and switches, with many more to the pilot's sides. These remain in most of the low-cost Mi-24 upgrades.

An armourer loads 12.7-mm (0.5-in) armament into the USPU-24 turret of an Mi-24. The standard gun of the Mi-24D and Mi-24V is the Yakoushev-Borzov YakB-12.7.

and the Israeli-proposed 'Hind' upgrade would use the Rafael Spike-ER.) The 1970s-vintage Shturm-V has a maximum range of 5 km (2.7 nm), but the new sighting-observation hardware to be integrated during upgrades would enable the crew to pick out and destroy targets from a greater distance, which would be safer in operations against the majority of the low-level battlefield air defences.

This is true for the Mi-24V and Mi-25, but the earlier Mi-24D 'Hind-D', still widely used in eastern Europe, and its export derivative the Mi-25, have been severely handicapped by the stringent employment limitations of their primary anti-tank weapon, the 9M17P Falanga-P (AT-2). This ATGM has a low speed, limited range (up to 4 km/2.2 nm) and relatively low probability of hit/kill; furthermore, stocks of the aged Falanga-P now have an unacceptably low reliability due to their time-expired and old-element base electronics.

'Hind' in the Second Chechen War

During the outset of the second Chechen campaign (1999-2000), Russian army aviation had a fleet of 32 Mi-24V/Ps deployed in the region, assigned to three groups of the Russian Army advancing to occupy Chechnya. There were also a certain number of helicopters at the main base at Mozdok, for use as reinforcements on an as-needed basis. Their main use was within the tactical aviation teams, which comprised two to four Mi-24s and two or three Mi-8s, and were often tasked to support the advance of mechanised rifle regiments and to operate closely with ground or airborne forward air controllers (FAC). Another type of mission, without FAC assistance, was 'free hunt-ing' or the search for targets of opportunity in certain designated areas (kill boxes) deep in rebel-held territory. In late 1999 and early 2000, free hunting accounted for some 30 per cent of all combat sorties flown by Russian Army Mi-24s.

As of late August 2000, when the main battles and anti-insurgency area clearing operations were over, it was reported that these Mi-24s had fired a total of 1,708 9M114 Shturm-V ATGMs (with only nine failures recorded), more than 85,000 S-8 80-mm (3.15-in) rockets and 89,850 rounds of 12.7-mm (0.5-in), 23-mm (0.9-in) and 30-mm (1.18-in) ammunition. During this time, 11 Mi-24s were lost and more than 40 suffered combat damage but were eventually returned to serviceable condition by the Russian Army's Mozdok-based field repair facility. The main causes of combat damage were 7.62-mm (0.3-in) and 5.45-mm (0.2-in) bullets fired from various Kalashnikov assault rifle and machine-gun derivatives, and on some occasions from 12.7-mm (0.5-in) and 14.5-mm (0.57-in) heavy machine-guns. 23-mm (0.9-in) ZU-23 truck-mounted twin-barrelled guns and ZSU-23-4 Shilka self-propelled systems with four-barrelled 23-mm (0.9-in) guns were also encountered occasionally, but no man-portable SAMs were launched against Mi-24s during this period. Nearly half of the write-offs during the combat operations in 1999 and 2000 were attributed to pilot error, mainly during final landing approach, and collisions with terrain resulting from inadequate pilot training for ultra-low-level operations, coupled with high levels of physical and mental stress.

Russian 'Hinds'

Experience in Afghanistan led to the Russian Mi-24 fleet being well protected against missile attack. This aircraft has an L-166V-11E Ispanka IR countermeasures turret behind the main rotor, upturned EVU infra-red suppression exhaust nozzles, and ASO-2V dispensers scabbed on to the fuselage sides.

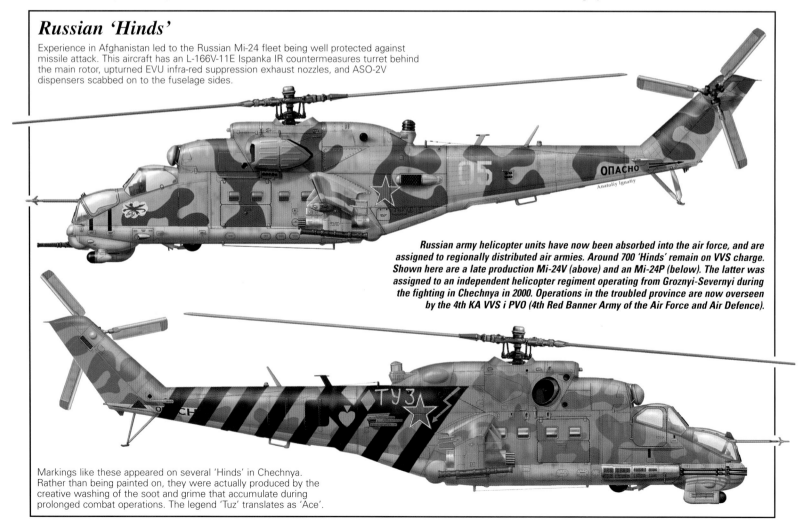

Russian army helicopter units have now been absorbed into the air force, and are assigned to regionally distributed air armies. Around 700 'Hinds' remain on VVS charge. Shown here are a late production Mi-24V (above) and an Mi-24P (below). The latter was assigned to an independent helicopter regiment operating from Groznyi-Severnyi during the fighting in Chechnya in 2000. Operations in the troubled province are now overseen by the 4th KA VVS i PVO (4th Red Banner Army of the Air Force and Air Defence).

Markings like these appeared on several 'Hinds' in Chechnya. Rather than being painted on, they were actually produced by the creative washing of the soot and grime that accumulate during prolonged combat operations. The legend 'Tuz' translates as 'Ace'.

Upgrade blocks

The block approach offered for the upgrade of Russian and export Mi-24 fleets has been designed by Mil and Rostvertol (the primary manufacturing organisation for the 'Hind') and encompasses a package of five 'building blocks' or modules that were promoted publicly for the first time in early 1999. All the airframe life extension and operational capability enhancement efforts offered by Mil Moscow Helicopter Plant for domestic and export customers are spread over Blocks 1 through 5. These can be carried out independently or together, depending on a customer's operational requirements and allocated budget.

Block 1 includes a comprehensive service life extension programme (SLEP) based on thorough inspection of the condition of each individual airframe. Main problems to be encountered include corrosion in certain places due to a low standard of maintenance and untidy storage, as well as fatigue cracking due to the very nature of inflight loading of the Mi-24's semi-monocoque fuselage structure.

Block 2 covers rotor system replacement, including the Mi-28's main rotor hub and composite blades as well as an X-shaped low-noise tail rotor. There is an option in this block to introduce the uprated Klimov TV3-117VMA (VK-2500) turboshaft, rated at 1790 kW (2,400 shp) in take-off, 2014 kW (2,700 shp) in emergency (OEI mode) and 1641 kW (2,200 shp) in maximum continuous mode; this would give additional performance improvements in 'hot-and-high' operating conditions.

Block 3 encompasses a host of airframe refinements such as shortened stub-wings with new DB-3UV pylons, and non-retractable landing gear. The latter is motivated by safe crash-landing requirements during low-level operations. Actual combat experience demonstrated that in an emergency Mi-24 pilots often do not have enough time to implement the undercarriage extension that is required for a safe landing. As a result, they often prefer to fly and fight at ultra-low level with the landing gear down, but such a configuration imposes severe speed restrictions. The fixed undercarriage proposed in Block 3 causes only an 11-km/h (6-kt) reduction in maximum level speed. The total weight reduction from all airframe refinements offered by Mil is said to be some 600 kg (1,320 lb), which, together with Block 2 enhancements, increases service ceiling by 300 m (985 ft) to 3100 m (10,170 ft) in standard conditions, and rate of climb to 12.4 m/s (40 ft/s).

Block 4 incorporates a host of weapons suite enhancements, the main one being the replacement of the 9M17P Falanga-P and 9M114 Shturm-V semi-automatic command line-of-sight ATGMs with the latter's much improved 9M120 Ataka-V (Attack) derivative, which was

purposely developed for the Mi-28 in the 1980s. The supersonic 9M120 missile has a maximum range of 5.8 km (3.13 nm) and is equipped with tandem warheads having an armour-penetration capability of up to 850 mm (33 in), compared to figures of 4 km (2.16 nm) and 500 mm (19.7 in) for its predecessor. Up to eight ATGMs can be carried on an APU-8/4-U launcher, attached to the new DB3-UV weapons pylons which are equipped with built-in hoists. The upgraded Mi-24 can carry 575-litre (126-Imp gal) underwing fuel tanks borrowed from the Mi-28.

For self-defence, anti-UAV and anti-helicopter operations, the 9M39 Igla-V (SA-18 'Grouse') air-to-air missile is offered in twin launcher packs. It has a range of up to 5.8 km (3.2 nm) and combines a very sensitive cooled IR seeker with a lethal warhead. An Ataka-V ATGM derivative, the 9M2200, equipped with a proximity fuse and blast-fragmentation warhead, is also offered in the air-to-air role, for use against helicopters and UAVs.

It is possible to replace the Mi-24V's YakB-12.7 four-barrelled machine-gun with a GSh-23L twin-barrelled cannon mounted in the NPPU-23 turret. Mil promotional materials indicate that the GSh-23's 23-mm (0.9-in) projectiles are 1.4 to 1.6 times more effective than 12.7-mm ammunition against individual targets. During area suppression fire, the turreted GSh-23 gun can saturate an area 2-2.5 times larger than the Mi-24V's YakB-12.7 can cover. The new weapons control system has a laser rangefinder, and a BVK-24 weapons control digital computer greatly enhances the precision of unguided weapons; the upgraded helicopter

retains the original VG-17 reflector gunsight, fed by the new digital ballistic computer. The upgraded 'Hind' can use the large S-13 122-mm (4.8-in) rockets, carried in five-round pods.

Block 5, the final and most expensive set of improvements offered by Mil, introduces day/night and adverse weather operating capability through NVG-compatible cockpit illumination, an advanced display system, precise navigation system (digital map is optional) and gyro-stabilised optronics system, integrated into a digital weapons control system.

The first 'Hind' prototype, featuring only the new rotor system, shortened stub-wings and fixed undercarriage, was flown officially for the first time on 4 March 1999. According to Mil, by 2001 a trio of upgraded Mi-24s was involved in the flight test programme. The first was tasked with testing the airframe and rotor system improvements; the second was used to test the uprated VK-2500 turboshafts; and the third machine, designated Mi-24VK-1, was involved in testing the new day/night observation-sighting hardware.

Mi-24PN – the first night proposal

The Mi-24PN is the most widely-publicised 'Hind' upgrade for the Russian Air Forces. A variant of the Mi-24P 'Hind-F', it is the first production version to have night ATGM capability while retaining the 30-mm (1.18-in) GSh-30-2 gun. It was in tests with Mil and Rostvertol between 2000 and 2003. Designated Mi-24PN (N for *nochnoy*, night capable), this simplified/low-cost upgrade features NVG-compatible cockpits and a BREO-24 avionics suite integrating one colour LCD screen in each

This former 'Berkuty' Mi-24V was the first aircraft to fly with the aerodynamic improvements envisaged in Blocks 2/3. It has the 'X' tail rotor, Mi-28N main rotors, fixed undercarriage and shortened stub wings. Its first flight in this guise took place at Panki on 3 March 1999.

cockpit (the co-pilot/gunner's cockpit has an additional, smaller LCD for navigation and communication systems). The front cockpit also has a precise navigation system with satellite navigation receiver. The avionics integrator for the Mi-24PN's BREO-24 is the Ramenskoye Instrument-making Design Bureau.

The Mi-24PN is equipped with the 9S47N Zarevo gyro-stabilised sighting system (developed by the Krasnodar Optical-Mechanical Plant), having an IR sensor coupled with a laser rangefinder and IR goniometer for use with the Shturm-V and Ataka ATGMs. It is installed onto a protruding 'chin' mount in the nose. Low-level flying at night is possible after a cockpit lighting adaptation for use with the OVN-1 night-vision goggles, permitting night flying down to 50 m (164 ft).

The helicopter's night ATGM employment was tested for the first time in late 2002. The radio guidance equipment of the standard Raduga-Sh guidance system is integrated with the Zarevo's IR-goniometer to facilitate night-time ATGM guidance.

Additional improvements such as non-retractable landing gear, shortened stub-wings and weapon pylons with built-in hoists were made to the Mi-24PN's airframe. It is still unclear whether more improvements – such as the lightened main rotor hub and the X-shaped tail rotor – will be fitted to follow-on Mi-24PNs.

The prototype was test-flown for the first time in July 2000. It was reported in late 2001 that two or three prototypes had been converted by Rostvertol, and two more pre-series conversions were rolled out in 2002 followed by four in 2003. Both prototypes and pre-series machines were used in the Mi-24PN's protracted trials.

According to a news release from Mil dated July 2003, the Mi-24PN's joint state trials were scheduled for completion by September 2003 and one example had already undergone state testing during spring and summer at the VVS Test Centre at Akhtubinsk in southern Russia. The same news release said that Rostvertol had already obtained a state order for an initial batch of eight Mi-24PN conversions: four units were expected to be upgraded by the end of 2003 and the rest in 2004.

The first group of five Mi-24PN production machines was commissioned by Russian army aviation in January 2004. They were taken on strength by a helicopter regiment reporting to the Russian Air Forces' 4th Army, stationed in southern Russia near the troubled republic of Chechnya (however, other sources say that some if not all of the delivered Mi-24PNs were put into service with the 334th Combat Training and Aircrew Conversion Centre at Torzhok to train the first group of front-line pilots in night operations and NVG employment). During the modernisation at Rostvertol the helicopters were cycled through main overhaul, making them good for another 1,000 flight hours or seven years of service.

According to the Russian Air Forces Deputy Commander-in-Chief, Lieutenant General Alexander Zelin, the night-capable Mi-24PN has attracted commercial interest from Venezuela, China and other countries. There was unconfirmed information from Russian news agencies that an undisclosed Mi-24 foreign customer had expressed strong interest in the Mi-24PN

upgrade and was closely following the upgraded helicopter's evaluation process by the Russian Air Forces. In early February 2004 this customer was named as Uganda, said to be interested in acquiring as many as six Mi-24PNs.

In Russian Air Forces service the Mi-24PN is to be followed by other Mi-24V/P derivatives, also night-capable but much more sophisticated, known as the Mi-24PK-2 and Mi-24VK-2 (K for *kruglosutochnoy*, day/night capable). These new versions feature the more modern KNEI-24N avionics suite integrated by Russkaya Avionika and are equipped with the capable and flexible OPS-24N observation-sighting system. An UOMZ GOES-342 gyro-stabilised system will enable Shturm-V/Ataka use during day and night.

Follow-on Russian upgrade efforts

In a 2001 interview with Moscow's authoritative military weekly, the *Independent Military Review* (*NVO*), Colonel General Vitaliy Pavlov, who headed Russian army aviation until his dismissal in late 2002, pointed out that costs of any fleet-wide Mi-24 replacement programme would be "prohibitively expensive" on account of the current weak Russian economy and the tight budgets to which military operations are subject. The as-yet untried Mi-28N and Ka-50N/52 – which feature somewhat unproven digital mission avionics – are being offered by their manufacturers at a base price equivalent to $US12 million, while an Mi-24V/P upgraded to the Mi-24VK-2/PK-2 standard would cost up to $US3 million a copy. The Mi-24VK-1 interim night-capable upgrade and life extension is believed to cost less than $US1 million per unit.

As Colonel General Pavlov intimated in this interview, the upgraded Mi-24 is going to be roughly equal in destructive power and weapons employment precision, day and night, to its nominated successors the Ka-50 and Mi-28. He also said that, in general, today's CAS/AA helicopter operations impose requirements first for good survivability, sufficient firepower, precise aiming and targeting capability.

Arguably, most if not all of these abilities would be well within the capability of a revitalised 'Hind'. Therefore, the Mi-24 upgrade is regarded by many authorities as the only cost-

Mi-24V 'Bort 63' (left) was the first 'Hind' to fly with the uprated VK-2500 (TV3-117VMA-SB3) engine (below). Its first VK-2500-powered flight was undertaken at Rostov-on-Don on 30 May 2000. Initially the power output was restricted to 2,200 shp (1641 kW) pending fitment of an uprated transmission.

Displayed at Paris in 1995 was this Mil/Rostvertol Mi-35M upgrade. It had a GSh-23L cannon, and the fixed undercarriage and 'X' tail rotor of later variations, but had a sensor/navigation suite developed by Sextant and Thomson TTD Optronique (now Thales), including a Chlio FLIR on the port side. This upgrade proved too expensive to garner more than passing interest, and was dropped in 1997.

effective, near-term, operational capability enhancement option for the Russian Air Forces' attack helicopter inventory. In its new guise, the 'Hind' is expected to provide warfighting capability far beyond that of the simple gunship/day-only anti-armour platform originally conceived in the 1970s.

It is believed that the cash-strapped Russian military chose the path that was least expensive and somewhat more modest in terms of performance improvements. The interim upgrade configuration encompasses only the basic airframe life-cycle and TBO extension modules, combined with a new digital mission avionics package to be integrated into the existing analog suite to provide an all-weather, day/night capability. As reported by Russian military sources in late 2002, as many as 200 low-hour Mi-24V/Ps have been earmarked for cycling through such an upgrade and will receive the OPS-24N avionics package from Russkaya Avionika (over 80 per cent of this package is identical to that used on the night-capable Mi-8MTKO assault/transport helicopter). In its definitivé production form, the OPS-24N works with an inexpensive ARINC 429 civilian-standard digital interface rather than the Mil-Std 1553B databus which is generally used in such upgrade projects. According to Russkaya Avionika officials, the chief reason for this is a significant reduction in development time and costs.

Mi-24VK-1 interim upgrade

The OPS-24N's initial version, as used in the Mi-24VK-1 (an interim upgrade), integrates the 460-mm (18.1-in) UOMZ GOES-321VMI gyro-stabilised electro-optical system. This comprises a FLIR sensor (a Swedish-made Agema THV1000 IR imager on the prototype/pre-production systems; Russian-made thermal imagers reportedly entered production in mid-2003) and a laser rangefinder, housed in a ball turret mounted on the starboard side of the nose. By the standards of contemporary Russian Air Forces equipment, the cockpit displays and precise navigation system are rather advanced. Both cockpits have black interiors and are NVG-compatible, optimised for use with Russian-made GEO-ONV-1 NVGs. The pilot's (rear) cockpit has a pair of IV-86-2 20 x 15-cm (8 x 6-in) landscape colour multi-func-

tion LCDs, while the front-seat co-pilot/gunner (CPG, known in Russia as the pilot-operator) has at his disposal only one display and new sensor/weapons control grips. As much as 80 per cent of the Mi-24's existing 'steam gauge' navigation, flight and engine control instruments are being retained to ease pilot transition to the new cockpit environment. Hands On Collective and Stick (HOCAS) controls may be introduced to further reduce pilot workload.

On the LCDs, navigation and weapons status information can be displayed along with IR images from the GOES-321VMI system, which is considered useful for both targeting and low-

level navigation tasks. Target ID range (tanks and armoured vehicles) provided by the system is said to be more than 4 km (2.2 nm). The FLIR has azimuth coverage of 230º (115º left and right) and elevation coverage of 60º up and 150º down. It provides two fields of view – wide (20º x 13.3º) and narrow (5º x 3.3º). The laser rangefinder has a maximum range of 5 km (2.7 nm) and can provide range measurement accuracy of 5 m (16.4 ft).

The relatively inexpensive GEO ONV-1 General III NVGs with 40º field of view (FoV) have been described by Colonel General Pavlov as a useful tool in the night-operating

Mi-24PN

The main elements of the Mi-24PN upgrade for existing Mi-24Ps are the addition of a Zarevo FLIR in the nose and the RPKB BREO-24 avionics suite, which includes a liquid-crystal display. The first modified aircraft have the fixed undercarriage and short wings and are known as Mi-24PN-1s. The new rotor system may also be added to the upgrade at a later date to produce the Mi-24PN-2.

On 28 January 2004 the first five Mi-24PNs (this is the prototype conversion) were handed over to the VVS's 344th TsBPiPLS AA, army aviation's evaluation centre at Torzhok. The aircraft were destined for service with the 4th Army, which oversees operations in Chechnya.

suite, particularly for take-off and landing operations from unlit sites and for low-level en-route navigation. However, General Pavlov maintains that night-vision goggles have ample operating restrictions, as they have been considered, in general, to be useless as aids for both guided and unguided weapons deployment. For such purposes, a high-tech but affordable gyro-stabilised system with precise auto-tracking and range-finding capabilities is required. The GOES-321VMI system, as said above, is an interim solution and provides targeting data that is reliable enough only for firing rockets, gun/gun pods and dropping free-fall bombs at night; this capability was thoroughly evaluated in 2002 and 2003 by the Russian Air Forces Flight Test Centre.

The Mi-24VK-1/VK-2/PK-2's navigational accuracy has been greatly increased by the new KNEI-24 navigation, flight management and display system. It integrates a highly-precise A-737-00 satellite navigation receiver unit (working with both the American GPS and Russian GLONASS systems) into the existing DISS-15D Doppler sensor. In order to limit upgrade package costs, no inertial navigation unit has been added; the precision and reliability demonstrated by the A-737-00 is deemed sufficient for low-level autonomous navigation (i.e., without

the use of ground navigation aids). Due to the new and very precise KNEI-24 and OPS-24N targeting system, the slow-speed helicopter can deliver free-fall bombs with great accuracy during the night and day, in bad weather, without the need for visual aiming. The first Mi-24V upgraded to the Mi-24VK-1 standard was test-flown in May 2001, and by mid-2002 five sets of OPS-24/KNEI-24 equipment had been supplied by Russkaya Avionika.

The Russian Air Forces are known to have also ordered an improved armour protection package for their upgraded Mi-24s. The necessity was highlighted in the 1999-2000 Chechen War, and particular emphasis is on improving crew protection from small-calibre high-speed projectiles and warhead fragments. There are no firm reports – only a number of useless company press releases – about the Russian Air Forces' definitive requirements in terms of Mi-24VK-2/PK-2 airframe/powerplant/rotor system enhancements such as those tested by Mil and Rostvertol in 1990-2001.

Night ATGM capability

The new equipment of the Russian Air Forces' definitive night-capable 'Hinds', designated Mi-24VK-2 and Mi-24PK-2, is almost identical with that of the Mi-24VK-1: they share all airframe and rotor system improvements, but the GOES-342 optronics system replaces the GOES-312VMI in the OPS-24N observation/sighting package. The new, much more sophisticated system is also provided by UOMZ. At

Designated Mi-35M1, this Mi-24V derivative first flew at Rostov-on-Don in May 1999. As well as fixed undercarriage and short-span wings, it had a GOES-321 FLIR turret added to the starboard side of the nose for trials, although it retained the Raduga sight. Tests with this aircraft led to the interim Mi-24VK-1 upgrade.

460 mm (18.1 in) in diameter, it integrates a number of elements. The FLIR, in the prototype and pre-series examples, is a SAGEM Iris with 288 x 4 HgCdTe LWIR detectors working in 8- to 12-µm wavelength; Russian-made devices are planned for use in the GOES-342 production examples. A Sony TV camera has a powerful zoom lens, laser rangefinder and thermal direction-finder (used for ATGM tracking and guidance, known also as an IR goniometer). Working together, they enable night-time Shturm-V and Ataka ATGM use in addition to the deployment of an array of unguided weapons. Detection range of tank-sized targets at night is 4 to 6 km (2.2 to 3.2 nm) and during the day is up to 10 km (5.4 nm); the laser rangefinder has a useful range of 10 km (5.4 nm). ATGM test firings using an Mi-24 equipped with the GOES-342 were demonstrated for the first time in 2001, according to Mil sources interviewed at the 2003 Le Bourget air show. The GOES-342 sensor ball can rotate through a 230º arc left and right in surveillance mode; in weapons control mode, rotation is restricted to 60º left and right; movement in elevation is 25º up and 115º down; and in precise aiming mode, movement is restricted to 15º up and 40º down.

The Mi-24VK-2 prototype was developed by Rostvertol and the Mi-24PK-2 by Mil, and both were scheduled to commence their flight tests in mid- or late 2003. However, as the authoritative Russian military news agency Interfax-AVN announced in late 2002, no funds were allocated in the 2003 defence budget for the commencement of production upgrade activity. Furthermore, all Mi-24 upgrade programmes have been proceeding at a notably slow pace since their commencement due to poor programme management, engineering difficulties and systematic underfunding for development, flight testing and commencement of the upgrade's production phase by Rostvertol.

Upgraded 'Hinds' for export

The Mi-35M displayed at Le Bourget in 2001 and Berlin in 2002 is the definitive export derivative of the revitalised 'Hind' which incorporates Block 1 through Block 5 enhancements but lacks the uprated turboshafts. The Mi-24VK-2 avionics and optronics equipment which has been adopted for the Mi-35M (Mi-35M-2) was purposely developed by Mil and Rostvertol on order from Rosoboronexport. The black-painted demonstrator features the BREO-24 avionics suite based on the OPS-24/KNEI-24 equipment proven in 2002 and 2003 on the Russian Air Forces' Mi-24VK-1 and Mi-24VK-2 prototypes.

There is no reliable information about any orders being placed for either newly-built helicopters or production conversions to the Mi-35M standard, and it is worth noting that until 2002 the sole prototype was used primarily for the ground testing of new systems, its first flight coming in mid- to late 2003. Such a notable delay in the flight test programme does not promote faith in the capability of the Russian companies to be considered reliable contractors for Mi-24 upgrades for export

customers. The Russian companies' lack of experience and expertise in new-generation digital avionics and the integration of night-vision equipment, plus the protracted trials schedules, prompted India and Algeria – both of which are generally considered significant and loyal clients for Russian-made weapons – to begin looking elsewhere during the mid- to late 1990s for more flexible and trusted avionics integrators offering proven solutions. Albeit not approved by Mil, these alternatives for comprehensive revitalisation of the Algerian and Indian 'Hind' fleets were offered at an affordable cost and on a tight schedule.

So far, the first night-capable Mi-24s known to be sold by Rostvertol to a foreign customer are four to six Mi-35s, either newly built or refurbished second-hand machines, that went to the Zimbabwean air arm in 1998. At least two of the helicopters are Mi-35Ps armed with 30-mm (1.18-in) guns. In 2000, they received US-made Inframetrics IRTV 445MGII thermal imaging systems with a turret-mounted ball installed on the port outer stub-wing pylon, and the associated cockpit display for IR image monitoring; there is also a video recorder capable of displaying target position via an onboard GPS receiver. The upgraded Mi-35s feature NVG-compatible cockpits and their navigation system is being enhanced with a Garmin 115L GPS receiver added to the DISS-15D Doppler sensor. The inexpensive IRTV 445MGII commercial, off-the-shelf thermal imaging system is described by Rostvertol promotional material as useful for anti-insurgency and patrol operations, and is said to be capable of small target identification at up to 4 km (2.2 nm).

Undoubtedly, the most significant Mil and Rostvertol commercial success of the early 2000s is the sale to the Cyprus National Guard of 12 Mi-35P improved gunships featuring NVG-compatible cockpits. No optronics systems are known to have been installed on them. These newly-built 'Hinds' in their overall gunmetal-grey colour scheme feature improved airframes with shortened stub-wings and eight-round Shturm-V/Ataka launchers. Delivered to Cyprus in 2001 and 2003, they apparently cost around or below $US5 million each.

It is worth noting that the ambitious Russian-French programmes revealed in the mid- and late 1990s to produce newly-built or converted machines from existing Mi-35 airframes using Western (predominantly French) digital avionics and observation/sighting equipment have so far failed to materialise. The chief reason cited for the lack of success of these marketing undertakings is the high price for such upgrade packages – both for equipment and integration/qualification – combined with the lack of interest from prospective customers, most of which operate under tight budgets. Between 1995 and 1997, several Mi-35M airframes were displayed at various exhibitions equipped with sophisticated Nadir 10 navigation system and NOCAS (Night Operation Capable Avionics System), jointly developed by Thales and Sextant Avionique. Built around the Thomson-CSF Optronics Chlio FLIR housed in a gyro-stabilised ball turret (installed on the port side of the nose), the NOCAS system also has a TMM 1410 display for FLIR imagery and navigation information, plus a VH 100 head-up display (HUD) and SMD LCD screen in both cockpits. However, no customers were found

Mi-24VK-1

The night-capable Mi-24VK-1 is an interim upgrade step pending development of the full Mi-24M/Mi-24VK-2. It has a new KNEI-24 avionics suite and GOES-321VMI electro-optical turret, also used by the Mi-8MTKO (right). The relatively unsophisticated turret replaces the old Raduga-F, which means that the Mi-24VK-1 gains night capability but cannot guide precision weapons. The first Mi-24VK-1 flew in May 2001. The modernisation concerns only the avionics, and does not include the airframe/dynamics upgrades that have been included in other packages.

for this rather expensive 'Hind' upgrade package, and co-operation with the French partners was terminated in 1997.

Never-ending proliferation

Between 1991 and 2003, no fewer than 140 Mi-24s, predominantly second-hand and little-used ones, were exported to over two dozen Third World nations as well as to the European states of Croatia, Serbia, Macedonia, Cyprus and Czech Republic. In 1998, the Serbian Special Operations Unit, subordinated to the State Security authority, was reported to have acquired a pair of late production Mi-24Vs from Russian sources. For most of these new

customers, the Mi-24D/V/P was a very capable weapons system, being their first dedicated attack helicopter type with true armour protection. Estimates indicate that between 1992 and 2003, Russia sold some 80 'Hinds' to over a dozen customers. The most important were Cyprus and Peru with 12 helicopters each, the latter introducing its newly-built Mi-35s in 1995. Ethiopia and Sudan are known to have acquired 10 'Hinds' each, delivered in 1999 and 2000/01, respectively. A number of sales were of newly-built airframes fitted with scavenged components and systems from old Mi-24s, as this proved to be a cheaper option for most African customers.

During the preceding decade, the newly exported 'Hinds' saw much use in many local conflicts, peacekeeping efforts and anti-insurgency operations around the globe. Most conflicts were essentially low-technology clashes (such as those in Sri Lanka and Sierra Leone) in which the Mi-24s' targets often lacked any sophisticated air defence, and thus the 'Hind' demonstrated fairly good results in numerous force projection missions. Weapons of choice were the inexpensive 57-mm (2.24-in) and 80-mm (3.15-in) rockets, 23-mm (0.9-in)/ 30-mm (1.18-in) gun pods/guns, and nose-mounted 12.7-mm (0.5-in) Gatling machine-gun, with little or no need for ATGM employment. Night operations were the exception rather than the rule during these conflicts.

Undoubtedly, the main driving force behind the renewed interest in the well-tried armoured gunship and the steady demand for the 'Hind' in Africa is the type's satisfactory warfighting capability in a Third World operational environment, coupled with a low price. The remarkably low price tag for newly-built or refurbished 'Hinds' from Rostvertol is possible due to the extremely low fixed manufacturing costs in Russia which result from a combination of very cheap labour, an old and inexpensive manufacturing technology base, ready availability of scavenged components (main gearbox, avionics and accessories) from retired Russian Air Forces or foreign Mi-24s, and an enormous production run in the preceding two decades with its impressive attendant economics of scale. Newly-built Mi-35Ps are reported to have been offered for $US4-5 million each, while 10- to 15-year-old second-hand examples fresh from major refurbishment are going for around $US1.5 million a copy, and in some cases even less. Seven Mi-35s, newly-built in 2002 and 2003 by Rostvertol for Czech Republic and delivered in lieu of part of Russia's trade debt, apparently had a total price of $US30 million, or $US4.3 million each. In September 2004, a pair of newly-built Mi-35Ps was delivered to Indonesian army aviation and follow-on orders are now expected to equip a full attack helicopter squadron.

Belarus and Ukraine are other major sources for cheap, second-hand Mi-24s – both refurbished and non-refurbished – that have sold well to Third World customers and some European states under UN embargo. These two CIS nations are thought to have exported more than 80 Mi-24s. Ukraine alone is believed to have sold in excess of 60 'Hinds': up to 20 Mi-24V/Ds to Croatia in the mid-1990s, 12 to Macedonia in 2001 (10 Mi-24Vs and two Mi-24Ks), and 14 to Algeria in 1999. Kyrgyzstan is another 'Hind' exporter and reportedly sold as many as 15 Mi-24s to India in 1995, most if not all of which were later refurbished by Rostvertol.

Israeli upgrade proposals

The wake-up call to Mi-24 export operators (as many as 600 Mi-24/25/35 export types are deemed suitable for various scales of upgrade) came from Israel Aircraft Industries. Its Mission 24 Mi-24 upgrade proposal was selected by the Indian Air Force in an order comprising 25 upgrade kits under a $US20 million contract signed in 1998. It proved to be a good advertisement with which to convince potential customers that a cost-effective alternative upgrade proposal exists, and was viewed as highly competitive to those offered by Russian and French companies. With an affordable and rapid integration of observation/sighting, navigation, self-defence and self-protection equipment proven in real-world operational conditions, the helicopter could perform well in the demanding CAS/AA role in a 21st century battlefield, including at night and in adverse weather.

IAI's Tamam electro-optical division was quick to offer an affordable upgrade package for the Mi-24 that required reduced development time and risk. The Indian Air Force contract covered prototype manufacture and testing in Israel, with production conversion to be undertaken at the customer's facilities. No airframe, flight control system, autopilot, powerplant, transmission or rotor system changes have been made by Tamam due to the

Mi-24PM/PK-2

When the 'full-spec' Mi-24M systems upgrade with GOES-342 turret is applied to the Mi-24P, the result is known as the Mi-24PM (army) or Mi-24PK-2 (design bureau). The VVS favours upgrading Mi-24Ps as they are for the most part younger than the Mi-24Vs which remain in service.

Mil/Rostvertol Mi-35M/Mi-24VK-2

Above: In the 'full-spec' Mi-35M and Mi-24VK-2/PK-2 upgrades the sensor turret is the GOES-342.

Both front and rear cockpits have IV-86-2 multi-function displays – two in the rear (above) and one in the front (below). The Mi-35M export model is offered with HOCAS controls.

Above: An important option for the Mi-35M is the replacement of the YakB-12.7 machine-gun by the much harder hitting GSh-23V water-cooled cannon.

Right: The avionics system of the Mi-35M and Mi-24VK-2/PK-2 is designed to support the employment of the 9M120 Ataka-V anti-tank missile, of which eight can be carried under each shortened stub wing. Another important weapon is the 9M39 Igla-V short-range air-to-air missile, two of which are seen here in their launching tubes under the inboard pylon. Note also the upturned heat-suppressing exhaust box.

complexity and costs of such rework and any subsequent required qualifications.

The Mission 24 upgrade package as sold to the Indian Air Force is built around a Mil-Std 1553B digital databus. The heart of the upgrade is a single mission computer developed with IAI MLM; it is a derivative of the model used in the US Air Force T-38 upgrade programme, in which IAI is the principal subcontractor. Mission 24 utilises Tamam's proven helicopter multi-mission optronic stabilised payload (HMOSP), which weighs around 30 kg (66 lb). It is a turret ball-mounted derivative of the combat-proven IAI Tamam night targeting system installed in the US Marine Corps' AH-1W Super Cobra and Israeli DF/AF Cobra attack helicopters. It provides day/night observation and targeting through TV and FLIR sensors with variable FoV (between 2.4° and 29.2° on the FLIR). The HMOSP can incorporate two types of FLIR: a scanning array of 4 x 480 cadmium-mercury-telluride detectors operating in the low-wavelength band, and a 320 x 240-element indium-antimony focal-plane array functioning at middle wavelengths. Monochrome or colour CCD TV cameras are included, together with a laser rangefinder, designator and pointer, plus a built-in auto-tracking unit that uses centroid and edge-tracking techniques.

The cockpits are NVG-compatible, and both crew members have the option to use IAI's advanced NVG set with built-in monocular display on which all necessary navigation and targeting information can be presented. Both cockpits feature a single multi-function display

(MFD) for TV, FLIR and targeting information, in addition to a keyboard and display unit for navigation and communication control. The CPG has control grips borrowed from the AH-1W, with all necessary sensor/weapons control switches and knobs; such devices, when combined with the MFD, can dramatically change work practices and reduce workload.

The HMOSP has been integrated with the Shturm-V ATGM SALOC guidance system through an IR goniometer and interface unit designed by IAI Tamam engineers, which has fully replaced the original old and bulky Raduga-F sighting/ATGM optical tracking system. The unit weighs more than 200 kg (440 lb). The Raduga-F's role for targeting and tracking both the target and missile was taken over by the HMOSP, with guidance commands being produced and transmitted to the missile through the existing equipment. Russian sources indicated in 2002 that Tamam experienced some guidance problems during Shturm-V test firings using the HMOSP system in place of Raduga-F. In order to solve the sensitive missile guidance problems, IAI contacted the Russian design authority for the Shturm, the KBP company of Tula, which provided important technical assistance. The contact was arranged through the Russian arms export agency Rosvoorouzhenie (the predecessor of Rosoboronexport, the only current Russian arms export agency). KBP expertise is believed to have been instrumental in solving the software/hardware, guidance and control problems associated with the HMOSP/Shturm-V assimilation on India's upgraded Mi-24s.

There are other types of ATGMs on offer for the Mission 24 system, such as Rafael's Spike-ER which has a maximum range of 7 km (3.8 nm) and employs 'fire-and-update' fibre-optic guidance. However, the Indian Air Force, which has ample stocks of Shturm-V missiles, preferred to limit the guided weapons integration work on its upgraded helicopters to the relatively cheap and well-proven Russian-made supersonic ATGM. The Shturm-V is still considered to be highly effective against older generation main battle tanks, such as the Chinese-made Type 59 and Type 69 – the chief potential target for Indian 'Hinds' in a future war with Pakistan. Integration of the indigenous Nag ATGM is known to have been earmarked for IAF Mission 24 machines at a later stage.

Navigation improvements introduced by IAI include a GPS receiver integrated into the existing DISS-15D Doppler sensor, and a three-dimensional digital map display. Both the HMOSP and YakB-12.7 gun are slaved to the pilot's line of sight through the use of a helmet-mounted sensor; the machine-gun can also be slaved to the HMOSP. A self-defence capability has been provided by IMI chaff/flare dispenser units and Elta radar/laser/missile warning systems. The total weight of these new systems is about 50 kg (111 lb).

It was reported that the production phase of the Indian Air Force Mi-35 upgrade was successfully running in 2001 or 2002. During the contract implementation phase, the IAF was tight-lipped about the upgrade details, and IAI has also been reluctant to disclose any details about the launch customer for its Mission 24

package. The upgraded helicopters, in overall light grey camouflage, were displayed publicly for the first time during the Aero India 2003 air show held in February 2003 in Bangalore.

Elbit Systems of Haifa, Israel, has also proposed a number of 'Hind' upgrades. The company has comprehensive expertise and experience in the upgrade business in general, and has one of the most aggressive marketing approaches in today's rather crowded defence upgrades arena. As identified by its engineering development team, which possesses enormous experience in battlefield helicopter upgrades, the main trends in any future Mi-24 upgrades are very short time to market, low risk, maximum integration of systems, and maximum utilisation of off-the-shelf hardware.

Elbit's preferred upgrade emphasises pilot situational awareness improvement, survivability enhancement, reduced aircrew workload with maximum 'head-out' operation, and maximum HOCAS controls employment. Such concepts were introduced and proved during the late 1990s on the Romanian Air Force Puma SOCAT upgrade, optimised for operations in a medium-to-high threat environment. Elbit's basic modular avionics package for a rotary-wing platform provides a day/night and adverse weather capability for the Mi-24 and enables its use in roles such as close air support, armed reconnaissance, air defence, anti-armour, escort and Combat SAR, in addition to the more conventional ones of assault transport, medevac and cargo lifting. It is centred around dual Mil-Std 1553B databuses and could include Elbit's own MIDASH (Modular Integrated Display And Sight Helmet) advanced helmet-mounted display and targeting system, highly capable TopLight or El-Op's COMPASS optronics systems. The latter weighs 45 kg (99 lb) and incorporates a gyro-stabilised, steerable turret with colour CCD TV camera, a third-generation FLIR operating in the low-wavelength band, and laser designator/rangefinder. Other components include fully NVG-compatible cockpit, hybrid GPS/INS navigation system, Western-standard navaids (VOR, ILS and DME), highly efficient self-protection suite, new radios, digital mapping module, and weapons interfaces. The MIDASH variant of Elbit's helmet-mounted sight and display family was designed especially for helicopter pilots

'212' is one of two Mi-24Ks serving with the Macedonian air force's 201 POHE (badge right). The reconnaissance equipment has been removed and they are now used as gunships. A modern reconnaissance capability may be restored as part of a wider plan to upgrade the Macedonian fleet, for which Elbit is seen as the most likely integrator.

and has a standard helmet body to which image intensifiers are attached to give a 50° x 40° FoV, providing flight and weapon-aiming information, including see-through binocular night imagery.

Elbit Systems adopted a unique approach to introducing night ATGM capability to the Mi-24, choosing to upgrade the Raduga-F sighting-missile guidance system rather than apply an all-new guidance system, thereby saving both development time and money. Shturm-V ATGM capability at night became possible due to the embedding of a miniaturised and relatively cheap CCD camera into the Raduga-F sighting system, and the upgraded system was dubbed 'Raduga by Night'. The CCD camera and a laser rangefinder are integrated with the upgraded helicopter's mission computer, enabling the processed and enhanced IR image of the target (from the Raduga-F) to be displayed on the CPG's display in the centre instrument panel. Raduga by Night's range is enough to provide a clear image of a tank-sized target from more than 11 km (6 nm).

Like its rival IAI, Elbit offers a number of Israeli and Western weapons systems for the Mi-24, including the Rafael Spike-ER ATGM and 70-mm (2.75-in) rocket pods.

An unconfirmed news release in January 2004 indicated that Elbit Systems has concluded (or is near concluding) a contract for upgrading some if not all of the Sri Lanka Air Force's Mi-24Ps, four of which were delivered newly-built in 1998, followed by three more (second-hand) examples in 2000. As well, it was reported that a contract for upgrading two Macedonian Air Force Mi-24Vs with high attack capability was near completion in January-February 2004.

South African 'Super Hinds'

Another successful upgrade, in both commercial and engineering terms, is that offered by the South African company Advanced Technologies and Engineering (ATE).

Its upgrade packages, 'Super Hind' Mk II and Mk III, were publicly revealed during the Africa Aerospace and Defence 2002 exhibition at Waterkloof in September 2002, where ATE's Mk III demonstrator ZS-BOI was on display.

The basic avionics/weapons modernisation is being offered by ATE in two different versions built around common avionics and weapons systems but featuring different levels of equipment sophistication to suit customers' operational requirements and, of course, budgets. ATE developed its Mi-24 upgrade package on the basis of the valuable experience and expertise gained during the Denel Rooivalk combat support helicopter development programme, for which the company was selected as avionics and system integrator.

ATE studied 'Hind' upgrade possibilities in 1996 and, understandably, it came to the same conclusions as the Russian and Israeli studies of the mid-/late 1990s. The chief possible developments outlined were night operation capability introduction, weapons accuracy and total firepower improvement, navigation and self-defence capability enhancements, and improvement to the logistics support and fleet management, which under the old Soviet/Russian service concepts were quite primitive. Like their counterparts at IAI Tamam, ATE engineers took the pragmatic decision to retain the Mi-24's basic analog avionics suite and to interface new digital mission avionics. However, if a customer wishes, a fully-digital system is an option.

The first Mi-24V to be used as a testbed was acquired at a bargain price from Ukraine in 1998 and received the civil registration ZU-BOI. An export order for 40 aircraft to be upgraded to the Mk III standard was signed in 1999 with

The front (pilot-operator's) cockpit has been extensively updated with AH-1W-style hand controls and a new screen display. Note also the monocular sight and control column.

The rear (pilot's) cockpit has a new MFD for targeting and tactical displays. The cockpit is NVG-compatible, and is equipped to support helmet-mounted sights.

Above: In the Mission 24 upgrade for the Indian Air Force (which supplied this airframe for the prototype conversion), the YakB-12.7 gun is retained, but it can be slaved to either the HMOSP or helmet-mounted sights.

Left: At the heart of the Mission 24's sensor suite is the HMOSP multi-sensor turret, fixed above the existing Raduga-F installation.

Right: Rafael's Spike-ER missile (centre pylon) is an option for Mission 24, alongside the existing Shturm-V (wingtip tubes).

Algeria and the first upgraded helicopters were delivered in 2000. A new order – for a smaller number of helicopters to be upgraded to the Mk III standard with additional airframe and equipment improvements, for an undisclosed customer – was announced by ATE in late 2002; it is believed that the customer for this derivative is once again Algeria, which intends to re-upgrade some of its earlier machines overhauled by ATE.

The ATE-developed 'Super Hind' core package is on offer in two main versions. The first, Mk II, aims to enhance the capability of the Mi-35P gun-armed helicopters (a certain number of which, new or refurbished, were sold to several African nations in the late 1990s and early 2000s); it retains the original Russian weapons. It could be a suitable and cost-effective Mi-35P upgrade solution for customers who have ample stocks of Shturm-V missiles and 30-mm (1.18-in) rounds. Mk II introduces only an observation/targeting and precise navigation package.

The second upgrade version, Mk III (as selected by the Algerian Air Force for 40-plus Mi-24D/Vs), features an entirely new weapons control system, replacement of the 12.7-mm (0.5-in) four-barrelled Gatling machine-gun by a 20-mm (0.787-in) gun, and replacement of the Falanga-P/Shturm-V ATGMs by the Kentron ZT35 Ingwe laser beam-riding missile. There is also an option for an agile Mk III derivative, dubbed 'Agile Hind', which would have much improved agility and manoeuvrability due to an extensive airframe/rotor system re-work.

The core system all three ATE upgrades is based on that developed by ATE for the Rooivalk, and comprises an ATE-produced mission computer that interfaces with various onboard systems and is responsible for all navi-gation/weapon delivery data processing; NVG-compatible cockpit and formation lights, as well as steerable infra-red landing light; and Kentron Cumulus Argos 550 gyro-stabilised multi-sensor system with TV-camera, FLIR, auto-tracker, and laser rangefinder/target designator. The nose-mounted Argos 550 system can rotate through 220° in the horizontal plane and +20°/-90° in elevation. Other elements incorporated into the core Mk II/Mk III systems include a head-up display; new NVG-compatible navigation displays in both cockpits, capable of providing position data as a Doppler fix, GPS fix or (more reliable and precise) a combined Doppler/GPS fix; new self-defence system with programmable Vinten chaff/flare dispenser units and control panel, installed in the pilot's cockpit; and a digital/optical rotor balancing and tracking facility to reduce vibration during low- and high-speed flight, thus improving comfort and weapons delivery precision as well as extending airframe/mission equipment life.

Archer sight and Armscor cannon

The 'Super Hind' Mk III package combines the core system with additional high-tech features. One is the Archer R2 helmet-mounted sight developed by Kentron, which is offered for both crew members and is useful for steering the IST Dynamics 20-mm (0.787-in) gun turret and cueing the Argus 550 multi-sensor system. Another is a high-rate-of-slew turret with the Armscor F2 20-mm gun (a licensed Giat Industries F2 model) with 840 rounds, housed in 'cheek' fairings protruding on both sides of the fuselage. The gun can be steered through 110° left/right and –50°/+15° in elevation, at a rate of 100° per second, and can be aimed through either the R550 system, Archer R2 HMS or the pilot's advanced HUD. The Kentron F2 20-mm gun has an impressive muzzle velocity of 1050 m/s (3,445 ft/s), a rate of fire of 750 rpm and an effective range of 3 km (1.6 nm). ATE claims that the combination of the Archer R2 HMS, robust turret and high-muzzle-velocity F2 gun can be deadly effective against air targets, making the integration of air-to-air missiles unnecessary.

One of the most important elements in the 'Super Hind' Mk III's operational capability enhancement package is the new Ingwe ATGM; a warload of eight missiles can be carried on two four-round launchers on the modified wingtips. This 127-mm (5-in) ATGM weighs 64 lb (29 kg), can be launched from 0.25 to 5 km (0.13 to 2.7 nm), and has an armour penetrating capability of up to 1000 mm (3.28 ft). Its laser beam-riding guidance method is highly resistant to countermeasures. In addition, the helicopter can carry a wide range of Russian- and South African-made rocket pods and free-fall bombs (with delayed fuses for a precise low-level delivery profile) – two or four weighing up to 500 kg (1,102 lb) each. The Mk III's enhanced package can also include a further improved and refined man-machine interface, digital HUD, new-generation Doppler sensor and, for NATO member states, a new IFF system. Also on the upgrade list are additional mission avionics components and systems, a digital autopilot/auto stabilisation system, and an advanced integrated communications suite.

The 'Agile Hind' is perhaps the most sophisticated Mi-24 upgrade package offered by ATE. It is aimed at producing a combat support helicopter with superior agility, manoeuvrability and power margins. Serge Vidal, the marketing manager of ATE's Helicopter Division, maintains that such a rotary-wing attack machine can easily be employed in accordance with

India displayed one of its IAI-upgraded Mission 24 'Hinds' at the Aero India show in 2003. The Indian Air Force has large numbers of Shturm-V missiles and these are retained as the primary armament for the modernised aircraft.

sophisticated Western attack helicopter tactics. Vidal points out that there is more to NATO compatibility than just the onboard IFF and radios. Interoperability, he says, can be truly achieved only if the helicopter can comply with NATO tactics. For the Mi-24, this means enough manoeuvrability to achieve nap-of-the-earth flight – and this is what ATE's follow-on upgrade is targeted at providing.

In order to achieve better agility, a comprehensive weight reduction programme was deemed necessary, so ATE stripped out an impressive 2000 kg (4,409 lb) of airframe empty weight. Company sources maintain that this can be achieved through replacing the old electrical, hydraulic and fuel systems with lighter and more reliable modern ones. As well, the existing armour plating can be replaced by lighter solutions that use composite and ceramic plating and by armoured crew seating. Additional weight reduction could be achieved through fixing the undercarriage in the down position, enabling the removal of surplus hydraulic systems and mechanical components.

ATE announced plans for new composite rotor blades (which in early 2004 were still in testing), new much more efficient and lightweight dust/sand engine intake filters, and IR exhaust suppressors. To prove the 'Agile Hind' airframe/rotor system improvements, in 1999 ATE acquired its second Mi-24V example from Ukraine for conversion as a testbed, which received the civil registration ZU-GAL.

ATE has designed a Western-style logistics support system, which focuses on TBO extension and transition to an 'on-condition' maintenance concept, new service documentation, spares, field services and expertise, as well as computer-aided training and maintenance.

SAGEM's upgrade proposal

Another Western company with a successful Mi-24 avionics upgrade is France's SAGEM, a major avionics and system manufacturer and integrator. The core system consists of an integrated modern suite of modular avionics including accurate and autonomous navigation, passive high-tech sensors and sights, 'glass' cockpit with map display and terrain avoidance system, advanced mission computers and night vision equipment.

At the 2001 Paris air show, the company displayed an Uzbekistan Air Force Mi-24P featuring a variety of digital systems borrowed from the Eurocopter Tiger and NH90 new-generation combat and support helicopters. Each cockpit is fitted with a 15 x 15-cm

(6 x 6-in) colour display and has NVG-compatible lightning for use with SAGEM's CN2H night-vision goggles. The highly precise Sigma 95L navigation system feeds inertial and GPS sensor inputs to the Mercator mapping module. A turret beneath the nose houses the modern Strix system, which was developed for the French Army Tiger HAP and has second-generation FLIR, CCD TV and laser rangefinder-designator. A proposed ground segment includes the MARS (Mission Analysis and Restitution System).

It was widely reported that in 2001 SAGEM won a contract to upgrade 12 Uzbekistan Air Force Mi-24Ps, in co-operation with the local aircraft manufacturer TAPOiCh of Tashkent. To develop its Russian-made helicopter upgrade activity further, in June 2003 SAGEM teamed with Mil and Rosoboronexport to offer an upgrade package for the Mi-24; it is being advertised as fully interoperable with NATO army aviation assets, and primary potential customers are the states of the Visegrad Four group (Czech Republic, Hungary, Poland and Slovakia) and Bulgaria.

New players in the upgrade field

In 2001, BAE Systems and Eurocopter announced their intentions to become two more significant players in the already crowded Mi-24 upgrade market. They both offer NATO compatibility and weapons/sighting/observation system packages for the East European states' Mi-24 fleets.

Since late 2001/early 2002, BAE Systems has put much effort into promoting the battlefield mission capability for the Mi-24 upgrade and NATO interoperability programmes in Central East European countries. Its Mi-24 upgrade promotional material claims that investing in capability means investing in the avionics systems – enhanced sensors, increased avionics system incorporation, and integration of the platform and mission avionics. BAE Systems proposed its upgrade for the first time in September 2001, and a company press release stated that the company was going to offer only proven off-the-shelf equipment. Its modular upgrade package is based around open architecture avionics using a Mil-Std 1553B databus which would provide room for further growth,

Having been hawked round the air shows and used for ground tests/demonstrations for some years, Rostvertol's Mi-35M demonstrator 'Yellow 77' eventually flew in late 2003. Hopes for upgrade orders from traditional Russian 'client' states and former Soviet republics are high.

ATE 'Super Hind' Mk III

Key features of the ATE Super Hind Mk III are the Armscor F2 20-mm cannon and Argos 550 multi-sensor turret in the nose (right), and the Kentron ZT35 Ingwe laser-guided missile (below), of which eight can be carried. The 'cheek' fairings house the ammunition for the hard-hitting cannon. Algeria was the first, and to date only, customer for th ATE upgrade, although the company is active in promoting its modification packages to other 'Hind' operators.

i.e., new weapons integration. The proposed avionics package is designed for full ICAO/NATO interoperability and compliance with NATO STANAG 4555, and can be supplied on a 'pick and mix' basis.

One option is the advanced Striker helmet-mounted display, already selected for the USMC AH-1Z upgrade. It comprises a light-weight flying helmet fitted with a pair of detachable image-intensified CCD cameras that may be removed for daylight operation. The cameras weigh 260 g (9 oz) each, have a 40° FoV and project onto the helmet visor a very high-resolution raster binocular image that is electronically combined with targeting and navigation symbology.

Another element in the BAE Systems' proposed upgrade package is the Titan 385 or Titan 485 multi-sensor turret, incorporating cutting-edge technology developed from more than 30 years' experience in combat operations worldwide. The Titan 385 combines a large-format General III gyro-stabilised FLIR (operating in the mid- and low-wavelength bands), CDD camera for day operations and laser rangefinder, installed to port in the nose. The mission suite also includes hybrid GPS/INS navigation system, NATO/ICAO-compatible navigation aids (VOR/ILS/MB/TACAN), advanced IFF, weather radar, state-of-the art jammers, chaff/flare dispensers and radar/laser/missile approach warning receivers, which would considerably improve the Mi-24's survivability in a medium-to-high threat environment. Particularly for battlefield survivability, BAE System proposes its HIDAS – a fully-integrated Defensive Aids System which it says is a modern attack helicopter's essential (albeit very expensive) piece of equipment, already proven on the British Army WAH-64D Apache.

Several types of ATGM are proposed, the chief ones being the AGM-114 Hellfire and Spike-ER/LR. As well, BAE Systems suggested replacement of the Mi-24D/V's 12.7-mm (0.5-in) four-barrelled machine-gun with an Oto Melara 20-mm (0.787-in) TM-197 three-barrelled gun.

In 2001, BAE Systems bid with the WZL-1 maintenance facility of Poland for a Polish Army Mi-24 upgrade, but with no result. In

mid-2003, BAE Systems was ranked among the prime bidders in the ongoing competition to upgrade 100-plus helicopters for the air arms of the Visegrad Four group nations. In order to demonstrate to potential customers its capability to upgrade the Mi-24, BAE Systems has acquired a former Russian Air Forces example from a private owner in the UK, which will be used as a company demonstrator vehicle. In mid-2003 the company started work on a proto-type which is slated to be ready for the 2004 Farnborough air show. BAE Systems plans to invest some $US5 million in the prototype upgrade, which company sources believe will remove as much as 90 per cent of technology risk. Talks are known to have been carried out

with MVZ Mil in mid-2003 regarding co-operation in the Mi-24 upgrade but, by February 2004, no definitive agreement had been signed.

East Europe's upgrade ambitions

In early 2002, the East European states of the so-called Visegrad Four (V4) group – Czech Republic, Hungary, Poland and Slovakia – decided to adopt a comprehensive joint upgrade and life extension of their 'Hind' fleets. On 30 May 2002, the defence ministers of the four countries signed a memorandum of understanding for the joint 'Hind' upgrade efforts, covering up to 106 Mi-24s (40 for Poland, 24 for Czech Republic, 28-32 for Hungary and 10-12 for Slovakia). Their original service life would

SAGEM's Uzbek upgrade

A 'prototype' conversion of SAGEM's Mi-24P upgrade for the Uzbekistan air force was displayed at Paris in June 2001. The French company has based much of the modification on sensors and equipment developed for the Eurocopter Tiger and NH90, including the undernose Nadia sensor ball which is mounted centrally under the chin (right). SAGEM is now officially linked with Mil and Rostvertol in offering NATO-compatible Mi-24 upgrades. This move overcomes one of the main stumbling blocks faced by other potential upgrade contractors, namely, withdrawal of support by the design authority.

BAE Systems upgrade

The 'Hind' upgrade package offered by BAE Systems focuses on NATO compatibility and integrated defences, in addition to improved navigation and combat effectiveness. This demonstrator (above) was displayed with a Titan multi-sensor turret ball, while a front cockpit model (right) shows the new screen display and hand controller proposed for the type. Weapons can include the Israeli Spike and the AGM-114 Hellfire. Aimed primarily at eastern European nations, the BAE upgrade was selected by Poland in February 2004 to proceed to prototype stage.

the upgrade work themselves, which was impossible because the work would involve sensitive NATO communications, targeting and identification technologies to which the Russian engineers could not have access.

Furthermore, at the 2003 Le Bourget air show, Rostvertol and Mil officials declared that they will not support any Mi-24 upgrade programmes led by Western, South African or Israeli companies, and will ban the supply of spare parts to operators of such helicopters.

A meeting of the V4 Ministers of Defence on 27 June 2003 eventually freed each member to sign a separate agreement with the Russian Federation and Rostvertol for fleet service support and for technical support during the development and testing of the Mi-24 prototype. Anticipating serious programme delays and even cancellation of the Mi-24 upgrade project, in early 2003 the WZL-1 facility and the Polish Air Force Technology Institute initiated joint development work on a Combat SAR variant for Polish army aviation, which has a requirement for three or four examples to be ready for service in 2004. This activity is independent of the main Mi-24 upgrade activity. The Mi-24 CSAR programmes include the installation of an enhanced self-defence suite, FLIR, SAR-optimised direction-finder equipment, and other mission avionics. WZL-1 was awarded a $US1.25 million contract for prototype work. In December 2003 it was announced that WZL-1 was awarded the long-expected contract to upgrade two Mi-24Vs to the CSAR variant, complying with the requirements of NATO Standardisation Agreement G 4555 dealing with minimum equipment packages for battlefield helicopters for attack operations in a low-threat environment. The upgraded helicopters, known as Mi-24CSAR, are to be taken on strength by the CSAR Group based at Pruszcz Gdanski which is expected to be formed in late 2004.

In late 2003 it was clear that the V4 group's joint upgrade had collapsed, although officially it still existed. The Czech Air Force is thought to be interested in some small upgrades to bring its older Mi-24Vs to the same standard as the Mi-35s delivered as payment of Russian debts in 2003. Slovakia, however, is still considering ways to co-operate with Poland. Poland itself issued a contract to BAE Systems in February 2004 covering the production of two prototype upgraded aircraft.

expire around 2006 and the helicopters were originally to be updated for another decade's service.

However, this rather ambitious programme, expected to exceed $US500 million, has proceeded very slowly. A technical agreement for the joint upgrade was signed in February 2003. This agreement authorised Poland to organise a tender for potential system integrators, which would have to co-operate with the WZL-1 maintenance facility of Lodz, Poland, to develop the prototype of the upgraded Mi-24. Companies which had expressed their willingness to participate in the tender in 2002 included BAE Systems, Eurocopter, Elbit Systems, IAI Tamam division, SAGEM and ATE. In the event of contract signature by the end of 2003, the prototype was to be test-flown in late 2004.

In early 2003, the four nations disagreed on the scale of the proposed upgrades in each country – and therefore on the eventual level of commonality, schedule of the project, and how

to move from prototype to production scale.

Then, in June 2003 Poland decided to drop its requirement for upgrading 40 helicopters and opted for the NATO minimum of 16 units, abandoning plans for 24 Mi-24Ds. New plans foresee upgrading as many as 13 Mi-24Ws (as the Mi-24V is known in Polish Army service), which are slated to receive NATO-interoperable avionics and will be used as all-weather attack helicopters. Three more will be upgraded to serve as CSAR platforms. The upgraded Mi-24s are intended to remain in service until 2018. The Slovak Air Force reduced to 10 the number of its Mi-24s to be upgraded, and Czech Republic and Hungary dropped theirs to 12-18.

A major hindrance for the Mi-24 upgrade programme is reaching a working agreement with Russia over the politically sensitive service life extension and spare parts delivery issues. According to unofficial sources from the Polish MoD, in April 2003 Russia set conditions that were unacceptable to the V4 group. Mil and Rostvertol aspired to carry out the majority of

Above: In 2003 the Czech air force received seven new 'Hinds' in the form of Mi-24V/35s delivered from Russia as part of a debt repayment deal. The Czechs are looking to upgrade around 12-18 'Hinds' to NATO-compatible standards, reduced from the 24 specified during the initial Visegrad Four discussions.

Left: Poland's 'Hinds' are being repainted in this all-over green scheme. Poland was the first to break from the V4 group by placing a contract for the prototype upgrade of two aircraft with BAE Systems. It is also modifying three aircraft for the CSAR mission.

There were some reports in 2002 that the Visegrad Four group attempted to invite Croatia and Ukraine to join the Mi-24 upgrade undertaking, thus sharing the benefits of the multinational approach and further reducing development expenses. However, V4 group expansion failed to materialise. The Croatian Air Force, whose Mi-24s were reported in early 2002 to have been grounded for three years, eventually elected to go ahead with only structural refurbishment and a minor avionics upgrade. Seven Croat Mi-24Vs were slated for the overhaul, which it was thought would most likely be carried out by the WZL-1 facility in Poland. However, in July 2003 Croatian Air Force Commander-in-Chief Brigadier General Victor Koprivnjak declared that the upgrade contract would go to Russian or Ukrainian companies, as only they had the necessary expertise and could offer an affordable price.

Bulgarian upgrade moves

In 2002/2003 the Bulgarian MoD prepared for an Mi-24D/V avionics upgrade and service life extension so that NATO-interoperable Bulgarian Air Force 'Hinds' could serve until about 2015. As many as 18 Mi-24s (12 late D variants and six V variants) were included in an upgrade that was estimated to cost between $US65 and $US70 million. BAE Systems, Eurocopter, IAI Tamam division, Elbit Systems (teamed with Lockheed Martin-Owego), ATE, Aviation Services (an Mi-24FM team from the Czech Republic with Flight Visions and Marconi), Eurocopter, SAGEM and Rosoboronexport (teamed with Mil and Rostvertol) all expressed interest in participating as avionics integrators and/or main contractors, but the tender procedure was delayed due to funding difficulties and organisational problems.

In early December 2003, the Bulgarian Minister of Defence was authorised to select a strategic partner to run this important project, valued in total between $US150 and $US200 million, without the need to organise an open tender. The leading contender appeared to be BAE Systems, which in 2002 and 2003 actively sought local partners for a large-scale offset

Ukraine maintains a sizeable 'Hind' fleet and is seeking to upgrade a number of its aircraft. In the light of ongoing joint efforts with Israel to upgrade L-39 trainers, the IAI Tamam Mission 24 'Hind' modernisation is the most likely candidate.

programme. However, the Bulgarian Air Force raised strong objections to the BAE Systems' offer, said to be a 'paper upgrade' with no prototype so far being demonstrated, and the Ministry of Defence eventually decided to go to the tender procedure, which was scheduled for announcement in early March 2004.

ATE has also been very active in Bulgaria, the company having formed a temporary (one-year) consortium with local maintenance company TEREM to undertake private-initiative-funded Mi-17 and Mi-24 upgrades. These will be used as company demonstrators for potential customers – chief among them, of course, being Bulgaria. The Mi-24 prototype, a phased-out Bulgarian Air Force Mi-24D serialled 123, is expected to be ready for ground and flight testing in May 2005.

SAGEM, in its turn, is trying to penetrate the Bulgarian market along with Mil Moscow Helicopter Plant and Rosoboronexport. Mil is known to have presented an independent bid to Bulgaria based exclusively around new-generation Russian-made avionics, night-vision equipment and weapons. However, sources say the bid has been deemed unacceptable.

CIS upgrade market

Ukraine is believed to be currently considering a bid by IAI Tamam to upgrade 50 to 100 of its 200-plus Mi-24s. This country, the second-largest in the CIS, has already established a good working relationship with Israel in the military aviation area. The main local contribu-

Bulgaria's delayed 'Hind' upgrade programme has attracted attention from BAE Systems, ATE and from the SAGEM/Mil/Rostvertol partnership. A clear and urgent requirement exists for NATO-compatible aircraft, but funds for such programmes are difficult to find.

tor to a Mil upgrade would undoubtedly be the Aviacon helicopter maintenance facility, based at Konotop. It is the largest of its kind in the CIS and is widely known among Third World Mi-24 operators as a source of readily available, cheap, refurbished Mi-24s and spare parts drawn from Ukrainian military inventory. There are also indications that SAGEM has been very active in Ukraine, promoting its avionics upgrade solutions. Budget constraints, however, could delay any upgrade process.

Belarus is another CIS state operating a sizeable 'Hind' fleet. It is expected to remain loyal to Russia, preferring the Mil/Rostvertol-proposed Mi-24VK-1/VK-2/PK-2 packages for 20 to 30 of its 70 or so Mi-24s. The primary facility for production upgrades and airframe refurbishment in such a case will be the Baranovichi-based 557 ARZ Company.

The same option – embracing Mil/Rostvertol or SAGEM Mi-24 upgrade proposals – may be taken up by other CIS states such as Turkmenistan, Kyrgyzstan and Kazakhstan. Other important Mi-24 upgrade markets which can be described as lying firmly within the Mil/Rostvertol/Rosoboronexport sphere of influence are those in Libya, Syria, Sudan and North Korea.

Alexander Mladenov

Ka-50/52
Kamov's 'Hokum' family

In applying its coaxial rotor concept to the demands of the battlefield attack mission, Kamov produced a helicopter unlike any other. The Ka-50 also incorporated a modern integrated weapon system, allowing it to be operated by a single pilot. Blessed with outstanding performance and agility, the aircraft outflew and outgunned its Mi-28 rival, and has entered limited service with the Russian Army. It also forms the basis of a growing family of two-seat derivatives with even greater capability.

By the mid-1970s, the Soviet Defence Ministry leadership had come to believe that the Mil Mi-24 'Hind' attack heli-copter (then the backbone of Soviet Army Aviation) did not meet Army requirements. The attempt to develop the type into a multi-role helicopter had led to increases in the aircraft's weight and size, and deficiencies in flight performance which, in turn, decreased its combat efficiency. In addition, late in 1972 the United States launched its Advanced Attack Helicopter (AAH) programme, resulting in such new combat aircraft as the Bell YAH-63 and the Hughes YAH-64. (The latter, designated Apache, was adopted for mass production and

The long-suffering 11th flying 'Hokum' is now in its third major incarnation, having originated as a standard Ka-50. It then became the Ka-52 prototype for the side-by-side two-seater, and is now in Ka-52K configuration, with nose-mounted sensor turret.

By the time the Ka-50 should have been entering large-scale production the Soviet Union was disintegrating and defence budgets were being slashed to lower than subsistence levels. Consequently, very few Ka-50s have been built and put into service, despite the obvious attractions of the type. Shown above is a production aircraft during flight test, while at right the sixth production aircraft (024) – in 'Black Shark' scheme – leads two later production machines in an air show flypast at MAKS'99.

in the mid-1980s entered the US Army inventory as its main combat helicopter.)

In light of this, on 16 December 1976 the Council of Ministers of the Soviet Union passed a resolution regarding the development of a new-generation combat helicopter that could be fielded with Soviet Army Aviation in the 1980s. The prospective helicopter's primary purpose was to destroy enemy materiel, particularly tanks on the battlefield and near the

forward edge of battle. The resolution also provided for competing proposals by the Kamov and Mil design bureaux, ensuring one could later be selected for series production. At the time of these programmes, both developers already had 30 years experience in designing rotary-wing aircraft.

When developing its advanced army combat helicopter, known as the Mi-28, Mil drew on both Soviet and foreign experience in operating

army aviation combat helicopters and opted for a single-rotor twin-seat machine. Flying the helicopter and employing the weapons were independent functions requiring a pilot and a weapons system operator, i.e., Mil adopted the same concept as the US AAH programme.

The Kamov design bureau – a dedicated developer of naval helicopters – had a wealth of experience from designing its complex Ka-25 and Ka-27 anti-submarine warfare helicopters,

Technical Briefing

Left: The third flying prototype (012) was essentially similar to the second aircraft, and also had a Mercury fairing in the upper nose section. It introduced the definitive fin arrangement without auxiliary side fins. Note that the gun is not fitted here, revealing the cut-out into which the weapon's swivelling mount was attached.

lapping. The V-50's estimated speed was 400 km/h (249 mph). In 1975-1976, during research for its future combat helicopter concept, Kamov designed the V-100, which would have featured lateral rotor positioning and a pusher propeller for propulsion. Both the V-50 and V-100 projects were daring for their times, but neither was destined to be realised.

V-80 concept features

The Kamov Helicopter Plant initiated design of its advanced combat machine, designated V-80 (aka Product 800), on the heels of the government directive in January 1977. The programme was run by the head of the design bureau, chief designer Sergei Mikheyev, later Designer General.

Various aerodynamic configurations were considered but Kamov's traditional coaxial configuration was retained, since it offered undeniable advantages. By comparison with a single-rotor configuration, the substantial reduction in power loss resulting from the deletion of a tail rotor provided a hefty increase in main rotor thrust. Coaxial rotors resulted in a greater hovering ceiling than did single rotors developing the same power. The aerodynamic symmetry and lack of cross-links within the control system simplified the act of flying the helicopter. Such a helicopter also offered less restriction regarding sideslip angles, angular speeds and acceleration over the whole speed range. The helicopter's compact size also meant lower moments of inertia, providing rapid and effective control.

Another fundamental aspect of the design was that it was a single-seater, in which the lack of a weapons operator was to be offset by a highly-automated sight/navigation suite. The feasibility of a single-seat combat helicopter was confirmed by the experience of attack aircraft and fighter-bombers, whose single crew members acted as both pilots and navigators/systems operators.

Kamov designers believed that if flying, target detection and tracking were automated, combining the functions of the pilot and weapons operator in a single person would be possible and would not cause an excessive psychological and physical strain. By the late 1970s, the state of the national helicopter industry was such that building these automatic systems was possible; even the Ka-25 and Ka-27 featured an automatic submarine search capability, automatic navigation and flight modes, automatic data exchange among helicopters operating as a team, etc.

Using just a single crew member would reduce the helicopter's weight and increase its flight performances. It would also cut the expense of personnel training and reduce casu-

which featured an ingenious and reliable coaxial rotor configuration. The bureau also had some experience in developing Army helicopters: in 1966, in a competition for a transport/combat helicopter, Kamov developed the Ka-25F (F = *frontovoy*, front line). Derived from the shipborne Ka-25 version, it was armed with series-produced weapons including 23-mm rotating automatic cannon, six Falanga anti-

tank guided missiles, six rocket pods and free-fall bombs. The Ka-25F had a crew of two and could carry eight assault troops in its cargo cabin. However, preference was given to Mil's Mi-24 based on its proposed engines and sighting systems, and its new Shturm ATGMs.

In 1969, in the last stage of that competition, the Kamov team offered a radically new design in the shape of the V-50 combat helicopter. The aircraft would have had two longitudinally-positioned rotors that rotated counterclockwise in the same plane – blade synchronisation would have prevented the blades from over-

The fifth prototype (015) was used heavily on firing trials, the aircraft being seen here firing rockets. The coaxial rotor layout of the Ka-50 allows precise and rapid aiming of the fixed weaponry such as rockets, and is also used for initial aiming of the cannon. Fine-tuned aiming of the gun is handled by a limited gun traverse angle.

alties in time of war, making an overall substantial reduction in the costs of supporting army aviation.

Developed by the Tula instrument-making design bureau (designer general Arkady Shipunov), the Vikhr anti-tank guided missile system was chosen to be the V-80's main weapons system. The Vikhr ATGM's most distinctive feature was its laser guidance system which, coupled with the automatic target-tracking system, ensured high precision irrespective of range. The missile's range exceeded that of the foreign Chapparal, Roland and Rapier anti-aircraft systems, and its impact and proximity fuses – plus powerful shaped-charge/fragmentation warhead – enabled the missile to destroy both armoured vehicles and aerial targets.

In designing the helicopter, special attention was paid to the choice of cannon, which eventually settled on the 2A42 30-mm single-barrelled cannon developed by the team at Tula headed by Vassily Gryazev. The cannon was initially intended for infantry fighting vehicles, so Kamov's designers faced the problem of mounting it on the helicopter in such a manner that it would retain its main feature – high accuracy – and make up for its main deficiency – heavy weight, compared to dedicated aircraft guns. It was decided to mount it on the starboard side close to the centre of gravity – the strongest part of the airframe. This would reduce the impact of the recoil on the airframe and provide maximum precision. The restriction on the cannon's horizontal angle of rotation was overcome by the coaxial-rotor helicopter's ability to turn at any speed, with an angular speed matching that of present-day aircraft cannon. Thus, the rough horizontal aiming of the cannon was achieved by turning the whole helicopter rather than the gun.

In addition to the ATGM system and cannon, it was desirable to outfit the helicopter with a range of other weapons. As a result, the V-80's weapons suite was bolstered by rocket pods, UPK-23-250 cannon pods, bombs and KMGU small bomb pods, with provision to mount air-to-surface and air-to-air missiles in the future.

Daytime optics

The V-80's launch-and-leave Shkval automatic TV/laser sighting system was developed by the Krasnogorsk-based Zenith Optics Mechanical Plant. It was developed in two variants – for the V-80 combat helicopter and the Sukhoi Su-25T attack aircraft. The Leningrad-based Electroavtomatika scientific production association was tasked with the development of the V-80's Rubicon unified sight/navigation/flight system.

One priority was to enhance the helicopter's survivability; configuration and systems' arrangement were chosen, assemblies designed

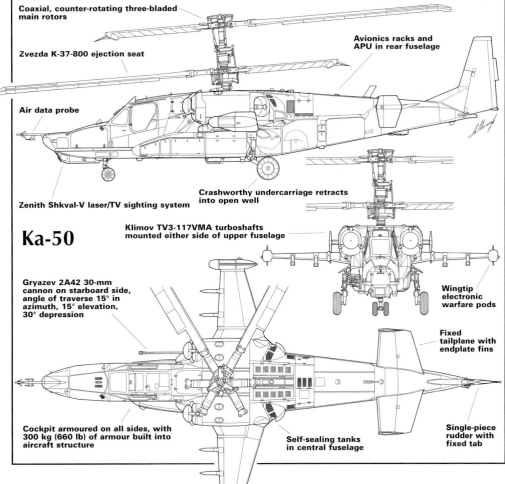

Coaxial, counter-rotating three-bladed main rotors

Zvezda K-37-800 ejection seat

Air data probe

Zenith Shkval-V laser/TV sighting system

Avionics racks and APU in rear fuselage

Crashworthy undercarriage retracts into open well

Klimov TV3-117VMA turboshafts mounted either side of upper fuselage

Ka-50

Gryazev 2A42 30-mm cannon on starboard side, angle of traverse 15° in azimuth, 15° elevation, 30° depression

Wingtip electronic warfare pods

Fixed tailplane with endplate fins

Single-piece rudder with fixed tab

Cockpit armoured on all sides, with 300 kg (660 lb) of armour built into aircraft structure

Self-sealing tanks in central fuselage

and structural materials tested all with this in mind. One advantage was that the helicopter lacked the very vulnerable tail rotor as well as the intermediate and tail reduction gearbox and control rods. The following measures were made to heighten survivability:

■ the engines were placed on both sides of the airframe, preventing them both being damaged with a single shot
■ the helicopter could fly on one engine in various modes
■ the cockpit was armoured and screened with combined steel/aluminium armour and armoured transparency
■ the hydraulic steering system compartment was armoured and screened
■ vital units were screened by less important ones
■ the self-sealing fuel tanks were filled with polyurethane
■ composites were used, thus preserving the helicopter's integrity if its load-carrying elements were damaged

■ the two-contour rotor-blade spar was developed
■ the diameter of the control rods was increased and most were positioned inside the armoured cabin
■ the powerplant and compartments adjacent to the fuel tanks were protected against fire
■ the transmission could operate faultlessly for 30 minutes with the oil system damaged
■ the power supply systems, control circuits, etc. were duplicated and placed on the sides of the airframe.

Armoured cockpit

The pilot, instruments, part of the control wiring and the sighting/navigation system were accommodated in the armoured cockpit. The armour consisted of spaced aluminium plates with a total weight of more than 300 kg (660 lb). The metal armour was fitted in the fuselage's load-bearing structure, which reduced the total weight of the helicopter. Tests at the GosNIPAS proving ground confirmed the

pilot's protection from shell fragments and shells of up to 23-mm calibre.

A unique feature of the V-80 was its rocket parachute ejection system. The helicopter emergency escape system, using the K-37-800 ejection seat, was developed by the Zvezda Scientific Production Association (chief designer Guy Severin). The pilot's safety was also increased by an undercarriage design capable of absorbing large loads in an emergency landing. The cockpit's internal volume was designed to shrink by no more than 10-15 per cent upon impact, while the fuel system incorporated fire prevention features.

A helicopter's combat effectiveness largely depends on its characteristics and ground maintenance facilities, issues that were considered at the early design stages of the V-80. Experts from the Defence Ministry NIIERAT Aircraft Operation and Maintenance Scientific and Research Institute actively participated in the work. While developing the helicopter's maintenance system, due consideration was given to

self-sustained deployment to unpaved airfields.

Thus, by the late 1970s, the Kamov design bureau had finalised the concept of its new combat helicopter – a coaxial single-seater with a wide variety of powerful weapons having a firing range that exceeded that of hostile air defence systems. It was expected to be fitted with functionally-integrated, highly-automated equipment that ensured high combat survivability and the pilot's survival in an emergency, and offered long-term deployment from unprepared locations. The helicopter was intended to operate as part of a reconnaissance/attack system comprising aerial and ground reconnaissance, surveillance, and target designation components.

Testing

In August 1980, the USSR Council of Ministers Presidium Commission on Military Industrial Issues decided to build two V-80 and two Mi-28 experimental prototypes in order to hold comparative tests. That same year, the

Ministry of Defence issued a common performance specification for both experimental helicopters.

The first V-80 prototype (Product 800-01, side number 010) left the Kamov Helicopter Plant in June 1982. On 17 June, for the first time, test pilot Nikolay Bezdetnov hovered the V-80, and on 23 July the helicopter made its maiden horizontal flight. V-80 no. 1 was designed to assess flight characteristics and try out the helicopter systems. In particular, it flew with tail assemblies of various forms, and without the wings. It was fitted with two TV3-117V turboshaft engines.

In August 1983, the second prototype (800-02, side number 011) was completed to test the onboard equipment, avionics and armament. It was powered by upgraded TV3-117VMA engines. For the first time, it was fitted with the Rubicon sighting/navigation system and NPPU-80 rotating cannon mount. The second aircraft flew for the first time on 16 August 1983.

As well as its strength against ground targets, demonstrated here in a rocket attack, the Ka-50 has a notable air-to-air capability, especially against other helicopters.

Just a little later than the V-80, the Mil design bureau began testing its two Mi-28 prototypes. The first helicopter (side number 012) made its first hovering on 10 November 1982, with the second prototype (side number 022) joining the trials in the autumn of 1983. Phase I of the V-80 and Mi-28 joint official comparative flight test programme began in December 1982 and ended in the autumn of 1984. Late in 1984, the Phase I assessment was made, which noted that many V-80 characteristics were superior to those of the Mi-28. In October 1984, the Minister of Aircraft Industry ordered V-80 series production preparations to be launched by the Arsenyev-based Progress Aircraft Plant in the Russian Far East, which at the time manufactured Mi-24 helicopters. Late in the year, flight trials under Phase II of the test programme assessed the V-80's and Mi-28's flight and

Ka-50 and Ka-52 specifications

	Ka-50	Ka-52
Engines	TV3-117VMA	TV3-117VMA
Take-off power, kW (hp)	2 x 1641 (2 x 2,200)	2 x 1641 (2 x 2,200)
Overall length, rotors turning, m (ft)	15.96 (52.36)	15.96 (52.36)
Rotors diameter, m (ft)	14.5 (47.57)	14.5 (47.57)
Height, m (ft)	4.93 (16.17)	4.93 (16.17)
Wing span, m (ft)	7.34 (24.08)	7.34 (24.08)
Empty weight, kg (lb)	7700 (16,975)	7600 (16,755)
Normal take-off weight, kg (lb)	9800 (21,605)	10400 (22,928)
Max take-off weight, kg (lb)	10800 (23,810)	11300 (24,912)
Max take-off weight for ferry, kg (lb)	–	11900 (26,235)
Combat load, kg (lb)	2300 (5,070)	2300 (5,070)
Internal fuel, kg (lb)	1460 (3,219)	1490 (3,285)
Fuel in drop tanks, kg (lb)	1720 (3,792)	1720 (3,792)
Max never exceed speed, km/h (mph)	350 (217)	350 (217)
Max speed in level flight, km/h (mph)	310 (193)	310 (193)
Cruising speed, km/h (mph)	270 (168)	270 (168)
Hovering ceiling, m (ft)	4000 (13,123)	3600 (11,811)
Service ceiling, m (ft)	5500 (18,045)	5000 (16,404)
Max rate of climb, m/s (ft/min)	10 (1,968)	8 (1,575)
Max g loading	3.5	3.0-3.5
Service range without drop tanks, km (miles)	455 (283)	455 (283)
Flight endurance without drop tanks, hours	2.4	2.4
Ferry range (with 4 drop tanks and 20-min reserve), km (miles)	1160 (721)	1120 (696)

Above: 22 was an early production Ka-50 assigned to the Torzhok centre. It was used for display work, for which a full 'Black Shark' scheme with jaws and shark fin tail markings was applied. It crashed in 1998, killing the centre's commander, Major-General Boris Vorobyov, who was also a renowned display pilot who had often demonstrated the Ka-50 at international shows.

Above: The cockpit of the standard 'daytime' Ka-50 is dominated by the large HUD, underneath which is a screen for displaying imagery from the Shkval-V system. Note the pull handles for the K-37-800 ejection seat.

combat performances in a more profound manner.

On 3 April 1985, test pilot Yevgeny Laryushin died in a crash of the V-80 no. 1. While descending quickly from low altitude to ground level in order to manoeuvre behind a terrain feature, his machine's main rotor blades crossed. The investigation revealed that the cause was the pilot exceeding the maximum allowed g load (it totalled -2g) rather than perceived deficiencies of the machine itself. Having poured over the investigation records, air force experts agreed to further tests.

The V-80's design was later modified to prevent the main rotor blades from crossing: the distance between the main rotors was increased, and the control system was fitted with a device increasing the load on the controls when the blades got too close. The tragic death of Yevgeny Laryushin dealt a heavy blow to the Kamov design bureau. His expertise, experience and instinct as a true aviator had greatly influenced the V-80's configuration.

In December 1985, in order to complete the flight performance evaluation programme, the third V-80 prototype (800-03, side number 012) was built with the Mercury low-level TV sighting system mock-up.

The Gorokhovets-based Main Rocket Artillery Directorate proving ground hosted the V-80 and Mi-28 flight trials in September 1985 to assess their combat capabilities within the framework of Phase II of the test programme. Flights were performed by test pilots of the Chkalov Air Force Scientific Research Institute, Colonel V. Kostin being the first military pilot to master the V-80.

These tests finished in August 1986. Results showed that the V-80 outperformed the Mi-28 in combat effectiveness owing to higher survivability, better flight characteristics (especially at high altitudes and temperatures), and wider weapons capabilities. During flights, the level of psycho-physical strain on the pilot was close to that on a fighter-bomber pilot but, in principle, it proved possible to combine the pilot's and navigator's functions.

The Defence Ministry Institutes concluded that the Kamov combat helicopter was more promising than the Mil. Nonetheless, a number of shortcomings were highlighted, the most serious being that the helicopter could not operate at night due to the limitations of the Mercury TV night-vision system. In accordance with the results of the comparative tests, it was recommended that Kamov improve the night-vision system, equip the V-80 with an airborne defence system, reduce the number of operations performed by the pilot while searching and attacking a target, and ensure the integration of the onboard equipment with ground and air reconnaissance systems.

Production launch

On 14 December 1987, the Council of Ministers of the USSR decided to halt development and to launch production of the V-80Sh-1 single-seat combat helicopter by the Progress plant in Arsenyev. The helicopter competition effectively ended. However, the same resolution provided for further Mi-28 development into the improved Mi-28A variant, production of which was launched at the Rostov Helicopter Plant (known today as Rostvertol JSC).

Under the resolution, the Kamov Helicopter Plant manufactured the fourth V-80 (800-04, side number 014) in March 1989, followed in April 1990 by the fifth (800-05, side number 015), which became the baseline version for future series production. Both aircraft were equipped for the first time with integral self-defence aids, i.e., the UV-26 passive countermeasures devices and a laser illumination warning system. The Rubikon system incorporated external target designation equipment. The analog weapons control system gave way to an advanced lightweight unit assembled

015 looses off a salvo of S-8 80-mm rockets (NURS) from the 20-round B-8V20A pods. Comprehensive firing campaigns have proven the Ka-50 to be a deadly accurate platform, at least in daylight.

Chechnya – baptism of fire

In December 2000, a strike/reconnaissance formation comprising two Ka-50 combat helicopters and one Ka-29 (for reconnaissance and target designation) arrived in Chechnya to join the ongoing Russian Army counter-terrorist operations in the northern Caucasus. The Ka-50s flew their first missions on 6 December.

Through January and February 2001 sorties against Chechen rebels included several weapons attacks – the first combat use of the Ka-50. The missions, which were largely accomplished in difficult mountainous terrain, reaffirmed the new machine's features, especially its high power-to-weight ratio and manoeuvrability, which exceed those of the Mi-24 by a considerable degree.

On 9 January, the pilot of a Ka-50, accompanied by a Mi-24, used S-8 rockets to destroy a rebel ammunition dump at the entrance to a gorge in the vicinity of the village of Komsomolskoye. On 6 February, operating in forested mountainous terrain south of the village of Tsentoroy, the strike/reconnaissance formation of two Ka-50s and the Ka-29 detected and eliminated with two Vikhr ATGMs a well-fortified rebel camp in a single pass from a distance of 3000 m (3,280 yards).

On 14 February the strike/reconnaissance formation conducted a search-and-destroy mission around the villages of Duba-Yurt and Khatunee. Operating over

Illustrating the effectiveness of the camouflage against a typical Russian background, a pair of Ka-50s follows a Ka-29 as they depart for the first combat deployment to Chechnya in November 2000. The Ka-29 operated as a reconnaissance/designation platform, in much the same role as that envisaged for the Ka-52.

difficult terrain, the team pinpointed and knocked out eight targets. During this operation the excellent magnification and resolution of the Shkval sighting system's TV channel was called upon.

While the two-month northern Caucasus stint of the two Ka-50s did little to tip the scale in favour of the federal forces in Chechnya, the deployment allowed the Ka-50 to demonstrate its capabilities in a real 'shooting' war. The combat experience gained has already proved useful for both refining the existing machine and in deriving new variants.

---

around a digital computer. With its K-37-800 ejection seat installed, V-80 no. 5 became the first rotary-wing aircraft in the world to boast a rocket/chute emergency escape system.

Four V-80 helicopters underwent development flight tests between July 1988 and June 1990. The no. 3 and no. 5 prototypes were used to hone the rotor system, control system, landing gear and external fuel tanks, assess flight performance and gauge the load factors affecting the machine in flight. Nos 2 and 4 prototypes evaluated weapons suites and fire control systems, avionics electromagnetic compatibility and the powerplant's gas-dynamic stability.

In 1990, the USSR Council of Ministers Commission on Military Industrial Issues authorised the manufacture of an initial batch of the helicopters, soon designated Ka-50, at the Arsenyev-based plant. The lead series-built helicopter (side number 018) took to the air on 22 May 1991 with test pilot N. Dovgan at the controls. The first stage of the Ka-50 state tests (the assessment of flight characteristics) was initiated in mid-1991 using prototypes nos 4 and 5. In January 1992, the lead production

Initial deliveries to the Russian Army were made to the Combat Training Centre at Torzhok, from where field trials began in November 1993. Further aircraft have been delivered to a regular unit in the Russian Far East.

Ka-50 was sent to the GLITs Russian Air Force State Flight Testing Centre for the second stage of state tests (the assessment of combat effectiveness), which started in February.

Soon, the Ka-50 entered the world arena. In March 1992, Designer General Sergei Mikheyev made a speech about the new helicopter at the international symposium in the United Kingdom, where the new designation of the helicopter – Ka-50 – was mentioned for the first time. In August 1992 the third Ka-50 prototype was revealed in flight during Mosaeroshow '92 at Zhukovskiy. The second production Ka-50 (side number 020) made its foreign debut at the Farnborough air show in September that year, where it topped the bill. Its rudder sported the image of a werewolf and an appropriate logo. By that time, the fifth prototype, painted black, had starred in a film called *Black Shark* – and that name has been associated with the Ka-50 ever since. The third production machine (side number 021) later sported a black shark on its rudder and wore the logo 'Black Shark'. Both it and the werewolf-adorned helicopter were showcased at the Le Bourget air show in France in June 1993. Following its debuts at Farnborough and Le Bourget, the Ka-50 was regularly seen at air and arms shows in Russia and abroad.

Ka-50s began field trials in November 1993 at the Torzhok-based Army Aviation Combat Training Centre, which had been provided with four production helicopters. The Centre's pilots and engineers made a substantial contribution to testing the Ka-50 and devising its tactics. Having mastered the new machine, the Centre's chief, Major-General Boris Vorobyov, flew the Ka-50 at international shows at Le Bourget, Dubai, Malaysia and Farnborough. He died in a crash in 1998, while testing a Ka-50 (side number 22) in the maximum allowable regime at Torzhok.

On 28 August 1995, the President of the Russian Federation authorised the fielding of the Ka-50 with the Russian Army. However, these helicopters have not yet replaced Mi-24 veterans. The collapse of the Soviet Union and a plunge in defence procurement resulted in a mere dozen machines built, compared to the several hundred planned to have been built by 2000. Three have been flown by the Torzhok-based Army Aviation Combat Training Centre. In 1999, a decision was taken to field the Ka-50 with a helicopter regiment in the Far Eastern Military District.

Night-capable Ka-50Sh

The Ka-50 single-seat combat helicopter was the forerunner of a family of army helicopters, of which the first production machines were able to operate only during the day. However, as far back as the late 1970s when the requirements of the Ka-50 were being devised, it was decided that the future combat helicopter should be fitted with aids enabling its employment around the clock and in adverse weather. Such aids could be night-vision goggles, stationary low-light television systems using special amplifiers and operating in very low light such as starlight, imaging infra-red (IIR) systems, or the only all-weather means – radar. Each system had its own demands.

Initially, the designers opted for the Mercury low-light TV system, mock-ups of which were installed in the second and third V-80 prototypes. There were plans to mount them on Mi-28 helicopters and Sukhoi Su-25T attack aircraft, as well.

At the same time, the debugging of the TpSPO-V helicopter IR imager was proceeding. It had been developed by the Geofizika Research and Production Association in Moscow and underwent trials on an Mi-24V

018 was the first production series Ka-50 (V-80Sh-1), but was subsequently modified to become the Ka-50Sh day/night demonstrator. In the first night-capable configuration to reach flying hardware stage, the Samshit-50 turret was mounted above the existing Shkval-V daytime optics suite.

The cockpit of 018 in its first Ka-50Sh incarnation was similar to that of a standard Ka-50, but reworked on the right-hand side to add a screen for Samshit-50 imagery.

prototype in 1986. A mock-up of its flight and sighting version, designated Stolb, was fitted to the fifth V-80 flight prototype under the protective glass cover of the Shkval-V system.

The first Soviet night-time surveillance and sighting systems were far from reliable, and their performance left much to be desired. The commission that assessed the Mi-28 and V-80 official comparative flight tests, which ended in August 1986, stressed that neither machine met the requirement for night-time operation set forth in the specification. Sixteen months later, when the government resolution dated 14 December 1987 announced the V-80 as the winner and authorised its series production, the Kamov design bureau was faced with upgrading the helicopter's avionics suite as soon as possible to make it capable of night-fighting.

However, it was roughly a decade before the emergence of the first night operations-capable version of the single-seat helicopter, designated Ka-50Sh. There were a number of reasons for the delay, the main one being that the Soviet Union lagged behind other industrial nations in night-time surveillance systems and sights for helicopters: for example, the US AH-64 Apache attack helicopter, fitted with the TADS/PNVS system featuring a FLIR flight and navigation sensor package, had been in production since 1984. This feet-dragging was exacerbated by the general economic crisis in the country and ensuing catastrophic slump in funding defence R&D efforts.

Refining the Mercury equipment, as well as developing other similar systems, was deemed pointless. Both domestic and foreign experience in this area proved that weight and size constraints prevented the night-vision TV systems from being installed in production tactical and army aviation aircraft – every extra kilometre of TV range would come at a prohibitive cost.

Infra-red imagers

This prompted the designers to shift their focus to developing and perfecting infra-red imaging systems. In 1993, the Kamov design bureau generated a draft design of the night-capable Ka-50. The Krasnogorsk plant launched development of the Shkval-N round-the-clock sighting system, which was to comprise an additional night-time capability wrapped around an infra-red imager designed by Geofizika (Moscow) and the State Institute for Applied Optics (Kazan). However, insufficient funding hampered progress, and in the mid-1990s Kamov decided on the temporary use of foreign-made equipment.

With Russian government approval, Kamov struck a deal with France's Thomson-CSF to buy several examples of its infra-red imagers for tests on the Ka-50. A pod-mounted imager was shown in 1995 under the wing of the tenth Ka-50 flying prototype (side number 020) during the MAKS '95 air show.

By the mid-1990s, the leading Russian manufacturer of optronics, the Urals Optico-Mechanical Plant (UOMZ) in Yekaterinburg, devised a concept of optronics for helicopters, aircraft and other vehicles, based on a line-of-sight stabilisation and control system using high-precision gyro sensors, ball bearings and a 3D torque engine. The UOMZ was able to quickly develop a range of efficient optronics systems, collectively known as gyro-stabilised optronics systems (the Russian acronym being GOES).

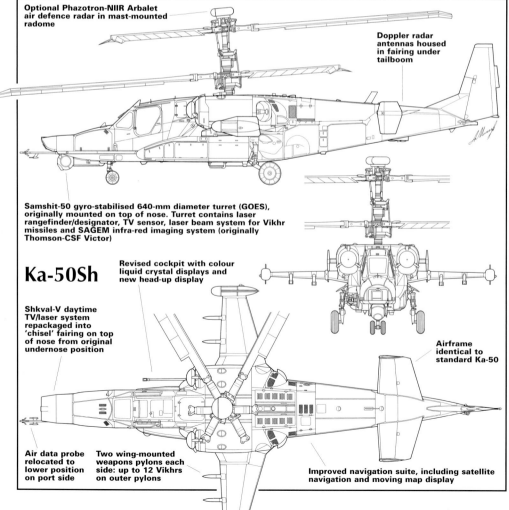

Optional Phazotron-NIIR Arbalet air defence radar in mast-mounted radome

Doppler radar antennas housed in fairing under tailboom

Samshit-50 gyro-stabilised 640-mm diameter turret (GOES), originally mounted on top of nose. Turret contains laser rangefinder/designator, TV sensor, laser beam system for Vikhr missiles and SAGEM infra-red imaging system (originally Thomson-CSF Victor)

Ka-50Sh

Revised cockpit with colour liquid crystal displays and new head-up display

Shkval-V daytime TV/laser system repackaged into 'chisel' fairing on top of nose from original undernose position

Airframe identical to standard Ka-50

Air data probe relocated to lower position on port side

Two wing-mounted weapons pylons each side: up to 12 Vikhrs on outer pylons

Improved navigation suite, including satellite navigation and moving map display

The GOES, which have several standard sizes (optical unit diameter of 640 mm/25 in, 460 mm/18 in or 360 mm/14 in), are designed as a ball moving in different axes. Inside the ball are one to five optronics modules operating as information channels: the daytime or low-light (dusk) TV channels, an infra-red imager, a laser target designator/rangefinder, a laser illumination warning device, a laser beam control system, ATGM infra-red detector, etc. Thus, the GOES offer surveillance and sighting systems with multi-channel operating capability while ensuring a single line-of-sight for all optronics modules, as well as a degree of spatial stability and the ability to traverse (±235° in azimuth and up to 160° in elevation) at high angular speed (up to 60° per second) and acceleration (up to 150° per second^2).

Samshit-50

One of the first UOMZ-built gyro-stabilised optronics systems was the Samshit-50, designed for the Ka-50. Early in 1997, it was fitted to the Ka-50's eighth flying prototype (the first production aircraft, side number 018) in its

The second Ka-50Sh configuration applied to demonstrator 018 reversed the positions of the primary sensors, so that the Shkval-V occupied a new chisel fairing in a reprofiled nose section. While this modification work was ongoing, the cockpit and navigation suites were also revamped with newer technology equipment. Note the four windows for the optical sensors in the Samshit-50 ball turret.

nose section above the optical port of the original Shkval-V daytime laser/TV system. The retrofitted machine was dubbed Ka-50Sh and its maiden flight was made by test pilot Oleg Krivoshein on 4 March 1997. Ten days later, the Ka-50Sh and a production Ka-50 (side number 22) from the Torzhok-based Army Aviation Combat Training Centre departed for the IDEX '97 arms show in Abu Dhabi (UAE), held between 16 and 20 March 1997. There, the daytime helicopter took part in demonstration flights and revealed for the first time its cannon and rockets, and made live anti-tank guided missile firings.

The Ka-50's Samshit-50 gyro-stabilised optronics system is a 640-mm (25-in) diameter ball with four optic windows and houses four

Right: At the 1999 MAKS show Kamov revealed yet another night-capable Ka-50 design with two nose-mounted GOES turrets. The smaller, upper turret houses optics to aid flying and navigation, while the larger, lower turret accommodates targeting sensors. The aircraft was the fourth prototype and was armed with four B-8 20-round rocket pods.

Below: Three colour LCDs dominate the cockpit of the later Ka-50Sh demonstrators (this is 014, the demonstrator for the two-turret configuration). The screens can be configured to display sensor imagery, navigation information or aircraft status data.

The Ka-52 Alligator was initially designed to perform a reconnaissance and attack-lead role, working with single-seat Ka-50s. This is the prototype (061), converted from an early production Ka-50. The aircraft was painted with 'Ka-50-2' titles during the initial phase of the attack helicopter proposal to Turkey.

major channels: a laser rangefinder/designator, a TV channel, a laser beam system to control Vikhr ATGMs and the Victor infra-red imager from Thomson-CSF. The equipment for night operations enables the machine to spot a tank-sized target at a range of 4 to 4.5 km (2.5 to 2.8 miles).

In addition to its optronics, the single-seat night-capable helicopter carried the Arbalet radar from Phazotron-NIIR Corporation, the antenna being housed in a mast-mounted fairing. Coupled with the upgraded self-defence suite, the radar alerts the pilot to possible enemy aircraft attack. The Ka-50Sh's improved flight and navigation suite was augmented with a satellite navigation receiver, while the original PA-4-3 automatic plotter with a paper map was ousted by a navigational LCD displaying a digital terrain map.

The aircraft was subsequently fitted with an advanced integrated open-architecture avionics suite based on multiplex data exchange channels, developed by the Ramenskoye Design Company. The cockpit management system was built around three colour LCDs and a modified head-up display (HUD). At the same time, the positions of the Shkval-V and Samshit-50 systems were altered, with the latter's ball moving downwards and the former's optic window moving upwards. The modified Samshit-50 system included an infra-red imager from SAGEM.

The updated Ka-50Sh was ready in June 1999 and displayed at the arms show in Nizhny Tagil, as well as at the MAKS '99 air show.

The Ka-50Sh's weapons suite matches that of the production daytime Ka-50, but the helicopter can fire its weapons (i.e., Vikhr ATGMs) round the clock owing to its night-vision surveillance and sighting capability. To counter aerial threats, the weapons suite was beefed up with R-73 or 9M39 Igla air-to-air missiles, while Kh-25ML semi-active laser-guided air-to-surface missile could also be carried.

To determine the best avionics suite configuration for the single-seat helicopter, in 1999 Kamov derived another prototype from the fourth Ka-50 flying prototype (side number 014), which was fitted with two gyro-stabilised optronics systems. Both are housed in the fuselage nose section, necessitating the removal of the Shkval-V system. The upper optronics system (GOES-520, with an optical unit diameter of 360 mm/14 in), has TV and IIR channels and is designed for flying and navigating, while the lower ball (GOES-330 with a 460-mm/18-in diameter) comprises the TV, IIR and laser channels and is intended to acquire, track and engage targets. To ensure night-time flight safety for all versions of the Ka-50, Kamov and the Orion Scientific Production Association suggested that crews be provided with OVN-1 night-vision goggles, which had been tested on Ka-50 helicopters in summer 1999 and been displayed at the MAKS '99 air show.

Ka-52 Alligator

In September 1994 at the Farnborough air show, it was announced that the Kamov company had produced a side-by-side twin-seat version from the baseline Ka-50 single-seat combat helicopter. As far back as 1984, when V-80 and Mi-28 comparative trials were in full swing, the Kamov design bureau proposed the development of a dedicated helicopter to conduct battlefield reconnaissance, provide target designation and support group attack helicopter operations. The system was supposed to be carried by the advanced Kamov V-60 helicopter that had also been designed in multi-role, utility and shipborne versions (it evolved into the current Ka-60 multi-role army aviation helicopter and the Ka-62 cargo/passenger variant). The system was intended to augment the combat efficiency of helicopter teams without introducing sophisticated and expensive surveillance and reconnaissance hardware.

The economic hardships that hit the nation in the late 1980s and dogged it throughout the 1990s significantly hampered the new helicopter's development programme. This prompted Kamov's Designer General to pursue mounting the reconnaissance and target designation system on a version of the production

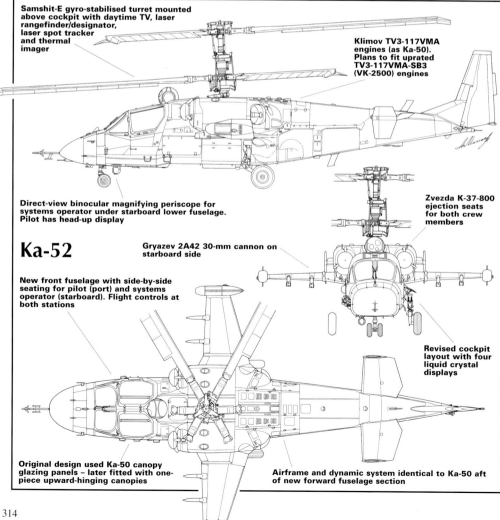

Samshit-E gyro-stabilised turret mounted above cockpit with daytime TV, laser rangefinder/designator, laser spot tracker and thermal imager

Klimov TV3-117VMA engines (as Ka-50). Plans to fit uprated TV3-117VMA-SB3 (VK-2500) engines

Direct-view binocular magnifying periscope for systems operator under starboard lower fuselage. Pilot has head-up display

Zvezda K-37-800 ejection seats for both crew members

Ka-52

Gryazev 2A42 30-mm cannon on starboard side

New front fuselage with side-by-side seating for pilot (port) and systems operator (starboard). Flight controls at both stations

Revised cockpit layout with four liquid crystal displays

Original design used Ka-50 canopy glazing panels – later fitted with one-piece upward-hinging canopies

Airframe and dynamic system identical to Ka-50 aft of new forward fuselage section

Ka-50 which, given that it retained its weapons suite, could not only conduct reconnaissance but also undertake independent combat missions, including those at night and in adverse weather.

A second crew member was needed to operate the optronics/radar reconnaissance suite. The systems operator was to be seated by the pilot's side, rather than in front of him as is the case with most army machines across the globe. The side-by-side seating arrangement was intended to facilitate co-operation between the crew in combat, especially in such demanding modes as terrain-following. It also meant that a number of instruments and controls did not have to duplicated.

Unveiled in September 1994 to the mock-up commission, the first version of the Ka-50 twin-seat reconnaissance/attack variant utilised as many of the production aircraft's components and systems as possible. The wide cockpit, with its angular outlines, reduced streamlining and did little to reduce radar signature. Therefore, the helicopter, a full-scale mock-up of which was displayed at the MAKS '95 show, was turned down by the mock-up commission; it suggested the twin-seater's fuselage nose section be reconfigured and the cockpit be provided with new glazing. This configuration was ready in mid-1996, when Kamov's experimental production facility began manufacturing the first Ka-52.

To this end, a decision was taken to employ the production Ka-50 (the 11th flying prototype) that used to have side number 021. Its nose section was removed up to frame 18 and work on assembling and attaching a new nose section began in the rig. Work was completed by November 1996, the machine having been fitted with several surveillance and sighting systems to select the best configuration. The Ka-52, which sported an all-black paint job and side number 061 (Product 806, no. 1), was

Above: The Ka-52 has slightly reduced performance compared with the Ka-50, but Kamov hopes to redress the balance by fitting uprated engines.

Right: The cockpit of the Ka-52 has four LCDs and a HUD for the pilot. The systems operator has a shrouded sight for the direct-view periscope system. Contrary to Western practice, Soviet tradition places the helicopter pilot in the left-hand seat. Kamov's Ka-60 is the first Russian helicopter to adopt a right-hand seat for the pilot.

unveiled to the media on 19 November 1996. On the eve of its presentation, the aircraft received a name of its own – Alligator – stencilled in large white letters on its left side.

Two-seat cockpit

According to the developer, the Ka-52 had 85 per cent commonality with the production Ka-50. The Alligator inherited the powerplant, rotor system, wing, empennage and landing gear intact from the baseline version. The central and tail sections remained unmodified. The main difference was a new nose section with a two-seat cockpit. The crew are seated side by side in K-37-800 ejection seats, the same seats as in the Ka-50, and enter the cockpit via the upwards-hinged canopy sections. Flight controls are provided at both crew stations. Instruments are updated, with most older needle-type instruments being replaced by four liquid-crystal displays (LCDs). Relevant flight and navigation data are fed to the pilot's HUD. The systems operator has a high-magnification optical binocular periscope

whose objective is housed by a spherical turret beneath the cockpit.

A 640-mm (25-in) diameter moving ball atop the upper fuselage forward of the rotor mast houses the Samshit-E gyro-stabilised optronics surveillance and sighting system. This comprises a daytime TV system, a French-made infra-red thermal imager, a laser rangefinder/designator and a laser spot detector. The first Ka-52 carried a swivelling mount below its chin, which accommodated the Rotor day/night surveillance and sighting system with two optical windows. One of the latter was used by the sensor for the Thomson-CSF Victor thermal imager. The Rotor was intended to be replaced in the improved radome by several modules of the Arbalet all-weather multi-mode day/night multi-function radar, including the antenna to detect ground targets. The other part of the system, designed to handle aerial threats, was to be mast-mounted in a pod above the rotors.

In addition to the entire weapons suite of the single-seat machine (i.e., the 30-mm 2A42

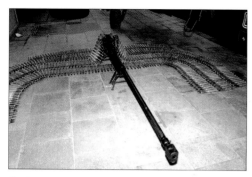

Designed for use on ground vehicles, the 2A42 cannon is heavy but extremely accurate. It is also fitted to the Ka-50/52's rival: the Mi-28 'Havoc'.

Two missile options for the Ka-50/52 are the R-73 air-to-air missile (left), and the Kh-25ML laser-guided air-to-surface missile (right).

This Ka-50 is armed with four Vikhr missiles on the lower mounts and two Igla-V AAMs. The Igla is a shoulder-launched SAM adapted for helicopter use.

The unusual mounting system for the Vikhr missiles is hinged at the rear, and can be lowered for missile launch. Note the caps which protect the missile launch tubes. The rocket pod is the standard B-8V20A.

Ka-52 ordnance options

The primary armament of 12 Vikhr ATGMs is carried on the outer of the two wing pylons. A range of other weaponry is available, such as rockets (including the massive 240-mm S-24), free-fall bombs (including FAB-100-120, FAB-500, RBK-250, RBK-500 and ZB-500), gun pods and Kh-25ML laser-guided missiles on APU-68-UM2 launchers. Defensive armament options are the R-73 air-to-air missile carried under the wing on an APU-62-1M rail or 9M39 Igla-V air-to-air missiles carried on dual launchers under the wingtip EW pods.

4 x 9M39 Igla-V AAM, 30-mm 2A42 cannon with 460 rounds

12 x Vikhr PTUR (ATGM), 4 x 9M39 Igla-V AAM, 30-mm 2A42 cannon with 460 rounds

12 x Vikhr PTUR (ATGM), 2 x B-8V20A pods with 40 S-8 80-mm rockets, 4 x 9M39 Igla-V AAM, 2A42 cannon

4 x B-8V20A pods with 80 S-8 80-mm rockets, 4 x 9M39 Igla-V AAM, 30-mm 2A42 cannon with 460 rounds

12 x Vikhr PTUR (ATGM), 2 x UPK-23-250 gun pods, 4 x 9M39 Igla-V AAM, 30-mm 2A42 cannon with 460 rounds

2 x UPK-23-250 gun pods, 2 x B-8V20A pods with 40 S-8 80-mm rockets, 4 x 9M39 Igla-V AAM, 2A42 cannon

2 x FAB-500 HE bomb (RBK-500 cluster bomb or ZB-500 FAE alternative), 4 x 9M39 Igla-V AAM, 2A42 cannon

4 x FAB-250 HE bomb (RBK-250 cluster bomb alternative), 4 x 9M39 Igla-V AAM, 30-mm 2A42 cannon

4 x KMGU weapons dispenser pod, 4 x 9M39 Igla-V AAM, 30-mm 2A42 cannon with 460 rounds

2 x B-13L5 rocket pods with 10 S-13 rockets, 4 x 9M39 Igla-V AAM, 30-mm 2A42 cannon with 460 rounds

4 x fuel drop tank, 4 x 9M39 Igla-V AAM, 30-mm 2A42 cannon with 460 rounds

cannon with a 280-rpm rate of fire, Vikhr laser beam-riding ATGM system, 80-mm rocket pods, gravity bombs, gun pods, etc.), the Ka-52 can carry Kh-25ML semi-active laser-guided air-to-surface missiles as well as R-73 'dogfighting' or 9M39 Igla-V air-to-air missiles. The same weapons equip the night-capable Ka-50Sh single-seater. The Ka-52's fully-redundant control system, coupled with the side-by-side seating arrangement, also makes it well-suited to training pilots for Ka-50 single-seaters.

Compared to that of the Ka-50, the twin-seater's flight performance is slightly down-graded. The systems operator's seat and the introduction of new systems increased take-off weight from 9800 kg (21,605 lb) to 10400 kg (22,928 lb) which, using the same powerplant, reduced hover ceiling from 4000 to 3600 m (13,123 to 11,811 ft) and service ceiling from 5500 to 5000 m (18,045 to 16,405 ft). The machine's rate of climb and maximum allow-able loading also dropped somewhat. In the future, Kamov plans to enhance the Ka-52's flight characteristics by installing more efficient VK-2500 (TV3-117VMA-SB3) engines, a joint development by the St Petersburg-based Klimov plant and Motor Sich JSC. The VK-2500 boasts 1865 kW (2,500 hp) for take-off and 2014 kW (2,700 hp) in emergency mode.

International debut

The first Ka-52 prototype was revealed at the Aero India '96 air show in Bangalore, even before it had begun flight trials. Upon its return home, preparations recommenced for its maiden flight, which was made by test pilot Aleksandr Smirnov on 25 June 1997. Following performance definition trials, the experimental Ka-52 was used to develop various surveillance and sighting suite configurations.

In 1999, it took part in demonstration and familiarisation flights in Turkey under the Ka-50-2 Erdogan programme to build an advanced helicopter for the Turkish Army (see below), and in spring 2001 it was remanufactured into the Ka-52K version to compete in a bid for the future combat helicopter for the Army of the Republic of Korea. That country plans to buy 36 combat helicopters from 2004, under a contract valued at some \$US1.8 billion. The Ka-52K faces competition from the US Boeing AH-64D Apache Longbow and Bell Helicopter Textron AH-1Z King Cobra.

The Ka-52K's surveillance and sighting equipment includes two gyro-stabilised optronics systems from the UOMZ, namely the nose-mounted GOES-342 fire-control optronics system with TV, laser and IIR channels, and the GOES-520 flight/navigation system housed in a spherical pod mounted under the cockpit, offset to port. Customers can order a weapons suite complemented by Western weapons, such as the French 20M621 750-round 20-mm cannon in an underbelly extendable turret instead of the indigenous 2A42 30-mm cannon, and standard NATO 2.75-in rockets in four 19-round pods (a total of 76 rockets) instead of the Russian-made S-8 rockets. In such a case, the Ka-52K's weapons suite retains the Ka-52's 16 Vikhr ATGMs and four Igla-V air-to-air missiles.

Korean authorities had planned to decide on a winner in November 2001, but the decision was delayed. The Ka-52 has one obvious edge over its US rivals, as South Korea has been operating 36 Kamov machines – multi-role Ka-32s – since the mid-1990s. However, given the strong US-Korea military and political links, the decision on the bid could prove to be polit-ically motivated.

Mounting the Samshit-E turret on the Ka-52's roof reduces its 'look' angle, but raises its sightline (for better terrain masking capability) and, more importantly, leaves the nose free for other sensors. Note the 2A42 cannon installation.

Right and below: The broad nose contours of the Ka-52 Alligator can be used to accommodate a variety of sensors, including the ground target portion of the Arbalet radar system. Other options are the Rotor optical system.

The Arbalet system consists of antennas located in a mast radome for air threats and nose radome (illustrated) for ground surveillance.

Meanwhile, the Progress plant in Arsenyev is prepared to launch the production of the Ka-52 for the Russian Army, and a few twin-seat airframes have been completed.

Ka-50-2 Erdogan

Another variant of the Ka-50 helicopter was developed for a tender issued by Turkey in late 1997. Under the ATAK programme, the Turkish Armed Forces expect to receive 145 modern gunships delivered up to 2010, the bulk of them licence-produced at a local TAI (Turkish Aerospace Industries) aircraft facility. Kamov is competing against the US Boeing AH-64D Apache Longbow and Bell AH-1Z King Cobra, joint French-German Eurocopter Tiger HCP and Italian Agusta A 129 Mangusta International helicopters.

Kamov responded to the tender with the Ka-50-2 two-seat multi-role helicopter, a derivative of the Ka-52 side-by-side all-weather combat helicopter. An important feature of the Ka-50-2 project was that it was developed in conjunction with the Lahav Division of Israel Aircraft Industries (IAI), which handles avionics development and integration.

IAI was chosen as a sub-contractor for several reasons. It has a wealth of experience in upgrading foreign-made – including Russian – aircraft by fitting them with up-to-date NATO-

Ka-52 with Arbalet, Samshit-E and Rotor

The Ka-52 airframe has been proposed with a variety of sensor fits according to customer requirements. The Samshit GOES system can mount a variety of sensors internally, all boresighted together. The Rotor system is another electro-optical unit, while Arbalet is a radar system housed in the nose and a mast-mounted radome. Additional optics, for flight/navigation aid, can be carried in a chin-mounted turret, as employed by the Ka-52K.

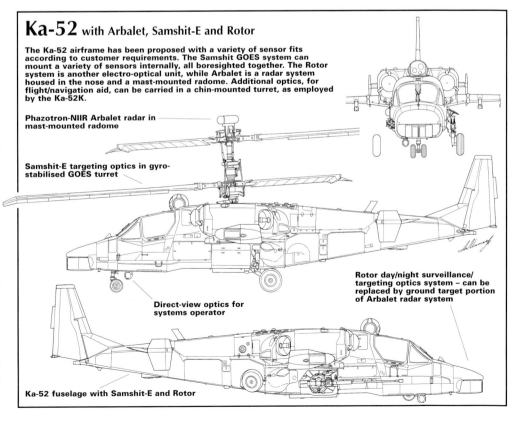

Phazotron-NIIR Arbalet radar in mast-mounted radome

Samshit-E targeting optics in gyro-stabilised GOES turret

Direct-view optics for systems operator

Rotor day/night surveillance/targeting optics system – can be replaced by ground target portion of Arbalet radar system

Ka-52 fuselage with Samshit-E and Rotor

The large box containers carried by Ka-50/52s can be used for general cargo carriage for deployment, or for housing test and recording equipment during weapons trials.

compliant avionics. It is very familiar with the Turkish market, having already upgraded the Turkish Air Force F-4E and F-5A/B fighters. Finally, IAI agreed to share the financial burden of the project.

During the first stage of the tender, completed in March 1999, Kamov demonstrated the Ka-50/52's performance and revealed some elements of the future avionics suite developed by Israel. The helicopter proved its worth in the Turkish environment, with inherent high temperatures and mountainous terrain, as well as its day/night capability. All five Turkish crews that piloted the Russian helicopters appreciated the machine.

The second stage of the tender, which began

in July 1999, compared the contenders' night performance and use of various weapons. The Ka-50-2 successfully completed demonstration flights in August. Its performance and avionics suite won high praise from local pilots who took an active part in its handling. Demonstration of the helicopter's firepower was another success – it fired the Vikhr anti-tank guided missiles, rockets and 30-mm cannon, hitting all of the targets.

Tandem cockpit requirement

At this stage, Turkey placed a number of additional requirements on the Ka-50-2, the most serious of which were reconfiguration of the side-by-side cockpit into a tandem one, replacement of the Russian 30-mm 2A42 cannon with a French 20-mm NATO-compliant flexible gun, and replacement of Russian 80-mm rockets with NATO-standard 70-mm

ones. Kamov prepared a number of proposals to meet these requirements, and by the September IDEF '99 exhibition a full-scale mock-up of a new helicopter had been built and delivered to Ankara. The new variant became known as the Erdogan (Turkish for warrior).

Kamov had been able to build this new machine so quickly due to the modular design of the Ka-50-2 – the nose part of the fuselage was simply cut off and replaced with a tandem one with a larger transparency area and less armour protection. Unlike in the Apache and Mangusta, the pilot was in the front seat and the operator in the rear, slightly above the pilot. The remainder of the helicopter fuselage, including the airframe, surfaces and assemblies, were left untouched. A 20-mm GIAT cannon was fitted to a mid-fuselage turret that was extendable after take-off. Many other requirements pertaining to the range of ammunition and equipment were also satisfied.

The Ka-50-2 avionics is of open architecture and is based on two R-3081 MDP processors and two Mil-Std-1553B-compliant databuses, one for the fire control system and one for the flight/navigation system. The main surveillance and sighting systems include the gyro-stabilised HMOPS consisting of FLIR and TV channels, a laser rangefinder and a laser ATGM guidance system, as well as NavFLIR and two IHS helmet-mounted target designators for each pilot. All information is displayed on four multi-function colour displays on the instrument panels.

The helicopter's flight/navigation system includes an INS/GPS navigation package and TACAN radio navigation system. Communications equipment comprises three VHF/UHF radios and a short-wave radio. Its electronic countermeasures suite consists of an Elint station, laser illumination sensors, an infra-red detector and a chaff/flare dispenser.

The Erdogan's primary weapons are its retractable belly-mounted 20-mm cannon in a turret, 12 Vikhr ATGMs (or 16 future foreign-made ATGMs), and 38 to 76 2.75-in rockets in two to four 19-round pods. Aerial threats could be handled by four Stinger AAMs.

The Ka-52K is a version of the Alligator on offer to the Republic of Korea Army to fulfil an outstanding attack helicopter requirement. The demonstrator is shown here armed with four Vikhr missiles on each wing. Alternative ATGMs could be integrated if a customer stated the requirement.

The main features of the Ka-52K demonstrator are the nose-mounted GOES-342 turret for the targeting optics, and the GOES-520 turret for flight aid/navigation under the port side of the forward fuselage. The demonstrator retains the 2A42 cannon, but Kamov can offer a French-built 20-mm cannon as an alternative.

The winner in the bid was determined in July 2000 when the Turkish government declared its intent to select the US-made King Cobra. Mention was made that the Russo-Israeli Kamov Ka-50-2 Erdogan remained on the short list and that the results of the tender were subject to reconsideration if the US failed to meet Turkish conditions.

The US and Turkey have yet to resolve their differences over technology transfer for licence-production of onboard computers and relevant software for the AH-1Z. In August 2001, the Pentagon announced that it would never allow the computer technology transfer and threatened to revoke the export licence. Ankara reciprocated with a sharp warning that the US stance could have an impact on both the AH-1Z acquisition and other joint military programmes. So, despite the official results of the tender, the Ka-50-2 still has some chances in Turkey. However, it is clear that Ankara's final decision will hinge on political expedience first and foremost.

Future Ka-50s

In 2001, the Kamov company announced its intention to develop another two-seat derivative of the Ka-50 helicopter. Like the Erdogan, it features the tandem configuration, but the cockpit design is believed to be different. Unlike the Ka-50-2, the new machine – designated Ka-54 – will feature a cockpit with much better armour protection, and the avionics and weapons suites will include advanced Russian-designed systems. The Ka-54 will be offered both to the Russian Army and foreign buyers.

The company is ready to develop other Ka-50 versions, as well, which could meet specific needs of demanding customers. The company guarantees that primary capabilities will be retained: unrivalled manoeuvrability, high reliability, flight safety and survivability, excellent combat efficiency. These qualities are grounded in the helicopter's unique coaxial rotor configuration, its ingenious and reliable design, and the top-drawer avionics and weapons suites, whose superiority has been proven by theoretical research, comparative trials and field operation.

Thomas Andrews

These two photos show Kamov's mock-up of the Ka-50-2 Erdogan proposal for Turkey. Unlike other gunships, the Ka-50-2's pilot occupies the front cockpit. The mock-up was displayed with standard Ka-50/52 weapons such as Vikhr and B-8V20A rocket pods, and also carried Vympel R-73 air-to-air missiles on wingtip launchers. If Turkey did adopt the type, Western equivalents would be substituted in most cases.

[illegible]e acknowledgments

[illegible] Randy Jolly. **8:** Randy Jolly, David Donald, Ted Carlson/Fotodynamics. **9:** US [illegible]r Force (two). **10:** US Air Force via Robert L. Lawson, Don Spering/AIR (two). **11:** Fairchild-Republic, Don Spering/AIR. **12:** Don Spering/AIR (two). **13:** via Robert L. Lawson (two). **14:** Jim Rotramel (three), Randy Jolly (two). **15:** Randy Jolly, Mal Gault, Jim Rotramel. **16:** Peter R. Foster, David Donald, US Air Force. **18:** Don Spering/AIR (two). **19:** Randy Jolly, Jeff Rankin-Lowe, US Air Force (two). **20:** David Donald, Mal Gault. **21:** US Air Force via David Donald, US Air Force. **22:** Randy Jolly (two), David Donald, US Air Force (two). **23:** Fairchild-Republic, US Air Force, David Donald (four), Jim Rotramel (two), Mal Gault. **24:** Peter R. Foster, David Donald, via Robert L. Lawson. **25:** Don Spering/AIR (three), Ben Knowles via Robert L. Lawson, Randy Jolly (three), David Donald. **26:** Peter R. Foster, US Air Force (two). **27:** Rick Llinares, Ted Carlson/Fotodynamics, Randy Jolly. **28:** David Donald, Jim Rotramel (two). **30:** Randy Jolly (two), Jeff Wilson. **31:** Yves Debay, Jeff Rankin-Lowe, Gary Frederick via Robert F. Dorr. **32:** 706th TFS, Randy Jolly (three), David Donald (five). **33:** Randy Jolly (three), 706th TFS (two), David Donald (three), Mal Gault. **34:** Yves Debay (two), Tim Ripley, Rick Llinares, Randy Jolly (two). **38:** Jim Rotramel, Randy Jolly (two). **39:** US Air Force (two), Ted Carlson/Fotodynamics, Jelle Sjoerdsma. **40:** Tim Ripley, Ted Carlson/Fotodynamics (two). **41:** Randy Jolly. **42:** USAF (four). **43:** via Clive Bennett, USAF (two). **44-46:** USAF. **47:** via Clive Bennett (two), USAF. **48:** USAF (two), Peter R. Foster, Peter R. March. **49:** USAF, Nate Leong, Peter R. March (two), Peter R. Foster. **50:** via Clive Bennett, Jamie Hunter/Aviacom, Peter R. March. **51:** Pete Becker, Peter R. Foster, USAF (two). **52-53:** Rick Llinares/Dash 2, Ottogalli, Marchetti, Maniago. **54:** Ted Carlson/Fotodynamics, Harry Gann. **55:** McDonnell Douglas, Randy Jolly. **56:** Randy Jolly, Chuck Lloyd/Dash 2. **57:** Rick Llinares/Dash 2. **58:** BAe via Michael Stroud. **59:** BAe via Michael Stroud, Rob Lea. **60:** Cpl John Cassidy/Strike Command. **61:** Rob Lea (two). **62:** Robert Hewson/Aerospace (three), Rob Lea (two). **64:** Rob Lea. **65:** BAe, Rob Lea (two). **66:** Ted Carlson/Fotodynamics. **67:** Chuck Lloyd/Dash 2, Randy Jolly. **68:** Ted Carlson/Fotodynamics. **70:** Randy Jolly, McDonnell Douglas. **71:** Randy Jolly. **74:** Ted Carlson/Fotodynamics, Bruce Trombecky. **75:** Chuck Lloyd/Dash 2 (two). **76:** Rob Lea (two). **77:** Cpl John Cassidy/Strike Command via Jon Lake, Rob Lea. **78:** BAe via Peter R. March (two). **79:** BAe via Peter R. March, Peter R. March (two). **80:** BAe, Cpl John Cassidy/Strike Command via Jon Lake. **81:** Cpl John Cassidy/Strike Command, Yves Debay. **82:** David Donald, Rick Llinares/Dash 2 (two). **84:** Yves Debay, Chuck Lloyd/Dash 2. **85:** Chuck Lloyd/Dash 2, Carl L. Richards. **86:** BAe via Salvador Mafé Huertas, Claudio Toselli. **87:** Salvador Mafé Huertas, McDonnell Douglas via Salvador Mafé Huertas. **88:** Luigino Caliaro, Hans Nijhuis, McDonnell Douglas. **89:** BAe via Salvador Mafé Huertas. **90:** Cpl John Cassidy/Strike Command (two), Peter R. March (two), Chuck Lloyd/Dash 2, Terry Senior, Salvador Mafé Huertas. **91:** BAe, David Donald (two), Carl L. Richards, Ted Carlson/Fotodynamics (two), Randy Jolly. **92:** Randy Jolly, BAe via Peter R. March. **93:** Peter B. Mersky (three). **94-95:** McDonnell Douglas. **96:** Sgt Rick Brewell/RAF PR, BAe. **97:** Matthew Olafsen, Ted Carlson/Fotodynamics. **98:** Boeing, Crown Copyright (three). **99:** USMC (two), Boeing. **100:** USMC (three), US Navy. **101:** USMC (three). **102:** US Navy (two), USMC (three). **103:** USMC, US Navy, Crown Copyright (three). **104:** Jamie Hunter/Aviacom, Neil Dunridge. **105:** USMC (two). **106-107:** Robert Hewson (two), Randy Jolly. **108:** Peter R. Foster. **109:** McDonnell Douglas (two). **110:** Lockheed (two), Boeing, Bell (two). **111-112:** Hughes. **113:** Hughes, US DoD, Aerospace. **114:** McDonnell Douglas, Hughes. **115:** Hughes (two). **116:** Randy Jolly, Hughes. **117:** Randy Jolly, Hughes. **118:** Hughes, US DoD. **119:** Greg Davis/FPI, McDonnell Douglas. **120:** Hughes, McDonnell Douglas (two). **121:** Rick Llinares/Dash 2. **122:** McDonnell Douglas (two). **123:** Jeremy Flack/API, McDonnell Douglas. **124:** Robert Hewson (two), John Gourley (four), David Donald (two), Jim Winchester, MATRA. **125:** Robert Hewson (seven), John Gourley (two), Jim Winchester. **126:** McDonnell Douglas (two). **127:** Randy Jolly, McDonnell Douglas. **128:** McDonnell Douglas, John Gourley. **129:** Rick Llinares/Dash 2. **130:** McDonnell Douglas (four). **131:** Randy Jolly. **132:** Robert Hewson. **133:** Robert Hewson, David Donald (two). **134-135:** McDonnell Douglas. **136-137:** Robert Hewson. **138:** Robert Hewson (two), McDonnell Douglas. **140:** Jeremy Flack/API, Rick Llinares/Dash 2. **141:** McDonnell Douglas. **142:** McDonnell Douglas, Rick Llinares/Dash 2, Yves Debay, Aerospace. **143:** Aerospace (three), Yves Debay, US DoD. **144:** Rick Llinares/Dash 2, Aerospace. **146:** John Gourley, Dougie Monk, Rick Llinares/Dash 2. **147:** McDonnell Douglas. **148:** Robert Hewson. **150:** Hughes, McDonnell Douglas (two), Ted Carlson/Fotodynamics. **151:** Yehuda Borovik/BIAF Magazine, McDonnell Douglas. **152:** Tim Ripley (two), McDonnell Douglas. **153:** Michael Stroud, McDonnell Douglas. **156:** Ted Carlson/Fotodynamics, Westland. **157:** Boeing (two), David Donald, Westland. **158:** McDonnell Douglas (three). **159:** Westland (two). **160-161:** Boeing. **162-163:** Ted Carlson/Fotodynamics. **164:** Ted Carlson/Fotodynamics (two), Robert Hewson. **165:** Robert Hewson, Ted Carlson/Fotodynamics. **166:** Robert Hewson. **167:** Ted Carlson/Fotodynamics (two). **168:** Peter Steinemann, Cees-Jan van der Ende. **169:** Yoshitomo Aoki (two), Yaso Niwa. **170:** via Robert Hewson (two). **171:** Shlomo Aloni (four). **172:** Peter Steinemann (two). **173:** Ted Carlson/Fotodynamics (two). **174:** Ted Carlson/Fotodynamics, US Marine Corps. **175-176:** US Navy. **177:** UK MoD (two). **178:** US Navy, Robert Hewson. **179-180:** US Navy. **181:** Robert Hewson (four). **182:** Ted Carlson/Fotodynamics, David Donald. **183:** Bell via Robert Hewson (two). **184:** Bell via Robert Hewson (two), Robert Hewson. **185:** Bell via Robert Hewson (two). **186:** Bell, Bell via Robert Hewson, US Marine Corps. **187:** Bell (two), Tom Kaminski. **188:** Jamie Hunter, Robert Hewson, Bell via Robert Hewson. **189:** Peter Steinemann, Bell, Peter R. Foster. **190:** Robert Hewson (three). **191:** Shlomo Aloni (four). **192:** Shlomo Aloni (four). **193:** Yaso Niwa, Peter R. Foster, Yoshitomo Aoki. **194:** Peter R. Foster (three), Peter Steinemann (two). **195:** Peter R. Foster, Cees-Jan van der Ende (three). **196:** Ted Carlson/Fotodynamics (five), Robert Hewson. **197:** Ted Carlson/Fotodynamics (four), Tom Kaminski (two). **198:** Sergei Skrynikkov. **199:** Robert Hewson. **200:** Sukhoi Design Bureau via Yefim Gordon, Emiel Sloot/STAS. **201:** Heinz Berger, Yefim Gordon. **202:** Yefim Gordon (three), Sukhoi Design Bureau via Yefim Gordon, Yefim Gordon archive (two). **203:** Martin Baumann, Yefim Gordon, Yefim Gordon archive. **204:** Sukhoi Design Bureau via Yefim Gordon (three). **205:** Yefim Gordon (two), Martin Salajka. **206:** Yefim Gordon, Alan Key/Key Aviation Photography, Yefim Gordon archive. **207:** Sukhoi Design Bureau via Yefim Gordon, Yefim Gordon. **208:** Chris Ryan, Yefim Gordon. **209:** Peter R. March. **210:** Yefim Gordon, Chris Ryan (two), Jon Lake, William Turner, Gábor Szekeres, Stefan Petersen, René van Woezik. **211:** Hans Nijhuis (seven), Martin Salajka, Tieme Festner. **212:** Yefim Gordon, Werner Greppmeir. **213:** Katsuhiko Tokunaga/DACT Inc. **214:** Yefim Gordon (three). **215:** Heinz Berger, Yefim Gordon, Robert Sant. **216:** Yefim Gordon archive, Yefim Gordon (two). **217:** Katsuhiko Tokunaga/DACT Inc, Robert Hewson. **219:** Martin Salajka, René van Woezik, Gert Kromhout. **220:** Jan Jørgensen, Alan Key/Key Aviation Photography. **221:** Katsuhiko Tokunaga/DACT Inc, Tieme Festner. **222:** Yefim Gordon archive, Simon Watson (five). **223:** Martin Baumann, René van Woezik. **224:** Chris Ryan, Hans Nijhuis. **225:** Chris Lofting, Peter R. Foster. **226:** Hans Nijhuis, Paul van Oers, Martin Baumann. **227:** Peter R. Foster, Marcus Fülber. **228:** René van Woezik. **229:** Georg Mader, Tieme Festner, Stefan Petersen. **230:** Chris Ryan, Tieme Festner. **231:** Jeroen M. Brinkman, Bulgarian AF via Robin Poldermann, Alexander Mladenov. **232:** Alexander Mladenov(two). **233:** Alexander Mladenov (two). **234:** Hans Nijhuis, Alan Key/Key Aviation Photography, Peter R. March. **235:** Hans Nijhuis, Heinz Berger. **236:** Robert Hewson, US DoD. **237:** Martin Baumann, Yefim Gordon. **240:** Sergey Skrynnikov, Alexander Mladenov. **241:** Sergey Skrynnikov, Aleksey Mikheyev. **242:** Sergey Skrynnikov, Piotr Butowski (three), Hugo Mambour. **243:** Sergey Sergeyev via Piotr Butowski, Piotr Butowski. **244:** Aleksey Mikheyev, Alexander Mladenov, Piotr Butowski, Hugo Mambour. **245:** Piotr Butowski (four). **246:** David Donald (two), Elbit/TAM. 247: Elbit/TAM, David Donald. **248:** Alexander Mladenov (two), Svilen Christov via Alexander Mladenov. **249:** Eugène Gadet, Alexander Mladenov, Piotr Butowski. **250-251:** Eddie De Kruyff (main), Robert Hewson (inset). **252:** Yefim Gordon Archive (two), David F. Brown. **253:** US DoD (inset). **254:** Yefim Gordon Archive (five). **255:** Yefim Gordon Archive (two). **256:** Yefim Gordon, Frank Rozendaal (two), Hugo Mambour, Paul Jackson, Chris Ryan. **257:** US DoD, Yefim Gordon Archive (two). **258:** Yefim Gordon Archive (three), Robert Hewson. **259:** Gabor Szekeres, Yefim Gordon Archive. **260:** Alexander Mladenov, Aerospace. **261:** Peter R. March, Jozef Gal (inset), Alexander Mladenov. **264:** Yefim Gordon Archive, Tieme Festner, Keith Wilson/SFB Photographic. **266:** Yefim Gordon Archive (two). **267:** Hugo Mambour, Frank Rozendaal. **268:** Stefan Peterson, Yefim Gordon Archive (two), Frank Rozendaal. **269:** Frank Spooner, GAMA/Frank Spooner. **270:** Yefim Gordon Archive (three), Peter Steinemann/Skyline APA. **271:** GAMMA/Frank Spooner (three). **272:** GAMMA/Frank Spooner, SIPA-Press/Rex Features. **273:** SIPA-Press/Rex Features (three). **274:** SIPA-Press/Rex Features, Yefim Gordon Archive (three), GAMA/Frank Spooner, Yefim Gordon Archive (two). **275:** SIPA-Press/Rex Features (two). **276:** Zoltan Buza (two). **277:** Peter Steinemann/Skyline APA, Eddie De Kruyff. **278:** GAMMA/Frank Spooner, Aerospace (two). **279:** Peter Steinemann/Skyline APA, Pushpindar Singh. **280:** Frank Rozendaal, Marcus Fülber, Jens Schymura. **282:** SIPA-Press/Rex Features, Paul O'Driscoll/REX Features, SIPA-Press/Rex Features. **283:** FANA/FAPLA via Vasco Henrique. **284:** ITAR-TASS va Dimitri Komissarov, GAMMA/Frank Spooner (two). **285:** Press Association, Tim Ripley. **286:** Yefim Gordon Archive (five), Paul Jackson (three). **287:** Sergey Sergeyev (two), Keith Wilson/SFB Photographic, Tieme Festner, David R. Hames, Georg Mader, Paul Jackson, Gabor Szekeres, Robert Hewson, Paul Jackson, Gabor Szekeres (two). **288:** Sergey Popsuevich, Rostvertol via Alexander Mladenov. **289:** Rostvertol via David Donald, Mikhail Kuznetsov. **290:** Alexander Mladenov (two). **291-292:** Piotr Butowski (two). **293:** David Donald (two), Piotr Butowski (two), David Willis. **294:** Rostvertol via Alexander Mladenov, Piotr Butowski, Alexander Mladenov. **295:** Piotr Butowski (two), Alexander Mladenov. **296:** David Willis (three), Piotr Butowski. **297:** Daniel J. March (three), Alexander Mladenov, Piotr Butowski. **298:** Alexander Mladenov (two). **299:** David Donald (three), IAI via Alexander Mladenov, Alexander Mladenov. **300:** David Willis (two), Rostvertol via Alexander Mladenov. **301:** Piotr Butowski (four). **302:** BAE Systems (two), Bronco Aviation (two). **303:** Alexander Mladenov, Sergey Popsuevich. **304-305:** Alexei Mikheyev. **306:** Kamov (three), Alexei Mikheyev. **307-312:** Alexei Mikheyev. **313:** Alexei Mikheyev (two), Sergey Sergeyev, Peter R. March. **314-316:** Alexei Mikheyev. **317:** Alexei Mikheyev (three), Phazotron. **318-319:** Alexei Mikheyev.